Duquesne University:

Spiritus Est Qui Vivificat

Gift
of
Harry T. Hutchinson

THEOLOGICAL
AND
RELIGIOUS
REFERENCE MATERIALS

THEOLOGICAL AND RELIGIOUS REFERENCE MATERIALS

Systematic Theology
and
Church History

G. E. Gorman and Lyn Gorman

with the assistance of Donald N. Matthews

Bibliographies and Indexes in Religious Studies, Number 2

Greenwood Press
Westport, Connecticut • London, England

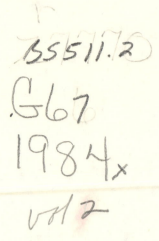

Library of Congress Cataloging in Publication Data

(Revised for volume 2)

Gorman, G. E.
 Theological and religious reference materials.

 (Bibliographies and indexes in religious studies,
ISSN 0742-6836 ; no. 1-   )
 Includes indexes.
 1. Bible—Bibliography. 2. Theology—Bibliography.
I. Gorman, Lyn. II. Title.
Z7770.G66 1984 [BS511.2]   016.2   83-22759
ISBN 0-313-20924-3 (lib. bdg.: v. 1)
ISBN 0-313-24779-X (lib. bdg.: v. 2)

Library of Congress Catalog Card Number: 83-22759
ISBN: 0-313-24779-X
ISSN: 0742-6836

First published in 1985

Greenwood Press
A division of Congressional Information Service, Inc.
88 Post Road West
Westport, Connecticut 06881

Printed in the United States of America

10 9 8 7 6 5 4 3 2 1

Contents

vi   Contents

Preface

> The first man I saw was of a meagre aspect,
> with sooty hands and face, his hair and beard
> long, ragged and singed in several places. His
> clothes, shirt, and skin were all of the same
> colour. He had been eight years upon a project
> for extracting sun-beams out of cucumbers, which
> were to be put into vials hermetically sealed,
> and let out to warm the air in raw inclement
> weather.
>
> (Swift, Gulliver's Travels III/5)

Some years ago we embarked on a project which seemed simple enough, the preparation of a basic guide to reference materials in theological and religious studies. At that time our editor at Greenwood Press hoped that we could expand the initial outline into a 450 page manuscript. In the end the publisher sought some guarantee that the project could be kept to four volumes. Gulliver's description of the Grand Academy of Lagado might well have included a theological bibliographer among those engaged in futile enterprises, for the cucumber extractor is as likely to meet with definitive success in his field as is the bibliographer of man's oldest discipline. Perhaps ironically this situation is the very raison d'être for a work of the type now in hand.

As John Trotti indicates in his introductory chapter for the first volume of this project,[1] religious studies and theology are among the most complex fields of human scholarship. Certainly these disciplines have the longest history of all scholarly endeavors, beginning with the earliest records of human activity and continuing unabated to the present. Furthermore, religion and theology as disciplines traditionally encompass far more than narrow

definitions would suggest, ranging from purely intellectual concerns of philosophical theory to the more concrete areas of history and literature and
to the practical fields of social ethics, psychology, education and politics.
Because religion covers such a wide range of man's interests and activities,
the literature in this field is perhaps the most exhaustive of all subjects.
Consequently, the sheer volume of material and the broad interests which
it encompasses mean that any attempt to exercise bibliographic control
requires a catholicity of knowledge and degree of stamina not usually associated with such activity. "To do his job properly, the bibliographer must
first have a thorough acquaintance with his subject. He must know the
primary texts well, and he must also have a command of the major reference
works in the field. He should be well acquainted with previous bibliographic
work on his author or subject and should have a solid understanding of previous trends in scholarship and criticism." [2] In addition to these requirements
the bibliographer must have a clear grasp of the significance of theological
bias. Because of the intensely subjective and personal nature of theological
inquiry, there has developed over the centuries a very complex language
in which each particular school defines terms according to its own views
and requirements. As Jeanette Lynn has said, "A mere opinion may often
be vested with importance in this field, when in another it would be of
only a passing interest." [3]

Given these traits and consequent criteria required for effective theological bibliography, one is consistently amazed that scholars optimistically
- or foolishly - devote time and effort to bibliographical activity at all, yet
every year sees the appearance of still more guides to theological literature.
Almost at random one can mention as examples such works as Barber's
The Minister's Library, Bollier's The Literature of Theology, Danker's Multipurpose Tools for Bible Study, McCabe's Critical Guide to Catholic Reference
Works, Walsh's Religious Bibliographies in Serial Literature. [4] Guides of
this type all share a common trait in limiting their coverage to specific
traditions, topics or audiences in theology. Barber and McCabe thus focus
on conservative Protestantism and Roman Catholicism respectively; Bollier
deals with basic reference works most often consulted by students and clergy;
Danker concentrates on the field of biblical studies, while Walsh covers
a specific form division within religious studies.

The present series of volumes differs from these and similar works
in several respects. First, the focus is international and interdenominational,
including works in all Western languages and from all traditions which are

likely to be consulted by students or scholars. While some users may look askance at the inclusion of general reference literature, as well as some material not generally regarded as theological in focus, we would remind them that works of this type can answer many basic questions which the more advanced and detailed reference books take for granted. Furthermore, students come to theology from a variety of disciplinary backgrounds, and what might seem unnecessarily repetitious to one will be totally new to another. Thus the student of history will already know about Historical Abstracts, while the chemist studying church history for the first time will not. For these reasons we have included a broad range of general reference works under the appropriate subject divisions. The second distinguishing feature of importance in this series is its multidisciplinary approach, covering the literature of biblical studies, systematic and dogmatic theology, church history and practical or applied theology. Third, the target audience of the series is not just students or clergy or scholars but all three categories. Fourth, our definition of reference materials is purposely broad, encompassing bibliographies, indexes, abstracts, encyclopedias, dictionaries, handbooks, manuals and basic textbooks or major topical surveys. These last two categories are generally excluded from guides to reference literature, yet for students they can be particularly useful in providing concise information or the general background needed to place ideas and events in context. The one main category of literature specifically overlooked in this guide is periodical articles, for the adequate treatment of such material (bibliographical essays and literature surveys in particular) would require another set of volumes. Fifth, we have not limited our treatment to titles recently published or of recognized superiority. Most libraries of any size contain reference works which are often very dated and which, according to critical opinion, are clearly inferior. Since such works are available for consultation, it would be unfair to ignore their existence; rather we have tried to indicate the caution required in approaching works of this type.

The intention of this fairly generous categorization is to provide a work which introduces students to the full range of reference materials likely to be required in theological or religious studies and available in academic libraries. For this class of user John Trotti's introductory chapter in the first volume should be required reading, for it carefully sets forth the attributes of each type of reference material and places the literature within the broad context of academic research. More advanced users, including research students, clergy and scholars, are also catered to, for the survey is not limited to basic reference materials but also includes research tools required for a range of specific scholarly needs. This is particularly true of bibliographies, indexes and certain types of dictionaries, while the more general encyclopedias and basic textbooks are suitable primarily for the less advanced user.

Aiming to meet the rather different requirements embodied in such a broad range of users always poses certain organizational difficulties. The most suitable arrangement for advanced users, and the most satisfactory from a classificatory viewpoint, is one which follows a rather detailed classification of disciplines/subjects/topics. However, this presents a some-what daunting prospect to the large body of student users unfamiliar with the niceties of theological and religious classification and may well dis-courage frequent use. In addition an intentionally broad subject arrangement encourages browsing by the neophyte theologian, and this is a prime con-sideration in a work which seeks to draw students into the maze rather than to reinforce barriers to understanding. Therefore, each volume follows a very broad subject division, with form subdivisions under each main subject. The more specific topical requirements of advanced students and scholars can be satisfied through the detailed author, title and subject indexes.

The four volumes which comprise this set are obviously interrelated in the sense that they deal with the same general discipline. However, by following the traditional fourfold division of theology (with the addition of comparative religion) we have sought to provide volumes which can be used independently of one another. Each volume, therefore, is a separate entity, with self-contained introductory remarks, cross referencing and indexes. Since students new to theological study generally begin their work with biblical studies in one form or another, the introductory chapter by John Trotti has been attached more appropriately to the biblical studies volume than to any other. Volume 1, then, treats general reference materials and biblical studies; Volume 2 covers systematic/doctrinal/moral theology and church history; Volume 3 deals with practical theology and related subjects in the social sciences. These three discrete but related titles are being published in rapid succession, probably within an eighteen month period. The fourth and final volume, dealing with comparative and non-Christian religions, will appear somewhat later.

In this second volume of the series we deal with the two broad areas of systematic theology and ecclesiastical history, together with certain theological topics which fall between doctrine and history. As the alphanumeric notation in Volume 1 ended with Section B, we have decided to continue with consecutive alphabetical indicators in this volume in order to avoid the duplication of entry notations between subjects. Because disciplines overlap and are never mutually exclusive, users are likely to consult more than one volume in the series; and it is with this in mind that we particularly wish to avoid any chance of confusion in notation. Section C, for example, deals with systematic theology, which we have interpreted to encompass doctrinal theology, dogmatics, apologetics, philosophy and moral theology or ethics. However, the last of these categories does not include pastoral aspects of ethical behavior, which are dealt with in the succeeding volume. Similarly, biblical theology has been treated in the preceding volume as part of biblical studies. Given this spread of subjects even within the most generous classification, it seems useful to avoid repeating entry numbers by the simple expedient of sequential alphabetical prefixes.

As indicated, systematic theology has been very broadly interpreted; the intention of this is to encourage student users to see the subject not as it is necessarily taught, as a series of discrete entities, but as a unified whole. In the same vein ecclesiastical history is a purposely broad category, encompassing patristics, the early church, medieval and modern periods plus denominational history under one umbrella. However, we have drawn the line at certain aspects of ancient and biblical history, which are discussed in the first volume. The 1500 entries found under systematics and church history are divided into three form categories: bibliographies, dictionaries, handbooks. As in the preceding volume, bibliographies are taken to include indexes and abstracting services; dictionaries encompass encyclopedic sets, while handbooks cover not only manuals and directories but also basic text-books and a representative range of general studies. The final two subject sections in this volume are arranged according to similar form divisions.

In the case of these last two main sections (missions/ecumenism and religious orders) we have decided that they fit uncomfortably into either systematics or history and so, despite our general insistence on the broadest possible categorization, include them as separate categories. Because missions and ecumenism are closely related subjects, they have been treated together, and the section on missions/ecumenism covers both theological and historical aspects within each of the three form divisions. Similarly religious orders cannot be dissociated from either doctrinal or historical aspects of theology, so both areas are treated in this final subject section. However, to those especially interested in monastic theology and spirituality, as well as religious orders generally, we must issue a warning. The literature of and about religious orders is so complex and overwhelming in quantity that our choice of entries has been far more selective and representative than in other sections. Most religious orders have a long tradition of scholarly reference literature which deserves detailed treatment in a separate volume; here we can only hint at the more significant titles which might lead one further into the field. The architectural aspects of religious orders will be treated in the next volume, which includes Christian architecture as part of liturgics. It must also be noted that in this section the form divisions cover bibliographies in one section and dictionaries plus handbooks in another, the latter combination having been chosen because of the comparatively small number of entries. In all four main sections we have sought to include works of all traditions, from the most conservative to the most liberal, as each approach to Christian doctrine and history has developed its own corpus of reference literature. In all sections items without annotations are those whose content we have been unable to verify or evaluate.

The three indexes in this volume are intended to cater to those who wish to approach the field by author, title or specific subject. The author index includes not only all named authors but also editors and translators, while the title index lists all known titles under which a work has appeared (reprints, British and American variants, original foreign language titles of translations). In both of these indexes the computer has necessitated certain departures from normal indexing procedures, particularly the exclusion of diacritical marks and the adoption of short titles for many works. The results, however, are still detailed enough for anyone seeking a work through the title or author approach. In the subject index we have tried to select specific terms and cross references which provide an alternative to the very broad subject categorization adopted in the main bibliography, although it has not been possible to index specific parts of books. Nevertheless, individual titles are given as many subject entries as required to indicate the content relevant to all types of theological inquiry.

No matter how accurate and complete one seeks to be in preparing a work of this magnitude omissions and errors are bound to occur. We trust, however, that these are few and that they do not detract from the intended usefulness of the volumes. Some will disagree with our classification of materials and may find certain inconsistencies in the arrangement of entries. We hope that such infelicities will be brought to our attention so that they may be corrected in any supplementary volumes. More general omissions regarding topics in religion, of course, can never be overcome in a work which aims to cover the entire field of religious studies. In order to deal with some of the more important areas omitted from this guide Greenwood Press has agreed to institute a new collection of volumes, originally to be called Topics in Religion: A Bibliographic Series but now entitled Bibliographies and Indexes in Religious Studies. This is intended to cover all aspects of religious studies which have as yet received inadequate bibliographic treatment. Initial volumes will deal with church and state in Eastern Europe, new religious movements, missions, the resurgence of Islam, pastoral counseling and related topics. We should be pleased to hear from those who believe that they have a subject worth including in the series. It is only by cooperative efforts of this kind that the many lacunae in theological and religious bibliography can be overcome effectively.

In preparing our own series of volumes we have had the extreme good fortune to secure the cooperation of several scholars and librarians and wish to aknowledge publicly our debt to them. Longest serving among our associates has been Donald N. Matthews of the Lutheran Theological Seminary in Gettysburg, who with consistent good humor and characteristic modesty has offered valuable advice on how to cope with the frustrations of broad classes of literature and over the years has provided several tons of photocopies (always within the law) for works not available to us. If anything can strain a friendship, this is it; however, we are happy to report that our relationship, now approaching its second decade, remains as close as ever. John B. Trotti of the Union Theological Seminary in Virginia has been foolish enough to accept the onerous task of providing a student oriented opening chapter to the work, and we are particularly grateful for his having done so despite recurring bouts of ill health and a heavy work load. The depth and informality of his wisdom have been a boon to generations of students in Richmond, and we are pleased that his insights are now available to a wider audience through the first volume in this series. Marilyn Brownstein of Greenwood Press, having inherited this project from her predecessor, has provided a wealth of helpful insights not only as an editor but also as one interested in religious studies. She is an invaluable asset to any author, being unwilling to say no in any but the most generous and constructive way. In addition, reference staff at the University of Sussex Library over the years have dealt, sometimes in puzzlement but always efficiently, with a bizarre range of requests arising from our search for some of the more elusive works in these volumes. Chris Wimlett, formerly of the University of Sussex Computing Centre and now of the University of St. Andrews, provided compassionate guidance and expert knowledge in our initially hesitant requests for computer assistance in compiling the indexes. The tedious hours needed to put these indexes on tape were found by Barbara E. Degenhardt, who not only performed her task quickly and efficiently but also assisted us in correcting errors and duplications in the text. To these individuals and many others we extend our sincere gratitude for their invaluable assistance, while retaining for ourselves the responsibility for all errors and omissions. We would remind these colleagues and all others who seek to understand and communicate the wisdom embodied in our religious heritage of the warning issued by Qoheleth so long ago: "Of making many books there is no end, and much study is a weariness of the flesh."

Notes

1   John B. Trotti, "Introduction to the Study and Use of Theological Literature," in G.E. Gorman and Lyn Gorman, Theological and Religious Reference Materials: General Resources and Biblical Studies (Westport, Conn.: Greenwood Press, 1984), pp. 3 - 26.

2   A.J. Colaianne, "The Aims and Methods of Annotated Bibliography," Scholarly Publishing 11 (1980): 324.

3   Jeannette Murphy Lynn, An Alternative Classification for Catholic Books (2nd rev. ed. by G.C. Peterson. Washington, D.C.: Catholic University of America Press, 1954), p. 17.

4   Cyril B. Barber, The Minister's Library (Grand Rapids, Mich.: Baker Book House, 1974); John A. Bollier, The Literature of Theology: A Guide for Students and Pastors (Philadelphia, Pa.: Westminster Press, 1979); Frederick W. Danker, Multipurpose Tools for Bible Study (3rd ed. St. Louis, Mo.: Concordia Publishing House, 1970); James P. McCabe, Critical Guide to Catholic Reference Works (2nd ed. Littleton, Colo.: Libraries Unlimited, 1980); Michael J. Walsh, comp., Religious Bibliographies in Serial Literature (Westport, Conn.: Greenwood Press; London: Mansell Publishing, 1981).

G.E. Gorman   Lyn Gorman
Ballarat College of Advanced Education   Creswick, Victoria

Feast of the Ascension, 1984

THEOLOGICAL
AND
RELIGIOUS
REFERENCE MATERIALS

C. Systematic/Doctrinal Theology and Ethics

C0001 Actualidad Bibliográfica de Filosofía y Teología: Selecciones de Libros San Francisco de Borja. Vol. 1- . Barcelona: Ediciones Mensajero for the Faculdades de Filosofía y Teología, San Francisco de Borja, 1964- ; semiannual.

This bibliographical serial includes a few articles, a section of reviews of books on theology and philosophy and shorter notes on titles received. The main review section is arranged alphabetically by author, and the notice section is arranged by subject. Books in Spanish, English, French and German are reviewed, and most entries are of fairly recent date. The bibliographical information is quite complete, and the second issue each year includes a full author index. This is a useful serial for those interested in recent continental works in particular, especially Roman Catholic titles. See also Archivo Teológico Granadino (C0007).

C0002 Adorno, Francesco. Il Pensiero Greco-Romano e il Cristianesimo: Orientamenti Bibliografici. Piccola Biblioteca Filosofica Laterza, Nuova Serie, no. 49. Bari: Laterza, 1970.

C0003 Albert, Ethel M.; Kluckhohn, Clyde; et al. A Selected Bibliography on Values, Ethics and Esthetics in the Behavioral Sciences and Philosophy, 1920-1958. Glencoe, Ill.: Free Press, 1959.

This annotated listing of some 2000 books and periodical articles is arranged by topic and includes an author index. For the period covered Albert is broadly indicative of the publications produced and lists a number of materials relevant to ethical and theological aspects of modern life, covering such areas as anthropology, psychology, sociology, government, economics and philosophy. See also Bibliography of Society (C0028).

C0004 American Theological Library Association. Liberation Theology, Black Theology and the Third World. Chicago, Ill.: American Theological Library Association, 1981.

Based on Religion Index One and Religion Index Two databases, this bibliography of approximately 1160 items has been printed in a looseleaf format. Similar in appearance to the regular Religion Index One issues with subject, author and book review indexes, this guide includes such topics as liberation theology, black theology, theology in Latin America, social change and the church, women's liberation. Covering books and articles, this is a significant and up to date guide to both theological and socio-economic aspects of the Third World. See also Facelina (C0066).

C0005 [no entry]

C0006 Andresen, Carl. Bibliographia Augustiniana. 2. Aufl. Darmstadt: Wissen-schaftliche Buchgesellschaft, 1973.

Using a classified arrangement, this 317 page bibliography lists books by or about St. Augustine. The preface is in German and Latin; the work is adequately indexed, but there are no annotations. Entries are taken from all periods, with special attention paid to more recent works from Europe. See van Bavel (C0016) for a more comprehensive but less up to date compila-tion. See also Lamirande (C0109) and Nebreda (C0136). A very basic bibliog-raphy on Augustine is available in Sciacca (C0180).

C0007 Archivo Teológico Granadino: Organo del Centro de Estudios Postriden-tinos de la Facultad de Teología de la Compañia de Jesús de Granada. Vol. 1- . Madrid: Instituto Francisco Suárez, Consejo Superior de Investigaciones Científ-icas; Granada: Facultad de Teología, 1938- ; annual.

Each volume of this Roman Catholic annual contains a substantial bibliog-raphy of theological books and articles in three sections: history of theology, 1500-1800; other works; index of authors and titles. The first two are subdivided into specific topics, and there is an outline of the subjects in the list of contents for each volume. The bibliographical reviews are generally detailed and evaluative, covering items mainly from Europe. Most titles are from the preceding two years and reflect all aspects of theological study. This is a very helpful survey of European theology which is little used in the English speaking world, no doubt because the reviews are in Spanish. See also Actualidad Bibliográfica (C0001).

C0008 Atiesmo e Dialogo. Vol. 1- . Vatican City: Secretariato per il Non-Credente, 1966- ;quarterly.

Following a collection of brief articles on questions of belief and the unbeliever, each issue includes a bibliography arranged under approximately ten subject headings. Both books and journals are covered, and the 300 entries in each issue provide only partial bibliographical data. This in-completeness is compounded by the lack of indexing, yet Atiesmo still provides better coverage of this interesting field than any other theological indexing service. Materials in most European languages are included.

C0009 Ayres, Samuel Gardiner. Jesus Christ Our Lord: An English Bibliography of Christology, Comprising over Five Thousand Titles Annotated and Classified. New York: A.C. Armstrong and Son, 1906.

Arranged in a classified sequence, this substantial bibliography of 502 pages lists both scholarly and devotional works on Christology. Emphasis is on publications of the nineteenth century. Titles are not annotated individually, but there are some annotations and notes at the beginning of each chapter. Ayres is a more substantial volume than Case (C0048) and serves somewhat more advanced requirements. See also Tavagnutti (C0185).

C0010 Baker, Frank, comp. Union Catalogue of the Publications of John and Charles Wesley. Durham, N.C.: Duke University, Divinity School, 1966.

Building on the earlier work by Green (C0077), this 230 page work attempts to provide a complete bibliography based on the catalogs of libraries with more than 100 eighteenth century works by the Wesleys. Titles are arranged chronologically with each entry listing its locations. There is a guide to abbreviations and a good subject index. See also Schmidt (C0177).

C0011 Baker, John Arthur, comp. A Select Bibliography of Moral Philosophy. Study Aids, vol. 9. Oxford: University of Oxford, Sub-Faculty of Philosophy, 1977.

This 144 page bibliography consists of a classified listing of books and articles for undergraduate and graduate students. Coverage includes morality, ethics and related topics. Although without annotations or indexes, Baker is a sound starting point for students unfamiliar with the philosophical aspects of ethics. See also Lineback (C0116).

C0012 Bastide, Georges. Ethics and Political Philosophy. French Bibliographical Digest, Series II, no. 34. New York: Cultural Center of the French Embassy, 1961.

This work was published in French as Morale et Philosophie Politique (Bibliographie Française Etablie à l'Intention Etrangère, tome 10. Paris: n.p., 1961). See also Matczak (C0128).

C0013 Bauer, Gerhard, comp. Towards a Theology of Development: An Annotated Bibliography. Geneva: Committee on Society, Development and Peace, 1970.

This 201 page bibliography is an important collection of titles dealing with theological aspects of the nature, process and purpose of economic and social development. It covers books, articles and reports in four main sections: aspects of development, idea of progress and development in philosophy, sources for a theology of development, towards a theology of development. Each section is divided into chapters and very specific subsections; within each the arrangement is generally by author. There are a few descriptive annotations, and the range of entries spans both secular and religious writings in most European languages. Basic and important works are indicated by an asterisk, and there is a list of abbreviations plus an author index. While the subject arrangement is not always as clear as it might be, this is the most substantial work of its kind and should be consulted by anyone interested in issues of development and theological or ethical topics related to these issues. See also Pigault (C0151).

C0014 Baumeister, Edmund J., comp. Booklist of the Marian Library. 2nd ed. Dayton, Ohio: Dayton University, Marian Library, 1949.

Listing nearly 11,000 works on Mary, this extensive bibliography covers titles in Latin, English and other European languages. Entries are arranged alphabetically by author; there is no subject index of the various aspects of Mariology treated in this otherwise valuable compendium. See also Bibliografía Mariana (C0021) and Tavagnutti (C0187).

C0015 Baumgardt, David. Philosophical Periodicals: An Annotated World List. Washington, D.C.: U.S. Library of Congress, General Reference and

Bibliography Division, 1952.

Drawing on Library of Congress holdings, this 89 page list includes periodicals from all areas and provides brief annotations. Frequency of publication, date of inception, editor, publisher and address are given for each title. An alphabetical index of titles is provided as a complement to the geographical arrangement of entries. Although now very dated in terms of relevant editorial data, this is a useful list for tracing titles of philosophical journals with marginal theological content. For a much more up to date listing see Hogrebe (C0089), which is also more current than Maison des Sciences de l'Homme (C0120).

C0016 Bavel, Tarsicius J. van. Répertoire Bibliographique de Saint Augustin, 1950-1960. Instrumenta Patristica, 3. Steenbrugis: St. Peter's Abbey, 1963.

This 991 page bibliography is a thorough and well annotated listing of books and articles published on St. Augustine between 1950 and 1960. The 5500 entries are arranged in a classified sequence, and there are author, subject and name indexes. Although limited in period and not covering works by St. Augustine, this is an important bibliography because of its thorough treatment. See Andresen (C0006) for a more up to date but less comprehensive bibliography. See also Lamirande (C0109) and Nebreda (C0136).

C0017 Bechtle, Thomas C., and Riley, Mary F. Dissertations in Philosophy Accepted at American Universities, 1861-1975. Garland Reference Library of the Humanities, vol. 112. New York: Garland Publishing Company, 1978.

This 537 page compilation is an author listing of more than 7500 doctoral dissertations accepted at 120 North American universities. For the most part only those works primarily concerned with philosophy and based in departments of philosophy have been included. There is a detailed subject index.

C0018 Bent, Ans J. van der. The Christian-Marxist Dialogue: An Annotated Bibliography, 1959-1969. Geneva: World Council of Churches, 1969.

This bibliography lists significant books, pamphlets and articles on the Christian-Marxist dialogue published during the preceding ten years in English, German, French, Italian and Spanish. Some older works are included for those interested in the historical context. An attempt has been made to select only objective works, excluding anti-communist and militant atheist materials. The books and articles are listed alphabetically by author under the relevant language division, with very brief annotations. A list of basic journals is provided. There is no index.

C0019 Benzing, Josef. Lutherbibliographie: Verzeichnis der Gedruckten Schriften Martin Luthers bis zu Dessen Tod. In Verbindung mit der Weimarer Ausgabe unter Mitarbeit von Helmut Claus. 3 pts. Bibliotheca Bibliographica Aureliana, Bd. 10, 16, 19. Baden-Baden: Librairie Heitz, 1965-1966.

The three parts of this chronological bibliography list the full range of Luther's writings from 1516 to his death. The first part covers complete editions, collections and specific publications issued between 1516 and 1523; the second part carries this forward to 1546; and the third consists of title and printer indexes, bibliography and title pages. As a guide to some

3700 primary documents by Luther this is a very thorough and useful compilation. See also Bigane (C0030).

C0020 Bibliografia Filosofica Italiana. Vol. 1- . Milan: Carlo Marzorati, 1951- ; annual.

Produced annually for publications issued at least two years previously, this bibliography of Italian books and articles on philosophy is sponsored by the Centro di Studi Filosofici Cristiani di Gallarate as a serial successor to bibliographies issued by the Istituto di Studi Filosofici (C0095, C0096). For readers of Italian this is an important bibliography of Roman Catholic philosophical thought, although it is not specifically Catholic in origin. See also Sciacca (C0181).

C0021 Bibliografía Mariana. Vol. 1- . Rome: Biblioteca Pontificia Faculta Teologica Marianum, 1948 - ; irregular.

This supplement to Marianum, which itself includes a listing of titles submitted for review plus notes on contents, provides a bibliography of books and articles on Mariology. It is international in coverage and attempts to be reasonably comprehensive. Subject and author indexes are provided, and a classified arrangement of entries is used. Unfortunately, there are no annotations, and coverage is not very comprehensive. The three volumes edited by Guiseppe Maria Besutti cover 1948-1951, 1951-1952, 1951-1957. See also Baumeister (C0014) and Tavagnutti (C0187).

C0022 Bibliografía Teológica Comentada. Vol. 1- . Buenos Aires. Instituto Superior Evangélico de Estudios Teológicos, 1973- ; annual.

For those interested in Latin American theology this bibliography is a sine qua non, as each year it lists some 5000 books and articles from more than 400 serials. Entries are arranged by broad subjects and subdivided into topics; all citations include basic bibliographical data, and there are a few abstracts as well. Indexes of authors, subjects and biblical references are provided in each volume. In most respects this service is reasonably current and provides an important source of information for those wishing to keep abreast of Latin American theological thinking.

C0023 Bibliographia Internationalis Spiritualitatis. Vol. 1- . Rome: Pontificio Istituto di Spiritualità, Edizioni dei Padri Carmelitani Scalzi, 1966- ; annual.

This comprehensive international bibliography of Christian, especially Roman Catholic, spirituality and related theology lists books and articles from nearly 500 Western journals. Entries are arranged in eight major subject areas and numerous subdivisions; these are outlined at the beginning of each volume, and there is an author index at the end of each compilation. Full bibliographical details are provided for each entry, and there are now nearly 7000 citations in each volume. This work is usefully international in scope and provides an excellent service for students of spirituality, although its coverage is up to four years behind. See also Dagens (C0058) and Metodio da Nembro (C0130).

C0024 Bibliographie de la Philosophie: Bulletin Trimestrial/Bibliography of Philosophy: Quarterly Bulletin. Vol. 1- . Paris: Librarie Philosophique J. Vrin, 1954- ; quarterly.

This bibliography supersedes that of the Institut International de Philosophie (C0093) and is essentially an abstracting journal limited to book materials, providing abstracts in the language of the original work but with English or French translations where necessary. The entries are arranged under ten subject headings, and in addition to abstracts very full bibliographical details are provided. Indexes of authors, titles and subjects appear in the final issue for each year. This is a most useful complement to the Philosopher's Index (C0146). Unfortunately, reprints, paperback works and translations receive only a bibliographical entry and not an abstract, but this is one of the few drawbacks to a service which otherwise provides valuable international coverage of philosophical literature.

C0025 Bibliographie Internationale de l'Humanisme et de la Renaissance. Vol. 1- . Geneva: Editions Aroz for the Fédération Internationale des Sociétés et Instituts pour l'Etude de la Renaissance, 1965- ; annual.

Now appearing in two parts, this annual bibliography lists books and articles from more than 2500 journals on (a) anonymous works and people of the Renaissance, (b) subjects of the Renaissance. The second part is arranged by subject, and there are indexes of names and subjects. Religion receives particularly strong coverage under its own heading. Although an important guide in its field because of the international coverage provided, this work is less up to date with every volume and now appears more than five years after the date of coverage. See also Gerlo (C0070).

C0026 Bibliographie Philosophie. Vol. 1- . Berlin: Zentralstelle für die Philosophische Information und Dokumentation, 1967- ; quarterly.

C0027 Bibliography of Philosophy. 4 vols. New York: Journal of Philosophy, 1934-1937.

Covering 1933-1936 and reprinted from the Journal of Philosophy, these annual classified lists are intended to include all scholarly philosophical literature published in English, French, German and Italian, with some items from other languages. Name indexes are provided. This collection is a useful compendium for the dates covered and includes a reasonable selection of materials on the philosophy of religion. See also de Brie (C0041).

C0028 Bibliography of Society, Ethics and the Life Sciences. Hastings-on-the-Hudson, N.Y.: Institute of Society, Ethics and the Life Sciences, 1973- ; annual.

Although less comprehensive and not as well indexed as Walters (C0204), coverage provided by this bibliography is very up to date and includes some brief annotations. The areas treated span a wide range of ethically complex topics of some concern to the churches and to Christian ethics. See also Albert (C0003).

C0029 Bibliotheek van Oude Schrijvers. Tevens Is Hier Bijgevoegd: Le Long, Chronologisch Register van Ned. Bijbeldrukken van 1477-1732. Rotterdam: Lindenbergs Boekhandel, Slaak 8, 1968.

This 121 page bibliography of early Dutch theological works is naturally strong on Reformed theology, but also includes some valuable philosophical titles, polemical materials and historical tracts.

C0030 Bigane, Jack, and Hagen, Kenneth. Annotated Bibliography of Luther

Studies, 1967-1976. Sixteenth Century Bibliography, no. 9. St. Louis, Mo.: Center for Reformation Research, 1977.

This guide to scholarly publications on Luther and his thought covers both books and articles published in German, English, French and the Scandinavian languages between 1967 and 1976. Entries are arranged alphabetically by author and include full bibliographical citations together with detailed annotations. While not exhaustive, this is an important guide for scholars of Luther and his thought. See also Benzing (C0019).

C0031 Biehl, Vincent Ferrer. John Henry Newman: A Bibliographical Catalogue of His Writings. Charlottesville, Va.: University of Virginia Press for the Bibliographical Society of the University of Virginia, 1978.

Although not covering works by Newman in other languages, this otherwise comprehensive bibliography lists all of Newman's writings and editions thereof. These are arranged in four sections: books, collections, pamphlets and postscripts; articles in periodicals and newspapers; works edited, translated or contributed to by Newman; posthumous publications. The introduction discusses Newman's relationships with his main publishers. There is a general index plus an index of poem titles and first lines. This is a valuable and reasonably complete guide to the writings of a prolific churchman.

C0032 Bleistein, Roman, ed. Bibliographie Karl Rahner: 1969-1974. Freiburg im Breisgau: Herder, 1974.

This 47 page bibliography supplements the earlier compilation by Bleistein and Klinger (C0033) with a chronological listing of Rahner's publications, interviews and Festschriften. There are analytical indexes of all items cited.

C0033 Bleistein, Roman, and Klinger, Elmar, eds. Bibliographie Karl Rahner: 1924-1969. Freiburg im Breisgau: Herder, 1969.

This bibliography contains a listing of 2040 writings by Rahner, covering everything from books and articles to interviews and reviews. Material is arranged chronologically, and there are analytical indexes. This and the supplement (C0032) are indispensible bibliographies for students of Rahner and his theology.

C0034 Bochenski, Innocentius M., ed. Einführungen in das Studium der Philosophie. 23 vols. Bern: A. Francke, 1948-1953.

This collection of twenty-three brief bibliographies by various authors on selected aspects or personalities of philosophy includes in each volume a basic selection of key titles felt to be important for those unfamiliar with the particular topic. The items listed are primarily twentieth century European works, which gives this series particular value as an alternative to the strong North American bias in most of the basic philosophical bibliographies. Individual titles in the series with some relevance to philosophical theology include Bochenski (C0035), Durr (C0062), Jolivet (C0099), Perler (C0143), Schäfer (C0176), Sciacca (C0180, C0181), Steenberghen (C0183) and Wyser (C0206, C0207).

C0035 Bochenski, Innocentius M., and Monteleone, Florenzo. Allgemeine Philosophische Bibliographie. Bibliographische Einführungen in das Studium der

Philosophie, Bd. 1. Bern: A. Francke, 1948.

This brief guide of 42 pages contains approximately 400 entries, the more important having brief annotations. The bibliography is arranged in two main sections, one on more inclusive bibliographies (pp. 12-25) and the other dealing with philosophy and related fields (pp. 26-40). The latter is arranged in seven sections according to type of publication (bibliographies, dictionaries, etc.). For students unfamiliar with the field this is a good starting point for learning about major reference sources, although the dated continental coverage may not appeal greatly to North American users. There is a name index.

C0036 Borchardt, C.F.A., and Vorster, Willem S., eds. South African Theological Bibliography/Suid-Afrikaanse Teologiese Bibliografie. Documenta, 22. Pretoria: University of South Africa, 1980.

This 398 page bibliography seeks to index all Festschriften and periodical literature published in South Africa and dealing with all aspects of theology. A detailed list of periodicals and other works used in the compilation is found at the beginning. The bulk of the work consists of a detailed classification of entries into very specific topics within eight major divisions. Within each topic the 5996 entries are arranged alphabetically by author or chronologically. The detailed table of contents is in English and Afrikaans, and there is an author index. As a guide to modern South African theological writings, both scholarly and popular, this is an indispensible bibliography. However, it does not cover all relevant serials and should be used with this in mind.

C0037 Borchardt, Dietrich Hans. How to Find Out in Philosophy and Psychology. The Commonwealth and International Library, Library and Technical Information Division. Oxford: Pergamon Press, 1968.

This 97 page work is similar to Koren (C0104), but intended more for the layman and undergraduate than the advanced student. Borchardt cites 186 works in nine chapters, and the information on each work is rather superficial. A more suitable bibliographical guide for beginning students is available in De George (C0059). See Higgins (C0086) for another basic work.

C0038 Bourke, Vernon Joseph. Thomistic Bibliography, 1920-1940. St.Louis, Mo.: The Modern Schoolman, 1945.

Issued as a supplement to volume 21 of The Modern Schoolman (C0134), this compilation continues the first edition of Mandonnet (C0122). It lists several thousand books and articles on St. Thomas and on Thomism in various languages, using a classified arrangement with adequate indexes. The entries are not annotated. A list of periodicals and collections consulted is located at the end of the work. See also Wyser's two bibliographies (C0206, C0207), which are much less comprehensive than this important compilation. For a continuation see Miethe (C0133).

C0039 Bowman, Mary Ann, comp. Western Mysticism: A Guide to the Basic Works. Chicago, Ill.: American Library Association, c. 1978.

This 113 page bibliography lists 532 English language books on the history, philosophy, practice and experience of mysticism. It also covers oriental mysticism in Western contexts and mystical expression in literature. The main section of the work lists books by and about the major mystics from 33 A.D. to modern times. There are very brief annotations and detailed indexes of authors/titles and subjects. Bowman omits a number of key works and includes others not suitable for a basic guide of this sort, but it is useful for the beginner. See also Sawyer (C0174).

C0040 Breit, Marquita, comp. and ed. Thomas Merton: A Bibliography. ATLA Bibliography Series, no. 2. Metuchen, N.J.: Scarecrow Press, 1974.

Covering 1957-1973, this bibliography is designed to facilitate research by listing in a single volume the numerous materials published by Merton. The 1801 items include books, articles, pamphlets, poems, translations and critical works on Merton. They are listed in two main divisions: primary and secondary sources, each with subdivisions. An index is provided. This is a useful work for specialist researchers. See also Dell'Isola (C0060).

C0041 Brie, G.A. de, ed. Bibliographia Philosophica, 1934-1945. 2 vols. Brussels: Editiones Spectrum, 1950-1954.

This comprehensive bibliography aims to list all philosophical literature (books, periodicals, book reviews) published in English and other European languages from 1934 to 1945. Volume 1, the Bibliographia Historiae Philosophiae (664 pp.), is arranged chronologically according to the lives of the philosophers of different historical periods and schools. Volume 2, the Bibliographia Philosophiae (798 pp.), lists publications treating philosophy in its doctrinal aspects in classified arrangement. There are 48,178 entries in all. A combined name index for both volumes is provided. Brie is a consolidation and expansion of the "Répertoire Bibliographique" from the Revue Philosophique de Louvain, now continued by the Répertoire Bibliographique de la Philosophie (C0161). See also Bibliographie de la Philosophie (C0024), which provides similar coverage of books in its abstracting service.

C0042 Brown, Marshall G., and Stein, Gordon. Freethought in the United States: A Descriptive Bibliography. Westport, Conn.: Greenwood Press, 1978.

Regarding freethought as a system without dogmatic assumptions and based on rational inquiry, this work is a chronological guide which covers European antecedents of American freethought to twentieth century developments in this field. Each of the four chapters begins with a bibliographical essay devoted to significant books on freethought history, periodicals, organizations and personalities of the particular period. In each case this is followed by a comprehensive bibliography. The appendixes discuss freethought among American ethnic groups and Canadians, major freethought collections in American libraries, theses and dissertations on the history and biography of freethought. Indexes treat authors and persons, titles, subjects.

C0043 Bulletin de Philosophie Médiévale. Vol. 1- . Louvain: Société Internationale pour l'Etude de la Philosophie Médiévale, 1959- ; annual.

Entitled simply Bulletin from 1959 to 1963, this publication is a guide to each year's bibliographical activity in medieval philosophy. Published titles, work in progress and doctoral dissertations (by country) are listed, and there are notes on relevant institutions. Indexes of names of medieval and modern authors are provided. See also Steenberghen (C0183) and Vasoli (C0200).

C0044 Bulletin Signalétique 519: Philosophie. Vol. 1- . Paris: Centre National de la Recherche Scientifique, 1961- ; quarterly.

Formerly the Bulletin Analytique: Philosophie between 1947 and 1955, this exhaustive classified index to periodical literature from around the world includes more than 3000 indicative abstracts in each quarterly issue. The abstracts are in French and present clear summaries of articles. Each issue includes a list of journals abstracted together with some locations, and there are indexes of concepts and names as well as authors. This is an important service which is reasonably up to date and which covers all aspects of philosophy, although there is not a section devoted specifically to the philosophy of religion. It is an excellent complement to the book coverage provided by Bibliographie de la Philosophie (C0024). See Philosophic Abstracts (C0147) for a series covering earlier periodical literature.

Periodicals C0045 Bulletin Thomiste. Vol. 1- . Paris: Editions du Cerf, 1924- ; annual.

Published between 1924 and 1930 as part of the Revue Thomiste (vols. 1-7) and since then as an annual supplement in parts, this bibliographical guide lists and analyzes a wide range of books and articles on St. Thomas, Thomism and Scholasticism. Coverage is international in scope but emphasizes French scholarship. Entries are arranged in a classified sequence, and there are indexes in each volume. Like many other serial bibliographies published in France and Italy this tends to record information which is rather dated. The Bulletin has been superseded by Rassegna di Letteratura Tomistica (C0160), which is equally behind in its coverage. See also Bourke (C0038), Mandonnet (C0122) and The Modern Schoolman (C0134).

C0046 Buzzard, Lynn Robert. Law and Theology: An Annotated Bibliography. Oak Park, Ill.: Christian Legal Society, 1979.

This descriptive bibliography focuses on monographs and periodical articles likely to be of most interest to students concerned with the interaction between law and theology. The entries represent a broad spectrum of religious and legal perspectives and tend to be more general than advanced researchers would find useful. A list of unannotated works relevant to the subject and a subject index complete the work, for which regular supplements are envisaged.

C0047 Calvin Theological Journal. Vol. 1- . Grand Rapids, Mich.: Calvin Theological Seminary, 1966- ; semiannual.

Each year one issue of this serial includes a bibliography of Calviniana covering books, parts of books, articles from periodicals and encyclopedias, theses and dissertations. The bibliography is arranged in seven sections, including bibliographies. Calvin's works, his life and work, theology, socioethical and political views, his influence, Calvinism. While not limited to theology, it is this field which is most adequately represented. Each section is subdivided into narrower topics where necessary, and most of them are then organized alphabetically by author. Full bibliographical details are provided for each item. While the bibliography aims to provide current coverage of publications, it also lists a considerable amount of retrospective material. A cumulation of these annual collections would be most useful; as it now stands, the bibliography should be consulted each year by those interested in Calvin studies, particularly as viewed by Anglo-American scholarship. See also Erichson (C0064), Kempff (C0103) and Niesel (C0139).

C0048 Case, Adelaide Teague. As Modern Writers See Jesus: A Descriptive Bibliography of Books about Jesus. Boston, Mass.: Pilgrim Press, 1927.

This 128 page bibliography provides longer annotations than Ayres (C0009) and covers both popular and scholarly titles. Most entries date from the early 1900s, so there is need for a revision. Indexes of titles and of authors are provided. For students of Christology and of the historical Jesus this is a useful beginning bibliography. See also Tavagnutti (C0185).

C0049 Chevalier, Cyr Ulysse Joseph. Catalogue Critique des Oeuvres de St. Thomas d'Aquin. Romans: Imprimerie R. Sibillat André, 1886.

See also Wyser (C0206) and Eschmann's bibliography in Gilson (C0468).

C0050 Choquette, Diane, comp. The Goddess Walks among Us: Feminist Spirituality in Thought and Action. Berkeley, Calif.: NRM Publications, 1981.

C0051 Church of England. National Assembly. Joint Board of Studies. Current Problems in the Understanding of Personal Responsibility: A Bibliography Selected from the Fields of Psychology, Sociology, Ethics and Theology. London: Church Information Office, 1960.

See also McLean (C0119).

C0052 Clouser, D. Danner, and Zucker, Arthur, comps. Abortion and Euthanasia: An Annotated Bibliography. Philadelphia, Pa.: Society for Health and Human Values, 1974.

Not an exhaustive annotated bibliography, this compilation focuses on ethical issues in particular. It is divided into two sections (abortion and euthanasia), with abortion receiving the more thorough coverage. See also Dollen (C0061) and Guérin (C0078) on abortion and Triche (C0193) on euthanasia.

C0053 Cohn, Margot, and Buber, Rafael. Martin Buber: A Bibliography of His Writings, 1897-1978. Munich: K.G. Saur; Jerusalem: Hebrew University, 1980.

Based on material in the Jewish National and University Library's Martin Buber Archives in Jerusalem, this compilation lists 1500 items published between 1897 and 1978. Arrangement is chronological in Latin, Cyrillic and Hebrew characters; notes and comments are in English except where Hebrew items are concerned. The four indexes (titles, themes, names and languages) greatly assist users and do much to overcome a somewhat awkward arrangement of entries. Cohn is particularly valuable in collecting writings which have appeared in a great variety of publications or which have been published several times. For students of Buber and of Jewish theology this is a very important compilation.

C0054 Cook, Blanche Wiesen; Chatfield, Charles; and Cooper, Sandi, eds. The Garland Library of War and Peace. 328 vols. New York: Garland Publishing Company, 1971.

This collection of 360 titles makes available a wide range of literature on the issue of war and peace, reprinting both significant books and pamphlets from around the world. The titles come from all periods and cover such topics as peace proposals, causes of war, arms control and religious positions on war. There is an author index, which lists a number of peace organizations. See also Hiebel (C0085), Overbeeke (C0141) and War, Peace and Violence (C0205).

C0055 Cottrell, Jack. History of Doctrine: Bibliography for Graduate Studies in the Cincinnati Bible Seminary. Cincinnati, Ohio: Cincinnati Bible Seminary, 1969.

C0056 Cottrell, Jack. Systematic Theology: Bibliography for Graduate Studies in the Cincinnati Bible Seminary. Cincinnati, Ohio: Cincinnati Bible Seminary, 1969.

See also Princeton Theological Seminary (C0156) and Pinnock (C0153).

C0057 [no entry]

C0058 Dagens, Jean. Bibliographie Chronologique de la Littérature de Spiritualité et de Ses Sources, 1501-1610. Paris: Desclée , De Brouwer, 1953 [c. 1952].

This chronologically arranged bibliography of 208 pages does not include annotations. An author index is provided. The period covered is important in the history of Christian spirituality, and Dagens provides a useful guide to the subject and to individual spiritual writers. See also Bibliographia Internationalis Spiritualitatis (C0023) and Metodio da Nembro (C0130).

C0059 De George, Richard T. The Philosopher's Guide to Sources, Research Tools, Professional Life and Related Fields. Lawrence, Kans.: Regents Press of Kansas, 1980.

This 220 page updating of A Guide to Philosophical Bibliography and Research (New York: Appleton-Century-Crofts, 1971) lists some 2000 sources, bibliographies and other reference tools for both beginning and more advanced students. Each section of the compilation is devoted to a specific type of material, including dictionaries, histories, source materials, bibliographies and serials, and there are numerous annotations. The introductory notes to each section are particularly useful for the beginner, as is the discussion of professional life. De George is well indexed by author, subject and title. This is probably the best work of its type which has the advantage of having been revised so recently. Less adequate guides have been prepared by Borchardt (C0037), Koren (C0104) and Totok (C0191).

C0060 Dell'Isola, Frank. Thomas Merton: A Bibliography. Rev. and expanded ed. Serif Series: Bibliographies and Checklists, no. 31. Kent, Ohio: Kent State University Press, 1975.

More substantial than Breit (C0040), this 220 page bibliography covers primary sources very thoroughly but also treats critical works and other studies about or by Merton.

C0061 Dollen, Charles. Abortion in Context: A Select Bibliography. Metuchen, N.J.: Scarecrow Press, 1970.

This bibliography covers English language materials (books and articles) with emphasis on those published between 1967 and 1969. The main theme is cultural and philosophical aspects of abortion, and selection of material is quite wide ranging, including marriage, family, contraception and the sexual revolution. Main entries are both by author and title, and an analytical index and list of sources are provided. See also Clouser (C0052) and Guérin (C0078).

C0062 Dürr, Karl. Der Logische Positivismus. Bibliographische Einführungen in das Studium der Philosophie, Bd. 11. Bern: A. Francke Verlag, 1948.

This brief (24 pp.), highly selective, annotated bibliography lists items under fourteen headings. A name index is included. Although not of direct value for students of philosophical theology, Dürr does list a limited number of items related to natural philosophy and ethics, as well as works by Wittgenstein and others, which have an obvious place in the understanding of this field. Most of the works are in languages other than English.

C0063 Erbacher, Hermann. Bibliographie der Fest- und Gedankschriften für Persönlichkeiten aus Evangelischer Theologie und Kirche 1881-1969. Veroffentlichungen der Arbeitsgemeinschaft für das Archiv- und Bibliothekswesen in der Evangelischen Kirche, 8. Neustadt an der Aisch: Degener, 1971.

See also Laurentius (C0112), Evangelische Theologie (C0065) and Vereinigung Evangelischer Buchhändler (C0201).

C0064 Erichson, Alfred, ed. Bibliographia Calviniana: Catalogus Chronologicus Operum Calvini: Catalogus Systematicus Operum Quae Sunt de Calvino, cum Indice Auctorum Alphabetico. Berlin: C.A. Schwetschke et Filium, 1900. Reprint. Nieuwkoop: B. De Graaf, 1960.

This 161 page bibliography is in two parts: the first lists works by Calvin; the second lists works on Calvin, published prior to 1900. An author index is provided. This is a useful work for those concerned with pre-twentieth century views on Calvin. For more recent material see Niesel's bibliography (C0139). See also Calvin Theological Journal (C0047).

C0065 Evangelische Theologie, 1935-1960: Systematisches Verzeichnis zum 225 Jährigen Bestehen des Verlages. Göttingen: Vandenhoeck und Ruprecht, 1960.

See also Erbacher (C0063), Laurentius (C0112) and Vereinigung Evangelischer Buchhändler (C0201).

C0066 Facelina, Raymond. Liberation and Salvation: International Bibliography, 1972-June 1973, Indexed by Computer/ Libération et Salut: Bibliographie Internationale, 1972-Juin 1973, Etablie par Ordinateur. RIC Supplément, no. 6. Strasbourg: CERDIC Publications, 1973.

Arranged alphabetically by author, this bibliography lists 467 items relevant to liberation theology. It is particularly strong on works stemming from black and Latin American religious thinking, listing books, parts of books and articles from a wide range of sources. Annotations are not provided, but the bibliographical citations are otherwise very complete. See also American Theological Library Association (C0004).

C0067 Facelina, Raymond, and Rwegera, Damien. African Theology: International Bibliography, 1968-June 1977, Indexed by Computer/ Théologie Africaine: Bibliographie Internationale, 1968-Juin 1977, Etablie par Ordinateur. RIC Supplément, no. 30. Strasbourg: CERDIC Publications, 1977.

This computer indexed bibliography is an international and ecumenical listing of 393 books and articles on African theology published from 1968 to 1977. Particular attention is given to materials produced in Africa by Africans, and a careful attempt has been made to avoid judging African theology. Although selective in content, this is an important bibliography in the context of increasing indigenization of Third World theology.

C0068 Fisher, William Harvey. Free at Last: A Bibliography of Martin Luther King, Jr. Metuchen, N.J.: Scarecrow Press, 1977.

With the exception of newspaper articles and foreign language materials this bibliography attempts to include all known works by or about Martin Luther King. The first section lists works by him; the second, works about him; the third, sources in which he is not the primary focus; the fourth, reviews of his writings. Brief, descriptive annotations are provided. There is an author index, which includes editors and compilers.

C0069 Gallagher, Donald, and Gallagher, Idella. The Achievement of Jacques and Raïssa Maritain: A Bibliography, 1906-1961. Garden City, N.Y.: Doubleday and Company, 1962.

This classified bibliography lists books, articles and chapters of books by or about the Maritains, each of whom is treated separately. In addition there are biographical sketches and introductory remarks on their thought. Particular attention is devoted to material in English and French, and there is a full subject index.

C0070 Gerlo, Aloïs, and Vervliet, Hendrik D.L. Bibliographie de l'Humanisme des Anciens Pays-Bas, avec une Répertoire Bibliographique des Humanistes et Poètes Néo-Latins. Instrumenta Humanistica, no. 3. Brussels: Presses Universitaires de Bruxelles, 1972.

This 546 page selective, classified bibliography contains about 5700 items. An index of names is provided. See also Bibliographie Internationale de l'Humanisme et de la Renaissance (C0025).

C0071 Gheddo, Piero. I Libri dell'Impegno: Bibliografia Introducciva alla Problematica del Terzo Mondo. Collana Quaderni Mani Tese, 1. Milan: Tipo-Lito M.E., [1971?].

See also American Theological Library Association (C0004) and Bauer (C0013).

C0072 Gianni, Andrea. Religious Liberty/Liberté Religieuse: International Bibliography, 1918-1978. RIC Supplément, no. 47-49. Strasbourg: CERDIC Publications, 1980.

This unannotated bibliography includes books and articles on religious liberty over the sixty year period covering juridical, sociological and historical (but not specifically theological) aspects. It is organized in eight sections which include general works, history of religious liberty and tolerance, religious liberty and the protection of minorities and works on particular countries. A list of specialist reviews on the subject, a list of relevant centres and institutes and an index of countries are included. The 114 pages of bibliography provide a substantial treatment of the subject. See also Le Leannec (C0114).

C0073 Gill, Athol. A Bibliography of Baptist Writings on Baptism, 1900-1968. Bibliographical Aids, no. 1. Rüschlikon-Zürich: Baptist Theological Seminary, 1969.

This 184 page bibliography is a comprehensive, classified listing of books, articles and reviews from around the world. There is an author index, index of authors reviewed and list of Baptist periodicals.

C0074 Gla, Dietrich. Systematisch Geordnetes Repertorium der Katholisch-Theologischen Litteratur, Welche in Deutschland, Osterreich und der Schweiz seit 1700 bis zur Gegenwart (1900) Erschienen Ist. Mit zahlreichen litterar-historischen und kritischen Bemerkungen und einem Personen- und Sachregister. 2 vols. Paderborn: Friedrich Schöningh, 1895-1904.

Arranged under 142 subject headings, Gla lists both books and articles. The first volume treats the general literature of theology and theological methodology, while the second covers apologetics, the church and related topics. Further volumes proposed for the series were never prepared. See also Korff (C0105).

C0075 Glorieux, Palémon. Répertoire des Maîtres en Théologie de Paris au XIIIe Siècle. 2 vols. Etudes de Philosophie Médiévale, 17-18. Paris: J. Vrin, 1933-1934.

This listing of 425 thirteenth century theologians is arranged according to religious orders, followed by the secular clergy. For each individual Glorieux provides a brief summary of his life, list of works with incipits, manuscripts and printed editions where the works are located and brief bibliography of relevant materials. For students and scholars of medieval French theology and its historical development this remains a helpful guide despite its age and some gaps in coverage.

C0076 Gothie, Daniel L. A Selected Bibliography of Applied Ethics in the Professions, 1950-1970: A Working Sourcebook with Annotations and Indexes. Charlottesville, Va.: University Press of Virginia, 1973.

This 176 page bibliography groups entries under such headings as "Business and management", "Law" and similar professions, with further subdivisions. Author and subject indexes are provided. For a more broadly based bibliography see Matczak (C0128).

C0077 Green, Richard. The Works of John and Charles Wesley: A Bibliography, Containing an Exact Account of All the Publications Issued by the Brothers Wesley, Arranged in Chronological Order, with a List of the Early Editions and Descriptive and Illustrative Notes. London: Methodist Publishing House, 1906.

First published in 1896, this predecessor of Baker (C0010) includes indexes to both titles and annotations. The bibliography purports to list all works by the Wesleys in chronological order. See also Schmidt (C0177).

C0078 Guérin, Daniel. Abortion: International Bibliography, 1973-June 1975, Indexed by Computer/ Avortement: Bibliographie Internationale, 1973-Juin 1975, Etablie par Ordinateur. RIC Supplément, no. 20. Strasbourg: CERDIC Publications, 1975.

This 51 page work contains 665 citations. See also Clouser (C0052) and Dollen (C0061).

C0079 Guerry, Herbert, ed. and comp. A Bibliography of Philosophical Bibliographies. Westport, Conn.: Greenwood Press, 1977.

This 332 page bibliography attempts to list all philosophical bibliographies published in all countries between 1450 and 1974. More than 2300 numbered entries, some of them annotated, are arranged alphabetically by individual philosophers and by subject. There are cross references, and an index is provided. This is one of the best modern philosophical bibliographies and is an excellent source of data on other bibliographies. More annotations would have increased the value of Guerry greatly. Many items not listed in the present undertaking but with marginal value in the field of philosophical theology may be traced in Guerry. See also Jasenas (C0097).

C0080 Gustafson, R.K. "The Literature of Christian Ethics, 1932-1956." M.Th. thesis, Union Theological Seminary in Virginia, 1957.

This valuable survey provides detailed annotations on approximately 200 major works in English on Christian ethics.

C0081 Haeghen, Ferdinand van der. Bibliotheca Erasmiana: Répertoire des Oeuvres d'Erasme. 3 vols. in 1. Ghent: Bibliothèque de l'Université de l'Etat, 1893. Reprint. 3 vols. in 1. Nieuwkoop: B. de Graaf, 1961.

This bibliography includes the works of Erasmus, his editions of other works and books containing abstracts of his works. See also Margolin (C0123-C0125).

C0082 Harvard University. Library. Philosophy and Psychology. 2 vols. Widener Library Shelflist, vols. 42-43. Cambridge, Mass.: Harvard University Press, 1973.

These volumes list nearly 59,000 books, periodicals and pamphlets concerning metaphysics in general, cosmology, ontology, epistemology, logic, esthetics and psychology. Volume 1 contains the classification schedule, the classified listing by call number and a chronological listing. Volume 2 contains the author and title listing. This is an important bibliography for those without recourse to substantial collections of philosophy. For a less complete catalog see University of Southern California (C0194).

C0083 Heintz, Jean Georges. Bibliographie des Sciences Théologiques. Cahiers de la Revue d'Histoire et de Philosophie Religieuses, no. 44. Paris: Presses Universitaires de France, 1972.

C0084 Hiebel, Jean Luc. Armed Forces and Churches/Forces Armées et Eglises: International Bibliography, 1970-1972, Indexed by Computer. RIC Supplément, no. 3. Strasbourg: CERDIC Publications, 1973.

This bibliography contains 401 entries on a topic not treated elsewhere with any degree of thoroughness.

C0085 Hiebel, Jean Luc. War, Peace and Violence: International Bibliography, 1973-1974, Indexed by Computer/Guerre, Paix et Violence: Bibliographie Internationale, 1973-1974, Etablie par Ordinateur. RIC Supplément, no. 18. Strasbourg: CERDIC Publications, 1975.

Containing 626 titles of books and articles on a topic of perennial interest to theologians, this 53 page bibliography covers both ethical and theological issues. It is arranged alphabetically by author and contains items representing all schools and from a variety of traditions. There is a keyword index. RIC Supplément, no. 67-68 (1982) is purported to list an additional 1761 items on this topic published between 1975 and 1981. See also Cook (C0054), Overbeeke (C0141) and War, Peace and Violence (C0205).

C0086 Higgins, Charles L. The Bibliography of Philosophy: A Descriptive Account. University of Michigan, Department of Library Science. Studies, no. 7. Ann Arbor, Mich.: Campus Publishers, 1965.

This 29 page guide provides a brief outline of the most important bibliographical tools in philosophy. It is a useful introduction for the beginning student, as is Borchardt (C0037).

C0087 Hillerbrand, Hans Joachim. Thomas Müntzer: A Bibliography. Sixteenth Century Bibliography, no. 4. St. Louis, Mo.: Center for Reformation Research, 1976.

This detailed bibliography of Thomas Müntzer covers primary and secondary literature published as books or articles in the major Western languages. The contents include sources, general studies, monographs, Thomas Müntzer in literature, addenda and an author index. In each bibliographical section entries are arranged chronologically according to date of publication.

C0088 Hoffmans, Jean. La Philosophie et les Philosophes: Ouvrages Généraux. Brussels: G. Van Oest et Compagnie, 1920. Reprint. Burt Franklin Bibliography and Reference Series, vol. 204. New York: Burt Franklin, 1968.

This 395 page bibliography lists works on philosophical subjects published from about the seventeenth to the early twentieth centuries. Titles are arranged according to the type of publication (dictionaries, histories, bibliographies, etc.) and do not extend to specialized monographs. Works in all Western languages are included. For beginning students with some knowledge of foreign languages this is a useful starting point for locating titles of general philosophical (and marginal theological value). See also Library Association (C0115) for a basic guide to English language materials.

C0089 Hogrebe, Wolfram; Kamp, Rudolf; and König, Gert. Periodica Philosophica: Eine Internationale Bibliographie Philosophischer Zeitschriften von den Anfangen bis zur Gegenwart. Kleine Philosophische Bibliographien aus dem Philosophischen Institut der Universität Düsseldorf, Bd. 2. Düsseldorf: Philosophia-Verlag, 1972.

This international listing of philosophical periodicals by title gives for each the country and place of publication, publisher, frequency, dates of publication with corresponding volume number for each year, changes of title, and special field of interest. Hogrebe is more up to date and more complete than Baumgardt (C0015) or Maison des Sciences de l'Homme (C0120).

C0090 Human Rights/Droits de l'Homme: International Bibliography, 1975-1981. RIC Supplément, no. 69. Strasbourg: CERDIC Publications, 1982.

Although covering only six years of publications, this unannotated bibliography on human rights contains 1186 entries. The first part comprises the listing of books, pamphlets and periodical articles. The second contains a general index (in English) with French, German, Spanish and Italian indexes referring back to the numbered headings of the general index. The material is primarily European in origin but deals with the subject worldwide, including many entries on Eastern Europe and Latin America.

C0091 Ibarra, Eduardo. Holy Spirit/Esprit Saint: International Bibliography, 1972-June 1974, Indexed by Computer. RIC Supplément, no. 14. Strasbourg: CERDIC Publications, 1974.

Containing 637 citations, this unannotated, numbered bibliography groups books and articles alphabetically by author under six headings: holy spirit: doctrine; holy spirit: church; pentecostalism; baptism in the spirit; charisms; and glossalalia. This is a useful tool for those studying recent spiritual manifestations in the Christian churches.

C0092 Institut des Etudes Augustiniennes. Fichier Augustinien/Augustine Bibliography. 4 vols. Boston, Mass.: G.K. Hall and Company, 1972.

The 63,000 entries in this author and subject catalog of nearly 2700 pages are a key source of bibliographical information on publications dealing with St. Augustine and related subjects. The collection is particularly strong on post-1940 materials, which is reflected in this listing. Emphasis is placed on the author catalog, which means that users will find it most convenient to adopt this approach in the first instance. Fichier Augustinien is an indispensible guide for advanced studies. See also Lamirande (C0109) and Nebreda (C0136), as well as Revue des Etudes Augustiniennes (C0165).

C0093 Institut International de Philosophie. Bibliographie de la Philosophie. 10 vols. Paris: Institut International de Philosophie, 1937-1953; semiannual and annual.

This bibliography, international in scope, lists books, periodical articles and doctoral dissertations. It was not published between 1939 and 1945 and has been superseded by Bibliographie de la Philosophie: Bulletin Trimestriel (C0024). The compilation aims at full coverage of books on philosophy and is arranged in sections, including social philosophy, philosophy of religion, reference books of various types. Entries for new works are annotated in the language of the original (English, French, German, Italian and Spanish) or in English or French. Individual issues are not indexed, but each annual volume includes a general index (authors and titles); indexes of publishers, preface writers, translators and authors cited; geographical index of publishers. For the period covered this is an indispensible bibliography with much valuable information on the philosophy of religion and related fields.

C0094 International Committee for Social Science Information and Documentation. International Bibliography of Political Science. Vol. 1- . International Bibliography of the Social Sciences. Chicago, Ill.: Aldine Publishing Company; London: Tavistock Publications, 1952- ; annual.

This useful but not essential guide for those with an interest in religion and politics covers periodicals, books and official publications in a classified sequence with entries arranged alphabetically by author. The classification scheme is outlined in the introduction, and there are both author and subject indexes. The annotations are full, often including English translations and indicative abstracts. There is also a list of the 1800 periodicals consulted, which includes abbreviations and place of publication. Although there are few citations relevant to religion, this is a useful guide to the field when used in conjunction with indexes which focus more particularly on religion. The two year publication delay can be a drawback to those who require immediate information.

C0095 Istituto di Studi Filosofici. Bibliografia Filosofica Italiana, 1850-1900. Rome: ABETE, 1969.

This 644 page bibliography follows the format of the Istituto's earlier work (C0096), covering the period indicated. Books and articles by and about Italian philosophers and published in Italy are arranged alphabetically by author. Since a fair percentage of nineteenth century Italian philosophy has a theological content, this can be a useful source of information for readers of Italian. See also Bibliografia Filosofica Italiana (C0020) and Sciacca (C0181).

C0096 Istituto di Studi Filosofici, et al. Bibliografia Filosofica Italiana del 1900 al 1950. 4 vols. Rome: Edizioni Delfino, 1950-1956.

This is an alphabetical author listing of books and articles by and about Italian philosophers published in Italy between January 1900 and December 1949. Anonymous and pseudonymous works are included in volume 4. A list of Italian periodicals is provided. It also contains Enrico Zampetti's Bibliografia Regionata delle Reviste Filosofiche Italiane del 1900 al 1955 which was published separately (Rome: Università, 1956). The bibliography is continued by the annual Bibliografia Filosofica Italiana (C0020). See Sciacca (C0181) for a basic introduction to Italian philosophical bibliography.

C0097 Jasenas, Michael. A History of the Bibliography of Philosophy. Studien und Materielen zur Geschichte der Philosophie. Hildesheim: G. Olms, 1973.

This moderately detailed bibliographic survey contains six chapters treating Renaissance bibliographies of philosophy, the rise of modern philosophy, bibliographies of German Aufklärung, post-Kantian bibliographies, the twentieth century (including current bibliographies, bibliographies and classification schemes, problems of current bibliographies), tradition and progress. There is a bibliography (pp. 138-149), an appendix dealing with major philosophical works discussed in standard histories and an index of names. Jasenas is particularly suited to the needs of librarians involved with philosophical documentation. See also Guerry (C0079).

C0098 Johnson, Alfred M. A Bibliography of Semiological and Structural Studies of Religion. Bibliographia Tripotamopolitana, no. 11. Pittsburgh, Pa.: Clifford E. Barbour Library, Pittsburgh Theological Seminary, 1979.

Limited to works available in a standard college or seminary library, this bibliography lists items which are even remotely related to the semiological or structuralist nature of religion. The 1893 monographs, essays and articles thus cover rhetorical criticism, semiotic studies, speech and discourse analysis and related fields. Items are arranged alphabetically by author. The final section lists recent works which include bibliographies on the subject and fourteen relevant journals.

C0099 Jolivet, Régis. Kierkegaard. Trans. by Olof Gigon. Bibliographische

Einführungen in das Studium der Philosophie, Bd. 4. Bern: A. Francke, 1948.

The three main sections of this basic 32 page bibliography include introduction (bio-bibliographical chronology, etc.), editions and translations of works, critical works of Kierkegaard arranged by subjects. A name index concludes the listing. For beginners interested in gaining basic insights into Kierkegaard's works this is a useful compilation.

C0100 Jones, Donald G. A Bibliography of Business Ethics, 1971-1975. Charlottesville, Va.: University Press of Virginia, 1977.

Composed primarily of English language materials published in the United States, this bibliography provides selective annotations and an author index. It is a continuation of Gothie (C0076).

C0101 Journal of Church and State. Vol. 1- . Waco, Tex.: J.M. Dawson Studies in Church and State of Baylor University, 1959- ; triannual.

As an adjunct to the main content of this journal, there is a regular bibliographical service entitled "Recent Doctoral Dissertations on Church and State". This is arranged alphabetically by author and provides details on title, university, date and pagination. Limited to American research and concentrating almost exclusively on American topics, this is a very up to date guide which can be a valuable time saver for those interested in this specific topic. See also Le Leannac (C0113), Menendez (C0129) and Metz (C0131).

C0102 Justice Ministries: Resources for Urban Mission. Vol. 1- . Chicago, Ill.: Institute on the Church in Urban-Industrial Society, 1978- ; quarterly.

Intended as an ecumenical service but with a clear North American and "liberal" bias, this journal consists primarily of lengthy abstracts on a very wide range of topics within the broad framework of urban-industrial mission and related ethical concerns. Included are such subjects as energy use, employment, housing, minorities, urban redevelopment. Although limited to materials in English, the types of publications surveyed include books, articles, conference papers, reports and reprints from a wide variety of sources. In most cases photocopies are available from the Institute. For those who require both information and document delivery in a field with a strong action orientation Justice Ministries performs a useful service.

C0103 Kempff, D. A Bibliography of Calviniana, 1959-1974. Wetenskaplike Bydraes van die Potchefstroomse Universiteit vir Christelike Hoër Onderwys. Reeks F: Instituut vir die Bevordering van Calvinisme; F3, Versamelwerke, no. 3. Potchefstroom: Institute for the Advancement of Calvinism; Leiden: E.J. Brill, 1975.

In many respects a sequel to Niesel (C0139), this work concentrates on post-1959 publications. The classified entries are arranged into two main parts ("Calvin" and "Calvinism") and subdivided into sections and subsections. The 4000 entries include books, chapters in books, articles, essays and Festschriften. There is an author index and a detailed table of contents in Afrikaans. In arranging entries by subject Kempff is careful to repeat items under each topic to which they relate. This is a useful guide to a wide range of publications and is particularly helpful in treating parts of books, Festschriften and other difficult materials. Coverage of periodicals is less adequate. See also Erichson (C0064) and <u>Calvin Theological Journal</u> (C0047).

C0104 Koren, Henry J. <u>Research in Philosophy: A Bibliographical Introduction to Philosophy and a Few Suggestions for Dissertations</u>. Pittsburgh, Pa.: Duquesne University Press, 1966.

In 203 pages Koren seeks to introduce graduate students in philosophy to the relevant bibliographical sources and tools. Aside from sections on classification and dissertation topics, the main parts treat philosophical books, periodical literature, encyclopedias and dictionaries, bibliographical tools. More adequate than either Borchardt (C0037) or Totok (C0191), this guide contains indexes of names and subjects. See also De George (C0059).

C0105 Korff, Heinrich, comp. and ed. <u>Bibliotheca Theologiae et Philosophiae Catholicae: Systematisches Verzeichnis von Deutschen Werken der Katholischen Theologie und Philosophie und einer Auswahl der Vorzüglichsten in Lateinischer Sprache Erschienenen Theol. und Philos. Werke des Auslandes von 1870-1897.</u> Munich: C. von Lama, 1897.

See also Gla (C0074) and McLean (C0118).

C0106 Kwiran, Manfred. <u>Index to Literature on Barth, Bonhoeffer and Bultmann.</u> Theologische Zeitschrift, Sonderband 7. Basel: Friedrich Reinhardt Verlag, 1977.

This index of material on Barth, Bonhoeffer and Bultmann provides for each theologian a chronological overview of his life, a list of dissertations on his theology and person, and indexes of persons and subjects important to the theological study of each man. The index of secondary literature is the main part of each section. Books and periodical articles are arranged alphabetically by author, entries are numbered and brief annotations are provided when the title does not indicate subject matter.

C0107 [no entry]

C0108 La Noue, George R., ed. <u>A Bibliography of Doctoral Dissertations Undertaken in American and Canadian Universities (1940-1962) on Religion and Politics.</u> New York: National Council of Churches of Christ in the U.S.A., Department of Religious Liberty, 1963.

This compilation is intended primarily for use by scholars and advanced students working on the relation between religion and politics. It is arranged in five main sections: philosophy and theory, foreign (subdivided by country), American national, American regional (including state and local), American constitutional and legal. Each numbered entry presents only the barest bibliographical detail, and there are no abstracts. Many of the entries are for dissertations begun but not completed at the time of compilation; it would be useful to have an updating which indicated whether these entries have come to fruition and whether similar work continues to be done. With its concentration on the American scene La Noue is of most value to scholars wishing to know retrospectively of doctoral research in religion and politics. See also Metz (C0132).

C0109 Lamirande, Emilien. <u>Un Siècle et Demi d'Etudes sur l'Ecclesiologie de Saint Augustin: Essai Bibliographique.</u> Paris: Etudes Augustiniennes, 1962.

This extract from the Revue des Etudes Augustiniennes of 1962 (C0165) presents in chronological order studies on St. Augustine's doctrine on the nature of the church and on his ecclesiology in a broad sense. The period covered is 1809-1954. The author attempted to verify all bibliographical citations; those not seen are indicated with an asterisk. Some entries are annotated. The bibliography is indexed by author and subject, which facilitates use of the chronological presentation. There is much of interest to theologians and historians as well as to those concerned with missiology, liturgics, pastoral theology, etc. See also Andresen (C0006), Institut des Etudes Augustiniennes (C0092), Nebreda (C0136), Sciacca (C0180) and van Bavel (C0016).

C0110 Lapointe, François H. Ludwig Wittgenstein: A Comprehensive Bibliography. Westport, Conn.: Greenwood Press, 1980.

This 297 page bibliography is the first monograph guide to Wittgenstein's writings to appear in English and the most comprehensive in any language. It includes a listing of his works, noting papers available in microform and lectures in private circulation. Other sections list critical books and reviews, as well as reviews of the books themselves, general philosophical studies which include some analysis of Wittgenstein, a listing of comparative studies arranged according to the other philosophers involved. A subject sequence and an author index conclude the work, which contains more than 2600 entries. This is an invaluable source of information for students of Wittgenstein.

C0111 Latin, Howard A. Privacy: A Selected Bibliography and Topical Index of Social Science Materials. Sponsored by the Earl Warren Legal Institute, University of California. South Hackensack, N.J.: F.B. Rothman, 1976.

In 93 pages this author listing covers books, journal articles, essays, symposia proceedings and similar materials from the social sciences relevant to the study of privacy. There is a topical subject index. While Latin is not particularly thorough in its coverage, there is as yet no alternative bibliography devoted to this important topic.

C0112 Laurentius, Hans, ed. Gesamtverzeichnis der Veröffentlichungen aus den Jahren 1946 bis 1970. Zusammengestellt von Willi Oltmanns. Berlin: Evangelische Verlagsanstalt, 1971.

See also Erbacher (C0065) and Vereinigung Evangelischer Buchhändler (C0201).

C0113 Le Leannec, Bernard. Church and State: International Bibliography, 1973-1977, Indexed by Computer/Eglise et Etat: Bibliographie Internationale, 1973-1977, Etablie par Ordinateur. RIC Supplément, no. 35-38. Strasbourg: CERDIC Publications, 1978.

This important sequel to Metz (C0131) contains 2173 entries of books and articles on church-state relations. It is international and comprehensive in its treatment, providing basic bibliographical details for each item. Arranged alphabetically by author, subject access is through the keyword index. It is understood that RIC Supplément, no. 59-60 contains 1585 entries on the same subject for 1978-1980. See also Journal of Church and State (C0101) and Menendez (C0131).

C0114 Le Leannec, Bernard. Religious Liberty: International Bibliography, 1968-1975, Indexed by Computer/Liberté Religieuse: Bibliographie Internationale, 1968-1975, Etablie par Ordinateur. RIC Supplément, no. 28. Strasbourg: CERDIC Publications, 1976.

This international bibliography on religious liberty contains 507 entries. See also Gianni (C0072).

C0115 Library Association, County Libraries Group. Readers' Guide to Books on Philosophy. 2nd ed. Comp. by Robert John Duckett. Readers' Guides, New Series no. 133. London: Library Association, 1974.

This basic bibliography lists titles under four headings: general philosophy, history of philosophy, philosophical systems, philosophical problems. In each section there are numerous subdivisions listing selected works alphabetically by author. Some entries have minimal abstracts, but most are not annotated. The titles listed provide some guidance for general readers completely unfamiliar with the field, but otherwise this bibliography has little value. For a basic guide to foreign language materials see Hoffmans (C0088).

C0116 Lineback, Richard H., Ethics: A Bibliography. Reference Library of the Humanities Series, vol. 65. New York: Garland Publishing Company, 1976.

See also Baker (C0011).

C0117 McCarthy, Joseph M. Pierre Teilhard de Chardin: A Comprehensive Bibliography. Garland Reference Library of the Humanities, vol. 158. New York: Garland Publishing Company, 1981.

See also Polgár (C0154) and Poulin (C0155).

C0118 McLean, George Francis, ed. An Annotated Bibliography of Philosophy in Catholic Thought, 1900-1964. Philosophy in the 20th Century: Catholic and Christian, vol. 1. New York: Frederick Ungar, 1967.

This bibliography lists some 13,000 books and articles on philosophy in a classified arrangement. Compiled as an aid to university students and general readers, McLean includes objective annotations and references to reviews. The history of philosophy is not treated, but coverage does extend from traditional areas of Roman catholic philosophy to such recent orientations as existentialism, personalism and phenomenology. Works both by and about Catholics are included. McLean is a thorough, basic reference tool. See also Korff (C0105) for a more theologically oriented compilation.

C0119 McLean, George Francis, ed. A Bibliography of Christian Philosophy and Contemporary Issues. Philosophy in the 20th Century: Catholic and Christian, vol. 2. New York: Frederick Ungar, 1967.

This 312 page bibliography lists some 4000 post-1930 books and articles in classified order. It covers a wide range of contemporary issues to which Roman Catholic philosophical literature has been directed. An author index is provided, and an appendix treats dissertations submitted to American Catholic universities. McLean is useful for students and academics in colleges and seminaries. See also Church of England (C0051) and Matczak (C0128).

C0120 Maison des Sciences de l'Homme. Service d'Echange d'Informations Scientifiques. Liste Mondiale des Périodiques Spécialisés, Philosophie/World List of Specialized Periodicals, Philosophy. Maison des Sciences de l'Homme. Service d'Echange d'Informations Scientifiques. Publications. Série C: Catalogues et Inventaires, tome 1. Paris: Mouton, 1967.

This 124 page listing covers 300 periodical titles of a scholarly nature which publish original articles and studies by specialists. Entries are arranged alphabetically by country and provide standard information on address, frequency, scope and cost. The compilation is more up to date than Baumgardt (C0015) but less so than Hogrebe (C0089). Indexes cover subjects, institutions and titles.

C0121 Maltby, Arthur. Religion and Science. Library Association Special Subject List, no. 46. London: Library Association, 1965.

This 36 page bibliography contains 236 numbered entries, some of which have brief annotations. The three sections cover pre-nineteenth century struggle between religion and science, nineteenth century struggle, religion and science in the twentieth century. Twenty-three English language periodicals are cited, and a name index is included. For beginning students interested in the history of the religion and science conflict this is a useful starting point.

C0122 Mandonnet, Pierre Félix, and Destrez, Jean. Bibliographie Thomiste. 2e éd. Rev. et completée par Marie Dominique Chenu. Paris: J. Vrin, 1960.

This bibliography lists 2219 selected books and articles in various languages with an index of authors and a list of periodicals cited. It is an excellent source of information and includes most of the significant pre-1960 studies on Aquinas and his thought. Both the Bulletin Thomiste (C0045) and Bourke (C0028) complement Mandonnet.

C0123 Margolin, Jean Claude. Douze Années de Bibliographie Erasmienne, 1950-1961. De Pétrarque à Descartes, 6. Paris: J. Vrin, 1963.

This brief bibliography lists books and articles on and by Erasmus which appeared in various languages during the period indicated. Detailed abstracts accompany each item. To complement the chronological listing, author and title indexes are provided. Together with Margolin's other bibliographies (C0124, C0125) this is a very thorough guide to Erasmian studies. See also Haeghen (C0081).

C0124 Margolin, Jean Claude. Neuf Années de Bibliographie Erasmienne, 1962-1970. De Pétrarque à Descartes, 31. Paris: J. Vrin; Toronto: University of Toronto Press, 1977.

See Margolin's 1963 bibliography (C0123) for a description of contents.

C0125 Margolin, Jean Claude. Quatorze Années de Bibliographie Erasmienne, 1936-1949. De Pétrarque à Descartes, 21. Paris: J. Vrin, 1969.

See Margolin's 1963 bibliography (C0123) for a description of contents.

C0126 Maria Assunta, ed. The Church in the World: A Bibliography Compiled by Students of the Course on the Church at Saint Mary's College, Notre

Dame, Indiana. Cincinnati, Ohio: CSMC Press, 1963.

C0127 Martínez Gómez, Luis. Bibliografía Filosófica Española e Hispano-americana, 1940-1958. Libros "Pensamiento". Serie: Difusión, no. 1. Barcelona: Juan Flors, 1961.

This is a classified listing of more than 10,000 books and articles previously listed in bibliographic sections of the Spanish philosophical journal Pensamiento. A name index is provided. For Spanish language philosophical works reflecting a conservative Roman Catholic theological viewpoint this listing can provide useful leads.

C0128 Matczak, Sebastian A. Philosophy: A Select, Classified Bibliography of Ethics, Economics, Law, Politics, Sociology. Philosophical Questions Series, no. 3. Louvain: Editions Nauwelaerts, 1970.

Part of a broader study embracing the whole of philosophy within its main branches and affiliated sciences, this volume covers ethics and other topics indicated in the title. Each chapter treats general studies, particular periods, special questions and periodicals. There are some brief annotations, and there is a substantial (pp. 281-308) index. There are about 3800 entries. For a similar work limited to professional ethics see Gothie (C0076). See also Bastide (C0012).

C0129 Menendez, Albert J. Church-State Relations: An Annotated Bibliography. Garland Reference Library of Social Science, vol. 24. New York: Garland Publishing Company, 1976.

This 126 page bibliography, although limited to books published in English since 1875, provides representative coverage of an important topic. Entries are classified under such topics as the Vatican in church-state relations and conversion to and from Catholicism. In addition to the nine main divisions, which are also subdivided, there is brief advice on how to stay informed in this area, as well as an index. See also Journal of Church and State (C0101), Le Leannec (C0113) and Metz (C0131).

C0130 Metodio da Nembro. Quattrocento Scrittori Spirituali. Centro Studi Cappuccini Lombardi Publicazioni, 18. Milan: Centro Studi Cappuccini Lombardi, 1972.

See also Bibliographia Internationalis Spiritualitatis (C0023) and Dagens (C0058).

C0131 Metz, René, and Schlick, Jean. Church and State/ Eglise et Etat: International Bibliography, 1972, Indexed by Computer. RIC Supplément, no. 2. Strasbourg: CERDIC Publications, 1973.

Containing 329 titles of articles and books arranged alphabetically by author, this is a useful guide to a representative range of materials on church and state relations issued during 1972. Substantial additions were made be Le Leannec (C0113). See also Menendez (C0129) and Journal of Church and State (C0101).

C0132 Metz, René, and Schlick, Jean. Politics and Faith: International Bibliography, 1972-June 1973, Indexed by Computer/Politique et Foi: Bibliographie Internationale, 1972-Juin 1973, Etablie par Ordinateur. RIC Supplément, no. 7.

Strasbourg: CERDIC Publications, 1973.

See also La Noue (C0108).

C0133 Miethe, Terry L., and Bourke, Vernon J. Thomistic Bibliography, 1940-1978. Westport, Conn.: Greenwood Press, 1980.

This continuation of Bourke's 1920-1940 bibliography (C0038) lists some 4000 items in more than ten languages. It includes work of historical scholarship on Aquinas as well as works by speculative Thomistic theologians. An initial survey of editions is followed by five subdivided chapters on the life, writings, teachings, doctrines and relations of St. Thomas; books and articles are included in a single sequence. The subject divisions in chapters are rather broad, and the lack of a subject index means that some patience is needed when using the work. There is a personal name index. This is a substantial contribution to Thomistic studies and should be consulted by students and scholars alike.

C0134 The Modern Schoolman: A Quarterly of Philosophy. Vol. 1- . St. Louis, Mo.: St. Louis University, College of Philosophy and Letters and Department of Philosophy, 1925- ; quarterly.

Including bibliographies of philosophical works published in North America, this journal focuses on the scholastic tradition of the Middle Ages and often contains useful bibliographical material in this field. For Thomistic bibliographies see Bourke (C0038), Mandonnet (C0122) and Wyser (C0207).

C0135 Müller, Karl, and Zimmermann, Marie. Mixed Marriage/Mariage Mixte: International Bibliography, 1960-June 1974, Indexed by Computer. RIC Supplément, no. 11. Strasbourg: CERDIC Publications, 1974.

This unannotated, numbered bibliography contains 942 entries on books and articles on mixed marriage published between the dates indicated, arranged alphabetically by author. The material is predominantly European, with German publications receiving especially good coverage. See also Pigault (C0152).

C0136 Nebreda del Cura, Eulogio. Bibliographia Augustiniana, seu Operum Collectio, Quae Divi Augustini Vitam et Doctrinam Quadentenus Exponunt. Rome: Cuore di Maria, 1928. Reprint. Dubuque, Iowa: William C. Brown Reprint Company, 1963.

This bibliography contains approximately 930 entries arranged by subject. The entries are annotated, and introductory remarks accompany each subject heading. There are topical, author and chronological indexes. This is a useful bibliography with helpful annotations. See also Institut des Etudes Augustiniennes (C0092) and Lamirande (C0109), as well as Revue des Etudes Augustiniennes (C0165), Andresen (C0006) and van Bavel (C0016).

C0137 Neue Zeitschrift für Systematische Theologie und Religionsphilosophie. Vol. 1- . Berlin: Walter de Gruyter und Kompagnie, 1959- ; triannual.

Each issue of this journal includes a Zeitschriftenschau, which abstracts a fairly limited number of journal articles in the field of systematic theology. The abstracts are reasonably detailed and clearly written. Emphasis is on continental, particularly German, scholarship of more advanced research and thought.

C0138 New Titles in Bioethics. Vol. 1- . Washington, D.C.: Georgetown University, Kennedy Institute of Ethics, Center of Bioethics Library, 1975- ; monthly.

See also Walters (C0204) and Bibliography of Society, Ethics and the Life Sciences (C0028).

C0139 Niesel, Wilhelm. Calvin-Bibliographie, 1901-1959. Munich: Christian Kaiser Verlag, 1961.

This important aid to the study of Calvinism lists books, parts of books and serial articles published during the period indicated. The four main divisions cover Calvin's life and work in general, specific periods and aspects of his life, influences from and on other countries and theologians, Calvin's theology. Each area is further subdivided as necessary, the theological section containing thirty-five divisions. Coverage of materials is international and wide ranging, providing an excellent guide to writings of the period. There is an author index. See also Erichson (C0064), Kempff (C0103) and Calvin Theological Journal (C0047).

C0140 Oko, Adolph S., comp. The Spinoza Bibliography. Published under the auspices of the Columbia University Libraries. Boston, Mass.: G.K. Hall and Company, 1964.

This is the most comprehensive bibliography available on all phases of Spinoza and his thought. It contains some 7000 entries on Spinoza's works in the original and in translation, as well as references to books, treatises and articles on Spinoza in many languages. The arrangement follows a detailed subject classification, and many entries carry scholarly annotations by Oko. This is an invaluable starting point for students seeking information on Spinoza.

C0141 Overbeeke, Addy P. Van. Gereformeerden over het Oorlogsvraagstuk: Bibliografisch Overzicht van het Denken van Gereformeerden over de Problemen van Oorlog en Vrede in de Jaren 1953-1968. Amsterdam: n.p., 1969.

This bibliography focuses on Dutch Reformed (Gereformeerde Kerken in Nederland) thinking on the issues of war and religion. See also Cook (C0054), Hiebel (C0085) and War, Peace and Violence (C0205).

C0142 Perini, David Aurelio. Bibliographia Augustiniana, cum Notis Biographicus. Scriptores Itali. 4 vols. Florence: Typografia Sordomuti, 1929-1938.

C0143 Perler, Othmar. Patristische Philosophie. Bibliographische Einführungen in das Studium der Philosophie, Bd. 18. Bonn: A. Francke Verlag, 1950.

This 44 page bibliography treats the main texts, histories and studies of the patristic philosophical tradition. The first part deals with general works on historical aspects of the subject, general texts, bibliographies and related materials. The second part contains sections on specific topics and individuals, including Greek and Latin writers of various centuries and regions, the Gnostics and the apostolic fathers. Books and articles are listed, but citations are basic and annotations almost nonexistent. The focus is on European works. A name index is provided.

C0144 The Philosopher's Index: A Retrospective Index to Non-U.S. English Language Publications from 1940. 3 vols. Bowling Green, Ohio: Philosophy Documentation Center, Bowling Green State University, 1978.

This retrospective supplement to the Index (C0146) covers articles in philosophy journals published between 1940 and 1966 and original philosophy books published between 1940 and 1978. Volumes 1 and 2 contain the subject index, while volume 3 contains the author index and full bibliographical citations together with brief abstracts. Together with the retrospective index to U.S. publications (C0145) this covers some 27,000 articles and 11,000 books.

C0145 The Philosopher's Index: A Retrospective Index to U.S. Publications from 1940. 3 vols. Bowling Green, Ohio: Philosophy Documentation Center, Bowling Green State University, 1978.

This retrospective supplement to the Index (C0146) covers articles in philosophy journals published between 1940 and 1966 and original philosophy books published between 1940 and 1976. Volumes 1 and 2 contain the subject index, while volume 3 contains the author index and full bibliographical citations together with brief abstracts. For earlier materials this is an important addition to the ongoing Index and should not be overlooked in information searches. For non-U.S. materials see the companion volume (C0144).

C0146 The Philosopher's Index: An International Index to Philosophical Periodicals. Vol. 1- . Bowling Green, Ohio: Philosophy Documentation Center, Bowling Green State University, 1967- ; quarterly.

Covering about 150 English language journals devoted to philosophy, this quarterly publication and its annual cumulation appear with admirable regularity due to computerized production. Reference is made from author or subject indexes to the full bibliographical entry, many of which include abstracts (beginning with volume 3). The bibliographical data presented at the back of each issue are admirably full and accurate, and many of the abstracts are prepared by the authors themselves in the language of the original article. Selected journals and related interdisciplinary publications in languages other than English are also covered, and a book review index is included. Material from The Philosopher's Index is incorporated into DIALOG, Lockheed Corporation's online computer search service. This allows inquirers to search the entire Index quickly and relatively inexpensively. Probably the most advanced reference tool of its kind, this compilation is of significant value to researchers in a wide range of philosophical and theological fields. See also the retrospective supplements (C0144, C0145). See also Répertoire Bibliographique (C0161).

C0147 Philosophic Abstracts. 16 vols. New York: Philosophical Library, 1939-1954.

This abstract journal provided abstracts in English of philosophical works published in various countries. An index was prepared for the first twelve years' issues, Decennial Index to Philosophical Literature, 1939-1950 (1952); this includes author, title and subject indexes. See also Bulletin Signalétique (C0044).

C0148 <u>Philosophical Books</u>. Vol. 1- . Leicester: Leicester University Press, 1960- ; trimestral.

Each issue of this serial contains descriptive and critical reviews of approximately two dozen works in English. Each review is about 100 words long and deals in depth with the content and value of the title in question. Miscellaneous collections and source books are summarized rather than reviewed. Although somewhat limited and dated in coverage, <u>Philosophical Books</u> is of some use to scholars unable to keep up with the output of philosophical books. See also <u>Philosophischer Literaturanzeiger</u> (C0149).

C0149 <u>Philosophischer Literaturanzeiger</u>. Vol. 1- . Meisenheim: Verlag Anton Hein, 1949- ; quarterly.

This international reviewing journal contains abstracts, notes and reviews of some 100 titles per annum. It is indexed by author, and volume 10 contains a cumulative index for the first ten volumes. Each volume covers more works in more languages than <u>Philosophical Books</u> (C0148), but there is little overlapping between the two; this undertaking is particularly useful for evaluating continental publications.

C0150 <u>Philosophy East and West: A Quarterly of Asian and Comparative Thought</u>. Vol. 1- . Honolulu, Hawaii: University Press of Hawaii, 1951- ; quarterly.

Each issue of this journal includes a section entitled "Current Periodicals", which is a brief listing of relevant articles arranged by periodical title and taken from an international range of serials. Particular attention is given to Eastern philosophies, with rather less focus on religions. Since the entry for a given article lacks both pagination and an abstract, the information provided is very limited. In addition coverage is not particularly comprehensive, so this current awareness service has rather limited value.

C0151 Pigault, Gérard. <u>Development and Justice/Développement et Justice: International Bibliography, 1972-1973, Indexed by Computer</u>. RIC Supplément, no. 12. Strasbourg: CERDIC Publications, 1974.

Containing 512 entries, this bibliography deals with development (particularly in relation to missions and in terms of commitment on the part of churches, communities and individuals), and with justice in the world (and links between justice and ideological and political lines of thought). The unannotated, numbered entries are arranged alphabetically by author in the two sections. Material listed is predominantly European and includes books and articles. See also Bauer (C0013).

C0152 Pigault, Gérard, and Rwegera, Damien. <u>Marriages in Sub-Saharan Africa: International Bibliography, 1945-1975, Indexed by Computer/Mariages en Afrique Sub-Saharienne: Bibliographie Internationale, 1945-1975, Etablie par Ordinateur</u>. RIC Supplément, no. 23-26. Strasbourg: CERDIC Publications, 1975.

This substantial bibliography contains 2212 entries. See also Müller (C0135).

C0153 Pinnock, Clark H. <u>A Selective Bibliography for the Study of Christian Theology</u>. Madison, Wisc.: Theological Students' Fellowship, [1974?].

This 12 page bibliography lists basic works on theology suitable for the beginner. See also Cottrell (C0056) and Princeton Theological Seminary (C0156).

C0154 Polgár, Láslό. Internationale Teilhard Bibliographie, 1955-1965. Freiburg im Breisgau: Alber, 1965.

The classified arrangement in this bibliography is used to present books and articles in all languages and includes translations of works by Teilhard. Contents notes are supplied where appropriate, and the guide is well indexed. See also Poulin (C0155), which covers much of the same ground. See also McCarthy (C0117).

C0155 Poulin, Daniel. Teilhard de Chardin: Essai de Bibliographie, 1955-1966. Québec: Presses de l'Université Laval, 1966.

This bibliography lists 352 books and articles by and about Teilhard, including books and phonograph records in preparation at the time of compilation. Some descriptive annotations and notes on contents are supplied, and an author index is provided. For coverage of almost the same period see Polgár (C0154). See also McCarthy (C0117).

C0156 Princeton Theological Seminary. Library. A Bibliography of Systematic Theology for Theological Students. Princeton Seminary Pamphlets, no. 2. Princeton, N.J.: Princeton Theological Seminary Library, 1949.

Aimed primarily at the beginning student, this 44 page bibliography is arranged alphabetically by author under twenty-five specific subject headings. It is restricted to works in English available at the time of compilation and contains neither index nor annotations. See also Cottrell (C0056) and Pinnock (C0153).

C0157 Rand, Benjamin, comp. Bibliography of Philosophy, Psychology and Cognate Subjects. 2 vols. New York: Macmillan Company, 1905. Reprint. 2 vols. New York: Peter Smith, 1949.

Although dated, this is an important bibliography. The first part lists general works; the second covers history of philosophy, with bibliographies of individual philosophers of all periods arranged alphabetically; the third covers systematic philosophy, logic, esthetics, philosophy of religion, ethics and psychology. Altogether some 70,000 articles and books are listed by Rand. This has also been published as part of Baldwin's dictionary (C0214), but there are no indexes in any of the imprints. See also Harvard University (C0082).

C0158 Rantanen, Liisa. Teologien Henkilöbibliografioita: Valikoima 1900-Luvulla Ilmestynyttä Kirjallisuutta. Theological Author Bibliographies. Helsingin Yliopiston Kirjaston Julkaisuja, no. 36. Helsinki: n.p., 1971.

C0159 Rassegna Bibliografica di Storia della Filosofia Ricavata dalle Riviste. Vol. 1- . Parma: Studium Parmense, 1968- ; annual.

This international listing of periodical articles, notes and reviews on the history of philosophy contains a general section and an alphabetical arrangement by name of the philosopher under consideration. Indexes of authors of articles and reviews and of authors of books reviewed are provided. See also Tobey (C0190) and Totok (C0192).

C0160 <u>Rassegna di Letteratura Tomistica</u>. Vol. 1- . Rome: Herder Editrice e Libreria, 1966- ; annual.

This continuation of <u>Bulletin Thomiste</u> (C0045) covers more than 250 periodicals dealing with St. Thomas, Thomism in general and related topics; the treatment of articles, book reviews and congresses in the bibliography is by broad subject and topical subdivisions. Each issue contains an index of authors and of subjects, as well as a list of contents and of abbreviations. Although <u>Rassegna</u> is not very up to date, covering as it does items published three years earlier as well as providing supplements to earlier volumes, it is the most comprehensive guide to Thomism and should be consulted by all students of scholastic philosophy and theology.

C0161 <u>Répertoire Bibliographique de la Philosophie</u>. Vol. 1- . Louvain-la-Neuve: Université Catholique de Louvain, Editions de l'Institut Supérieur de Philosophie, 1949- ; quarterly.

Essentially an expansion and continuation of the "Répertoire Bibliographique" in <u>Revue Philosophique de Louvain</u>, this serial provides a comprehensive guide to philosophical books and articles issued in various countries. The first issue of each volume is essential reading, as it contains an introduction to the coverage and arrangement of materials, a list of periodicals and their abbreviations, an outline of the subject arrangement used. The next two issues contain only bibliography, and the fourth issue contains the "Répertoire des Comptes Rendus", indexes and a list of contents. The subject listing is subdivided into the various branches of philosophy, including the philosophy of religion, patristics, medieval philosophy, moral philosophy. Publications are usually listed within three years of their appearance, and the citations are full and accurate. As a very comprehensive philosophical bibliography, this work is an important and well arranged reference tool; the introductory and concluding issues to each volume are particularly useful aids in insuring that information is retrieved as completely and as quickly as possible. See also de Brie (C0041) and <u>The Philosopher's Index</u> (C0146).

C0162 <u>Review of Metaphysics: A Philosophical Quarterly</u>. Vol. 1- . Washington, D.C.: Catholic University of America, Philosophy Education Society, 1947- ; quarterly.

Although the <u>Review</u> is not essentially a bibliographical or indexing service, it does list in each issue a number of articles together with abstracts from a representative range of philosophical journals. Subject and author indexes are not provided, which in practice limits the reference value of this publication. Many of the serials treated here are also covered by <u>The Philosopher's Index</u> (C0146).

C0163 <u>Revista Augustiniana de Espiritualidad</u>. Vol. 1- . Logroño: Revista Augustiniana de Espiritualidad, 1960- ; triannual.

Each issue of this journal, which in fact appears less frequently than triannually, includes a "Revista de Revistas de Espiritualidad", which is arranged alphabetically by journal title and provides a list of current contents for each one. Approximately 100 titles dealing with spirituality are covered, with Portuguese and Spanish publications being predominant. This work provides very current coverage of serials not indexed elsewhere so should be regarded as an important guide for students of Christian spirituality. See also <u>Bibliographia Internationalis Spiritualitatis</u> (C0023).

C0164 <u>Revue d'Histoire de la Spiritualité</u>. Vol. 1- . Paris: Revue d'Histoire de la Spiritualité, 1920- ; quarterly.

Originally published as <u>Revue d'Ascétique et de Mystique</u> and suspended temporarily at the end of 1977, this serial includes a "Bulletin d'Histoire de la Spiritualité" in each issue. The bibliographical bulletin consists of literature surveys for medieval, modern and contemporary eras; these cover books and articles on all aspects of Christian spirituality in an historical context. Only publications of francophone countries are listed in the surveys, which are not annotated and have been in existence only since 1977. For the preceding twelve years the <u>Revue</u> carried an annual "Bibliographie Française d'Histoire de la Spiritualité", which listed materials in a classified sequence. In earlier volumes there were also literature surveys on specific topics, but most bibliographical value of a clearly predictable nature will be gained from the current historical surveys. However, the cumulative indexes for 1920-1949, 1950-1960 and 1961-1977 have not yet incorporated these surveys. Without an annual or even biennial index the reference value of this work is limited. Furthermore, coverage is not nearly current enough for up to date bibliographical searching.

C0165 <u>Revue des Etudes Augustiniennes</u>. Vol. 1- . Paris: Institut des Etudes Augustiniennes, 1955- ; quarterly.

This continuation of the <u>Année Théologique Augustinienne</u>, which was published between 1940 and 1954, regularly carries a bibliographical section entitled "Bulletin Augustinien". This provides a listing of journal articles and books on St. Augustine and on aspects of systematic theology and philosophy related to Augustinian thought. Coverage extends to a wide range of materials and focuses on European publications. The treatment could be more up to date and more adequate from a philosophical viewpoint. See also Institut des Etudes Augustiniennes (C0092), Lamirande (C0109) and Nebreda (C0136).

C0166 <u>Revue des Sciences Philosophiques et Théologiques</u>. Vol. 1- . Paris: Librairie Philosophique J. Vrin, 1907- ; quarterly.

At least half of each issue of this journal is devoted to bibliographical information, which is arranged in three sections. The "Bulletin" is devoted to a specific topic in each issue and provides a detailed literature survey plus bibliographical references. The "Recension des Revues" presents lists of contents from recent periodical issues plus brief annotations, and the "Notices Bibliographiques" record short reviews of recent publications. All materials are indexed at the end of each volume, but this is only a partial help in coping with the eclectic content and arrangement. Subject coverage includes items in theology, philosophy, history and related areas of ecclesiastical interest, but there is no clear indication as to the scope of this subject spread. All of the materials are Western European in origin, and descriptions are in French. Approximately 100 serials are surveyed in the "Recension des Revues", but otherwise it is difficult to quantify the coverage provided by this publication. From a bibliographical standpoint it is clearly of mixed value.

C0167 Riedl, John Orth, <u>et al.</u>, comps. <u>A Catalogue of Renaissance Philosophers (1350-1650)</u>. Milwaukee, Wisc.: Marquette University Press, 1940.

This bio-bibliography of Western philosophers from Dante to Nicholas Malebranche provides brief biographical and critical information and a list of written works for each. Arrangement is by schools with an alphabetical author index. It is a convenient reference tool for the period concerned and includes many theologians of importance in Renaissance philosophy.

C0168 Riesenfeld, Harald, and Riesenfeld, Blenda, eds. Repertorium Lexicographicum Graecum: A Catalogue of Indexes and Dictionaries to Greek Authors. Coniectanea Neotestamentica, no. 14. Stockholm: Almqvist and Wiksell, 1954.

This brief (95 pp.) compilation lists the standard reference tools for classical and post-classical Greek authors. See also Voumvlinopoulos (C0202).

C0169 Riss, Paul; Roellig, Harold; and Wahschal, Francis. A Guide to Christian Thought for the Lutheran Scholar: Annotated Bibliography. New York: n.p., 1962.

C0170 Risse, W. Bibliographia Logica: Verzeichnis der Druckschriften zur Logik mit Angabe Ihrer Fundorte. Vol. 1- . Hildesheim: G. Olms Verlagsbuchhandlung, 1965- .

Each volume contains several thousand entries arranged chronologically and includes locations in German and other libraries. The first two volumes treat the subject historically (1472-1800, 1800 to the present); later volumes cover types of materials (Zeitschriftenartikel, Logikhandschriften, etc.). Each volume is indexed by authors and subjects.

C0171 Robertson, D.B. Reinhold Niebuhr's Works: A Bibliography. Boston, Mass.: G.K. Hall and Company, 1979.

This detailed bibliography on Reinhold Niebuhr opens with two chapters which chronologically list the books and collections of shorter writings and sermons by him. Chapter 3, again chronologically arranged, lists Niebuhr's numerous periodical articles. The final chapter deals with writings about Niebuhr and represents a major attempt to list the widest possible range of sources about the man and his thought. There is an index to periodical articles by Niebuhr and writings about him. This is an indispensible guide to a seminal figure in American theology.

C0172 Roszak, Betty, comp. Science and Parascience: A Select Bibliography. Berkeley, Calif.: NRM Publications, 1978.

C0173 Sapsezian, A., comp. Bibliografia Teológica en Língua Portuguêsa. São Paulo: Associação de Seminários Teológicos Evangélicos, 1968.

C0174 Sawyer, Michael E. A Bibliographical Index of Five English Mystics: Richard Rolle, Julian of Norwich, the Author of the Cloud of Unknowing, Walter Hilton, Margery Kempe. Bibliographia Tripotamopolitana, no. 10. Pittsburgh, Pa.: Clifford E. Barbour Library, Pittsburgh Theological Seminary, 1978.

Covering materials published through 1976, this 126 page guide provides separate treatment for each mystic listed in the title. Each part covers editions of the person's works, modern studies, theses, dissertations, journal articles, reference sources. The listings are not limited to English language publications and provide representative coverage of documents by and about historically significant mystical writers. See also Bowman (C0039).

C0175 Schäfer, Odulf. Bibliographia de Vita, Operbus et Doctrina Johannis Duns Scoti, Doctoris Subtilis ac Mariani: Saec. XIX-XX. Rome: Herder, 1955.

This large scale undertaking lists more than 4500 books and articles in all major languages. More important titles include content analysis, but most entries are not annotated. Both name and subject indexes are provided in this important bibliographical guide to Duns Scotus. For an introductory bibliography beginners should consult Schäfer's shorter work (C0176).

C0176 Schäfer, Odulf. Johannes Duns Scotus. Bibliographische Einführungen in das Studium der Philosophie, Bd. 22. Bern: A. Francke, 1953.

This brief (34 pp.) bibliography presents entries in three sections: aids to the study of Duns Scotus, his life and works, his philosophy. There is a name index. For students new to the field this is a suitable introductory bibliography; others will want to consult Schäfer's larger compilation (C0175).

C0177 Schmidt, Martin. John Wesley: A Theological Bibliography. Trans. by Norman P. Goldhawk. 2 vols. London: Epworth Press, [1962]; New York: Abingdon Press, 1963 [c. 1962].

See also Baker (C0010) and Green (C0077).

C0178 Scholars' Choice: Significant Current Theological Literature from Abroad. No. 1- . Richmond, Va.: Union Theological Seminary in Virginia, 1960- ; semiannual.

This selective checklist of foreign books on all aspects of theology is chosen by a panel of some fifty scholars and attempts to indicate the most significant works in each theological discipline. The emphasis is on German Protestant literature, but British, Scandinavian and French titles are also listed; particular emphasis is on systematic, ethical and doctrinal literature. Scholars' Choice is primarily a union listing of titles held by nine libraries but is also useful for bibliographical browsing. There is a cumulative list of titles from the first fifteen issues.

C0179 Schooyans, Michel. Bibliographie Philosophique de Saint Albert le Grand (1931-1960). Separata da Revista da Universidade Catòlica de São Paulo, vol. 21, fascs. 37-38. São Paulo: Universidade Catòlica de São Paulo, 1961.

This bibliography of works on Albertus Magnus concentrates on philosophical studies published between 1931 and 1960.

C0180 Sciacca, Michele Federico. Augustinus. Trans. by Ernst Schneider. Bibliographische Einführungen in das Studium der Philosophie, Bd. 10. Bern: A. Francke, 1948.

Comparable to Wyser's bibliographies of Aquinas (C0206, C0207), this international listing presents approximately 250 entries in fourteen sections. Both books and articles are included, and there is a chart of St. Augustine's writings. An author index is provided. This is a useful but somewhat dated starting point for Augustinian studies. See van Bavel (C0016) for a more recent bibliography, but one which does not cover works by Augustine. Sciacca lists items by and about Augustine. See also Lamirande (C0109).

C0181 Sciacca, Michele Federico. Italienische Philosophie der Gegenwart. Trans. by Ernst Schneider. Bibliographische Einführungen in das Studium der Philosophie, Bd. 7. Bern: A. Francke, 1948.

In 36 pages Sciacca lists bibliographical aids, periodicals and works on individual philosophical systems. There are a few annotations, although the work is primarily a list of titles intended to help in locating rather than evaluating individual items. There is an author index. For an ongoing guide to Italian philosophy see Bibliografia Filosofica Italiana (C0020).

C0182 Sell, Irene L. Dying and Death: An Annotated Bibliography. New York: Tiresias Press, 1977.

The 506 annotated items in this selective bibliography are arranged in three sections: articles (328 items), books (71 titles), audio-visual aids (53 items). In each section materials are listed by author, and there are author and title indexes. Many items useful for the counselor or pastor are listed.

C0183 Steenberghen, Fernand van. Philosophie des Mittelalters. Trans. by Ernst Schneider. Bibliographische Einführungen in das Studium der Philosophie, Bd. 17. Bern: A. Francke, 1950.

This 52 page bibliography is arranged in four sections and contains entries for works by or on various medieval philosophers and movements. There are only occasional annotations; a name index is provided. See Vasoli (C0200) for a more substantial guide to the same period. See also Bulletin de Philosophie Médiévale (C0043).

C0184 Stegmüller, Friedrich. Repertorium Commentariorum in Sententias Petri Lombardi. 2 vols. Würzburg: F. Schöningh, 1947.

This is a comprehensive list of medieval doctoral theses which took the form of commentaries on the Sentences of Peter Lombard. Authors are listed alphabetically, with the incipit and explicit for each author's commentary on each of the four books of the Sentences, and editions and manuscripts are indicated. Anonymous commentaries are listed by libraries where they can be found. Indexes of first words, authors, scribes and professors are provided in volume 2. For additions and corrections see Victorin Doucet's 128 page supplement, Commentaires sur les Sentences (Florence: Typ. Colegii S. Bonaventurae, 1954).

C0185 Tavagnutti, Mario Sigismondo. Christologische Bibliographie: Verzeichniss der über den Göttlichen Heiland Jesus Christus von 1837 bis 1890 Erschienenen Werke, Predigten und Andachtsbücher mit Besonderer Berucksichtigung der Herz-Jesu-Verehrung. Systematisch nach Materien Geordnet und mit Einem Autorem-Register. Katholisch-Theologische Bücherkunde der Letzten Fünfzig Jahre, Bd. 2. Vienna: Drescher und Compagnie, 1891.

See also Ayres (C0009) and Case (C0048).

C0186 Tavagnutti, Mario Sigismondo. Hagiographia: Verzeichniss der über Jesus Christus, die Jungfrau Maria, Heilige, Selige, Päpste und Sonstige Ehrwürdige und Fromme Personen von 1830 bis 1890 Erschienenen Lebensbeschreibungen, Systematisch nach Materien Geordnet und mit Einem Stich- und Schlagwörter sowie Einem Autoren-Index. 2. Aufl. Katholisch-Theologische Bücherkunde der Letzten Fünfzig Jahre, Bd. 1. Vienna: Drescher und Compagnie, 1891.

C0187 Tavagnutti, Mario Sigismondo. Mariologische Bibliographie: Verzeichniss der Wichtigsten über die Allersel. Jungfrau und Gottesmutter Maria von 1837 bis 1890 Erschienenen Werke, Predigten und Andachtsbücher mit Besonderer Berücksichtigung der Rosenkranz-Verehrung. Systematisch nach Materien Geordnet und mit einem Autoren-Register. Katholisch-Theologische Bücherkunde der Letzten Fünfzig Jahre, Bd. 3. Vienna: Drescher und Compagnie, 1891.

See also Baumeister (C0014) and Bibliografía Mariana (C0021).

C0188 Teologia. Vol. 1- . Milan: Facolta Teologica dell'Italia Settentrionale, 1976- .

This journal includes a specialized bibliography on methodological issues in theology in every fourth issue. References are taken from about 130 theological journals, especially European publications. This is an important source of information on this area.

C0189 [no entry]

C0190 Tobey, Jeremy L. The History of Ideas: A Bibliographical Introduction. 4 vols. Santa Barbara, Calif.: Clio Books, 1975-1979.

This guide to the development of philosophy, religion, esthetics and scientific thought from classical antiquity is both a useful introductory text and an authoritative bibliographical reference work. For a compilation less wide ranging and more closely tied to philosophy see De George (C0059), which has a similar introductory focus in its bibliographical coverage. See also Rassegna Bibliografica (C0159) and Totok (C0192).

C0191 Totok, Wilhelm. Bibliographischer Wegenweiser der Philosophischen Literatur. Frankfurt am Main: V. Klostermann, 1959.

Similar to Borchardt (C0037) and Koren (C0104), this 35 page outline guide to philosophical literature is arranged in eight sections (including abstracts, dictionaries, bibliographies, etc.). There are very few entries, but all are analyzed and annotated briefly. For a more suitable work in English see De George (C0059).

C0192 Totok, Wilhelm. Handbuch der Geschichte der Philosophie. 3 vols. Frankfurt am Main: V. Klostermann, 1964- .

Covering material published since 1920, this is a comprehensive international bibliography arranged by topics and subtopics. Volume 1 covers ancient, Indian, Chinese and Greco-Roman philosophy; volume 2, Middle Ages; and volume 3, modern times. In each volume the topics covered include philosophy of religion and ethics; there are no annotations, but substantial introductions adequately survey each main period. There are author and subject indexes for each volume. Totok is a thorough and well researched compendium containing many useful entries relevant to philosophical theology. See also Varet (C0199), Tobey (C0190) and Rassegna Bibliografica (C0159).

C0193 Triche, Charles W., and Tirche, Diane Samson. The Euthanasia Controversy, 1812-1974: A Bibliography with Select Annotations. Troy, N.Y.: Whitston Publishing Corporation, 1975.

This list of approximately 1350 titles includes books, periodical articles and newspaper reports. Books are arranged by author; periodical articles, by subject. There is an author index to this guide which deals with a topic of special significance to the church. See also Walters (C0204), which covers this area on a regular basis. See also Clouser (C0052).

C0194 University of Southern California. Hoose Library of Philosophy. Catalog of the Hoose Library of Philosophy. 6 vols. Boston, Mass.: G.K. Hall and Company, 1968.

This catalog of an important philosophical library contains about 100,000 entries for 37,000 volumes. There is a single alphabetical sequence for authors, titles and subjects. As a bibliography this collection is less complete and not as up to date as the Harvard University catalog (C0082), but it is a widely representative guide to works on the philosophy of religion, metaphysics, ethics, the German schools and related areas of interest to theologians.

C0195 Vajda, Georges. Judische Philosophie. Bibliographische Einführungen in das Studium der Philosophie, Bd. 19. Bern: A. Francke, 1950.

This 40 page guide consists of five sections which deal first with general study aids and then with specific topics (rabbinical thought, Middle Ages, Jewish mysticism, Jewish philosophy in modern times). A name index is provided.

C0196 Valeske, Ulrich. Votum Ecclesiae. Munich: Claudius Verlag, 1962.

Based on a thesis presented to the University of Göttingen, this study includes a substantial interconfessional bibliography on ecclesiology.

C0197 Van Vlack, Philip W.; Sewrey, Charles L.; and Nielsen, Charles E. Economic Ethics Bibliography: Ethical Studies. Brookings, S. Dak.: Agricultural Experiment Station, South Dakota State University, 1964.

C0198 [no entry]

C0199 Varet, Gilbert. Manuel de Bibliographie Philosophique. 2 vols. Logos: Introduction aux Etudes Philosophiques, tome 9. Paris: Presses Universitaires de France, 1956.

Listing both books and journal articles in various languages, this comprehensive annotated bibliography follows a systematic arrangement by period. Volume 1 covers ancient and Christian philosophy up to Kant; volume 2 treats modern philosophical schools and contains a detailed index (pp. 923-1045). The first chapter in volume 1 deals with encyclopedic reference works. Varet is very useful as a bibliography of Christian philosophy and of its influence on modern philosophers. See also Totok (C0191).

C0200 Vasoli, Cesare. Il Pensiero Medievale: Orientamenti Bibliografici. Piccolo Biblioteca Filosofica Laterza, 70. Bari: Laterza, 1971.

This 301 page bibliographic guide cites both editions and critical studies of major and minor medieval writers. For a more basic bibliographical guide to the medieval period see Steenberghen (C0183). See also Bulletin de Philosophie Médiévale (C0043).

C0201 Vereinigung Evangelischer Buchhändler. Das Evangelische Schrifttum: Ein Systematisches Verzeichnis. Gesamtausg. Stuttgart: Verbandssortiment Evangelischer Buchhändler, 1969.

This 519 page catalog/bibliography covers Protestant theology. See also Erbacher (C0063), Evangelische Theologie (C0065) and Laurentius (C0112).

C0202 Voumvlinopoulos, Georges E. Bibliographie Critique de la Philosophie Grecque depuis la Chute de Constantinople à Nos Jours, 1453-1953. Athens: Imprimerie de l'Institut Français d'Athènes, 1966.

This 236 page bibliography includes writings by and about Greek philosophers since the mid-fifteenth century. See also Riesenfeld (C0168).

C0203 Wainwright, William J. Philosophy of Religion: An Annotated Bibliography of Twentieth Century Writings in English. Garland Reference Library of the Humanities, vol. 3. New York: Garland Publishing Company, 1978.

Aimed primarily at advanced students and scholars interested in philosophical problems, this 776 page bibliography lists more than 1100 monographs and articles in eight sections: divine attributes, arguments for the existence of God, problem of evil, mysticism and religious experience, miracles, faith and revelation, religious language, the justification of religious belief. The annotations are clear and descriptive, providing adequate details of content and argument. There is an index of authors, editors and reviewers. Wainwright is admirably suited for students with some background in the philosophy of religion and who are interested in more advanced work on the topics indicated.

C0204 Walters, LeRoy. Bibliography of Bioethics. Vol. 1- . Detroit, Mich.: Gale Research Company, 1975- ; annual.

Issued by the Center for Bioethics of the Kennedy Institute, Georgetown University, this important subject bibliography lists books, journal and newspaper articles, essays in books, legal materials, films and audio cassettes. It is concerned with the ethical aspects of health care, contraception, abortion, population, reproductive technologies, genetic intervention, mental health therapies, human experimentation and organ transplants, death and dying. It is confined to English language materials and is becoming more up to date with each volume. The aim is to be comprehensive for all English language materials, whether out of print or currently available. Index aids to the compilation include a thesaurus, title and author indexes and a list of periodicals consulted. For academics, counselors, clergy and medical practitioners this is a most important bibliographical guide to all aspects of bioethics. See also Bibliography of Society, Ethics and the Life Sciences (C0028) and New Titles in Bioethics (C0138).

C0205 War, Peace and Violence/Guerre, Paix et Violence: International Bibliography, 1975-1981. RIC Supplément, no. 67-68. Strasbourg: CERDIC Publications, 1982.

Although covering only six years of publications, this unannotated bibliography contains 1761 entries. The first part comprises the listing of books, pamphlets and periodical articles. The second contains a general index (in English) with French, German, Spanish and Italian indexes referring back to the numbered headings of the general index. The material is primarily European. See also Cook (C0054) and Hiebel (C0085).

C0206 Wyser, Paul. Thomas von Aquin. Bibliographische Einführungen in das Studium der Philosophie, Bd. 13/14. Bern: A. Francke, 1950.

Arranged in three main sections (aids and collected works, life and work, philosophy), this bibliography employs analytical subject headings to cover both works by and about Aquinas. There are no annotations, but an author index is provided in Wyser's Der Thomismus (C0207). The 900 entries in this work are only representative of the field but provide a good starting point for Aquinas research. See also Bourke (C0038).

C0207 Wyser, Paul. Der Thomismus. Bibliographische Einführungen in das Studium der Philosophie, Bd. 15/16. Bern: A. Francke, 1951.

This 120 page continuation of Thomas von Aquin (C0206) contains two sections (history of Thomism, systematics of Thomism), which contain approximately 1500 entries devoted to books and articles on Thomistic philosophy. The author index (pp. 103-119) covers both this work and the earlier one. See also Bourke (C0038).

SYSTEMATIC/DOCTRINAL THEOLOGY AND ETHICS: DICTIONARIES

C0208 Abbagnano, Nicola. Dizionario di Filosofia. Turin: Unione Tipografico-Editrice Torinese, 1961.

The 2000 entries in this Italian dictionary explain the various applications of terms succinctly and clearly. Some articles are fairly lengthy and provide the depth of detail more often associated with encyclopedic works. Particularly helpful for readers wishing to translate terms is the listing of equivalent words in French, English and German together with Greek or Latin origins where applicable. See also Enciclopedia Filosofica (C0238).

C0209 Alès, Adhémar d', ed.-in-chief. Dictionnaire Apologétique de la Foi Catholique, Contenant les Preuves de la Verité de la Religion et les Reponses aux Objections Tirées des Sciences Humaines. 4e éd. 4 vols. Paris: G. Beauchesne et Ses Fils, 1925-1929.

Containing long, signed articles, this work attempts to reconcile faith and science and to present answers to objections raised against the teachings of the Church. Bibliographies accompany the articles. This product of the Modernist controversy is now somewhat dated. See also Loth (C0263).

C0210 Algermissen, Konrad, et al., eds. Lexikon der Mariekunde. Vol. 1- . Regensburg: Friedrich Pustet Verlag, 1957- .

Focusing on the Blessed Virgin Mary, this work contains articles on the theological, artistic, moral and historical aspects of Mariology and also includes much useful data on many ideas associated with her veneration. Bibliographies following each article are representative of the more substantive Western studies in this field. The firm of Harrassowitz has assumed responsibility for publishing the remaining volumes, but nothing has appeared since the fifth fascicle in 1961. See also Attwater (C0213), Enciclopedia Mariana (C0239) and Roschini (C0287).

C0211 Ancilli, Ermanno, ed.-in-chief. Dizionario Enciclopedico di Spiritualità. 2 vols. Rome: Studium, 1975.

This scholarly and detailed dictionary of spirituality covers various schools of thought, biographies of prominent spiritual leaders and practitioners, key concepts and trends in the spiritual life. Most articles include bibliographies of works in Italian, English and other languages. Less detailed than Viller (C0301), this is suitable for a wide range of users able to read Italian.

C0212 Apel, Max, and Ludz, Peter. Philosophisches Wörterbuch. 6. Aufl. Sammlung Göschen, 2202. Berlin: Walter de Gruyter und Kompagnie, 1976.

See also Brugger (C0226), Eisler (C0236) and Hoffmeister (C0255).

C0213 Attwater, Donald, comp. A Dictionary of Mary. New York: P.J. Kenedy, 1956; London: Longmans, Green and Company, 1957.

This 312 page work aims to provide Catholic and non-Catholic readers with a quick reference in nontechnical language to aspects of the life, significance and veneration of Mary. Organizations, shrines, devotions and legends are included, as well as doctrines. There is no bibliography. See also Algermissen (C0210), Enciclopedia Mariana (C0239) and Roschini (C0287).

C0214 Baldwin, James Mark, ed. Dictionary of Philosophy and Psychology, Including Many of the Principal Conceptions of Ethics, Logic, Aesthetics, Philosophy of Religion, Mental Pathology, Anthropology, Biology, Neurology, Physiology, Economics, Political and Social Philosophy, Philology, Physical Science and Education, and Giving a Terminology in English, French, German and Italian. New ed. with corrections. 3 vols. in 4. New York: Macmillan Company, 1925. Reprint. 3 vols. in 4. Gloucester, Mass.: Peter Smith, 1949-1957.

As the first encyclopedia on its subject in English, Baldwin is now dated but retains value as a concise reference work on a variety of philosophical topics. Coverage is not exhaustive but representative of the field as perceived in the latter years of the nineteenth century. The signed articles include many bibliographies, and brief biographies of deceased figures are provided. French, German and Italian equivalents of English terms used in entries are included, and there are indexes of foreign terms used in the articles (Greek and Latin among them). The first two volumes contain the dictionary and indexes; volume 3 contains Rand's bibliography (C0157). See also Edwards (C0235), which is a much more up to date encyclopedia devoted specifically to philosophy.

C0215 Bardy, Gustave. Enciclopedia Cristologica. Multiformis Sapientia. Alba: Ediziones Paoline, 1960.

This scholarly and relatively detailed volume of 1245 pages includes both the dogmatic aspects of Christology and the influence of Christ on various aspects of society, thought and the arts. Material is organized in a classified arrangement, and each section includes numerous lengthy bibliographies. Originally published in 1935 in a French edition, this Italian version includes much revised material and is a useful reference volume for those seeking information on Christology as perceived in the pre-Vatican II Roman Catholic tradition. See also Bardy (C0216).

C0216 Bardy, Gustave, and Tricot, A., eds. Le Christ: Encyclopédie Populaire des Connaissances Christologiques. Avec le concours de René Aigrain. Paris: Bloud et Gay, 1932.

See also Bardy (C0215).

C0217 Bigler, Vernon. Key Words in Christian Thinking: A Guide to Theological Terms and Ideas. New York: Association Press, 1966.

See also Lord (C0262).

C0218 Blaise, Albert. Dictionnaire Latin Français des Auteurs Chrétiennes. Revu spécialment pour le vocabulaire théologique par Henri Chirat. Strasbourg: Le Latin Chrétien; Turnhout: Brepols, 1954.

This 913 page dictionary contains non-classical words and meanings used from the first to the seventh centuries. It is particularly concerned with theological terms. The definitions are illustrated by quotations, with references to the sources.

C0219 Blanc, Elie. Dictionnaire de Philosophie Ancienne, Moderne et Contemporaine, Contenant Environ 4000 Articles Disposé par Ordre Alphabétique, dans le Cours de l'Ouvrage, Complété par Deux Tables Méthodiques. Paris: P. Lethielleux, 1909. Reprint. New York: Burt Franklin, 1972.

Including the three supplements to the 1906 edition, this dictionary contains brief definitions of abour 4000 terms, schools of thought and prominent personalities in the field of philosophy. It is often recommended as a classic standard dictionary but has only marginal relevance to philosophical theology. Blanc has some use as a guide to philosophy in general but should not be used in place of the other continental dictionaries which are more up to date. See also Foulquié (C0245), Julia (C0257) and Lalande (C0261).

C0220 Bouyer, Louis. Dictionary of Theology. Trans. by Charles Underhill Quinn. New York: Desclée Company, 1965.

First published in French as Dictionnaire Théologique (2e éd. Tournai: Desclée, 1963), this English translation contains articles of varying length which attempt to provide concise definitions of theological terms as well as a precise synthesis of Catholic doctrine. The approach is clear and nontechnical, and the definitions reflect a moderate theological position on most issues. An appendix lists articles topically as in the sequence of doctrines presented in the Apostles' Creed. Somewhat more traditional than Rahner (C0279), this is nonetheless a useful Catholic compendium.

C0221 Bradley, John P., ed. Encyclopedic Dictionary of Christian Doctrine. 3 vols. The Catholic Layman's Library, vols. 7-9. Gastonia, N.C.: Good Will Publishers, 1970.

See also Carbone (C0228).

C0222 [no entry]

C0223 Brewer, Ebenezer Cobham. <u>A Dictionary of Miracles, Imitative, Realistic</u> <u>and Dogmatic.</u> Philadelphia, Pa.: J.B. Lippincott Company, 1885. Reprint. Detroit, Mich.: Gale Research Company, 1966.

> Regarded as the definitive work in its field for some time, this volume aims to provide impartial information on a particular mode of religious thought, without entering into questions of the historical truth of the miracles recorded. Three parts examine miracles of saints in imitation of scripture miracles; realistic miracles, founded on a literal interpretation of scripture; and miracles to prove Roman Catholic dogmas. A full descriptive table of contents and an index make reference easy. Preliminary matter includes details of ecclesiastical symbols, saints of the nineteenth century, dates of ecclesiastical customs, etc. A brief list of sources is included.

C0224 Brink, H., ed.-in-chief. <u>Theologisch Woordenboek.</u> Assistant eds.: G. Kreiling, A.H. Maltha and J.H. Walgrave. 3 vols. Roermond, J.J. Romen, 1952-1958.

C0225 Brugger, Walter, ed. <u>Philosophical Dictionary.</u> Trans. and ed. by Kenneth Baker. Spokane, Wash.: Gonzaga University Press, 1972.

> This English translation and adaptation of Brugger (C0226) covers all of Western philosophy with more than 400 articles explaining key philosoph- ical concepts. The bibliographies have been omitted, but new articles dealing with contemporary Anglo-American philosophical concerns have replaced some entries of more interest to continental, particularly German, users.

C0226 Brugger, Walter, ed. <u>Philosophisches Wörterbuch.</u> 13. Aufl. Philosophie in Einzeldarstellungen, 1. Erganzungband. Freiburg im Breisgau: Herder, 1967.

> This philosophical dictionary includes an outline of the history of philosophy from ancient times to the present. The main part of the work explains terms and concepts briefly and clearly; bibliographies offer suggestions for further reading. For those with knowledge of German this is a most acceptable basic dictionary; English readers should consult the revision and translation (C0225). See also Apel (C0212), Eisler (C0236) and Hoff- meister (C0255).

C0227 Burnaby, John. <u>Christian Words and Christian Meanings.</u> New York: Harper and Brothers; London: Hodder and Stoughton, 1955.

> The chapters in this 160 page book, originally delivered as lectures, treat eight pairs of basic words in the Christian vocabulary (faith and knowledge, love and incarnation, sin and judgment, etc.). The origins of the words in secular use, their development by biblical writers and their modern use are discussed in a brief and illuminating manner. This is a valuable work for the student.

C0228 Carbone, Carlo, and Roncuzzi, Alfredo. <u>Piccolo Dizionario della Dottrina</u> <u>Cattolica.</u> Rome: C. Colombo, [1953].

> See also Bradley (C0221).

C0229 <u>A Catholic Dictionary of Theology: A Work Projected with the Approval</u> <u>of the Catholic Hierarchy of England and Wales.</u> Vol. 1- . London: Thomas Nelson and Sons, 1962- .

Projected in four or five volumes and intended to serve as a companion to A Catholic Commentary on Holy Scripture, this excellent theological encyclopedia concentrates on doctrine as presented in scripture and tradition, thereby largely ignoring such ancillary areas as canon law. Material is arranged alphabetically by subject and exhibits a strong pastoral and practical emphasis. Most articles include references to sources and bibliography. Although only one volume appeared before Vatican II, there is some evidence that more recent theological developments have been ignored by the contributors. Overall, however, this is an admirable work for the student with some theological training and fills a gap between basic and advanced guides. See also Rahner (C0280).

C0230 Crooks, George Richard, and Hurst, John Fletcher. Theological Encyclopaedia and Methodology; on the Basis of Hagenbach. New York: Phillips and Hunt; Cincinnati, Ohio: Walden and Stowe, 1884.

Based on Karl R. Hagenbach's German work, this volume aims to outline the importance, nature and history of the four divisions of theological study - exegetical, historical, systematic and practical theology. In addition, the first part contains a general encyclopedia on theology in relation to other disciplines, leading tendencies in theological thought since the early church, and related aspects. A detailed table of contents, a bibliography of English and American literature and a list of histories of Christian churches in the United States are included in this useful handbook for the theological student. See also Harrison (C0250).

C0231 Cuénot, Claude. Nouveau Lexique Teilhard de Chardin. Etudes et Recherches sur Teilhard de Chardin. Paris: Editions de Seuil, 1968.

This lexicon supplies definitions and examples from the writings of Teilhard of terms peculiar to his philosophical system. Scholars have found Cuénot particularly free from interpolations drawn from related systems, which means that this reference work follows Teilhard more closely than other studies. The definitions are as clear as can be expected and do much to illuminate a unique philosophical system. Much less detailed is Hubert Cuyper's Vocabulaire Teilhard de Chardin: Lexique, Citations, Références (Carnets Teilhard, 5-6. Paris: Editions Universitaires, 1963), which defines only major terms.

C0232 Davidson, Gustav. A Dictionary of Angels, Including the Fallen Angels. New York: Free Press; London: Collier-Macmillan, 1967.

Including a substantial bibliography (pp. 363-387), this 387 page work comprises the dictionary proper (pp. 1-334) of about 7000 brief entries, followed by thirty-three appendixes. There are also many illustrations. The brief definitions include references to other sources. This is a thorough handbook on the subject.

C0233 Deferrari, Roy Joseph, and Barry, M. Inviolata. A Lexicon of St. Thomas Aquinas Based on the "Summa Theologica" and Selected Passages of His Other Works. 5 vols. Washington, D.C.: Catholic University of America Press, 1948-1953.

This monumental undertaking is a complete dictionary/concordance of all works used in the Summa and selected other works by St. Thomas, giving the English meanings together with appropriate Latin quotations and indications of exact sources. The Latin entry word is followed by the genitive form, part of speech, meanings and references. An abbreviated edition (1115 pp.) is available under the title, A Latin-English Dictionary of St. Thomas Aquinas Based on the "Summa Theologica" and Selected Passages of His Other Works (Boston, Mass.: St. Paul Editions, 1960). The unabridged volumes are essential guides for advanced students of Aquinas and his thought. See Stockhammer (C0295) for a limited concordance to a wider range of writings by St. Thomas; Schütz (C0292) falls between Defarrari and Stockhammer.

C0234 Duncan, Archibald Sutherland; Dunstan, Gordon Reginald; and Welbourn, Richard Burkewood, eds. Dictionary of Medical Ethics. Executive ed.: J.A. Rivers. London: Darton, Longman and Todd, 1977.

C0235 Edwards, Paul, ed.-in-chief. The Encyclopedia of Philosophy. 8 vols. New York: Macmillan Company; London: Collier-Macmillan, 1967. Reprint. 8 vols. in 4. New York: Macmillan Company, 1973.

Broader in scope than Baldwin (C0214), this useful reference work covers not only Eastern and Western philosophy but also main points of contact with other disciplines, including concepts of moral reformers and religious thinkers. The nearly 1500 signed articles, contributed by an international group of some 500 scholars, are long, full and include bibliographies. They are arranged alphabetically by subject. There is an extensive analytical index which should be consulted. This encyclopedia is recommended for its valuable secular views on the contribution of theology to philosophy. For a philosophical encyclopedia of a somewhat less "secular" nature see Enciclopedia Filosofica (C0238).

C0236 Eisler, Rudolf. Handwörterbuch der Philosophie. 2. Aufl. Hrsg. von Richard Müller-Frienfels. Berlin: E.S. Mittler und Sohn, 1922. Reprint. Mikrobuch, nr. 1. Düsseldorf: Microbuch- und Film Gesellschaft, 1949.

First published in 1913, this condensation of Eisler's three volume work (C0237) is useful where short and concise articles are required. Bibliographies are included for further reference. In general this is a suitable dictionary for basic inquiries. For similar German language dictionaries see Apel (C0212), Brugger (C0226) and Hoffmeister (C0255) among others.

C0237 Eisler, Rudolf. Wörterbuch der Philosophischen Begriffe, Historisch-Quellenmässig. 4. Aufl. Hrsg. unter Mitwirkung der Kantgesellechaft. 3 vols. Berlin: E.S. Mittler und Sohn, 1927-1930.

First published in 1889, this important work for advanced study contains lengthy definitions with bibliographies on philosophical terms and concepts. The articles trace the use, meanings and treatment of words through the writings of philosophers. A detailed list of books is provided at the end of volume 3 (pp. 695-906). For a condensed version see Eisler's Handwörterbuch (C0236); for a new edition see Ritter (C0285). See also Ziegenfuss (C0306).

C0238 Enciclopedia Filosofica. 2. ed. 6 vols. Florence: G.C. Sansoni, 1968-1969.

Compiled under the auspices of the Centro di Studi Filosofici Cristiani di Gallarate and first published in 1957-1958 (4 vols. Venice: Istituto per la Collaborazione Culturale), this scholarly Italian work containing signed articles and updated bibliographies treats philosophical concepts and related matters in a variety of fields. There are many biographical articles as well. Volume 6 includes indexes of theoretical concepts, historical developments, terms or names referred to in the text but not used as entries. For readers of Italian this encyclopedia is a suitable alternative to Edwards (C0235), providing a sound continental outline of philosophy in all aspects. For a smaller Italian dictionary see Abbagnano (C0208).

C0239 Enciclopedia Mariana, "Theotócos". Trans. by Francisco Aparicio. Colección Mariana, 21. Madrid: Ediciones Studium, 1960.

A translation from the second Italian edition, this classified encyclopedia covers the full range of relevant topics, such as history of Mariology, Marian dogmas, spirituality, influence on art, literature, music, etc. Useful bibliographies and author and subject indexes are included. See also Algermissen (C0210), Attwater (C0213) and Roschini (C0287).

C0240 Exeler, Adolf, and Scherer, Georg, eds. Glaubersinformation: Sachbuch zur Theologischen Erwachsenenbildung. Freiburg im Breisgau: Herder, [1971].

C0241 Ferguson, John. An Illustrated Encyclopaedia of Mysticism and the Mystery Religions. New York: Seabury Press; London: Thames and Hudson, 1977.

This useful source of basic information contains brief articles on names, terms and movements in various orms of mysticism. Such peripheral areas as demonology, magic and witchcraft are excluded, as Ferguson seeks to cover only the main fields associated with mysticism. There is a helpful bibliography of secondary sources (pp. 217-227) for further study. See also Gaynor (C0246) and Viller (C0301).

C0242 Ferm, Vergilius Ture Anselm, ed. Encyclopedia of Morals. New York: Philosophical Library, 1956; London: Peter Owen, 1957. Reprint. New York: Greenwood Press, 1969.

First published in 1945, this individualistic work treats both moral theory as propounded by various philosophers and religions as well as moral behavior, particularly from an anthropological viewpoint. Bibliographies are appended to articles, and there are adequate cross references. A name index is included, but the lack of subject or title indexes is a drawback from a reference viewpoint. In some cases Ferm's own views color the content and detract from the objectivity expected in such a work. See also Henry (C0253) and Macquarrie (C0267).

C0243 Fernandez-Garcia, Mariano. Lexicon Scholasticum Philosophico-Theologicum in quo Termini, Definitiones, Distinctiones et Effata seu Axiomaticae Propositiones Philosophiam ac Theologiam Spectantes a B. Ioanne Duns Scoto Exponontur, Declarantur, Opera et Studio. 2 folios. Ad Claras Aquas (Quaracchi): Ex Typographia Collegii S. Bonaventurae, 1910.

This detailed three part lexicon of scholastic philosophy treats speculative grammar, definitions of terms and general principles. There are indexes to each part, giving Fernandez-Garcia current reference value despite its date of publication. For students and researchers engaged in scholastic studies this is an important reference work. See also Wuellner (C0305).

C0244 Flew, Antony Newton Garrard, ed. consultant. A Dictionary of Philosophy. New York: St. Martin's Press, 1979.

This 351 page dictionary for both students and scholars is a concise, well organized and adequately detailed guide to all aspects of philosophy. The thirty-three contributors, although focusing on Anglo-American philosophical topics, provide information on a broad range of philosophical systems, terms, concepts and theories. Some of the entries provide too little information, and there are no bibliographies. In general, however, Flew is a very useful compendium for those who want brief definitions of philosophical terms and individuals. See also Runes (C0289) and Lacey (C0260), the latter being closest to Flew in content and scope.

C0245 Foulquié, Paul. Dictionnaire de la Langue Philosophique. Avec la collaboration de Raymond Saint-Jean. 2e éd. Paris: Presses Universitaires de France, 1969.

This dictionary lists approximately 1500 words arranged in groups according to the main root word and including cross references from derivative forms. Each entry gives etymology and definitions, indicating various areas of usage, synonyms and examples from philosophical literature. References to sources are included, but the quotations are not dated, and there is no bibliography of source material. For theologians engaged in linguistic aspects of philosophical study this is a useful reference work. See also Blanc (C0219) and Julia (C0257).

C0246 Gaynor, Frank, ed. Dictionary of Mysticism. New York: Philosophical Library, 1953.

This brief dictionary of 206 pages consists of alphabetically arranged entries of terms used in religious mysticism, esoteric philosophy, occultism, psychical research, spiritualism, alchemy, astrology and oriental philosophies. More than 2200 terms are defined, many for the first time in an English language compendium. The definitions are very brief and often inadequate for basic requirements, but there are bibliographical references for further reference. See also Ferguson (C0241) and Viller (C0301).

C0247 Grooten, Johan, and Steenbergen, G. Jo. eds. New Encyclopedia of Philosophy. With the cooperation of K.L. Bellon et al. Trans., ed. and rev. by Edmond van den Bossche. New York: Philosophical Library, 1972.

This 468 page translation of Filosofisch Lexicon provides clear definitions of philosophical terms and ideas, and information on their historical origins and development within various Western systems of thought. This is a useful source for theology students requiring philosophical background, but its coverage tends to be limited: philosophers within the Eastern Christian tradition have been largely neglected. See also Lacey (C0260) and Runes (C0289).

C0248 Gutmann, James. Philosophy A to Z. Based on the work of Alwin Diemer et al. Trans. by Salvatore Attanasio. Universal Reference Library. New York: Grosset and Dunlap, 1963.

Based on Das Fischer Lexikon, Enzyklopädie des Wissenschafts: Band 2: Philosophie (Frankfurt am Main: Fischer Bücherei, 1958), this dictionary contains lengthy articles on major philosophical topics. Each entry is very full and detailed, providing key data for those unfamiliar with the scope of philosophical concerns. Bibliographies are included. See also Ward (C0302).

C0249 Hanselmann, Johannes. Kleines Lexikon Kirchlicher Begriffe. Munich: Claudius Verlag, 1969.

Although covering all aspects of Christianity, it is in the area of systematic theology that this 211 page dictionary is most useful. It defines key terms and concepts in clear, general language suitable for the beginning student. Occasionally a German Protestant bias is evident, but for the most part definitions are brief and objective.

C0250 Harrison, Everett Falconer, ed.-in-chief. Baker's Dictionary of Theology. Associate ed.: Geoffrey W. Bromiley. Consulting ed.: Carl F.H. Henry. Grand Rapids, Mich.: Baker Book House; London: Pickering and Inglis, 1960.

This 566 page dictionary by evangelical Protestants includes terms from philosophy, systematics and various sects in an attempt to acquaint readers with areas of disagreement in modern theological discussion. The alphabetically arranged entries are concise and often include bibliographies. For those seeking information on theological concepts particularly as placed in their biblical context according to conservative Protestant views, this is a helpful dictionary. See also Crooks (C0230).

C0251 Harvey, Van Austin. A Handbook of Theological Terms. New York: Macmillan Company, 1964; London: Allen and Unwin, 1966 [c. 1964].

This widely used handbook provides concise and competent definitions of 350 theological terms. Entries are drawn from basic systematic and philosophical issues, and an attempt is made to show how words have been used at different times. Both Protestant and Catholic views are given in many cases, which makes Harvey a useful work for comparing traditions. Articles are arranged in systematic clusters and present some bibliographical material within the text. This is a sound work for students at both beginning and advanced levels. See also Richardson (C0284).

C0252 Healey, Francis G. Fifty Key Words in Theology. Richmond, Va.: John Knox Press; London: Lutterworth Press, 1967.

This Protestant guide provides basic and succinct explanations of such terms as "existentialism", "predestination" and "transcendence". It is intended for beginning students and general readers with no knowledge of the field and is particularly suitable for popular teaching situations rather than academic instruction. See also Lord (C0262) and Schultz (C0291).

C0253 Henry, Carl Ferdinand Howard, ed. Baker's Dictionary of Christian Ethics. Grand Rapids, Mich.: Baker Book House, 1973. Reprint. Grand Rapids, Mich.: Baker Book House, 1978.

This dictionary by a number of evangelical Protestants in Europe and the United States attempts to explain the biblical ethic, its impact on culture and relevance to modern ethical issues. The signed articles are arranged alphabetically, and some include brief bibliographies. Although wider in scope than Macquarrie (C0267), this work is less useful because of its rigid approach and narrow interpretation of ethical issues. For students and clergy in the conservative Protestant tradition this dictionary has limited value; it should not be consulted for scholarly inquiries. See also Ferm (C0242).

C0254 Höffe, Otfried, ed. Lexikon der Ethik. In Zusammenarbeit mit Max-imilian Forschner et al. Munich: C.H. Beck'sche Verlagsbuchhandlung, 1977.

Aimed essentially at the student, this general dictionary of ethics treats topics in individual, social, political and religious ethical systems. Some of the broader entries are lengthy and discursive, often with useful bibliog-raphies for those able to read German. The shorter entries provide basic definitions of key terms in scholarly but nontechnical language. See also Hörmann (C0255).

C0255 Hörmann, Karl. Lexikon der Christlichen Moral. Innsbruck: Tyrolia Verlag, 1969.

Consisting of 1392 columns, this work contains long scholarly articles by thirty-nine Austrian contributors. There are cross references and bibliog-raphies which include publications in all Western languages. This is a useful work for its treatment of current issues in moral theology and for its extensive bibliographies. See also Höffe (C0254).

C0256 Hoffmeister, Johannes. Wörterbuch der Philosophischen Begriffe. 2. Aufl. Die Philosophische Bibliothek, Bd. 225. Hamburg: Felix Meiner, 1955.

First published in 1944 and based on an earlier work of the same title by Friedrich Kirchner and Carl Michaelis (6. Aufl. Leipzig: E. Meiner, 1911), this dictionary contains concise articles on philosophical terms and concepts. There are some bibliographical references but no biographical entries. This is a standard German language work which offers adequate definitions of standard concepts but without any particular attention to philosophical theology. See also Apel (C0212), Brugger (C0226) and Eisler (C0236).

C0257 Julia, Didier. Dictionnaire de la Philosophie. Les Dictionnaires de l'Homme du XXe Siècle. Paris: Larousse, 1964.

Intended for the layman or beginning student, this 320 page dictionary provides clear and precise definitions, explanations and biographies. See also Blanc (C0219), Foulquié (C0245) and Lalande (C0261).

C0258 Kahane, Ernest, et al., eds. Dictionnaire Rationaliste. Paris: Editions de l'Union Rationaliste, 1964.

Although less comprehensive than McCabe (C0265, C0266), this work contains more detailed information on key aspects of rationalism. Some of the entries are very lengthy, and much biographical material is included.

C0259 [no entry]

C0260 Lacey, Alan Robert. A Dictionary of Philosophy. London: Routledge and Kegan Paul, 1976.

Intended for the layman and beginning student, this 239 page dictionary concentrates on common terms and concepts in philosophy. Each entry provides both a definition and an indication of the problems normally associated with the concept. The work is clearly written and includes cross references as well as some bibliographies. Lacey is comparable to Grooten (C0247) and Runes (C0289) in intent and content. It is a useful complement to Flew (C0244), which is rather better in its coverage of biographies and non-Western religions.

C0261 Lalande, André, ed. Vocabulaire Technique et Critique de la Philosophie. 10e éd. Paris: Presses Universitaires de France, 1967.

First published in parts in the Bulletin de la Société Française de Philosophie, this large work provides definitions of philosophical concepts and terms with reference to their use by philosophers and notes on the evolution of their present meaning. German, English and Italian equivalents of terms are provided, and there are numerous footnotes and bibliographic citations. See also Blanc (C0219), Foulquié (C0245) and Julia (C0257).

C0262 Lord, Eric, and Whittle, Donald Carey Grenfell. A Theological Glossary. Oxford: Religious Education Press, 1969.

In 134 pages this basic work lists major terms and movements in theology and provides simple definitions for those unfamiliar with this field. See also Bigler (C0217), Healey (C0252) and Schultz (C0291).

C0263 Loth, Bernard, and Michel, Albert. Dictionnaire de Théologie Catholique, Contenant l'Exposé des Doctrines de la Théologie Catholique, Leurs Preuves et Leur Histoire: Tables Générales. 3 vols. Paris: Letouzey et Ané, 1951-1972.

This synthesis of material from Vacant (C0299) is a commentary on, supplement and index to the main encyclopedia. It provides a synthesis of data under alphabetically arranged headings but also adds new information where appropriate. Loth is an indispensible guide to a major Catholic encyclopedia. See also Alès (C0209) and Rahner (C0279-C0281).

C0264 McCabe, Joseph, comp. A Biographical Dictionary of Ancient, Medieval and Modern Freethinkers. Girard, Kans.: Haldeman-Julius Publications, 1945.

C0265 McCabe, Joseph, comp. A Biographical Dictionary of Modern Rationalists. London: Watt and Company, 1920.

Including some personalities living at the time of compilation, this biographical dictionary contains about 2000 brief, factual entries. Although McCabe is suitably broad in its interpretation of "rationalist", it does include some individuals not generally placed in this category. The entries are very short, providing only the most basic biographical data suitable for general inquiries.

C0266 McCabe, Joseph. A Rationalist Encyclopaedia: A Book of Reference on Religion, Philosophy, Ethics and Science. 2nd ed. London: Watts, 1950.

First published in 1948, this rationalist dictionary covers philosophy, ethics and religion in its broad view of the field. Some biographical sketches are provided, as are references to relevant literature. See also Kahane (C0258).

C0267 Macquarrie, John, ed. A Dictionary of Christian Ethics. Philadelphia, Pa.: Westminster Press; London: SCM Press, 1967.

This standard dictionary contains signed articles by eighty scholars from all the Christian traditions and does not attempt to represent a particular line of thought. The articles cover basic ethical concepts, ethical systems, non-Christian ethics, traditional biblical and theological ethics, ethical problems of the modern world and similar areas. All of the topics are presented solely from the point of view of their ethical content or influence and represent a moderate, pragmatic approach which gives Macquarrie a refreshing objectivity. Brief bibliographies are included in this valuable reference volume. See also Stoeckle (C0296).

C0268 Menchaca, José A. Diccionario Bio-Bibliográfico de Filosofos. Publicaciones de la Universidad de Deusto, Sección de Filosofia. Bilbao: El Mensajero del Carazón de Jesús, 1965.

For each author treated this detailed work presents a biographical note, bibliographies in which he is covered, a list of the author's writings and their translations, a list of studies on the author. See also American Catholic Philosophical Association (C0318), Directory of American Philosophers (C0427), International Directory of Philosophy and Philosophers (C0535) and Runes (C0289).

C0269 Mosse, Walter M. A Theological German Vocabulary: German Theological Key Words Illustrated in Quotations from Martin Luther's Bible and the Revised Standard Version. New York: Macmillan Company, 1955; New York: Octagon Books, 1968.

Intended as a German-English theological vocabulary for students of theological German, this brief dictionary contains basic theological expressions indispensible for reading theological texts. In principle the selection of entries is limited to words and phrases current in writing of the nineteenth and twentieth centuries. Accompanying many of the terms are brief quotations indicating the biblical context, although it is impossible to tell from which versions the quotations are taken. An asterisk next to a German word in the definitional synonym list after a main entry indicates that that word is also treated as a main entry. Although a German-English synonym list rather than a dictionary, this is a valuable reference tool for quick reference.

C0270 Nauman, St. Elmo. The New Dictionary of Existentialism. New York: Philosophical Library, 1971.

This dictionary provides precise definitions of the technical terms of existentialism, using material from major existentialists in philosophy and psychology. Biographies are included, as well as bibliographies.

C0271 Neuhäusler, Anton Otto. Grundbegriffe der Philosophischen Sprache. Grundbegriffe der Fachsprachen. Munich: Ehrenwirth Verlag, 1963.

This basic dictionary contains about 500 main entry terms and provides English, French and Italian equivalents in addition to brief definitions in German. Useful bibliographies accompany each entry. Appended is a classified list of topics treated. See also Abbagnano (C0208).

C0272 Noack, Ludwig. Philosophiegeschichtliches Lexikon: Historisch-Bibliographisches Handwörterbuch zur Geschichte der Philosophie. Stuttgart: F. Frommann, 1968.

See also Brugger (C0226), Eisler (C0237) and Ritter (C0285).

C0273 Odell, Robin, and Barfield, Tom, comps. A Humanist Glossary. London: Pemberton, 1967.

This collection of clear and simple definitions of some 100 terms is intended primarily to aid humanists in their reading and in discussions.

C0274 [no entry]

C0275 Palazzini, Pietro. Dictionarium Morale et Canonicum. 4 vols. Rome: Officium Libri Catholici, 1962-1968.

Prepared by Italian scholars, this detailed encyclopedic work is based on traditional church teachings, papal instructions and Vatican II. The signed articles conclude with bibliographies devoted entirely to non-English materials. The articles cover all aspects of moral theology, ethical issues and Christian ethics from a moderate and balanced Roman Catholic view-point. This is a useful reference work which falls between the strictly traditionalist and enthusiastically liberal Roman Catholic approaches; it is suitable for inquiries at many levels. See also Rauch (C0282), Roberti (C0286) and Rossi (C0288).

C0276 Parente, Pietro; Piolanti, Antonio; and Garofalo, Salvatore. Dictionary of Dogmatic Theology. Trans. by Emmanuel Doronzo. Milwaukee, Wisc.: Bruce Publishing Company, 1951.

Translated from Dizionario di Teologia Dommatica (2. ed. Rome: Editrice Studium, 1945), this 310 page dictionary contains brief articles on philo-sophical thought and Catholic dogma. References to ancient and modern authors are included. Although originally intended for the layman, it contains useful material for the theological student.

C0277 Peters, Francis Edwards. Greek Philosophical Terms: A Historical Lexicon. New York: New York University Press; London: University of London Press, 1967.

Intended for the intermediate student of Greek philosophy and arranged in thirty-six sections, this lexicon defines a few hundred key concepts quite fully but without recourse to obscure language. There are numerous cross references, textual citations referring to the Greek philosophers and an English-Greek index of some 500 terms.

C0278 La Philosophie, Les Idées, les Oeuvres, les Hommes. Paris: Centre d'Etude et de Promotion de la Lecture, 1969.

This dictionary of contemporary philosophy contains nine lengthy signed articles on key topics such as existentialism and psychoanalysis, and briefer treatment of some 400 terms and philosophers. An index of English terms with their French equivalents is provided. See also Julia (C0257).

C0279 Rahner, Karl, ed. Encyclopedia of Theology: The Concise Sacramentum Mundi. New York: Seabury Press, 1975.

This volume contains revisions of the major articles on theology, biblical studies and related topics primarily from Sacramentum Mundi (C0280).

Although bibliographies are not included in this work it is nonetheless useful as a basic encyclopedia of Christian theology for the student and layman.

C0280 Rahner, Karl, et al. eds. Sacramentum Mundi: An Encyclopedia of Theology. 6 vols. New York: Herder and Herder; London: Burns and Oates, 1968-1970.

This international encyclopedia has also appeared in five other European languages, which is an indication of its widespread popularity. The compilation is based on the work of more than 600 Roman Catholic theologians and attempts to present current developments in all areas of theology; it is based on modern investigations of key themes in the various theological disciplines, and the articles, all of substantial length, include bibliographies and cross references. Because there are approximately 1000 articles, many of which overlap to some degree, it is important to consult the general index in volume 6. Especially interesting for the various approaches and backgrounds evident in the treatment of particularly sensitive issues, this encyclopedia perhaps lacks the objectivity sought in such works. Nevertheless, it remains the best large scale guide to current thinking among liberal Roman Catholics and should be consulted by students of all theological disciplines. A single volume condensation is available (C0279) for those without access to the full work. See also A Catholic Dictionary of Theology (C0229).

C0281 Rahner, Karl, and Vorgrimler, Herbert. Concise Theological Dictionary. Ed. by Cornelius Ernst. Trans. by Richard Strachan. Freiburg im Breisgau: Herder, 1965; London: Burns and Oates, 1966.

Based on the German original, Kleines Theologisches Wörterbuch (5. Aufl. Herder Bücherei, Bd. 108/109. Freiburg im Breisgau: Herder, 1965), this dictionary contains short articles on the concepts of Roman Catholic dogmatic theology. References to biblical and ecclesiastical texts are provided, but there are no bibliographies as such. Nevertheless, this is a sound guide to modern theological views and usefully complements Bouyer (C0220). A second and thoroughly revised edition, Dictionary of Theology (New York: Crossroad Publishing Company, 1981) incorporates considerable material generated by Vatican II, which the first edition does not. The explanations remain brief but lucid, providing excellent reference data for users at various levels.

C0282 Rauch, Wendelin, ed. Lexikon des Katholischen Lebens. Unter Schriftleitung von Jakob Hommes. Freiburg im Breisgau: Herder, 1952.

This collection of more than 800 articles deals with a wide range of contemporary moral problems from a traditional Roman Catholic viewpoint. Each article is written in clear, nontechnical German for the nonspecialist. Issues are treated succinctly and concisely. Each article includes a brief bibliography, and there is a classified bibliography for the entire work. A classified index greatly facilitates the location of information scattered throughout the volume. This work is now dated but provides enough basic data to retain usefulness for less advanced reference purposes. See also Palazzini (C0275), Roberti (C0286) and Rossi (C0288).

C0283 Reich, Warren, T., ed.-in-chief. Encyclopedia of Bioethics. 4 vols. New York: Free Press, 1978.

This comprehensive source of information on ethical and social issues in the health professions, life sciences, medicine and health care is designed for both students and researchers. For those interested in issues of particular concern to the church there is good coverage of euthanasia, birth control, abortion, death and similar topics. The alphabetically arranged entries summarize historical developments and the current state of individual topics in a very clear and nontechnical manner. Ethical problems and theories, religious traditions, basic concepts and principles and interdisciplinary approaches are all treated concisely but thoroughly. To allow for the various approaches applicable to a given topic each entry is often composed of several distinct articles, which is a valuable feature of this work. Each article is followed by a selective bibliography, and cross references are provided where necessary. Reich is a valuable guide to a field of growing importance and should retain its usefulness for some time.

C0284 Richardson, Alan, ed. A Dictionary of Christian Theology. Philadelphia, Pa.: Westminster Press; London: SCM Press, 1969.

This 364 page dictionary is concerned primarily with contemporary theological issues and with the interdisciplinary relationships in theology. The alphabetically arranged entries provide brief but informative notes on a wide range of terms, and there are both cross references and bibliographies. Richardson is not intended as an exhaustive dictionary and is most suitable for laymen and less advanced students. The views expressed are objective and moderate in tone, providing clear and nontechnical information of a philosophical and dogmatic nature. See also Harvey (C0251).

C0285 Ritter, Joachim, ed. Historisches Wörterbuch der Philosophie. Völlig neubearb. Ausg. In Verbindung mit Günther Bien et al. Vol. 1- . Darmstadt: Wissenschaftliche Buchgesellschaft, 1971- .

This complete revision of Eisler's Wörterbuch (C0237) is a scholarly and up to date compilation, containing concise and lucid contributions by more than 700 scholars. Some entries in the older work have been omitted altogether; some have been expanded, and much new material has been added to provide an important reference work for advanced study. The articles cover philosophical terms and concepts, giving their meaning and tracing their use through history. References to sources and bibliographies are included in this valuable encyclopedic guide suitable for advanced students with knowledge of German. When completed, Ritter will contain seven volumes plus a separate index volume; interim lists of articles and authors are appended to existing volumes. See also Ziegenfuss (C0306).

C0286 Roberti, Francesco, comp. Dictionary of Moral Theology. Ed. under the direction of Pietro Palazzini. Trans. from the 2nd Italian ed. under the direction of Henry J. Yannone. Westminster, Md.: Newman Press; London: Burns and Oates, 1962.

This translation of Dizionario di Teologia Morale (2. ed. Rome: Editrice Studium, 1957) aims to present moral theology and all aspects of practical theology which influence the conduct of daily life. It includes problems of psychology, medicine, sociology, international law and similar topics, as well as the standard concerns of moral theology. There are entries for leading moral theologians of the past, and a lengthy bibliography is included. This English translation is slightly dated, but a fourth Italian edition (2 vols. Rome: Editrice Studium, 1968) has been prepared which takes account of Vatican II decisions and which reflects a more relaxed Catholic view on many issues. The entries in the 1962 English translation are detailed and clearly written, although the strong continental emphasis may deter many English language users from using Roberti. The work is suitable for less advanced reference inquiries. See also Palazzini (C0275), Rauch (C0282) and Rossi (C0288).

C0287 Roschini, Gabriele Maria. Dizionario di Mariologia. Rome: Editrice Studium, c. 1961.

This 517 page dictionary provides biographies of famous Mariologists, an article on "Bibliographia Mariana" and articles with bibliographies. It is similar in approach to the Enciclopedia Mariana (C0239). See also Algermissen (C0210) and Attwater (C0213).

C0288 Rossi, Leandro, and Valsecchi, Ambrogio, eds. Dizionario Enciclopedico di Teologia Morale. 3. ed. Rome: Edizioni Paolini, [c. 1974].

This substantial dictionary of 1274 pages contains lengthy articles by Italian and other specialists in the Roman Catholic tradition. While the emphasis is on traditional moral principles, these are discussed in the light of recent Roman Catholic thinking. This work provides useful insights into current Catholic approaches to important moral doctrines, concepts and issues. The articles are arranged in topical sections, and most entries provide detailed treatment of their subjects, including bibliographical references. See also Palazzini (C0275), Rauch (C0282) and Roberti (C0286).

C0289 Runes, Dagobert David. The Dictionary of Philosophy. 15th ed. New York: Philosophical Library, 1960.

This dictionary is designed for teachers, students and laymen and contains signed articles which give concise definitions of philosophical terms from all branches and schools of ancient, medieval and modern philosophy. Not all of the definitions are as accurate as they might be, but for the beginning student this is an acceptable reference work. See also Grooten (C0247), Lacey (C0260) and Urmson (C0298).

C0290 Schmidt, Heinrich. Philosophisches Wörterbuch. 16. Aufl. Kröners Taschen-ausgabe, Bd. 13. Stuttgart: A. Kröner, 1961.

Originally published in 1935, this standard German language dictionary contains entries ranging from very brief definitions to lengthy articles. There are approximately 2000 entries, and most of them include bibliograph-ies. In contrast to Brugger's Roman Catholic approach (C0226), Schmidt is clearly non-Christian; this can serve as an interesting and useful correc-tive to philosophical attitudes which are uncritically Christian. See also Noack (C0272).

C0291 Schultz, Hans Jürgen, ed. Theologie für Nichttheologen: ABC Protestant-ischen Denkens. 3 vols. Gütersloher Taschenausgaben, Bd. 46-48. Gütersloh: Gütersloher Verlagshaus, 1969.

This popularly written encyclopedic dictionary seeks to provide basic definitions in simple and nontechnical language. Schultz presents Protestant views on a wide range of theological topics for the general reader. See also Healey (C0252), Lord (C0262) and Stewart (C0294).

C0292 Schütz, Ludwig. Thomas-Lexikon; Sammlung, Ubersetzung und Erklarung der in Sämtlichen Werken des Hl. Thomas von Aquin Verkommenden Kunstaus-drücke und Wissenschaftlichen Ausspruche. 2. Aufl. Paderborn: Friedrich Schöningh, 1895. Reprint. New York: Frederick Ungar Publishing Company, 1957.

Although covering some works attributed to St. Thomas but now known to be spurious, this dictionary of Thomistic terminology is a useful compilation which gives definitions of some substance in German and includes references to their appearance in major works. See also Stockhammer (C0295) and Deferrari (C0233).

C0293 Simcox, Carroll Eugene. The Words of the Creeds: A Brief Dictionary of Our Faith. Cincinnati, Ohio: Forward Movement Publications, 1960.

C0294 Stewart, William. 50 Key Words: The Church. Richmond, Va.: John Knox Press, 1970.

See also Healey (C0252), Lord (C0262) and Schultz (C0291).

C0295 Stockhammer, Morris, ed. Thomas Aquinas Dictionary. New York: Philosophical Library; London: Vision, 1965.

Based on the 1882 edition of Opera Omnia and the two English translations by Joseph Rickaby, this work is a concordance or index to the major works of Aquinas rather than a dictionary. Arranged by subject, Stock-hammer provides quotations from Aquinas to illustrate terms and concepts of interest to the modern reader. Coverage is very selective and altogether less satisfactory than Deferrari's Lexicon (C0233) but does have the ad-vantage of drawing on a wider range of writings by St. Thomas. It is most suitable for less advanced students. See also Wuellner (C0305).

C0296 Stoeckle, Bernhard, ed. The Concise Dictionary of Christian Ethics. New York: Seabury Press, 1979.

This dictionary contains brief articles by various contributors on eighty-five alphabetically arranged subjects from "abstinence" to "world". It offers basic guidelines for Christians concerned with the fundamentals of ethics. Some articles were translated from German for this collection. See also Macquarrie (C0267).

C0297 Torres Calvo, Angel, ed. Diccionario de Textos Sociales Pontificos. 2. ed. Biblioteca "Fomento Social". Madrid: Cía. Bibliográfica Española, 1962.

This massive tome of 1948 pages contains an alphabetical arrangement by subject of quotations from papal documents on social problems. Refer-ences to complete texts, summaries of contents and in some cases complete quotations are given. Coverage extends from Pope Leo XIII to Pope John XXIII. Indexes are provided.

C0298 Urmson, James Opie, ed. The Concise Encyclopedia of Western Philos-ophy. 2nd ed. London: Hutchinson, 1975.

Initially published in 1968, this encyclopedia is a nonscholarly work intended for the general reader. It contains a series of alphabetically arranged articles by some fifty experts, mainly British, on the main philosophical concepts, including definitions of terms and brief biographies. Although lacking an index, Urmson contains numerous cross references, an extensive bibliography and notes on the contributors. Similar to Runes (C0289), this work is suitable for basic inquiries but should be used with caution, as some definitions are somewhat inaccurate or misleading

C0299 Vacant, Alfred; Mangenot, Joseph-Eugène; and Amann, Emile, eds. Dictionnaire de Théologie Catholique, Contenant l'Exposé des Doctrines de la Théologie Catholique, Leurs Preuves et Leur Histoire. 15 vols. in 30. Paris: Letouzey et Ané, 1909-1950.

Much more exhaustive in treatment than any of the English language encyclopedias prepared from a Roman Catholic standpoint, this impressive work contains long, authoritative articles and excellent bibliographies. Vacant is particularly thorough on topics and names in scholastic and medieval philosophy, and it clearly fills the need for detailed reference works in these areas. More recent information on topics treated in earlier volumes is frequently included under allied subjects in later volumes, so for a full awareness of the spread of a topic it is necessary to consult the guide prepared by Loth and Michel (C0263). Other sets within the Encyclopédie des Sciences Ecclésiastiques (of which Vacant is a part) would have benefitted from similar treatment to make their coverage more up to date. The Table Analytique compiled in 1929 covers only the first nine volumes of the dictionary. This is a sound and thorough guide to Catholic theology which should be consulted by those requiring detailed information provided in a traditional framework. See also Alès (C0209) and Rahner (C0279-C0281).

C0300 Valle, Florentino del. Diccionario de Moral Profesional, Según los Documentos Pontificios. Biblioteca "Fomento Social". Madrid: Cía. Bibliográfica Española, 1962.

C0301 Viller, Marcel; Cavallera, F.; and Guibert, J. de, eds. Dictionnaire de Spiritualité, Ascétique et Mystique, Doctrine et Histoire. Continué par A. Rayez, A. Derville et A. Solignac. Vol. 1- . Paris: G. Beauchesne, 1932- .

Issued in fascicles and under various editors, this ongoing compilation offers long, signed articles with bibliographies and references to sources. Approximately half complete, Viller will be a massive reference encyclo-pedia unrivalled in its field and should remain a standard guide for many decades. Roman Catholic in orientation, it covers concepts of spiritual theology and explains their origins and development. The spiritual history by century for each country of the world is covered in detail, including treatment of individual schools of spirituality and major and minor figures relevant to spiritual life. For students of this field Viller is an indispensible reference tool. See also Ancilli (C0211), Ferguson (C0241) and Gaynor (C0246).

C0302 Ward, Keith. Fifty Key Words in Philosophy. London: Lutterworth Press, 1968; Richmond, Va.: John Knox Press, 1969.

This helpful guide to ideas central to philosophical discussion contains articles ranging from 300 to 800 words in length on fifty terms used in philosophy. Cross references, a chronological list of philosophers men-tioned and an index of philosophical expressions used in the articles help to make this a useful, brief reference work, particularly for teachers, clergy and students. See also Gutmann (C0248).

C0303 Wiener, Philip P., ed. Dictionary of the History of Ideas: Studies of Selected Pivotal Ideas. 5 vols. New York: Charles Scribner's Sons, 1973-1974.

This multi-volume work provides an intellectual history of such selected "ideas" as human nature, esthetics, religion, philosophy and historiography. An analytical table arranges articles into seven major areas, and a list of 311 articles follows. Volume 5 is a detailed index, which assists the user in tracing individuals and concepts throughout the collection. There are extensive bibliographies. Wiener's thematic approach can be somewhat confusing, but the excellent index eases consultation considerably. See also Adler (C0311), which is similar in intention and arrangement. See also Edwards (C0235) and Ziegenfuss (C0306).

C0304 Wörterbuch zum Religionsunterricht: Für Alle Schularten und Schulstufen. Freiburg im Breisgau: Herder, 1976.

C0305 Wuellner, Bernard. A Dictionary of Scholastic Philosophy. 2nd ed. Milwaukee, Wisc.: Bruce Publishing Company, 1966.

Designed primarily for undergraduates or those needing a basic understanding of the terminology of scholasticism, this dictionary gives brief explanations and definitions of terms with some references to sources. Arranged alphabetically, with cross references, it includes charts and diagrams, a guide to abbreviations and a bibliography. See also Fernandez-Garcia (C0243) and dictionaries of Thomism by Stockhammer (C0295) and others.

C0306 Ziegenfuss, Werner, ed. Philosophen-Lexikon: Handwörterbuch der Philosophie nach Personen. Unter Mitwirkung von Gertrud Jung. 2 vols. Berlin: Walter de Gruyter und Kompagnie, 1949-1950.

This biographical dictionary of philosophers of all periods and from all countries places emphasis on philosophy since Hegel and includes individuals living at the time of compilation. Intended to replace Rudolf Eisler's Philosophen-Lexikon (Berlin: E.S. Mittler und Sohn, 1912), this work contains longer articles, additional names and material. Bibliographies are included with most of the articles, which clearly outline each subject's thought and contribution to the field. See also Eisler (C0237) and Ritter (C0285).

SYSTEMATIC/DOCTRINAL THEOLOGY AND ETHICS: HANDBOOKS

C0307 Abell, Aaron Ignatius. American Catholic Thought on Social Questions. The American Heritage Series, vol. 58. Indianapolis, Ind.: Bobbs-Merrill, 1968.

This volume contains a selection of writings by Roman Catholics, organized in four main sections: conditions of Catholic growth; the emergence of Catholic social liberalism; social education and organization; and the new pluralism. A selected bibliography is provided. One of a series on the American experience, this work provides useful documentary material on the topic covered. See also Cronin (C0404) and Williams (C0738).

C0308 Adam, Alfred. <u>Lehrbuch der Dogmengeschichte</u>. Vol. 1- . Gütersloh: G. Mohn, 1965- .

This history of dogma is projected in three volumes, the first covering the early period to the rise of Islam; the second, the Middle Ages and Reformation; the third, from the Reformation to the present. It is designed as a text for students, and contains an appropriate selection of references and useful bibliographies at the end of chapters. Each volume treats major tenets of dogma (the trinity, Christology, etc.) in an objective historical manner and is ideally suited to guide beginning students through the basic phases of dogmatic development. A vast array of factors, individuals, developments and events is treated concisely and clearly. For students able to read German Adam is a significant reference tool. See also Seeberg (C0676).

C0309 Adams, David Stow. <u>A Handbook of Christian Ethics</u>. Edinburgh: T. and T. Clark, 1925.

This scholarly textbook covers the full range of ethics, both individual and social, from a largely practical rather than a theoretical viewpoint. See also Ward (C0725).

C0310 Adams, Hampton. <u>Vocabulary of Faith</u>. St. Louis, Mo.: Bethany Press, 1956.

This 124 page book contains twelve chapters, each on an important concept of Christian theology, including revelation, faith, Christ, God, atonement and redemption. It is intended as an aid to the layman, in setting out the church's message in simple terms.

C0311 Adler, Mortimer, J., ed.-in-chief. <u>The Great Ideas: A Syntopicon of "Great Books of the Western World"</u>. 2 vols. Great Books of the Western World, vols. 2-3. Chicago, Ill.: Encyclopaedia Britannica, 1952.

Including a substantial bibliography (pp. 1143-1217) in volume 2, this wide ranging survey in summary form is useful for those without a background in philosophy. While the <u>Syntopicon</u> covers many fields and philosophy only selectively, it allows beginners to grasp bare essentials of key philosophical works quickly and easily. See also Wiener (C0303), which provides more detailed summaries.

C0312 Ahlstrom, Sydney E., ed. <u>Theology in America: The Major Protestant Voices from Puritanism to Neo-Orthodoxy</u>. The American Heritage Series, no. 73. Indianapolis, Ind.: Bobbs-Merrill Company, 1967.

Containing selections from the writings of influential personalities, this sourcebook also develops fresh ideas about theology in America in the author's introduction. A useful bibliography and biographical introductions to particular documents add to the value of this collection for students and scholars who wish to refer to important sources of American Protestant thought. For a complementary interpretation see Dillenberger (C0426).

C0313 Aland, Kurt. <u>Hilfsbuch zum Lutherstudium</u>. Bearb. in Verbindung mit Ernst Otto Reichert und Gerhard Jordon. 3. Aufl. Witten: Luther Verlag, 1970.

> This 677 page compendium enumerates alphabetically all of Luther's writings, then provides information on the content of each of the various collected editions (for nineteenth-twentieth century editions and for sixteenth-eighteenth century editions). This is an excellent reference tool for students of Luther's works.

C0314 Alexander, Anthony F. College Apologetics. Chicago, Ill.: H. Regnery Publishing Company, [1954].

> See also Linden (C0566).

C0315 Alexander, Anthony F. College Dogmatic Theology. Chicago, Ill.: H. Regnery Publishing Company, 1962.

> See also Kaiser (C0538) and Smith (C0687).

C0316 Althaus, P. Grundriss der Ethik. 2. Aufl. Grundrisse zur Evangelischen Theologie. Gütersloh: C. Bertelsmann, 1953.

> See also Søe (C0689).

C0317 Alves, Reuben A. A Theology of Human Hope. New York: Corpus Books, [1971, c. 1969].

> This basic study within the framework of liberation theology explores the meaning of salvation in strongly immanental terms. Alves is concerned to develop a theological language consistent with the new consciousness of an oppressed community, and to put forward a genuinely radical theology of conflict, struggle and hope. The style of the work has been criticized for lacking coherence. See also Moltmann (C0597).

C0318 American Catholic Philosophical Association. Directory of Members. Ed. 1- . Washington, D.C.: American Catholic Philosophical Association, 1968- .

> This work provides brief biographical data and publications for members of the Association. See also Directory of American Philosophers (C0427), International Directory of Philosophy and Philosophers (C0535), Menchaca (C0268) and Runes (C0661).

C0319 Aquinas, Thomas. Summa Theologiae: Latin Text and English Translation, Introduction, Notes, Appendices and Glossaries. 60 vols. New York: McGraw-Hill Book Company, 1964-1976.

> Of the many available editions of the Summa, this is the most scholarly and detailed. Substantial introductory sections and extensive notes accompany the Latin and English text. Every volume stands on its own for reference purposes, as each contains appendixes on doctrinal issues, philosophical glossary and index. This version must be regarded as the most suitable for advanced scholarly inquiries. See also Deferrari (C0420) for an index and Farrell (C0442), Glenn (C0474) and Grabmann (C0481) for general surveys of the Summa.

C0320 Armstrong, Arthur Hilary, ed. The Cambridge History of Later Greek and Early Medieval Philosophy. Cambridge: Cambridge University Press, 1967.

Intended in some ways as a continuation of Guthrie (C0493), this survey is designed to show how Greek philosophy evolved in relation to its contacts with Judaism, Christianity and Islam. Coverage extends from the fourth century B.C. to St. Anselm (twelfth century A.D.), and the discussion is detailed without being unnecessarily loaded with facts. There is a select bibliography arranged by chapters (pp. 670-691); indexes cover ancient and medieval works mentioned in the text, subjects and Greek terms. This is a sound reference volume which provides data often missing in other works on medieval Christian philosophy. See also Maurer (C0594).

C0321 Aróstegui, Antonio. Doctrina Social de la Iglesia. 3. ed. Salamanca: Anaya, 1969.

See also Berna (C0348) and Sobreroca Ferrer (C0688).

C0322 Aulén, Gustaf Emanuel Hildebrand. Christus Victor: An Historical Study of the Three Main Types of the Idea of the Atonement. Authorised trans. by A.G. Hebert. American ed. New York: Macmillan Company, 1960.

This translation of Aulén's Olaus Petri lectures delivered in Uppsala in 1930 presents an interpretation of the history of the idea of the atonement. It is particularly useful in its distinction between Anselmian, humanistic and classic ideas of the atonement. The English translation has been slightly revised, providing a now somewhat dated account by an eminent Swedish dogmatic theologian. See also Grillmeier (C0484), Pannenberg (C0620) and Watlington (C0727).

C0323 Aulén, Gustaf Emanuel Hildebrand. The Faith of the Christian Church. Trans. from the 5th Swedish ed. by Eric H. Wahlstrom. Philadelphia, Pa.: Muhlenberg Press, [c. 1960].

Also called the "second English edition" (London: SCM Press, 1961), this 403 page summary of Christian theology covers faith, scripture and tradition, the Lord's Supper, and related topics. There is an ecumenical theme throughout. New references have brought this well known work on doctrine up to date. See also De Wolf (C0419).

C0324 Badcock, Francis John. The History of the Creeds. 2nd ed. New York: Macmillan Company; London: SPCK, 1938. Reprint. Nedeln: Kraus Reprint, 1980.

See also Curtis (C0411), Kelly (C0544) and Schaff (C0664).

C0325 Baelz, Peter R. Christian Theology and Metaphysics. Philadelphia, Pa.: Fortress Press; London: Lutterworth Press, 1968.

This work attempts to provide an answer to the question: to what are we referring when we talk about God? It also outlines the metaphysical theology which the answer implies. The audience for which the book is intended is not entirely clear, for although it contains technical words and allusions to philosophers and theologians, it does not show all the rigor required by trained philosophers and theologians. See also Baillie (C0326), Cobb (C0393) and Copleston (C0402).

C0326 Baillie, John. The Interpretation of Religion: An Introductory Study of Theological Principles. New York: Charles Scribner's Sons, 1928. Reprint. New York: Abingdon Press, 1965.

Reprinted on various occasions, this study of the nature of religion includes detailed consideration of methodological issues. The first part focuses on the nature of theology, its scope, its relation to other disciplines and critiques of various approaches to the study of theology and religion. The second part treats various theories of religion and considers basic questions regarding belief, the conception of God, etc. An index is provided. Although dated, this work is valuable to the student, particularly for its survey of various approaches to theology. References are provided in plentiful footnotes. See also Baelz (C0325), Cobb (C0393) and Jennings (C0536).

C0327 Bainton, Roland Herbert. Christian Attitudes toward War and Peace: A Historical Survey and Critical Re-evaluation. New York: Abingdon Press, 1960.

This work surveys Christian experience in relation to war, including chapters on the origins of the crusading idea in the OT, and war and peace in the NT, up to the present. The author takes the position of a Christian pacifist in the concluding chapters. The work contains an impressive bibliographical apparatus, and much stimulating material on an issue of current concern.

C0328 Baker, Frank, ed. The Works of John Wesley. Oxford: Clarendon Press, 1975- .

This new critical edition of Wesley attempts to identify all of his quotations and contains extensive introductory material and notes. Divided into units of "cognate material", each section of the proposed thirty-four volumes is by a different editor, including such scholars as Gerald R. Cragg. An essential feature is the bibliography which outlines historical settings of over 450 items published by Wesley and his brother, as well as offering full analytical data for identifying each of the 2000 editions published during Wesley's lifetime. An index is supplied for each unit.

C0329 Bancroft, Emery Hubert. Christian Theology, Systematic and Biblical. 2nd ed. Ed. by Ronald B. Mayers. Grand Rapids, Mich.: Zondervan Publishing House, 1976.

See also Berkhof (C0346) and Buswell (C0374).

C0330 Bangs, Carl Oliver. German-English Theological Word List. Rev. ed. Kansas City, Mo.: n.p., 1962.

This 16 page listing contains over 500 noncognate terms used in theology, philosophy, church history, Bible or biblical criticism, ethics and related fields. Words from the works of key writers are included. Arrangement is alphabetical (by German word) with very brief English equivalents, printed in two columns. Although not claiming to be an exhaustive dictionary, this is a handy quick reference for more commonly used terms for theology students or others without a knowledge of German. For a basic grammar see Manton (C0587).

C0331 Banner, William Augustus. Ethics: An Introduction to Moral Philosophy. New York: Charles Scribner's Sons, 1968.

Intended as an introduction for beginners, this brief work presents the author's views on certain fundamental problems in ethics, then summarizes and comments upon the ethical views of the Greeks, Christians, Utilitarians, Existentialists, etc. A glossary clarifies terms for the beginning student, and extensive footnotes provide guidance to primary sources. Some ethical positions with which the author is not in sympathy do not receive adequate treatment for an introductory work. See also Frankena (C0455), Garner (C0462), Garnett (C0463) and Pepper (C0624),

C0332 Barnette, Henlee H. Introducing Christian Ethics. Nashville, Tenn.: Broadman Press, 1961.

This work offers an introduction to Christian ethics, paying attention to the biblical basis and role of the Holy Spirit. The first part examines the basic principles of Christian morality; the second applies Christian moral principles in areas such as marriage, race relations and economic issues. Written by a Southern Baptist, it compresses much material into a brief space and provides a useful resource book. It does not attempt to consider the contributions of philosophy to the development of ethical theory. See also Robinson (C0655).

C0333 Barth, Karl. Church Dogmatics. Authorized trans. by G.T. Thomson. Ed. by Geoffrey W. Bromiley and T.F. Torrance. 5 vols. in 14. Edinburgh: T. and T. Clark, 1936-1969; New York: Charles Scribner's Sons, 1936-1970.

This multivolume evangelical exposition of systematic theology covers the doctrines of the word of God, God, creation, reconciliation. The indispensible fifth volume includes a full index to the preceding parts plus exegetical selections for the church year. Together with Brunner (C0371) Barth offers the most comprehensive and detailed attempt to restate the "neo-orthodox" position in scholarly and theologically intricate language. Barth is clearly the more comprehensive of the two and with the invaluable index volume serves as an excellent reference work for advanced students of Protestant dogmatic theology. For condensations see the translations by Bromiley (C0334) and Thomson (C0335).

C0334 Barth, Karl. Church Dogmatics: A Selection. Trans. and ed. by Geoffrey W. Bromiley. Edinburgh: T. and T. Clark, 1961.

In 262 pages Bromiley seeks to indicate the essence of Barth's major work, following the same outline. This is a useful condensation for the beginning student but should not be used as a substitute for the full Church Dogmatics (C0333) for detailed study or reference purposes. See also Barth's Dogmatics in Outline (C0335).

C0335 Barth, Karl. Dogmatics in Outline. Trans. by G.T. Thomson. New York: Harper and Brothers; London: SCM Press, 1949. Reprint. London. SCM Press, 1957; New York: Harper and Brothers, 1959.

This work, first published as Dogmatik im Grundriss (Zollikon-Zürich:

Evangelischer Verlag, 1947) is based on a series of lectures delivered at the University of Bonn in 1946. It is organized around the Apostles' Creed and presents the basic elements of Christian doctrine in relatively nontechnical language for the beginner. This is a useful introduction to Barthian theology for those about to study his Church Dogmatics (C0333). See also Barth's selection by Bromiley (C0334).

C0336 Barth, Karl. Evangelical Theology: An Introduction. Trans. by Grover Foley. New York: Holt, Rinehart and Winston; London: Weidenfeld and Nicolson, [1963]; Garden City, N.Y.: Doubleday and Company, 1964.

This translation of Einführung in die Evangelische Theologie (Zürich: ENZ-Verlag, 1962) contains the lectures delivered prior to Barth's retirement from the chair of theology in the University of Basel in 1962. They give Barth's views on the nature, basis and method of an evangelical theology and on its place in relation to certain key concepts. No technical apparatus is included, nor are there any indexes. Nonetheless, this is an important introduction to Barth's thought for teachers and students of theology. See also Bloesch (C0354) and Bornkamm (C0360).

C0337 Barth, Karl. Protestant Theology in the Nineteenth Century: Its Background and History. London: SCM Press; Valley Forge, Pa.: Judson Press, [1973, c. 1972].

This translation of Die Protestantische Theologie in 19. Jahrhundert serves as an introduction both to nineteenth century theology and to Barth's own theology. The translation includes additional features such as essays on eighteenth century theology and on nineteenth century theologians omitted in the original. Although somewhat dated in approach, this English version provides a valuable addition to the translated corpus of Barth. See also Tillich (C0708).

C0338 Barth, Karl. The Teaching of the Church Regarding Baptism. Trans. by Ernest A. Payne. London: SCM Press, 1948.

In this analysis Barth presents the biblical evidence for immersion and for "believer baptism".

C0339 Bartmann, Bernhard. Précis de Théologie Dogmatique. Trans. of 8th ed. by Marcel Gautier. 7th ed. 2 vols. Mulhouse: Editions Salvator, 1951.

This detailed general survey of dogmatic theology covers formal principles, God, the Trinity, creation and redemption in volume 1 and grace, the church, sacraments and eschatology in volume 2.

C0340 Bartsch, Hans Werner. Handbuch der Evangelisch-Theologischen Arbeit, 1938 bis 1948. Evangelischer Schriftendienst Supplementband, 1. Stuttgart: Evangelisches Verlagswerk, [1949].

C0341 Bennett, John Coleman. Christian Ethics and Social Policy. New York: Charles Scribner's Sons, 1946.

This excellent treatment is based on Oldham's middle axioms and seeks to set forth guiding norms of value in a Christian view of social policy. This is neither a textbook nor a reference volume, but the lucid exposition of a normative standard of Christian social ethics gives Bennett a leading place among handbooks and standard treatises. See also Bennett's later work (C0342) and Winter (C0742).

261
B 471

C0342 Bennett, John Coleman, ed. Christian Social Ethics in a Changing World: An Ecumenical Theological Inquiry. New York: Association Press, 1966.

Prepared under the sponsorship of the Department Church and Society of the World Council of Churches for the 1966 conference, this collection of working papers provides an excellent summary and overview of modern social ethics and ethical issues from a wide range of Christian traditions. There are numerous bibliographical citations. See also Bennett's earlier work (C0341).

C0343 Bennett, John Coleman. Christianity and Communism Today. Rev. ed. New York: Association Press, 1965.

Originally published as Christianity and Communism (New York: Association Press, 1948; London: SCM Press, 1949), this key work provides a lucid description of the overlapping interests and basic differences between the two systems. It is concise and nontechnical, and is intended for students and other young people. There is no index, but the table of contents provides adequate guidance to this brief work. See also West (C0736).

230
B51 2

C0344 Berkhof, Louis. The History of Christian Doctrines. Grand Rapids, Mich.: Wm. B. Eerdmans Publishing Company, 1949. Reprint. Grand Rapids, Mich.: Baker Book House, 1975.

This work was first published as Reformed Dogmatics, Historical Volume (Grand Rapids, Mich.: Wm. B. Eerdmans Publishing Company, 1937).

C0345 Berkhof, Louis. Manual of Reformed Doctrine. Grand Rapids, Mich.: Wm. B. Eerdmans Publishing Company, 1933.

See also Berkhof's Reformed Dogmatics (C0346).

C0346 Berkhof, Louis. Reformed Dogmatics. 2nd ed. Grand Rapids, Mich.: Wm. B. Eerdmans Publishing Company, 1941.

This work was also published as Systematic Theology by the same publisher. See also Bancroft (C0329), Buswell (C0374) and Heppe (C0513).

C0347 Berkouwer, Gerrit Cornelius. Studies in Dogmatics. Trans. by James E. Davison. 12 vols. Grand Rapids, Mich.: Wm. B. Eerdmans Publishing Company, 1952-1955.

BT7L4
B4

Translated from the author's Dutch series, Dogmatische Studiën, this thorough survey by a noted exponent of conservative Protestantism covers faith and sanctification, providence of God, faith and justification, person of Christ, general revelation, faith and perseverance, divine election, man in the image of God, the work of Christ, sacraments, sin, the return of Christ. Each of the twelve volumes is devoted to one of these dogmatic themes. The discussion is well balanced, with acknowledgements of post-Vatican II contributions of the Roman Catholic Church, and sensitive awareness of bodies such as the World Council of

Churches. Ample footnotes offer access to a broad range of relevant literature.

C0348 Berna, Angel, et al. Doctrina Social Católica. 2. ed. Madrid: Instituto Social Leon XIII, 1966.

This 595 page survey provides more substantial coverage than Aróstegui (C0321). See also Sobreroca Ferrer (C0688).

C0349 Bertman, Martin A. Research Guide in Philosophy. Consulting ed.: Carl Kalvelage. Morristown, N.J.: General Learning Press, 1974.

This research guide for undergraduate students contains chapters on research methods, use of the library, selective bibliography, glossary of terms and related material essential for those just beginning the study of philosophy. It is clearly written and logically presented, serving as an excellent starting point for students new to the field. See also the two works by Matczak (C0592, C0593).

C0350 Bethge, Eberhard. Dietrich Bonhoeffer: Man of Vision, Man of Courage. Trans. by Eric Mosbacher et al. Ed. by Edwin Robertson. New York: Harper and Row, 1970.

Published in Britain as Dietrich Bonhoeffer: Theologian, Christian, Contemporary (London: William Collins and Son, 1970), this 567 page biography, translated from the German edition of 1967, provides a definitive treatment of Bonhoeffer's life, and of his work as a theologian and Christian. The lengthy work is thoroughly documented, and is an invaluable resource for students of Bonhoeffer.

C0351 Bethune-Baker, James Franklin. An Introduction to the Early History of Christian Doctrine to the Time of the Council of Chalcedon. [9th ed.] London: Methuen and Company, [1951]. Reprint. London: Methuen and Company, 1962.

First published in 1903 and reprinted on many occasions, this older work retains value for its clarity of presentation and useful word studies of key concepts. It offers to the student of the history of Christian doctrine a narrative treatment, supplemented by detailed footnotes. An index facilitates use of this thorough introductory study. See also Daniélou (C0413) and Kelly (C0545).

C0352 Bettoni, Efram. Duns Scotus: The Basic Principles of His Philosophy. Trans. and ed. by Bernardine Bonansea. Washington, D.C.: Catholic University of America Press, 1961.

This introductory study provides a concise exposition of Duns Scotus' philosophical thought, presenting the basic principles of his system against their doctrinal background. There are three parts which are further subdivided: the man and his works; Duns Scotus' thought; Duns Scotus in history and Catholic thought. A useful bibliography and an analytic index are provided. Author's and translator's footnotes supplement the text. See also Gilson (C0472).

C0353 Bird, Herbert S. Theology of Seventh Day Adventism. Grand Rapids, Mich.: Wm. B. Eerdmans Publishing Company, 1961.

This brief volume (137 pp.) provides a critique of Seventh Day Adventist theology from a conservative viewpoint. Adventist views on the Bible, man, Christ, salvation, the Sabbath and Christian conduct are treated. It is primarily of interest to fundamentalist and conservative Christians.

C0354 Bloesch, Donald G. Essentials of Evangelical Theology. 2 vols. San Francisco, Calif.: Harper and Row, 1978-1979.

This American analysis of past and contemporary evangelical Protestantism is an important contribution to the understanding of this tradition. It is also a useful source of information on the beliefs and dogmas expressed in evangelical theology. Volume 1 deals with God, authority and salvation; volume 2, with life, ministry and hope. See also Barth (C0336) and Thielicke (C0703).

BC15
B643

C0355 Bochenski, Innocentius M. A History of Formal Logic. Trans. and ed. by Ivor Thomas. Notre Dame, Ind.: University of Notre Dame Press, 1961.

Including an extensive bibliography of several thousand entries, this thorough and detailed history covers both periods (ancient, scholastic, classical) and types of logic.

C0356 Bock, Paul. In Search of a Responsible World Society: The Social Teachings of the World Council of Churches. Philadelphia, Pa.: Westminster Press, 1974.

This volume provides an introduction to the social teachings of the World Council of Churches, some background for understanding them, and includes many of the teachings themselves. A historical review of trends in ecumenical social thought, 1925-1970, is included. A selected bibliography (pp. 243-244) and an index are provided. This is a useful work on non-Roman Catholic thought in this area.

BV1758.2
B5713

C0357 Böckle, Franz. Fundamental Concepts of Moral Theology. Trans. by William Jerman. New York: Paulist Press, 1968.

See also Curran (C0409).

C0358 Bois, Jacques; Boisset, Jean; and Mehl, Roger. Le Problème de la Morale Chrétienne. Les Problèmes de la Pensée Chrétienne, tome 3. Paris: Presses Universitaires de France, 1948.

See also Rémy (C0646).

C0359 Bonhoeffer, Dietrich. Ethics. Ed. by Eberhard Bethge. Trans. by Neville Horton Smith. New York: Macmillan Company, 1962; London: William Collins Sons, 1964.

204
B7142

This translation of Ethik follows the sixth German edition of 1963, although Bethge's foreword is not translated. This is regrettable since the foreword explained the significance of the reorganization of material in part 1, Bonhoeffer's treatment of Christian ethics. This is presented chronologically according to the development of Bonhoeffer's thought. Part 2 contains occasional ethical pieces. An index is provided, although it is inferior to the German version. See also Brunner (C0370).

C0360 Bornkamm, Heinrich. The Heart of the Reformation Faith: The Funda-mental Axioms of Evangelical Belief. Trans. by John W. Doberstein. New York: Harper and Row, 1965.

This brief (126 pp.) work sets out the major themes of the Protestant Reformation in a straightforward manner: Luther's theology of the cross, the meaning of the Church, Reformation views of God, man, life and death, etc. It is of particular relevance to Protestant readers seeking a summary treatment of the theme. See also Barth (C0336) and Brunner (C0371).

C0361 Bourke, Vernon Joseph. Ethics: A Textbook in Moral Philosophy. With a new introduction and an updated, enlarged bibliography. Christian Wisdom Series. New York: Macmillan Company, 1966.

This textbook is in two parts, the first dealing with moral principles (the nature of ethics, moral law and ethics, conscience and moral obliga-tion, etc.); the second, with ethical problems (right action in regard to others, justice, etc.). There is a general bibliography (pp. 479-484), and an index is provided. See also Callan (C0378).

C0362 Bourke, Vernon Joseph. History of Ethics. Garden City, N.Y.: Double-day and Company, 1968.

The five parts in this 432 page history deal with Greco-Roman ethics, patristic and medieval ethics, early modern ethics, modern theories and contemporary ethics. Notes, a bibliography (pp. 353-417) and a detailed index add to the reference value of this scholarly survey. See also Dittrich (C0429) and MacIntyre (C0580).

C0363 Bouyer, Louis. Christian Humanism. Trans. by A.V. Littledale. West-minster, Md.: Newman Press, 1959 [c. 1958].

C0364 Bouyer, Louis. Christian Initiation. Trans. by R. Foster. New York: Macmillan Company; London: Burns and Oates, 1960.

Intended as an initiation into Christian truth and life, this brief work contains eight chapters on "the discovery of" the spiritual, God, the divine word, the living church, the cross and the resurrection, the euchar-ist, the new life, eternal life. There is neither bibliography nor index. See also Di Brandi (C0424).

C0365 Bouyer, Louis, et al. History of Christian Spirituality. 3 vols. New York: Desclée Company; London: Burns and Oates, 1963-1969.

This translation of Histoire de la Spiritualité Chrétienne provides a comprehensive manual and reference book, covering the various schools or periods. Bibliographical notes and chapters on the literature of various topics provide guides to more detailed research. There are indexes of subjects, biblical references, ancient and modern authors. The first volume treats the spirituality of the NT and the fathers. See also Pourrat (C0632) and Williams (C0739).

C0366 Bréhier, Emile. The History of Philosophy. Trans. by Joseph Thomas. 7 vols. Chicago, Ill.: University of Chicago Press, 1963-1969.

This translation of Bréhier's classic work, Histoire de la Philosophie (of which there is a ninth edition published in Paris by Presses Universitaires de France, 1967-), is the standard treatment of philosophical history from ancient times to the mid-twentieth century. Selective bibliographies are included. Although lacking a theological orientation, Bréhier provides a useful survey; particularly helpful is volume 3, dealing with the Middle Ages and Renaissance. For a work more closely attuned to philosophical theology see Copleston (C0401) or Fischl (C0449). See also Gilson (0471) and Rivaud (C0650) for surveys with a clear Christian bias.

C0367 Brennan, Joseph Gerard. The Meaning of Philosophy: A Survey of the Problems of Philosophy and of the Opinions of Philosophers. 2nd ed. New York: Harper and Row, 1967.

See also Matczak (C0592).

C0368 Bromiley, Geoffrey William. Introduction to the Theology of Karl Barth. Grand Rapids, Mich.: Wm. B. Eerdmans Publishing Company, 1979.

Following the framework of Church Dogmatics (C0333), this sympathetic introduction provides a concise summary of Barth's theology as well as suggested lines of investigation and further study. It concludes with a brief but thoughtful critique. This is an excellent contribution to the literature on Barth's major statement of Christian theology and is suitable for beginning students.

C0369 Brown, Colin. Philosophy and the Christian Faith: A Historical Sketch from the Middle Ages to the Present Day. Chicago, Ill.: InterVarsity Press; London: Tyndale Press, 1969.

This 319 page survey of major thinkers and schools of thought from medieval times to the 1960s concentrates on the relation between philosophy and the Christian faith. There are many footnote and appendix references to further reading, which adds to the value of the work as a survey volume. The bibliography (pp. 291-309) and much of the content indicate that Brown is intended primarily for the beginner, especially one more interested in "faith" than in philosophical theology or the philosophy of religion. See also Gilson (C0470) and Lee (C0560).

C0370 Brunner, Heinrich Emil. The Divine Imperative: A Study in Christian Ethics. Trans. by Olive Wyon. Philadelphia, Pa.: Westminster Press, 1947; London: Lutterworth Press, 1951.

This systematic study of ethics by Brunner is a standard Protestant interpretation, translated from the 1932 publication, Das Gebot und die Ordnungen: Entwurf einer Protestantisch-Theologischen Ethik (2. Aufl.). It is in three main parts: the problem; the divine command; the orders. A substantial body of notes and appendixes, including important discussions of, for example, socialism, is provided, as is an index. See also Bonhoeffer (C0359).

C0371 Brunner, Heinrich Emil. Dogmatics. Trans. by Olive Wyon. 3 vols. London: Lutterworth Press, 1949-1962; Philadelphia, Pa.: Westminster Press, 1950-1962. Reprint. 3 vols. Philadelphia, Pa.: Westminster Press, 1978-1980.

The three volumes of this widely used guide cover God; creation and redemption; church, faith and consummation. As a clear exponent of neo-orthodoxy, Brunner seeks to indicate the essence of this position within a traditional dogmatic framework. Detailed tables of contents are provided in each volume, with subject, name and scripture reference indexes. See also Barth (C0333) and Bornkamm (C0360).

C0372 Brunner, Heinrich Emil. Justice and the Social Order. Trans. by Mary Hottinger. New York: Harper and Brothers, 1945; London: Lutterworth Press, 1949.

Reflecting on justice in the political, economic, international and family orders, this work is concerned with establishing a knowledge of justice as a basis for action. The first part is concerned with principles (justice and equality, individualism and collectivism, etc.). The second applies principles to practice. Full notes follow the main text, and an index is provided. See also Ferré (C0447) and Gardner (C0461).

C0373 Burr, John R., ed. Handbook of World Philosophy: Contemporary Developments since 1945. London: Aldwych Press, 1980.

Primarily geographical in orientation, this 641 page compendium consists of twenty-eight signed articles covering all of the major philosophical countries or describing the present situation in large geographical or cultural blocs (e.g., Africa, Islam). These articles vary from continuous descriptions of influences and patterns to subdivided sections giving detailed analytical accounts of movements or individuals. There is also a useful list of philosophical associations and associated publications. Indexes are provided for subjects and individual philosophers. Introductory bibliographies for further study accompany most articles. In general Burr is useful for students seeking summaries of movements, concepts or the work of individual philosophers; it also has some value for the specialist in describing philosophical activity in non-Western countries, but in most cases the geographical framework is not particularly relevant to the scholar. See also Institut International de Philosophie (C0534) and Klibansky (C0548).

C0374 Buswell, James Oliver. A Systematic Theology of the Christian Religion. 2 vols. Grand Rapids, Mich.: Zondervan Publishing House, 1962-1963.

This is a scholarly study from a conservative viewpoint. Main sections focus on soteriology, eschatology, etc. Parts of the work have been criticized for unclear interpretation and poor organization. See also Bancroft (C0329) and Berkhof (C0346).

C0375 Cahn, Zvi. The Philosophy of Judaism: The Development of Jewish Thought throughout the Ages, the Bible, the Talmud, the Jewish Philosophers and the Cabala until the Present Time. New York: Macmillan Company, 1962.

Covering much the same ground as Guttmann (C0495), this 524 page work provides a story of Judaism rather than its philosophy proper. It treats the biblical and talmudic eras and the era of philosophers. There are many biographical sketches of the rabbinic sages, and the work is useful for its breadth of coverage of the history of Judaism. See also Husik (C0531).

201
C136

C0376 Caird, John. An Introduction to the Philosophy of Religion. New ed. Glasgow: J. Mackhose and Sons, 1901. Reprint. New York: AMS Press, 1970.

Based on the Croall Lecture delivered in Edinburgh in 1878-1879, this 343 page introductory work develops a philosophy of religion in ten chapters. These examine issues such as objections to the scientific treatment of religion, proofs of the existence of God, the relation of morality and religion. Bibliographical references are provided in footnotes, and a detailed table of contents provides adequate guidance in the absence of an index. This provides a thorough nineteenth century approach to the subject.

C0377 Calcagno, Francesco Saverio. Theologia Fundamentalis. Cursus Theologicus, vol. 1. Naples: M. d'Auria, S. Sedis Apostolycae Typographus, 1948.

See also Hervé (C0515).

C0378 Callan, Charles Jerome. Moral Theology: A Complete Course Based on St. Thomas Aquinas and the Best Modern Authorities. Rev. and enlarged by Edward P. Farrell. 2 vols. New York: Joseph F. Wagner, 1958.

This careful revision of a standard Roman Catholic work is particularly useful for its many definitions, which are clear without being overly simple. There is a thorough index to the terms and concepts discussed in the text but no bibliography. Some of the material is clearly pre-Vatican II in content, but this remains a useful if basic reference work for beginners. See also Bourke (C0361).

262
C167

C0379 Calvez, Jean-Yves, and Perrin, Jacques.   The Church and Social Justice: The Social Teaching of the Popes from Leo XIII to Pius XII, 1878-1958. Trans. by J.R. Kirwan. Chicago, Ill.: H. Regnery Publishing Company; London: Burns and Oates, 1961.

This is a full and detailed survey of pontifical documents issued under Leo XIII, Pius X, Benedict XV, Pius XI and Pius XII. Particular moral problems are addressed out of this continuing tradition, and this collection allows comparisons to be made quickly and easily. There is a useful bibliography for more detailed study. See also Fremantle (C0457) and Harte (C0507).

BX9420
I65
1960

C0380 Calvin, John. Institutes of the Christian Religion. Trans. by Ford Lewis Battles. Ed. by John T. McNeill. 2 vols. The Library of Christian Classics, vols. 20-21. Philadelphia, Pa.: Westminster Press, 1960; London: SCM Press, 1961 [c. 1960]. Reprint. 2 vols. Edinburgh: T. and T. Clark, 1981.

Including detailed biblical, author and subject indexes, this excellent English translation is notable for its lucid, concise and clear style.

C0381 Cannon, William Ragsdale. The Theology of John Wesley, with Special Reference to the Doctrine of Justification. Nashville, Tenn.: Abingdon-Cokesbury Press, 1946.

Including a bibliography (pp. 257-273) and index, this 284 page guide to Wesley's theological system examines the problem of salvation as Wesley faced it, the theology which emerged, and the English evangelical revival of the eighteenth century as the context. The two parts focus on the development and formulation of the doctrine of justification, and theological and ethical concepts arising from that doctrine. The work is thoroughly documented. See also Schmidt (C0625).

C0382 Carmody, John. Theology for the 1980's. Philadelphia, Pa.: Westminster Press, 1980.

This work summarizes major theological trends of the 1970s, both Catholic and Protestant, in a concise and objective manner. Carmody then suggests key areas for theological reflection and investigation in the 1980s, including science, secularization, nature, world religions, society, self, divinity and recent NT studies. This is a useful summary volume for those seeking an overview of recent theological interests. See also Ferm (C0445).

C0383 Carol, Juniper Benjamin, ed. Mariology. 3 vols. Milwaukee, Wisc.: Bruce Publishing Company, 1955-1957.

This comprehensive collection covers theological, historical and other aspects of Mariology in a series of contributions by specialists. Bibliographies are provided for each chapter, and there is an author index in the final volume. See also Doheny (C0430), Du Manoir de Juaye (C0431) and Sträter (C0695).

C0384 Cassilly, Francis Bernard. Religion: Doctrine and Practice. Chicago, Ill.: Loyola University Press, 1958.

See also Litton (C0567) and O'Collins (C0612).

C0385 Catholic Students Mission Crusade. CSMC Study Guide [to] Concilium Library. Cincinnati, Ohio: CSMC Press, 1967- .

This series of study guides is designed for use with Concilium (C0395) and is keyed to the topics treated in each volume of this topical series.

C0386 Cavallera, Ferdinand, comp. Thesaurus Doctrinae Catholicae, ex Documentis Magisterii Ecclesiastici, Ordine Methodico. Paris: G. Beauchesne et Ses Fils, 1920.

This 794 page collection of the teachings of the Church comprises extracts from documents, papal and conciliar, arranged in traditional theological divisions. Chronological and subject indexes are included. This is a standard Roman Catholic sourcebook. See also Denzinger (C0421).

C0387 Cave, Alfred. An Introduction to Theology: Its Principles, Its Branches, Its Results and Its Literature. 2nd ed. Edinburgh: T. and T. Clark, 1896.

This classic nineteenth century introduction to the full range of Protestant theology is arranged in a series of topical or disciplinary chapters, each of which provides an overview of the field plus a bibliography. Most substantial is the section on biblical theology (pp. 240-423); other sections are adequate but less detailed. The bibliographies list both basic and advanced works in English, French and German. Cave, despite its dated quality, continues to serve as a useful introductory volume for students of traditional Protestant theology. See also Clarke (C0390) and Hodge (C0522).

C0388 Chenu, Marie Dominique. <u>Toward Understanding St. Thomas</u>. Trans. with authorized corrections and bibliographical additions by Albert M. Landry and Dominic Hughes. The Library of Living Catholic Thought. Chicago, Ill.: H. Regnery Publishing Company, 1964.

This valuable introduction to the life, times, works and intellectual milieu of St. Thomas includes references for further study and bibliographical data up to 1964. The first part sets the context for St. Thomas' work and provides information on his language, vocabulary, the literary forms of his work and similar aspects. The second part comprises chapters on specific works. Information on technical words, abbreviations, etc. and a list of proper names are included. See also Gilson (C0468), Grenet (C0483) and Pieper (C0626).

C0389 Childs, James M. <u>Christian Anthropology and Ethics</u>. Philadelphia, Pa.: Fortress Press, 1978.

This work examines the contribution of eschatological theology to contemporary understanding of humanity and the explication of Christian ethics. It contains useful material on the relationship between ethical theory and the nature and destiny of persons. It is not particularly easy to use, as its language tends to be rather complex. See also Moltmann (C0597).

C0390 Clarke, William Newton. <u>An Outline of Christian Theology</u>. 12th ed. New York: Charles Scribner's Sons, 1902. Reprint. 12th ed. New York: Charles Scribner's Sons, 1927.

Reprinted at various times, this work provides an introduction on sources of Christian theology, before giving detailed treatment of the Christian conception of God, man, sin, Christ, the Holy Spirit and the divine life in man and things to come. A detailed table of contents and an index are provided. This is a useful but dated guide for the beginner interested in a traditional Protestant approach. See also Hagenbach (C0499), Cave (C0387) and Hodge (C0522).

C0391 Clarkson, John F., et al., eds. <u>The Church Teaches: Documents of the Church in English Translation</u>. St. Louis, Mo.: B. Herder Book Company, 1955.

Prepared by members of St. Mary's College, Kansas, this collection of translations includes documents frequently used for theology courses. References to Denziger (C0421) are given, where there are references to complete texts from which the excerpts are drawn. Classified and subject indexes are provided. Although a useful sourcebook, Clarkson has been largely superseded by the translation of Denzinger (C0422).

C0392 <u>Classics of Western Spirituality: A Library of the Great Spiritual Masters</u>. Vol. 1- . New York: Paulist Press, 1978- .

Projected in sixty volumes, this ecumenical series presents new translations of major spiritual works by Catholic, Orthodox, Protestant, Jewish, Islamic and American Indian writers. Each volume is devoted to one writer, containing selections from his most notable works, a substantial introduction, a bibliography for further study and a detailed index. For those interested in ascetical and spiritual theology this should prove to be a valuable collection and reference set.

C0393 Cobb, John B. Living Options in Protestant Theology: A Survey of Methods. Philadelphia, Pa.: Westminster Press, 1962.

This 336 page survey of methods in Protestant doctrinal theology has an American, liberal Protestant perspective, and is limited to theologians who have published major works since the Second World War. The three parts examine natural theology, theological positivism and theological existentialism; within each part the methodology of individual theologians is studied. A bibliography (pp. 324-331) and an index are included. See also Baelz (C0325), Baillie (C0326), Sontag (C0690) and Senarclens (C0678).

C0394 Collins, James Daniel. A History of Modern European Philosophy. Milwaukee, Wisc.: Bruce Publishing Company, 1954. Reprint. Milwaukee, Wisc.: Bruce Publishing Company, 1965.

Designed primarily for Roman Catholic students of philosophy, this history covers the lives of eighteen modern European philosophers. Critical bibliographies of their works and studies of them are included, as is an index. For the personalities treated this is a useful and well written history which clearly pinpoints areas of importance for philosophical theology. See also Maréchal (C0588).

C0395 Concilium: Theology in an Age of Renewal. Vol. 1- . Glen Rock, N.J.: Paulist Press, 1965- .

Each volume in this series covers a theological area which has attracted substantial modern interest among Roman Catholics or which has significant ramifications for this tradition. Each volume consists of a collection of essays and a bibliographical section which together seek to provide a broad overview of the theme in question. This is a widely respected series which provides an excellent means of keeping abreast of current Catholic thought. See also the CSMC Study Guide (C0385).

C0396 Cone, James H. A Black Theology of Liberation. C. Eric Lincoln Series in Black Religion. Philadelphia, Pa.: J.B. Lippincott Company, 1970.

This basic work relates black religion and the black search for liberation (particularly in the United States) to the work of contemporary theological reflection. Black power, informed by a virile black theology of liberation, is seen as the only means of giving credibility and purpose to the Christian faith in the black community. This is a serious discussion of theological tasks and structure from a leading black theologian.

C0397 Congar, Yves Marie Joseph. A History of Theology. Trans. and ed. by Hunter Guthrie. Garden City, N.Y.: Doubleday and Company, 1968.

See also Danielou (C0415) and Otten (C0617).

C0398 Conn, Harvie M. Contemporary World Theology: A Layman's Guide. 2nd ed. Nutley, N.J.: Presbyterian and Reformist Publishing Company, 1974 [c. 1973].

See also Hobbs (C0520) and Guthrie (C0492).

C0399 Conway, John Donald. What They Ask about Morals. Notre Dame, Ind.: Fides Publishers, 1960.

This question and answer guide to such issues of moral theology as conscience, sin, vices and virtues and church regulations is geared to the needs of those who instruct Roman Catholic laity. Both the issues and their treatment are very objectively and openly treated. There is a classified index, making this 370 page survey a useful reference volume.

C0400 Copleston, Frederick Charles. Aquinas. Baltimore, Md.: Penguin Books, 1955.

This 263 page introduction focuses on Aquinas' philosophy, providing a clear account of the structure of his system. The six chapters treat aspects such as God and creation; man, body and soul; and man, morality and society. There are three pages of bibliographical notes and an index. Although intended for the general reader, this contains much that will interest the specialist. See also Gilson (C0468) and Lynch (C0575).

C0401 Copleston, Frederick Charles. A History of Philosophy. 9 vols. London: Burns and Oates, 1947-1974.

Available under various imprints and in a new edition for some volumes, this lucid and scholarly history by a noted Roman Catholic philosopher is the most extensive recent survey in English and is especially valuable for those studying Western philosophy in relation to theology. Each volume contains an extensive bibliography and an index. This is an important reference work for inquiries at various levels because of its objective approach and wealth of detail. Fischl (C0449) is a German language equivalent, while Bréhier (C0366) is equally wide ranging but less attuned to the history of philosophical theology. See also Gilson (C0470).

C0402 Copleston, Frederick Charles. Religion and Philosophy. New York: Barnes and Noble, 1974.

This two part work comprises five lectures delivered in Dundee in 1969 and reprints of five articles originally published in the Heythrop Journal in 1960-1961. The lectures argue that transcendent metaphysics have a religious character and provide the context for argument in the historical relations between philosophy and religion. The articles develop the argument that metaphysics can embody a religious impulse. This is a considered contribution by a distinguished historian of philosophy. See also Baelz (C0325).

C0403 Copleston, Frederick Charles. Religion and the One: Philosophies East and West. London: Search Press, 1982.

This study of the metaphysical One or "metaphenomenal ultimate reality" reviews this concept as treated by the major philosophical systems: Taoist, Buddhist, Hindu, Islamic, Greek, Christian and modern Western. It compares ideas about the One in relation to the world and to the self and examines the connections of metaphysics with ethics, mysticism, sciences and religion. Although at times lacking the clarity required in works of this sort, Copleston is a useful volume for those interested in metaphysical aspects of the philosophy of religion or comparative philosophy. See also Flew (C0453) and Smart (C0686).

C0404 Cronin, John Francis. Catholic Social Principles: The Social Teaching of the Catholic Church Applied to American Economic Life. Milwaukee, Wisc.: Bruce Publishing Company, 1950.

Each topic or chapter in this volume is preceded by excerpts from papal documents stating principles which are then explained. Bibliographical references for each chapter and an annotated bibliography for the entire work are provided. See also Abell (C0307) and Williams (C0738).

C0405 Cuénot, Claude. Pierre Teilhard de Chardin: Leben und Werk. Freiburg im Breisgau: Walter, 1966.

Including an extensive bibliography (pp. 713-796), this masterful survey of the life and work of a leading philosopher/theologian is well documented and provides an authoritative treatment suitable for students able to read German. See also Murray (C0602).

C0406 Cunliffe-Jones, Hubert. Christian Theology since 1600. Studies in Theology, [no. 66]. London: Gerald Duckworth and Company, 1970.

This 172 page study compresses a wealth of material into four chapters, each covering a century. For the earlier periods, subject are dealt with mainly by school or movement of thought; for the twentieth century, individual theologians are given more particular consideration. This provides a valuable summary for the student who requires a brief, compressed treatment of the subject. See also Lohse (C0569).

C0407 Cunliffe-Jones, Hubert, and Drewery, Benjamin, eds. A History of Christian Doctrine; in Succession to the Earlier Work of G.P. Fisher Published in the International Theological Library Series. Edinburgh: T. and T. Clark, 1978; Philadelphia, Pa.: Fortress Press, 1980.

This 601 page survey presents a series of topical chapters by such noted scholars as Lampe, Ware, Knowles, Rupp, Parker and Buick Knox. The chapters include treatment of the patristic period, Eastern Christianity, the Middle Ages, Reformation period, major Reformers, the seventeenth century and the modern era. Each area is treated thoroughly but occasionally in a fairly discursive manner; the chapters are densely written and provide an excellent array of basic factual data together with standard interpretations. Unfortunately, there are few notes and no bibliographies, but indexes of names and subjects give reference value to the work. As a single volume survey, Cunliffe-Jones is a useful textbook and reference guide for the less advanced student. See also the original work by Fisher (C0450) and McGiffert (C0579).

C0408 Curran, Charles E. New Perspectives in Moral Theology. Notre Dame, Ind.: Fides Publishers, 1974. Reprint. Notre Dame, Ind.: University of Notre Dame Press, 1976.

See also Regan (C0644).

C0409 Curran, Charles E. Themes in Fundamental Moral Theology. Notre Dame, Ind.: University of Notre Dame Press, 1977.

This collection of essays on the methodology of theological ethics covers such topics as church law, utilitarianism, consequentialism and moral theology from a Roman Catholic viewpoint. It provides a useful base for the reformulation of Catholic moral theology. See also Böckle (C0357).

C0410 Curtis, Charles J. The Task of Philosophical Theology. New York: Philo-sophical Library, 1964.

This work defines a number of classic Christian notions in the categories of Alfred North Whitehead, and examines traditional theological ideas in the light of process philosophy. Whitehead's life and thought are examined and basic theological ideas such as Christ, death, judgment and prayer analyzed. Whiteheadian terminology is explained in an appendix. There is no index. See also Nicholls (C0606) and Ross (C0658).

C0411 Curtis, William Alexander. A History of Creeds and Confessions of Faith in Christendom and Beyond, with Historical Tables. Edinburgh: T. and T. Clark, 1911; New York: Charles Scribner's Sons, 1912.

This survey of creeds includes extensive quotations from the documents themselves. Although the historical analysis is less authoritative than Kelly (C0544), this remains a sound reference work for the beginner. Historical tables, bibliographies and an index add to the reference value of Curtis. See also Badcock (C0324) and Schaff (C0664).

C0412 Dailey, Robert H. Introduction to Moral Theology. New York: Bruce Publishing Company, 1970.

See also Hörmann (C0525).

C0413 Daniélou, Jean. A History of Early Christian Doctrine before the Council of Nicaea. 2 vols. Philadelphia, Pa.: Westminster Press; London: Darton, Longman and Todd, 1964-1973.

Initially published in volume 1 as The Development of Christian Doctrine before the Council of Nicaea, this translation of Histoire des Doctrines Chrétiennes avant Nicée (2 vols. Paris: Desclée de Brouwer, 1958-1961) presents a rather sympathetic survey of early Christian doctrine as influenced by Hellenistic thought and culture. Each volume includes a substantial bibliography, textual indexes and a general index. Daniélou is a substantial survey written from a Roman Catholic viewpoint and has noteworthy reference value because of its factual content and ex-cellent indexes. See also Bethune-Baker (C0351) and Kelly (C0545).

C0414 Daniélou, Jean. The Theology of Jewish Christianity. Trans. and ed. by John A. Baker. The Development of Christian Doctrine before the Council of Nicaea, vol. 1. Chicago, Ill.: H. Regnery Company; London: Darton, Longman and Todd, 1964.

This comprehensive study of 446 pages translated from the French original traces the transition of theology from its semitic form and structure to the Greek synthesis. The theology, organization and practice of the various groups studied is examined in this valuable contribution on ante-Nicene theology. Helpful footnotes, a glossary of technical terms and a subject index are included. For students of early Christian theology this is an important survey of such topics as angelology, soteriology, eschatology, sacraments, piety and asceticism.

C0415 Daniélou, Jean; Couratin, A.H.; and Kent, John. Historical Theology. The Pelican Guide to Modern Theology, vol. 2. Harmondsworth: Penguin Books, 1969.

This 384 page work contains three examples of how historical theology is conducted. The section by Daniélou catalogs early Christian writings, with bibliographic information about new editions and new interpretations. The second by Couratin surveys the history of the baptismal and euchar- istic liturgies. The third by Kent considers post-1930 work by historians of the period since the Reformation. Thus the volume will appeal to a mixed audience, including students of patristics, those interested in the modern liturgical movement, historians and theologians. See also Congar (C0397). For a similar Protestant work see Pelikan (C0622).

C0416 Daujat, Jean. L'Ordre Social Chrétien. Paris: G. Beauchesne et Ses Fils, 1970.

See also Gestel (C0466) and Lubac (C0572).

C0417 Davies, Brian. An Introduction to the Philosophy of Religion. London: Oxford University Press, 1982.

This comprehensive and clearly written introduction concentrates on the central question of the existence of God and covers most topics usually dealt with by the philosophy of religion: verification and falsifica- tion, religious language, the problem of evil, arguments for God's exis- tence, religious experience, the concept of God, morality and religion, miracles, life after death. Davies makes his own views known but care- fully examines other approaches for the student unfamiliar with the discipline. The work is well indexed and is one of the more objective and readable introductions in its field. Because each topic is covered so concisely and thoroughly, this volume is also a useful reference work for the beginner and more advanced student alike. See also Ross (C0657).

C0418 Davis, Henry. Moral and Pastoral Theology. 7th ed. Rev. and enlarged by L.W. Geddes. 4 vols. Heythrop Series, no. 2. New York: Sheed and Ward, 1958.

This standard Roman Catholic work covers the traditional range of topics with frequent bibliographical references, excerpts from pertinent church documents and detailed treatment of the pastoral aspects of moral problems. Each volume includes an index. While this edition has been criticized for inadequate updating, it is a sound, if somewhat dated and conservative, work which serves a number of basic reference needs quite adequately. See also Häring (C0497).

C0419 De Wolf, Lotan Harold. A Theology of the Living Church. New York: Harper and Brothers, 1953.

This 383 page statement of Christian theology is written from a moderate- ly liberal Protestant viewpoint. Its coverage is broad and the methodology easy to follow. It is well documented, with an extensive bibliography, and could be used as a beginner's textbook or by educated Christians. See also Aulén (C0323) and Gollwitzer (C0476).

C0420 Deferrari, Roy Joseph, and Barry, M. Inviolata. A Complete Index of the "Summa Theologica" of St. Thomas Aquinas. Baltimore, Md.: [n.p.], 1956.

Prepared in conjunction with the author's lexicon (C0233), this concordance or index verborum is based on the Leonine edition of the Summa (Rome: Apud Sedum Commissionis, 1882-1948). It lists every word in the text except common forms such as et, cum, qui and inflected forms and supplies accompanying words to show the context. References are to numbered articles in the text, making this useful with any edition. See also Farrell (C0442).

C0421 Denzinger, Heinrich Joseph Dominik. Enchiridion Symbolorum, Definitionum et Declarationum de Rebus Fidei et Morum Quod Funditus Retractavit; Auxit, Notulis Ornavit Adolfus Schönmetzer. 33rd ed. Barcelona: Herder, 1965.

This handbook of sources and texts on which Roman Catholic dogma and moral teachings are based contains excerpts arranged in chronological order. Full references to the complete works are provided, and there are classified and alphabetical indexes. The collection does not include scriptural quotations. See also Deferrari's translation (C0422) and Cavallera (C0386).

C0422 Denzinger, Heinrich Joseph Dominik. The Sources of Catholic Dogma. Trans. by Roy J. Deferrari from the 30th ed. of Enchiridion Symbolorum. St. Louis, Mo.: Herder, 1957.

This 653 page translation of Denzinger's Enchiridion Symbolorum (C0421) presents in chronological order translations of Catholic documents, papal and others, on which Catholic dogma is based. It covers the period to Pius XII. Bibliographical notes and systematic and alphabetical indexes are included. The translation has been criticized as theologically weak. See also Clarkson (C0391).

C0423 Dewar, Lindsay. An Outline of Anglican Moral Theology. London: A.R. Mowbray and Company, 1968.

This work provides an outline of Anglican, as contrasted with Roman Catholic, moral theology, dealing in turn with such concepts as human conduct, punishment and forgiveness, and the nature of authority. It is intended both for the clergy and laity, and is written in a straightforward manner. Bibliographical references are included in notes, and an index is provided. See also Mortimer (C0599).

C0424 Di Brandi, Herman A. Introduction to Christian Doctrine. New York: Morehouse-Barlow Company, c. 1976.

This work provides a very brief (90 pp.) introduction to the subject. See also Bouyer (C0364).

C0425 Diem, Hermann. Dogmatics. Trans. by Harold Knight. Philadelphia, Pa.: Westminster Press, 1959.

This work examines the debate between NT and dogmatics scholars on the question of exegesis and systematics, covering the work of such theologians as Barth, Bultmann and Käsemann. It is a constructive continental contribution to discussion of problems in theology, and is appropriate to both the scholar and parish minister.

C0426 Dillenberger, John, and Welch, Claude. Protestant Christianity Interpreted through Its Development. New York: Charles Scribner's Sons, 1954.

Designed as a college textbook, this 340 page work sets out Protestant beliefs in the context of history, with a more theological than historical emphasis. It contains a wealth of clearly presented material, although it has been criticized for some omissions and misinterpretations. It was written at the request of the Committee on Research of the National Council of Religion in Higher Education. For a useful collection of documents see Ahlstrom (C0312).

C0427 Directory of American Philosophers. Ed. 1- . Bowling Green, Ohio: Bowling Green State University, Philosophy Documentation Center, 1962- ; biennial.

Published under various imprints, this directory provides an alphabetical listing by state or province, then by institution, for United States and Canadian universities (in separate sections). Philosophy faculty members at each institution are listed. Indexes of philosophers and of institutions are provided. For a worldwide listing see the international companion directory (C0535), and for a Roman Catholic listing see American Catholic Philosophical Association (C0318). See also Menchaea (C0268) and Runes (C0661).

C0428 Dirksen, Cletus Francis. Catholic Social Principles. St. Louis, Mo.: Herder, 1961.

See also McKenzie (C0581).

C0429 Dittrich, Ottmar. Geschichte der Ethik: Die Systeme der Morale von Altertum bis zur Gegenwart. 4 vols. Leipzig: F. Meiner, 1926-1932.

Although the fourth volume on the Reformation was completed only through part 1, this remains the standard basic history of ethics. It covers the discipline thoroughly, accurately and in some detail, providing inquirers with an excellent source of data on all aspects of the history of ethics. There are profuse footnote references, excellent bibliographies and detailed subject indexes. Dittrich is an indispensible reference work in its field. See also MacIntyre (C0580) and Bourke (C0362).

C0430 Doheny, William Joseph, and Kelly, Joseph Patrick, comps. Papal Documents on Mary. Milwaukee, Wisc.: Bruce Publishing Company, [1954].

This collection comprises the texts of documents on Mary issued from 1849 to 1953. Arrangement is chronological with an index. See also Carol (C0383), Du Manoir de Juaye (C0431) and Sträter (C0695).

C0431 Du Manoir de Juaye, Hubert, ed. Maria: Etudes sur la Sainte Vierge. 7 vols. Paris: G. Beauchesne et Ses Fils, 1949-1964.

This comprehensive, scholarly collection treats various aspects of Mariology, including doctrine, history and devotion, in great detail. Bibliography plays a major role throughout each volume. This is a key reference work for both advanced and beginning students, providing both factual and brief interpretive information in depth. A proposed index volume will be of inestimable value in locating data, which are scattered throughout the work. See also Carol (C0383), Doheny (C0430) and Sträter (C0695).

C0432 Dudáš, Cyril. Conspectus Theologiae Moralis. Bratislava: Spolok sv. Vojtecha, 1966.

See also Gury (C0488).

C0433 Dulles, Avery. A History of Apologetics. Theological Resources. New York: Corpus Books; London: Hutchinson and Company, 1971.

This 307 page survey provides a historical account of twenty centuries of writing which has contributed to the defence of Christianity against criticism from various quarters. The format follows six major chronological periods (NT, patristic, medieval, sixteenth-eighteenth centuries, nineteenth, twentieth centuries). The references to writers on apologetics range from allusions to title of book and author to several paragraphs on the more important writers. While providing a useful resource, this work does not attempt to develop a theory of apologetics, and it has been criticized for some omissions. See also Werner (C0732).

C0434 Dulles, Avery. Revelation Theology: A History. New York: Herder and Herder; London: Burns and Oates, 1969.

In 192 pages Dulles provides a well written, thorough and comprehensive theological treatment of the concept of revelation. The work offers good coverage of a broad range of theologians and philosophers who have written on the subject throughout history.

C0435 Duméry, Henry. Philosophie de la Religion: Essai sur la Signification du Christianisme. 2 vols. Bibliothèque de Philosophie Contemporaine. Morale et Valeurs. Paris: Presses Universitaires de France, 1957.

See also Sertillanges (C0679).

C0436 Dyck, Arthur J. On Human Care: An Introduction to Ethics. Nashville, Tenn.: Abingdon Press, 1977.

This work sets out to introduce ethics as a discipline, to consider what ethics offers as guidance for practical understanding and medical decision making and to introduce appropriate concepts and methods. Discussion focusing on particular issues such as euthanasia is helpful, although possibly more so for medical students than for students of ethics. See also Häring (C0498), Kenny (C0546) and McFadden (C0578).

C0437 Ebeling, Gerhard. Dogmatik des Christlichen Glaubens. Vol. 1- . Tübingen: J.C.B. Mohr, 1979.

See also Fritzsche (C0459) and Luthardt (C0573).

C0438 Ebeling, Gerhard. The Study of Theology. Trans. by Duane A. Priebe. Philadelphia, Pa.: Fortress Press, c. 1978.

This translation of Studium der Theologie is concerned particularly with the question of the unity and wholeness of theology, and examines the connections between various aspects (church history, social sciences, practical theology, etc.). Although intended for anyone interested in the basic principles of theology, this study is more suitable for the advanced than for the beginning student. See also Elert (C0439).

C0439 Elert, Werner. The Christian Ethos. Trans. by Carl J. Schindler. Philadelphia, Pa.: Muhlenberg Press, 1957.

This translation of Elert's work presents, from the Lutheran viewpoint, a comprehensive discussion of the Christian ethos, ranging from topics such as creation, eschatology and psychology to liturgics. This is an important reference work, although in the English version the bibliography is inferior to that in the original, and scholarly footnotes have been omitted. See also Ebeling (C0438).

C0440 Evans, Gillian, ed. A Concordance to the Works of St. Anselm. Prepared at the Literary and Linguistic Computing Centre at the University of Cambridge. 4 vols. Millwood, N.Y.: Kraus International Publications, 1982.

Based on Franciscus Salesius Schmitt's S. Anselmi Cantuariensis Archiepiscopi Opera Omnia and R.W. Southern's Memorials of St. Anselm, this detailed concordance provides full context for most words, with common particles and conjunctions treated in word list form with line and page references only. Evans covers all of St. Anselm's works, thus providing an indispensible research tool for philosophers and theologians.

C0441 Fanfani, Amintore. Catechism of Catholic Social Teaching. Trans. by Henry J. Yannone. Westminster, Md.: Newman Press, 1960.

See also Masse (C0591).

C0442 Farrell, Walter. A Companion to the "Summa". 4 vols. New York: Sheed and Ward, 1938-1942.

This handy reference work is a commentary on the Summa arranged in the same order and following the same numbering system as the original. Farrell attempts to reduce the thought and language of St. Thomas to a popular level, thereby providing an excellent tool for the beginning student. Each volume contains an index. See Glenn (C0474) and Grabmann (C0481) for much more basic compilations.

C0443 al Faruqi, Isma'il Ragi A. Christian Ethics: A Historical and Systematic Analysis of Its Dominant Ideas. Montreal: McGill University Press, 1967; The Hague: Djambatan, 1968.

This Moslem work on Christian dogma and ethics includes a lengthy introduction on the principles of dialogue between religions. This is followed by analysis of the ethic of Jesus and of the Christian view of man, church and society. It is thoroughly documented, and there are indexes of subjects, biblical quotations and authors and book titles.

C0444 Feiner, Johannes; Trütsch, Josef; and Böckle, Franz, eds. Theology Today. Trans. by Peter White and Raymond H. Kelly. 2 vols. Milwaukee, Wisc.: Bruce Publishing Company, 1965- .

First published as Fragen der Theologie Heute (Einsiedeln: Benziger, 1958), this collection consists of individual topical chapters by specialists. Each chapter seeks to indicate the current state of thought on the topic and to summarize the essence of particular movements from a Roman Catholic perspective. Useful bibliographies are also provided. Feiner is helpful for students who wish to have a brief, overall survey

of specific theological topics as viewed in mid-century. See also Macquarrie (C0584) and Schilling (C0669).

C0445 Ferm, Deane W. Contemporary American Theologies: A Critical
Survey. New York: Seabury Press, 1981.

This brief and clearly written work provides useful introductory guidance
on the main features of recent theological thought in America. Ferm
surveys in very concise but informative fashion the main lines and key
variants of such theologies as secular, black, liberationist and feminist.
The book also outlines the new directions being taken by Roman Catholic
and evangelical theologians. This is a good starting point for basic reference or study requirements. See also Carmody (C0382).

C0446 Ferré, Nels Frederick Solomon. Basic Modern Philosophy of Religion.
New York: Charles Scribner's Sons, 1967.

Written as a textbook, this work offers a critical and comprehensive
understanding and assessment of religion. It concentrates on Judeo-Chris-
tian theism since the sixteenth century, including an examination of
belief in God and arguments for God's existence and discussion of meta-
religious thought. This raises important contemporary issues in religious
thought, and its clear style and coverage make it a suitable text for
philosophy of religion courses. See also Flew (C0453), Hick (C0516),
Hudson (C0529) and Smart (C0686).

C0447 Ferré, Nels Frederick Solomon. Christianity and Society. Reason
and the Christian Faith, vol. 3. New York: Harper and Brothers, 1950.
Reprint. Essay Index Reprint Series. Freeport, N.Y.: Books for Libraries
Press, 1970.

This discussion of the bearing of the Christian faith on social solutions
is presented in three main parts: the eternal purpose and the historic
process; the church and the world; concrete considerations. The last
treats issues such as Christian perspectives on war, on property and
on education. An index is provided. The theme is that Christianity provides the right key to practical problems. See also Brunner (C0372)
and Gardner (C0461).

C0448 Field, Benjamin. The Student's Handbook of Christian Theology.
New ed. Ed. by John C. Symons. New York: Phillips and Hunt; Cincinnati,
Ohio: Cranston and Stowe, [1887]. Reprint. Freeport, Pa.: Fountain Press,
1952.

First published in 1868 and long a standard work in Methodist circles,
this handbook provides comprehensive doctrinal definitions in twenty
chapters devoted to the main tenets of Christian belief. Although the
approach is quite old fashioned, the content remains valuable for students
who seek detailed explanations of a very traditional nature. For a broader
view see Halverson (C0501).

C0449 Fischl, Johann. Geschichte der Philosophie. 5 vols. Christliche Philosophie in Einzeldarstellung. Graz: A. Pustet and Verlag Styria, 1948-1954.

This comprehensive reference history, similar in scope to Bréhier (C0366)
or Copleston (C0401), is arranged by individuals with bibliographies

and detailed indexes in each volume. Fischl is a useful reference work for basic philosophical inquiries by theological students, as it outlines clearly and briefly the key points in the thought of major thinkers. See also Ueberweg (C0718).

C0450 Fisher, George Park. History of Christian Doctrine. 2nd ed. The International Theological Library, vol. 4. Edinburgh: T. and T. Clark, 1916. Reprint. 2nd ed. Edinburgh: T. and T. Clark, 1949.

This work was first published by Charles Scribner in 1896. It has been superseded in part by Seeberg (C0676) and more completely by Cunliffe-Jones (C0407). See also McGiffert (C0579).

C0451 Fletcher, Joseph Francis. Moral Responsibility: Situation Ethics at Work. Philadelphia, Pa.: Westminster Press; London: SCM Press, 1967.

Covering the same ground as Situation Ethics (C0452), this collection of fourteen essays, mostly reprints of articles which predate Fletcher's major work, discusses particular situations for ethical decision making. The coverage of situations is very broad and largely avoids theoretical issues, but it does bring vital issues of Christian ethics into question very clearly. This is not a reference work but should be used to illuminate the more theoretical content of Situation Ethics.

C0452 Fletcher, Joseph Francis. Situation Ethics: The New Morality. Philadelphia, Pa.: Westminster Press, 1966.

See also Lehmann (C0562) and Pike (C0627).

C0453 Flew, Antony Garrard Newton. God and Philosophy. New York: Harcourt, Brace and World; London: Hutchinson, 1966.

This work develops and examines a case for Christian theism and sets out to contribute to the philosophy of religion. It discusses alleged incoherences in the concept of God, the invalidity of arguments for divine existence, the problem of evil and flaws in the freewill argument, etc. Arguments are presented clearly and vigorously. It is a useful basis for study in philosophy of religion courses. See also Copleston (C0403), Ferré (C0446), Hick (C0516) and Smart (C0686).

C0454 Ford, John Cuthbert, and Kelly, Gerald. Contemporary Moral Theology. 2 vols. Westminster, Md.: Newman Press, 1958-1963.

See also Lanza (C0558).

C0455 Frankena, William K. Ethics. 2nd ed. Prentice-Hall Foundations of Philosophy Series. Englewood Cliffs, N.J.: Prentice-Hall, 1973.

This widely used introduction is a standard textbook for students new to the field of ethics. Frankena clearly outlines the scope, principles and development of ethical thinking in a scholarly and thorough manner. A brief bibliography (pp. 117-119) is useful for further study, and his Introductory Readings (C0456) offers primary source materials to support the text. See also Banner (C0331), Garner (C0462), Garnett (C0463) and Pepper (C0624).

C0456 Frankena, William F., and Granrose, John T., eds. Introductory Readings in Ethics. Englewood Cliffs, N.J.: Prentice-Hall, 1974.

> While collections of readings generally have little reference value, this volume is slightly different in being correlated with Frankena's introductory textbook (C0455). Here he presents a selection of primary source materials which illustrate, substantiate and clarify various points and aspects of the basic work.

C0457 Fremantle, Anne Jackson, ed. The Social Teachintgs of the Church. New York: New American Library, 1963.

> This volume comprises complete texts or selections from thirteen major encyclicals from Pope Leo XIII to Pope John XXIII. It introduces the student quickly and easily to Catholic social teaching. A thorough subject index facilitates use of the work. See also Calvez (C0379), Fullam (C0460), Harte (C0507) and Husslein (C0532).

C0458 Fries, Heinrich, ed. Handbuch Theologischer Grundbegriffe. Unter Mitarbeit zahlreicher Fachgelehrter. 2 vols. Munich: Kösel Verlag, 1962-1963.

> This concise guide aims to elaborate fundamental theological concepts and to describe their significance in the Roman Catholic tradition. It contains lengthy articles on biblical origins, history and current topics related to the concepts in question. Lengthy bibliographies are supplied for most articles and provide useful guidance on German language publications for further study. A subject index is included in volume 2. See also Scheeben (C0666) and Schmaus (C0671).

C0459 Fritzsche, Hans Georg. Lehrbuch der Dogmatik. 2 vols. Göttingen: Vandenhoeck und Ruprecht, 1964-1967.

> See also Ebeling (C0437) and Luthardt (C0573).

C0460 Fullam, Raymond B., comp. and ed. The Popes on Youth: Principles for Forming and Guiding Youth from Popes Leo XIII to Pius XII. New York: D. McKay Company, 1956.

> This subject arrangement of selections from papal statements on youth includes references to complete texts in English and the original language. An index of titles and subjects is provided. See also Fremantle (C0457), Harte (C0507) and Husslein (C0532).

C0461 Gardner, Edward Clinton. Biblical Faith and Social Ethics. New York: Harper and Row, 1960.

> This useful introductory volume deals with the development of Christian ethics, guiding principles (theological foundations) and Christian ethics in society (sex and marriage, love and justice, economic and political life, race relations). It is mainly concerned with theological ethics, and with their application to major areas of society; it provides extensive treatment of the Bible in relation to these concerns. See also Brunner (C0372), Ferré (C0447) and Ramsey (C0641).

C0462 Garner, Richard T., and Rosen, Bernard. Moral Philosophy: A Systematic Introduction to Normative Ethics and Meta-Ethics. New York: Macmillan

Company, 1967.

This introductory work discusses normative ethics, including summaries of different theories, related nonnormative questions (relativism and freedom) and meta-ethics. It provides a useful summary of different approaches for the beginning student, and suggests exercises and provides helpful bibliographies after each chapter. An index is included. See also Banner (C0331), Frankena (C0455), Garnett (C0463) and Pepper (C0624).

C0463 Garnett, Arthur Campbell. Ethics: A Critical Introduction. New York: Ronald Press Company, 1960.

This introductory work provides a survey of ethics in primitive society and among the great religions of the world, a historical and critical discussion of ethical issues, and selections dealing with such issues as authority and liberty, property rights, marriage and the family (by contributors ranging from Nietzsche to Schweitzer, Bertrand Russell to Pope Pius XI). It is especially useful for students wishing to review the development of philosophical ethics in the West. See also Banner (C0331), Frankena (C0455), Garner (C0462) and Pepper (C0624).

C0464 Gautier, Jean. Some Schools of Catholic Spirituality. With the assistance of Eugene Masure et al. Trans. by Kathryn Sullivan. New York: Desclée Company, 1959.

This translation of La Spiritualité Catholique is a selective survey of the spirituality of the major religious orders, the Imitation of Christ and contemporary French spirituality. It is not particularly strong on the theological bases of the various schools. Some bibliographical references are provided, but there is no index.

C0465 Gerstner, John H. The Theology of the Major Sects. Grand Rapids, Mich.: Baker Book House, 1960.

In 206 pages Gerstner provides much useful information on the theology of such groups as the Seventh Day Adventists, Jehovah's Witnesses, Christian Scientists, Theosophists, Mormons and Spiritualists. However, the analysis is not especially objective, as the author clearly regards the various sects as aberrations from an evangelical Protestant viewpoint. A bibliography (pp. 191-201) is provided, and there are author and subject indexes. Appendixes include tables showing doctrines by sect and vice versa, brief definitions of sects and a glossary of terms used by the sects.

C0466 Gestel, Constant Julius Ferdinand van. La Doctrine Sociale de l'Eglise. 3e éd. Brussels: Pensée Catholique, 1964.

See also Daujat (C0416) and Lubac (C0572).

C0467 Gilson, Etienne Henry. The Christian Philosophy of St. Augustine. Trans. by L.E.M. Lynch. New York: Random House, 1960; London: Victor Gollancz, 1961.

Including a substantial bibliography (pp. 367-383), this classic Roman Catholic study of St. Augustine's philosophy is translated from Introduction à l'Etude de Saint Augustin (2e éd. Paris: Vrin, 1943). Three main parts examine the search for God through understanding and through the will and contemplating God in His works. Detailed notes and two indexes (analytical and proper names) are provided. For a concordance to St. Augustine see Lenfant (C0563).

C0468 Gilson, Etienne Henry. The Christian Philosophy of St. Thomas Aquinas. With a catalogue of St. Thomas's works by I.T. Eschmann. Trans. by L.K. Shook. New York: Random House, 1956; London: Victor Gollancz, 1957.

This translation, with a few revisions and additions, of Le Thomisme (5e éd. Paris: Vrin, 1948) provides a full and thorough discussion of St. Thomas' philosophy. The order of the volume follows St. Thomas' own theological order: God, nature, morality. Detailed notes and extensive bibliographical information are provided. Eschmann's catalog and notes (pp. 381-439) contain ninety-eight entries and detailed annotations which give full information on various editions and translations. For a similar bibliographical survey see Chevalier (C0049). See also Chenu (C0388), Pieper (C0626), Lynch (C0575) and Copleston (C0400).

C0469 Gilson, Etienne Henry. Elements of Christian Philosophy. Garden City, N.Y.: Doubleday and Company, 1960. Reprint. Westport, Conn.: Greenwood Press, 1978.

See also Toinet (C0712).

C0470 Gilson, Etienne Henry. History of Christian Philosophy in the Middle Ages. New York: Random House; London: Sheed and Ward, 1955. Reprint. Westminster, Md.: Christian Classics, 1972.

This authoritative Roman Catholic treatment is arranged chronologically from Justin Martyr to Nicholas of Cusa. Based on La Philosophie au Moyen Age, des Origines Patristiques à la Fin du XIVe Siècle (2e éd. Paris: Payot, 1944), the English version is a full reworking of the original and remains a standard work for the student. An extensive bibliography (pp. 552-804) covers every name and topic mentioned in the text, and an index of authors and historians is provided. Gilson is far more detailed than Steenberghen (C0693) but is not for the absolute beginner. See also Maurer (C0594) and Leff (C0561).

C0471 Gilson, Etienne Henry, gen. ed. A History of Philosophy. 4 vols. New York: Random House, 1962-1966.

This comprehensive survey by noted Roman Catholic scholars is arranged in biographical order, although the emphasis is on doctrine and theory rather than personalities. A general bibliography for each period and for each philosopher is provided, including editions of works and critical annotations on works about them. Each volume is indexed. This is a useful reference work for college students. See also Copleston (C0401) and Bréhier (C0336).

C0472 Gilson, Etienne Henry. Jean Duns Scot: Introduction à Ses Positions Fondamentales. Etudes de Philosophie Médiévale, tome 42. Paris: J. Vrin, 1952.

This insightful introductory study is based mainly on the Commentaries of Peter Lombard and focuses on Duns Scotus' basic philosophical and theological ideas. It does not offer any particular system but attempts to see the man through one of his works. References to other works are included in the notes. See also Bettoni (C0352).

C0473 Gilson, Etienne Henry. The Spirit of Thomism. New York: P.J. Kenedy, 1964.

This brief (127 pp.) volume contains the 175th Anniversary Fenwick Lectures in Philosophy, delivered by the author under the auspices of the Department of Philosophy of Georgetown University. They focus on critical points of St. Thomas' doctrine. Notes follow the four chapters. There is no index. See also Chenu (C0388), Grenet (C0483) and Pieper (C0626).

C0474 Glenn, Paul Joseph. A Tour of the "Summa". St. Louis, Mo.: B. Herder Book Company, 1960.

Thus survey presents a condensed paraphrase of the essential teachings found in the Summa, retaining the original numbering system employed by St. Thomas. It is a highly readable compilation particularly suited for beginners, review work and basic reference inquiries. More detailed guidance is available in Farrell (C0442). See also Grabmann (C0481).

C0475 Glorieux, Palémon. La Littérature Quodlibétique. 2 vols. Bibliothèque Thomiste, 5, 21. Paris: J. Vrin, 1925-1935.

Published under two imprints (also Saulchoir: Revue des Sciences Philosophiques et Théologiques), this two volume work lists the relevant authors, includes a brief sketch of the life of each one and outlines his quodlibetal questions with subdivisions as appropriate. Manuscripts recording the full texts are indicated.

C0476 Gollwitzer, Helmut. An Introduction to Protestant Theology. Philadelphia, Pa.: Westminster Press, 1982.

Very much in the tradition of Barth, this 235 page introduction discusses the nature of theology as an academic discipline, as a science of inquiry and as a servant of faith. It is a sound starting point for the beginner, providing a clear view of traditional Protestant theology. See also De Wolf (C0419).

C0477 Gonzalez, Justo L. A History of Christian Thought. 3 vols. Nashville, Tenn.: Abingdon Press, 1970-1975.

Covering the beginnings to Chalcedon, Augustine to the Reformation and Reformation to the twentieth century, these three volumes are intended to serve as a general introduction. They were originally written for seminary students in Latin America, but were revised for an English speaking audience. They are well organized, and sufficiently well documented to guide more detailed research. See also Heick (C0510).

C0478 Goodspeed, Edgar Johnson. Index Apologeticus sive Clavis Iustini Martyris Operum Aliorumque Apologetarum Pristinorum. Leipzig: J.C. Hinrichs Buchhandlung, 1912.

Goodspeed provides a concordance of Greek Christian apologetic literature.

C0479 Gorman, Robert. Catholic Apologetical Literature in the United States (1784-1858). Catholic University of America Studies in Church History, vol. 28. Washington, D.C.: Catholic University of America Press, 1939.

Prepared as a doctoral thesis, this history covers books, pamphlets and tracts published in defence of the Roman Catholic Church for the period indicated. The works included are listed in an appendix.

C0480 Grabmann, Martin. Die Geschichte der Katholischen Theologie seit dem Ausgang der Vaterzeit. Freiburg im Breisgau: Herder, 1933.

This 368 page study begins with an excellent survey of sources and literature of the history of theology and includes an analysis of the role of patristics in medieval theology. The bulk of the work contains a study of theology as it developed in the middle ages; Grabmann ably outlines the major developments and movements, clearly indicating their key points. For students able to read German this is a valuable handbook of use for basic reference needs. For Catholic surveys of later periods see Hocedez (C0521) and Werner (C0733).

C0481 Grabmann, Martin. Introduction to the "Theological Summa" of St. Thomas. Trans. from the 2nd German ed. by John Stanislaus Zybura. St. Louis, Mo.: B. Herder Book Company, 1930.

See also Farrell (C0442) and Glenn (C0474).

C0482 Grandmaison, Léonce de. Le Dogme Chrétien: Sa Nature, Ses Formules, Son Développement. 3e éd. Paris: G. Beauchesne et Ses Fils, 1928.

This 332 page work provides an analysis from a Roman Catholic viewpoint.

C0483 Grenet, Paul Bernard. Thomism: An Introduction. Trans. by James F. Ross. New York: Harper and Row, 1967.

See also Chenu (C0388), Gilson (C0473) and Pieper (C0626).

C0484 Grillmeier, Alois, Christ in Christian Tradition. Trans. by John Bowden. 2nd ed. Vol. 1- . Atlanta, Ga.: John Knox Press; London: A.R. Mowbray and Company, 1975- .

First published in 1965, this Roman Catholic survey of Christology covers the apostolic age to 451 in volume 1 and provides an analysis which is both thorough and up to date. The treatment is thoroughly ecumenical, making use of current scholarly insights from various traditions in order to offer a judicious critique of the development of Christology. Covering such areas as the birth of Christology, kerygma, theology and dogma, Grillmeier presents factual and interpretive data in a manner highly suitable to advanced students, particularly those interested in such topics as Athanasian orthodoxy, Cappadocian Christology, theology of the hypostatic union and related issues, all of which are dealt with clearly and objectively. See also Aulén (C0323), Pannenberg (C0620) and Watlington (C0727).

C0485 Grisez, Germain Gabriel. Beyond the New Theism: A Philosophy of Religion. Notre Dame, Ind.: University of Notre Dame Press, [1975].

This sophisticated work develops an argument for the existence of an uncaused cause beginning from the existence of contingent entities in the world of experience. It is rather too complex for the college student studying philosophy of religion; for advanced students or teachers it is more appropriate in level of approach but it neglects some key thinkers who have shaped contemporary religious thought and does not provide any new perspective on recent theology.

C0486 Gruezmacher, Richard Heinrich, comp. Textbuch zur Deutschen Systematischen Theologie und Ihrer Geschichte vom 16. bis 20. Jahrhundert. 4 Aufl. Hrsg. von Gerhard G. Muras. 2 vols. Quellen Handbuch der System-atischen Theologie, Bd. 1-2. Gütersloh. C. Bertelsmann, 1955-1961.

See also Herbst (C0514) and Ritschl (C0649).

C0487 Guerry, Emile Maurice. The Social Doctrine of the Catholic Church. Trans. by Miriam Hederman. New York: Alba House, 1961.

This work is a translation of La Doctrine Sociale de l'Eglise, Son Actual-ité, Ses Dimensions, Son Rayonnement (Paris: Bonne Presse, 1957). See also Lubac (C0572).

C0488 Gury, Jean Pierre. Theologia Moralis. Ed. 5. Ed. by Tommaso Angelo Iorio. 3 vols. Naples: M. d'Auria, 1960-1961.

This is a classic textbook on Roman Catholic moral theology. See also Dudáš (C0432).

C0489 Gustafson, James M. Christ and the Moral Life. New York: Harper and Row, 1968.

In this study Gustafson discusses the Christian ethical heritage with reference to three substantive problems in ethics: the nature of the good, the nature of the moral agent, the criteria of moral action. The work contains a penetrating analysis of a wide range of materials from the NT to recent theologians, particularly modern Protestant thinkers. It is a thorough and systematic approach, suitable to serious students of the field. See also Piper (C0628).

C0490 Gustafson, James M. Christian Ethics and the Community. Philadelphia, Pa.: Pilgrim Press, 1971.

This is a collection of ten essays, nearly all published previously between 1965 and 1970. They examine aspects such as Christian ethics in America, various issues involved in the situational ethic debate of the mid-1960s, and the substantive concerns of ethical reflection; they also illustrate developments in the author's own ethical method. They form a useful collection of stimulating studies on the subject.

C0491 Gustafson, James M. Theology and Christian Ethics. Philadelphia, Pa.: United Church Press, 1974.

See also Sellers (C0677) and Thielicke (C0704).

C0492 Guthrie, Shirley Caperton, Jr. Christian Doctrine: Teachings of the Christian Church. Richmond, Va.: CLC Press, 1968.

Produced as part of the Covenant Life Curriculum sponsored by John Knox Press, this survey of the teachings of organized Christianity is planned around the Apostles' Creed. In a clear and conversational style Guthrie presents the beliefs of Protestantism more as possible views than as religious dogmas. For students with little or no background in theology this is a suitable beginning work. See also Hobbs (C0520) and Conn (C0398).

C0493 Guthrie, William Keith Chambers. A History of Greek Philosophy. 5 vols. Cambridge: Cambridge University Press, 1962-1978.

B171
G83

This scholarly survey covers the earlier pre-Socratics and the Pythagoreans (volume 1),pre-Socratic tradition (volume 2), fifth century B.C. (volume 3), Plato (volumes 4-5). In each volume Guthrie adequately discusses both movements and individuals, including analysis of major writings. There are numerous citations and footnote references, and each volume contains an index of passages, a subject index and a bibliography. Guthrie contains a wealth of factual data and is well indexed for reference purposes. For those requiring information on the Greek background to Christian philosophy this is an indispensible work. For a continuation see Armstrong (C0320). See also Marías Aquilera (C0589) and Windelband (C0740) for shorter histories of the period.

C0494 Gutiérrez Garcia, José Luis. Conceptos Fundamentales en la Doctrina Social de la Iglesia. 4 vols. Colección Documental de Ciencias Sociales, 1. Madrid: Centro de Estudios Sociales del Valle de los Caidos, 1971.

C0495 Guttmann, Julius. Philosophies of Judaism: The History of Jewish Philosophy from Biblical Times to Franz Rosenzweig. Trans. by David W. Silverman. New York: Holt, Rinehart and Winston; London: Routledge and Kegan Paul, 1964.

B154
G813

This translation, based on a Hebrew translation of 1951 of the original German version published in 1933, is primarily concerned with the philosophy of Judaism. It covers religious development of Judaism in antiquity, medieval and modern Jewish religious philosophy. See also Cahn (C0375) and Husik (C0531).

C0496 Hägglund, Bengt. History of Theology. Trans. by Gene L. Lund. St. Louis, Mo.: Concordia Publishing House, 1968.

This 425 page translation of Teologins Historia: En Dogmhistorisk Oversikt (3. uppl. Lund: Gleerup, 1966) provides a reasonably comprehensive, nontechnical survey of the history of Christian doctrine from the Fathers to Bultmann. Written from a Lutheran and European perspective, it does, however, give inadequate treatment to some Roman Catholic developments and to the history of Christian thought in the United States. Nonetheless, this is a clearly written, useful introductory work for the student. See also Klotsche (C0550).

BX1754
H313

C0497 Häring, Bernhard. The Law of Christ: Moral Theology for Priests and Laity. Trans. by Edwin G. Kaiser. 3 vols. Westminster, Md.: Newman Press, 1961-1966.

Recognized as a watershed in Roman Catholic moral theology, these three volumes clearly indicate the need for ethics to be in dialogue with fundamental theology, biblical theology, ascetical theology and canon law. They also provide a firm foundation for substantive dialogue with the Protestant ethical tradition. Haring's approach is by way of the scriptures, the fathers and the liturgy rather than via a restatement of dogmatic principles. As a detailed handbook, this is a scholarly and thoroughly documented work which includes a bibliography in each section and an index in each volume. For Catholics and others this is one of the best multi-volume handbooks cum reference works and should be used for inquiries at various levels. For a much more traditional but equally thorough Roman Catholic approach see Davis (C0418).

C0498 Häring, Bernhard. Medical Ethics. Ed. by Gabrielle L. Jean. Slough: St. Paul Publications, 1972; Notre Dame, Ind.: University of Notre Dame Press, 1973.

With its extensive bibliography (pp. 219-235) and wide survey of all aspects of medical ethics this is a most useful work for students of the subject and others. See also Dyck (C0436), Kenny (C0546) and McFadden (C0578).

C0499 Hagenbach, Karl Rudolf. A Text-Book of the History of Doctrines. The Edinburgh translation of Carl W. Buch. Rev. with large additions from the 4th German ed. and other sources by Henry Brynton Smith. 2 vols. New York: Sheldon and Company; Boston, Mass.: Gould and Lincoln, 1861-1862.

This textbook remains useful in providing a compressed statement of the main points of doctrine, supported by quotations from original sources, for the period from the apostolic age to the mid-nineteenth century. Periods are classified as the age of apologetics, the age of polemics, the age of systematic theology, etc. Detailed tables of contents are provided in each volume, with an index in volume 2. References to English and American literature have been included in this edition, and Smith's substantial additions to Hagenbach are indicated by brackets. For a similar Protestant treatment see Clarke (C0390).

C0500 Hall, Thor, ed. A Directory of Systematic Theologians in North America. Waterloo, Ontario: Council on the Study of Religion in cooperation with the University of Tennessee at Chattanooga, 1977.

This 183 page directory of theologians in North America provides basic factual data about Roman Catholic and Protestant academics and researchers in this field. The 580 entries include data on year of birth, higher education, teaching career, representative publications, research interests, current projects, religious affiliation and current address.

C0501 Halverson, Marvis, and Cohen, Arthur, A., eds. A Handbook of Christian Theology: Definition Essays on Concepts and Movements of Thought in Contemporary Protestantism. Cleveland, Ohio: World Publishing Company; Glasgow: William Collins Sons and Company, 1958. Reprint. Cleveland, Ohio: World Publishing Company, 1962.

This useful introductory compendium contains more than 100 essays on major theological concepts and seeks to illustrate emerging emphases in Protestant thought. Most essays include a brief bibliography. Representing American and continental Protestant views, this is not an exhaustive handbook but provides substantial commentary on key concepts for students at various levels. See also Hordern (C0526) and for a more traditional approach Field (C0448).

C0502 Halverson, William H. A Concise Introduction to Philosophy. New York: Random House, 1967.

See also Windelband (C0741).

BL625
H25
1970

C0503 Happold, Frederick Crossfield. Mysticism: A Study and an Anthology. Baltimore, Md.: Penguin Books, 1963.

See also Stace (C0692) and Tanquerey (C0698).

230
H289L

C0504 Harnack, Adolf von. History of Dogma. Trans. from the 3rd ed. by N. Buchanan. 7 vols. Boston, Mass.: Little, Brown and Company, 1899-1903. Reprint. 7 vols. in 4. New York: Dover Publications, 1961.

This classic Protestant survey of Christian dogma and its evolution treats the major events, movements and circumstances very objectively and extremely thoroughly. Although many subsequent investigators have discounted Harnack's basic thesis, this work with its useful scholarly apparatus of footnotes, bibliographies and index continues to serve as a sound reference guide and textbook. For the German version see C0505; for a single volume summary see Mitchell (C0506).

C0505 Harnack, Adolf von. Lehrbuch der Dogmengeschichte. 4 Aufl. 3 vols. Tübingen: J.C.B. Mohr (Paul Siebeck), 1909-1910. Reprint (as 5 Aufl.). 3 vols. Tübingen: J.C.B. Mohr (Paul Siebeck), 1931-1932.

See also the standard English translation by Buchanan (C0504).

BT21
H27
1957L

C0506 Harnack, Adolf von. Outlines of the History of Dogma. Trans. by Edwin Knox Mitchell. Boston, Mass.: Beacon Press, 1957.

This reprint of the authorized English translation of 1893 represents the author's attempt to summarize in one volume his work on dogma. The two main parts examine the rise of and development of ecclesiastical dogma; within each part are books, chapters and sections. The detailed table of contents to some extent compensates for the lack of an index. This is an important work for students of this influential Protestant historiographer, and provides a much shorter version than his multi-volume History of Dogma (C0504).

262.8
H324

C0507 Harte, Thomas Joseph. Papal Social Principles: A Guide and Digest. Milwaukee, Wisc.: Bruce Publishing Company, 1956.

The major papal documents on social problems are arranged under twelve broad subject divisions with an outline, introduction and bibliography supplied for each document. An index of titles and subjects is provided. See also Fremantle (C0457), Fullam (C0460) and Husslein (C0532).

C0508 Hawkins, Denis John Bernard. Christian Ethics. The Twentieth Century Encyclopedia of Catholicism, vol. 58. Section 5: The Life of Faith. New York: Hawthorn Books, 1963.

This brief work examines the main features which distinguish a specifically Christian ethic from a purely philosophical morality. Twelve chapters cover issues such as the crisis of morals, the gift of wisdom, the basis of Christian sexual ethics, Christianity and war, and Christianity and politics. A select bibliography is included, and a full table of contents compensates for the lack of an index. See also Jone (C0537).

C0509 Hazelton, Roger. New Accents in Contemporary Theology. New York: Harper and Row, c. 1960. Reprint. Westport, Conn.: Greenwood Press, 1979.

Based on lectures at Columbia University in 1958, this work analyzes new accents in theology in relation to the arts, science, philosophy, ecumenism and other contemporary concerns. It includes an index, although it is rather inconsistent in coverage of proper names. This theological critique of current developments is stimulating, although the intended audience is not entirely clear, probably those with some knowledge of theology. See also Kliever (C0549).

C0510 Heick, Otto William. A History of Christian Thought. 2 vols. Philadelphia, Pa.: Fortress Press, 1965-1966.

This successor to the two volume work of the same title by Neve (Philadelphia, Pa.: United Lutheran Publication House, 1943-1946) is characterized by improved arrangement and style and by updated bibliographies. It provides a valuable guide which should be supplemented by more detailed works on particular periods. Volume 1 covers ancient, medieval and Reformation periods; volume 2 takes coverage into the twentieth century. The work has been criticized for its neglect of Eastern Orthodox theology, and for some bibliographical omissions. See also Shedd (C0682), Tillich (C0707) and Gonzalez (C0477).

C0511 Hendry, George Stuart. The Holy Spirit in Christian Theology. Rev. ed. Philadelphia, Pa.: Westminster Press, [1965].

This careful analysis of the basic issues involved in the doctrine of the Holy Spirit focuses on five specific relations: the Holy Spirit and Christ; the Holy Spirit and God; the Holy Spirit and the church; the Holy Spirit and the Word; and the Holy Spirit and the human spirit. The work shows thorough familiarity with Roman Catholic and Protestant historical theology, while stressing the use of scripture as the basis for any reform.

C0512 Henry, A.M., ed.-in-chief. Theology Library. Trans. by William Storey et al. 6 vols. in 7. Chicago, Ill.: Fides Publishing Association, 1954-1958.

This translation of Initiation Théologique contains essays by more than forty contributors on major areas of theology; it is intended to introduce beginners to the full spectrum of systematic and dogmatic theology, and this is reflected in both the content and level of detail. The essays provide useful introductory material on theological issues within the following areas: introduction to theology, God, virtues, Christ, sacraments. For Roman Catholic readers this is a useful starting point, and it includes glossaries, bibliographies and indexes for reference purposes. The main drawback to Henry is the somewhat uneven coverage of topics and the rather eclectic approach to the theological system.

C0513 Heppe, Heinrich Ludwig Julius. Reformed Dogmatics Set Out and Illustrated from the Sources. Rev. and ed. by Ernst Bizer. Trans. by G.T. Thomson. London: Allen and Unwin, 1950.

This is the English translation of a work which appeared originally in German in 1861 and was revised and reissued in 1934. It provides a systematic account of classical Calvinist doctrine, with many passages from sixteenth and seventeenth theologians. This is an important textbook for students of historical theology in providing a compendium of classical Calvinist teaching, and for students of dogmatics. See also Berkhof (C0346) and Hoeksema (C0524).

C0514 Herbst, Wolfgang, comp. Quellen zur Geschichte des Evangelischen Gottesdienstes von der Reformation bis zur Gegenwart. Göttinger Theologische Lehrbücher. Göttingen: Vandenhoeck und Ruprecht, [1968].

See also Gruezmacher (C0486) and Ritschl (C0649).

BX1751
H4 1957+

C0515 Hervé, Jean Marie. Manuale Theologiae Dogmaticae. 4 vols. Paris: Berche et Pagis, 1951-1953.

Consisting of different editions for each volume in this printing, Hervé provides a traditional Roman Catholic survey of dogmatic theology. The first volume covers revelation and the Christian tradition generally; the second, God and the trinity, creation, the incarnate word; the third, grace of Christ, theological virtues, the sacraments in general; the fourth, individual sacraments. For those who want broadly based information without excessive detail this remains a sound Roman Catholic guide; it is particularly useful on the sacraments as traditionally viewed within this tradition. See also Calcagno (C0377) and Tanquerey (C0697).

BL51
H494

C0516 Hick, John. Philosophy of Religion. Foundations of Philosophy Series. Englewood Cliffs, N.J.: Prentice-Hall, 1973.

This introductory work covers western and eastern religions, and provides a readable account of major issues. The bulk of the text deals with the Judaic-Christian religious tradition, but there are also chapters on the Indian belief in reincarnation and on conflicting truth claims in the world's major religions. See also Ferré (C0446), Hudson (C0529) and Smart (C0686).

C0517 Higgins, Thomas J. Basic Ethics. Milwaukee, Wisc.: Bruce Publishing Company, 1968.

See also Hudson (C0528).

C0518 Hillerdal, Gunnar. Kirche und Sozialethik. Gütersloh: G. Mohn, 1963.

This is a translation of the Swedish Kyrke och Socialetik. See also Rasmussen (C0642).

C0519 Hirsch, Emanuel. Ethos und Evangelium. Berlin: Walter de Gruyter und Kompagnie, 1966.

This detailed ethical survey of thirty chapters consists of three main parts: Die Antinomien des Ethos, Ethische Ansicht der geschichtlichen

Gemeinschaft, Fragen und Gestalten des individuellen Ethos. Within each of these sections Hirsch provides a series of chapters dealing with the main concepts and key issues of Christian ethics. For those able to read German this is a useful introduction to the field. It also has some reference value because of the very specific topics dealt with in each chapter. See also Hirsch (C0715).

C0520 Hobbs, Herschel H. A Layman's Handbook of Christian Doctrine. Nashville, Tenn.: Broadman Press, [1974].

This 142 page handbook for general readers provides a conservative Protestant guide to Christian doctrine. Questions of doctrine are dealt with clearly but often too simply. See also Guthrie (C0492) and Conn (C0398).

C0521 Hocedez, Edgar. Histoire de la Théologie au XIXe Siècle. 3 vols. Museum Lessianum. Section Théologique, nos. 43-45. Brussels: Editions Universelles, 1947-1952.

This history of theology as viewed from a continental Roman Catholic viewpoint provides concise but detailed treatment of the major movements, personalities and events. The three volumes cover 1800-1831, 1831-1870, 1878-1903. Each chapter is subdivided into brief topical or historical sections for ease of reference, and extensive bibliographies follow each chapter. For students of nineteenth century European theology this remains a sound, if somewhat biased, survey and reference source. For other Catholic surveys see Grabmann (C0480) and Werner (C0733).

C0522 Hodge, Archibald Alexander. Outlines of Theology. New York: R. Carter and Brothers, 1879. Reprint. Grand Rapids, Mich.: Wm. B. Eerdmans Publishing Company, 1949.

Available in many reprints, this standard Presbyterian survey contains forty-three chapters on topics such as predestination, original sin, faith, justification, and the sacraments. There is neither an index nor bibliography. Extracts from the principal confessions, creeds and classical theological writers are appended to some chapters. It was written as a textbook for theological students. See also Cave (C0387), Clarke (C0390) and Shedd (C0681).

C0523 Hodge, Charles. Systematic Theology. 3 vols. New York: Charles Scribner and Company; London: Thomas Nelson and Sons, 1872-1873. Reprint. 3 vols. Grand Rapids, Mich.: Wm. B. Eerdmans Publishing Company, 1960.

Available in many reprints, this Presbyterian outline of systematic theology provides a thorough treatment. Volume 1 deals with theism, the nature and attributes of God, the trinity, the divinity of Christ and related aspects. Volume 2 focuses on man, and on soteriology. Volume 3 continues examination of concepts such as faith, justification, the law, and contains a section on eschatology. Footnote references are provided, and each volume has a detailed table of contents. See also Kuyper (C0556). For a Lutheran treatment of similar quality see Pieper (C0625).

C0524 Hoeksema, Herman. Reformed Dogmatics. Grand Rapids, Mich.: Reformed Free Publishing Association, 1966.

This 917 page survey covers the entire field of systematic theology as formulated within the conservative Protestant tradition. A detailed content analysis and a subject index add to the reference value of this work. Extensive use of untranslated Latin and Dutch tends to narrow the range of readers able to use the work with ease. See also Berkhof (C0346) and Heppe (C0513).

C0525 Hörmann, Karl. An Introduction to Moral Theology. Trans. by Edward Quinn. Westminster, Md.: Newman Press, 1961.

Intended primarily for laymen studying theology, this work describes the main characteristics of the Roman Catholic Church's teaching. There are two main parts: general principles of morality; the moral life. Bibliographies are given at the end of each chapter, and an index is provided. See also Dailey (C0412).

C0526 Hordern, William. A Layman's Guide to Protestant Theology. Rev. ed. New York: Macmillan Company, 1968.

This clear and simply written exposition of Protestant theology sketches the historical background of contemporary theology, as well as providing more detailed treatment of Barth, Niebuhr, Tillich, Bultmann and Bonhoeffer, and a survey of recent developments. It is suitable for beginners in its clear and interesting coverage of the topic. See also Halverson (C0501).

C0527 Horton, Walter Marshall. Christian Theology: An Ecumenical Approach. Rev. ed. New York: Harper and Brothers, 1958.

This 304 page textbook in systematic theology analyzes eight major concerns (Christianity, the knowledge of God, the nature of God, God and the world, God and man, Christ the Saviour, the church and the means of grace, and Christian hope) in terms of the underlying universal human problem, and of a universal Christian answer. Ecumenical aspects are emphasized. The work has been criticized for giving too little attention to Eastern Orthodoxy.

C0528 Hudson, William Donald. Modern Moral Philosophy. Garden City, N.Y.: Doubleday and Company; London: Macmillan and Company, 1970.

This basic guide summarizes recent English language moral philosophy and places emphasis on theories of meaning as they pertain to moral discourse. Together with Frankena (C0455) this is both a useful introduction and a basic reference handbook. See also Higgins (C0517).

C0529 Hudson, William Donald. A Philosophical Approach to Religion. New York: Barnes and Noble; London: Macmillan and Company, 1974.

This carefully argued study systematically applies stringent criteria to some of the fundamentals of religious belief, concluding that such belief is in principle tenable. It has been criticized for its reliance on the concept of a language game. It tends to focus on questions about rather than within religious belief. See also Ferré (C0446), Lewis (C0564) and Smart (C0686).

C0530 Hughes, Philip Edgcumbe. Theology of the English Reformers. London:

Hodder and Stoughton, 1965; Grand Rapids, Mich.: Wm. B. Eerdmans Publishing Company, [1966, c. 1965].

This 283 page volume quotes extensively from the Reformers, with some commentary by the author. The selections are arranged under headings such as "justification", "ministry" and "sacraments". Treatment reflects the author's Protestant viewpoint.

C0531 Husik, Isaac. A History of Medieval Jewish Philosophy. New York: Macmillan Company, 1916. Reprint. New York: Meridian Books, 1958.

This standard survey is a useful reference point for those without much background knowledge. The 1958 reprint includes a bibliography updated in both 1930 and 1941 reprints. See also Cahn (C0375) and Guttmann (C0495).

C0532 Husslein, Joseph Casper, comp. Social Wellsprings. 2 vols. Milwaukee, Wisc.: Bruce Publishing Company, 1940-1942.

The complete texts of thirty-two of the most significant social encyclicals of Pope Leo XIII and Pope Pius XI are presented in volumes 1 and 2 respectively, with an introduction and bibliography for each document. Topics include marriage, the family, politics and government. An index is provided in each volume. See also Fremantle (C0457), Fullam (C0460) and Harte (C0507).

C0533 Index Thomisticus: Sancti Thomae Aquinatis Operum Omnium Indices et Concordantiae in Quibus Verborum Omnium et Singulorum Formae et Lemmata cum Suis Frequentiis et Contextibus Variis Modis Referentur; quaeque Auspice Paulo VI Summo Pontifice Consociata Plurium Opera atque Electronico IBM Automato Usus Digessit Robertus Busa. Vol. 1- . Stuttgart-Bad Cannstatt: Frommann-Holzboog, 1974- .

Projected in thirty volumes, this massive undertaking contains a series of indexes and concordances to all works by St. Thomas or attributed to him. The concordances are divided by parts of speech and provide full quotations in context plus references for each word and form. The indexes list references to his works in coded form, which is not always easy to decipher. Nevertheless, Index Thomisticus is unquestionably an essential reference tool for all advanced research work on St. Thomas.

C0534 Institut International de Philosophie. Philosophy in the Mid-Century: A Survey. Ed. by Raymond Klibansky. 4 vols. Florence: La Nuova Italia, 1958-1959.

Published under the auspices of Unesco, this compilation surveys developments in philosophy between 1949 and 1955, although the dates are expanded where necessary. Volume 3 covers the philosophy of value, of history and of religion. The contributions are in French or English and include selective bibliographies. For information on the state of the philosophy of religion in mid-twentieth century thought this is a useful survey. For a continuation see Klibansky's later work (C0548); see also Burr (C0373).

C0535 International Directory of Philosophy and Philosophers. Ed. 1- . Bowling Green, Ohio: Bowling Green State University, Philosophy Documentation

Center, 1965- ; quadrennial.

This directory comprises a list of international philosophical organizations and a list arranged by country or territory, giving colleges and universities (with names of members of philosophy staffs), institutes and research centers, philosophical associations and societies, philosophy journals and publishers specializing in philosophical works. Part 1 lists international organizations; part 2, entries by country. See also American Catholic Philosophical Association (C0318) and Directory of American Philosophers (C0427), as well as Menchaca (C0268) and Runes (C0661).

C0536 Jennings, Theodore W., Jr. Introduction to Theology: An Invitation to Reflection upon the Christian Mythos. Philadelphia, Pa.: Fortress Press, c. 1976.

This introductory work aims to clarify the nature and tasks of theology. The first part examines theological reflection and its content and process, the second discusses the dialectic of theological reflection, and the third aspects of theological enquiry such as revelation and faith. There is neither bibliography nor index. This is a suitable description of a particular approach to theological reflection for the student of theology. See also Baillie (C0326).

C0537 Jone, Heribert. Moral Theology. Trans. and adapted to the laws and customs of the United States of America by Urban Adelman. 16th ed. Westminster, Md.: Newman Press, 1956.

This Roman Catholic work provides brief but clear treatment of moral questions in a wide range of areas, including definitions, distinctions and examples to help clarify and illuminate various issues. An index is provided. See also Hawkins (C0508) and Slater (C0684).

C0538 Kaiser, Edwin G. Sacred Doctrine: An Introduction to Theology. Westminster, Md.: Newman Press, 1958.

See also Alexander (C0315).

C0539 Karmirēs, Iōannēs Nikolaou. Dogmatica et Symbolica Monumenta Orthodoxae Catholicae Ecclesiae. 2 vols. Athens: n.p., 1952-1953. Reprint. 2 vols. Graz: Akademische Druck-- und Verlagsanstalt, 1968.

These two volumes examine aspects of the Eastern Church such as symbols, liturgies and various key statements on, for example, relations with Protestants and Roman Catholics. It is of interest to those seeking easy access to the original texts (which are quoted together with notes and introductions). A bibliography is provided. See also Karmirēs' Synopsis (C0540) and Lossky (C0571), Meyendorff (C0596) and Platon (C0629).

C0540 Karmirēs, Iōannēs Nikolaou. A Synopsis of the Dogmatic Theology of the Orthodox Church. Trans. by George Dimopoulos. [n.p.]: Christian Orthodox Edition, [c. 1973].

Available in several languages, this 120 page translation of the classic work by John Kamiris provides a valuable summary of the theology of the Orthodox Church. See also his Dogmatica (C0539), Lossky (C0571), Meyendorff (C0596) and Platon (C0629).

C0541 Die Katholische Sozialdoktrin in Ihrer Geschichtlichen Entfaltung. 4 vols. Aachen: Scientia Humana Inst., 1976.

This very thorough compilation contains documents in Latin and German from 1431 to 1976 which deal with social issues. Papal documents, conciliar statements and related materials are reproduced in full. These are arranged by subject, and there are detailed indexes of names, documents and subjects. See also Utz (C0719).

C0542 Kaufmann, Gordon D. Systematic Theology: A Historicist Perspective. New York: Charles Scribner's Sons, 1969 [c. 1968].

This 543 page survey of major topics in systematic theology proposes a viewpoint that "understands the world in historical terms, and man in terms of the radical implications of his historicity." There are four main parts covering the Christian understanding of ultimate reality, of the world, of man and of the redeemed life. It is a well written, thorough attempt to do justice to the Christian tradition and to modern knowledge and to set out a full scale systematic theology.

C0543 Keely, Robin, ed. Eerdman's Handbook to Christian Belief. Grand Rapids, Mich.: Wm. B. Eerdmans Publishing Company, 1982.

C0544 Kelly, John Norman Davidson. Early Christian Creeds. 3rd ed. New York: D. McKay Company; London: Longmans, Green and Company, 1972.

This is a standard work for more advanced students and scholars. See also Badcock (C0324), Curtis (C0411) and Schaff (C0664).

C0545 Kelly, John Norman David. Early Christian Doctrines. 4th ed. London: Adam and Charles Black, 1968.

This thorough treatment of Christian doctrine from the apostolic era to the Council of Chalcedon is intended for students and others interested in an outline account of theological development in the church of the fathers. There are many quotations from theologians of the time, and sources are indicated in footnotes. Brief bibliographies are appended to the chapters, and an index is provided. See also Bethune-Baker (C0351) and Daniélou (C0413).

C0546 Kenny, John Paulinus. Principles of Medical Ethics. 2nd ed. Westminster, Md.: Newman Press, 1962.

Intended to provide moral guidance in the medical and nursing professions, this textbook, which was developed from lectures given to pre-medical and nursing students, begins with a chapter on the fundamental principles of morality. It then treats issues such as professional rights and duties, morals and marriage, the administration of baptism in hospital practice, etc. A reading list follows each section, and there are references and a bibliography at the end of the book. An index is provided, and there are six appendixes containing various codes of ethics and directives for Catholic hospitals. This is a useful single volume introduction in the field. See also Dyck (C0436), Häring (C0498) and McFadden (C0578).

C0547 Kieffer, George H. Bioethics: A Textbook of Issues. Reading, Mass.: Addison-Wesley Publishing Company, 1979.

B804
C57
V.3 only
(PHEN.
CENTER)

C0548 Klibansky, Raymond, ed. Contemporary Philosophy: A Survey. 4 vols. Florence: La Nuova Italia Editrice, 1968-1971.

This continuation of Philosophy in the Mid-Century (C0534) covers esthetics, ethics, law, religion and politics in volume 4. The forty-eight contributions in this substantial (695 pp.) volume include extensive bibliographies, and there are indexes of subjects and persons. For the period covered this is a useful survey which conveys the essence of current thinking in scholarly but nontechnical language. See also Burr (C0373).

C0549 Kliever, Lonnie D. The Shattered Spectrum: A Survey of Contemporary Theology. Atlanta, Ga.: John Knox Press, 1981.

This examination of theology since the Second World War focuses on six prominent schools, including theologies of secularity, process and liberation. The ideas of each movement's chief spokesmen and the movement's overall strengths and weaknesses are summarized. See also Hazelton (C0509).

C0550 Klotsche, Ernest Heinrich. The History of Christian Doctrine. With additional chapters by John Theodore Mueller and David P. Scaer. Rev. ed. Grand Rapids, Mich.: Baker Book House, 1979.

This Protestant history of Christian doctrine treats four periods: the rise and development of doctrine in the patristic age, developments in the scholastic period, development and fixation of doctrine through the Reformation and Counter-Reformation, and aspects of doctrine in the modern era. There is a detailed table of contents (but no index) and references to works for further study are included. See also Hägglund (C0496).

BX1758
K6
,919X

C0551 Koch, Anton. A Handbook of Moral Theology. Adapted and ed. by Arthur Preuss. 5 vols. St. Louis, Mo.: B. Herder Book Company, 1918-1924.

The five volumes of this traditional Roman Catholic explication of moral theology cover methodology, literature, subject, norm and object; sin and the means of grace; man's duties to self, God and other men. For a German language treatment see Schilling (C0668). See also Tillmann (C0710).

C0552 Koenker, Ernest Benjamin. Great Dialecticians in Modern Christian Thought. Minneapolis, Minn.: Augsburg Publishing House, 1971.

This work develops the theme that theology should foster dialectical thought about God, the world and man, to examine contradictions and reveal identities in opposing views, and to look toward a final synthesis. Ten post-Reformation thinkers are studied: Luther, Pascal, Kierkegaard, Barth, Elert, Bodhme, Hegel, Tillich, Heidegger and Bultmann. The book is of interest for its survey of the above, as much as for its vigorous defence of the need for dialectical thinking. See also Mackintosh (C0582).

C0553 Kreck,Walter. Grundfragen der Dogmatik. Einführung in die Evangel-ische Theologie, Bd. 3. Munich: C. Kaiser Verlag, 1970.

See also Pannenberg (C0619).

C0554 Kress, Robert. A Rahner Handbook. Atlanta, Ga.: John Knox Press, 1982.

This 118 page handbook provides guidance on studying Rahner and uses biographical data and primary sources to offer insights into his thought. A bibliography (pp. 107-108), an appendix on how to read Rahner and an index are also provided. This is a useful work for students about to study this theologian. See also Vorgrimler (C0723).

C0555 Küng, Hans. The Church. Trans. by Ray and Rosaleen Ockenden. London: Burns and Oates, 1967; New York: Sheed and Ward, 1968 [c. 1967].

Clearly not intended as a textbook or reference work, this seminal study by Küng nevertheless serves both functions. It is a comprehensive survey of the doctrine of the church and covers everything from biblical exegesis to contemporary doctrinal statements. Küng carefully discusses the differing polity of Roman Catholic and Protestant traditions in ecumenical perspective. This work is recommended not only as a significant Roman Catholic study but also as a general textbook on ecclesiology for students of all traditions. It is well indexed for reference requirements.

C0556 Kuyper, Abraham. Principles of Sacred Theology. Trans. by J. Hendrik de Vries. New York: Charles Scribner's Sons, 1898. Reprint. Grand Rapids, Mich.: Wm. B. Eerdmans Publishing Company, 1954.

Based on Kuyper's Encyclopaedie der Heilige Godgeleerdheid (3 vols. Amsterdam: J.A. Wormser, 1894) and including part of volume 1 and all of volume 2, this is a useful supplement to Hodge (C0523). The analysis is from a Calvinistic viewpoint, and includes a review of the history of theology, as well as a history of the name, idea and conception of theological encyclopedia. The main part treats the place of theology among the sciences and the nature of theology as a science. An index is provided.

C0557 Landgraf, Artur Michael. Dogmengeschichte der Frühscholastik. 4 parts in 8 vols. Regensburg: Friedrich Pustet Verlag, 1952-1956.

This work provides an extensive survey of the history of early scholastic theology.

C0558 Lanza, Antonio, and Palazzini, Pietro. Principles of Moral Theology. Trans. by W.J. Collins. Vol. 1- . Boston, Mass.: St. Paul Editions, 1961- .

See also Ford (C0454).

C0559 Lawson, John. Comprehensive Handbook of Christian Doctrine. Englewood Cliffs, N.J.: Prentice-Hall, 1967.

This handbook occupies a middle ground between elementary introductions to theology and more detailed technical discussions of theological issues. It treats the historical development of Christian doctrine as well as focusing on divisions of thought within Christianity. This is a useful contribution for the serious, nonprofessional reader. See also Macquarrie (C0583).

C0560 Lee, Francis Nigel. <u>A Christian Introduction to the History of Philos-</u><u>ophy</u>. University Series: Historical Studies. Nutley, N.J.: Craig Press, 1969.

See also Brown (C0369) and Gilson (C0470).

C0561 Leff, Gordon. <u>Medieval Thought: St. Augustine to Ockham</u>. Baltimore, Md.: Penguin Books, 1958.

Available in various imprints, this concise introduction to the special nature of the medieval philosophical outlook is an excellent guide for students new to the field. The period is treated in three parts, with valuable introductory chapters to each part. The work has been criticized on some points of detail. See also Armstrong (C0320), Gilson (C0470) and Maurer (C0594).

C0562 Lehmann, Paul Louis. <u>Ethics in a Christian Context</u>. New York: Harper and Row; London: SCM Press, 1963.

This volume comprises three main parts: Christian faith and Christian ethics; Christian and philosophical thinking about ethics; and the question of conscience. A bibliography (pp. 367-370) and indexes of biblical references, names and subjects are included. See also Fletcher (C0452).

C0563 Lenfant, David. <u>Concordantiae Augustinianae; sive, Collectio Omnium</u> <u>Sententiarum quae Sparsim Reperintur in Omnibus S. Augustini Operibus.</u> <u>Ad Instar Concordantiarum Sacrae Scripturae</u>. 2 vols. Paris: D. and G. Cram-oisy, 1656-1665.

For a basic study of St. Augustine see Gilson (C0467).

C0564 Lewis, Hywel David. <u>Philosophy of Religion</u>. Teach Yourself Books. London: English Universities Press, 1965.

This clear and comprehensive introductory work, designed for self instruc-tion, deals with religion and ethics, revelation and authority and other major issues in this area. Carefully chosen examples and various aids to understanding make this a most instructive work for the beginner. Lists of books for further reading provide guidance to more detailed research on each topic covered. See also Hudson (C0529).

C0565 Lillie, William. <u>An Introduction to Ethics</u>. 3rd ed. With a new bibliog-raphy. New York: Barnes and Noble; London: Methuen and Company, 1961.

This introductory book for beginners includes material on twentieth century moral philosophers. The various concepts are discussed and contributions of different theorists summarized. There are helpful sugges-tions for further reading (pp. 329-339), and an index is provided. See also Mabbott (C0576).

C0566 Linden, James V., and Costello, William T. <u>The Fundamentals of</u> <u>Religion</u>. Chicago, Ill.: Loyola University Press, 1956.

This 344 page textbook is useful for those requiring a Roman Catholic approach to apologetics. See also Alexander (C0314).

C0567 Litton, Edward Arthur. <u>Introduction to Dogmatic Theology</u>. New ed. Ed. by Philip E. Hughes. London: J. Clarke, 1960.

See also Cassilly (C0384) and O'Collins (C0612).

C0568 Lohr, Charles H. Thomas Aquinas, "Scriptum super Sententiis": An Index of Authorities Cited. Amersham: Avebury Publishing Company, 1980.

As the first published index to Aquinas' Sentences of Peter Lombard, this 391 page work greatly facilitates the study of Aquinas' use of individual sources and his attitude towards doctrinal tradition. The seven sections list all citations .of scripture, works of Lombard, Augustine, Aristotle, Dionysius and other authors, as well as sects, heresies and quidams.

C0569 Lohse, Bernhard. A Short History of Christian Doctrine. Trans. by F. Ernest Stoeffler. Philadelphia, Pa.: Fortress Press, 1966.

This 304 page translation of Epochen der Dogmengeschichte (Stuttgart: Kreuz Verlag, c. 1963), which itself is now in a third edition, presents a general discussion of doctrinal development throughout the history of the church. Lohse treats the major doctrines and dogmas without placing undue emphasis on his own theological interpretation, which is that of German Protestantism. Both historical and doctrinal elements are explained clearly and succinctly , making this an ideal single volume history for reference purposes. A bibliography, including English titles, and an index are provided. See also Cunliffe-Jones (C0406) and Tillich (C0707).

C0570 Long, Edward LeRoy. A Survey of Christian Ethics. New York: Oxford University Press, 1967.

This survey of historical and contemporary approaches in Christian ethics considers the varieties and functions of ethical discourse, the formulation of the ethical norm, the implementation of ethical decisions and issues of analysis and evaluation. Bibliographical references are provided in notes, and an index is included. The work attempts to be comprehensive, covering a considerable amount of material. See also Waddams (C0724).

C0571 Lossky, Vladimir. Orthodox Theology: An Introduction. Trans. by Ian and Ihita Kesarcodi-Watson. Crestwood, N.Y.: St. Vladimir's Seminary Press, 1978.

Originally intended as a course in dogmatic theology, this work investigates the fundamental questions of Orthodox theology (creation, original sin, etc.). Bibliographical references are included, although there is no separate bibliography; nor is there an index. See also the works by Karmirēs (C0539, C0540), Meyendorff (C0596) and Platon (C0629).

C0572 Lubac, Henri de. Catholicisme: Les Aspects Sociaux du Dogme. Foi Vivante, tome 13. Paris: Editions du Cerf, 1965.

This Roman Catholic work examines the social aspects of the church's teaching, considers some implications (including the role of Christianity in history), and examines the contemporary theological situation and the teachings of the church on the individual and society. Detailed notes and references accompany the text. There is no index, but the table of contents provides some guidance. See also Daujat (C0416), Gestel (C0466) and Guerry (C0487).

C0573 Luthardt, Christoph Ernst. Kompendium der Dogmatik; Gegenwarts-gemäss Gestaltet. 13. Aufl. Ed. by Robert Jelke. Heidelberg: Jedermann Verlag, 1948.

This classic German Lutheran treatment of dogmatic theology surveys the entire field broadly and succinctly for a student audience. Following a useful introductory section and a brief overview of the history of dogmatics, there are six sections describing the various facets of dog-matic theology. God, man, Christ, redemption and sanctification, the church and other topics are all dealt with briefly but clearly in a very traditional way. The table of contents fully outlines the chapters, and there is an index. For students able to read German and Latin Luthardt is a remarkably useful reference volume which adequately states the traditional Protestant view. See also Eberling (C0437) and Fritzsche (C0459).

C0574 Luther, Martin. Luther's Works. Ed. by Jaroslav Jan Pelikan and Helmut T. Lehmann. 55 vols. Philadelphia, Pa.: Fortress Press, 1955.

Begun by Concordia Publishing House, this definitive English translation includes all of Luther's writings from commentaries and sermons to polemical texts and letters.

C0575 Lynch, Lawrence E. A Christian Philosophy. New York: Charles Scrib-ner's Sons, 1968.

This book is in fact an introduction to the philosophy of St. Thomas Aquinas. It examines epistemology, especially the relationship between philosophy and theology, anthropology, and philosophic knowledge of God. Some of the concerns of modern philosophers such as Sartre, Russell and Heidegger are compared with St. Thomas' treatment of similar issues. This is a readable, nontechnical introductory work, with a misleadingly general title. See also Gilson (C0468) and Copleston (C0400).

C0576 Mabbott, John David. An Introduction to Ethics. Hutchinson University Library: Philosophy. London: Hutchinson, 1966.

This introductory volume for beginners discusses various concepts in moral philosophy and different theories. References are used sparingly in the text, but brief bibliographies are given after each chapter. An index is provided. For those who have not studied philosophy or ethics this is a helpful, compact work. See also Lillie (C0565).

C0577 McCabe, Herbert. What Is Ethics All About? Washington, D.C.: Corpus Books, 1969.

This 215 page textbook for students new to the field of Christian ethics seeks to bridge the gap between principalist and situationalist approaches represented by Thielicke (C0704) and Fletcher (C0452). McCabe suggests that three guidelines are decisive in ethical decision making: meaning (creation), law (exodus), love (resurrection); within this threefold frame-work it is possible to make moral judgments which both take into account

Christian tradition and reflect the need to be situationally flexible. Although brief, this is a clear and lucid exposition of a moderate approach to Christian ethics. See also Wassmer (C0726).

C0578 McFadden, Charles Joseph. Medical Ethics. 6th ed. Philadelphia, Pa.: F.A. Davis Company, 1967.

This work is concerned with the application of moral principles to medicine, and was written particularly for the medical profession. It treats issues such as contraception, abortion, sterilization, as well as broader questions of human rights and the rights of the patient in the spiritual order. Appendixes include various formal statements regarding ethics and medicine, and an index is provided. See also Dyck (C0436), Häring (C0498) and Kenny (C0546).

C0579 McGiffert, Arthur Cushman. A History of Christian Thought. 2 vols. New York: Charles Scribner's Sons, 1932-1933. Reprint. New York: Charles Scribner's Sons, 1947.

Treating the development of Christian thought from its NT beginnings to the time of Erasmus, this work is designed for students. Volume 1 covers from Jesus to John of Damascus; volume 2, the West from Tertullian to Erasmus. It is carefully documented, providing adequate guidance for further research. Each volume contains a substantial bibliography and an index. See also Cunliffe-Jones (C0407), Fisher (C0450) and Workman (C0743).

C0580 MacIntyre, Alasdair C. A Short History of Ethics. New York: Macmillan Company, 1966; London: Routledge and Kegan Paul, 1967.

This introductory work treats the history of ethics from the Greek philosophers to modern moral philosophy, paying particular attention to certain individuals (Plato, Kant, etc.). There are few bibliographical references, but an index is provided. For the undergraduate this is a suitable introduction. See also Dittrich (C0429) and Bourke (C0362).

C0581 McKenzie, Leon. Designs for Progress: An Introduction to Catholic Social Doctrine. Boston, Mass.: St. Paul Editions, 1968.

See also Dirksen (C0428) and Masse (C0591).

C0582 Mackintosh, Hugh Ross. Types of Modern Theology: Schleiermacher to Barth. New York: Charles Scribner's Sons; London: Nisbet and Company, 1937. Reprint. Welwyn: Nisbet and Company, 1962.

Available in several reprints, this helpful survey provides a critical assessment of the theology of Schleiermacher, Hegel, Ritschl, Troeltsch, Kierkegaard and Barth. Although Mackintosh has been superseded in many respects, it remains a sound introduction for students seeking basic guidance on the theological work of these individuals. See also Koenker (C0552) and for a more conservative interpretation Ramm (C0639).

C0583 Macquarrie, John. Principles of Christian Theology. 2nd ed. New York: Charles Scribner's Sons; London: SCM Press, c. 1977.

One of the few Anglican surveys of systematic theology, this 544 page textbook seeks to present the main themes, contemporary views and modern currents of theology in an objective and ecumenical manner. See also Lawson (C0559).

C0584 Macquarrie, John. Twentieth-Century Religious Thought: The Frontiers of Philosophy and Theology, 1900-1960. New York: Harper and Row; London: SCM Press, 1963.

B804
M25
1971

This clearly organized handbook identifies types, trends and authors of recent and contemporary thought. The bulk of the work consists of short summaries of the thought of approximately 150 theologians and philosophers, arranged in three major phases, with subdivisions into schools of thought. Each chapter includes a summary and criticism, and introductory and concluding chapters make the patterns clear. This work covers a wide area, providing a wealth of information. Its value is as a comprehensive reference book rather than an in depth analysis. See also Feiner (C0444) and Schilling (C0669).

C0585 Mainelli, Vincent P., comp. Social Justice. Official Catholic Teachings, vol. 4. Wilmington, N.C.: Consortium Books, 1978.

BX1753
5625

Covering social justice in its broadest sense, Mainelli presents the texts of various official Catholic documents from a variety of sources. The items are numbered in topical sections and indexed by subject. This is an informative collection of source materials which includes both older and more modern documents. It is a revision of Social Justice! The Catholic Position (Washington, D.C.: Consortium Books, 1975). See also Masse (C0591).

C0586 Maloney, George A. A History of Orthodox Theology since 1453. Belmont, Mass.: Nordland Publishing Company, 1976.

BX320.
M84

This 388 page history examines the development of Orthodox theology in five separate traditions: Russian, Greek, Serbian, Bulgarian, Rumanian. It provides a sound analysis and excellent condensation of major trends for the beginner. Additional bibliographical references are given in notes, although there is no composite bibliography.

C0587 Manton, J.D. Introduction to Theological German. 2nd ed. Grand Rapids, Mich.: Wm. B. Eerdmans Publishing Company; London: Tyndale Press, 1973.

This course in theological German is aimed at the student with no previous knowledge of the language. Each chapter presents the basic grammar clearly, simply and concisely, placing emphasis on the rapid acquisition of reading skills. A vocabulary list, grammatical tables and an index are provided for quick reference. This is a very useful and effective text for those who wish to acquire basic theological German in a very short time. For a German-English word list see Bangs (C0330).

C0588 Maréchal, Joseph. Précis d'Histoire de la Philosophie Moderne: De la Renaissance à Kant. Avec supplément bibliographique de 1933 à 1949. Museum Lessianum, Section Philosophique, no. 16. Brussels: L'Edition Universelle; Paris: Desclée de Brouwer, 1951.

B79
M3x

Maréchal treats each philosopher of the period, giving biography, major teachings in summary form and bibliographical data. General introductions to movements and periods are also provided, again with bibliographies. Useful indexes are included, and the bibliographies have been updated to 1949 in this edition. For information on modern thinkers with some relevance to philosophical theology this is a useful compendium. Although originally projected as a multivolume work, Maréchal never proceeded beyond this single volume. See also Collins (C0394).

C0589 Marías Aquilera, Julián. History of Philosophy. Trans. by Stanley Appelbaum and Clarence C. Strowbridge. New York: Dover Publications, 1967.

This translation of Historia de la Filosofía (22. ed. Madrid: Revista de Occidente, 1966) provides a clear and readable account of philosophy from the pre-Socratics to existentialism and beyond. Full details on the systems of all major and many minor philosophers are included to make this a valuable reference work. An adequate bibliography is also provided (pp. 469-487). See also Guthrie (C0493), Armstrong (C0320) and other works for more detailed coverage of limited periods.

C0590 Martin, James Alfred. The New Dialogue between Philosophy and Theology. New York: Seabury Press; London: Adam and Charles Black, 1966.

This work summarizes the work of various writers on philosophy and theology. The main focus is on the impact of the rise of British analytical philosophy on the philosophy of religion. The summaries of writers such as Russell, Wittgenstein, Flew and Ryle are brief, but form a useful introductory collection for the theological student, although the work has been criticized for neglecting the influence of existentialist and naturalist philosophies upon theological work. See also Sontag (C0691).

C0591 Masse, Benjamin Louis. Justice for All: An Introduction to the Social Teaching of the Catholic Church. Milwaukee, Wisc.: Bruce Publishing Company, 1964.

This provides an introduction to the social teaching of the Roman Catholic church written against an American background. It is intended for the general reader, aiming to bridge the gap between papal social documents and those Catholics concerned with contemporary socio-economic issues. Topics such as religion and economics, property rights, wages and justice, industrial relations, and rich and poor nations are treated. A bibliographical note and an index are provided. See also Fanfani (C0441), McKenzie (C0581) and Mainelli (C0585).

C0592 Matczak, Sebastian A. Philosophy: Its Nature, Methods and Basic Sources. Philosophical Questions Series, 4. New York: Learned Publications; Louvain: Editions Nauwelaerts, 1975.

See also Bertman (C0349) and Matczak's other work (C0593).

C0593 Matczak, Sebastian A. Research and Composition in Philosophy. 2nd ed. Philosophical Questions Series, 2. Louvain: Editions Nauwelaerts, 1971.

See also Bertman (C0349) and Matczak's other work (C0592).

B721
N37

C0594 Maurer, Armand Augustine. Medieval Philosophy. A History of Philosophy, vol. 2. New York: Random House, 1962.

This work provides clear summaries on the main medieval philosophers, with notes and bibliography (pp. 380-426). It is designed as an introduction for the educated layman or the undergraduate student. Five main parts treat the age of the fathers, the coming of the schoolmen, the age of the schoolmen, the modern way, and the Middle Ages and Renaissance philosophy. An index is provided. See also Armstrong (C0320), Gilson (C0470) and Leff (C0561).

C0595 Mehl, Roger. Pour une Ethique Sociale Chrétienne. Cahiers Théologiques, tome 56. Neuchâtel: Editions Delachaux et Niestlé, 1967.

BX320.2
M47

C0596 Meyendorff, Jean. Byzantine Theology: Historical Trends and Doctrinal Themes. New York: Fordham University Press, 1974; London: A.R. Mowbray and Company, 1975.

Including a basic bibliography (pp. 229-237), this 243 page survey presents a synthesis of Byzantine Christian thought. The first part provides a history of Byzantine Christian thought; the second covers doctrinal themes. It is well documented, clearly written, and useful as a text on the subject. See also the works by Karmirēs (C0539, C0540), Lossky (C0571) and Platon (C0629).

C0597 Moltmann, Jürgen. Theology of Hope. New York: Harper and Row; London: SCM Press, 1967.

This seminal analysis views Christian eschatology from the standpoint of the resurrection of Christ, providing a major statement of an eschatological theology which emphasizes the critical effect of Christian hope upon the thought, institutions and conditions of life. In 342 pages Moltmann has done much to recapture the biblical emphasis on eschatology as an essential and creative aspect of the future. In terms of both content and impact Theology of Hope is bound to be an essential guide for students of modern theology for many years. See also Alves (C0317) and Childs (C0389).

C0598 Monzel, Nikolaus. Katholische Soziallehre. Hrsg. von Trude Herweg, unter Mitarbeit von Karl Heinz Grenner. 2 vols. Cologne: J.P. Bachem, 1965-1967.

See also Welty (C0731).

C0599 Mortimer, Robert Cecil. The Elements of Moral Theology. New York: Harper and Brothers, 1960.

This volume is intended as a simple introduction to moral theology, especially for Anglican readers, and as a starting point for the compilation of an Anglican manual of moral theology. It treats such concepts as conscience, faith, hope, love, justice. A general index and an index of quotations are provided, but there is no bibliography. See also Dewar (C0423).

C0600 Moss, Claude Beaufort. The Christian Faith: An Introduction to Dogmatic Theology. New York: Morehouse-Gorham Company; London: SPCK, 1943.

Reprint. London: SPCK, 1944.

This 488 page introduction to dogmatic theology is a precursor of Macquarrie (C0583) in approach and tone. It is intended chiefly for members of Anglican churches. The seventy-six chapters cover aspects such as arguments for the existence of God, atonement, revelation, church and state, the holy eucharist, ordination, marriage and creeds. There are few references to authorities other than scriptural. An index is included.

C0601 Murray, J. Principles of Conduct: Aspects of Biblical Ethics. Grand Rapids, Mich.: Wm. B. Eerdmans Publishing Company; London: Tyndale Press, 1957.

Using the "biblico-theological method", this work attempts to state some of the most important biblical principles of conduct, for example, the sanctity of life. The organic unity of the process of divine revelation in the OT and NT is emphasized. See also Barnette (C0332) and Robinson (C0655).

C0602 Murray, Michael H. The Thought of Teilhard de Chardin: An Introduction. New York: Seabury Press, 1966.

This work presents a careful examination of Teilhard's thought, based upon his published and unpublished writings, presented systematically. In addition, there are chapters on his response to the secularism of the modern world and on his methodology. This is appropriate as an introductory volume. For an index to eleven French editions of works by Teilhard one should consult Paul L'Archevêque, Teilhard de Chardin: Index Analytique (Québec: Presses de l'Université Laval, 1967). See also Cuénot (C0405).

C0603 Neuner, Joseph, and Dupuis, Jacques, eds. The Christian Faith in the Doctrinal Documents of the Catholic Church. Westminster, Md.: Christian Classics, 1975.

This updating of Neuner and Roos (C0604) includes characteristic texts of Vatican II and post-conciliar documents. Arrangement is by subject. There is a chronological table of documents, and biblical, name and subject indexes are provided. There is also a concordance with other editions of church documents. This is generally not as complete as Denzinger (C0421), although it includes some post-conciliar documents not in that volume.

C0604 Neuner, Josef, and Roos, Heinrich. The Teaching of the Catholic Church As Contained in Her Documents. Ed. by Karl Rahner. Trans. by Geoffrey Stevens. Cork: Mercier Press, 1966; Staten Island, N.Y.: Alba House, 1967.

This translation of the 1938 publication entitled Der Glaube der Kirche in den Urkunden der Lehrverkündigung, which is now available in an eighth edition (Neubearb. von Karl Rahner und Karl-Heinz Weger. Regensburg: Friedrich Pustet Verlag, 1971), contains a selection of documents, not including those from Vatican II. Arrangement is by subject, with an index and references to Denzinger (C0421).

C0605 Neve, Jürgen Ludwig. Introduction to the Symbolical Books of the

Lutheran Church: A Historical Survey of the Oecumenical and Particular Symbols of Lutheranism, an Outline of Their Contents and an Interpretation of Their Theology on the Basis of the Doctrinal Articles of the Augsburg Confession. 2nd ed. Columbus, Ohio: Lutheran Book Concern, 1926.

> First issued as Introduction to Lutheran Symbolics in 1917, this work treats the symbolical writings on which the system of Lutheran theology rests. It is intended for use as a textbook in Lutheran theological seminaries in the United States. The main body of the work provides a commentary on the Augsburg Confession; briefer sections cover the Apostles', Nicene and Athanasian Creeds, and other key documents of the Lutheran tradition. A descriptive table of contents, an index and some bibliographical references are included. See also Preus (C0635), Schlink (C0670) and Schmid (C0674).

C0606 Nicholls, William. Systematic and Philosophical Theology. The Pelican Guide to Modern Theology, vol. 1. Harmondsworth: Penguin Books, 1969.

> This 364 page guide to developments in systematic and philosophical theology over the previous fifty years is intended for the general reader rather than the specialist. It tends to concentrate on German Protestant theologians at the expense of the Catholic tradition, and although primarily for British readers neglects other theologians such as Temple. See also Curtis (C0410) and Ross (C0658).

C0607 Niebuhr, Reinhold. An Interpretation of Christian Ethics. New York: Meridian Books, 1956.

> First published in 1935 as a collection of lectures which expressed general support for the purposes of the social gospel as expounded by Rauschenbusch (C0643), this work is concerned with the issue of how to derive a social ethic from the absolute ethic of the Gospels. The eight chapters include sections on criticism of Christian orthodoxy and of Christian liberalism. Brief notes and an index conclude the volume.

C0608 Niebuhr, Reinhold. The Nature and Destiny of Man. 2 vols. Gifford Lectures, 1939. New York: Charles Scribner's Sons; London: Nisbet and Company, 1941-1943.

> These two volumes comprise the author's first and second series of Gifford lectures on human nature and human destiny from the perspective of Christian faith. Such aspects as individuality in modern culture, the relevance of the Christian view of man and original sin and man's responsibility are treated. Indexes to both volumes are provided. This is an important study which is based on the conviction that there are resources in the Christian faith for an understanding of human nature which have been lost in modern culture.

C0609 Noort, Gerardus Cornelius van. Dogmatic Theology. Trans. and ed. by John J. Castelot and William R. Murphy. Vol. 1- . Westminster, Md.: Newman Press, 1955- .

> See also Regan (C0645).

C0610 Nygren, Anders. Agape and Eros. Trans. by Philip S. Watson. Philadelphia, Pa.: Westminster Press, 1953.

This work examines the history of the two themes, <u>agape</u> and <u>eros,</u> throughout the development of Christian thought. From its particular perspective, it provides an interesting view of the history of dogma. It has been criticized for making too rigid a separation between the two ideas.

C0611 Nygren, Anders. <u>Meaning and Method: Proleg omena to a Scientific Philosophy of Religion and a Scientific Theology; Authorized Translation.</u> Trans. by Philip S. Watson. London: Epworth Press, 1972.

Including a substantial bibliography (pp. 387-401), this 412 page study examines the proper nature of theology and philosophy. It includes analyses of metaphysical and scientific philosophy, of objectivity, of different forms of scientific argumentation, etc. The coverage is wide ranging, and the argument stimulating; the level of treatment is suitable for the more advanced researcher. See also Richmond (C0647) and Smart (C0685).

C0612 O'Collins, Gerald. <u>Foundations of Theology</u>. Chicago, Ill.: Loyola University Press, 1971.

This 211 page volume examines questions of theological procedure, concepts of revelation, of faith, history and salvation history; it contains an exposition and critique of the work of Pannenberg and Downing; and, finally, it duscusses the roots of Christian confession (the resurrection and the Jesus of history). This is a perceptive discussion of important issues for theology by a Roman Catholic theologian. However, by focusing mainly on issues arising from German discussion, other schools of thought are somewhat neglected. See also Cassilly (C0384), Litton (C0567) and Ott (C0616).

C0613 O'Collins, Gerald. <u>Fundamental Theology</u>. New York: Paulist Press, c. 1981.

C0614 Olafson, Frederick A. <u>Principles and Persons: An Ethical Interpretation of Existentialism.</u> Baltimore, Md.: Johns Hopkins University Press, 1967.

This brief survey of Western moral philosophy evaluates the ethical claims of existential or phenomenological writers, concentrating on the issues of value, choice and moral freedom. For those unfamiliar with existentialism and its major exponents this is a useful starting point for locating basic data. See also Roberts (C0652), and for an existentialist dictionary Nauman (C0270).

C0615 Olson, Arnold Theodore. <u>This We Believe: The Background and Exposition of the Doctrinal Statement of the Evangelical Free Church of America.</u> Minneapolis, Minn.: Free Church Publications, 1961.

C0616 Ott, Ludwig. <u>Fundamentals of Catholic Dogma</u>. 6th ed. Ed. by James Canon Bastible. Trans. by Patrick Lynch. St. Louis, Mo.: Herder and Herder, 1964.

This translation of <u>Grundriss der Katholischen Dogma</u> (6. Aufl. Freiburg im Breisgau, 1963) contains statements of doctrine and explanations of the foundations of the teachings of the Catholic Church. It provides a useful basic outline, without offering detailed treatment of speculative aspects of doctrine. See also O'Collins (C0612).

BT2/
O8x

C0617 Otten, Bernard John. A Manual of the History of Dogmas. 2 vols. St. Louis, Mo.: B. Herder Book Company, 1917-1918. Reprint. 2 vols. St. Louis, Mo.: B. Herder Book Company, 1925.

See also Congar (C0379).

C0618 Palmer, Paul F., ed. Sources of Christian Theology. 3 vols. Westminster, Md.: Newman Press, 1955-1966; London: Longmans, Green and Company, 1957-1966.

This series is designed to present in English translation and in topical arrangement the basic texts and documents which have shaped Roman Catholic theological teaching. Volume 1 covers the sacraments and worship (liturgy and doctrinal development of baptism, confirmation and the eucharist); volume 2, the sacraments and forgiveness (the history and doctrinal development of penance, extreme unction and indulgences); and volume 3, Christ and His mission (Christology and soteriology). Documents are selected from early liturgies, the fathers, the councils and official pronouncements of the Holy See. Selections from the writings of Protestant reformers are included to illustrate differing viewpoints. There are indexes in each volume. See also Textus et Documenta (C0702).

C0619 Pannenberg, Wolfhart. Grundfragen Systematischer Theologie. Gesammelte Aufsätze. Göttingen: Vandenhoeck und Ruprecht, 1967.

See also Kreck (C0553).

BT20
BP3/3

C0620 Pannenberg, Wolfhart. Jesus, God and Man. Trans. by Lewis L. Wilkins and Duane A. Priebe. Philadelphia, Pa.: Westminster Press; London: SCM Press, 1968.

One of the most creative modern studies of Christology, this work investigates major christological themes from the historicity of the resurrection to the coming of the Kingdom. In 415 pages Pannenberg seeks to cover all of the basic approaches and provides his own detailed and often controversial analysis of Christology. For advanced students this work has particular value in its survey of christological thought. This translation is particularly true to the German original, Grundzüge der Christologie (2. Aufl. Gütersloh: G. Mohn, 1966 [c. 1964]). See also Aulén (C0323), Grillmeier (C0484) and Watlington (C0727).

C0621 Pelikan, Jaroslav Jan. The Christian Tradition: A History of the Development of Doctrine. Vol. 1- . Chicago, Ill.: University of Chicago Press, 1971- .

BT20
P43

Projected in five volumes, this detailed survey of the development of Christian doctrine covers the emergence of the Catholic tradition (A.D. 100-600), the spirit of Eastern Christendom (600-1700), the growth of medieval theology (600-1300), the reformation of church and dogma (1300-1700), Christian doctrine and modern culture since 1700. Each volume covers the allocated period in a series of well devised chapters which deal adequately and fairly with the subject matter. Pelikan utilizes a system of marginal notes to indicate relevant primary sources which substantiate the discussion; the abbreviations in these notes are clearly set forth in a preliminary listing of abbreviations, authors and texts for each volume. Also included are excellent bibliographies of selected secondary works and indexes of biblical passages and subjects for each volume. For reference and as a series of advanced textbooks Pelikan is bound to become a major work in the history of doctrinal development.

C0622 Pelikan, Jaroslav Jan. Historical Theology: Continuity and Change in Christian Doctrine. Theological Resources. New York: Corpus Books; London: Hutchinson and Company, 1971.

Seeking to elucidate the theological and methodological assumptions which underlie modern theological scholarship, this 228 page volume discusses in five chapters the problem of doctrinal change, the evolution of historical theology, the present task of the history of dogma, the historiography of doctrine and historical theology as a theological discipline. Each chapter is further subdivided and presents a scholarly and clearly argued overview of the field together with copious notes, bibliography and index. Both as a textbook and a reference volume this is a valuable introductory work. See also Pelikan's The Christian Tradition (C0621) for a history of the development of Christian doctrine. See also Werner (C0735).

C0623 Pendleton, James Madison. Christian Doctrines: A Compendium of Theology. Philadelphia, Pa.: American Baptist Publication Society, 1906. Reprint. Valley Forge, Pa.: Judson Press, 1971.

First published in 1878, this volume discusses the main subjects of systematic theology, drawing on the work of many writers in the field. The thirty chapters cover topics such as the trinity, creation, angels, the person of Christ, justification and baptism. It is of interest as a nineteenth century compendium. See also Roark (C0651).

C0624 Pepper, Stephen Coburn. Ethics. The Century Philosophy Series. New York: Appleton-Century-Crofts, 1960.

This work focuses on the application of general value concepts to the particular problems of ethics. It examines principal types of ethical theory and suggests ways of reconciling major empirical theories. This provides useful summaries of various approaches, and suggestions for further reading (pp. 337-342) are of value for the student. An index is provided. See also Banner (C0331), Frankena (C0455), Garner (C0462) and Garnett (C0463).

C0625 Pieper, Franz August Otto. Christian Dogmatics. 4 vols. St. Louis, Mo.: Concordia Publishing House, 1950-1957.

Including an excellent index prepared by Walter W.F. Albrecht in volume 4, this work distills four decades of classroom teaching, lecturing and writing by a Lutheran theologian. The index, by subjects, authors and scriptural passages, provides a kind of digest of Pieper's dogmatics. See also Hodge (C0523) for an earlier Presbyterian treatment of similar depth.

C0626 Pieper, Josef. Guide to Thomas Aquinas. Trans. by Richard Winston and Clara Winston. New York: Pantheon Books, 1962.

This guide and introduction aims to present a portrait of Aquinas as he concerns philosophical minded persons today. It does not attempt to provide a detailed biography nor a systematic interpretation of his doctrines. It is based on a series of university lectures. There are twelve chapters, described in an analytical table of contents, quite extensive notes and an index. See also Chenu (C0388), Gilson (C0468) and Grenet (C0483).

C0627 Pike, James Albert. Doing the Truth: A Summary of Christian Ethics. New ed. New York: Macmillan Company, 1965; London: Victor Gollancz, 1966.

This work examines the relationship between believing and doing, and Christian ethics as a way of deciding matters. The sixteen chapters consider issues such as freedom and responsibility, worship and evangelism, and the ethics of business and profession. There is neither bibliography nor index. See also Fletcher (C0452).

C0628 Piper, Otto A. Christian Ethics. Nelson's Library of Theology. London: Thomas Nelson and Son, 1970.

This is essentially an expository volume which sets out the subject matter of the field: method, theological foundations, form of moral action, institutions of the moral order, etc. Short chapters on politics, economics, family, and other issues relevant to Christian ethics are included. There are few footnotes; a brief bibliography is provided. See also Gustafson (C0489).

C0629 Platon. The Orthodox Doctrine of the Apostolic Eastern Church; or, A Compendium of Christian Theology. To Which Is Prefixed an Historical and Explanatory Essay on General Catechism; and Appended, a Treatise on Melchisedec. Trans. by G. Potessaro. London: Whittaker and Company, 1857. Reprint. New York: AMS Press, [1969].

See also the works by Karmirēs (C0539, C0540), Lossky (C0571) and Meyendorff (C0596).

C0630 Plattel, Martin G. Social Philosophy. Trans. by Henry J. Koren. Duquesne Studies. Philosophical Series, vol. 18. Pittsburgh, Pa.: Duquesne University Press, 1965.

C0631 Pohle, Joseph. Lehrbuch der Dogmatik. Neuarbeitet von Josef Gummersback. 10. Aufl. Vol. 1- . Wissenschaftliche Handbibliothek: Eine Sammlung Theologischer Lehrbücher. Paderborn: Ferdinand Schöningh, 1952- .

C0632 Pourrat, Pierre. Christian Spirituality. Trans. by William Henry Mitchell, S.P. Jacques and Donald Attwater. 4 vols. Westminster, Md.: Newman Press, 1953-1955.

This history of Christian spirituality covers the period from the early church to the beginning of the twentieth century. It is a readable, handy reference work, with extensive bibliographical notes to each chapter and an index in each volume. The first two volumes cover the period to the end of the Middle Ages. See also Bouyer (C0365) and Williams (C0739).

C0633 Premm, Matthias. Dogmatic Theology for the Laity. Staten Island,

N.Y.: Alba House, 1967.

See also Premm's larger work in German (C0634).

C0634 Premm, Matthias. Katholische Glaubenskunde: Ein Lehrbuch der Dogmatik. 4 vols. in 5. Vienna: Herder, 1951-1955.

See also Premm's basic survey (C0633).

C0635 Preus, Robert D. The Theology of Post-Reformation Lutheranism: A Study of Theological Prolegomena. St. Louis, Mo.: Concordia Publishing House, 1970.

This is a comprehensive study of Lutheran orthodoxy from the late sixteenth to the early eighteenth century, surveying the origin and development of theological prolegomena and dogmatics during the period. Preus writes with sympathy for the dogmaticians of orthodoxy. The work is based on thorough study of original sources. See also Neve (C0605), Schlink (C0670) and Schmid (C0674).

C0636 Prümmer, Dominicus M. Handbook of Moral Theology. Trans. by Gerald F. Shelton. Ed. by John Gavin Nolan. New York: P.J. Kenedy, 1957.

Based on the same author's Manuale Theologiae Moralis (C0637), this small handbook includes basic information on the key areas of moral theology and on basic ethical issues. It is much less satisfactory than the complete Manuale, as a great deal of pertinent material is either omitted or condensed too rigorously. For quick reference at a fairly basic level by those seeking traditional Roman Catholic views the Handbook has some limited value.

C0637 Prümmer, Dominicus M. Manuale Theologiae Moralis: Secundum Principia s. Thomae Aquinatis, in Usum Scholarum. Ed. 14. Recognita a Joachim Overbeck. 3 vols. Barcelona: Herder, 1960.

This comprehensive and detailed work deals with all aspects of moral theology in a competent but uncomplicated manner. Coverage is advanced but nontechnical, and the scholarly apparatus is provided in full. Volume 1 contains a detailed bibliography, while volume 3 carries the general index. This is a valuable reference work for clergy, students and scholars; it reflects the traditional Roman Catholic viewpoint. For a more liberal approach see Häring (C0497). See also Prümmer's Handbook (C0636), which is based on the Manuale, and Tanquerey (C0700).

C0638 Raeymaeker, Louis de. Introduction à la Philosophie. 6e éd. Louvain: Publications Universitaires de Louvain; Paris: B. Nauwelaerts, 1967.

This work includes a survey of Western philosophy and its history, which includes footnote biographical data. More important is the guide to philosophical literature, covering organizations, introductions, biographical dictionaries, encyclopedias and dictionaries, histories, editions of texts, commentaries and manuals, bibliographies. Major works include annotations, and there is a name index. For readers of French this guide to the literature covers most of the basic information sources. Others will prefer De George (C0059) and similar English works. An English translation exists under the title, Introduction to Philosophy

(New York: Joseph Wagner, 1948), but is not as up to date as the sixth French edition.

C0639 Ramm, Bernard Lawrence. A Handbook of Contemporary Theology. Grand Rapids, Mich.: Wm. B. Eerdmans Publishing Company, 1966.

This conservative Protestant handbook of 141 pages seeks to explain contemporary theological terminology. Although often lacking objectivity, it does adequately describe key concepts of major contemporary theologians. Particular attention is focused on the work of Kierkegaard, Barth, Brunner, Bultmann, Tillich and Reinhold Niebuhr. Only theological concepts are treated, and entries are relatively well documented but lack bibliographies. See also Mackintosh (C0582).

C0640 Ramsey, Ian T. Christian Ethics and Contemporary Philosophy. New York: Macmillan Company; London: SCM Press, 1966.

This collection of signed articles and discussions of certain topics deals with questions of morality and religion, duty and God's will, moral decisions, and towards a concept of Christian morality. Notes on the contributors and an index are provided. Some bibliographical references are given in footnotes. See also Lehmann (C0562).

C0641 Ramsey, Paul. Basic Christian Ethics. New York: Charles Scribner's Sons, 1954.

This work on basic Christian ethics discusses concepts such as Christian liberty, Christian vocation and human nature. There are suggestions for further reading (pp. 389-394) and indexes of authors and subjects and of OT and NT passages cited. See also Gardner (C0461).

C0642 Rasmussen, Albert Terrill. Christian Social Ethics: Exerting Christian Influence. Englewood Cliffs, N.J.: Prentice-Hall, 1956.

This study is concerned with the problem of Christian response to various influences and situations. The eleven chapters examine issues such as relating faith to social action, steps in building a church of influence, and exerting influence in politics. There is a detailed table of contents, and an index is provided. Suggestions for practical measures include a list of community projects. See also Hillerdal (C0518).

C0643 Rauschenbusch, Walter. A Theology for the Social Gospel. New York: Macmillan Company, 1917. Reprint. New York: Abingdon Press, 1960.

Available in several reprints, this volume is based on the Taylor Lectures delivered at the Yale School of Religion. The nineteen chapters cover topics such as consciousness of sin, the social gospel and personal salvation, and baptism and the Lord's supper. There is neither index nor bibliography, although some footnote references are given. See also Niebuhr (C0607).

C0644 Regan, George M. New Trends in Moral Theology: A Survey of Fundamental Moral Themes. New York: Newman Press, 1971.

See also Curran (C0408).

C0645 Regan, James Wilfred; Henry, John A.; and Donlan, Thomas C. A Primer of Theology. Vol. 1- . Dubuque, Iowa: Priory Press, 1954- .

See also Noort (C0609).

C0646 Rémy, Pierre. Foi Chrétienne et Morale. Paris: Le Centurion, 1973.

See also Bois (C0358).

C0647 Richmond, James. Theology and Metaphysics. The Library of Philosophy and Theology. New York: Schocken Books; London: SCM Press, 1970.

This clear and systematic exposition of recent discussion on the philosophy of religion includes developments in natural theology, the philosophy of Barth and of Wittgenstein, analysis of religion by Schleiermacher, Aquinas and others, and thorough treatment of the British analytic tradition. The inadequacies of positivism are indicated. The work has been criticized for confusing natural theology and metaphysical theology. See also Nygren (C0611) and Smart (C0685).

C0648 Rickaby, Joseph John. Index to the Works of John Henry Cardinal Newman. London: Longmans, Green and Company, 1914.

This subject index to Newman's works is based on the Longman editions and provides thorough coverage of the literature under broad categories. Because the indexing is fairly general, Rickaby can be frustrating to use when very specific topics are sought; therefore, it is less suitable for advanced research work than for basic inquiries.

C0649 Ritschl, Otto. Dogmengeschichte des Protestantismus. 4 vols. Leipzig: J.C. Hinrichs'sche Buchhandlung, 1908-1927.

Published under various imprints, this multivolume survey of Protestant dogma focuses primarily on biblicism, traditionalism, orthodoxy and syncretism. While the focus is on Lutheran orthodoxy, Ritschl ranges widely across the Protestant tradition and provides a useful, if dated, survey of theological thought in historical perspective. The work is clearly arranged, well indexed and copiously footnoted, making it an adequate reference work for students familiar with continental Protestant history. For a more limited survey see Herbst (C0514); see also Gruezmacher (C0486).

C0650 Rivaud, Albert. Histoire de la Philosophie. 5 vols. in 6. Logos. Introduction aux Etudes Philosophiques, tome 6. Paris: Presses Universitaires de France, 1948-1968.

Written from a Roman Catholic viewpoint, this detailed history covers the origins of philosophy to scholasticism, scholasticism to the classical period, the classical period, French and English philosophy from 1700 to 1830, German philosophy in the nineteenth and twentieth centuries. From the standpoint of philosophical theology Rivaud's volumes on earlier periods are particularly relevant. Each chapter includes a bibliography, and each volume is indexed by name only. Brehier (C0366) and similar European works follow much the same pattern as Rivaud, which for theological students has the advantage of a Christian orientation.

C0651 Roark, Dallas M. The Christian Faith. Nashville, Tenn.: Broadman Press, 1969.

This work, intended particularly for the undergraduate student, covers the main Christian concepts, paying attention to philosophical and theological influences. Brief summaries of relevant schools of thought are provided. There is no index. There is evidence of the author's Baptist commitment and the assumption of biblical authority in the work. See also Pendleton (C0623).

C0652 Roberts, David Everett. Existentialism and Religious Belief. Ed. by Roger Hazelton. New York: Oxford University Press, 1957. Reprint. New York: Oxford University Press, 1959.

This discussion of the nature, development and influence of existentialism contains an introductory chapter on general characteristics of existentialists, followed by discussion of six representative thinkers (Pascal, Kierkegaard, Heidegger, Sartre, Jaspers and Marcel). Written from a Christian viewpoint, this is a concise, insightful and learned study which provides a good introduction to the subject for the serious student. See also Olafson; for an existentialist dictionary see Nauman (C0270).

C0653 Robertson, John Mackinnon. A History of Freethought, Ancient and Modern, to the Period of the French Revolution. 4th ed. 2 vols. London: Watts and Company, 1936. Reprint. 2 vols. London: Dawsons, 1969.

This chronologically arranged history includes a bibliography and an index (partly analytical). Although clearly biased in favor of the subject and in places lacking clarity, this older work is a standard history and reference tool. For a continuation see Robertson's work on the nineteenth century (C0654).

C0654 Robertson, John Mackinnon. A History of Freethought in the Nineteenth Century. 2 vols. New York: G.P. Putnam's Sons; London: Watts, 1929. Reprint. 2 vols. London: Dawsons, 1969.

This classic history continues the author's work on the earlier period (C0653).

C0655 Robinson, Norman Hamilton Galloway. Groundwork of Christian Ethics. Grand Rapids, Mich.: Wm. B. Eerdmans Publishing Company; London: William Collins Sons, 1971.

Concerned with understanding of the moral life which is intrinsic to Christian faith rather than with particular ethical problems, this work discusses various aspects of ethics and theology. There are appendixes on Tillich's ethical thought and on agape, eros and nomos. An index is provided. See also Barnette (C0332) and Murray (C0601).

C0656 Rommen, Heinrich A. The Natural Law: A Study in Legal and Social History and Philosophy. Trans. by Thomas R. Hanley. St. Louis, Mo.: B. Herder Book Company, 1947.

This introductory work deals with the history of the idea of natural law, beginning with the legacy of Greece and Rome, and with its philosophy and content. Bibliographical references are provided in footnotes, and there is an index.

C0657 Ross, James F. Introduction to the Philosophy of Religion. New York: Macmillan Company, 1969.

This work by a Roman Catholic philosopher examines aspects of the philosophy of religion such as faith and reason, and the problem of evil. See also Davies (C0417).

C0658 Ross, James F. Philosophical Theology. Indianapolis, Ind.: Bobbs-Merrill, 1969.

This 326 page introduction by a Roman Catholic philosopher is firmly grounded in natural theology within the scholastic tradition. In this work Ross retains the form of detailed scholastic arguments and distinctions and much of the content of that tradition as well. This is most apparent in the discussion of such traditional issues as the existence of God, the problem of evil and reasons for the creation of the world. Although the metaphysical approach lacks appeal among many students, this is a sound and modern introduction to the scholastic form and content of philosophical theology. See also Nicholls (C0606) and Curtis (C0410).

C0659 Rouët de Journel, Marie Joseph, and Dutilleul, Joseph, comps. Enchiridion Asceticum: Loci SS. Patrum et Scriptorum Ecclesiasticorum ad Ascesim Spectantes. 5th ed. Barcelona: Herder, 1958.

This collection of passages selected from the Greek and Latin church fathers includes references to sources, and a subject index is provided. Greek works are printed in Greek and Latin.

C0660 [no entry]

C0661 Runes, Dagobert David, ed. Who's Who in Philosophy. New York: Philosophical Library, 1942.

Covering only Anglo-American philosophers and much stronger on the latter group, this 293 page dictionary presents biographical data and bibliographies of the published works and periodical articles of philosophers living in 1942. There are very few entries relevant to philosophical theology. For current guides see American Catholic Philosophical Association (C0318), Directory of American Philosophers (C0427), International Directory of Philosophy and Philosophers (C0535) and Menchaca (C0268).

C0662 Sacrae Theologiae Summa, Iuxta Constitutionem Apostolicam "Deus Scientiarum Dominus". 4 vols. Biblioteca de Autores Cristianos, vols. 61-62, 73, 90. Madrid: La Editorial Católica, 1950-1953.

This work covers all areas of dogmatic theology, providing brief introductions and full bibliographies for each topic. Each volume contains an index, and there is a general index in the final volume. See also Scheeben (C0666).

C0663 Sahakian, William S. Philosophies of Religion. Cambridge, Mass.: Schenkman Publishing Company, 1965.

See also Thomas (C0705).

C0664 Schaff, Philip, comp. Bibliotheca Symbolica Ecclesiae Universalis. The Creeds of Christendom; with a History and Critical Notes. 6th ed. of vol. 1, 4th ed. of vols. 2-3. 3 vols. New York: Harper and Brothers, 1919. Reprint. Grand Rapids, Mich.: Baker Book House, n.d.

BT990
S4
1966t

First published in 1877, this standard work describes the history of creeds and includes a critical appraisal of each one from a Protestant standpoint. Volume 1 traces the history of creeds according to church or denomination and includes many bibliographical references. Volume 2 treats the creeds of the Greek and Latin churches in their original languages with English translations in parallel columns and a useful subject index. The final volume deals with the creeds of evangelical Protestant churches, again in the original language with a parallel English translation and a full subject index. Schaff continues to be a very functional collection, particularly when used in conjunction with more analytical works by Kelly (C0544) and others. While the appraisals are often somewhat biased, the collection of documents gives this work current reference value for a wide range of users. See also Curtis (C0411) and Badcock (C0324).

C0665 Schaff, Philip. Theological Propaedeutic: A General Introduction to the Study of Theology, Exegetical, Historical, Systematic and Practical, Including Encyclopaedia, Methodology and Bibliography; a Manual for Students. 7th ed. New York: Charles Scribner's Sons, 1907.

The first such work written specifically for American theological students, this classic tome includes interesting introductory and bibliographical materials on all areas of theological study. A bibliography entitled "A Ministerial Library" by Samuel Macauley Jackson (pp. 539-596) is arranged in the order of Schaff's discussion. Topical and author indexes are provided.

C0666 Scheeben, Matthias Joseph. Handbuch der Katholischen Dogmatik. 6 vols. Gesammelte Schriften, Bd. 3-7. Freiburg im Breisgau: Herder, 1943-1961.

230
G724

Each volume of this detailed survey exists in either a second or third edition and provides a most thorough guide to dogmatic theology in a traditional Roman Catholic vein. The volumes treat all aspects expected in a full handbook of this sort and are clearly written with theological students in mind. Each volume contains a detailed list of contents in outline form, and each section of text includes numerous references to further reading, footnotes, bibliographies and additional reference apparatus. Particularly useful are the frequent references to writings of the church fathers and medieval scholastics. One of the most ambitious Roman Catholic outlines of recent decades, Scheeben is an important reference compendium for students at various levels. See also Fries (C0458), Schmaus (C0671) and Sacrae Theologiae Summa (C0662).

C0667 Schilling, Otto. Grundriss der Moraltheologie. 2. Aufl. Freiburg im Breisgau: Herder, 1949.

See also Werner (C0734).

C0668 Schilling, Otto. Handbuch der Moraltheologie. 2. Aufl. 2 vols. Stuttgart: Schwabenverlag, 1952-1954.

See also Koch (C0551).

C0669 Schilling, Sylvester Paul. Contemporary Continental Theologians.
Nashville, Tenn.: Abingdon Press; London: SCM Press, 1966.

> This careful survey of 288 pages examines eleven scholars and their
> particular theological contribution: Barth, Diem, Hromádka, Bultmann,
> Gogarten, Ebeling, Schlink, Wingren, Congar, Rahner and Nissiotis.
> They are grouped under five headings (theologies of the word of God,
> theologies of existence, neo-Lutheran theology, Roman Catholic theology,
> and Eastern Orthodox theology). This is a valuable introduction to the
> thought of these contemporary European theologians. See also Feiner
> (C0444) and Macquarrie (C0584).

C0670 Schlink, Edmund. Theology of the Lutheran Confessions. Trans. by
Paul F. Koehneke and Herbert J.A. Bouman. Philadelphia, Pa.: Muhlenberg
Press, 1961.

> This translation of Theologie der Lutherischen Bekenntnisschriften includes
> a bibliography, index and notes. The work is based on lectures delivered
> in the 1930s, and represents a useful study for theological students
> of Lutheranism. See also Neve (C0605), Preus (C0635) and Schmid (C0674).

C0671 Schmaus, Michael. Dogma. Trans. by Ann Laeuchli, William McKenna
and T. Patrick Burke. 6 vols. New York: Sheed and Ward, 1968- .

> This translation of Der Glaube der Kirche: Handbuch Katholischer Dog-
> matik (2 vols. Munich: Max Huebner Verlag, 1969-1970) presents a fresh
> approach to systematic theology, incorporating significant developments
> since Vatican II. The six volumes cover God in revelation, God and
> creation, Jesus Christ, the Church, Christian anthropology, and the
> ultimate realities, attempting to interpret Catholic faith and theology
> in an intelligible way for modern man. The work is intended for priests,
> students and teachers of theology. See also Fries (C0458) and Scheeben
> (C0666).

C0672 Schmaus, Michael. Katholische Dogmatik. 6. Aufl. 8 vols. Munich:
Max Huebner Verlag, 1960-1963.

> Following the traditional Roman Catholic structure of dogmatic theology,
> Schmaus discusses in detail the various formulations of dogma both
> historically and conceptually. Although conservative in tone, this is an
> excellent and thorough scholarly survey which covers the entire field
> of dogmatic theology in a manner suitable for advanced students. Biblical
> passages, church fathers, modern thinkers and Protestant theologians
> are all cited in the text, which displays a sound grasp of ancient and
> modern developments. See also Scheeben (C0666).

C0673 Schmaus, Michael, et al., eds. Handbuch der Dogmengeschichte.
Vol. 1- . Freiburg im Breisgau: Herder, 1951- .

> Issued in fascicles and projected in four volumes, this work is also
> available in English as The Herder History of Dogma (Vol. 1- . New
> York: Herder and Herder, 1974-). The various parts cover both specific
> theological doctrines (Christology, Mariology, etc.) and broader themes
> such as belief in the Middle Ages. Each section or fascicle is by a

specialist and provides a detailed, scholarly survey of the topic from a Roman Catholic viewpoint. Biblical texts, early writers and modern scholars are all cited accurately; completed volumes index these citations as well as subjects, and the contents are clearly outlined at the beginning of each volume. Schmaus is an important compendium for reference purposes, as it treats all aspects of dogma in their historical context. See also Turmel (C0717).

C0674 Schmid, Heinrich Friedrich Ferdinand. The Doctrinal Theology of the Evangelical Lutheran Church Verified from the Original Sources. Trans. by Charles Augustus Hay and Henry Eyster Jacobs. 3rd ed. Rev. by Henry Eyster Jacobs and Charles Augustus Hay. Philadelphia, Pa.: Lutheran Publication Society, [1899]. Reprint. Minneapolis, Minn.: Augsburg Publishing House, 1961.

First published in 1843, this sourcebook of Lutheran dogmatics was an important influence in the mid-nineteenth century revival of conservatism. It follows the orthodox Lutheran "Loci" arrangement of material, with expository comments and excerpts from the symbolical books and major sixteenth and seventeenth century dogmaticians. This is an important sourcebook of Lutheran orthodoxy. See also Neve (C0605), Preus (C0635) and Schlink (C0670).

C0675 Schmidt, Martin. John Wesley: A Theological Biography. Trans. by Norman P. Goldhawk. 3 vols. New York: Abingdon Press; London: Epworth Press, 1963-1973.

This study, by a major Lutheran theologian, is based on thorough examination of Wesley's sermons, diaries, letters and treatises, and includes extensive notes and references to a wide range of reading. The coverage of theological aspects is somewhat variable, with volume 2 containing thematic essays on Wesley as preacher, theological writer, pastor, educationalist, etc. Extensive summaries of relevant writings by Wesley are included. This is an important biographical study for researchers and students. See also Cannon (C0381).

C0676 Seeberg, Reinhold. Text-Book of the History of Doctrines. Trans. by Charles Ebert Hay. 2 vols. Philadelphia, Pa.: Lutheran Publication Society, c. 1905. Reprint. 2 vols. in 1. Grand Rapids, Mich.: Baker Book House, 1961.

This translation of Lehrbuch der Dogmengeschichte (3. Aufl. 4 vols. in 5. Leipzig: A Deichert, 1913-1923) closely resembles Harnack (C0505) in attempting to cover all periods of the history of dogmatic theology from a German Protestant viewpoint. Volume 1 covers the ancient church; volume 2, the medieval and modern church. A scholarly work, thoroughly documented in many footnotes, this is suitable for the theology student and pastor. See also Adam (C0308).

C0677 Sellers, James Earl. Theological Ethics. New York: Macmillan Company, 1966.

This brief but instructive introduction is organized around four loci (stance, wisdom, action, fulfillment); coverage is general but reasonably comprehensive, providing a sound background for beginners. For advanced work and detailed reference needs in this field one should consult Thielicke (C0704). See also Gustafson (C0491).

C0678 Senarclens, Jacques de. Heirs of the Reformation. Trans. and ed. by Geoffrey W. Bromiley. The Library of History and Doctrine. Philadelphia, Pa.: Westminster Press, 1964 [c. 1959].

This study of theological method assesses the attitudes to revelation and to Christ of three theologies: Roman Catholicism, liberal Protestantism and evangelical (that is, Reformation theology as interpreted by Barth). It tends to neglect post-Vatican II developments in Roman Catholicism, and focuses on French and Swiss representatives of neo-Protestantism, while drawing conclusions in line with the evangelical tradition. See also Cobb (C0393).

C0679 Sertillanges, Antonin Gilbert. Le Christianisme et les Philosophies. 2e éd. 2 vols. Paris: Aubier, Editions Montaigne, 1939-1941.

See also Duméry (C0435).

C0680 Shaw, John Mackintosh. Christian Doctrine: A One-Volume Outline of Christian Belief. London: Lutterworth Press, 1953.

This volume examines the doctrines of God, man and sin, redemption, the Christian life, and life after death. An adequate index is provided, and there are footnotes; there is no bibliography. Suitable for the minister, student or teacher of theology, and for educated laymen, this is a readable introduction and guide to systematic theology written from a reformed Presbyterian viewpoint. For a similar treatment see Stevens (C0694).

C0681 Shedd, William Greenough Thayer. Dogmatic Theology. 3 vols. New York: Charles Scribner's Sons, 1888-1894. Reprint. 3 vols. Grand Rapids, Mich.: Zondervan Publishing House, 1953.

See also Hodge (C0522).

C0682 Shedd, William Greenough Thayer. A History of Christian Doctrine. 14th ed. 2 vols. New York: Charles Scribner's Sons, 1902.

This survey of the development of Christian doctrine follows particular themes in each of its seven main divisions (history of apologies, of trinitarianism, of anthropology, of soteriology, etc.). Sources are indicated at the beginning of each main division. Although detailed tables of contents are provided for each volume there are no indexes. This is a thorough, now dated, conservative treatment of the subject. See also Heick (C0510) and Tillich (C0707).

C0683 Simons, Menno. The Complete Writings of Menno Simons. Ed. by John Christian Wenger. Trans. by Leonard Verduin. Scottsdale, Pa.: Herald Press, 1966.

First published in 1956, this substantial volume contains translations of Menno Simons' books and tracts (pp. 31-1018) and letters and other writings (pp. 1019-1070). A brief biography (by Harold S. Bender) is also included, as well as a list of locations of Menno Simons's writings in various editions, and an index. Within the two sections material is ordered chronologically. This is an essential collection for researchers concerned with early Anabaptist history and thought.

C0684 Slater, Thomas. A Manual of Moral Theology for English-Speaking Countries. With notes on American Legislation by Michael Martin. New York: Benziger Brothers, 1908.

See also Jone (C0537).

C0685 Smart, Ninian. The Phenomenon of Religion. Philosophy of Religion Series. New York: Herder and Herder; London: Macmillan and Company, 1973.

This work is concerned with the technique, methodology, hermeneutics and epistemology of the study of religion as well as with the phenomenon of religion itself. The nature and object of the study of religion, the nature of myth and possible conflicts between being religious and studying religions are examined in turn. This presents an approach of interest to philosophers of religion and members of divinity schools and theological seminaries. See also Nygren (C0611) and Richmond (C0647).

C0686 Smart, Ninian. The Philosophy of Religion. Studies in Philosophy, vol. 19. New York: Random House, 1970.

This work includes consideration of questions arising out of Eastern and other religions, in addition to the main issues in philosophy of religion based on Western traditions. It takes a broader approach than that based on linguistic analysis. After discussion of the concept of religion, it considers questions about understanding and meaning and issues about truth. The final chapter is devoted to some theories of religion. An index is provided. See also Copleston (C0403), Ferré (C0446), Flew (C0453) and Hick (C0516).

C0687 Smith, George Duncan, ed. The Teaching of the Catholic Church: A Summary of Catholic Doctrine. 2nd ed. London: Burns and Oates, 1963.

This useful reference work contains essays on theological issues, contributed by various authors. Marginal notes are provided, although there is no bibliography. An index is included. See also Alexander (C0315).

C0688 Sobreroca Ferrer, Luis Antonio, comp. La Doctrina Social de la Iglesia: Textos Pontificos Sistematizados, 1878-1967. 3. ed. Colección Biblioteca Mensajero, 8. Bilbao: Mensajero, 1967.

See also Arostegui (C0321) and Berna (C0348).

C0689 Søe, Niels Hansen. Christliche Ethik: Ein Lehrbuch. 3. Aufl. Munich: Chr. Kaiser Verlag, 1965.

Following a traditional German Protestant approach, Søe presents the various aspects of Christian ethics in a manner suitable for the student without prior knowledge of the field. The text is logically and clearly presented, arguing the various ethical viewpoints objectively and succinctly. Frequent reference is made to biblical and modern literature, but footnotes are kept to a minimum. For the beginner able to read German this is a useful starting point. See also Althaus (C0316).

C0690 Sontag, Frederick. The Future of Theology: A Philosophical Basis for Contemporary Protestant Thought. Philadelphia, Pa.: Westminster Press, 1968.

> Based on lectures delivered in Rome in 1966-1967, this work surveys contemporary theologies and philosophical sources, discusses the possibility of a distinctively American approach to theology, and the ecumenical issue of the relationship of Protestant and Roman Catholic theologies, and stresses the need for a realistic, pluralistic philosophical basis for Protestant theology. The book contains stimulating material for clergy and for courses in the philosophy of religion. See also Cobb (C0393).

C0691 Sontag, Frederick. How Philosophy Shapes Theology: Problems in the Philosophy of Religion. New York: Harper and Row, 1971.

> This substantial (495 pp.) examination of philosophy in relation to religion includes examples of the interrelations between the two, consideration of writings of six seminal philosophers and theologians (Origen, Augustine, Bonaventure, Luther, Hegel, Kierkegaard) and twelve studies of significant religious concepts (faith, God, salvation, etc.). See also Martin (C0590).

C0692 Stace, Walter Terence. Mysticism and Philosophy. Philadelphia, Pa.: J.B. Lippincott Company, 1960.

> This 349 page study provides a useful treatment of the thought of both Eastern and Western mystics, and combines modern concern for philosophical and linguistic analysis with a broad interest in all the major religions. It is readable and covers a wealth of material. See also Happold (C0503).

C0693 Steenberghen, Fernand van. Histoire de la Philosophie. Période Chrétienne. Louvain: Publications Universitaires, 1964.

> Covering the end of the fifth century to the end of the twelfth century, this 196 page guide is a suitable summary for those requiring basic data on movements, concepts and developments of the period. The brief bibliography includes both sources for research work and items for further reading. For a work in the same Roman Catholic mold but in English see Gilson (C0471).

C0694 Stevens, William Wilson. Doctrines of the Christian Religion. Grand Rapids, Mich.: Wm. B. Eerdmans Publishing Company, 1967.

> This textbook of sixteen chapters covers the traditional doctrines of systematic theology as formulated by conservative Protestants. It is suitable for theology students. For a similar treatment see Shaw (C0680).

C0695 Sträter, Paul. Katholische Marienkunde. 3 vols. Paderborn: F. Schöningh, 1947-1952.

> Consisting of topical sections by specialists on Mariology, this collection covers sources of Marian doctrine, meaning and significance of the various doctrines, spiritual aspects of Mariology and similar topics. Each section includes a bibliography for further reference, and a full index is provided. For those unfamiliar with Mariology but with sub-

stantial theological knowledge this is a valuable reference collection and textbook. See also Carol (C0383), Doheny (C0430) and Du Manoir de Juaye (C0431).

230
T767&

C0696 Tanquerey, Adolphe. Brevior Synopsis Theologiae Moralis et Pastoralis. Ed. 10. Paris: Desclée, 1933.

First published in 1913, this once standard Roman Catholic work is now quite dated. In historical terms it retains some reference value, but more up to date reference needs are met by Häring (C0497), among others. The fuller work by Tanquerey (C0700) is also quite dated but provides more complete information than this abbreviated volume.

BX1751
T313
1959

C0697 Tanquerey, Adolphe. A Manual of Dogmatic Theology. Trans. by John J. Byrnes. 2 vols. New York: Desclée Company, 1959.

This translation of Brevior Synopsis Theologiae Dogmaticae (Ed. 7. Paris: Desclée, 1931; New York: Benziger Brothers, 1943) includes updated text and bibliography. It is a classic pre-Vatican II work on dogmatic theology, with useful bibliographical data on sources and modern commentaries. An index is provided for each volume. See also Hervé (C0515).

248
T167

C0698 Tanquerey, Adolphe. The Spiritual Life: A Treatise on Ascetical and Mystical Theology. 2nd ed. Trans. by Herman Branderis. New York: Desclée Company, 1961.

This 750 page work covers the general principles of the spiritual life as conceived in the traditional manner. There are separate bibliographies for each chapter as well as a general bibliography arranged by period. See also Happold (C0503).

Bx1751
T2
/457

C0699 Tanquerey, Adolphe. Synopsis Theologiae Dogmaticae ad Mentem S. Thomas Aquinatis Hodiernis Moribus Accommodata. Ed. 26. 3 vols. New York: Benziger Brothers, 1949-1950.

This is a classic pre-Vatican II work on dogmatic theology, with copious bibliographical data. See also the shorter version (C0700).

C0700 Tanquerey, Adolphe. Synopsis Theologiae Moralis et Pastoralis ad Mentem S. Thomae et S. Alphonsi Hodiernis Moribus Accommodata. Ed. 12. 3 vols. Paris: Desclée, 1936-1943.

First published in 1922-1926 this classic Roman Catholic guide to moral theology is now very dated. However, there are few works which cover the field more adequately from a traditional Catholic viewpoint, and for this reason Tanquerey retains its significance as a reference guide. It should not be used by students or clergy interested in current attitudes; for those studying past moral attitudes this is a significant work. See also Tanquerey's abridged volume (C0699) and Prümmer (C0637).

C0701 Textus et Documenta in Usam Exercitationum et Praelectionum Academarum. Series Philosophica, no. 1- . Rome: Pontificia Universita Gregoriana, 1932- .

This series contains source material with commentaries, notes and bibliography. The texts are those of theologians, philosophers and the fathers, as well as official church documents. See also the Series Theologica (C0702).

C0702 Textus et Documenta in Usam Exercitationum et Praelectionum Academarum. Series Theologica, no. 1- . Rome: Pontificia Universita Gregoriana, 1932- .

This is a companion to the Series Philosophica (C0701) and provides a collection of source materials on various aspects of systematic, dogmatic and moral theology. It includes extracts from major theological treatises of the Roman Catholic Church plus selections from various theologians of the past and more recent periods. Commentaries, notes and bibliographies are provided to assist the beginner. See also Palmer (C0618).

C0703 Thielicke, Helmut. The Evangelical Faith. Trans. by Geoffrey W. Bromiley. 3 vols. Grand Rapids, Mich.: Wm. B. Eerdmans Publishing Company; Edinburgh: T. and T. Clark, 1974-1982.

This translation of Der Evangelische Glaube: Grundzüge der Dogmatik provides both a critical examination of contemporary theology and an attempt to develop a theology that can serve proclamation. This is an important work by a contemporary Lutheran theologian. See also Bloesch (C0354), Barth (C0336) and Tillich (C0709).

C0704 Thielicke, Helmut. Theological Ethics. Trans. by William H. Lazareth. 2 vols. Philadelphia, Pa.: Fortress Press, 1966-1969; London: Adam and Charles Black, 1968-1969.

This translation of Theologische Ethik (3 vols. Tübingen: J.C.B. Mohr, 1951-1964) is the basic Lutheran study of theological ethics, as well as being one of the most detailed studies of the field in any discipline. Thielicke's intention is to give a Christian interpretation of human and historical reality in a comprehensive and systematic way; to do this he discusses in volume 1 (foundations) three main subjects: Christian ethics in the age of secularism, the foundational principles of ethics, man's relation to the world. In volume 2 (politics) the main subjects include political ethics in the modern world, the nature of the state, borderline situations, the theological debate on church and state, the message of the church to the world. Each section is subdivided into a number of small units clearly outlined in the contents pages. The discussions are detailed and scholarly without being dry, and there are numerous bibliographical footnotes. Each volume includes indexes of authors, biblical passages, names and subjects. For students, researchers and clergy this is an important reference volume matched in its field perhaps only by Häring (C0497) among the Roman Catholic works. See also Sellers (C0677) and Gustafson (C0491).

C0705 Thomas, George Finger. Religious Philosophies of the West. New York: Charles Scribner's Sons, 1965.

This clear, nontechnical study of fifteen religious philosophers from Plato to Tillich is useful for understanding the major philosophers of the Western religious tradition. An introduction and an epilogue, which deals with present tendencies such as analytic philosophy and religious and atheistic existentialism, are included. As a primarily historical study, concerned with philosophical aspects rather than the place of each philosopher studied in the history of doctrine this provides a valuable contribution. See also Sahakian (C0663).

C0706 Thomas, William Henry Griffith. The Principles of Theology: An Introduction to the Thirty-Nine Articles. London: Longmans, Green and Company, 1930. Reprint (as 4th ed.). London: Church Bookroom Press, 1951.

This work provides an evangelical Anglican interpretation of the subject.

C0707 Tillich, Paul Johannes Oskar. A History of Christian Thought. 2nd ed. Ed. by Carl E. Braaten. New York: Harper and Row; London: SCM Press, 1968.

Based on Tillich's 1953 lectures at Union Theological Seminary (New York), the six parts of this survey cover the Greco-Roman background, early church, Middle Ages, Roman Catholicism from Trent to the present, theology of the Protestant reformers and the development of Protestant theology. Each section is subdivided into specific theological schools or topics, and there are indexes of names and subjects. This is a valuable and reasonably objective survey for both beginners and more advanced students. See also Heick (C0510) and Shedd (C0682).

C0708 Tillich, Paul Johannes Oskar. Perspectives on 19th and 20th Century Protestant Theology. Ed. by Carl E. Braaten. New York: Harper and Row; London: SCM Press, 1967.

This posthumously published collection comprises Tillich's lectures on the history of Christian thought given at the University of Chicago Divinity School in 1963. They cover the period from the Enlightenment to the present and refer to many men and movements, with particular emphasis on the nineteenth century. This book is of particular interest in understanding Tillich's theology as well as providing an introductory coverage of modern Protestant theological developments. See also Barth (C0337) and Welch (C0730).

C0709 Tillich, Paul Johannes Oskar. Systematic Theology. 3 vols. Chicago, Ill.: University of Chicago Press, 1951-1963. Reprint. 3 vols. in 1. Chicago, Ill.: University of Chicago Press, 1967.

Together with Barth (C0336) Tillich is the most influential Protestant systematic theologian of the twentieth century. His Systematic Theology offers a comprehensive and orderly philosophical system in five parts: "Reason and Revelation", "Being and God", "Existence and the Christ", "Life and the Spirit", "History and the Kingdom of God". Throughout this work Tillich uses a method of correlation whereby in the light of an analysis of the ambiguities of existence he shows that the solutions to these ambiguities exist in certain theological symbols. Particularly valuable in this approach is Tillich's categorical consistency which allows one to come to grips with his analysis more readily than in many other systems. Although frequently criticized for its immanental approach, this system has had a profound impact on liberal Protestant theology and for this reason cannot be overlooked. The detailed table of contents and index, especially in the 1967 reissue, make this work admirably suitable for quick reference. See also Thielicke (C0703).

C0710 Tillmann, Fritz, ed. Handbuch der Katholischen Sittenlehre. Unter

Mitarbeit von Theodor Steinbüchel und Theodor Müncker. 3rd ed. 5 vols. in 7. Düsseldorf: Patmos Verlag, 1947-1953.

See also Koch (C0551).

C0711 Tixeront, Joseph. History of Dogmas. Trans. from the 5th French ed. by Henry L. Brianceau. 2nd ed. 3 vols. St. Louis, Mo.: B. Herder Book Company, 1920-1926. Reprint. 3 vols. St. Louis, Mo.: B. Herder Book Company, 1923-1930.

See also Turmel (C0717).

C0712 Toinet, Paul. Existence Chrétienne et Philosophie: Essai sur les Fondaments de la Philosophie Chrétienne. Présence et Pensée. Paris: Editions Montaigne, 1965.

See also Gilson (C0469).

C0713 Trempelas, Panagiōtēs Nikolaou. Dogmatique de l'Eglise Orthodoxe Catholique. Traduction par Pierre Dumont. Vol. 1- . Paris: Desclée, De Brouwer; Chevetogne: Edition de Chevetogne, 1966- .

This textbook on Orthodox theology includes reference to many patristic sources, and represents a traditional approach to the subject. See also Lossky (C0571).

C0714 Trillhaas, Wolfgang. Dogmatik. 2. Aufl. Sammlung Töpelmann, 1. Reihe: Die Theologie im Abriss, Bd. 3. Berlin: Alfred Töpelmann, 1967.

The eight major parts in this conventional study outline the basic components of dogmatic theology in a straightforward, uncomplicated fashion for the less advanced student able to read German. The thirty-three chapters and their subdivisions are clearly set forth in the table of contents, while the indexes (pp. 561-581) treat biblical passages, names and subjects very fully. Trillhaas covers the subject succinctly and without being unnecessarily technical, making this work useful both as a basic text and a reference manual.

C0715 Trillhaas, Wolfgang. Ethik. 3 . Aufl. De Gruyter Lehrbuch. Berlin: Walter de Gruyter und Kompagnie, 1970.

See also Hirsch (C0519).

C0716 Troeltsch, Ernst. The Social Teaching of the Christian Churches. Trans. by Olive Wyon. 2 vols. London: Allen and Unwin, 1956; New York: Harper and Brothers, 1960.

This important work seeks to place the social teachings of the church in their historical context by tracing the interaction of religious ideas, community formation and cultural environment. While Troeltsch's liberal Protestant views often color his analysis, this is a significant attempt to understand Christian social ethics in historical perspective and contains a great deal of information not found elsewhere.

C0717 Turmel, Joseph. Histoire des Dogmes. 6 vols. Paris: Rieder, 1931-1936.

See also Schmaus (C0673) and Tixeront (C0711).

C0718 Ueberweg, Friedrich. History of Philosophy, from Thales to the Present Time. Trans. from the 4th German ed. by George S. Morris. 2 vols. New York: Charles Scribner's Sons, 1892.

Reprinted many times and available under several imprints, this translation of Grundriss der Geschichte der Philosophie is an important reference work covering ancient, medieval and modern philosophy. Unfortunately the English translation is much less up to date than later German editions (12. Aufl. Hrsg. von Karl Praechter. 5 vols. Berlin: E.S. Mittler und Sohn, 1923-1928. Reprint. 5 vols. Basel: Benno Schwabe and Company, 1951-1953). The English version also lacks the bibliographies, which are a special feature of the original. The English condensation covers early Christian and patristic philosophy clearly but briefly, serving as a basic reference guide to be supplemented by data from the preferred German editions or Fischl (C0449), among others. See also Windelband (C0740) and Wulf (C0745).

C0719 Utz, Arthur Fridolin. Sozialethik: Mit Internationaler Bibliographie. Vol. 1- . Sammlung Politeia, Bd. 10. Heidelberg: F.H. Kerle, 1958- .

Intended to trace the history and content of social ethics from a Roman Catholic viewpoint, this is both a detailed handbook and a reasonably wide ranging bibliography. The first volume (Die Prinzipien der Gesellschaftslehre) of 520 pages contains more than 100 pages of bibliography, which is arranged by subject and covers works published up to 1955. Utz does not limit his discussion or sources to Roman Catholic ethics but tries to survey all of social ethics regardless of provenance. The first volume indicates that his approach is too ambitious for one individual; nevertheless, the bibliographical content of the work is of particular value and should not be overlooked by students interested in modern European ethical thought and its historical antecedents. As a handbook, Utz has been surpassed by several newer works of both Roman Catholic and Protestant origin. See also Die Katholische Sozialdoktrin (C0541).

C0720 Vann, Gerald. Morals and Man. Rev. ed. New York: Sheed and Ward; London: William Collins Sons, 1960.

This revised version of the work first published in 1937 is in two parts: theory and essays in application. It presents a Dominican's defence of Thomistic moral philosophy, with an emphasis on personalism and support for such developments as less centralization and specialization in education, and more local autonomy in politics. This is a challenging exposition of the need for a unifying philosophy of life. For a more substantial work in the same vein see Tanquerey (C0700).

C0721 Vasoli, Cesare. La Filosofia Medioevale. Storia delle Filosofia, 2. Milan: Feltrinelli, 1961.

This 707 page study includes an extensive bibliography. See also Leff (C0561), Vignaux (C0722) and Weinberg (C0728).

C0722 Vignaux, Paul. Philosophy in the Middle Ages: An Introduction. Trans. by E.C. Hall. New York: Meridian Books; London: Burns and Oates, 1959.

This small but profound survey is translated from the third French edition of Philosophie au Moyen Age. The six chapters proceed chronologically from St. Anselm, Abelard, St. Bernard through the intellectual environment of the thirteenth century, to John Duns Scotus and William of Ockham, and, finally, aspects of thought in the fourteenth and fifteenth centuries. A bibliography (pp. 215-218) and index are included. See also Leff (C0561), Vasoli (C0721), Weinberg (C0728) and Wulf (C0745).

C0723 Vorgrimler, Herbert. Karl Rahner: His Life, Thought and Works. Trans. by Edward Quinn. Glen Rock, N.J.: Paulist Press; London: Burns and Oates, [1966].

This 96 page translation of Karl Rahner: Leben, Denken, Werke (Munich: Manz, 1963) provides a Roman Catholic treatment of Rahner's life and basic questions of his theology. Notes and a bibliography conclude the brief study of the important modern Catholic theologian. See also Kress (C0554).

C0724 Waddams, Herbert Montague. A New Introduction to Moral Theology. Rev. ed. London: SCM Press, 1972.

This introductory volume, written particularly for clergy and theological students, covers the main problems of moral theology (conscience, justice and punishment, the sanctity of life, etc.). Appendixes include technical terms used in moral theology and suggestions for further reading (pp. 233-236). An index is provided. See also Long (C0570).

C0725 Ward, Keith. Ethics and Christianity. New York: Humanities Press; London: Allen and Unwin, 1970.

This work focuses on the fundamental characteristics of Christian ethics, discussing duty and the will of God, ethics and Christian authority, and justice and redemption. Bibliographical references are included in the notes, and an index is provided. See also Adams (C0309).

C0726 Wassmer, Thomas A. Christian Ethics for Today. Contemporary College Theology Series. Milwaukee, Wisc.: Bruce Publishing Company, 1969.

See also McCabe (C0577).

C0727 Watlington, Amanda G., comp. Christ Our Lord. Official Catholic Teachings, vol. 1. Wilmington, N.C.: Consortium Books, 1978.

Like other volumes in the series Watlington presents a collection of papal, conciliar and other documents which reflect official Catholic views, in this case on the lordship of Christ in the church. The texts are numbered and indexed by subject. This is a sound compilation for the beginning theological student and saves much time when official views are sought. See also Aulén (C0323), Grillmeier (C0484) and Pannenberg (C0620).

C0728 Weinberg, Julius Rudolph. A Short History of Medieval Philosophy. Princeton, N.J.: Princeton University Press, 1964.

This 304 page survey analyzes the leading philosophical ideas of selected medieval Christian thinkers and provides comparatively comprehensive

chapters on Islamic and Jewish thought. Medieval authors of systems
of thought are treated chronologically. A bibliography, which does
not include all the editions cited in the text, is provided. The main
value of Weinberg is as an introductory survey on key philosophers
of the period. See also Leff (C0561), Vasoli (C0721) and Vignaux (C0722).

C0729 Welch, Claude. In This Name: The Doctrine of the Trinity in Contemporary Theology. New York: Charles Scribner's Sons, 1952.

Published in Britain as The Trinity in Contemporary Theology (London:
SCM Press, 1953), this 313 page study provides an expository and critical
survey of various views of the Trinity held in the nineteenth and twentieth centuries. The historical presentation is arranged topically, and
the position of many key theologians is examined. The author also gives
his own interpretation of the doctrine of the Trinity. This is both a
comprehensive survey and a constructive approach to the subject, of
particular interest to the theologian.

C0730 Welch, Claude. Protestant Thought in the Nineteenth Century. Vol. 1- .
New Haven, Conn.: Yale University Press, 1972- .

This valuable contribution to the understanding of nineteenth century
theology attempts to view Protestant thought as nearly as possible
as a whole, covering the German, British and American scenes. It is
clearly written, and is suitable for theology students. See also Tillich
(C0708).

C0731 Welty, Eberhard. A Handbook of Christian Social Ethics. Trans. by
Gregor Kirstein. Rev. and adapted by John Fitzsimons. Vol. 1- . Freiburg
im Breisgau: Herder, 1960- .

This translation of Herder's Sozialkatechismus consists of questions
and answers on Catholic social teachings, using quotations from papal
documents and other sources together with extended commentary.
Each volume includes an annotated, critical bibliography and an index.
The first volume deals with man and society; the second, with the
structure of the social order. See also Monzel (C0598).

C0732 Werner, Karl. Geschichte der Apologetischen und Polemischen Literatur
der Christlichen Theologie. 5 vols. Regensburg: G.J. Manz, 1862-1889.

This work has been published under varying imprints and is available
in later editions for some volumes. See also Dulles (C0433).

C0733 Werner, Karl. Geschichte der Katholischen Theologie seit dem Tridenter
Konzil bis zur Gegenwart. 2. Aufl. Munich: R. Oldenbourg, 1889.

For other Roman Catholic surveys see Grabmann (C0480) and Hocedez
(C0521).

C0734 Werner, Karl. System der Christlichen Ethik. 2 vols. Regensburg:
Verlagsanstalt, 1888. Reprint. 2 vols. in 3. Frankfurt: Minerva Verlag, 1970.

See also Schilling (C0667).

C0735 Werner, Martin. The Formation of Christian Dogma: An Historical

Study of Its Problem.Trans. by S.G.F. Brandon. New York: Harper and Brothers; London: Adam and Charles Black, 1957.

Essentially a rewritten and abbreviated version of Die Entstehung des Christlichen Dogmas Problemgeschichtlich Dargestellt (2. Aufl. Tübingen: Katzmann, 1954), this 352 page study provides a good account of major turning points in early doctrinal history through to the fourth century, with a summary of later history. However, its approach is somewhat dated, largely ignoring the work of Barth and Brunner, for example. There are copious references to the literature of early Christian history. See also Pelikan (C0622).

C0736 West, Charles C. Communism and the Theologians: Study of an Encounter. New York: Macmillan Company, 1963.

Based on a doctoral dissertation completed at Yale University in 1958, this work studies the reactions to Communism of such noted theologians as Brunner, Hromádka, Tillich, Barth and Reinhold Niebuhr. In addition, there is an introductory chapter on "Communism as the enemy", and a concluding chapter on the Christian encounter with Communism. Subject and name indexes are provided. See also Bennett (C0343).

C0737 White, Reginald E.O. Christian Ethics: The Historical Development. Atlanta, Ga.: John Knox Press, 1981.

First published in 1980 as The Insights of History, this 442 page study provides a survey of Christian ethics from Augustine to Bultmann. It includes helpful critiques of a variety of ethical positions. A bibliography (pp. 379-384) and an index are included. For those wanting a readable, historical approach this is a useful survey. See also Bourke (C0362).

C0738 Williams, Melvin J. Catholic Social Thought: Its Approach to Contemporary Problems. New York: Ronald Press Company, 1950.

Although it has been criticized for some important omissions, this extensive bio-bibliography of British and American Catholic social theorists is an excellent source of information on a number of major and lesser known personalities. A classified bibliography and an index of names are included. See also Abell (C0307) and Cronin (C0404).

C0739 Williams, Rowan. Christian Spirituality: A Theological History from the New Testament to Luther and St. John of the Cross. Atlanta, Ga.: John Knox Press, 1980.

This work examines the ways in which a succession of saints has responded to the call of the goal of the Christian life, interpreted here as wholeness. See also Bouyer (C0365) and Pourrat (C0632).

C0740 Windelband, Wilhelm. A History of Philosophy; with Especial Reference to the Formation and Development of Its Problems and Conceptions. Trans. by James H. Tufts. 2nd ed. New York: Macmillan Company, 1901. Reprint. New York: Macmillan Company, 1956.

This translation of Geschichte der Philosophie provides thorough coverage of the field from the pre-Socratics through the neo-Platonists and early

Christians. Although less comprehensive than Marías Aquilera (C0589), it contains much valuable material which is often hidden in the author's verbose prose style. See also Armstrong (C0320), Guthrie (C0493) and Ueberweg (C0718).

C0741 Windelband, Wilhelm. An Introduction to Philosophy. Trans. by Joseph McCabe. New York: H. Holt, 1921; London: T.F. Unwin, 1923.

This introduction seeks to provide a general view of philosophical problems and to explain the tendencies of the various attempts to solve them. Two main parts focus on theoretical problems (questions of knowledge) and on axiological problems (questions of value). A full, descriptive table of contents and an index are provided. See also Halverson (C0502).

C0742 Winter, Gibson. Elements for a Social Ethic: Scientific and Ethical Perspectives on Social Process. New York: Macmillan and Company, 1966.

this work argues for a style of social ethics which can be cultivated by theologians and social scientists in collaboration. Problems of the social sciences are discussed; the development of a science of the social world is proposed; finally, the relationship between ethics and society, the questions of social policy are considered. A bibliography (pp. 287-293) is included. This contains stimulating material for sociological theorists, social philosophers and theologians. See also Bennett (C0341).

C0743 Workman, Herbert Brook. Christian Thought to the Reformation. New York: Charles Scribner's Sons; London: Gerald Duckworth and Company, 1911. Reprint. London: Gerald Duckworth and Company, 1947.

Particularly useful for its emphasis on the role of philosophy and science in the development of Christian thought, this study surveys a broad time span, with nine chapters on aspects such as the person of Christ, the Dark Ages, the medieval mystics and the schoolmen. A bibliography (pp. 245-252) and an index are included, the former not attempting to cover original sources. See also McGiffert (C0579).

C0744 Wuellner, Bernard. Summary of Scholastic Principles. Chicago, Ill.: Loyola University Press, 1956.

This work outlines the principles of scholastic disciplines with reference to their occurrence in the writings of St. Thomas and occasionally in contemporary sources. It is a valuable basic work for students new to the field and also serves as a useful reference guide to scholasticism. An index is provided. See also Wulf (C0746).

C0745 Wulf, Maurice Marie Charles Joseph de. History of Medieval Philosophy. Trans. by Ernest C. Messenger. 3 vols. New York: Thomas Nelson and Sons; New York: Dover Books, 1952.

Based on the sixth French edition of Wulf's classic work, Histoire de la Philosophie Mediévale (4 vols. Louvain: Institut Supérieur de Philosophie; Paris: J. Vrin, 1934-1947), this scholarly and well documented survey provides detailed information on movements, concepts and ideas important in medieval philosophy. While coverage extends to the entire medieval period, the thirteenth century receives particularly detailed treatment. Arrangement is chronological for the most part, and there are copious footnote references plus full chapter bibliographies, the latter intended in part to update Ueberweg (C0718). See also Leff (C0561) and Vignaux (C0722).

C0746 Wulf, Maurice Marie Charles Joseph de. <u>Scholasticism Old and New:</u> <u>An Introduction to Scholastic Philosophy, Medieval and Modern.</u> Trans. by P. Coffey. New York: Benziger Brothers, 1907; Dublin: M.H. Gill, 1910.

Reprinted as <u>An Introduction to Scholastic Philosophy, Medieval and</u> <u>Modern Scholasticism Old and New</u> (New York: Dover Publications, 1956), this classic survey covers the methodology, metaphysics, evolution, decline and revival of scholasticism. See also Wuellner (C0744).

D. Church History

D0001 Abbott, Wilbur Cortez. A Bibliography of Oliver Cromwell: A List of Printed Materials Relating to Oliver Cromwell, together with a List of Portraits and Caricatures. Cambridge, Mass.: Harvard University Press, 1929.

> This 551 page bibliography lists material on Cromwell published between 1597 and 1928.

D0002 Aland, Kurt; Peschke, Erhard; and Schmidt, Martin, eds. Bibliographie zur Geschichte des Pietismus, im Auftrag der Historischen Kommission zur Erforschung des Pietismus. Vol. 1- . Berlin: Walter de Gruyter und Kompagnie, 1972- .

D0003 Allison, William Henry. Inventory of Unpublished Material for American Religious History in Protestant Church Archives and Other Repositories. Carnegie Institution of Washington Publication, no. 137. Washington, D.C.: Carnegie Institution of Washington, 1910. Reprint. New York: Kraus Reprint, 1965.

> This 254 page bibliography describes material relevant to American religious history deposited in archives of governing bodies of Protestant churches and of Protestant missionary societies, in libraries of theological colleges, seminaries, historical societies and the like. The local collection forms the basis for the arrangement which is alphabetical by state, town and repository/institution. Although dated this inventory provides a useful guide for researchers on Protestant religious history in America, particularly at the local level. See also Mode (D0172).

D0004 Altaner, Berthold. Patrology. Trans. by Hilda C. Graef. 2nd ed. New York: Herder and Herder, 1961.

> Based on the fifth edition of Patrologie: Leben, Schriften und Lehre der Kirchenvater, which also exists in an eighth edition (Freiburg im Breisgau: Herder, 1978), this extensive bibliographical work includes comments on the lives, writings and teachings of the fathers. It has also been translated into French, Spanish and Italian. Similar to Barden-

hewer (C0342-D0345), this has the advantage of being more up to date, although Quasten (D0675, D0676) provides more detail and more thorough coverage of the field. See also Stewardson (D0208).

D0005 Altholz, Josef Lewis. Victorian England, 1837-1901. Conference on British Studies, Bibliographical Handbooks. Cambridge: Cambridge University Press for the Conference on British Studies, 1970.

The 2500 entries in this bibliography are arranged by subject and include both books and articles, with emphasis on publications of scholarly utility. A list of abbreviations, explanatory notes and an index of authors, editors and translators are provided. Bibliographical data are basic but adequate for most purposes; annotations are few and tend to be evaluative rather than descriptive. Religious history (pp. 61-70) is covered less thoroughly than in similar works by Altschul (D0006) and Levine (D0161) in the same series, but this is still a useful starting point for advanced students of the period.

D0006 Altschul, Michael, comp. Anglo-Norman England, 1066-1154. Conference on British Studies Bibliographical Handbooks. Cambridge: Cambridge University Press for the Conference on British Studies, 1969.

This 83 page bibliography lists and comments upon the most important books, articles and editions of texts (with the exception of literature per se) relevant to all aspects of Anglo-Norman England. Special attention is paid to recent trends in investigation and research, and a significant proportion of the material comes from the 1950s and 1960s. Entries are arranged under fourteen subject headings, with religious history (pp. 49-62) receiving the most extensive treatment. Bibliographical citations are not complete but do provide enough information to allow one to identify or locate a given item; citations are included infrequently and give minimal information. There is an index of authors, editors and translators. A list of abbreviations and brief explanatory notes are found at the beginning of the compilation.

D0007 America: History and Life. Vol. 1- . Santa Barbara, Calif.: American Bibliographical Center-Clio Press, 1964- ; five per annum in two parts.

Covering publications from around the world on North American history and current life, this work consists of two main parts. Part A (three per annum) contains article abstracts and citations from more than 2000 periodicals. Each issue provides full citations and very informative abstracts. Part B contains an index to book reviews and appears twice annually. Quinquennial indexes are also produced. This is an important source of information for church historians, as American religion receives broadly representative and up to date coverage. For treatment of pre-1964 titles see Historical Abstracts (D0129), which no longer covers America.

D0008 American Historical Association. Guide to Historical Literature. Chairman of the Board of Editors: George Frederick Howe. New York: Macmillan Company, 1961.

This 962 page bibliographical guide is a standard work for students in all areas of historical study. The annotated bibliographies by specialists are arranged in broad subject and country groups, and within these

a form arrangement is followed wherever possible. Bibliographies, encyclopedias, dictionaries, histories, biographies and similar categories are
covered. The history of religions, including Christianity, is treated
adequately for the beginner. See also Coulter (D0074) and Day (D0084).

D0009 The American Historical Review. Vol. 1- . Washington, D.C.: American
Historical Association, 1895- ; five per annum.

With as much as three quarters of each issue devoted to book lists
and reviews, AHR is an important bibliography for those interested
in all aspects of church history. Book reviews show a clear European
bias, but coverage does extend to other areas as well. Particularly
comprehensive is the treatment of modern Europe. In addition to the
reviews there is a reasonable listing of books and articles in "Other
Recent Publications". The July number indexes both reviews and books
listed during the year, and a cumulative index is issued every ten years.
See also The English Historical Review (D0092) and Revue Historique
(D0195) for periodicals which focus more directly on European history.
All three are useful tools for retrospective bibliographical searching.

D0010 Analecta Bollandiana: Revue Critique d'Hagiographie. Vol. 1- . Brussels:
Société des Bollandistes, 1882- ; semiannual (four issues published as two).

Prepared by the compilers of the Acta Sanctorum (D0306, D0388),
this review is devoted primarily to hagiographical articles of scholarly
interest. There is also a much smaller bibliographical section, consisting
of a Bulletin des Publications Hagiographiques, a list of books received
and a collection of indexes and contents lists. The Bulletin contains
signed reviews and short book notices, while the list of received books
covers both lives of the saints and major scholarly works. There are
also occasional catalogs devoted to manuscript collections. Saints treated
in the reviews or catalogs are listed in the annual Index Sanctorum,
which also has regular cumulations. Although there are often lengthy
delays in the coverage of new books, virtually all scholarly works in
the field are treated eventually, making this an indispensible guide
to hagiographical titles. See also the other bibliographies published
by the Société (D0035-D0037).

D0011 L'Année Philologique: Bibliographie Critique et Analytique de l'An-
tiquité Greco-Latine. Vol. 1- . Paris: International Society of Classical
Bibliography, 1924- .

Particularly valuable as a guide to topics in Greco-Roman and Hellenistic
history and to works about or by Greek and Latin authors (both pagan
and Christian), this bibliography lists books, book reviews and articles
from around the world but with a strong European focus. The text
is in a variety of Western languages, and summaries are provided in
English, French and German. Within its field this is an essential tool
but lacks the currency one would prefer in such a work. See also Buchwald (D0054).

D0012 Annual Bibliography of British and Irish History. Vol. 1- . Brighton:
Harvester Press for the Royal Historical Society, 1975- ; annual.

Covering all aspects of British and Irish history, entries are arranged
chronologically by historical topic; each period is subdivided by subject

divisions (including religion). Entries provide only author and title details plus bibliographical references, and there is a subject index. This compilation usefully gathers information from a number of journals, most of them standard historical serials, thus providing a useful service for those interested in the history of the British Isles. The coverage of religion is not especially thorough, but again it provides some help to those who otherwise would have to scan a number of journals for potentially relevant items. See also Berkowitz (D0029).

D0013 Annual Bulletin of Historical Literature. Vol. 1- . London: Historical Association, 1910- ; annual.

Focusing primarily on Europe, especially Britain, this annual guide contains a narrative discussion of selected books and serials, which is arranged by period and topic (including religion). It provides a useful overview of current research, indicating the content and scope of items selected for coverage. The Bulletin does not aim to be comprehensive but seeks instead to survey general trends in research; within this framework it provides a useful guide to work in religious history. Bibliographical details, especially for periodicals, leave much to be desired, and there is no subject index to accompany the index of authors. See also Historical Abstracts (D0129) and Historische Zeitschrift (D0130).

D0014 Annuarium Historiae Conciliorum: Internationale Zeitschrift für Konziliengeschichtsforschung. Vol. 1- . Paderborn: Ferdinand Schöningh Verlag, 1969- ; semiannual.

This journal is devoted primarily to scholarly articles on all aspects of conciliar history, and it also contains a bibliographical section on the same subject. The bibliography contains up to 150 citations in each issue and is arranged by subject. In most respects this is not a particularly useful service both because of the very limited coverage provided and because of the fairly dated inclusion of citations. For most purposes students of conciliar affairs should instead consult the Bulletin of Medieval Canon Law (D0056). See also Sawicki (D0199).

D0015 Archaeological Bibliography for Great Britain and Ireland. Vol. 1- . London: Council for British Archaeology, 1950- ; annual.

This guide to archeological materials relating to the British Isles from the earliest times to 1600 covers items published in archeological journals, general periodicals, books and monographs. Entries are presented in two sections; the topographical division is essentially an alphabetical index arranged by period and county, and this refers the user to fuller entries in the alphabetical author listing, which provides full bibliographical details for each item. Although the coverage is often three years behind, this is a usefully comprehensive guide for students interested in early British religious history and the history of religious buildings. See also British Archaeological Abstracts (D0050) for more detailed entries on the same topic.

D0016 Archief voor de Geschiedenis van de Katholieke Kerk en Nederland. Vol. 1- . Nijmegen: Dekker and van de Vegt, 1959- ; semiannual.

The second issue of each volume contains a bibliography of publications (both books and articles) on the church history of the Low Countries, especially Holland. This is arranged primarily on a geographical basis, with the addition of general and bibliographical sections; within each section entries are listed alphabetically by author, and there is a combined index to the entire volume. Most items listed are in Flemish and English, providing a very useful survey of both books and serials (approximately three dozen) for students of this field. See also Bibliotheca Catholica Neerlandica (D0033).

D0017 Archiv für Kirchengeschichte von Böhmen-Mähren-Schlesien. Vol. 1- . Königstein: Institut für Kirchengeschichte Böhmen-Mähren-Schlesien, 1967- ; irregular.

Issued approximately annually or biennially, this journal focuses on the history of the church in Bohemia and Silesia. Following the usual articles, expositions and reviews, there is a bibliographical section arranged by broad subjects and then alphabetically by author. Most materials listed are in German or Czech, and the seven journals covered each year yield approximately 100 entries. There are no indexes. This is a useful, if somewhat limited, guide to a topic and journals not well covered elsewhere.

D0018 Archiv für Reformationsgeschichte, Beiheft: Literaturbericht/Archive for Reformation History. Supplement: Literature Review. Vol. 1- . St. Louis, Mo.: American Society for Reformation Research; Gütersloh: Gütersloher Verlagshaus Gerd Mohn, 1972- ; annual.

This supplement to the Archiv für Reformationsgeschichte, which has been appearing since 1904, is an annual annotated index to periodicals, books and dissertations on all aspects of Reformation history. Entries are arranged in a classified subject sequence; there is a list of headings and geographical regions in each issue, which helps to compensate for the lack of annual indexes. A quinquennial index to volumes 1-5 contains indexes of authors, of people discussed and of places. This broadly based survey covers such subjects as sixteenth century European church history, the Reformation and Counter-Reformation, cultural and political aspects of the period, major Protestant reformers (Luther, Zwingli, Calvin). These subjects are complemented by a parallel series of country and regional subdivisions. The signed abstracts or annotations are in English or German and cover publications in all European languages. Because it provides reasonably up to date coverage of a wide range of materials and caters to a variety of user approaches, this is a helpful bibliography of Reformation history. See also Center for Reformation Research (D0063) and The Sixteenth Century Journal (D0202).

D0019 Archivo Vatican. Bibliografia dell'Archivo Vaticano. A cura della Commissione Internazionale per la Bibliografia dell'Archivo Vaticano. Vol. 1- . Vatican City: Presso l'Archivo Vaticano, 1962- .

This extensive and very thorough bibliography of works about the contents of the Vatican Archives is arranged by author and by document. It lists both books and articles in various languages which deal with items in a collection of unique importance for advanced research in Roman Catholic history. See also Boyle (D0049) and Fink (D0472).

D0020 Archivum Historiae Pontificiae. Vol. 1- . Rome: Pontificia Universitas Gregoriana, Facultas Historiae Ecclesiasticae, 1963- ; annual.

Following a collection of scholarly articles and book reviews on papal history in general, each annual issue contains a very substantial bibliography in six major sections on the popes, history of the papacy, Christian archeology, art and liturgy, church councils, theological problems relating to the papacy. Most of the sections are arranged chronologically with subdivisions under the name of each pope, and these divisions vary according to the topics of the period in question. The bibliography includes articles, monographs, encyclopedias, Festschriften and dissertations, covering materials from Europe, North America and Latin America and emanating from all traditions. There are very full author and subject indexes to the numbered entries in each volume, and this is particularly important in view of the complex arrangement of materials. Detailed instructions for use are provided, and these should be consulted by all users wishing to achieve the full benefits of this valuable guide. The major drawback is the rather delayed appearance of each volume (approximately two years following the dates covered), yet for research on the history and theology of the papacy this is a most valuable bibliographical tool.

D0021 Association Internationale des Etudes Byzantines. Dix Années d'Etudes Byzantines: Bibliographie Internationale, 1939-1948. Paris: Secrétariat de l'Association: Ecole des Hautes Etudes, 1949 [i.e., 1950].

This bibliography of works published between 1939 and 1948 lists books plus articles from some 250 journals on such topics as Byzantine history, archeology, art, literature and philology. Entries are arranged by country and then by subject. Author and subject indexes are provided.

D0022 Atiya, Aziz Suryal. The Crusades: Historiography and Bibliography. Bloomington, Ind.: Indiana University Press, 1962.

This 170 page bibliography covers materials in several languages. Monographs, periodical literature and collections of source material are listed in classified order. A brief essay on the historiography of the crusades is included. See also Mayer (D0168).

D0023 Atkinson, Ernest Edwin. A Selected Bibliography of Hispanic Baptist History. Nashville, Tenn.: Southern Baptist Convention, Historical Commission, 1981.

See also Whitley (D0227).

D0024 Bainton, Roland Herbert, and Gritsch, Eric W. Bibliography of the Continental Reformation: Materials Available in English. 2nd ed. Hamden, Conn.: Archon Books, 1972.

First published in 1935, this 220 page bibliography is designed for those limited to the English language. In classified arrangement it covers Luther, Calvin and related reformers, the Anabaptists, Roman Catholic reform, Erasmus and Arminius. Brief annotations are provided for books and periodicals. There is a detailed list of contents but no index. See also Center for Reformation Research (D0063).

D0025 Baker, Derek, ed. The Bibliography of the Reform, 1450-1648, Relating to the United Kingdom and Ireland for the Years 1955-70. Comp. by D.M. Loades, J.K. Cameron and Derek Baker for the British Sub-Commission,

Commission Internationale d'Histoire Ecclésiastique Comparée. Oxford: Basil Blackwell, 1975.

This 242 page complement to the International Committee of Historical Sciences publication, Bibliographie de la Réforme (D0139), is arranged geographically to cover England and Wales, Scotland, Ireland. Each section opens with a list of journals and society publications consulted in tracing works published between 1955 and 1970. This is followed by the bibliographies, which are arranged according to form: books and parts of books, bibliographies and dictionaries, academic journals, society and occasional publications, reviews, completed theses. The lists are adequately detailed and widely representative of publications in the field. However, busy researchers will not appreciate the lack of indexes.

D0026 Baumgart, Winfried. Bücherverzeichnis zur Deutschen Geschichte. Hilfsmittel, Handbücher, Quellen. Deutsche Geschichte, 14. Frankfurt am Main: Ullstein Verlag, 1971.

Based on the same author's Bibliographie zum Studium des Neueren Geschichte, this selective bibliography of German history treats most aspects and all periods of the subject. Particularly helpful is the inclusion of general reference works with historical content. The church is treated adequately for the beginner in this volume, which is suitable when one is devising a first bibliography. For a more detailed approach see Dahlmann (D0078).

D0027 Beers, Henry Putney. Bibliographies in American History: Guide to Materials for Research. Rev. ed. New York: H.W. Wilson Company, 1942. Reprint. Paterson, N.J.: Pageant Books, 1959.

This classified listing of nearly 12,000 bibliographies treats many areas of American history, among them religion. For bibliographies published before 1942 Beers is a very comprehensive guide to separate works, manuscripts, titles in progress and analytics. Many of the items are not listed elsewhere. For older works see Larned (D0157, D0158).

D0028 Bell, S. Peter. Dissertations on British History, 1815-1914: An Index to British and American Theses. Metuchen, N.J.: Scarecrow Press, 1974.

This useful index of theses is divided into five main subject divisions, one of which is ecclesiastical history; these divisions are further divided as required in order to group the 2300 entries into suitable topics. Bell includes doctorates submitted to British and American universities and British master's theses. There are indexes of authors, persons, places and subjects. As a retrospective guide to research on early modern Britain, Bell is most suitable for scholars.

D0029 Berkowitz, David Sandler. Bibliotheca Bibliographica Britannica; or, Bibliographies in British History: A Manual of Bibliographies of Bibliography, and of Bibliographies, Catalogues, Registers, Inventories, Lists, Calendars, Guides, Reference Aids, Directories, Indices, etc.; Collected and Classified for the Use of Researchers in British History. Vol. 1- . Waltham, Mass.: [Brandeis University], 1963- .

See also Annual Bibliography (D0012).

D0030 Bibliographia Patristica: Internationale Patristische Bibliographie. Vol. 1- . Berlin: Walter de Gruyter for the Patristische Komision der Akademien der Wissenschaften in der Bundesrepublik Deutschland, 1959- ; annual.

Covering books, articles and dissertations, this compilation is arranged in a classified subject order and is subdivided alphabetically by author. The areas treated include not only writings of the fathers themselves but also such topics as NT, doctrine, philosophy, exegesis, creeds, hagiography. Although a volume may contain 3000 entries, many of these are repeated under various subjects. Each volume covers a specific year but can be up to seven years late in appearing, which is a very serious handicap. Nevertheless, Bibliographia Patristica is the most detailed work in its field and should be used by those who do not require immediate information on publications. See also Altaner (D0004) and Stewardson (D0208).

D0031 Bibliographie Annuelle de l'Histoire de France. Vol. 1- . Paris: Centre National de la Recherche Scientifique, 1953- ; annual.

Covering all topics related to French history, this classified bibliography includes a section devoted to religious history in particular. This is further divided into specific topics and generally lists more than 1000 books and articles, mostly French. Each entry lists author and title together with essential bibliographical details. There are excellent subject and author indexes for each volume. Although items are listed approximately two years after they have appeared, this remains an important bibliographical guide to the religious history of France for both students and scholars. See also Bibliothèque Nationale (D0038-D0040) and Caron (D0060).

D0032 Bibliographie zur Deutschen Geschichte. Vol. 1-Vol. 33. Leipzig: B.G. Teubner, 1889-1931; annual.

Issued by various publishers as an annual supplement to the Historische Vierteljahrschrift, this bibliography lists publications issued between 1889 and 1927 on German history. It is arranged by subject and is indexed by author. Coverage extends to books, articles and pamphlets and includes references to reviews of many titles. As a general bibliography, this is useful for historians of the German church who are searching for older publications. It is a helpful precursor of the Jahresberichte zur Deutschen Geschichte (D0143), which covers publications issued from 1925 onwards. See also Dahlmann (D0078).

D0033 Bibliotheca Catholica Neerlandica, Impressa 1500-1727. The Hague: Martinus Nijhoff, 1954.

This 669 page bibliography is a chronologically arranged guide to Roman Catholic works published in The Netherlands. Because many significant historical works were published in the Low Countries during the period indicated, this is an important guide to a major corpus of writings. See also Archief voor de Geschiedenis (D0016).

D0034 Bibliotheca Celtica: A Register of Publications Relating to Wales and the Celtic Peoples and Languages. Vol. 1- . Aberystwyth: National Library of Wales, 1909- ; annual with some variations.

Using the Library of Congress classification, this listing of materials on all aspects of Celtic life in Europe concentrates particularly on Wales and in this respect is a unique guide to a very specific field. Within the classification religion is treated as an individual topic, covering both pre-Christian and Christian aspects. Books, articles and book reviews are included, and coverage appears to be limited to the years indicated in each volume title. However, the appearance of each can be four years late. For students of the Celtic, especially Welsh, church this is a helpful bibliography. See also Bonser (D0045).

D0035 Bibliotheca Hagiographica Graeca. 3. ed. Ed. by François Halkin. 3 vols. and supplement. Subsidia Hagiographica, nos. 8a, 47. Brussels: Société des Bollandistes, 1957-1969.

This third edition of a standard work updates the listing of Greek hagiographical manuscripts and documents in a thorough, detailed and scholarly fashion. It includes a substantial number of items not listed elsewhere and is an essential bibliographical work for scholars and advanced students of hagiographical literature. Arrangement is alphabetical by names of saints and includes literature related to the lives of the saints written in Greek. The supplement of 1969 includes appendixes and useful tables. For recent discoveries and corrections see Analecta Bollandiana (D0010).

D0036 Bibliotheca Hagiographica Latina Antiquae et Mediae Aetatis. 2 vols. and supplement. Subsidia Hagiographica, nos. 6, 12. Brussels: Société des Bollandistes, 1898-1911. Reprint. 3 vols. Brussels: Société des Bollandistes, 1949.

This bibliography on the saints is arranged alphabetically by names of individuals and lists all literature on their lives and works written in Latin before the sixteenth century. The first two volumes are paginated continuously, and the supplement adds many items not included in the original compilation. For advanced students of hagiography this is a most valuable work which is a standard bibliographical guide in its field. See also the preceding (D0035) and following (D0037) entries. For additions see Analecta Bollandiana (D0010).

D0037 Bibliotheca Hagiographica Orientalis. Ed. by Paulus Peeters. Subsidia Hagiographica, no. 10. Brussels: Société des Bollandistes, 1910. Reprint. Brussels: Société des Bollandistes, 1954.

This work, like those devoted to Greek (D0035) and Latin (D0036) hagiographical writings, is arranged alphabetically by names of saints and includes biographical and other sources in Oriental languages. For a very specialized topic this is a most thorough and detailed bibliographical guide. See Analecta Bollandiana (D0010) for additions.

D0038 Bibliothèque Nationale. Département des Imprimés. Catalogue de l'Histoire de France. 11 vols., index, 6 supplements. Paris: Firmin Didot et Cie, 1855-1895.

This classified catalog of various types of publications on pre-1875 French history is divided into fifteen subject areas and 904 subclasses. Volume 5 covers religious history in great detail and is an important source of bibliographical information for students of French ecclesiastical history. The two indexes (D0039, D0040) of authors and titles are necessary additions to the series. None of the supplements adds to the coverage of religion. For coverage of later years see Caron (D0060) and Bibliographie Annuelle (D0031).

D0039 Bibliothèque Nationale. Département des Imprimés. Catalogue de l'Histoire de France. Table des Auteurs. Paris: Firmin Didot et Cie, 1895.

This 798 page index is an essential tool for users of the main series (D0038).

D0040 Bibliothèque Nationale. Département des Imprimés. Catalogue de l'Histoire de France. Table Générale Alphabétique des Ouvrages Anonymes. 15 vols. Paris: Firmin Didot et Cie, 1905-1932.

The first four volumes contain the table des noms de personnes, while the remaining volumes provide the table des noms de lieux. For the main catalog see Bibliothèque Nationale (D0038).

D0041 Billington, Ray Allen. Guides to American History Manuscript Collections in Libraries of the United States. New York: Peter Smith, 1952.

Reprinted from the Mississippi Valley Historical Review (vol. 38, no. 3), this 30 page bibliographical guide lists guides to manuscript collections in national depositories, university and public libraries, historical societies and private collections to which members of the public have access. The two part arrangement treats (1) federal depositories and (2) state depositories and single depositories.

D0042 Bindoff, Stanley Thomas, and Boulton, James T., eds. Research in Progress in English and History in Britain, Ireland, Canada, Australia and New Zealand. New York: St. Martin's Press; London: St. James Press, 1976.

This new edition of Research in Progress in English and Historical Studies in the Universities of the British Isles attempts to include not only university based research but also private projects; it sensibly broadens coverage to certain Commonwealth countries which traditionally undertake significant research related to English literature and history. As a guide to current research, Bindoff should appear much more frequently. The present volume is now too dated to serve more than retrospective search needs.See also Current Research (D0077).

D0043 Boehm, Eric H., and Adolphus, Lalit, eds. Historical Periodicals: An Annotated List of Historical and Related Serial Publications. Santa Barbara, Calif.: Clio Press, 1961.

This 618 page annotated list contains more than 4500 current titles, arranged by area and country and covering history and related fields. The four sections treat history in general, auxiliary disciplines, local history, related fields. Entries in the first two sections are especially detailed, indicating title and subtitle, frequency, date of origin, publisher and editor, subject coverage, existence of summaries and indexes, subscription rates. Other sections provide only the most basic data on titles, but coverage is very broad indeed. Like Caron (D0059), however, Boehm is only representative of the field and should not be treated as a complete or up to date directory. See also Kramm (D0153).

D0044 Boehmer, Eduard. Bibliotheca Wiffeniana: Spanish Reformers of Two Centuries from 1520; Their Lives and Writings, According to the Late Benjamin B. Wiffen's Plan and with the Use of His Materials. 3 vols. Strasbourg: K. Trübner, 1874-1904. Reprint. 3 vols. Burt Franklin Bibliographical and Reference Series, no. 32. New York: Burt Franklin, [1971?].

D0045 Bonser, Wilfrid. An Anglo-Saxon and Celtic Bibliography, 450-1087. 2 vols. Oxford: Basil Blackwell, 1957.

This 574 page bibliography lists nearly 12,000 items from 422 periodicals, collected works and Festschriften. The twelve topical sections include one on religion, where much valuable material of historical interest is listed. Bonser is very closely classified and includes an indispensible outline of the classification to facilitate use; the latter compensates for the lack of an index. This is a usefully broad guide for students of early British history and church expansion. See also Bibliotheca Celtica (D0034).

D0046 Booty, John E., ed. The Godly Kingdom of Tudor England: Great Books of the English Reformation. Wilton, Conn.: Morehouse-Barlow, c. 1981.

See also Levine (D0161) and Read (D0187).

D0047 Bowditch, John, and Grew, Raymond, comps. and eds. A Selected Bibliography on Modern French History, 1600 to the Present. Assisted by Roger Geiger. Ann Arbor, Mich.: Xerox University Microfilms, 1974.

Following a somewhat inconsequential listing of Xerox Microfilm publications on French history, Bowditch lists approximately 1200 American university dissertations in this subject. Entries are listed by topic and include basic bibliographical data. There is an author index. This listing is useful for postgraduate students working on French church history, which is treated in passing. See also Pagès (D0179).

D0048 Boyce, Gray Cowan, comp. and ed. Literature of Medieval History, 1930-1975: A Supplement to Louis John Paetow's "Guide to the Study of Medieval History". Sponsored by the Mediaeval Academy of America. 5 vols. Millwood, N.Y.: Kraus International Publications, 1981.

This important supplement to Paetow (D0178) is a comprehensive bibliography of 55,000 works on every aspect of medieval life and culture published between 1930 and 1975. The set is divided into three parts, each of which is subdivided into a total of 3000 categories. Part 1 lists general reference works providing an overview of the Middle Ages, including bibliographies, encyclopedias, handbooks, collections, atlases and guides on all relevant subjects and geographical areas. Part 2 (General History of the Middle Ages) is arranged chronologically and then geographically. Part 3 lists publications concerning life and culture of the period, including theology, philosophy, literature, music, art and language. Boyce is international in scope, listing items in their original language and providing full bibliographical citations. Author and subject indexes are provided in this essential work for scholars and advanced students of the medieval era. See also Caenegem (D0057).

D0049 Boyle, Leonard E. A Survey of the Vatican Archives and Its Medieval Holdings. Subsidia Mediaevalia, 1. Toronto: Pontifical Institute of Medieval

Studies, 1972.

This two part work deals with the holdings of the Vatican Archives, their location and main chronological and topical contents down to this century in part 1; and in part 2 provides a historical account of the thousands of volumes of Vatican, Avignon and Lateran Registers. This is an invaluable tool for the researcher in making accessible these sources in a practical way. Much of the illustrative material is from English and Irish sources, making the work particularly relevant to an Anglo-Saxon audience. See also Archivo Vaticano (D0019).

D0050 British Archaeological Abstracts. Vol. 1- . London: Council for British Archaeology, 1967- ; semiannual.

Arranged by broad subject categories and further subdivided by period and topic, this work lists articles from some 200 journals on British archeology. Each issue contains approximately two dozen entries of interest to religious studies; each citation includes bibliographical data plus a brief abstract, and there are author and subject indexes for each issue. For those interested in pre-Christian and early Christian Britain or in particular buildings this is a useful source of information. See also Archaeological Bibliography (D0015).

D0051 Brown, Lucy M., and Christie, Ian R. Bibliography of British History, 1789-1851. Issued under the direction of the American Historical Association and the Royal Historical Society of Great Britain. Oxford: Clarendon Press, 1977.

This 759 page bibliography contains 4782 entries for books, journal articles, collections of source materials, etc., usually with brief annotations and with some cross references. A chapter on ecclesiastical history is included. There are main entry and subject indexes. For other periods see Graves (D0109), Read (D0187), Davies (D0081), Pargellis (D0181) and Hanham (D0120).

D0052 Bruggeman, J., and Ven, Adrianus Johannes van de. Inventaire des Pièces d'Archives Françaises Se Rapportant à l'Abbaye de Port-Royal des Champs et Son Cercle et à la Resistance contre la Bulle Unigenitus et à l'Appel (Ancien Fonds d'Amersfoort). Archives Internationales d'Histoire des Idées, 54. The Hague: Martinus Nijhoff, 1972.

Focusing on Jansenism and the resulting papal bull, Unigenitus, this 450 page bibliography lists more than 7000 items in the Fonds d'Amersfoort archives which deal with this subject. It is a valuable guide to an important movement in the church and is well indexed by author and name. See also Willaert (D0229).

D0053 Buchholz, Peter. Bibliographie zur Alteuropäischen Religionsgeschichte, 1954-1964. Literatur zu den Antiken Rand- und Nachfolgekulturen in Aussermediterranean Europa unter Besonderer Berücksichtigung der Nichtchristlichen Religionen. Arbeiten zur Frühmittelalterforschung, Bd. 2. Berlin: Walter de Gruyter und Kompagnie, 1967.

D0054 Buchwald, Wolfgang; Holweg, Armin; and Prinz, Otto, eds. Tusculum-Lexikon: Griechischer und Lateinischer Autoren des Altertums und des Mittelalters. Munich: Heimeran Verlag, 1963.

Although brief, this lexicon is a sound bibliographical dictionary which lists authors, their dates, main works, references to editions of their texts and translations of these works. Several of the authors are of interest to students of early church thought and history. Buchwald's main value lies in its identification of original works, as the translations are generally not listed for the convenience of English language readers. See also L'Année Philologique (D0011).

D0055 Bulletin de la Société de l'Histoire du Protestantisme Français. Vol. 1- . Paris: Société de l'Histoire du Protestantisme Français, 1853- ; quarterly.

Limited to the history of Protestant Christianity in France, this work includes in each issue a literature survey, which consists of reviews of books and abstracts of periodical articles. The reviews are usually quite current, but the number of article abstracts is very limited. No systematic arrangement is used, but as the only bibliographical service in its field, this service cannot be ignored by advanced students.

D0056 Bulletin of Medieval Canon Law. Vol. 1- . Berkeley, Calif.: University of California, Institute of Medieval Canon Law, 1971- ; annual.

Devoted to the history of canon law and of the church's councils, this journal includes in each issue a substantial bibliographical section. This is arranged by subject and lists books, periodical articles, Festschriften, parts of encyclopedias and reviews of works cited in earlier issues. Coverage is relatively up to date and provides basic bibliographical data (plus occasional abstracts) needed to trace a given item. An index of names is provided in each issue. In addition there are occasional bibliographical articles and lists intended to update Sawicki (D0199). For canon lawyers, historians of the conciliar movement and related topics this is an indispensible bibliographical journal which is much wider in its coverage than Annuarium Historiae Conciliorum (D0014).

D0057 Caenegem, R.C. van. Guide to the Sources of Medieval History. With the collaboration of François Louis Ganshof. Europe in the Middle Ages: Selected Studies, vol. 2. Amsterdam: North Holland Publishing Company, 1978.

This revision and expansion of Encyclopedie van de Geschiedenis der Middeleeuwen is arranged in five sections, each of which contains several chapters describing a broad range of sources for medieval studies. The five sections cover typology of sources, libraries and archives, major collections, reference works, auxiliary sciences. Within the sections van Caenegem treats all areas of medieval studies, concentrating primarily on European sources of information and indicating very clearly their scholarly value. A detailed table of contents and an index of names and anonymous titles complete the work, which is a useful complement to the many bibliographies on medieval Europe with a strong anglophone bias. See also Boyce (D0048).

D0058 Cahiers de Civilisation Médiévale Supplement. Vol. 1- . Poitiers: Centre d'Etudes Supérieures de Civilisation Médiévale, 1958- ; annual.

Issued until 1969 as part of the journal, this bibliography provides detailed coverage of books and articles on European history during the high Middle Ages (tenth-twelfth centuries). Some attention is also paid to publications on Byzantine, Islamic and Middle Eastern history of the period. The annual author index is supplemented by a quinquennial index of names, places and texts. While not to be ignored by students of the medieval church, Cahiers is not as current or as comprehensive in its treatment of non-European publications as one might hope. See also Chevalier (D0068) and Le Moyen Age (D0175).

D0059 Caron, Pierre, and Jaryc, Marc. World List of Historical Periodicals and Bibliographies. Oxford: International Committee of Historical Sciences, 1939 [i.e. 1940].

This listing of more than 3000 historical periodicals surveys a wide range of relevant titles, providing data on content, coverage and similar items. Like Boehm (D0043) this is only representative of the field but has value as a starting point for those searching for journals in history. It is important to note that additions appear annually in the International Bibliography of Historical Sciences (D0136); this is useful but tedious in terms of tracing titles. These supplements should be collected to form a new edition of Caron. See also Kramm (D0153).

D0060 Caron, Pierre, and Stein, Henri. Répertoire Bibliographique de l'Histoire de France. Publication de la Société Française de Bibliographie, subventionnée par la Confédération des Sociétés Scientifiques Françaises, à l'aide des fonds alloués par le Parlement. 6 vols. Paris: A. Picard et Fils, 1923-1938.

This useful bibliography of French history to 1914 covers publications issued between 1920 and 1931 in various languages. Books and articles are treated in the classified arrangement, and there are both place and name indexes. For a continuation see Bibliographie Annuelle (D0031).

D0061 Case, Shirley Jackson, ed. A Bibliographical Guide to the History of Christianity. Comp. by Shirley Jackson Case et al. Chicago, Ill.: University of Chicago Press, 1931. Reprint. New York: Peter Smith, 1951.

This judicious selection of 2512 representative titles in church history is arranged in classified order with a combined author and subject index. Coverage extends to the church in the Western hemisphere, as well as to the growth of Christianity in Africa, Asia and the Pacific. Each topical chapter includes numerous subdivisions, and brief annotations frequently accompany entries, which encompass both articles and books. Case is now rather dated but still contains useful material for less advanced needs. For briefer works see Chadwick (D0067) and Whitney (D0228).

D0062 Catholic Historical Review: Official Organ of the American Catholic Historical Association. Vol. 1- . Washington, D.C.: Catholic University of America Press, 1915- ; quarterly.

Although not essentially an indexing service, each issue of this journal includes a brief index of recent periodical literature from a wide range of sources. The entries are arranged by subject (major historical periods and some regions), and within each subject articles are listed by title. There are no annotations, but full bibliographical details are provided for each entry. All aspects of Roman Catholic history are covered, and data are drawn from current historical and theological journals, as well as from standard journals devoted to ecclesiastical history.

Although there are no indexes, this is a quite up to date service which provides historians of the Catholic Church with much useful bibliographical information. See also Ellis (D0089, D0090) and Kenneally (D0150).

D0063 Center for Reformation Research. The Center for Reformation Research Microform Holdings from All Periods: A General Finding List. 8 vols. Sixteenth Century Bibliography, nos. 12-19. St. Louis, Mo.: Center for Reformation Research, 1977-1979.

This guide to microform holdings of nearly 10,000 primary documents of printed works from late medieval to early modern European history is a significant contribution to the bibliography of Reformation history. It includes most printed titles in the Center's collection and is arranged alphabetically by main entry, providing for each a short title, publication information and Center catalog number. Items already listed in previous issues of the series are not included, but there are references to the issues in which such works are indexed. Documents may be consulted at the Center or, in some cases, through inter-library loan. This is an extremely useful bibliography for scholars, as it is based on an indispensible collection of Reformation documents which frequently are not available even in major libraries. See also Bainton (D0024).

D0064 Center for Reformation Research. Early Sixteenth Century Roman Catholic Theologians and the German Reformation: A Finding List of CRR Holdings. Sixteenth Century Bibliography, no. 2. St. Louis, Mo.: Center for Reformation Research, 1975 [c. 1974].

This 55 page listing of the Center's microform holdings treats biographies and bibliographies of twenty-one theologians, including Cajetan, Eck, Emser, Hosius and Pigge. Entries are arranged alphabetically by author, and each listing opens with a sentence or two of identifying remarks on the particular theologian. This is followed by a listing of the man's works in chronological order, and every entry includes title, place of publication, printer, date of publication, call number of the Center's microfilm or microcard holding. For advanced students and scholars this is a useful bibliography/finding list of important Roman Catholic controversialists whose works are often difficult to trace.

D0065 Center for Reformation Research. Evangelical Theologians of Württemberg in the Sixteenth Century: A Finding List of CRR Holdings. Sixteenth Century Bibliography, no. 3. St. Louis, Mo.: Center for Reformation Research, 1975.

This finding list/bibliography lists selected works by a number of important Württemberg theologians (Brenz, Andreae, Osiander, Heerbrand, Schnepf) together with certain official publications by the government and theologians of Württemberg. All of the works are important sources for the study of Lutheranism in its early development and of the early years of evangelical ecclesiastical life in Germany. Works are listed by author, and for each person a brief historical note is provided. Titles are arranged chronologically under each author, and bibliographical data include title, place of publication, printer, date and Center microfilm or microcard call number. As many of the works are generally unavailable, this is a very useful bibliography for advanced students and scholars of the German Reformation. See also the Center's Gnesio-Lutherans, Philippists and Formulators (D0066) and Edmond (D0088).

D0066 Center for Reformation Research. Gnesio-Lutherans, Philippists and Formulators: A Finding List of CRR Holdings. Sixteenth Century Bibliography, no. 8. St. Louis, Mo.: Center for Reformation Research, 1977.

This highly specialized bibliography is devoted to the works of various theologians involved in conflicts over issues within German Lutheranism during the mid-sixteenth century, with special attention devoted to issues leading up to the Formula of Concord. Works are listed alphabetically by author and then chronologically by date of publication. Bibliographical data include title, place of publication, printer, date and Center call number. Only dates are provided after each author's name; because many of them are very obscure figures, it would have been useful to have basic historical notes as appear in other Center bibliographies. Nevertheless, this bibliography is of obvious importance for specialists in the history of early Lutheranism. See also the Center's Evangelical Theologians of Württemberg (D0065), Edmond (D0088) and Green (D0114).

D0067 Chadwick, Owen. The History of the Church: A Select Bibliography. 3rd ed. Helps for Students of History, no. 66. London: Historical Association, 1973.

First published in 1923, this annotated, classified bibliography contains some 700 entries in five sections (general works, early, medieval, Reformation and Counter-Reformation, modern church). Chadwick is a valuable guide for the beginner, including numerous additional references in the annotations and adequately treating a wide range of basic titles. Usage, however, is hampered by the lack of author and subject indexes. For a more detailed work see Case (D0061); see also Whitney (D0228).

D0068 Chevalier, Cyr Ulysse Joseph. Répertoire des Sources Historiques du Moyen Age. Nouv. éd. 2 vols. in 4. Paris: Alphonse Picard et Fils, 1894-1907. Reprint. 4 vols. New York: Kraus Reprint, 1959-1960.

This set consists of two subseries, each in two volumes: Bio-Bibliographie and Topo-Bibliographie. The first part, originally issued in nine fascicles between 1903 and 1907, is an alphabetical listing of names with very brief biographical data plus a full bibliography for each individual, concentrating on works about the person, his influence and thought. The bibliographies do not include works by the personalities. Chevalier's bio-bibliography is one of the most complete guides to medieval personalities up to 1500 and should be regarded as a standard reference for anyone interested in the medieval church or its theology. The second part, Topo-Bibliographie, is also in two volumes and is a guide to place names and topics, again providing brief descriptive annotations plus rather full bibliographies. While not used as frequently as the first two volumes, these again contain much information of value to the medievalist and should not be overlooked by more advanced students. Both common and more esoteric names, places and topics are covered in this important set. See also Cahiers (D0058) and Pontifical Institute of Mediaeval Studies (D0183).

D0069 Christ, Karl. Romische Geschichte, eine Bibliographie. Unter Mitwirkung von Reinhard Anders et al. Darmstadt: Wissenschaftliche Buchgesellschaft, 1976.

This guide to twentieth century writings on the history of the Roman world through the fifth century A.D. covers books, articles and some dissertations. The emphasis is on German writings, but some attention is given to work from other countries as well. The broad topical arrangement is supplemented by a detailed subject index. Christ is suitable primarily for advanced students of the late biblical period.

D0070 Christie, Ian R. British History since 1760: A Select Bibliography. Helps for Students of History, no. 81. London: Historical Association, 1971.

This 56 page bibliography provides guidance to standard works covering the period 1760-1970 and selected monographs. After two general sections on bibliographies and periodicals and general series and general works organization is by period. An analytical guide is also provided, including references to religious history, and there is an author index. Brief annotations accompany some of the entries. See also Elton (D0091).

D0071 Clavis Patrum Graecorum. Vol. 1- . Turnhout: Brepols, 1974- .

As a catalog of the Corpus Christianorum: Series Graeca (D0409), this series of volumes when completed will provide an excellent bibliography on each writer. It lists not only relevant works by the Greek writers but also various editions and translations together with additional bibliography. For students and scholars of the patristic period this is an important reference tool. See also Dekkers (D0085).

D0072 Comité Français de Sciences Historiques. La Recherche Historique en France de 1940 à 1965. Paris: Centre National de la Recherche Scientifique, 1965.

This classified bibliography of French historical writings issued between 1940 and 1965 covers all areas and fields. General sections on research, theses and journals precede the classified listing, which provides thorough treatment of work produced during a specific period. Church history is covered within the scope of this work, which is useful for advanced students and scholars. See also Bibliographie Annuelle (D0031).

D0073 Committee for a New England Bibliography. Bibliographies of New England History. Vol. 1- . Boston, Mass.: G.K. Hall and Company, 1976- .

Intended to include volumes for each New England state plus guides to manuscript and other sources and a concluding volume on the entire region, this series of bibliographies covers books, series and journal articles. There are indexes of authors, subjects and geographical locations to supplement the alphabetical arrangement of entries. Given the significant religious history of most of the states, this is likely to be an important bibliographical resource for advanced students of regional church history.

D0074 Coulter, Edith Margaret, and Gerstenfeld, Melanie. Historical Bibliographies: A Systematic and Annotated Guide. Berkeley, Calif.: University of California Press, 1935. Reprint. New York: Russell and Russell, 1965.

Although limited to older bibliographies, this 206 page guide retains value for its very clear annotations of many works of interest to the beginning church historian. The lists are arranged by subject and then by region. Coulter should not be used without reference to the many bibliographies which treat newer works of use to students. See also Day (D0084) and American Historical Association (D0008).

D0075 Crouch, Milton, and Raum, Hans, comps. Directory of State and Local History Periodicals. Chicago, Ill.: American Library Association, 1977.

Limited to titles being published at the time of compilation, this state-by-state listing includes a wide range of lesser known state and local history periodicals which frequently deal with church history at the parochial level. Information on available indexes is included with each brief citation on the scope, content and coverage of the publication. A title index is provided.

D0076 Crouzel, Henri. Bibliographie Critique d'Origène. Publié avec le concours du Centre National de la Recherche Scientifique de France. Instrumenta Patristica, 8. The Hague: Martinus Nijhoff, 1971.

This 685 page bibliography lists chronologically (from 1468) editions and works on Origen arranged in alphabetical order by author. A section on ancient writers is included. This scholarly work is indispensible for those working on this specialized area, and especially for historians of exegesis. See also Farina (D0094).

D0077 Current Research in British Studies by American and Canadian Scholars. Vol. 1- . Dallas, Tex.: SMU Press for the Conference on British Studies, 1969- ; quadrennial.

Arranged by period and then broadly by subject, this basic register of current research lists only the author, university affiliation and research title for each project. The author index includes addresses. Because this listing does not provide project abstracts, it is useful only as a point of contact for scholars and advanced students. The infrequent publication schedule makes much of the information rather dated. An annual or biennial guide with fuller data would be of much greater value. See also Bindoff (D0042).

D0078 Dahlmann, Friedrich Christoph, and Waitz, Georg. Dahlmann-Waitz: Quellenkunde der Deutschen Geschichte; Bibliographie der Quellen und der Literatur zur Deutschen Geschichte. 10. Aufl. Unter Mitwirkung zahlreicher Gelehrter. Hrsg. im Max-Planck-Institut für Geschichte von Hermann Heimpel und Herbert Geuss. Vol. 1- . Stuttgart: A. Hiersemann, 1965- .

Projected in six volumes and expected to cover events to the end of 1945, this new edition of Dahlmann lists works published through 1960. While many more entries are included, especially for non-German publications, much of the material in the ninth edition is not repeated; this means that students will want to consult both editions. The general outline of this edition is the same as its predecessor, and church history receives very adequate treatment. For a more basic bibliography see Franz (D0098). Otherwise Dahlmann should be used as the starting point for the bibliography of German history, which includes substantial coverage of ecclesiastical affairs.

D0079 Daniel, David P. The Historiography of the Reformation in Slovakia. Sixteenth Century Bibliography, no. 10. St. Louis, Mo.: Center for Reformation

Research, 1977.

This basic introduction to the spread of Lutheranism in Slovakia concentrates on more recently published materials dealing with the historiography of the subject. In the essay Daniel discusses a wide range of publications which have been ignored primarily because of their inaccessibility.

D0080 Davies, Alun Grier. Modern European History, 1494-1788: A Select Bibliography. Helps for Students of History, no. 68. London: Historical Association, 1967.

This is a very basic bibliography of the period, listing some 200 secondary works suitable for the beginner. Arranged in nineteen topical or country sections, Davies focuses on works in English which provide general surveys of broad topics. Indexes are not provided. For general coverage of the modern period see Roach (D0196).

D0081 Davies, Godfrey, ed. Bibliography of British History: Stuart Period, 1603-1714. Issued under the direction of the American Historical Association and the Royal Historical Society of Great Britain. 2nd ed. Ed. by Mary Frear Keeler. Oxford: Clarendon Press, 1970.

This revision of a work first published in 1928 lists 4350 books, journals, collections and similar materials. In most cases indicative annotations are provided, and there are numerous cross references. Entries are arranged broadly by subject (including ecclesiastical history), and the subjects are divided into narrower topics. Within church history coverage includes Anglicanism, Nonconformity, Roman Catholicism, Huguenots, Quakers, nuns, Unitarianism and Judaism. Within each of these topics Keeler lists bibliographies, sources and later works. An extensive table of contents and very full index of authors and subjects combine to make this an easy work to consult. Keeler is an indispensible bibliography for advanced students and scholars of the Stuart period. For other periods see Brown (D0051), Graves (D0109), Hanham (D0120), Pargellis (D0181) and Read (D0187). For the seventeenth century see Gerould (D0103) and Sachse (D0198).

D0082 Davis, Godfrey Rupert Carless. Medieval Cartularies of Great Britain: A Short Catalogue. London: Longmans, Green and Company, 1958.

This important guide to the location of monastic and other cartularies in both public and private hands is arranged in two parts: cartularies of religious houses, secular cartularies. Religious cartularies are listed alphabetically by location, and for each item a basic bibliographical description is provided. The two indexes treat present owners and former owners. For scholars and research students using primary sources this is a valuable finding tool.

D0083 Davis, Ralph Henry Carless. Medieval European History, 395-1500: A Select Bibliography. 2nd ed. Helps for Students of History, no. 67. London: Historical Association, 1968.

First published in 1963, this 48 page bibliography provides narrative commentary on some 600 items in twenty-two sections, none of which is devoted more than marginally to ecclesiastical topics. Nevertheless,

Davis has some value as a general guide for the beginning student unfamiliar with key works in European history of the medieval period. There is an author index. For an ongoing indexing service see International Medieval Bibliography (D0141).

D0084 Day, Alan Edwin. History: A Reference Handbook. Hamden, Conn.: Linnet Books; London: Clive Bingley, 1977.

This 354 page guide to reference works defines the form widely enough to include bibliographies, atlases, biographical works, textbooks, collections of texts and similar materials. Day provides basic information on each item cited and is useful both for students new to history and for more advanced investigators looking for reference works in specific fields. See also Coulter (D0074) and Poulton (D0185).

D0085 Dekkers, Eligius. Clavis Patrum Latinorum Qua in Novum Corpus Christianorum Edendum Optimas Quasque Scriptorum Recensiones a Tertulliano ad Bedam. Opera usas qua rem praeparuit et ivuit Aemilius Gaar. Editio altera. Sacris Erudiri, 3.2. Bruges: St. Peter's Abbey, [1961].

First published in 1951, this compendium is essentially a catalog or prospectus of the Corpus Christianorum series (D0410). It is arranged in fifteen chronological sections and lists the most acceptable edition of each patristic text by author. For each entry there are notes on where the text appears and where manuscripts of the text are analyzed. There are three indexes: index nominum et operum, index systematicus, initia. For scholarly research in patristics, Dekkers is an essential index and guide to relevant primary literature. See also Clavis Patrum (D0071).

D0086 Deutsches Archiv für Erforschung des Mittelalters. Vol. 1- . Cologne: Böhlau Verlag, 1937- ; semiannual.

Originally entitled Deutsches Archiv für Geschichte des Mittelalters, this bibliography of books and periodical articles on medieval studies uses a topical arrangement and includes brief annotations of entries. It usefully updates Monumenta Germania Historica (D0174) by dealing to a large extent with the Middle Ages in Germany, treating historical, social and cultural topics in some depth. See also Holtzmann (D0131), Lorenz (D0163) and Wattenbach (D0223).

D0087 Doctoral Dissertations in History. Vol. 1- . Washington, D.C.: American Historical Association, Institutional Services Program, 1976- ; semiannual.

This successor to List of Doctoral Dissertations uses a chronological and geographical arrangement to cover both completed and ongoing research on ancient, medieval and modern history. Each section lists work in progress before completed dissertation, and a brief abstract accompanies each entry. This element is a great time saver, but enough additional information is provided if one wants to contact a researcher. This is a useful complement to Dissertation Abstracts International. An author index appears in each issue. See also Current Research (D0077).

D0088 Edmond, John Philip, comp. Catalogue of a Collection of Fifteen Hundred Tracts by Martin Luther and His Contemporaries, 1511-1598. Bibliotheca Lindesiana Collations and Notes, no. 7. [Aberdeen], 1903. Reprint. Burt Franklin Bibliography and Reference Series, no. 79. New York: Burt

Franklin, [1965?].

See also <u>Lutherjahrbuch</u> (D0164) and Center for Reformation Research (D0065, D0066).

D0089 Ellis, John Tracy. <u>A Guide to American Catholic History</u>. Milwaukee, Wisc.: Bruce Publishing Company, 1959.

This 147 page bibliography comprises a classified and annotated list of more than 800 titles, including dissertations. It is arranged in sections such as diocesan, sectional and parish history; biographies, correspondence and memoirs; religious communities; education; periodicals. Supplementary sections list manuscript depositories, historical associations and relevant periodical titles. Each entry is numbered, and there is a full author, title and subject index. Overall this work covers its limited field reasonably well, but there are gaps in the coverage of more recent American Catholic historical developments. See also Ellis' earlier work (D0090) and Kenneally (D0150).

D0090 Ellis, John Tracy. <u>A Select Bibliography of the History of the Catholic Church in the United States</u>. New York: the Declan X. McMullen Company, 1947.

This earlier version of the same author's <u>Guide</u> (D0089) is a 96 page bibliography which includes material on American Catholic history and on American history in general for students new to the field. There are fewer and less up to date entries than in the later volume, but this remains a marginally useful guide for the beginner. See also Kenneally (D0150) and Vollmar (D0221).

D0091 Elton, Geoffrey Rudolph. <u>Modern Historians on British History, 1485-1945: A Critical Bibliography, 1945-1969</u>. London: Methuen and Company, 1970; Ithaca, N.Y.: Cornell University Press, 1971 [c. 1970].

Based on a literature survey first published in Sonderheft 3 of <u>Historische Zeitschrift</u> (D0130), this series of thirteen chapters presents bibliographical essays on sources, centuries, social and intellectual history, Scotland and Ireland. In the century chapters the church receives some attention, as it does in the history of ideas; ecclesiastical topics, however, are not a strong point of the work. The narrative is clear and objective, presenting evaluations and criticisms in a straightforward manner; bibliographical footnotes appear at the bottom of each page. There are indexes of authors and editors and of subjects. For those interested in historiography or in a general survey of works written between 1945 and 1969 Elton is a useful starting point. See also Christie (D0070).

D0092 <u>The English Historical Review</u>. Vol. 1- . London: Longmans, Green and Company, 1886- ; quarterly.

Half of the <u>EHR</u> regularly consists of book reviews and a listing of other publications. Although relatively few titles are reviewed in detail, the shorter notices and inclusion of other publications give this journal some value as a guide to recent historical literature in all fields. There is an annual author index of books reviewed. See <u>The American Historical Review</u> (D0009) for more comprehensive coverage in the same format.

D0093 Fallon, Maura. Church of Ireland Diocesan Libraries. Dublin: Library Association of Ireland, 1959.

This short account of Anglican diocesan libraries in Ireland includes a list of the most important holdings in each library together with a bibliography of related publications. The latter was also published in An Leabharlann (vol. 17). Fallon is useful for students of Irish church history, especially at the diocesan and parochial level.

D0094 Farina, Raffaele. Bibliografia Origeniana, 1960-1970. Biblioteca del "Salesianum", 77. Turin: Società Editrice Internazionale, 1971.

This bibliography presents thematically publications of the ten year period on Origen. An author index is provided. The coverage illustrates the broad area over which Origen's work is of interest, from patristics in general to biblical exegesis in particular. This is an invaluable bibliography for the specialist researcher. See also Crouzel (D0076).

D0095 Farrar, Clarissa Palmer, and Evans, Austin Patterson. Bibliography of English Translations from Medieval Sources. Records of Civilization: Sources and Studies, no. 39. New York: Columbia University Press, 1946.

This 534 page compilation lists nearly 4000 translations of medieval documents in alphabetical author order. Full bibliographical details and historical notes are provided for each item, and there is an index to the entire volume. For students of medieval literature, history, philosophy and theology Farrar can be a useful source of information. See also Ferguson (D0096) for a supplement.

D0096 Ferguson, Mary Anne. Bibliography of English Translations from Medieval Sources, 1943-1967. Records of Civilization: Sources and Studies, no. 88. New York: Columbia University Press, 1974.

This supplement to Farrar (D0095) lists 1980 items from the period indicated and includes both books and articles which contain English language translations of medieval documents. The entries are arranged by author, and there is an author/subject index. This is a helpful bibliography for the historian and student who wishes to consult materials on a wide range of topics related to church history.

D0097 Franklin, Alfred. Les Sources de l'Histoire de France. Notices Bibliographiques et Analytiques des Inventaires et des Recueils de Documents Relatifs à l'Histoire de France. Paris: Firmin Didot et Cie, 1877. Reprint. Nedeln: Kraus Reprint, 1967.

Although now rather dated, Franklin remains useful as a guide to the contents of many important French historical collections, including Catalogue de l'Histoire de France, Collection des Documents Inédits Relatifs à l'Histoire de France, Bibliothèque de l'Ecole des Chartes and several others. See also Bibliothèque Nationale (D0038-D0040).

D0098 Franz, Günther. Bücherkunde zur Deutschen Geschichte. Munich: R. Oldenbourg, 1951.

Limited primarily to post-1930 publications, this 279 page bibliography is a selective guide to works on German history of all periods. It includes titles in various languages and is a suitable starting point for students new to the subject but proficient in European languages. For a more thorough treatment see Dahlmann (D0078).

D0099 Franz, Günther. Bücherkunde zur Weltgeschichte vom Untergang des Römischen Weltreiches bis zur Gegenwart. Unter Mitwirkung von Ludwig Alsdorf et al. Munich: R. Oldenbourg, 1956.

Particularly useful as a guide to European history and publications, this general survey includes selective bibliographies on various historical periods. Some entries include very brief annotations. For students seeking literature on continental history not specifically limited to ecclesiastical matters this 544 page bibliography is of some value. See also Harvard University (D0124).

D0100 Freidel, Frank Burt, ed. Harvard Guide to American History. Rev. ed. With the assistance of Richard K. Showman. 2 vols. Cambridge, Mass.: Belknap Press, 1974.

This 1290 page successor to Oscar Handlin's Harvard Guide covers monographs, journals, primary and secondary sources of information on American history. Volume 1 is arranged topically and emphasizes economic, social and cultural history plus biography; volume 2 is a chronological listing of materials. The entries are not annotated, but full indexes of names and subjects are provided. Freidel is marginally useful for the theological student who requires general historical information on America. See also Harvard University (D0121).

D0101 Gandilhon, René. Bibliographie Générale des Travaux Historiques et Archéologiques Publiés par les Sociétés Savantes de la France, Dressée sous les Auspices du Ministère de l'Education Nationale. Sous la direction de Charles Samaran. 5 vols. Paris: Imprimerie Nationale, 1944-1961.

Continuing the earlier works by Lasteyrie (D0159, D0160), this compilation deals with local historical society publications issued between 1910 and 1940. Gandilhon follows the general outline of its predecessors and again serves as a valuable guide to works difficult to trace elsewhere.

D0102 García y García, Antonio; Cantelar Rodríguez, Francisco; and Nieto Cumplido, Manuel. Catálogo de los Manuscritos e Incunables de la Catedral de Córdoba. Bibliotheca Salmanticensis, 6: Estudios, 5. Salamanca: Universidad Pontificia, 1976.

The important collection treated in this guide consists of 171 manuscripts and some 500 incunabula which are valuable sources of information on political and intellectual history of the medieval era. Each item is provided with a descriptive annotation. There are indexes of incipits, incunabula, authors and titles.

D0103 Gerould, James Thayer, comp. Sources of English History of the Seventeenth Century, 1603-1689, in the University of Minnesota Library, with a Selection of Secondary Material. University of Minnesota Bibliographical Series, no. 1. Minneapolis, Minn.: University of Minnesota Press, 1921.

See also Davies (D0081). For the previous period see Levine (D0161) and Read (D0187); for seventeenth to eighteenth century coverage see Grose (D0117).

D0104 Ghirardini, Lino Lionello. Saggio di una Bibliografia dell'età Matildico-Gregoriana (1046-1122). Deputazione di storia patria per le antiche provincie Modenesi. Biblioteca, Nuova Serie, no. 14. Modena: Aedes Muratoriana, 1970.

D0105 Gillett, Charles Ripley, comp. and ed. Catalogue of the McAlpin Collection of British History and Theology. 5 vols. New York: Union Theological Seminary, 1927-1930.

Covering 1500-1700, this catalog of more than 15,000 entries is particularly rich in pamphlets and similar materials on British theology of the period. Entries are arranged chronologically and then alphabetically by author for each year. Full bibliographical details are provided for each item; volume 5 contains a detailed index of authors and anonymous publications. While extensive additions to the collection mean that a new edition of the catalog is long overdue, this remains an excellent bibliography of theology and its historical aspects as seen from the British viewpoint during two religiously important centuries. See also Harvard University (D0122).

D0106 Gliozzo, Charles A., comp. A Bibliography of Ecclesiastical History of the French Revolution. Bibliographia Tripotamopolitana, no. 6. Pittsburgh, Penn.: Pittsburgh Theological Seminary, Clifford E. Barbour Library, [1972].

This selective bibliography emphasizes the religious history of Paris, with other references to provincial areas. Arrangement is alphabetical by author or title if the author is unknown. Journal articles are included in the citations, which are not annotated. This provides a helpful listing for specialized research on this particular period.

D0107 Gomme, George Laurence, ed. Index of Archaeological Papers, 1665-1890. Published under the direction of the Congress of Archaeological Societies in union with the Society of Antiquaries. London: A. Constable and Company, 1907.

Limited primarily to British archeology and including some reference to early Christian sites, this 910 page author index covers the contents of ninety-four English archeological periodical titles and transactions of local antiquarian societies. In terms of both dates and type of material indexed this is a useful guide for the advanced student. The lack of a subject index, however, is a major drawback. For a continuation see Index of Archaeological Papers (D0133).

D0108 [no entry]

D0109 Graves, Edgar B., ed. A Bibliography of English History to 1485: Based on "The Sources and Literature of English History from the Earliest Times to about 1485" by Charles Gross. Issued under the sponsorship of the Royal Historical Society, the American Historical Association and the Mediaeval Academy of America. Oxford: Clarendon Press, 1975.

This successor to Gross' Sources and Literature of English History (2nd ed. London: Longmans, Green and Company, 1915. Reprint. New York: A.M. Kelly, 1970) is an 1103 page survey of the printed materials related to the political, legal, social and economic history of England to 1485. It includes both older standard works and newer publications which provide modern interpretations and specialized bibliographies. Entries are closely classified, and the coverage of social history is particularly thorough. The extensive index makes rapid consultation very easy. Like its predecessor Graves is an excellent bibliography of the period for advanced students. See also Berkowitz (D0029).

D0110 Great Britain. Historical Manuscripts Commission. Guide to the Reports of the Royal Commission on Historical Manuscripts, 1911-1957. 3 vols. London: Her Majesty's Stationery Office, 1966.

These three volumes continue the index of persons in the following index (D0111), which deals with reports issued between 1870 and 1911. It serves the same research needs as the earlier collection.

D0111 Great Britain. Historical Manuscripts Commission. A Guide to the Reports on Collections of Manuscripts of Private Families, Corporations and Institutions in Great Britain and Ireland Issued by the Royal Commissioners for Historical Manuscripts. 2 vols. in 3. London: His Majesty's Stationery Office, 1914-1938.

Part 1 contains a topographical index; part 2, an index of persons. The latter is an alphabetical index of names which provides references to the reports in which a letter or document connected with the individual is listed. This is suitable for advanced research requirements and can save a great deal of time when one is trying to trace personalities mentioned in Commission reports. For a continuation see the preceding entry (D0110), which carries coverage forward to 1957.

D0112 Great Britain. Public Record Office. Guide to the Contents of the Public Record Office. 3 vols. London: Her Majesty's Stationery Office, 1963-1968.

Essentially a revision and updating of M.S. Giuseppi's Guide to the Manuscripts Preserved in the Public Record Office, this compendium covers legal records and related documents in volume 1, state papers and departmental records in volume 2, documents transferred from 1960 to 1966 in volume 3. It is suitable primarily for church historians interested in documents related to political and legal aspects of English ecclesiastical history. See also U.S. Library of Congress (D0213).

D0113 [no entry]

D0114 Green, Lowell C. The Formula of Concord: An Historiographical and Bibliographical Guide. Sixteenth Century Bibliography, no. 11. St. Louis, Mo.: Center for Reformation Research, 1977.

Prepared for beginning and advanced scholars, this guide to the Formula of Concord and its early development is arranged in six parts: historical orientation, Melancthonian problem, how to study the Formula, listing of secondary literature, special problems in interpretation, additional references. Especially valuable are the sections on studying the Formula and on problems in interpretation, both of which present a wide range of useful references. See also Lutherjahrbuch (D0164).

D0115 Green, Richard. Anti-Methodist Publications Issued during the Eighteenth Century: A Chronologically Arranged and Annotated Bibliography.

A Contribution to Methodist History. London: C.H. Kelly, 1902. Reprint. Burt Franklin Bibliography and Reference Series, vol. 491. New York: Burt Franklin, 1973.

See also Wesley Historical Society Proceedings (D0226).

D0116 Griffin, Appleton Prentiss Clark. Bibliography of American Historical Societies (the United States and the Dominion of Canada). 2nd ed. [Washington, D.C.: Government Printing Office, 1907]. Reprint. Detroit, Mich.: Gale Research Company, 1966.

This index to publications issued by general and local history societies in America up to 1905 is arranged alphabetically by society and lists the full contents of each relevant publication. There is an author/subject index and a biographical index. Griffin is a most useful index to literature which has some value for church historians but which has little bibliographical coverage elsewhere for the period in question. Subsequent years are treated in Writings on American History (D0223) and in the Annual Magazine Subject Index.

D0117 Grose, Clyde Leclare. A Select Bibliography of British History, 1660-1760. Chicago, Ill.: University of Chicago Press, 1939. Reprint. New York: Octagon Books, 1967.

This valuable bibliography is a detailed and well organized guide to writings on Restoration Britain. It is divided by periods (general, 1660-1760; 1660-1688; 1689-1714; 1715-1760) and follows a classified arrangement indicated in the very full table of contents. Books and articles are treated, and important works are starred. The annotations are particularly informative. This is an indispensible guide for students of the period and contains much of value for the church historian. See also Davies (D0081), Gerould (D0103) and Sachse (D0198).

D0118 Grundmann, Herbert. Bibliographie zur Ketzergeschichte des Mittelalters (1900-1966). Sussidi Eruditi, 20. Rome: Edizioni di Storia e Letteratura, 1967.

This 93 page bibliography of medieval sects is useful for researchers interested in this specific area.

D0119 Guth, DeLloyd J., comp. Late Medieval England, 1377-1485. Conference on British Studies Bibliographical Handbooks. Cambridge: Cambridge University Press, 1976.

In 143 pages Guth provides a usefully representative guide to 2500 books, articles and texts on all aspects of late medieval English history. The fourteen chapters include one devoted to religious history, which contains citations on a wide range of publications of interest to the intermediate or advanced student. Bibliographical data are adequate for most purposes, and infrequent evaluations indicate the usefulness of titles. There is an author/translator/editor index. For the preceding period see Wilkinson (D0230).

D0120 Hanham, H.J., comp. and ed. Bibliography of British History, 1851-1914. Issued under the direction of the American Historical Association and the Royal Historical Society of Great Britain. Oxford: Clarendon Press, 1976.

This 1606 page volume lists 10,829 items which a student of the period is most likely to consult, which make clear the scope of contemporary printed materials or which indicate the range of available biographical and bibliographical publications. Items are organized by subject and then by type of material or topic. The chapter on churches (pp. 387-463) covers general works, Anglicans, Nonconformists, Roman Catholics, Jews and various other groups. The bibliographical information is complete for each entry, and there are some annotations and cross references. A detailed author and subject index completes the work. Hanham is an excellent bibliography for the beginner and more advanced student of modern British church history. See also Graves (D0109), Davies (D0081), Pargellis (D0181) and Brown (D0051) for similar treatment of different periods. See also Havighurst (D0125).

D0121 Harvard University. Library. American History. 5 vols. Widener Library Shelflist, nos. 9-13. Cambridge, Mass.: Harvard University Library, 1967.

Like other sets in this collection, American History consists of a classified listing, an alphabetical listing and a chronological listing of a wide range of publications. American history is broadly interpreted and includes all aspects of the development of America, including the role of Christianity. For students embarking on the study of this field this is an excellent starting point for information on a wide range of basic and specialized publications issued over a long period. See also Freidel (D0100).

D0122 Harvard University. Library. British History. Classification Schedule, Classified Listing by Call Number, Chronological Listing, Author and Title Listing. 2 vols. Widener Library Shelflist, vols. 53-54. Cambridge, Mass.: Harvard University Library, 1975.

This valuable bibliography for students at various levels lists more than 45,000 works on British history. Coverage is both broad and detailed, providing references to materials on most aspects of British history on many levels. It is especially recommended for those unfamiliar with the range of materials likely to be useful in studying British history in its various manifestations. See also Gillett (D0105) and Writings on British History (D0234, D0235).

D0123 Harvard University. Library. Church History Periodicals: Classified Listing by Call Number. Widener Library Shelflist. Cambridge, Mass.: Harvard University Library, 1966.

D0124 Harvard University. Library. General European and World History: Classification Schedule, Classified Listing by Call Number, Chronological Listing, Author and Title Listing. Widener Library Shelflist, no. 32. Cambridge, Mass.: Harvard University Library, 1970.

This 959 page bibliography lists some 37,000 titles on world history and the history of Europe in general. Scholarly journals are included. The whole field from medieval to modern times is covered. This is suitable primarily for those unfamiliar with the range of titles available in history. Especially noteworthy for church historians is the section on the crusades. See also Coulter (D0074) and Franz (D0099).

D0125 Havighurst, Alfred F., comp. Modern England, 1901-1970. Conference on British Studies Bibliographical Handbooks. Cambridge: Cambridge University

Press, 1976.

This 109 page bibliography lists books, articles and texts relevant to modern English history. Following brief sections devoted to bibliographies; catalogs, guides and handbooks; and general surveys, Havighurst uses a subject arrangement to list items. Religious history receives reasonable treatment, with key books and major articles listed alphabetically by author. Skeletal bibliographical citations sometimes include brief annotations, and there is an index of authors, editors and translators. Havighurst is suitable for students beyond the beginning level. See also Hanham (D0120).

D0126 Hillerbrand, Hans Joachim. A Bibliography of Anabaptism, 1520-1630. Elkhart, Ind.: Institute of Mennonite Studies, 1962.

This translation of Bibliographie des Taufertums, 1520-1630 (Gütersloh: Gütersloher Verlagshaus Gerd Mohn, 1962) contains 4665 entries for works on and by sixteenth century Anabaptists, arranged according to areas, persons and topics. Locations are listed for many items; the work was compiled on the basis of collections in the United States and Europe. An exhaustive index of titles and authors is provided, and a section on sources is especially useful to the scholar. This is an invaluable reference work for specialist historical research on this topic and period. Hillerbrand has updated this edition in the sequel (D0127).

D0127 Hillerbrand, Hans Joachim. A Bibliography of Anabaptism, 1520-1630: A Sequel, 1962-1974. Sixteenth Century Bibliography, no. 1. St. Louis, Mo.: Center for Reformation Research, 1975.

This sequel to Hillerbrand's earlier bibliography (D0126) contains more than 500 titles which appeared between 1962 and 1974, with a few which were omitted from the earlier work. The same arrangement is followed, with numbering of entries following on from the 1962 publication. The research covered is primarily North American, with some European contributions.

D0128 Hinz, James A., comp. A Handlist of the Printed Books in the Simmlersche Sammlung (Complete Imprints from Volumes 1-155): Manuscript Collection in the Microfilm Library of the Center for Reformation Research, the Original Located in the Zentralbibliothek in Zürich. Rev. ed. 2 vols. Sixteenth Century Bibliography, nos. 6-7. St. Louis, Mo.: Center for Reformation Research, 1976.

This important bibliography lists 685 works of significance in the study of Swiss church history, particularly the Reformation era. It is based on the collection of Johann Simmler, which contains much early printed material not available elsewhere. The two volumes are arranged chronologically according to period covered by the documents, and there is a list of works cited plus an author index in the second volume. A useful introduction in the first volume describes the contents of Simmler's collection. See also Center for Reformation Research (D0063) and Zwingliana (D0236).

D0129 Historical Abstracts: Bibliography of the World's Periodical Literature. Vol. 1- . Santa Barbara, Calif.: ABC-Clio, 1953- ; quarterly.

Covering modern history (1775-1914) in part A and the twentieth century in part B, this major abstracting service treats all aspects of history and related fields. The two parts together provide coverage of approximately 2200 serial titles, which are arranged alphabetically within three broad sections. The citations and abstracts are clearly presented and provide essential information for those interested in religious history. Each issue includes a detailed subject index (which incorporates both geographical and biographical descriptors) and an author index; these are cumulated annually in the winter issue. Although Historical Abstracts no longer covers North America, it remains an essential reference work for students of modern history and provides valuable coverage of the church and religions generally in a fairly up to date fashion.

D0130 Historische Zeitschrift. Vol. 1- . Munich: R. Oldenbourg, 1859- ; bimonthly.

This widely respected scholarly journal includes a significant amount of bibliographical material in each issue in the form of book reviews and notices. The reviews are arranged by periods and countries; both these and the book notices cover a broad range of historical literature from around the world. Information on each title is detailed and scholarly, but often works are not listed until several years after publication. Book reviews in each volume are indexed, and there are cumulative indexes for volumes 1-56, 57-96, 97-130. In addition Historische Zeitschrift includes a separately published and independently numbered Sonderheft. These supplements survey several thousand historical works by country and period. The selections are made by specialists and include much of interest to church historians, especially those working on European topics. See also Annual Bulletin of Historical Literature (D0013).

D0131 Holtzmann, Robert. Deutschlands Geschichtsquellen im Mittelalter: Die Zeit der Sachsen und Salier. Neuausgabe, besorgt von Franz Josef Schmale. Vol. 1- . Cologne: Böhlau Verlag, 1967- .

Based in part on Wattenbach's Deutschlands Geschichtsquellen im Mittelalter bis zur Mitte des Dreizehnten Jahrhunderts, Holtzmann treats issues of medieval German history (900-1125) in the first two volumes plus topics related to Italy (1050-1125) and England (900-1135) in the third volume, which also includes appendixes to the first two volumes. Bibliographical data are reasonably complete and accurate, providing information on a wide selection of materials of value for advanced research in German history. See also Deutsches Archiv (D0086) and Lorenz (D0163), as well as Wattenbach (D0223-D0225).

D0132 Holtzmann, Walther, and Ritter, Gerhard, eds. Die Deutsche Geschichtswissenschaft im Zweiten Weltkrieg: Bibliographie des Historischen Schrifttums Deutscher Autoren 1939-1945, Hrsg. im Auftrag des Verbandes der Historiker Deutschlands und der "Monumenta Germaniae Historiae". 1 vol. in 2. Marburg: Simons Verlag, 1951.

This 149 page bibliography covers German writings in two parts: prehistory and ancient history; medieval and modern history. It is useful in covering works of the war years not covered in other listings. An author index is included. Holtzmann is a valuable supplement to the International Bibliography of Historical Sciences (D0136).

D0133 Index of Archaeological Papers Published 1891-1910. 20 vols. London: A. Constable and Company, 1892-1914; annual.

This annual continuation of Gomme (D0107) indexes by author various English archeological periodicals and transactions of local antiquarian societies. Each volume also includes a subject index through which it is quite simple to trace works dealing with early Christian sites in Britain. The content of each volume is generally limited to the year indicated, although a periodical newly added to the list in a given year is indexed back to 1891 as well. The Index is a helpful guide to material which otherwise might go unnoticed and is useful as a scholarly bibliography.

D0134 Index to Book Reviews in Historical Periodicals. Metuchen, N.J. Scarecrow Press, 1976- ; annual.

Covering approximately 100 English language historical periodicals, this annual service indexes book reviews in history and related disciplines. As with the journals themselves, titles are representative of a wide range of topics and viewpoints; although the reviews can appear long after a book's publication, the Index itself is a useful time saver for those who scan reviews as a means of keeping up with recent scholarship. Entries are arranged by author, with a title index. See also Reviews in American History (D0192) and Reviews in European History (D0193).

D0135 Indice Histórico Español: Bibliografia Histórica de España e Barcelona. Vol. 1- . Barcelona: Universidad de Barcelona, Centro de Estudios Históricos Internacionales, 1953- ; trimestral.

This useful index combines historiographical and bibliographical articles with extensive lists of published literature on Spanish history. The lists consist of detailed abstracts of accurately cited publications. There are annual indexes of authors and subjects. While volumes are not published until five or six years after the date of coverage, this is the most thorough work of its kind on Spanish history, including religious history.

D0136 International Bibliography of Historical Sciences. Ed. for the International Committee of Historical Sciences. Vol. 1- . Munich: K.G. Saur Verlag, 1926- ; irregular.

Published under various imprints since its inception and rarely produced on an annual basis as intended, this selective, classified listing of historical books, articles and other materials includes political, economic, social and religious aspects of history in its coverage. Publications are classified primarily by period and topic, and the classes include such topics as the early church and modern religious history. There are no annotations, but both name and geographical indexes are provided. Since the work appears three to four years after the date of coverage, it should be used only as a retrospective guide to a selective range of publications with some bearing on church history. See also Caron (D0059) and Holtzmann (D0132).

D0137 International Committee of Historical Sciences, ed. Bibliographie Internationale des Travaux Historiques Publiés dans les Volumes de "Melanges", 1880/1939-1940/1950/International Bibliography of Historical Articles in Festschriften and Miscellanies. Etablie avec le concours des comités nationaux sous la direction de Hans Nabholz par Margarethe Rothbarth et Ulrich Helfen-stein. 2 vols. Paris: Armand Colin, 1955-1965.

This bibliography covers 1880-1939 in volume 1, 1940-1950 in volume 2. Works are grouped by country, with a classified index and a name index; volume 2 has additional indexes covering the contents of the entire work. This is a useful guide to material otherwise difficult to locate. See also Historical Abstracts (D0192) and Koner (D0152).

D0138 International Committee of Historical Sciences. Commission Inter-nationale d'Histoire Ecclésiastique Comparée. Bibliographie de Cartographie Ecclésiastique. Vol. 1- . Leiden: E.J. Brill, 1968- .

D0139 International Committee of Historical Sciences. Commission Inter-nationale d'Histoire Ecclésiastique Comparée. Bibliographie de la Réforme, 1450-1648: Ouvrages Parus de 1940 à 1955. 7 pts. Leiden: E.J. Brill, 1958-1970.

Covering materials published between 1940 and 1955 on the Reformation, this bibliography lists books, dissertations and articles. Each of the seven fascicles deals with publications from specific countries, and nearly all European countries have been covered. Although this geographical arrangement is somewhat unusual, the bibliography is a valuable guide to literature of some importance for advanced students of Reformation history. Adequate indexes are provided for most parts. For a similar guide to Britain see Baker (D0025). See also Center for Reformation Research (D0063).

D0140 International Guide to Medieval Studies: A Quarterly Index to Period-ical Literature. Vol. 1- . Darien, Conn.: American Bibliographic Service, 1961- ; quarterly.

This alphabetical author listing of periodical articles includes cumulative author and subject indexes plus a book review index. See also International Medieval Bibliography (D0141) and Williams (D0231).

D0141 International Medieval Bibliography. Vol. 1- . Leeds: University of Leeds, School of History, 1967- ; semiannual.

Arranged by subject and then by geographical region, this index includes articles from some 650 journals and from Festschriften, collections and conference proceedings. Each entry is provided with the necessary bibliographical data, and there is an author and subject index. This compila-tion is especially useful for its coverage of medieval church history and theology in Europe, Byzantium and Russia. It is very up to date in coverage and forms an excellent supplement to information provided in Revue d'Histoire Ecclésiastique (D0194).

D0142 Jacobs, Phyllis M., comp. History Theses, 1901-70: Historical Research for Higher Degrees in the Universities of the United Kingdom. London: University of London, Institute of Historical Research, 1976.

This comprehensive guide to British theses contains more than 7600 entries arranged in a classified sequence with author and subject indexes. This is not a cumulation of lists issued by the Institute of Historical Research (D0217, D0218) but in fact contains verified citations and so is more accurate than the annual guide. For a highly accurate and detailed guide to the titles, authors and repositories of theses approved during the period indicated, Jacobs cannot be bettered. For a similar work on North America see Kuehl (D0154).

D0143 Jahresberichte der Deutschen Geschichte. 7 vols. Breslau: Priebatsch, 1920-1926; annual.

This is a very thorough annual survey of German historical publications issued between 1918 and 1924. Covering these dates, it fits nicely between the Jahresberichte der Geschichtswissenschaft (D0144) and Jahresberichte für Deutsche Geschichte (D0145).

D0144 Jahresberichte der Geschichtswissenschaft; im Auftrage der Histor-ischen Gesellschaft zu Berlin. 36 vols. Berlin: E.S. Mittler und Sohn, 1880-1916; annual.

This international bibliography of works published between 1878 and 1913 is a useful guide to continental, especially German, historical liter-ature for a period not well covered in other bibliographies. It is continued by the Jahresberichte für Deutsche Geschichte (D0145).

D0145 Jahresberichte für Deutschen Geschichte. Bd. 1-Bd. 15/16; n.F. Bd. 1- . Leipzig: K.F. Koehler, 1927-1942; Berlin: Akademie Verlag, 1949- ; annual.

Initially prepared in two parts annually (Bibliographie and Forschungs-berichte), this compilation is now devoted entirely to bibliography. It lists writings on German history from the earliest period through the Second World War, and is a usefully up to date general bibliography which often lists titles relevant for students of German church history. For pre-1925 publications see Bibliographie zur Deutschen Geschichte (D0032).

D0146 Keiling, Hanns Peter, comp. The Formation of the United Church of Christ (U.S.A.): A Bibliography. Bibliographia Tripotamopolitana, no. 2. Pittsburgh, Pa.: Pittsburgh Theological Seminary, Clifford E. Barbour Library, [1970].

This classified listing of 1655 items concentrates on primary source materials, including denominational records, committee minutes, individual statements, letters, pamphlets, court records, interviews and published documentation (books, articles, newspaper reports). An index of persons is included. Since the United Church of Christ was formed in 1957 from a merger of the Congregational Christian Churches and the Evangelical and Reformed Church, Keiling is useful as a guide to all three denomina-tions.

D0147 Kellaway, William, comp. Bibliography of Historical Works Issued in the United Kingdom, 1957-60. Comp. for the Seventh Anglo-American Conference of Historians. London: University of London, Institute of Historical Research, 1962.

This 236 page bibliography lists 3801 items in classified order and treats many titles relevant to church history in Europe and elsewhere. Like Kellaway's other compilations (D0148, D0149) this is a sound guide to works published during a brief period and is useful for retrospective searching. Entries are not annotated.

D0148 Kellaway, William, comp. Bibliography of Historical Works Issued in the United Kingdom, 1961-1965. Comp. for the Eighth Anglo-American Conference of Historians. London: University of London, Institute of Historical Research, 1967.

Reflecting the increased publishing activity of the early 1960s, this sequel to Kellaway's 1957-1960 compilation (D0147) lists 4883 unannotated items on all aspects of history. Coverage includes sections on world history; European history: Byzantium, the crusades and Middle Ages; other regions of the world.

D0149 Kellaway, William, comp. Bibliography of Historical Works Issued in the United Kingdom, 1966-1970. Comp. for the Ninth Anglo-American Conference of Historians. London: University of London, Institute of Historical Research, 1972.

Following the format of the two preceding entries (D0147, D0148), this compilation lists 5315 items on all aspects of history. Taken together, Kellaway's works provide very sound bibliographical guidance on British historical publications issued between 1957 and 1970.

D0150 Kenneally, Finbar. United States Documents in the Propaganda Fide Archives: A Calendar. Academy of American Franciscan History, First Series, vol. 1- . Washington, D.C.: Academy of American Franciscan History, 1966- .

This important catalog of documents in the Propaganda Fide Archives includes a broad range of materials on American ecclesiastical history, ranging from papal bulls to letters on various matters. Each item is given a reference location plus an indication of content. The volumes are thoroughly indexed. Kenneally is a valuable reference tool for students of American Roman Catholic history. See also Ellis (D0089, D0090).

D0151 Kenney, James Francis. The Sources for the Early History of Ireland: An Introduction and Guide. Volume One: Ecclesiastical. Records of Civilization: Sources and Studies, no. 11. New York: Columbia University Press, 1929.

Reprinted as The Sources for the Early History of Ireland: Ecclesiastical; an Introduction and Guide (New York: Octagon Books, 1966), this work contains 659 annotated entries divided among eight chronological chapters on Irish history up to 1170. A general bibliography and a subject index are included. Kenney is an older work which lists many basic sources which continue to be valuable for students of early Irish church history.

D0152 Koner, Wilhelm David. Repertorium über die vom Jahre 1800 bis zum Jahre 1850 in Akademischen Abhandlungen, Gesellschaftsschriften und Wissenschaftlichen Journalen auf dem Gebiete der Geschichte und Ihrer Hülfswissenschaften Erschienenen Aufsätze. 2 vols. in 1. Berlin: Nicolai, 1852-1856.

This is a bibliography of articles on historical subjects which have appeared in some 500 periodicals and society publications in various languages. A subject index is provided. A separate section lists biographical articles arranged alphabetically. This is only of interest for old material (published between 1800 and 1850). See also International Committee of Historical Sciences (D0137).

D0153 Kramm, Heinrich. Bibliographie Historischer Zeitschriften, 1931-1951. 3 pts. Marburg: Otto Rasch, 1952-1954.

Arranged by country and limited to European coverage, this bibliography is subdivided under each region by subject (bibliography, ecclesiastical history, etc.). It includes details of historical periodicals current between 1939 and 1951 and serves as a marginally useful, retrospective bibliography for students of European church history. There are indexes of titles and of places of publication.

D0154 Kuehl, Warren F. Dissertations in History: An Index to Dissertations Completed in History Departments of United States and Canadian Universities, 1873-1970. 2 vols. Lexington, Ky.: University of Kentucky Press, 1965-[1972].

This listing is restricted to dissertations completed for history departments and for which a doctorate was awarded. Volume 1 covers 1873-1960, containing 7600 titles; volume 2 covers 1961-June 1970, with approximately 5900 entries. Arrangement is alphabetical by author, with a detailed subject index. There is no indication of publication information. This is a useful tool for specialized study, especially by postgraduate students. See also List of Doctoral Dissertations (D0162); for a similar work on British universities see Jacobs (D0142).

D0155 Kuhlicke, Frederick Williams, and Emmison, Frederick George, eds. English Local History Handlist: A Select Bibliography and List of Sources for the Study of Local History and Antiquities. Ed. for the Local History Committee of the Historical Association. 4th ed. Helps for Students of History, no. 69. London: Historical Association, 1969.

This collection of brief lists is very useful for the student unfamiliar with local history sources. The 1600 entries are arranged by subject, including topography, church, genealogy, biography, folklore, societies, yearbooks and bibliographies. Citations are accurate, and some annotations are provided. This is a suitable bibliography for the beginner.

D0156 Langlois, Chalres Victor, and Stein, Henri. Les Archives de l'Histoire de France. Manuels de Bibliographie Historique, 1. Paris: A. Picard, 1891-1893. Reprint. Nedeln: Kraus Reprint, 1966.

This guide to source materials for the study of French history covers archives in France and elsewhere, listing the special interests and major collections of various archives and manuscript collections. Langlois has obvious value for the advanced research student. See also Bibliothèque Nationale (D0038-D0040), Caron (D0060) and Bibliographie Annuelle (D0031).

D0157 Larned, Josephus Nelson, ed. The Literature of American History: A Bibliographical Guide in Which the Scope, Character and Comparative Worth of Books in Selected Lists Are Set Forth in Brief Notes by Critics of Authority. Contributors: Charles M. Anderson et al. Ed. for the American Library Association. Boston, Mass.: Houghton Mifflin Company for the American Library Association, 1902. Reprint. Columbus, Ohio: Long's College Book Company, 1953.

Although now a very dated compilation, Larned lists a wide range of interesting source materials and other documents in a classified sequence.

Research students will find the notes on source material and records of continuing value. There is an alphabetical author and subject index. See also the Library of Congress annual bibliography (D0213) and the two year supplement by Wells (D0158).

D0158 Larned, Josephus Nelson, ed. The Literature of American History: Supplement for 1900 and 1901. Ed. by Philip Patterson Wells. Boston, Mass.: Houghton Mifflin Company for the American Library Association, 1902. Reprint. Columbus, Ohio: Long's College Book Company, 1953.

This is a two year supplement to Larned (D0157) and covers the same type of material but with less attention to primary sources.

D0159 Lasteyrie du Saillant, Robert Charles. Bibliographie Annuelle des Travaux Historiques et Archéologiques Publiés par les Sociétés Savantes de la France, Dressée sous les Auspices du Ministère de l'Instruction Publique. Avec la collaboration d'Alexandre Charles Philippe Vidier. 3 vols. in 9 pts. Paris: Imprimerie Nationale, 1906-1914.

This continuation of Lasteyrie (D0160) consists of nine annual parts containing nearly 43,000 analyticals of items published between 1901 and 1910. There is a general index of societies in the final part, and an author and a subject index at the end of volume 1, number 1 for entries in that part only. Despite the inadequate indexing, this compilation has the same reference value as the original set. For a continuation see Gandilhon (D0101).

D0160 Lasteyrie du Saillant, Robert Charles. Bibliographie Générale des Travaux Historiques et Archéologiques Publiés par les Sociétés Savantes de la France, Dressée sous les Auspices du Ministère de l'Instruction Publique. 6 vols. Paris: Imprimerie Nationale, 1888-1918.

Although lacking an author or subject index, Lasteyrie is a valuable guide to the publications of French historical societies issued before 1901. It is arranged alphabetically by département, town and then society. In addition to more general information on the societies there is full coverage of the titles, dates and contents of their publications. There is an index of societies in the final volume, which is important given the division of material into pre-1886 (volumes 1-4) and 1886-1900 (volumes 5 and 6). For continuations see Lasteyrie (D0159) and Gandilhon (D0101). All of these compilations are important bibliographies for students of local church history in France, as many of the societies have issued publications relevant to this subject.

D0161 Levine, Mortimer, comp. Tudor England, 1485-1603. Conference on British Studies Bibliographical Handbooks. Cambridge: Cambridge University Press for the Conference on British Studies, 1968.

Including a list of abbreviations, explanatory notes and an index of authors, editors and translators, this 115 page bibliography is a classified listing of 2360 publications on Tudor history. Coverage extends to printed sources, surveys, monographs, articles and bibliographies. Citations include basic bibliographical information, and many of the entries have brief annotations. Religious history (pp. 67-88) receives excellent treatment. Although less comprehensive than Read (D0187), this is a very helpful guide for the advanced student. See also Booty (D0046).

D0162 List of Doctoral Dissertations in History Now in Progress or Completed at Universities in the United States. Washington, D.C.: American Historical Association, 1947- ; irregular.

This useful listing for postgraduate students, which succeeds earlier compilations by the Carnegie Institution of Washington, is arranged by fields and includes author and university indexes. By listing work in progress the List provides a necessary complement to the completed dissertations indexed in Dissertation Abstracts International. See also Kuehl (D0154).

D0163 Lorenz, Ottokar. Deutschlands Geschichtsquellen im Mittelalter seit der Mitte des Dreizehnten Jahrhunderts. 3 Aufl. In Verbindung mit Arthur Goldmann. 2 vols. Berlin: W. Hertz, 1886-1887. Reprint. 2 vols. Graz: Akademische Druck- und Verlagsanstalt, 1966.

Together with Wattenbach (D0223), this survey offers a very comprehensive guide to medieval German historiography for advanced students and scholars. Lorenz begins with the middle of the thirteenth century, providing thorough critical coverage of a wide range of printed materials relevant to the medieval church and society in Germany. See also Holtzmann (D0131) and Deutsches Archiv (D0086).

D0164 Lutherjahrbuch: Organ der Internationalen Lutherforschung. Vol. 1- . Göttingen: Vandenhoeck und Ruprecht, 1919- ; annual.

This yearbook, following a collection of articles, conference reports and book reviews in each volume, contains a Lutherbibliographie, which concentrates particularly on Luther and the German Reformation but with some attention to related topics in other countries as well. The entries are arranged by subject and include full bibliographical details. Books, book reviews, journal articles and theses are all listed; coverage is international, and titles in languages other than German or English are provided with translations. For the specific field treated this is an indispensible bibliography. See also Archiv für Reformationsgeschichte (D0018) and Edmond (D0088).

D0165 Macgregor, Malcolm Blair. The Sources and Literature of Scottish Church History. Glasgow: J. McCallum and Company, 1934.

This is a classified and annotated bibliography of both primary and secondary materials. It includes biographical sketches of outstanding personalities in Scottish religious history from the earliest times. This is a useful guide to the history of various denominations in Scotland up to the twentieth century.

D0166 Madoz, José. Segundo Decenio de Estudios sobre Patrística Española, 1941-1950. Estudios Onienses Ser. 1, vol. 5. Madrid: Ediciones FAX, 1951.

This 209 page sequel to Madoz's 1931-1940 survey in the Revista Española de Teologia (1941) lists and discusses important books and articles dealing with the Spanish patristic age (from the beginnings of Spanish Christianity to Carolingian times) which appeared between 1941 and 1950. Some works in European languages other than Spanish are included. This is an indispensible bibliography for students of this subject.

D0167 Matthews, William, comp. British Diaries: An Annotated Bibliography of British Diaries Written between 1442 and 1942. Berkeley, Calif.: University of California Press, 1950.

This 339 page bibliography provides brief descriptions of published and unpublished diaries by a wide range of personalities.

D0168 Mayer, Hans Eberhard. Bibliographie zur Geschichte der Kreuzzüge. Hannover: Hahnsche Buchhandlung, 1960.

Including both books and periodical articles published before 1958, Mayer lists some 5400 items on the crusades in Western languages, Hebrew, Chinese and Arabic. The classified arrangement includes the church and provides excellent coverage for more advanced research requirements. For a more basic guide see Atiya (D0022).

D0169 Meister, Aloys, ed. Grundriss der Geschichtswissenschaft, zur Einführung in das Studium der Deutschen Geschichte des Mittelalters und der Neuzeit. 13 vols. in 2 series. Leipzig: B.G. Teubner, 1906-1923.

This series of specialized volumes for advanced students and researchers deals with the techniques of historical method and with various phases of medieval and modern German history. Although neither series has been completed, individual volumes provide much valuable information on historical interpretation. Meister is most useful for the student of medieval German history. See also Deutsches Archiv (D0086).

D0170 Miller, Helen, and Newman, Aubrey. Early Modern British History, 1485-1760: A Select Bibliography. Helps for Students of History, no. 79. London: Historical Association, 1970.

This 42 page bibliography is intended to introduce students to the best recent secondary works available on the period concerned. Collections of selected documents are also included. Material is listed in twelve sections which include bibliographies, general surveys, religion (pp. 18-22) and thought. The 600 unannotated entries are presented chronologically within sections. An index of authors is included. This is a useful bibliography for works published between 1940 and 1970. See also Levine (D0161), Davies (D0081) and Grose (D0117).

D0171 Milward, Peter. Religious Controversies of the Jacobean Age: A Survey of Printed Sources. Lincoln, Neb.: University of Nebraska Press, 1978.

This sequel to Milward's Religious Controversies of the Elizabethan Age: A Survey of Printed Sources (Lincoln, Neb.: University of Nebraska Press, 1977) covers conflicts during the reign of King James I (1603-1625). The five broad subject areas into which the work is arranged include Anglican and Puritan, schisms among separatists, Catholics and the king, Catholic and Anglican, fragments of controversies. Each section combines commentary and historical background with a chronological listing of key publications, each of which is placed in context. Author and title indexes complete the work, which is useful for students of early seventeenth century church history in England. For general British history of the period see Gerould (D0103); see also Davies (D0081).

D0172 Mode, Peter George. Source Book and Bibliographical Guide for American Church History. Menasha, Wisc.: George Banta Publishing Company, 1921. Reprint. Boston, Mass.: J.S. Canner, 1964.

In 735 pages this annotated listing of printed materials covers items which Mode regards as the most significant items in American church history. In particular attention focuses on contributions which the church has made to society and the ways in which this institution has adjusted to the American environment. The documents are from the seventeenth century through the early twentieth century. Each chapter begins with a bibliographic essay on primary and secondary sources. Eleven chapters are devoted to the colonies, nine to various religious bodies, the remainder to topics such as mission societies, the Civil War and westward expansion. A subject index is provided. Although old, this remains a most useful source. See also Allison (D0003).

D0173 Molinier, Auguste Emile Louis Marie, et al. Les Sources de l'Histoire de France depuis les Origines jusqu'en 1815. 3 pts in 18 vols. Manuels de Bibliographie Historique, 2-5. Paris: A. Picard et Fils, 1901-1935.

This extensive critical bibliography of printed sources for French history is arranged in chronological parts and volumes and then topically. The three main parts cover from the origins to 1494, 1494-1610, 1610-1715. The first and third parts include detailed indexes, but the second has only a provisional index of authors. While the church is well covered throughout, there is particularly thorough treatment of the wars of religion in volume 3 of the second part. For those seeking thorough bibliographical coverage of French history, Molinier is highly recommended despite its age, which is being overcome in part by Les Sources de l'Histoire de France (D0206). See also Bibliothèque Nationale (D0038-D0040).

D0174 Monumenta Germaniae Historica. Hochschulschriften zur Geschichte und Kultur des Mittelalters 1939 bis 1972/74: (Deutschland, Osterreich, Schweiz). Zusammengestellt von Mitarbeiten der Monumenta Germaniae Historica. 3 vols. Hilfsmittel, Bd. 1. Munich: Monumenta Germaniae Historica, 1975.

This classified listing of 8400 dissertations from the countries and period indicated in the title includes research on all aspects of medieval history and culture, with religion receiving particularly good coverage. Volume 3 consists of author and subject indexes.

D0175 Le Moyen Age: Revue d'Histoire et de Philologie. Vol. 1- . Brussels: La Renaissance du Livre, 1880- ; quarterly.

Devoted to medieval European history, literature and thought, this periodical includes, in addition to articles and book reviews, a two part bibliography in each issue. The first is a series of literature surveys; the second, a list of periodical articles by subject. The literature surveys are devoted primarily to books, and both sections cover publications of the preceding year in major European languages. While the subject coverage is broad, the arrangement of materials is not geared to theological requirements but does treat a significant number of topics of interest to both church historians and theologians. See also Cahiers de Civilisation Médiévale (D0058) and Speculum (D0205).

D0176 Mullins, Edward Lindsay Carson. A Guide to the Historical and Archaeological Publications of Societies in England and Wales, 1903-1933. Comp. for the Institute of Historical Research. London: Athlone Press, 1968.

This 850 page complement to Writings on British History (D0234) lists and indexes books and articles issued by more than 400 national and local societies in England and Wales between 1903 and 1933. Materials are listed under the sponsoring society, and there is an author index plus an excellent subject index. For advanced students hoping to trace somewhat fugitive publications on local British history, many of them relevant to church history, this is a valuable compilation. See also University of London (D0216).

D0177 Pacaut, Marcel. Guide de l'Etudiant en Histoire Médiévale. Paris: Presses Universitaires de France, 1968.

An important guide for the beginner in medieval history, Pacaut is both a classified bibliography and a manual on the study of medieval society. The bibliography includes critical assessment of useful works and also lists suitable reference tools, including encyclopedias, dictionaries, atlases and similar categories. For more thorough coverage see Chevalier (D0068) and Paetow (D0178).

D0178 Paetow, Louis John. A Guide to the Study of Medieval History. Prepared under the auspices of the Mediaeval Academy of America. Rev. and corrected ed. with errata comp. by Gray Cowan Boyce and an addendum by Lynn Thorndike. New York: F.S. Crofts and Company, 1931. Reprint. Millwood, N.Y.: Kraus International Publications, 1980.

Long regarded as the most useful bibliographical survey of medieval history, Paetow is a critical guide to more than 1000 reference works on both general and specific topics. It covers original sources, secondary works, topical outlines and recommended reading, providing critical and scholarly details for each title. This compilation is an indispensible, if somewhat dated, guide to medieval history and is available in several reprints. For a complete revision and updating see Boyce (D0048). See also Chevalier (D0068).

D0179 Pagès, Georges; Cahen, Léon; and Jaryc, Marc, eds. Bibliographie Critique des Principaux Travaux Parus sur l'Histoire de 1600 à 1914 en 1932 et 1933-35. Publiée par le Comité de Direction de la Revue d'Histoire Moderne. 3 vols. Publications de la Société d'Histoire Moderne. Série des Instruments de Travail. Paris: Maison du Livre Français, 1935-1937.

Devoted to works on French history published in the early 1930s, this substantial bibliography includes titles in French, English, German and other languages. However, coverage of non-French language titles varies from volume to volume, and the treatment is somewhat uneven. For those doing research in post-sixteenth century French history this is a useful starting point for tracing publications issued during the years in question. Church history is treated to some degree. See also Bowditch (D0047).

D0180 Palumbo, Pier Fausto. Bibliografia Storica Internazionale, 1940-1947; con una Introduzione sullo Stato degli Studi Storici durante a Dopo la Seconda Guerra Mondiale. Biblioteca Storica, 2. Rome: Edizioni del Lavoro, 1950.

This 241 page bibliography lists publications, including periodical articles, by broad period, subdivided by subject. The long introductory section outlines the course of historical studies in various countries during and after the Second World War. There are author and subject indexes.

D0181 Pargellis, Stanley McCrory, and Medley, D.J., eds. Bibliography of British History: The Eighteenth Century, 1714-1789. Oxford: Clarendon Press, 1951.

This 642 page bibliography lists 4558 books, articles, pamphlets and documentary sources on various aspects of British history for the period in question. The classified arrangement of material includes a substantial section on ecclesiastical history, which is subdivided into major topics. The bibliographical citations are accurate and provide adequate information for most needs; annotations are indicative of both content and current value of items. There is a detailed author index. Pargellis, because of its thoroughness and broad coverage, is indispensible for the advanced student despite its age. For the early modern period see Miller (D0170).

D0182 Pollen, John Hungerford, ed. Sources for the History of Roman Catholics in England, Ireland and Scotland from the Reformation Period to That of Emancipation, 1533 to 1795. Helps for Students of History, no. 39. New York: Macmillan Company; London: SPCK, 1921.

See also Recusant History (D0189).

D0183 Pontifical Institute of Mediaeval Studies. Dictionary Catalog of the Pontifical Institute of Mediaeval Studies. 5 vols. Boston, Mass.: G.K. Hall and Company, 1972.

Arranged according to the Library of Congress classification, this catalog includes entries for approximately 83,000 items. It is especially strong in canon law, church history, patristics, philosophy and theology of the medieval period. This is a very important bibliography for advanced students. See also Chevalier (D0068), Paetow (D0178) and Potthast (D0184).

D0184 Potthast, August. Bibliotheca Historica Medii Aevi. Wegweiser durch die Geschichtswerke des Europäischen Mittelalters bis 1500. Vollständiges Inhaltsverzeichniss zu "Acta Sanctorum" Boll.-Bouquet-Migne, Monum. germ. hist. Muratori-Rerum britann. scriptores, etc.; Anhang-Quellenkunde für die Geschichte der Europäischen Staaten Während des Mittelalters. 2nd ed. 2 vols. Berlin: W. Weber, 1896. Reprint. 2 vols. Graz: Akademische Druck- und Verlagsanstalt, 1954-1957.

This two part classification of the primary sources of medieval history contains an index to printed texts of documents written between A.D. 375 and 1500, and an alphabetical list of medieval authors with an identifying phrase, references to biographies and a list of written works indicating manuscripts, translations, editions and commentaries. There are some inaccuracies and omissions. A revision of this large undertaking was begun by an international group of historians in 1962; see Repertorium Fontium Historiae (D0190). See also Pontifical Institute of Mediaeval Studies (D0183).

D0185 Poulton, Helen J. The Historian's Handbook: A Descriptive Guide to Reference Works. With the assistance of Marguerite S. Howland. Norman,

Okla.: University of Oklahoma Press, 1972.

This bibliography of reference sources for the beginner comments on approximately 1000 items in a series of eleven chapters dealing largely with types of materials, including bibliographies, encyclopedias, dictionaries, biographies, primary sources and other categories. Where necessary the chapters are subdivided by countries, and in most cases the bias is towards American undergraduate requirements. A general index and a title index facilitate rapid use. See also Coulter (D0074) and Day (D0084).

D0186 Quaker History. Vol. 1- . Swarthmore, Pa.: Swarthmore College, Friends Historical Library, 1902- ; semiannual.

Originally entitled Friends' Historical Association Bulletin, this specialized journal includes a bibliographical section, "Articles in Quaker Periodicals". This is limited to material printed in the handful of major Quaker journals and concentrates primarily on the history and biography of this denomination. Each entry includes both bibliographical details and a brief annotation. Coverage is quite current, and there are quinquennial cumulative indexes.

D0187 Read, Conyers, ed. Bibliography of British History: Tudor Period, 1485-1603. Issued under the direction of the American Historical Association and the Royal Historical Society of Great Britain. 2nd ed. Oxford: Clarendon Press, 1959.

This 624 page classified and annotated bibliography is an essential reference tool for advanced students and scholars. It is a very comprehensive work and includes materials, both books and articles, published up to 1957. The 6543 entries are arranged by subject, including religious history; citations are accurate and full, and there are numerous informative annotations. An author index is provided. For a complementary but less detailed bibliography see Levine (D0161). See also Booty (D0046).

D0188 Recently Published Articles. Vol. 1- . Washington, D.C.: American Historical Association, 1976- ; trimestral.

Originally published as a regular feature in the American Historical Review, this classified bibliography lists current articles which have appeared in a very wide range of historical periodicals. Bibliographical data are sufficient for reference purposes and allow one to locate articles quickly. Coverage is not limited to a specific area, so this service is a useful way for historians interested in a broad range of topics to keep abreast of current writings in their field. The section on American history cumulates annually into Writings on American History (D0233). See also International Committee of Historical Sciences (D0137).

D0189 Recusant History. Vol. 1- . London: Catholic Record Society, 1951- ; biannual.

Begun as Biographical Studies, this journal since 1972 has carried a section entitled "Newsletter". This bibliographical survey is a continuation of T.A. Birrell's Newsletter for Students of Recusant History, which ceased publication with no. 9 in 1970. The "Newsletter" appears in the spring issue each year and consists of five sections: bibliography (historical), bibliography (literary), theses, manuscripts, important sales. The historical bibliography is subdivided by broad period, and the listing of theses is divided into work in progress and completed research. The bibliographies are based on periodical holdings of the Institute of Historical Research at London University and are limited to the period from Elizabeth I to the first Vatican Council. Largely British in focus, the brief lists are fairly useful for those interested in British Catholic history but are rather limited in scope and somewhat dated. There is a biennial cumulative index to the journal. See also Pollen (D0182).

D0190 Repertorium Fontium Historiae Medii Aevi: Primum ab Augusto Potthast Digestum, nunc Cura Colegii Historicorum e Pluribus Nationibus Emendatum et Auctum. Vol. 1- . Rome: Istituto Storico Italiano per il Medio Evo, 1962- .

This revision of Potthast (D0184) includes both additions and corrections, as well as greatly expanded treatment of Oriental sources. The first volume, which follows the general outline of the first section in the original, is an alphabetical listing of sets of chronicles, miscellanies and other collections of sources; it includes full bibliographical data and explanatory material in Latin. Volumes 2 and 3 contain "Fontes" A to C. These sections contain a repertory of medieval writings arranged by author or title and entries include notes plus references to manuscripts, translations, editions and commentaries. In these sections coverage extends to theology, philosophy, literature and other areas relevant to medieval history. See also Chevalier (D0068) and Paetow (D0178).

D0191 Reuss, Jeremias David. Repertorium Commentationum a Societatibus Litteratiis Editarum. Secundum Disciplinarum Ordinem, t. 8.: Historia. Göttingen: Dieterich, 1810. Reprint. Burt Franklin Bibliography and Reference Series, no. 29. New York: Burt Franklin, 1961.

This 674 page index covers the publications of learned societies of various countries up to 1800. It uses classified arrangement with an author index. This is a valuable tool for the specialist.

D0192 Reviews in American History. Vol. 1- . Baltimore, Md.: Johns Hopkins University Press, 1973- ; quarterly.

Each issue of this review journal contains a number of critical review essays dealing with topically related titles in American history and ancillary subjects. Most of the coverage is of current history, but some attention is given to the history of American religious groups. Because of its general and somewhat unpredictable coverage, Reviews is not an indispensible awareness service for the church historian. Consultation is facilitated by the annual author/title/reviewer index, which indicates the occasional item of interest to students of American church history. See also Index to Book Reviews (D0134) and Reviews in European History (D0193).

D0193 Reviews in European History: A Journal of Criticism; the Renaissance to the Present. Vol. 1- . New York: Burt Franklin Publishing Company, 1974-197?; quarterly.

Covering a broad spectrum of professional and nonfiction publications, including teaching materials, this quarterly review journal includes lengthy analyses of recently published titles on all aspects of European history.

Coverage has not been consistently current, and titles relevant to church history have not always received adequate coverage. Otherwise, however, this serial has served as a useful bibliographical guide for those interested in topics with some bearing on the church in Europe. See also Reviews in American History (D0192) and Index to Book Reviews (D0134).

D0194 Revue d'Histoire Ecclésiastique. Vol. 1- . Louvain: Université Catholique de Louvain, Bibliothèque de l'Université, 1900- ; quarterly.

Covering all fields of church history from NT times to the present and focusing particularly on the Roman Catholic tradition, this wide ranging journal includes a separately paged "Bibliographie" intended to form an independent volume. This is nearly as long (800 pp.) as the main part of the journal each year and is arranged in four sections plus numerous subdivisions on the historical sciences, sources, historical studies and citations of reviews for listed books. More than 1000 journal titles are treated, and each volume contains some 11,000 entries for articles and books from around the world. In each section books precede periodical articles, both of which are listed alphabetically by author and include full citations. In terms of scope, arrangement and clarity of presentation this is an important current bibliography on ecclesiastical history. The lack of indexes means that consultation can be time consuming, but the inclusion of references to book reviews of listed titles is a particular advantage. This serial is recommended particularly to those interested in European church history, especially Roman Catholicism.

D0195 Revue Historique. Vol. 1- . Paris: Presses Universitaires de France, 1876- ; quarterly.

Like its counterpart American and British publications (D0009, D0092), this general historical journal includes a substantial number of book reviews, book notices and periodical information in each issue. Some coverage is given to church history, although most titles are rather dated by the time they are reviewed or listed.

D0196 Roach, John Peter Charles, ed. A Bibliography of Modern History. London: Cambridge University Press, 1968.

Intended as a bibliographical supplement to The New Cambridge Modern History (D0640), this 388 page compilation covers the periods 1493-1648, 1648-1793 and 1793-1945 in three sections. Arrangement is by subject within each period. There are brief annotations, and an index of personal names (excluding authors) and of countries is provided. The main emphasis is on books in English and the better known Western sources; manuscript sources and most periodical articles are excluded. This bibliography represents the work of over 170 scholars.

D0197 Rouse, Richard H. Serial Bibliographies for Medieval Studies. Assisted by J.H. Claxton and M.D. Metzger. Publications of the Center for Medieval and Renaissance Studies, no. 3. Berkeley, Calif.: University of California Press, 1969.

This classified listing of 283 bibliographies in serial form covers national and regional publications, archival listings, periodicals and bibliographical annuals. All items deal with current literature in medieval studies and are grouped according to fields of interest. The annotations are brief but informative, and there are numerous cross references. Indexes of titles and editors complete the work, which is a useful tool for the beginning graduate student.

D0198 Sachse, William Lewis, comp. Restoration England, 1660-1689. Conference on British Studies Bibliographical Handbooks. Cambridge: Cambridge University Press for the Conference on British Studies, 1971.

Containing 2350 entries, this 115 page bibliography lists a wide range of books and articles under fifteen headings common to the series as a whole. Religious history (pp. 69-83) is quite well covered and provides information on a representative selection of older as well as newer publications. Basic bibliographical data are occasionally accompanied by brief annotations. A list of abbreviations, explanatory notes and index of authors, editors and translators are provided. This is a suitable bibliography for advanced users. See also Davies (D0081).

D0199 Sawicki, Jacobus Theodorus. Bibliographia Synodorum Particularium. Monumenta Iuris Canonici Series C: Subsidia, vol. 1. Vatican City: S. Congregatio de Seminariis et Studiorum Universitatibus, 1967.

This international bibliography lists more than 3400 items in all European languages on synods and councils of the Roman Catholic Church. The two part arrangement lists collections and histories of general and ecumenical councils and of local synods and councils. Within each section the arrangement is alphabetical, and there are indexes of names, places and subjects. Despite its lack of annotations Sawicki is a useful starting point for students of conciliar history. See also Annuarium Historiae Conciliorum (D0014) and Bulletin of Medieval Canon Law (D0056).

D0200 Schmale, Franz Josef. Deutschlands Geschichtsquellen im Mittelalter. Unter der Mitarbeit von Irene Schmale-Ott und Dieter Berg. Vol. 1- . Darmstadt: Wissenschaftliche Buchgesellschaft, 1976- .

Beginning coverage with the death of Kaiser Henry V, this new series is intended to supersede the sixth edition of Wattenbach (D0223-D0225).

D0201 Schottenloher, Karl. Bibliographie zur Deutschen Geschichte im Zeitalter der Glaubensspaltung, 1517-1585. 2. Aufl. 7 vols. Stuttgart: Anton Hiersemann, 1956-1966.

This comprehensive bibliography of the Reformation era in Germany lists both books and articles, including not only contemporary works but also later studies of the period. The volumes are arranged topically, covering personalities, rulers, territories, movements and similar subjects. Under each subject the bibliographical entries are very brief but provide enough information for one to trace the indicated sources without undue difficulty. The volumes are extremely well indexed for reference purposes. Together with Wolf (D0232) this work forms an indispensible bibliography of the German Reformation. See also Center for Reformation Research (D0064-D0065).

D0202 The Sixteenth Century Journal: A Journal for Renaissance and Reformation Students and Scholars. Vol. 1- . Kirksville, Mo.: The Sixteenth Century Journal, 1970- ; semiannual.

From a bibliographical viewpoint the main advantage of this serial lies in its book review and notice sections, which provide a rather current source of information on publications relevant to the Reformation in particular. However, these are not systematically arranged or indexed sections and should be used only as an adjunct to established review or indexing services which cover this period inter alia. See also Archiv für Reformationsgeschichte (D0018).

D0203 Smith, Dwight La Vern, ed. Afro-American History: A Bibliography. Clio Bibliography Series, vol. 2. Santa Barbara, Calif.: ABC-Clio Press, [1974].

This collection of 2274 abstracts is based on material from volumes 0-10 (1954-1972) of America: History and Life. The reprinted items deal with Afro-American history and are arranged in a classified sequence. There is an author/subject index. This is a useful collection for those doing retrospective bibliographical work in Afro-American history, as it includes some information related to the church. See also U.S. National Archives (D0215).

D0204 Les Sources de l'Histoire de France, des Origines à la Fin du XVe Siècle. Refonte de l'ouvrage d'Auguste Emile Louis Marie Molinier. Entreprise sous la direction de Robert Fawtier. Vol. 1- . Paris: Editions A. et J. Picard, 1971- .

Expected to be completed in eight or nine volumes, this revision of part 1 of Molinier (D0173) provides a much needed updating of the period to 1494. Arrangement is similar to that of the original work, and bibliographical coverage is as thorough. See also Bibliographie Annuelle (D0031) and Caron (D0060).

D0205 Speculum: A Journal of Medieval Studies. Vol. 1- . Cambridge, Mass.: Mediaeval Academy of America, 1926- ; quarterly.

Essentially a scholarly journal, Speculum also includes a regular section devoted to book reviews, books received and irregular bibliographies of periodical literature. It is a useful retrospective guide to publications on all aspects of medieval studies. See also Cahiers de Civilisation Médiévale (D0058) and Le Moyen Age (D0175).

D0206 Spence, Thomas Hugh. Catalogues of Presbyterian and Reformed Institutions. I. As Historical Sources. II. In the Historical Foundation. Montreat, N.C.: Historical Foundation Publications, 1952.

See also Trinterud (D0212).

D0207 Steck, Francis Borgia. A Tentative Guide to Historical Materials on the Spanish Borderlands. Philadelphia, Pa.: The Catholic Historical Society of Philadelphia, 1943. Reprint. Burt Franklin Research and Source Work Series, vol. 670. Geography and Discovery, vol. 12. New York: Burt Franklin, 1971.

This 106 page bibliography of scholarly books and articles covers all American territories once controlled by Spain, including Louisiana to 1803, Florida to 1814, Texas to 1836, New Mexico, Arizona and California to 1846. The annotations are brief and descriptive. Despite the lack of indexes, this is a useful guide for advanced students of a specialized historical field. It is especially valuable as a bibliography of Roman Catholic mission history.

D0208 Stewardson, Jerry L. A Bibliography of Bibliographies on Patristics. Evanston, Ill.: Garrett Theological Seminary Library, 1967.

This 52 page bibliography describes and lists the main bibliographical sources for patristics. Arrangement is by subject in fourteen sections, with some cross references. Asterisks are used to indicate particularly important bibliographies. The annotations are detailed, and the work includes periodicals. It does not attempt to cover bibliographies of Armenian, Ethiopian, Georgian or Arabic literature, and coverage of Syriac material is not exhaustive. Quasten (D0675, D0676) provides references in these areas. See also Altaner (D0004).

D0209 Stokes, Lawrence D. Medieval and Reformation Germany (to 1648). Helps for Students of History, no. 84. London: Historical Association, 1972.

Aimed particularly at students limited to works in English, this narrative bibliography treats some 1400 books and articles on Germany. The six main sections cover bibliographies (including essential German works), geography, general surveys, origins to 800 A.D., 800-1500, 1500-1648. Most of the works discussed are major scholarly or reference volumes plus key survey articles. An author index is provided. This is an excellent starting point for the beginner. See also Holtzmann (D0131), Lorenz (D0163), Wattenbach (D0223-D0225) and Schottenloher (D0201).

D0210 [no entry]

D0211 Tomasi, Silvano, and Stibili, Edward C. Italian Americans and Religion: An Annotated Bibliography. New York: Center for Migration Studies, 1978.

This unique bibliography on the religious experience of Italians in America covers the early period of Italian missionaries, mass migration of the nineteenth and early twentieth centuries, the contemporary period. The first section lists major archives and describes their contents. The second part, which is divided into five sections, provides brief annotations of bibliographies, serials, theses and dissertations, parish histories, books and articles. Most of the 1158 entries are in the final section, and an author/subject index is provided.

D0212 Trinterud, Leonard J., comp. A Bibliography of American Presbyterianism during the Colonial Period. Presbyterian Historical Society Publication Series, vol. 8. Philadelphia, Pa.: Presbyterian Historical Society, 1968.

This bibliography lists 1129 primary source documents from colonial presbyteries or synods, indicating their location in selected libraries. An author index is included. See also Spence (D0206).

D0213 U.S. Library of Congress. Descriptive Cataloging Division, comp. and ed. The National Union Catalog of Manuscript Collections. Vol. 1- . Hamden, Conn.: Shoe String Press, 1962- ; annual.

For those requiring access to primary documentation in church history this catalog is an indispensible finding list. It reproduces cards of manuscript collections in more than 1000 repositories in the United States. Each entry indicates the number of items, physical format and description, scope and content, location, access, finding tools, microfilm copies. Indexes produced at irregular intervals cover names, places, subjects and periods. For a similar guide to Great Britain see the Public Record Office (D0112).

D0214 U.S. Library of Congress. General Reference and Bibliography Division. A Guide to the Study of the United States of America: Representative Books Reflecting the Development of American Life and Thought. Prepared under the direction of Roy P. Basler by Ronald Henry Mugridge and Blanche Pritchard McCrum. Washington, D.C.: Library of Congress, 1960.

This 1193 page bibliography includes a chapter on religion in the development of American life. Descriptive annotations are provided for most works listed, which in general are aimed at students new to the field of American church history. There is a combined author/title/subject index. See also America (D0007).

D0215 U.S. National Archives and Records Service. Black Studies: Select Catalog of National Archives and Records Service Microfilm Publications. Washington, D.C.: National Archives, 1973.

Listing only documents available on microfilm, this catalog is arranged by record group and describes in detail a wide range of materials important in the study of black history. Churches, sects and various religious movements figure prominently in the collection, making it an interesting guide for students of black American church history. See also Smith (D0203).

D0216 University of London. Institute of Historical Research. Guide to the Historical Publications of the Societies of England and Wales. 13 vols. Bulletin of the Institute of Historical Research, Supplements 1-13. London: Longmans, Green and Company, 1930-1948.

This incomplete guide lists issues of society publications for the years 1929-1946. In itself it is not a particularly useful compilation, but there is in preparation a full treatment of the societies, their publications and an index. Mullins (D0176) lists the contents of the thirteen supplements. See also Writings on British History (D0234, D0235).

D0217 University of London. Institute of Historical Research. Historical Research for University Degrees in the United Kingdom. 14 vols. Bulletin of the Institute of Historical Research, Supplements 1-14. London: Longmans, Green and Company, 1933-1953.

Until succeeded by Theses Completed and Theses in Progress (D0218), this compilation covered these two areas. It is now largely of retrospective value, indicating postgraduate research topics in all historical fields from 1931 to 1952. See also Jacobs (D0142).

D0218 University of London. Institute of Historical Research. Historical Research for University Degrees in the United Kingdom: Theses Completed. List no. 15- . London: University of London, Institute of Historical Research, 1954- ; annual.

This register, together with Theses in Progress (London: University of London, Institute of Historical Research, 1954- ; annual), was published as a supplement to the Bulletin of the Institute of Historical Research until 1967. Now a separate publication, it is arranged by period and country and lists thesis title, researcher, supervisor, university and degree. There are author and subject indexes. It is primarily of interest to post-graduate researchers seeking information on recently completed theses, including those in church history. See also Jacobs (D0142).

D0219 University of North Carolina at Chapel Hill. Library. Humanities Division. Medieval and Renaissance Studies: A Location Guide to Selected Works and Source Collections in the Library of the University of North Carolina at Chapel Hill and Duke University. Prep. under the supervision of Louise McG. Hall. Chapel Hill, N.C.: University of North Carolina, 1974.

Updating the 1967 edition by including a 15 page Addenda II, this biblio-graphical guide covers the entire range of medieval and Renaissance studies. Like the Harvard University shelflist (D0124) this is a general bibliography of use primarily to less advanced students.

D0220 Vekené, Emile van der. Bibliographie der Inquisition: Ein Versuch. Hildesheim: Georg Olms Verlag, 1963.

This 323 page bibliography lists 1950 numbered items and is arranged chronologically from 1483 to 1961. It includes works in all Western lan-guages and attempts to provide representative coverage of publications related to the Inquisition. The location of copies in European libraries is indicated, but annotations are not provided. An author and title index is included, but there is no subject index.

D0221 Vollmar, Edward R. The Catholic Church in America: An Historical Bibliography. 2nd ed. New York: Scarecrow Press, 1963.

Superseding the first edition of 1956, this 399 page bibliography covers the history of the Roman Catholic Church in America between 1850 and 1961. Arranged alphabetically by author, it lists books, articles, theses and dissertations. While the last two categories are limited to items submitted at Catholic universities, this guide is the most comprehen-sive in its field and should be consulted by anyone interested in the history of American Catholicism. Although annotations are not provided, bibliographical information is reasonably complete, and there is a subject index. Coverage is broader than that provided by Ellis (D0090).

D0222 Von Oeyen, Robert R. Philippine Evangelical Protestant and Indepen-dent Catholic Churches: An Historical Bibliography of Church Records, Publications and Source Material Located in the Greater Manila Area. Asian Center, University of the Philippines Bibliography Series, no. 1. Quezon City: University of the Philippines, Asian Center, 1970.

D0223 Wattenbach, Wilhelm. Deutschlands Geschichtsquellen im Mittelalter: Deutsche Kaiserzeit. Hrsg. von Robert Holtzmann. 4 pts in 1 vol. Tübingen: M. Matthiessen, 1948.

First published under the authorship of Wattenbach in 1848, this volume and the two following titles together form a very important bibliographical guide to printed materials on German history. This revision by Holtzmann covers 900-1050, while Levison (D0224) and Buchner (D0225) treat Germany from early times to the Treaty of Verdun in 843. As a listing of works on German history to 1050, Wattenbach is indispensible for advanced students, since it covers many titles of value in ecclesiastical research. See also Holtzmann (D0131), Schmale (D0200) and Wolf (D0232).

D0224 Wattenbach, Wilhelm. Deutschlands Geschichtsquellen im Mittelalter: Vorzeit und Karolinger. Bearb. von Wilhelm Levison und Heinz Löwe. Weimar: H. Böhlaus Nachfolger, 1952-1953.

Like the Holtzmann revision of Wattenbach (D0131) this is an indispensible bibliographical guide for advanced students of German history. Here coverage extends to 843.

D0225 Wattenbach, Wilhelm. Deutschlands Geschichtsquellen im Mittelalter: Vorzeit und Karolinger. Beiheft: Das Rechtsquellen. Von Rudolf Buchner. Weimar: H. Böhlaus Nachfolger, 1953.

See also the Levison-Löwe revision (D0224) of Wattenbach.

D0226 Wesley Historical Society Proceedings. Vol. 1- . Newcastle-upon-Tyne: Wesley Historical Society, 1897- ; triannual.

Since 1976 this guide to Methodist history has included an annual bibliography of books, articles and dissertations. It is arranged alphabetically by author or editor and includes only the most basic bibliographical information (usually title and date). Coverage is not especially comprehensive but does provide a representative listing of British and American works on Methodist history, with passing attention to evangelical Protestantism as well. Because there is neither a subject arrangement nor a subject index, use of this compilation is not particularly easy. However, it does provide a reasonable indication of writings on Methodist history and should be regarded as one of the better guides to this large and important denomination. If more up to date analytical coverage could be provided, the bibliography in Proceedings could become an essential guide for scholars and others interested in Methodism. See also Green (D0115).

D0227 Whitley, William Thomas, comp. A Baptist Bibliography; Being a Register of the Chief Materials for Baptist History, Whether in Manuscript or in Print, Preserved in Great Britain, Ireland and the Colonies. Comp. for the Baptist Union of Great Britain and Ireland. 2 vols. London: Kingsgate Press, 1916-1922.

Arranged chronologically, this bibliography covers 1526-1776 in volume 1 and 1777-1837 in volume 2, with addenda covering 1613-1653. Indexes treat anonymous pamphlets, authors, places and subjects. Bibliographical citations provide adequate details for most purposes. The location of titles in thirty-one libraries, mainly British, is also indicated. In its time Whitley was a valuable guide. See also Atkinson (D0023).

D0228 Whitney, James Pounder. A Bibliography of Church History. The Historical Association Leaflet no. 55. London: Historical Association, 1923.

This 44 page guide covers general church history in part A and English church history in part B. See also Chadwick (D0067).

D0229 Willaert, Léopold. Bibliotheca Janseniana Belgica: Répertoire des Imprimés Concernant les Controverses Théologiques en Relation avec le Jansénisme dans les Pays-Bas Catholiques et le Pays de Liège aux XVIIe et XVIIIe Siècles. 3 vols. Bibliothèque de la Faculté de Philosophie et Lettres de Namur, fasc. 4, 5, 12. Namur: n.p., 1949-1951.

Limited to works by Belgians, printed in Belgium or dealing with Belgium, this bibliography lists more than 1400 books and articles on Jansenism. It also includes the names of libraries with notable collections in thie field. Arranged chronologically, the volumes cover 1476-1679, 1680-1738, 1739-1950. This is a unique guide to the Jansenist heresy and is indispensible for students of this movement. See also Bruggeman (D0052).

D0230 Wilkinson, Bertie, comp. The High Middle Ages in England, 1154-1377. Conference on British Studies Bibliographical Handbooks. Cambridge: Cambridge University Press, 1978.

Like other volumes in the series, this 130 page bibliography seeks to list major books, important articles plus significant editions of texts relevant to all aspects of the period. The fourteen sections cover various historical subjects, including religion. The 2259 entries provide essential bibliographical information and, on occasion, evaluative notes. There is an author/translator/editor index. Because of its broad and representative coverage, Wilkinson is most suitable for students without extensive knowledge of English medieval history. For treatment of earlier and later periods see Altschul (D0006) and Guth (D0119).

D0231 Williams, Harry Franklin. An Index of Medieval Studies Published in Festschriften, 1865-1946, with Special Reference to Romanic Material. Berkeley, Calif.: University of California Press, 1951.

This 165 page index of 5000 items from approximately 500 volumes of Festschriften covers medieval history, philosophy, art, customs and similar topics. Included are a list of Festschriften, an index of authors and a subject index. This is a helpful guide to literature not indexed elsewhere. See also International Guide to Medieval Studies (D0140) and International Medieval Bibliography (D0141).

D0232 Wolf, Gustav. Quellenkunde der Deutschen Reformationsgeschichte. 3 vols. in 4. Gotha: F.A. Perthes, 1915-1923. Reprint. 3 vols. in 2. Hildesheim: Georg Olms Verlagsbuchhandlung, 1965.

The three volumes in this comprehensive bibliographical treatment of the German Reformation cover the pre-Reformation era, Reformation in general and history of the ecclesiastical Reformation. The final volume includes indexes of authors and titles. The detailed discussion of resources is very carefully classified into major subjects, topics and narrow subdivisions; these are outlined in the list of contents. The commentary by Wolf indicates the context, content and significance of each work in a thorough and detailed manner. This is an essential guide for advanced students and provides an excellent complement to Schottenloher (D0201).

D0233 Writings on American History, [   ]: A Subject Bibliography of Articles. Washington, D.C.: Americn Historical Association; Millwood, N.Y.: Kraus International Publications, 1905- ; irregular.

Published with slightly variant titles and by several different publishers, this irregularly produced (but supposedly now annual) bibliography now appears under the aegis of the two bodies noted above. The 1981 publication covers books and articles published in 1979-1980 and uses a topical arrangement supplemented by an author index. Citations are based on information derived from lists in the American Historical Review and provide full bibliographical details on items dealing with all aspects of American history. Although there is not a detailed subject index, Writings is a prime source of information for the advanced student and scholar of American church history. Earlier volumes vary greatly in coverage and arrangement so should be consulted with care. See also Griffin (D0116) and Recently Published Articles (D0188).

D0234 Writings on British History. London: Jonathan Cape for the Royal Historical Society, 1937- ; irregular.

The sets produced to date in this series vary widely in periods covered: 1934-1945, 1946-1948, 1949-1951, 1952-1954, 1955-1957, 1958-1959, 1960-1961, 1962-1964, 1965-1966. Regardless of this unevenness and the fact that there is currently a fifteen year lag in coverage, this is an important guide to literature, both books and articles, on British history. Treatment is comprehensive, thorough and international; the 1965-1966 volume lists some 6000 items from around the world. A classified arrangement by area, period and subject is followed, which makes consultation fairly rapid. The church, religious history and related areas are well covered, making this a significant aid for retrospective bibliographical searching. For treatment of 1901-1933 publications see the following entry (D0235). See also Annual Bibliography (D0012) and Mullins (D0176).

D0235 Writings on British History, 1901-1933: A Bibliography of Books and Articles on the History of Great Britain from about 400 A.D. to 1914 Published during the Years 1901-1933 Inclusive, with an Appendix Containing a Select List of Publications in These Years on British History since 1914. 5 vols. in 7. London: Jonathan Cape for the Royal Historical Society, 1968-1970.

Providing retrospective coverage of writings published prior to the beginning of the annual series of the same title (D0234), this classified bibliography of books and articles treats general works and auxiliary sciences, the Middle Ages, Tudor and Stuart periods, the eighteenth century and 1815-1914. For comprehensive treatment of historical writings published between 1901 and 1933 this is a most valuable guide which includes much information of interest to the church historian. See also Annual Bibliography (D0012).

D0236 Zwingliana: Beiträge zur Geschichte Zwinglis der Reformation und des Protestantismus in der Schweiz. Vol. 1- . Zürich: Verlag Berichthaus Zürich for the Zwingliverein, 1897- ; semiannual.

Alternate issues of this journal include a bibliography on historical aspects of the Reformation in Switzerland, which is arranged in four sections (bibliography, collective studies, original texts, monographs) alphabetically by author. In addition to bibliographical information each entry includes a brief abstract. Although limited in the extent of its coverage, this is a helpful guide to work on Zwingli and other aspects of the Swiss Reformation. There is a quinquennial index which includes the bibliography. See also Hinz (D0128).

CHURCH HISTORY: DICTIONARIES

D0237 Adams, James Truslow. Concise Dictionary of American History. Advisory ed.: Thomas Childs Cochran. Ed. by Wayne Andrews. New York: Charles Scribner's Sons, 1962.

This condensation of Adams' multivolume work, itself superseded by the Ketz edition (D0287), is useful for basic inquiries. Some of the material remains unchanged from the original work, but many articles have been abbreviated or omitted altogether. There are no bibliographies, but the index is very full. See also Martin (D0297).

D0238 Aldea Vaquero, Quintín; Marín Martínez, Tomás; and Vives, José Gatell, eds. Diccionario de Historia Eclesiástica de España. 4 vols. Madrid: Instituto Enrique Flórez, Consejo Superior de Investigaciones Científicas, 1972-1975.

This interesting encyclopedia contains lengthy articles on the entire range of Roman Catholic history in Spain. Major events, significant topics, important personalities and key geographical regions are all covered in some detail. Most articles include bibliographical notes. This is an important guide for those studying the history of Iberian Catholicism.

D0239 American Catholic Historical Society of Philadelphia. Records: Index, Vols. 1-31, 1884-1920. Philadelphia, Pa.: American Catholic Historical Society, 1924.

The Records of the Society cover a wide range of personalities important in the history of American Catholicism, as well as significant events and movements. The Index, in turn, not only provides access to these names and terms but also provides brief information on each one; in this respect it servies as a useful, basic dictionary of Catholicism in America.

D0240 Andresen, Carl, et al., eds. Lexikon der Alten Welt. Redaktion: Klaus Bartels und Ludwig Huber. Zurich: Artemis Verlag, 1965.

Including material on early Christianity in its coverage of the ancient world, Andresen contains nearly 250 articles on all aspects of ancient history. There are numerous bibliographies and cross references. Chronologies, a list of abbreviations, list of place names and index of Greek and Latin terms are provided. This compilation is suitable for students of the NT and patristic periods. See also Pauly (D0303, D0304).

D0241 Anstruther, Godfrey. The Seminary Priests: A Dictionary of the Secular Clergy of England and Wales, 1558-1850. Vol. 1- . Durham: Ushaw College; Ware: St. Edmund's College, [1969]- .

Volume 1 covers clergy of the Elizabethan period (1558-1608), while succeeding volumes cover 1603-1659, 1660-1715, 1716-1800. It is assumed that the final volume will cover 1801-1850. The introduction to volume 1 includes a critical survey of manuscript sources. Based on careful research, this is a useful guide to this specific area of study.

D0242 Attwater, Donald, comp. A Dictionary of Saints; Based on Butler's "Lives of the Saints", Complete Ed. New York: P.J. Kenedy; London: Burns and Oates, 1958.

This 280 page dictionary is similar in content to Attwater's Penguin Dictionary (D0245), which is more up to date in terms of scholarship. In addition to basic biographical data, this 1958 volume includes for each saint an index reference to the fuller treatment in Butler (D0377); this is perhaps the most important aspect of Attwater.

D0243 Attwater, Donald, comp. A Dictionary of the Popes from Peter to Pius XII. London: Burns, Oates and Washbourne, 1939.

This biographical dictionary is a chronologically arranged guide to 258 popes and provides extensive details for more important names with correspondingly less information for not so well known figures. For each pope a portrait is provided, and there is also an index. Attwater is more detailed than Kühner (D0289) and is a sound guide for students of papal history.

D0244 Attwater, Donald. Martyrs from St. Stephen to John Tung. New York: Sheed and Ward, 1957.

This 236 page dictionary covers more than sixty individuals and groups of martyrs and provides basic information on the lives and work of each martyr listed. A bibliography of sources (pp. 226-236) is also included. This is a good but basic reference work for those interested in this particular hagiographical category.

D0245 Attwater, Donald. The Penguin Dictionary of Saints. Baltimore, Md.: Penguin Books, 1965.

In this 362 page dictionary a short glossary of useful hagiographical terms precedes the alphabetical listing of more than 750 saints. Data for each individual are concise, accurate and generally adequate for basic reference requirements. The factual information covers the saints' lives, works, feast days, dates of canonization and symbols in arts. See also Coulson (D0263) and Farmer (D0274).

D0246 Attwater, Donald. Saints of the East. New York: P.J. Kenedy, 1963.

This 190 page survey provides brief biographies of two dozen Eastern saints who lived before the split with Rome. Although it lacks the detail and scholarship which one would expect in a work by Attwater, this guide remains one of the few reliable biographical surveys in English devoted to Eastern hagiography.

D0247 Auty, Robert, et al., eds. Lexikon des Mittelalters. Bd. 1- . Munich: Artemis Verlag, [1977].

Projected in six volumes, this substantial international guide to the Middle Ages covers persons, places, terms, events, movements and other areas of relevance to medieval history and thought. It covers the period from 300 to 1500, concentrating essentially on the European scene. It is published in parts, and those issued to date display thorough and scholarly coverage.

D0248 Avery, Catherine B., ed. The New Century Italian Renaissance Encyclopedia. Editorial consultants: Marvin B. Becker and Ludovico Borgo. New York: Appleton-Century-Crofts, [1972].

Primarily a biographical dictionary, this 978 page guide covers religion, politics, art and literature in Italy from 1265 to 1564. Ecclesiastical affairs are well represented in the selection of personalities, and there are numerous cross references. The lack of bibliographies and indexes detracts from the usefulness of Avery, which is suitable for general inquiries.

D0249 Avi-Yonah, Michael, and Schatzman, Israel, eds. Illustrated Encyclopaedia of the Classical World. New York: Harper and Row, [1975]; Maidenhead: Sampson Low, 1976.

Aimed at students and general readers who are not trained in the classics, this dictionary contains some 2300 articles on Greek and Roman history, religion, philosophy, personalities, geography, sites and society. The articles are concise and clearly written, and some include brief bibliographies. There is an index of names, terms and subjects; this covers items which are not main entries. See also Seyffert (D0309) and Warrington (D0315).

D0250 Bacci, Antonio. Varia Latinitatis Scripta. Ed. 4. Vol. 1- . Rome: Societas Libraria Studium, 1963- .

Volume 1, Lexicon Vocabularum quae Difficilius Latine Reduntur, is an excellent tool for historians and theologians working with the Latin texts of papal documents, for it concentrates on providing the Latin equivalents of modern words. The second volume, Inscriptiones, Orationes, Epistulae, deals similarly with the indicated categories of documents. Bacci should be consulted by anyone working with primary source materials and seeking an aid in translation.

D0251 Barker, William Pierson. Who's Who in Church History. Old Tappan, N.J.: Fleming H. Revell Company, 1969. Reprint. Grand Rapids, Mich.: Baker Book House, 1977.

This 319 page dictionary treats more than 1500 individuals of particular importance in church history as viewed from a conservative Protestant standpoint. It includes theologians, popes, kings, missionaries, educators and similar types of personalities, concentrating particularly on the Protestant tradition. Each entry provides dates and a summary of the person's achievements in a fairly uncritical fashion. Nevertheless, Barker is of some use to general readers wishing to have basic information on a selected range of historical figures. See also Bautz (D0253), Jamieson (D0284) and Moyer (D0301).

D0252 Baudrillart, Alfred. Dictionnaire d'Histoire et de Géographie Ecclés-

iastiques. Continué par A. de Meyer et Etienne van Cauwenbergh. Vol. 1- .
Paris: Letouzey et Ané, 1912- .

Part of the Encyclopédie des Sciences Ecclésiastiques, this work has
been appearing in parts since 1909 (although volume 1 is dated 1912).
Coverage extends to all subjects in the history of Roman Catholicism
from the beginning to the present. Geographical material includes separate
articles on towns and other divisions, indicating the connection with
ecclesiastical history, present ecclesiastical status, list of its religious
institutions and similar information. Also included are biographical articles
on all important and some less significant figures in the Roman Catholic
Church, members of other churches who have had an influence on Roman
Catholicism, ecclesiastical and theological writers, saints in the Russian
and other churches, ecclesiastical musicians and artists and many other
types of personalities. The signed articles and ample bibliographies help
to make this encyclopedic potpourri a significant source of information
on topics often ignored in other compilations. Earlier volumes are somewhat dated but still retain historical value.

D0253 Bautz, Friedrich Wilhelm, ed. Biographisch-Bibliographisches Kirchen-
lexikon. Bd. 1- . Hamm: Verlag Trangott Bautz, 1975- .

This work contains substantial articles and bibliographies on notable
figures in all fields who have had some impact on ecclesiastical affairs
and the church generally. For each entry the biographical data are quite
adequate, providing both basic facts and contextual interpretations;
the bibliographies are detailed and international in coverage. The main
drawback of this work is its wide interpretation of what is relevant
to Christianity, for it means that far too many fields are touched upon
and none is dealt with comprehensively. Political figures, theologians,
popes, artists, writers, controversialists, reformers, philosophers and
others from all periods and regions are treated by Bautz. On the other
hand this interdisciplinary and ecumenical approach means that such a
work will have a broad appeal and should become an important reference
guide for a wide spectrum of users able to read German. See also Barker
(D0251).

D0254 Bleiberg, Germán, ed. Diccionario de Historia de España. 2. ed. 3 vols.
Madrid: Ediciones de la "Revista de Occident", [1968-1969].

First published as a two volume work in 1952, this substantial dictionary
consists of relatively lengthy articles on all aspects, topics, events and
personalities important in Spanish history. Living persons are not included,
but otherwise coverage is admirably wide ranging for most basic reference
needs. The final volume includes a lengthy bibliography (pp. 1083-1111),
a chronology and a collection of maps. For Spanish ecclesiastical history
see Aldea Vaquero (D0238).

D0255 The Book of Saints: A Dictionary of Persons Canonized or Beatified
by the Catholic Church. Comp. by the Benedictine monks of St. Augustine's
Abbey, Ramsgate. 5th ed. New York: Thomas Y. Crowell, 1966.

Published in Britain as The Book of Saints: A Dictionary of Servants
of God Canonized by the Catholic Church (5th ed. London: Adam and
Charles Black, 1966), this 740 page dictionary provides concise and highly
accurate biographical data on some 2200 saints. The fifth edition includes

entries for individuals beatified or canonized during the preceding twenty-five years but excludes the calendar of saints. The sources of information used in collecting data are clearly documented for further study. This is one of the most useful hagiographical dictionaries available for basic reference inquiries, particularly where information is sought concerning the Roman Catholic martyrology or saints with a British connection. See also The Encyclopedia of Catholic Saints (D0270).

D0256 Bowden, Henry Warner. Dictionary of American Religious Biography. Advisory ed.: Edwin S. Gaustad. Westport, Conn.: Greenwood Press, 1977.

Containing 425 biographical sketches of individuals who have helped shape the American religious experience, this 572 page dictionary is a factual and scholarly compendium of value to a wide range of users. It is broadly representative of American religion and for each person provides basic factual information, vital statistics, interpretive judgments and a compact bibliography. More than 3000 sources are cited, and there are appendixes on denominational affiliation and place of birth. A general subject index greatly facilitates the use of this volume, which is an excellent source of information for both church historians and theologians, as well as for those involved in other disciplines where religion is a factor.

D0257 Brauer, Jerald C., ed. The Westminster Dictionary of Church History. Philadelphia, Pa.: Westminster Press, 1971.

This 887 page dictionary seeks to provide introductory definitions and explanations of major facts, movements, events and individuals in church history. Particularly strong is coverage of nineteenth and twentieth century American church history, and there is a clear emphasis on institutional developments. Brauer is Protestant in orientation but deals objectively and factually with all periods and traditions. Most articles are fairly brief, and longer entries include bibliographies. This work is useful for basic data on a wide range of topics, although more substantial coverage is available in Cross (D0418).

D0258 Cappelli, Adriano. Lexicon Abbreviaturarum: Dizionario di Abbreviature Latine Ed Italiane Usate nelle Carte e Codici Specialmente del Medio-Evo Riprodotte con Ottre 14,000 Segni Incisi, con l'Aggiunta di Uno Studio Sulla Brachigrafia Medioevale, un Prontuario di Sigle Epigrafiche, l'Antica Numerazione Romana Ed Arabica Ed i Segni Indicanti Monete, Pesi, Misure, etc. 6. ed. Milan: Hoepli, 1961.

Abbreviations, signs, symbols, numbers and similar sigla are all covered in this useful handbook for the medievalist. Where appropriate, definitions are provided for entries. There is also a bibliography of other works on abbreviations. See also Pelzer (D0305).

D0259 Carruth, Gorton, et al., eds. The Encyclopedia of American Facts and Dates. 6th ed. With a supplement of the 70's. New York: Thomas Y. Crowell, [1972].

This chronologically arranged guide to American history covers, in columnar format, politics and related areas; arts; science, education, religion and philosophy; society, folklore and pasttimes. The sixth edition is a reprint of the fifth edition and its index plus a supplement and separate index covering 1970-1971. For those who want basic facts rather than full explanations Carruth is of some reference value. Coverage of religion is adequate but not extensive. See also Johnson (D0285).

D0260 Cary, Max, et al., eds. The Oxford Classical Dictionary. Oxford: Clarendon Press, 1949.

This standard work is a useful guide to Greek and Roman names, subjects, customs, arts, culture, philosophy and related topics. It includes entries for prominent Christians of the classical era, and there are bibliographies incorporated in many articles. The entries are brief but informative and provide an unexpected source of useful data for a wide range of theological inquiries. For a second edition see Hammond (D0278).

D0261 Chéruel, Pierre Adolphe. Dictionnaire Historique des Institutions, Moeurs et Coutumes de la France. 8e éd. 2 vols. Paris: Hachette et Cie, 1910.

This is a useful dictionary of pre-nineteenth century French history. See also Lalanne (D0290).

D0262 Collison, Robert Lewis. Dictionary of Dates. [Rev. ed.] New York: Transatlantic Arts, [1967]. Reprint. [1st ed.] Westport, Conn.: Greenwood Press, 1969.

Also published as Newnes Dictionary of Dates (2nd ed. London: Newnes, [1966]), this chronology consists of an alphabetical listing (pp. 11-278) of personal and place names, events and similar entries together with their dates and also a listing by month and day (pp. 281-428) of major events in history. See also Keller (D0286) and Haydn (D0280).

D0263 Coulson, John, ed. The Saints: A Concise Biographical Dictionary. New York: Hawthorn Books; London: Burns and Oates, 1958.

This 496 page dictionary contains brief sketches of the lives of 2230 saints; these are arranged alphabetically by the anglicized form of Christian name. The entries vary greatly in length and content, but for the most part data are adequate for basic reference inquiries. Numerous cross references, a calendar of feast days and list of references for further reading all add to the usefulness of Coulson, which compares favorably with Attwater (D0245). See also Delaney (D0265).

D0264 Daremberg, Charles Victor; Saglio, Edmond; and Pottier, Edmond, eds. Dictionnaire des Antiquités Grecques et Romaines d'après les Textes et les Monuments. 5 vols. in 10. Paris: Hachette et Cie, 1877-1919.

Originally issued in fifty-three fascicles and printed as a complete set at various dates, this highly respected encyclopedia covers most fields associated with the study of classical antiquity. Literature and biography are not covered, but religion receives adequate attention. The articles are detailed and scholarly and provide excellent bibliographical references. There are indexes of authors, subjects, Greek words and Latin words. For students requiring an in-depth reference work in this field, Daremberg is an indispensible compendium. For a German language work see Pauly (D0304).

D0265 Delaney, John J. Dictionary of Saints. Garden City, N.Y.: Doubleday and Company, 1980.

This up to date compendium of 5000 saints is useful both for the scholar and general reader. Entries vary from several lines to more than a column, providing accurate though not original or new information. A worthwhile introduction, ample cross references, an appendix listing saints as patrons and saints' symbols in art, a chronological chart of popes and world rulers and Byzantine and Roman calendars including locally honored saints all add to the usefulness of the volume. Saints are listed alphabetically under surnames. For lengthier accounts see Butler (D0377). See also Attwater (D0242, D0245) and Coulson (D0263).

D0266 [no entry]

D0267 DuBoulay, Francis Robin Houssemayne, comp. A Handlist of Medieval Ecclesiastical Terms. Local History Series, no. 9. London: National Council of Social Service for the Standing Conference for Local History, 1952.

This handlist of some 500 terms is intended primarily for beginning students and amateur historians doing research which involves the use of parochial or diocesan records. The terms are defined briefly and clearly, with frequent inclusion of references to other works which provide more detailed information. For those unfamiliar with medieval records this is a suitable starting point; others will find Latham (D0294) of more value.

D0268 Dunan, Marcel, gen. ed. Larousse Encyclopedia of Modern History from 1500 to the Present Day. Trans. by Delano Ames. English advisory ed.: John Roberts. New York: Harper and Row; London: Paul Hamlyn, 1974.

See also Morris (D0299).

D0269 Dunbar, Agnes Baillie Cunninghame. A Dictionary of Saintly Women. 2 vols. London: G. Bell and Sons, 1904-1905.

Although this work is based primarily on the Acta Sanctorum (D0388), it does not include the most significant female saints but rather those of whom bizarre tales can be told. For each woman Dunbar provides a brief biographical sketch, facts about the attendant cult and related symbolism, sources of information. An index of surnames is provided. Except for the rather unorthodox criteria for selecting entries, this is a helpful guide for those who lack access to Acta Sanctorum.

D0270 The Encyclopedia of Catholic Saints. 12 vols. Philadelphia, Pa.: Chilton Books, 1966.

Based on Robert Morel's Les Saints de Tous les Jours (Paris: Le Club du Livre Chrétien), this encyclopedia is arranged according to the calendar and deals with a single month in each volume. Biographies are provided for the major saint of each day, and lesser saints are merely listed. An index is provided in volume 12. This work is neither comprehensive nor detailed in content so should be consulted only where more substantial hagiographical encyclopedias are not available. See also The Book of Saints (D0255) and Holweck (D0281).

D0271 Encyclopedia of Living Divines and Christian Workers of All Denomina-

tions in Europe and America; Being a Supplement to Schaff-Herzog Encyclopedia of Religious Knowledge. New York: Funk and Wagnalls, 1887.

See also Barker (D0251).

D0272 Engelbert, Omer. The Lives of the Saints. Trans. by Christopher
and Anne Jackson Fremantle. New York: D. McKay Company; London: Thames
and Hudson, [1951].

Arranged according to the church calendar, this 532 page dictionary
provides brief biographical articles on major saints and also mentions
minor figures together with dates and place of birth. An index assists
users in locating specific entries. For more detailed treatment see Butler
(D0377).

D0273 Everyman's Dictionary of Dates. 6th ed. Rev. by Audrey Butler.
New York: E.P. Dutton and Company; London: J.M. Dent and Sons, [c. 1971].

First published in 1911, this standard guide provides a wide range of
facts, figures, chronologies, lists and tables under alphabetically arranged
headings. It is a widely consulted work for general reference purposes
and should be used with this in mind. Theological students will find
the dictionary useful for background information on historical areas
indirectly related to church history. See also Collison (D0262) and Haydn
(D0280).

D0274 Farmer, David Hugh. The Oxford Dictionary of Saints. Oxford: Clarendon Press, 1978.

Including bibliographical references and an index, this 435 page collection
treats saints which have been particularly venerated in the British Isles.
It includes many Celtic saints not listed in geographically less limited
guides but whose authenticity is open to question. Still, Farmer is scholarly
rather than hagiographical and provides basic factual information needed
to identify and place in context the various individuals listed. See also
Baring-Gould (D0343), Doble (D0436, D0437) and O'Hanlon (D0648),
all of which treat British saints.

D0275 Feret, Pierre. La Faculté de Théologie de Paris et Ses Docteurs
les Plus Célèbres. 8 vols. Paris: A. Picard et Fils, 1894-1904.

This biographical dictionary of an important theological faculty covers
the twelfth-fifteenth centuries (volumes 1-4) and sixteenth-seventeenth
centuries (volumes 5-8). The data on individual theologians are succinct
and clearly presented but in some cases require supplementing with
more recent studies. See also the sequel by Feret (D0276).

D0276 Feret, Pierre. La Faculté de Théologie de Paris et Ses Docteurs
les Plus Célèbres. Epoque Moderne. 7 vols. Paris: A. Picard et Fils, 1900-1910.

Covering the sixteenth (volumes 1-2), seventeenth (volumes 3-5) and
eighteenth (volumes 6-7) centuries, this sequel to Feret's earlier work
(D0275) includes "phases historiques" and "revue litteraire" for each
century. This is useful not only as a biographical directory to a specific
category of personalities but also for having a theological focus.

D0277 Fines, John. <u>Who's Who in the Middle Ages</u>. London: Anthony Blond, 1970.

Focusing primarily on Western Europe, Fines provides biographical sketches of 101 medieval personalities from various spheres (including the church). The notes on each person are scholarly, evaluative and nontechnical; but the choice of people is too selective to give Fines a primary place among biographical dictionaries of the period. There is an index of proper names.

D0278 Hammond, Nicholas Geoffrey Lemprière, and Scullard, Howard Hayes. <u>The Oxford Classical Dictionary</u>. 2nd ed. Oxford: Clarendon Press, 1970.

This successor to Cary (D0260) is a standard work in its field and provides excellent data and bibliographical notes on personalities and themes of historico-religious significance. For students of the NT, the intertestamental period and very early church Hammond can be a valuable reference source for basic factual information. Particularly useful is the extensive coverage of early Christian writers.

D0279 Hastings, James, ed. <u>Dictionary of the Apostolic Church</u>. With the assistance of John Alexander Selbie and John Chisolm Lambert. 2 vols. New York: Charles Scribner's Sons; Edinburgh: T. and T. Clark, 1915-1918.

Reprinted many times, most recently with <u>The Dictionary of Christ and the Gospels</u> as <u>Dictionary of the New Testament</u> (4 vols. Grand Rapids, Mich.: Baker Book House, 1973), this remains a valuable historico-geographical treatment of events, people and places important in the early church. It is a companion set to Hasting's other dictionary noted above and serves as a useful reference compendium on the later NT era.

D0280 Haydn, Joseph Timothy. <u>Haydn's Dictionary of Dates and Universal Information Relating to All Ages and Nations</u>. By the late Benjamin Vincent. Rev. and brought up to date by eminent authorities. 25th ed. London: Ward Lake, 1910; New York: G.P. Putnam's Sons, 1911. Reprint. Grosse Point, Mich.: Scholarly Press, 1968.

This general historical dictionary consists of alphabetically arranged headings under which various facts are listed chronologically. As a broadly based guide to historical data, Haydn is most useful for its European, especially British, content. Little attention is given to ecclesiastical matters <u>per se</u>. See also <u>Everyman's Dictionary</u> (D0273) and Little (D0295).

D0281 Holweck, Frederick George. <u>A Biographical Dictionary of the Saints, with a General Introduction on Hagiology</u>. St. Louis, Mo.: B. Herder Book Company, 1924. Reprint. Detroit, Mich.: Gale Research Company, 1969.

This Roman Catholic dictionary includes many personalities who have been sanctified by other traditions; in this sense it is a useful ecumenical guide to hagiography. The entries reflect careful and judicious scholarship and provide basic biographical data plus key sources of information. See also <u>The Encyclopedia of Catholic Saints</u> (D0270).

D0282 Howat, Gerald Malcolm David, gen. ed. <u>Dictionary of World History</u>. London: Thomas Nelson and Sons, 1973.

The 20,000 entries in this substantial dictionary cover people, events, movements, institutions and other factors in history. The notes on individuals are particularly useful for factual data, but for the church historian other aspects treated in Howat are less relevant and not always as accurate as expected. As a general historical dictionary, this work is of marginal reference value in ecclesiastical history. See also Langer (D0292).

┌0283 Hurwitz, Howa.d Lawrence. An Encyclopedic Dictionary of American History. New York: Washington Square Press, [1968].

The articles in this 882 page dictionary cover events, movements, major personalities, organizations and significant books in American history. Bibliographies are not provided, but there is an adequate index. For the beginning student or nonspecialist Hurwitz is useful as a first point of reference. For the student of church history Hurwitz need be consulted only when basic information on secular topics is required. See also Johnson (D0285) and Morris (D0298).

D0284 Jamieson, Robert. Cyclopaedia of Religious Biography: A Series of Memoirs of the Most Eminent Religious Characters of Modern Times, Intended for Family Reading. London: J.J. Griffin and Company; Glasgow: R. Griffin and Company, 1853.

This work contains biographies of eminent Christians belonging to almost every religious denomination, selected on the basis of being widely known because of their written works or activities. Entries are in quite discursive narrative form. This is a source of limited value for mid-nineteenth century religious biography. See also Barker (D0251).

D0285 Johnson, Thomas Herbert. The Oxford Companion to American History. In consultation with Harry Wish. New York: Oxford University Press, 1966.

Although remarkably poor in its coverage of topics in church history, this dictionary is useful for its general treatment of political, social, cultural and economic affairs. In nearly 5000 brief articles Johnson covers people, places, events and movements important in understanding most aspects of American history. Some longer articles include references and an appendix deals with the United States Constitution and its amendments. See also Hurwitz (D0283) and Morris (D0298).

D0286 Keller, Helen Rex. Dictionary of Dates. 2 vols. New York: Macmillan Company, 1934.

Based in part on Haydn (D0280), this compilation presents world history by date; it is arranged by country and then chronologically in separate parts for the old and new worlds. Events and related information are presented clearly and very concisely. Like other chronologies Keller is useful mainly as an indicator of events which occurred similtaneously with major ecclesiastical movements or trends. See also Collison (D0262) and Everyman's Dictionary (D0273).

D0287 Ketz, Louise Bilebof, managing ed. Dictionary of American History. Rev. ed. 8 vols. New York: Charles Scribner's Sons, 1976.

This complete revision of James Truslow Adams' Dictionary of American

History (2nd ed. 7 vols. New York: Charles Scribner's Sons, 1942-1963) contains 7200 new, updated or completely rewritten entries. It contains clear, concise articles on broad subjects and narrower topics in all areas of American history, although the coverage of religion is inadequate for more advanced students. There are numerous cross references and brief bibliographies for most entries. Volume 8 contains a detailed analytical index which is extremely helpful in tracing scattered information. For more basic requirements one should consult Adams' Concise Dictionary of American History (D0237). See also Martin (D0297).

D0288 Kraft, Heinrich. Kirchenväter Lexikon. Munich: Kösel Verlag, 1966.

This 509 page dictionary was first published as volume 5 of Texte der Kirchenväter. See also Lampe (D0291).

D0289 Kühner, Hans. Encyclopedia of the Papacy. Trans. by Kenneth J. Northcott. New York: Philosophical Library, [1958]; London: Peter Owen, [1959].

This translation of Lexikon der Päpste von Petrus bis Pius XII (Zürich: W. Classen, 1956) provides brief biographical sketches, historical background and significant dates for all popes to Pius XII. It is a good source of information for quick reference requirements, but in 249 pages it cannot provide the same detail as Mann (D0604) or von Pastor (D0656). See also Attwater (D0243).

D0290 Lalanne, Ludovic. Dictionnaire Historique de la France, Contenant pour l'Histoire Civile, Politique et Littéraire, la Biographie; La Chronologie les Assemblées Politiques, les Parlements, les Droits et Usages Féodaux des Notices sur les Principales Familles Nobles, le Blason, les Institutions et Etablissements Artistiques, Littéraires, Politiques et Scientifiques; La Liste des Académiciens; pour l'Histoire Militaire, les Guerres, les Ordres de Chevalerie, les Institutions et les Etablissements Militaires, etc.; pour l'Histoire Religieuse, les Conciles, les Institutions, les Usages et les Dignités Ecclésiastiques, les Ordres Monastiques, etc. 2e éd. 2 vols. Paris: Hachette et Cie, 1877. Reprint. 2 vols. Burt Franklin Bibliography and Reference Series, vol. 144. New York: Burt Franklin, [1968].

Like Chéruel (D0261) this is a useful handbook for French history before the nineteenth century. Lalanne deals with the persons, places and institutions related to the topics indicated in the title, providing brief factual articles suitable for basic reference requirements. The treatment of religious history, while not outstanding, is suitably objective.

D0291 Lampe, Geoffrey William Hugo, ed. A Patristic Greek Lexicon. 5 pts. Oxford: Clarendon Press, 1961-1967.

Generally regarded as the most important lexicon for patristic literature, Lampe sets out to interpret the theological and ecclesiastical vocabulary of Greek Christian authors from Clement of Rome to Theodore of Studium. It is not intended to replace Liddell and Scott's standard Greek lexicon but to supplement it by concentrating on the fuller range of patristic literature only marginally covered by this earlier work. Each entry includes a full definition and many references to patristic writers. There is a full list of authors and their works together with abbreviations (pp. xi-xiv). See also Kraft (D0288).

D0292 Langer, William Leonard, comp. and ed. An Encyclopedia of World History, Ancient, Medieval and Modern, Chronologically Arranged. 5th ed. Boston, Mass.: Houghton Mifflin Company, 1972.

This general historical dictionary focuses primarily on political history and provides useful outlines of events and movements to 1970. The maps, tables and other aids helpfully summarize the main trends in world history. For students who wish to place ecclesiastical events in their secular context Langer can be a useful guide. The New Illustrated Encyclopedia of World History (2 vols. New York: H.N. Abrams; London: Thames and Hudson, 1975) is virtually unchanged except in illustrative content. See also Howat (D0282).

D0293 Larned, Josephus Nelson. The New Larned History for Ready Reference, Reading and Research; the Actual Words of the World's Best Historians, Biographers and Specialists; a Complete System of History for All Uses, Extending to All Countries and Subjects and Representing the Better and Newer Literature of History. Rev. ed. Ed.-in-chief: D.E. Smith. Associate eds.: Charles Seymour et al. 12 vols. Springfield, Mass.: C.A. Nichols Publishing Company, 1922-1924.

First published in 1893-1895 as History for Ready Reference, this diction-ary of world history is arranged alphabetically by subject. Under each heading the entries consist primarily of extracts from other sources together with additional facts and definitions. The extracts include full bibliographical references to the original sources. While Larned is not devoted specifically to church history, it does provide information on many ancillary areas of importance in the study of ecclesiastical history. See also Langer (D0292).

D0294 Latham, Ronald E., ed. Revised Medieval Latin Word-List from British and Irish Sources. London: Oxford University Press for the British Academy, 1965.

Based on the Medieval Latin Word-List from British and Irish Sources edited by J.H. Baxter and Charles Johnson in 1934 and last reprinted in 1962, this very useful glossary concentrates on Latin words which are non-classical in either form or meaning. Each entry consists of a number of elements, including the Latin word, variant or synonymous forms, English equivalents, and dates. There are also numerous cross references. The notes on arrangement of entries, a list of abbreviations and a select bibliography precede the main part of the work, which is an invaluable guide for those using medieval Latin texts of various types. See also DuBoulay (D0267).

D0295 Little, Charles Eugene. Cyclopedia of Classified Dates, with an Exhaus-tive Index, for the Use of Students of History, and for All Persons Who Desire Speedy Access to the Facts and Events Which Relate to the Histories of the Various Countries of the World, from the Earliest Recorded Dates. New York: Funk and Wagnalls, 1900. Reprint. New York: Funk and Wagnalls, 1905.

Arranged by country and then by period and subject (including the church), this chronology provides an unusual approach to the dates of major events in history. Although a detailed index (pp. 1163-1454) is provided, Little remains a difficult tool to consult and for this reason is less highly regarded than other chronologies. See also Haydn (D0280).

D0296 Low, Sidney James Mark, and Pulling, Frederick Sanders. The Dictionary of English History. New ed. Rev. by Fossey John Cobb Hearnshaw et al.
London: Cassell and Company, 1928.

First published in 1884, this historical dictionary for the general reader
contains brief entries on topics, personalities and events in English history.
Brief bibliographies, now rather dated, accompany most articles. Low
is adequate for general historical topics but is not suitable for details
of ecclesiastical affairs or figures. For British history see Steinberg
(D0313).

D0297 Martin, Michael Rheta, and Gelber, Leonard. The New Dictionary
of American History. New York: Philosophical Library, 1952.

This dictionary attempts to provide a ready reference source on American
history, including political and military events, economics, social welfare,
literature, education. Biographical studies of prominent personalities
are included. There are useful cross references in many of the entries
which are around 100 words in length on average. See also Adams (D0237)
and Ketz (D0287).

D0298 Morris, Richard Brandon, ed. Encyclopedia of American History.
Bicentennial ed. Associate ed.: Jeffrey Brandon Morris. New York: Harper
and Row, 1976.

More a chronological guide than a dictionary of events, this work is in
three parts: basic chronology of major political and military events
to 1970, topical chronology (including thought and culture), biographical
sketches of 500 notable personalities. There are no bibliographies or
references to sources. Morris is of marginal value to church historians
seeking data on secular events of a given period. See also Hurwitz (D0283)
and Johnson (D0285).

D0299 Morris, Richard Brandon, and Irwin, Graham W., eds. Harper Encyclopedia of the Modern World: A Concise Reference History from 1760 to
the Present. New York: Harper and Row, 1970.

This dictionary of world history is arranged in two parts: "basic chronology"
deals with political, military and diplomatic history by geographical
regions; "topical chronology" covers economic, social, cultural and intellectual history. In each section data are presented concisely and accurately,
but there is little information of a specifically religious nature. However,
Morris is useful for general historical details. See also Langer (D0292)
and Dunan (D0268).

D0300 Mourre, Michel. Dictionnaire d'Histoire Universelle. 2 vols. Paris:
Editions Universitaires, [1968].

This dictionary, while concentrating on political movements and institutions, does deal to some extent with events, people and places in other
spheres. The articles, some of which include bibliographies, present
concise factual information of continuing reference value. For students
able to read French and without access to the larger English language
dictionaries with a European focus, Mourre can be a useful guide to

historical events and personalities. See also Howat (D0282) for an English
language work.

D0301 Moyer, Elgin Sylvester. The Wycliffe Biographical Dictionary of
the Church. Rev. ed. Ed. and additional text by Earl Cairns. Chicago, Ill.:
Moody Press, 1982.

Entitled Who Was Who in Church History in the original edition, this 449
page revision contains brief biographical sketches of more than 2000
religious leaders, both Christian and non-Christian, who have been influential in the history of the church. Particular emphasis is placed on individuals of the nineteenth and twentieth centuries, especially those important
in Protestant circles. An outline of church history and a chronological
index are included. Entries are arranged alphabetically. The work would
have benefited from bibliographical references; nonetheless it is suitable
for teachers and general readers. See also Barker (D0251).

D0302 Ollard, Sidney Leslie; Crosse, Gordon; and Bond, Maurice Francis, eds.
A Dictionary of English Church History. 3rd ed. New York: Morehouse-Gorham;
London: A.R. Mowbray and Company, [1948].

First published in 1912, this dictionary covers only the provinces of
Canterbury and York. It consists of signed articles on specific topics,
personalities and events in the areas of history, doctrine, liturgy, ritual,
vestments, architecture, theological controversies and movements. Written
from an Anglo-Catholic viewpoint, it provides interesting insights into a
wide range of fields related to the history of Anglicanism.

D0303 Pauly, August Friedrich von. Der Kleine Pauly: Lexikon der Antike.
Auf der Grundlage von Pauly's Real-Encyclopädie der classischen Altertums-
wissenschaft unter Mitwirkung zahlreicher Fachgelehrter. Hrsg. von Konrat
Julius Fürchtegott Ziegler und Walther Sontheimer. 5 vols. Stuttgart: Alfred
Druckenmüller Verlag, 1964-1975.

This abridged version of Pauly (D0304) takes account of recent advances
in scholarship and includes updated bibliographies. The articles tend
to be condensations of entries in the parent work and often include
references to the longer articles for those who wish additional information.
In most respects this work meets the same needs as Pauly-Wissowa.
"Nachträge" are found in volumes 1 and 3. See also Andresen (D0240).

D0304 Pauly, August Friedrich von. Paulys Real-Encyclopädie der Classischen
Altertumswissenschaft. Neue Bearb. begonnen von Georg Wissowa. Unter
Mitwirkung von Wilhelm Kroll und Karl Mittelhaus. Hrsg. von Konrad Ziegler.
33 vols. in 49 pts. Supplementary vol. 1- . Stuttgart: Alfred Drückenmuller,
1894- .

Originally published by Metzler in Stuttgart, this impressive compendium
consists of two main sequences: 1. Reihe covering A-Q and completed
in 1963, 2. Reihe covering R-Z and completed in 1967. Supplementary
volumes, which are still being published, are geared to the main set,
making Pauly-Wissowa extremely difficult to use. Nevertheless, the
patient user is well rewarded, as the coverage of classical literature,
history, antiquities, biography and related areas is unsurpassed. The
"Nachträge und Berichtigungen" which appear in many volumes are listed
in volume 23. For advanced students and scholars of classical-biblical

relationships Pauly is an indispensible guide. For a condensed version one should consult Der Kleine Pauly (D0303). See also Reallexikon für Antike und Christentum (D0306).

D0305 Pelzer, Auguste. Abréviations Latines Médiévales: Supplement au "Dizionario di Abbreviature Latine", Ed. Italiane de Adriano Cappelli. 2. éd. Louvain: Publications Universitaires; Paris: Béatrice-Nauwelaerts, 1966.

This supplement to Cappelli (D0258) covers both new and additional symbols as well as additional definitions where appropriate.

D0306 Reallexikon für Antike und Christentum: Sachwörterbuch zur Aus-einandersetzung des Christentums mit der Antiken Welt. In Verbindung mit Franz Joseph Dölger und Hans Lietzmann und unter besonderer Mitwirkung von Jan Hendrik Wasznik und Leopold Wenger. Hrsg. von Theodor Klausner. Vol. 1- . Stuttgart: K.W. Hiersemann, 1950- .

Published initially from Leipzig and employing the services of various cooperating editors, this German encyclopedia of the classical world and early Christianity (up to the sixth century A.D.) contains scholarly, signed articles, some of which are quite lengthy, with bibliographies. Entries are both factual and interpretive, providing a valuable source of information for students of the classical world and early Christianity. See also Pauly (D0303, D0304).

D0307 Roeder, William S. Dictionary of European History. New York: Philo-sophical Library, [1954].

This alphabetically arranged dictionary contains concise information on major events and prominent personalities in European history from 500 A.D. to the early twentieth century. Roeder is reasonably accurate but lacks the depth of information required by advanced students. Ecclesiastical history is not a strong point of the work, which is useful only for data on secular history.

D0308 Routh, Charles Richard Nairne, gen. ed. Who's Who in History. 5 vols. Oxford: Basil Blackwell and Mott, 1960-1975.

Published under various imprints (volume 5 in New York by Harper and Row, 1975), this work is aimed particularly at the general reader and seeks to provide a portrait of the specific period to which each volume is devoted (55 B.C.-1485 A.D., 1485-1603, 1603-1714, 1714-1789, 1789-1837). Coverage is limited to Britain, and each volume is by a different specialist. Approximately 200-300 individuals are dealt with chronologically within each period. For each personality the biographical details seek to indicate his particular role and place in history, and these are supported by references to the relevant standard biographies. While not focusing particularly on church history, Routh does treat a number of figures relevant to this aspect of history and is of some use to the beginning student. Each volume is provided with a detailed index.

D0309 Seyffert, August Oskar. A Dictionary of Classical Antiquities: Myth-ology, Religion, Literature, Art. Rev. and ed. by Henry Nettleship and John Edwin Sandys. New York: Macmillan Company, 1891. Reprint. New York: Meridian Books, 1956; London: Allen and Unwin, 1957.

This compact dictionary of 716 pages covers all aspects of the classical world briefly and succinctly. Terms are defined adequately for the beginner, and there are both cross references and references to sources. A general index is provided. For those seeking information on various aspects of the biblical milieu Seyffert is a useful reference volume. See also Avi-Yonah (D0249) and Warrington (D0315).

D0310 Smith, William, and Cheetham, Samuel, eds. Dictionary of Christian Antiquities; Being a Continuation of the "Dictionary of the Bible". 2 vols. Boston, Mass.: Little, Brown and Company; London: John Murray, 1875-1880. Reprint. 2 vols. New York: Kraus Reprint, 1968.

Published with a slightly different subtitle in the British edition, this work contains long, signed articles on matters connected with church organization from the beginning to the age of Charlemagne: officers, legislation, discipline, revenue, social life, ceremonial, music, vestments, architecture, art and symbolism. The coverage does not extend to topics covered by the companion work (D0311). There are exact references to many sources and bibliographies of continuing value. Overall Smith may be regarded as a useful compilation for students requiring broadly based background data on a wide range of ecclesiastical topics. It should not be consulted for precise or current information. See also Reallexikon für Antike und Christentum (D0306).

D0311 Smith, William, and Wace, Henry. A Dictionary of Christian Biography, Literature, Sects and Doctrines during the First Eight Centuries. 4 vols. Boston, Mass.: Little, Brown and Company; London: John Murray, 1877-1887. Reprint. New York: AMS Press, 1967; Nedeln: Kraus Reprint, c. 1979.

This companion to Smith's Dictionary of Christian Antiquities (D0310) aims to treat all persons connected with the church to the age of Charlemagne about whom anything is know, all literature connected with them and controversies about doctrine and discipline in which they engaged. Emphasis is on the fathers, and special attention is paid to subjects and people in English, Scottish and Irish history. Articles are signed, and there are some bibliographies containing predominantly Protestant works. This has appeared in a single volume condensation entitled Murray's Dictionary of Christian Biography; there is also a revision of the entire work edited by Wace and Piercy (D0314).

D0312 Souter, Alexander, comp. A Glossary of Later Latin to 600 A.D. Oxford: Clarendon Press, 1949. Reprint. Oxford: Clarendon Press, 1957.

This supplement to standard Latin dictionaries such as that by Lewis and Short focuses on developments in the language between 180 and 600 A.D. It is thus useful for those reading the works of St. Augustine, Gregory the Great and Cassiodorus, among others. Each word in the dictionary includes a brief definition and in many cases the part of speech, Greek derivation and reference to a work in which the word appears. A list of authors quoted and abbreviations precedes the dictionary proper.

D0313 Steinberg, Sigfrid Henry, and Evans, Ivor H., eds. Steinberg's Dictionary of British History. 2nd ed. London: Edward Arnold, 1970; New York: St. Martin's Press, 1971.

This revision of A New Dictionary of British History covers ecclesiastical, political, economic, legal, administrative and constitutional history in brief but adequate entries for basic reference purposes. Biographies are not dealt with, and bibliographies are not provided. Steinberg interprets "British" to include the Commonwealth. For British church history this is an acceptable general compendium.

D0314 Wace, Henry, and Piercy, William C., eds. A Dictionary of Christian Biography and Literature to the End of the Sixth Century A.D., with an Account of the Principal Sects and Heresies. Boston, Mass.: Little, Brown and Company; London: John Murray, 1911.

This revised and abridged version of Smith (D0311) adds later references but does not supersede the earlier work, which is still useful for its long articles, coverage of minor names and of the seventh and eighth centuries. This abridged edition includes bibliographies.

D0315 Warrington, John. Everyman's Classical Dictionary, 800 B.C.-A.D. 337. 2nd ed. New York: E.P. Dutton Company; London: J.M. Dent and Company, 1969.

This 537 page dictionary deals with a broad range of persons and subjects from the classical world. In the case of writers (including philosophers) Warrington lists useful editions and translations of their works. For students of the early NT and patristic eras this is a useful dictionary for basic information. See also Seyffert (D0309), which is more comprehensive.

CHURCH HISTORY: HANDBOOKS

D0316 Acta Sanctorum Quotquot Toto Orbe Coluntur, Vel a Catholicis Scriptoribus Celebrantur Quae ex Latinis et Graecis, Aliarumque Gentium Antiquis Monumentis Collegit, Digessit, Notis Illustravit Johannes Bollandus Servata Primigenia Scriptorum Phrasi. Ad. Acta Sanctorum Supplementum. Volumen Complectens Auctaria Octobris et Tabulas Generales. Scilicet Ephemerides et Indicem Alphabeticum Decem Priorum Mensium. Cura et Opere L.M. Rigollot. 2 vols. Paris, 1875.

This work is a supplement to Carnandet (D0388).

D0317 Adams, James Truslow, ed.-in-chief. Atlas of American History. Rev. ed. Ed. by Kenneth T. Jackson. New York: Charles Scribner's Sons, [1978].

Designed to supplement Adams' Dictionary of American History (D0287), this compilation contains 198 chronologically arranged maps together with a full table of contents and index of place names. Maps are clearly arranged to show military history, population growth and geographical expansion from the early explorations to modern times. The revised edition includes maps of utopian experiments, abolition of slavery and other topics of interest in the history of American Christianity, but in general Adams should be used as an atlas of secular aspects of American history. See also Lord (D0593) and Paullin (D0658).

D0318 Addison, James Thayer. The Episcopal Church in the United States, 1789-1931. New York: Charles Scribner's Sons, 1951. Reprint. Hamden, Conn.: Archon Books, 1969.

In five main parts this volume deals chronologically with the history of the Episcopal Church in the United States for the period indicated. A table of dates in English church history, 1558-1799, is provided, as well as a list of books (pp. 382-386) referred to in the notes, and an index. This work usefully provides adequate background on Anglicanism in England prior to its beginnings in North America. See also Albright (D0321) and Manross (D0605).

D0319 Ahlstrom, Sydney E. A Religious History of the American People. New Haven, Conn.: Yale University Press, 1972.

This massive work of 1158 pages seeks to set American religious history within the larger context of world history. Ahlstrom provides detailed but concise data on the major movements, developments and personalities of American Christianity in a manner which is objective and factual. Extensive bibliographies (pp. 1097-1128) add greatly to the reference value of this survey, and a full index is included. See also Gaustad (D0490), Hudson (D0541), Mead (D0614), Olmstead (D0650) and Smith (D0712).

D0320 Albers, Petrus Henricus. Manuel d'Histoire Ecclésiastique. Adaptation de la seconde édition hollandaise par René Hedde. Nouvelle éd. revue par Paulin Jouet. 2 vols. Paris: J. Gabalda et Cie, 1939.

Covering the entire history of the church, this manual is a translation of Handboek der Algemeen Kerkgeschiedenis. Each period is treated clearly and succinctly, providing adequate footnotes and bibliographical references for further study. Although Roman Catholic in bias, Albers is a sound introduction for students new to the study of church history. See also de Jong (D0552).

D0321 Albright, Raymond Wolf. A History of the Protestant Episcopal Church. New York: Macmillan Company, 1964.

In many ways a successor to Manross (D0605), this 406 page history covers the period from the first Anglican settlements in America to 1963. Useful bibliographical sketches are included, as well as discussion of important themes. There is a wealth of factual material in the volume. See also Addison (D0318).

D0322 Alekseev, Vasilii Ivanovich. Materials for the History of the Russian Orthodox Church in the U.S.S.R. Vol. 1- . [East European Fund) Mimeographed Series, nos. 61, 70- . New York: Research Program on the U.S.S.R., 1954- .

D0323 Alzog, Johannes Baptist. Manual of Universal Church History. Trans. with additions from the 9th and last German ed. by F.J. Pabisch and Thomas S. Byrne. 3 vols. Cincinnati, Ohio: R. Clarke Company, 1903.

This encyclopedic Roman Catholic history of the church covers all periods to the end of the nineteenth century. Individual bibliographies are provided for each epoch and subdivision. Numerous chronological tables and a full index add to the reference value of Alzog, which is useful as a fact book and basic reference work. See also Bihlmeyer (D0360) and Kirsch (D0560).

D0324 Anderson, Charles S. Augsburg Historical Atlas of Christianity in the Middle Ages and Reformation. Minneapolis, Minn.: Augsburg Publishing House, [1967].

The thirty-two maps in this atlas cover Christian history between 590 and 1648. Each topical map is accompanied by an explanatory text suitable for beginning students.

D0325 Armstrong, Maurice Whitman; Loetscher, Lefferts Augustine; and Anderson, Charles A. The Presbyterian Enterprise: Sources of American Presbyterian History. Philadelphia, Pa.: Westminster Press, 1956.

This collection contains letters, journals, diaries, periodical articles, minutes and other documents illustrating the history of American Presbyterianism from 1706 to 1956. An appendix of documents quoted and an author/subject index are included. See also Sweet (D0729).

D0326 Atiya, Aziz Suryal. A History of Eastern Christianity. Notre Dame, Ind.: University of Notre Dame Press; London: Methuen and Company, 1968.

This classic study deals with non-Greek Eastern churches, including Copts, Maronites, churches of Antioch, Armenia, South India and the vanished churches of Carthage, Nubia and Pentapolis. Copious bibliographical footnotes and a select bibliography are included. Written by a member of the Coptic Church, this is nonetheless an objective study which adds substantially to knowledge of this subject. See also Harder (D0522), Neale (D0638) and Schmemann (D0700).

D0327 Aubert, Roger, et al. Die Kirche in der Gegenwart. Vol. 1- . Handbuch der Kirchengeschichte, Bd. 6. Freiburg im Breisgau: Herder, 1971.

See also Heussi (D0531) and Schmidt (D0702).

D0328 Ayer, Joseph Cullen. A Source Book for Ancient Church History, from the Apostolic Age to the Close of the Conciliar Period. New York: Charles Scribner's Sons, 1913. Reprint. New York: AMS Press, 1970.

Covering early church history to 787 A.D., this is a standard collection of sources which is of special value to students new to the field. Selected sources are arranged by period and then by topic within each era. Short annotations on the accuracy and authority of individual texts are included, as are indications of where additional materials may be found. An index is provided. See also Fremantle (D0480), Kee (D0554) and Stevenson (D0722).

D0329 Ayerst, David, and Fisher, A.S.T. Records of Christianity. Vol. 1- . New York: Barnes and Noble; Oxford: Basil Blackwell and Mott, 1971- .

This collection of source materials seeks to provide the nonspecialist with background information on the particular period covered in each volume. Thus volume 1 on Christianity in the Roman Empire includes extracts from various contemporary sources, including items by both secular and religious figures. Chapters are arranged topically and present brief extracts from standard translations or versions chosen to give students some insight into the thinking of those who shaped the period. Volume 2 on Christendom covers the fifth to the fourteenth centuries and follows the same pattern as the first volume. Each compilation stands on its own and includes a detailed table of contents, charts and maps, illustrations, and indexes of biblical references, places, persons and subjects. See also Barry (D0345), Bettenson (D0354) and Kidd (D0557).

D0330 Bainton, Roland Herbert. <u>The Age of the Reformation</u>. Princeton, N.J.: Van Nostrand, 1956.

This 191 page account of the Reformation is in two parts. The first provides an interpretive account; the second contains selected readings organized under twelve headings (Luther's early development, Calvinism, the Catholic Reformation, etc.). A bibliography (pp. 186-188) and an index add to the value of this handy history and sourcebook. See also Elton (D0459), Hillerbrand (D0537) and Sykes (D0730).

D0331 Bainton, Roland Herbert. <u>Christendom: A Short History of Christianity and Its Impact on Western Civilization</u>. 2 vols. New York: Harper and Row, [1966].

Originally published as <u>The Horizon History of Christianity</u> (New York: American Heritage Publishing Company, 1964) and also available as <u>The Penguin History of Christianity</u> (Harmondsworth: Penguin Books, 1968), this history provides a well organized and readable account for the undergraduate student. Volume 1 covers the period from the birth of Christ to the Reformation, volume 2 from the Reformation to the present. Each volume contains selected bibliographies, illustrations and an index. The many subheadings make the volumes easily usable for quick reference purposes. See also Latourette (D0568) and Walker (D0748).

D0332 Bainton, Roland Herbert. <u>Early Christianity</u>. Princeton, N.J.: Van Nostrand, 1960.

This brief work by an eminent church historian tells the history of Christianity during its first five centuries in part 1. Part 2 contains a collection of documents and readings arranged topically (the Church and society, the empire and the Church, etc.). A bibliography (pp. 179-182), a chronological table of emperors, church fathers and events, and an index add to the reference value of this handy interpretive history and sourcebook. See also Chadwick (D0395), Conzelmann (D0408), Davies (D0422), Frend (D0481) and Wand (D0749).

D0333 Bainton, Roland Herbert. <u>The Reformation of the Sixteenth Century</u>. Boston, Mass.: Beacon Press, c. 1952. Reprint. Boston, Mass.: Beacon Press, 1959.

In thirteen chapters this volume treats such aspects of the Reformation as Luther's reform, Anabaptism, Calvinism, and the Reformation and the political, economic and domestic spheres. A bibliography (pp. 262-268) and an index are included. See also Chadwick (D0398), Grimm (D0504) and Hillerbrand (D0534).

D0334 Bainton, Roland Herbert. <u>Women of the Reformation in Germany and Italy</u>. Minneapolis, Minn.: Augsburg Publishing House, 1971.

This useful study contains brief biographical sketches of sixteen women who played a prominent role in both Protestant and Roman Catholic reform movements. It is popular in tone, but given a lack of scholarly material on this subject will be of interest to students as well as the general public, and the notes and bibliographies provide guidance for further research.

D0335 Baker, Derek, ed. The Materials, Sources and Methods of Ecclesiastical History: Papers Read at the Twelfth Summer Meeting and Thirteenth Winter Meeting of the Ecclesiastical History Society. Studies in Church History, vol. 11. New York: Barnes and Noble; Oxford: Basil Blackwell, 1975.

The topics treated in this collection include particular documents or types of documents; methodology and historiography; the contribution of archeological, socio-linguistic and socio-cultural techniques to church history; the place and role of the contemporary church historian. Although somewhat eclectic in content, this is an invaluable compendium for the advanced student about to embark on historical research. See also Woolley (D0766).

D0336 Baker, Robert Andrew. The Southern Baptist Convention and Its People, 1607-1972. Nashville, Tenn.: Broadman Press, 1974.

This 477 page history provides a well organized account of Southern Baptist associations, conventions, leading figures, disputes, struggles for political and religious liberty and activities up to the 1970s. Much statistical information is included, particularly for the nineteenth and twentieth centuries. See also Olson (D0651) and Torbet (D0739).

D0337 Baker, Robert Andrew. A Summary of Christian History. Nashville, Tenn.: Broadman Press, [1959].

D0338 Baldwin, Marshall Whithed, ed. Christianity through the Thirteenth Century. New York: Harper and Row, 1970.

This collection contains documents in English which illustrate Christian life during four periods: the early patristic age, the Carolingian era, the tenth through mid-twelfth centuries, the high middle ages (1150-1300). Each section presents material on a wide range of topics of interest to the student, and brief bibliographies are provided for further study. An index of subjects and personalities is provided. See also Bettenson (D0354).

D0339 Baldwin, Marshall Whithed. The Medieval Church. Ithaca, N.Y.: Cornell University Press, 1953.

This 124 page volume provides a concise introduction to the religious life and political organization of the middle ages. Narrative essays cover an interesting range of topics from Christian origins in Israel to the evolution of thought in the medieval church. It is a useful starting point for students unfamiliar with Christianity in the middle ages. See also Volz (D0746).

D0340 Bardenhewer, Otto, et al., eds. Bibliothek der Kirchenväter: Eine Auswahl Patristischer Werke in Deutscher Übersetzung. [Neue Aufl.] 81 vols. Munich: Kösel-Pustet, 1911-1938.

This work was published in two series of sixty-one and twenty volumes respectively. See also Texte und Untersuchungen (D0734) and Testimonia (D0733).

D0341 Bardenhewer, Otto. Geschichte der Altkirchlichen Literatur. 2. Aufl. 5 vols. Freiburg im Breisgau: Herder, 1913-1932. Reprint. 5 vols. Darmstadt: Wissenschaftliche Buchgesellschaft, 1962.

A leading work in its field, this coverage of Eastern and Western literature to the end of the fifth century is arranged by author, with biographical data, quotations and bibliographies which are particularly useful for older studies. A semi-analytical name index is provided for each volume. See also Schanz (D0697).

D0342 Bardenhewer, Otto. Patrology: The Lives and Works of the Fathers of the Church. Trans. from the 2nd ed. by Thomas J. Shahan. Freiburg im Breisgau and St. Louis, Mo.: Herder, 1908.

This useful reference manual intended primarily for seminarians provides three types of material for each of the fathers: a brief bibliographical sketch; a general statement about his writings, their character and doctrines; a bibliography, indicating complete editions, selections and separate works, translations, works about each individual. This is a useful guide to older works in the field, and there is a third edition which has not yet been translated from the German. See also Altaner (D0004), Cayré (D0393), Quasten (D0675) and Tixeront (D0737).

D0343 Baring-Gould, Sabine, and Fisher, John. The Lives of the British Saints: The Saints of Wales and Cornwall and Such Irish Saints As Have Dedications in Britain. 4 vols. London: C.J. Clark for the Honourable Society of Cymmrodorion, 1907-1913.

Like Butler (D0376) in its uncritical acceptance of both historical and legendary hagiographical data, this comprehensive British guide includes a useful, scholarly introduction to the subject. This is followed by an alphabetically arranged series of lives, which include biographical and bibliographical information of some depth. Baring-Gould relies heavily on primary sources, and many of these are quoted. Illustrations cover symbols, maps, saints themselves and genealogical tables. The work is well indexed. See also the two works by Doble (D0436, D0437) and the volume by O'Hanlon (D0648).

D0344 Baring-Gould, Sabine. The Lives of the Saints, with Introduction and Additional Lives of English Martyrs, Cornish, Scottish and Welsh Saints, and a Full Index to the Entire Work. Rev. ed. 16 vols. Edinburgh: J. Grant, 1914.

First published in 1872-1882, this standard work is arranged day by day throughout the year, providing biography, illustrations, information on source and history of the cult, and attempting to distinguish fact from legend. Volume 16 is an appendix volume containing indexes. The revised edition has been published in various imprints. The work is now quite dated but remains an interesting hagiographical compendium which provides particularly good coverage of pre- and post-Reformation British saints. See also Butler (D0376) and Delehaye (D0426).

D0345 Barry, Colman James, ed. Readings in Church History. 3 vols. West-minster, Md.: Newman Press, 1960-1965.

This representative collection of primary materials illustrates important events in all periods of church history from the beginning to the present. It includes many of the treaties, decrees, addresses, reports, papal bulls, encyclicals and selections from other writings which have influenced the course of ecclesiastical history. Readings are grouped chronologically, and references to both original documents and translations are provided. Volume 1 includes a useful reference table to standard textbooks in church history. See also Ayerst (D0329), Bettenson (D0354) and Kidd (D0557).

D0346 Batiffol, Pierre Henri. Le Catholicisme des Origines à Saint Léon. 4 vols. Paris: J. Gabalda et Compagnie; Paris: Librairie Lecoffre, 1909-1924.

Published under various imprints, each volume in this series exists in a different edition. The collection as a whole is intended as an apologetic study of the origin and history of the church to 451. Although clearly written and adequate in its detailed coverage of the period, the views expressed often lack objectivity and a sound basis in historical fact. There are many useful bibliographical references. For a more balanced Roman Catholic survey one should consult Jedin (D0548), Bilhmeyer (D0360) or McSorley (D0600).

D0347 Baudot, Jules Leon, and Chaussin, Leon, eds. Vies des Saints et des Bienheureux selon l'Ordre du Calendrier, avec l'Historique des Fêtes par les RR. PP. Bénédictins de Paris. 13 vols. Paris: Letouzey et Ané, 1935-1959.

Similar in content to Butler (D0376), this is a chronologically arranged guide to saints as they appear in the church calendar. Each saint is pro-vided with a lengthy biographical sketch based on the Acta Sanctorum (D0388) or similar sources; bibliographical information is provided after each article. The final volume contains supplementary information related to moveable feasts of the church year and indexes.

D0348 Baur, Ferdinand Christian. Geschichte der Christlichen Kirche. 5 vols. Tübingen: L.F. Fues, 1863-1877. Reprint. 5 vols. Leipzig: Zentralantiquariat der D.D.R., 1969.

See also Krüger (D0562).

D0349 Bayerischer Schulbuch Verlag. Grosser Historischer Weltatlas. [5. Aufl.] Pt. 1- . Munich: Bayerischer Schulbuch Verlag, 1972- .

Following the pattern of earlier editions, the parts in this very well produced collection of maps cover prehistory, ancient and medieval history, modern history since 1500. Each part appears separately and contains a detailed index of place names plus a full table of contents. While the work is in German, the excellent cartography and map reproduction make this a very pleasant work to use. It is worth consulting by those with a general interest in the broad aspects of history around the world. Religious topics are dealt with in passing, and they are usefully placed in the context of wider events. See also Stier (D0723). Less detailed but more suitable for English language readers are the atlases by van der Meer (D0615, D0617), Muir (D0633), Rand McNally (D0679) and Shepherd (D0710).

D0350 Beck, Hans Georg. Kirche und Theologische Literatur im Byzantinischen Reich. Handbuch der Altertumswissenschaft, 12. Abt.: Byzantinisches Handbuch, 2. T., 1. Bd. Munich: Beck, 1959.

This substantial 835 page compendium covers such aspects of the Eastern Church as organization and government; liturgics, hymnology, hagiography; theology, and the history of Byzantine theological literature. It focuses on the period from Justinian to 1453. A wealth of bibliographical information is included. For readers of German this is an indispensible source for the period concerned.

D0351 Benedict, David. A General History of the Baptist Denomination in America and Other Parts of the World. 2 vols. Boston, Mass.: Lincoln and Edmands, 1813. Reprint. Freeport, N.Y.: Books for Libraries Press, 1971.

Reprinted many times, this early nineteenth century history of the Baptists attempts to provide general coverage, although some individual churches have been given more detailed treatment than others. The work is mainly of interest from an historical point of view. For a work with a more specifically American focus see Torbet (D0739).

D0352 Bengtson, Hermann. Introduction to Ancient History. Trans. from the 6th ed. by R.I. Frank and Frank D. Gillard. Berkeley, Calif.: University of California Press, 1970.

This standard survey of ancient history is a translation of Einführung in die Alte Geschichte in which the first part consists of lengthy essays on broad areas of historiography. The second part contains a detailed bibliography arranged according to the Cambridge Ancient History (D0379, D0452). Bengtson is useful for the student pursuing studies in ancient Near Eastern history and early biblical history.

D0353 Bergendorff, Conrad John Immanuel. The Church of the Lutheran Reformation: A Historical Survey of Lutheranism. St. Louis, Mo.: Concordia Publishing House, 1967.

This survey is well organized and readable. It does not include footnotes, but there is a bibliography of works in several languages. It is suitable as a handbook on Lutheran history, theology and practice for students, although it has been criticized for omitting reference to some important sources. See also Mackinnon (D0597).

D0354 Bettenson, Henry Scowcroft, ed. Documents of the Christian Church. 2nd ed. London: Oxford University Press, 1963. Reprint. London: Oxford University Press, 1967.

First published in 1943, this standard collection of writings illustrates the development of Christianity and its doctrines by including relatively few documents in full instead of brief selections from many sources. The translations are lucid and readily understood by the beginner, for whom this is a useful single volume alternative to The Library of Christian Classics (D0584) and similar multivolume collections. Part 1 is arranged according to doctrines and covers writings to 451; part 2 is arranged chronologically and covers from Chalcedon to the recent past. Appendixes list councils of the church, and both an index and a bibliography are provided. See also Ayerst (D0329), Baldwin (D0338), Barry (D0345) and

Kidd (D0557).

D0355 Bettenson, Henry Scowcroft, ed. and trans. The Early Christian Fathers: A Selection from the Writings of the Fathers from St. Clement of Rome to St. Athanasius. London: Oxford University Press, 1956. Reprint. London: Oxford University Press, 1969.

As a selection from key writings of the early fathers, Bettenson manages to touch upon most of the essential teachings by this seminal group of churchmen. Material is arranged topically to allow students to compare viewpoints and developments quite easily. See also Bettenson's The Later Christian Fathers (D0356), as well as Musurillo (D0636), Staniforth (D0717) and Wiles (D0759).

D0356 Bettenson, Henry Scowcroft, ed. and trans. The Later Christian Fathers: A Selection from the Writings of the Fathers from St. Cyril of Jerusalem to St. Leo the Great. London: Oxford University Press, 1970.

Following the same topical format as The Early Christian Fathers (D0355), Bettenson provides significant extracts from key writings of Ambrose, Jerome, Augustine and other fathers. A wide range of historical and theological issues is touched upon in this collection, which is a useful compendium for students.

D0357 Biblia Patristica: Index des Citations et Allusions Bibliques dans la Littérature Patristique. Vol. 1- . Paris: Editions du Centre National de la Recherche Scientifique, 1975- .

Prepared in cooperation with the Centre d'Analyse et de Documentation Patristique in Strasbourg, this computer produced index offers correspondence tables arranged according to books of the OT and lists in abbreviated form the following information: biblical book, chapter and verse, relevant patristic author, his book, chapter, paragraph and line in which the relevant OT passage is mentioned. The first volume covers the origins to Clement of Alexandria and Tertullian; the second volume treats the third century (excluding Origen).

D0358 Bibliotheca Sanctorum. 13 vols. Rome: Istituto Giovanni XXIII nella Pontificia Università Lateranense, 1961-1970.

More scholarly than Butler (D0376) but less detailed than the Acta Sanctorum (D0388), this substantial compendium contains lengthy bio-bibliographical articles on the lives, influence, thought and writings of the saints. Data are presented clearly and with some attention to historical detail; the bibliographies are especially valuable for further study. This work is most useful for those who want fairly detailed information.

D0359 Bibliothèque des Ecoles Françaises d'Athènes et de Rome. Vol. 1- . Paris: E. de Boccard, 1877- .

Produced under varying imprints, this compendium consists of three series which contain the regestae of thirteenth and fourteenth century popes. Series 2 is devoted to registers of thirteenth century pontiffs; series 3, to letters of fourteenth century popes. As yet there is no index to the contents.

D0360 Bihlmeyer, Karl. <u>Church History</u>. Rev. by Hermann Tüchle. Trans. from the 13th German ed. by Victor E. Mills. 3 vols. Westminster, Md.: Newman Press, 1958-1966.

BR145
B573

Covering the ancient church to the seventh century in volume 1, 692-1517 in volume 2 and 1517-1960 in the final volume, this is a comprehensive general history written from a Roman Catholic perspective. Each chapter covers basic events, movements and personalities briefly and concisely, and excellent bibliographies for further study accompany each topic. Each volume is separately indexed, and there are tables of popes, emperors and kings. See also Alzog (D0323), Hughes (D0542) and Kirsch (D0560).

D0361 Bithell, Jethro, ed. <u>Germany: A Companion to German Studies</u>. [5th ed.] London: Methuen and Company, 1955.

DD61
P28
1955x

This handbook for the beginning student is not limited to the history of Germany but also covers literature, art and culture. The historical coverage provides useful basic bibliographies and introductory remarks on various periods, many of them significant for students of German church history. For more detailed works on German history see Gebhardt (D0491) and Grotefend (D0508).

D0362 Bossy, John. <u>The English Catholic Community, 1570-1850</u>. London: Darton, Longman and Todd, 1975.

See also Watkin (D0751).

D0363 Boüard, Alain de. <u>Manuel de Diplomatique Française et Pontificale</u>. 2 vols. Paris: A. Picard, 1929-1952.

The two volumes in this standard manual cover diplomatique générale and l'acte privé. See also Bresslau (D0368), Giry (D0493) and Prou (D0670).

D0364 Boulenger, Auguste. <u>Histoire Générale de l'Eglise</u>. 3 vols. in 9. Lyon: E. Vitte, 1931-1950.

Consisting of various editions for some volumes, this Roman Catholic history is more objective and factual than Mourret (D0632). It covers the entire history of the church without focusing excessively on a particular country or movement. Each section is very clearly outlined for quick reference, and both bibliographies and references are particularly comprehensive. For a French work written from the Protestant viewpoint see Fargues (D0466).

BX7676
B7
1961x

D0365 Braithwaite, William Charles. <u>The Beginnings of Quakerism</u>. 2nd ed. Rev. by Henry J. Cadbury. Cambridge: Cambridge University Press, 1955.

This second edition of a work first published in 1912 provides an intensive study of the first years of Quakerism up to 1660, based on research into the original sources. It contains additional references and a new appendix in the form of additional notes which bring bibliographical references up to date. Maps and an index are included. This is a detailed and scholarly work suitable for advanced students and scholars. See also Braithwaite's later work (D0366).

BX7676
B75
1961

D0366 Braithwaite, William Charles. <u>The Second Period of Quakerism</u>. 2nd ed.

Prepared by Henry J. Cadbury. Cambridge: Cambridge University Press, 1961.

See also Braithwaite's work on earlier Quaker history (D0365). For biographical data on nineteenth century Quakers see Joseph Joshua Green, ed. Quaker Records; Being an Index to "The Annual Monitor", 1813-92, Containing over 200,000 Obituary Notices of Members of the Society of Friends, Alphabetically and Chronologically Arranged (London: Hicks, 1894).

D0367 Brauer, Jerald C. Protestantism in America: A Narrative History. Rev. ed. Philadelphia, Pa.: Westminster Press, [1965]; London: SCM Press, 1966.

This narrative history of American Protestantism provides introductory treatment of the subject suitable for the beginning student or layman. See also Gaustad (D0490), Handy (D0519), Hudson (D0540) and Mead (D0614).

D0368 Bresslau, Harry. Handbuch der Urkundenlehre für Deutschland und Italien. 3. Aufl. 2 vols. Berlin: Walter de Gruyter und Kompagnie, 1958.

This handbook and the accompanying index (D0369) provide a thoroughly documented and admirably detailed introduction to the study of German and Italian diplomatics. For advanced students doing research which involves either type of documentation this is an important manual. See also Boüard (D0363) and Giry (D0493).

D0369 Bresslau, Harry. Handbuch der Urkundenlehre für Deutschland und Italien. Register zur 2. und 3. Aufl. Zusammengestellt von Hans Schulze. Berlin: Walter de Gruyter und Kompagnie, 1960.

This is an invaluable index to Bresslau's Handbuch (D0368).

D0370 Bright, William. The Age of the Fathers; Being Chapters in the History of the Church during the Fourth and Fifth Centuries. 2 vols. London: Longmans, Green and Company, 1903. Reprint. 2 vols. New York: AMS Press, [1970].

Intended for the general reader as well as the student, this work is based on Dr Bright's lectures delivered to generations of Oxford students. An index is included. See also Gwatkin (D0511), Kidd (D0558) and McGiffert (D0596).

D0371 Brown, Peter Robert Lamont. Augustine of Hippo: A Biography. Berkeley, Calif.: University of California Press; London: Faber and Faber, 1967.

Although less detailed than van der Meer (D0616), this biography provides quite comprehensive coverage. The approach is both chronological and topical, with the relatively brief chapters focusing on an important theme, issue or event of Augustine's life and thought. The historical context is covered ably. This is an important volume for anyone doing detailed work on Augustine.

D0372 Bryce, James Bryce. The Holy Roman Empire. New ed. New York: Macmillan Company, 1904. Reprint. London: Macmillan and Company, 1956.

Reprinted on several occasions, this classic study discusses the survival of the Roman idea in church and state from Charlemagne to Napoleon.

More generally, it is a sound survey of the medieval outlook and its ramifications. A detailed table of contents, chronological tables, notes, a list of further reading and an index supplement the main text.

D0373 Bucke, Emory Stevens, et al. gen. eds. The History of American Methodism. 3 vols. New York: Abingdon Press, 1964.

This collection of writings by some forty contributors describes the relationship of Methodism and the nation, the contribution of Methodism to American culture, the connection between the American spirit and Methodism, and related issues. There is a wealth of material for researchers and students. See also Norwood (D0644).

D0374 Burke, John Bruce, and Wiggins, James F. Foundations of Christianity: From the Beginnings to 1650. New York: Ronald Press Company, 1970.

This book is intended to provide a straightforward, concise introductory text presenting the foundations of Christianity within the historical context. A general bibliography (pp. 307-308) and an index follow the thirteen chapters which treat broad themes such as Eastern Christianity, the papacy, the Reformation era. See also Frankforter (D0478) and Manschreck (D0606).

D0375 Burleigh, John H.S. A Church History of Scotland. London: Oxford University Press, 1960.

Designed for the general reader, this 456 page history offers a comprehensive overview of the Church of Scotland from its early antecedents (St. Columba) to the present. The chapters are clearly presented and avoid complexities of historical argument. A selective bibliography, detailed index and diagram of church divisions and reunions complete the work.

D0376 Butler, Alban. The Lives of the Saints. Ed., rev. and supplemented by Herbert Thurston. 12 vols. London: Burns, Oates and Washbourne, 1926-1938.

First published in the eighteenth century, this standard work plus the 1949 supplementary volume prepared by Attwater is the best known English language guide to hagiography. It relies heavily on the Acta Sanctorum (D0388) and consists of one volume for each month of the year. Within each volume Butler presents a brief biographical account of each saint's life together with critical commentary, brief bibliography and homiletical or devotional notes. The 1926-1938 revision seeks to indicate legendary content of the traditional lives as well as historically accurate information and for this reason is to be preferred over earlier editions or reprints. Attwater's Dictionary of Saints (D0242) may be used as an index to Butler, which should be used less for its historical accuracy than for its traditional hagiographical content. For an additional 1000 names see the four volume revision by Thurston and Attwater (D0377).

D0377 Butler, Alban. Lives of the Saints. Complete ed. Ed. and rev. by Herbert Thurston and Donald Attwater. 4 vols. New York: P.J. Kenedy, 1956. Reprint. 4 vols. New York: P.J. Kenedy, 1962.

Based on the revision of Butler by Thurston (D0376), this compilation contains 2565 entries and lacks the expository content of the original. Otherwise it follows the pattern of Butler and contains indexes in each volume plus a general index in volume 4. This is a useful reference work for basic inquiries and should be regarded as more comprehensive than the twelve volume work because of the inclusion of 1000 additional names. For more specialized and detailed requirements see Acta Sanctorum (D0388) and publications of the Bollandists (D0035-D0037). See also Baudot (D0347).

D0378 Cadden, John Paul. The Historiography of the American Catholic Church, 1785-1943. Studies in Sacred Theology, no. 82. Washington, D.C.: Catholic University of America Press, 1944.

Based on a doctoral dissertation, this 122 page work treats developments in American Catholic historiography and pays particular attention to major historians who have contributed to this field. As such, Cadden is an important guide for advanced students of ecclesiastical historiography and for bibliographical requirements should be used in conjunction with Ellis (D0455) and Vollmar (D0221).

D0379 The Cambridge Ancient History. 17 vols. New York: Macmillan Company; Cambridge: Cambridge University Press, 1923-1939.

Especially valuable for advanced students and scholars of the biblical period, this excellent history covers Egypt, Babylon, the Hittites, Assyria, Athens, Macedonia, Hellenistic monarchies and the rise of Rome. Chapters are by noted specialists and provide detailed, factual accounts of specific periods. Full bibliographies and indexes accompany each volume. Twelve volumes of text are supplemented by five volumes of plates. A third edition (D0452) has been appearing in fascicles since 1961 and in completed volumes since 1970; when completed, this will replace the original set as an indispensible reference tool. See also Bengtson (D0352).

D0380 The Cambridge Medieval History. Planned by John Bagnall Bury. Ed. by Henry Melville Gwatkin et al. 8 vols. New York: Macmillan Company; Cambridge: Cambridge University Press, 1911-1936.

Particularly valuable for its coverage of the Christian Roman Empire, the Eastern Roman Empire and the papacy, this authoritative history is an important reference source. The chapters are by specialists and are filled with detailed, accurate and objective analyses of events, movements and personalities. With the bibliographies and indexes this is a significant tool for the advanced student of medieval Christianity. Volume 4 on the East appeared in a second edition in 1966-1967; the second part of this revision deals with the church. For a greatly condensed version of the full work see Charles William Previté Orton, The Shorter Cambridge Medieval History (2 vols. Cambridge: Cambridge University Press, 1952).

D0381 The Cambridge Modern History. Planned by John E.E.D. Acton. Ed. by Adolphus William Ward et al. 13 vols. and atlas. New York: Macmillan Company; Cambridge: Cambridge University Press, 1902-1912.

This important work is a valuable reference history because of its authoritative factual survey of events from the Renaissance to the nineteenth century. Each volume is lucidly written, providing detailed analyses of personalities, events and movements in all areas of history. The bibliographies are especially noteworthy. Volume 13 contains useful tables and an extensive index to the entire set. It has not been replaced by The New Cambridge Modern History (D0640).

D0382 Cameron, Kenneth Walter. American Episcopal Clergy: Registers of Ordinations in the Episcopal Church in the United States from 1785 through 1904, with Indexes. Hartford, Conn.: Transcendental Books, [1970].

D0383 Cameron, Richard Morgan, comp. The Rise of Methodism: A Source Book. New York: Philosophical Library, 1954.

This 397 page volume presents selected writings on Methodism in the eighteenth century, with particular emphasis on the works of John and Charles Wesley. Dates and sources are indicated, and useful comments are included. There are notes and a bibliography of early books on Methodism.

D0384 Campbell, Thomas Joseph. Pioneer Laymen of North America. 2 vols. New York: The America Press, 1915.

This popular work contains detailed lives of about fifteen explorers, traders, politicians and soldiers, together with portraits and a general bibliography.

D0385 Campbell, Thomas Joseph. Pioneer Priests of North America, 1642-1710. 3 vols. New York: Fordham University Press, 1908-1919.

This popular work provides brief lives of the early Jesuits and other priests who worked among the Iroquois, Hurons and early colonists in North America. There is no bibliography.

D0386 Campenhausen, Hans von. The Fathers of the Greek Church. Trans. by Stanley Godman. New York: Pantheon Books, 1959; London: Adam and Charles Black, [1963].

This 170 page translation of Griechische Kirchenväter contains sketches of the life and work of twelve important Greek fathers of the church. It provides a good general introduction to patrology, presenting each of these writers' personalities, intellectual aims and achievements within the context of their times. See also Cross (D0418).

D0387 Campenhausen, Hans von. The Fathers of the Latin Church. Trans. by Manfred Hoffmann. London: Adam and Charles Black, [1964].

Published in America as Men Who Shaped the Western Church (New York: Harper and Row, 1964), this translation of Lateinische Kirchenväter covers the personalities and teachings of seven individuals who had a major impact on the Western church: Tertullian, Lactantius, Ambrose, Jerome, Augustine, Ambrose and Boethius. The bibliographies include English language works. See also Cross (D0418).

D0388 Carnandet, Jean Baptiste. Acta Sanctorum Quotquot Toto Orbe Coluntur, vel a Catholicis Scriptoribus Celebrantur Quae ex Latinis et Graecis, Aliarumque Gentium Antiquis Monumentis Collegit, Digessit, Notis Illustravit Johannes Bollandus Servata Primigenia Scriptorum Phrasi. Operam et studium continulit Godefridus Henschenius. Editio novissima, curante Joanne Carnandet. 85 vols in 67. Paris: V. Palme, 1863-1931.

The Society of Bollandists, a group of Belgian Jesuits organized in 1651 to publish materials on the lives of the saints, began their important

work after several false starts with the Acta Sanctorum. Earlier versions
had been begun in 1643 in Antwerp by J. Bollandus, continued by G.
Henschenius. This is the definitive version, which won immediate scholarly
acceptance on publication and has continued to appear in various forms.
Potthast's Bibliotheca Historica Medii Aevi (2. Aufl., 1896, Bd. 1, pp. xxxii-
xxxiii) provides a fuller description of the series). The main set contains
the acts or lives of the saints, reprinted from sources in European libraries.
Each includes annotations and commentary on the manuscripts, lists
of variants in texts of different editions and a commentary which tries
to solve problems in chronology, geography, history and interpretation.
The lives are arranged in the order of occurrence of their feasts in the
calendar year. This edition is the primary reference tool for hagiographical
studies. See also the two supplements (D0316, D0637), Butler (D0376)
and Delehaye (D0426).

D0389 Carpenter, Spencer Cecil. Church and People, 1789-1889: A History
of the Church of England from William Wilberforce to "Lux Mundi". London:
SPCK, 1933. Reprint. London: SPCK, 1959.

This work provides a balanced analysis of many aspects of nineteenth
century church life, including but not concentrating exclusively on the
Oxford Movement and its aftermath. For treatment of earlier centuries
see Carpenter (D0390) and Moorman (D0631).

D0390 Carpenter, Spencer Cecil. The Church in England, 597-1688. London:
J. Murray, [1954].

Based on primary sources and on some modern specialist studies, this
work tells the story of the English Church to the end of the Stuart period,
emphasizing "how the English people took what was done and what they
made of it." Some bibliographical references are included, and an index
is provided. For more general coverage see Moorman (D0631).

D0391 Cavallera, Ferdinandus, comp. Patrologiae Cursus Completus Accurante
J.P. Migne. Paris: Fratres Garnier Editores, 1912. Micro-reprint. [Tumba:
International Documentation Center, n.d.].

Like Hopfner (D0539) this is a useful index to Migne's Series Graeca
(D0623).

D0392 Cave, Roy Clinton, and Coulson, Herbert H., eds. A Source Book
for Medieval Economic History. Milwaukee, Wisc.: Bruce Publishing Company,
1936.

This 467 page collection of English translations of medieval documents
contains many items with a bearing on the economic history of the church.
As such, it is a valuable guide for students of a neglected area of church
history. A basic bibliography of other works is included for further study.

D0393 Cayré, Fulbert. Manual of Patrology and History of Theology. Trans.
by H. Howitt, 3 vols. Paris: Society of St. John the Evangelist, Desclée and
Company, 1936-1940.

This translation of Patrologie et Histoire de la Théologie which exists
in a fourth edition (Paris: Desclée et Cie, 1947-1950) covers all topics
related to the history of Catholic theology in volume 1 (the apostolic

fathers to 461) and volume 2 (the end of the patristic period to St. Francis de Sales), and the history of spirituality in volume 3 (the sixteenth to nineteenth centuries). Arrangement is bio-bibliographical covering each author in chronological order. The work is intended for seminarians. It provides very comprehensive coverage of the subject. See also Bardenhewer (D0342), Quasten (D0675) and Tixeront (D0737).

D0394 Ceillier, Remi. Histoire Générale des Auteurs Sacrés et Ecclésiastiques Qui Contient Leur Vie, le Catalogue, la Critique, le Jugement, La Chronologie, l'Analyse et le Denombrement des Différentes Editions de Leurs Ouvrages; Ce Qu'ils Renferment de Plus Interessant sur le Dogme, sur la Morale et sur le Discipline de l'Eglise; l'Histoire des Conciles et les Actes Choisis des Martyrs. Nouv. éd. 14 vols. in 15. Paris: L. Vivès, 1858-1863.

This large work, arranged chronologically, contains the lives and commentaries on the works of writers from OT times to the end of the thirteenth century. Articles are quite long and thoroughly documented. Lengthy extracts from works of the authors are provided, together with contemporary criticism. Indexes are included in each volume, and a two volume general index has been compiled by Rondet (D0686). See also Labriolle (D0565), Monceaux (D0629), Rose (D0687) and Schanz (D0697).

D0395 Chadwick, Henry. The Early Church. The Pelican History of the Church, vol. 1. Harmondsworth: Penguin Books, 1967.

This account of the history of the church from its origins to the time of Justinian is well written, concise and primarily descriptive. Emphasis is given to great theologians and theological controversies which are treated in their historical context. A useful bibliography and an index are supplied. This survey of a complex subject is relevant to the student, pastor and layman. See also Bainton (D0332), Conzelmann (D0408), Davies (D0422), Frend (D0481) and Wand (D0749).

D0396 Chadwick, Henry, and Chadwick, Owen, gen. eds. The Oxford History of the Christian Church. Vol. 1- . Oxford: Clarendon Press, 1976- .

Projected in twenty volumes, this comprehensive series will cover all areas and aspects of church history in scholarly detail. The first two volumes are Robert Handy's (D0519) and Owen Chadwick's The Popes and European Revolution. For a shorter work see Chadwick (D0397).

D0397 Chadwick, Owen, gen. ed. The Pelican History of the Church. 6 vols. Harmondsworth: Penguin Books, 1964-1972.

Also published by Eerdmans and Hodder and Stoughton, this excellent survey includes volumes by Henry Chadwick (D0395), Southern (D0714), Cragg (D0415), Vidler (D0743) and Owen Chadwick himself (D0398). Together these volumes provide a broad and uncontroversial overview of church history from its beginnings to the recent past. The works are suitable as basic texts or for quick reference. For a more substantial work see Chadwick (D0396).

D0398 Chadwick, Owen. The Reformation. The Pelican History of the Church, vol. 3. Harmondsworth: Penguin Books, 1964. Reprint: Harmondsworth: Penguin Books, 1972.

This well written treatment of the Reformation covers the period to 1650 in England, slightly earlier in other European countries. It places somewhat more emphasis on English events. An excellent bibliography and an index are provided. This is a useful textbook for college students and a very readable history for the educated layman. See also Bainton (D0333), Grimm (D0504) and Hillerbrand (D0534).

D0399 Chadwick, Owen. The Victorian Church. 3rd ed. 2 vols. An Ecclesiastical History of England, vols. 7-8. London: Adam and Charles Black, 1971- .

This masterful history of the church in nineteenth century England naturally focuses on the Anglican Church but also treats nonconformity and Roman Catholicism to some degree. The first volume covers 1829-1859; the second, 1860-1901. The lengthy but adequately subdivided chapters in each volume treat major personalities, political activities, theological and ecclesiastical issues, social developments. Thus such topics as the Whig reform of the church, Oxford Movement, science and religion, diocesan affairs and the working class are discussed in some detail. While chronology is not always followed in the treatment of such topics, Chadwick does provide a fairly complete and detailed picture of the period. The analysis is thorough, objective and clearly presented throughout, providing data in a highly readable format for students at all levels. Footnotes accompany the text, and there are detailed bibliographies and indexes for each volume. See also Carpenter (D0389).

D0400 The Christian Centuries: A New History of the Catholic Church. Ed. committee: Louis J. Rogier et al. Vol. 1- . New York: McGraw Hill Book Company; London: Darton, Longman and Todd, 1964- .

Also available in French (Nouvelle Histoire de l'Eglise) and German (Geschichte der Kirche), this history of the Roman Catholic Church by a team of specialists seeks particularly to place events and movements in the context of world history. In many ways it approaches an historico-sociological study of the church and in so doing places interesting emphasis on an otherwise standard chronicle. Each volume includes lengthy bibliographies and multiple indexes for reference purposes. For a more traditional survey see Daniel-Rops (D0419).

D0401 Church Historians; Including Papers on Eusebius, Orosius, St. Bede the Venerable, Ordericus Vitalis, Las Casas, Baronius, Bollandus, Muratori, Moehler, Lingard, Hergenroether, Janssen, Denifle, Ludwig von Pastor. With foreword and index by Peter Keenan Guilday. American Catholic Historical Association Papers, vol. 1. New York: P.J. Kenedy, 1926.

This collection of essays provides biographical sketches and commentaries on the work of fifteen important church historians. Critical bibliographies of works by and about them are provided, as is an index. For students of ecclesiastical historiography this is a most helpful compendium.

D0402 Clark, George, gen. ed. The Oxford History of England. 2nd ed. 15 vols. Oxford: Clarendon Press, 1939-1965.

This standard history consists of substantial introductions to the various periods of English history and includes excellent critical bibliographies. Each volume is very well indexed and clearly outlined in the table of contents. Particularly trustworthy from an ecclesiastical viewpoint are the volumes by Powicke (1216-1307), Mackie (1485-1558), Davies (1603-1660) and Clark (1660-1714). Only half of the volumes exist in a second edition, which means that some can be rather dated in terms of current scholarship. Overall, however, the series is admirable both for study or reference purposes, particularly in cases where students wish to place the English church in its wider historical context.

D0403 Clark, George Kitson. Guide for Research Students Working on Historical Subjects. 2nd ed. Cambridge: Cambridge University Press, 1968. Reprint. Cambridge: Cambridge University Press, 1969.

Written for research students about to start work on historical subjects. Clark consists of eight chapters dealing very briefly and basically with the objects of research, choice of subject, preparation required, reviewing and presenting the evidence, notes. Appendixes treat books on historical research, sources of information, working tools. This 63 page introduction should be used by the beginning researcher as a general overview of the research process.

D0404 Clio: Introduction aux Etudes Historiques. Nouv. éd. 13 vols. Paris: Presses Universitaires de France, 1947-1953.

For the neophyte historian able to read French this is an interesting series of introductory works which ably describe in general the various periods of history from a European viewpoint. The first nine volumes cover historical periods, while remaining volumes deal with art, texts and documents, geography (in the form of an atlas) and chronology. See also Mann (D0603).

D0405 Cole, Stewart Grant. The History of Fundamentalism. New York: R.R. Smith, 1931. Reprint. Hamden, Conn.: Archon Books, 1963.

Focusing on the theme of conflict, this volume examines aspects such as the impact of secularism upon Christianity, current conflict within the Protestant Church, and conflict beyond the church. A bibliography (pp. 341-352) and an index are included. This work will be of most interest to Protestant readers seeking an interpretive approach.

D0406 Commager, Henry Steele, ed. Documents of American History. 9th ed. New York: Appleton-Century-Crofts, [1973].

This work contains a broad selection of documents on American history from 1492 to mid-1973 arranged chronologically and indexed by topic and personal name. Useful introductory notes include reference to other sources. This is an invaluable compendium for the student who requires ready access to key primary materials.

D0407 Commager, Henry Steele, and Morris, Richard Brandon, eds. New American Nation Series. Vol. 1- . New York: Harper and Row, 1954- .

Projected in forty-three volumes, this massive series is to consist of both chronological and topical volumes. Titles published to date provide scholarly and detailed surveys of the various periods of American history, concentrating on historical narrative rather than topical analysis. The display of factual data, inclusion of bibliographies and adequate indexes make these volumes suitable for general reference purposes. Church history is not a strong point of the series. See also Winsor (D0765),

D0408 Conzelmann, Hans. History of Primitive Christianity. Trans. by John F. Steely. Nashville, Tenn.: Abingdon Press, 1973.

This 190 page translation of Geschichte der Urchristentums (Grundrisse zum Neuen Testament, Bd. 5. Göttingen: Vandenhoeck und Ruprecht, 1969) treats the history of Christianity from its inception to approximately 100 A.D. The thirteen chapters discuss sources, chronology, the primitive community, Hellenistic Christianity, Paul and his communities, etc. A brief essay on history and the idea of history, a discussion of the emergence of the NT canon and two appendixes are also included. Although intended for the nonspecialist, the book contains material relevant to more specialized research. It has been criticized for a preoccupation with Paul. See also Bainton (D0332), Chadwick (D0395), Davies (D0422), Frend (D0481) and Wand (D0749).

D0409 Corpus Christianorum: Series Graeca. Vol. 1- . Turnhout: Typographi Brepols, 1977- .

Together with the Latin series (D0410), this massive work is designed to supersede Migne (D0623). It provides new critical texts or the best of those extant of the Greek fathers, and follows the critical catalog of Dekkers (D0085).

D0410 Corpus Christianorum: Series Latina. Vol. 1- . Turnhout: Typographi Brepols, 1953- .

Together with the Greek series (D0409), this massive work is designed to supersede Migne (D0624). It provides new critical texts or the best of those extant of the Latin fathers, and follows the critical catalog of Dekkers (D0085). Volumes are not issued in numerical sequence. When complete, this should serve as the fullest possible collection of writings by the Latin fathers. See also Corpus Scriptorum Ecclesiasticorum Latinorum (D0412).

D0411 Corpus Scriptorum Christianorum Orientalum. Curantibus I.B. Chabot et al. Vol. 1- . Louvain: Sécretariat du Corpus Scriptorum Christianorum Orientalum, 1903- .

Published under various imprints, this collection is arranged in sections (Ethiopic, Arabic, Armenian, Coptic, Syriac, etc.) and contains writings in the original languages with Latin or modern language translations. Each text is accompanied by an introduction, notes and bibliography. This is a monumental collection. For a smaller selection from the same languages see Graffin (D0498, D0499).

D0412 Corpus Scriptorum Ecclesiasticorum Latinorum. Editum consilio et impensis Academiae Litterarum Caesareae Vindobonensis. Vol. 1- . Vienna: C. Geroldi Filium, 1866- . Reprint. Vol. 1- . New York: Johnson Reprint Corporation, 1966- .

Widely recognized as an important collection of Latin patristic texts, CSEL is intended to cover all authors to the end of the seventh century. The highly accurate texts are accompanied by lengthy introductions and bibliographical notes. Indexes of names, places and subjects are provided.

See also Migne (D0624).

D0413 Cotton, Henry. Fasti Ecclesiae Hibernicae: The Succession of the Prelates and Members of the Cathedral Bodies of Ireland. 6 vols. Dublin: Hodges and Smith, 1848-1878.

Although limited to bishops and cathedral clergy and superseded in part by Leslie (D0576-D0583), this remains a valuable collection for students of Irish Anglicanism. The first four volumes cover Munster, L einster, Ulster and Connaught; volume 5 contains corrections, additions, illustrations and indexes. The final volume is a supplement by Charles Philip Cotton, carrying information forward to disestablishment in 1870. See also Swanzy (D0727).

D0414 Cox, John Charles. The Parish Registers of England. London: Methuen and Company, 1910. Reprint. Totowa, N.J.: Rowman and Littlefield; Wakefield: E.P. Publishing, 1974.

Much less wide ranging than Tate (D0732), this volume deals quite thoroughly with the history of parish registers and especially with their role in illuminating customs and life of the period. Cox provides numerous citations to substantiate his discussion and is a sound starting point for those about to embark on research requiring the use of parish registers. See also Ker (D0555).

D0415 Cragg, Gerald R. The Church and the Age of Reason, 1648-1789. [Rev. ed.] The Pelican History of the Church, vol. 4. Harmondsworth: Penguin Books, [1970].

This straightforward work provides a sound introductory study for the student. Geographically coverage extends to Europe, Russia and the New World. A bibliographical note (pp. 285-288) and an index are included. For the later period see Vidler (D0743).

D0416 Creed, John Martin, and Boys Smith, John Sandwith, eds. Religious Thought in the Eighteenth Century, Illustrated from Writers of the Period. Cambridge: Cambridge University Press, 1934.

Including brief biographical sketches, this 301 page study concentrates particularly on natural religion but also touches upon church-state relations and study of the Bible. See also Livingston (D0589).

D0417 Crittenden, Christopher, and Godland, Doris, comps. and eds. Historical Societies in the United States and Canada: A Handbook. Washington, D.C.: American Association for State and Local History, 1944.

Somewhat dated in content, this 261 page handbook provides descriptive and historical information on 1467 national, local and general historical societies in North America. Notes on society publications are included. The main list of 904 entries is supplemented by 564 entries at the end of lists for each state. Crittenden is most useful as a guide to local historical societies, many of which have an interest in local parish history. See also Directory of Historical Societies (D0435) for regular updatings.

D0418 Cross, Frank Leslie. The Early Christian Fathers. Studies in Theology. London: Gerald Duckworth and Company, 1960.

Useful as a quick introduction to the early fathers and their works, this volume deals individually with each personality and summarizes the thought of each school in terms of geographical location. Brief bibliographies refer to key works and to more complete bibliographies for advanced requirements. See also von Campenhausen (D0386, D0387).

D0419 Daniel-Rops, Henri. History of the Church of Christ. Trans. by Audrey Butler et al. 10 vols. New York: E.P. Dutton and Company; London: J.M. Dent and Sons, 1957-1969.

With many of the volumes reprinted on various occasions, this translation of Histoire de l'Eglise du Christ is a somewhat popularly written series which seeks to express a traditional Roman Catholic view of Christian history. Focusing especially on France and Italy, Daniel-Rops provides useful summaries of various pontificates and their relationship with secular states. Chapters in each chronological volume are clearly written and provide minimal scholarly apparatus. Selected bibliographies, historical tables and subject indexes accompany each title in the series. This is a suitable reference work for the beginning student. For a newer survey see The Christian Centuries (D0400).

D0420 Dannenfeldt, Karl H. The Church of the Renaissance and Reformation: Decline and Reform from 1300 to 1600. Church in History Series. St. Louis, Mo.: Concordia Publishing House, [1970].

This 144 page introductory survey gives more attention to the latter part of the period covered, providing only little discussion of the fourteenth and fifteenth centuries. It is written in a straightforward manner suitable for the nonspecialist reader. See also Dickens (D0431), Elton (D0460), Major (D0601) and Spitz (D0716).

D0421 Davies, Horton. Worship and Theology in England. 5 vols. Princeton, N.J.: Princeton University Press, 1961-1975.

Highly regarded for its balanced treatment of a significant and difficult topic, this scholarly study follows a chronological arrangement: 1534-1603, 1603-1690, 1690-1850, 1850-1900, 1900-1965. In each volume Catholic, Anglican and Protestant developments are dealt with fully and objectively. Footnotes, bibliographies and indexes of persons and places accompany each volume. The final volume includes a subject index as well.

D0422 Davies, John Gordon. The Early Christian Church. New York: Holt, Rinehart and Winston; London: Weidenfeld and Nicolson, 1965.

Covering the first five centuries of the church, this 314 page work provides a balanced, readable, carefully arranged treatment. Apart from the first chapter, all others are divided into sections on background, sources, expansion and development, beliefs, worship, social life. This is a useful volume for students and contains much of interest to the general reader. See also Bainton (D0332), Chadwick (D0395), Conzelmann (D0408), Frend (D0481) and Wand (D0749).

D0423 Davies, Rupert Eric, and Rupp, Ernest Gordon, gen. eds. A History of the Methodist Church in Great Britain. Vol. 1- . London: Epworth Press, 1965 [i.e. 1966]- .

Projected as a three volume survey plus a volume of source materials, this collection is intended to provide a comprehensive history of Methodism in Britain from its origins to the present. Volume 1, dealing with the eighteenth century, includes a bibliography of primary and secondary sources and indexes of subjects, names and places.

D0424 Deanesly, Margaret. A History of the Medieval Church, 590-1500. 9th ed. London: Methuen, 1969.

In 283 pages this work provides a basic introduction to the history of medieval Christianity from Gregory the Great to the Renaissance. It focuses on social and personal aspects rather than political, aiming to give some idea of the medieval attitude towards life, religion and the church, the faith and ideals of medieval churchmen, and of the working of the church system of the time. A select book list (pp. 266-269), lists of major events, of popes, of emperors and kings and of archbishops of Canterbury are provided, as well as two maps and an index. Based on sound knowledge of the period, this study is suitable both for the general reader and for the theological student. See also Southern (D0714).

D0425 Deanesly, Margaret. The Pre-Conquest Church in England. 2nd ed. An Ecclesiastical History of England, vol. 1. London: Adam and Charles Black, [1963].

This volume in the Dickinson series (D0434) covers Christian history in England from the second to the eleventh century, providing a sound, readable treatment which stresses personalities rather than institutions. It deals with Celtic Christianity, the mission of St. Augustine, the age of Theodore, etc. The final chapter is devoted to religion and lay people in the late Old English period. Some specialized matters are considered, and technical information on the early meaning of certain terms is included. The work shows thorough attention to sources. It is intended for the educated general reader. See also Deanesly's other work (D0424) for the succeeding period.

D0426 Delehaye, Hippolyte. The Legends of the Saints. Trans. by Donald Attwater. New York: Fordham University Press; London: Geoffrey Chapman, 1962.

This successor to the 1907 translation by Mrs. V.M. Crawford entitled The Legends of the Saints: An Introduction to Hagiography is a new translation of the fourth edition of Les Légendes Hagiographiques (Subsidia Hagiographica, no. 18a. Brussels: Société des Bollandistes, 1955). It is a substantial introduction to the application of historical criticism to hagiography and in seven chapters covers general ideas, the production of legend, the work of the hagiographer, classification of hagiographical texts, dossier of a saint, pagan memories and survivals, some hagiographical errors. Each chapter includes useful notes. There is no subject index, but a detailed table of contents and index of saints give the work added reference value. This is a very helpful volume for students and historians using hagiographical sources and covers all topics likely to be required by the less experienced investigator. A memoir and bibliography on Delehaye conclude the volume. See also Butler (D0376) and Carnandet (D0388). For a biographical dictionary of saints see Otto Wimmer, Handbuch der Namen und Heiligen, mit Einer Geschichte des Christlichen Kalenders (Innsbruck: Tyrolia Verlag, 1956).

D0427 Delorme, Jean. Chronologie des Civilisations. [3. éd.] Paris: Presses Universitaires de France, 1969.

First published in 1949, this work presents chronological tables from 3000 B.C. to 1969 A.D. Sources of information are clearly indicated, and there is a full index. See also Collison (D0262) and Keller (D0286).

D0428 Delorme, Jean. Les Grandes Dates du Moyen Age. 3. éd. Paris: Presses Universitaires de France, 1970.

See also Mas-Latrie (D0612) and Storey (D0724).

D0429 Denholm-Young, Nöel. Handwriting in England and Wales. Cardiff: University of Wales Press, 1954.

Similar in intention to Hector (D0527), this guide for students of British history and literature seeks to explain the handwriting encountered in manuscripts from various periods. It also gives some attention to the dating and geographical origin of manuscripts. There is a useful bibliography (pp. 86-93) which lists works of value for more detailed study. This is a useful starting point for the student embarking on research utilizing primary documents in English history generally. See also Emmison (D0462), Martin (D0609) and Newton (D0641).

D0430 Devreesse, Robert. Introduction à l'Etude des Manuscrits Grecs. Paris: Librairie C. Klincksieck, 1954.

Although in French, this is an invaluable introduction to the study of Greek manuscripts for anyone able to read French even with difficulty. The first part deals with paper, handwriting, transmission of texts and ancient libraries. The second part describes extant manuscripts by topic, including Bible, liturgies and numerous other subjects.

D0431 Dickens, Arthur Geoffrey. The Age of Humanism and Reformation: Europe in the Fourteenth, Fifteenth and Sixteenth Centuries. Englewood Cliffs, N.J.: Prentice-Hall, [1972].

This 290 page survey describes the development of European civilization, treating thought, religion, art and politics. It usefully treats Christianity as one aspect of a wider cultural milieu, showing how it evolved in relation to other areas of life. See also Dannenfeldt (D0420), Elton (D0460), Major (D0601) and Spitz (D0716).

D0432 Dickens, Arthur Geoffrey. The Counter Reformation. London: Thames and Hudson, 1968; New York: Harcourt, Brace and World, [1969].

In 215 pages this popularly written and very well illustrated history of the Catholic reformation provides sound treatment by an authority on the Reformation era. There are useful insights in the area of social history, and a generally objective study of the Counter-Reformation. For a collection of documents see Olin (D0649).

D0433 Dickens, Arthur Geoffrey. The English Reformation. Rev. ed. London: William Collins Sons and Company, 1967.

Making excellent use of research findings current at the time of writing, this 374 page history relates conditions which made possible and encouraged religious reform in England, describes the development of Protestantism and indicates how this affected society at large. The writing is concise, methodical and illuminating. See also Elton (D0458), Hughes (D0543) and Parker (D0655).

D0434 Dickinson, John Compton, gen. ed. An Ecclesiastical History of England. London: Adam and Charles Black, 1961- .

Extremely slow in appearing, the volumes so far published include Deanesly (D0425) and Chadwick (D0399), which are excellent surveys of specific periods and useful as textbooks and reference volumes. See also Stephens (D0720).

D0435 Directory of Historical Societies and Agencies in the United States and Canada. Ed. 1- . Nashville, Tenn.: American Association for State and Local History, 1956- , triennial.

This triennial updating of Crittenden (D0417) generally lists some 2500 North American historical societies, providing details of address, secretary, staff, foundation date, membership, libraries and museums, publications and opening arrangements. This is most useful for students of local history.

D0436 Doble, Gilbert Hunter. Lives of the Welsh Saints. Ed. by Daniel Simon Williams. Cardiff: University of Wales Press, 1971.

This detailed guide to the lives of five early Welsh saints includes substantial historical data plus excellent bibliographical notes. See also Baring-Gould (D0343, D0344).

D0437 Doble, Gilbert Hunter. Saints of Cornwall. [Ed. by Donald Attwater]. 5 vols. Chatham: Parrett and Neves, 1960-1970.

First published in pamphlet form as the Cornish Saints Series, this edited version is arranged geographically and treats each Cornish saint within the locality normally associated with him. Biographical and bibliographical information together with selected excerpts from source materials are provided for each saint. While not essentially a scholarly tool, this collection does provide useful biographical data to supplement Baring-Gould (D0343, D0344).

D0438 Dölger, Franz, and Schneider, Alfons Maria. Byzanz. Wissenschaftliche Forschungsberichte, Geisteswissenschaftliche Reihe, Bd. 5. Bern: A. Francke, 1952.

Devoted to Byzantine studies published between 1938 and 1950, this 328 page survey covers history, literature and language in the first section and art in the second. Useful bibliographical footnotes accompany the text, and each section includes an author index. For students of Eastern church history and early Christian art this is a useful guide to publications from a limited period.

D0439 Donaldson, Gordon. The Scottish Reformation. Cambridge: Cambridge University Press, 1960.

This 242 page study covers the period from 1560, with particular emphasis on administrative changes through to the end of the sixteenth century. Based on original sources, this is a scholarly and objective work, of value to students of the church in Scotland.

D0440 [no entry]

D0441 Dowley, Tim, ed. Eerdman's Handbook to the History of Christianity. Grand Rapids, Mich.: Wm. B. Eerdmans Publishing Company, 1977.

With contributions by more than seventy scholars, this handbook describes the development of Christianity from its beginnings to the present in seven chapters. Each chapter contains numerous subdivisions in which important movements and personalities are portrayed. The work is more popular than scholarly in tone and pays particular attention to the development of evangelical Protestantism. There are numerous illustrations and charts, but the work lacks footnotes and bibliography. An index of personal names is provided. In general this is of use primarily to teachers and pupils rather than to university or seminary students.

D0442 Duchesne, Louis Marie Oliver. Early History of the Christian Church from Its Foundation to the End of the Fifth Century. Trans. from the 4th ed. 3 vols. London: Lohn Murray, 1909-1924; New York: Longmans, Green and Company,1922-1924. Reprint. 3 vols. London: John Murray, 1950-1951.

Long a standard Roman Catholic survey of early church history, this frequently reprinted set covers the following periods: the Roman Empire to the end of the third century in volume 1; the great persecution to the end of the fourth century in volume 2; the church in the days of Theodosius I to the end of the fifth century in volume 3. An index is included in each volume, together with a detailed table of contents. For a later Protestant survey see Lietzmann (D0586).

D0443 Duchesne, Louis Marie Olivier. Le Liber Pontificalis: Text, Introduction et Commentaire. 3 vols. Paris: E. de Boccard, 1955-1957.

Also published in Paris by E. Thorin and E. de Boccard between 1886 and 1957, this is generally recognized as the most complete edition of Liber Pontificalis. It is a collection of papal biographies from St. Peter to 891 and includes a list of "accomplishments" by each pope. It is based on material compiled by biographers of the seventh to fifteenth centuries and, although slightly hagiographical in tone, is a valuable collection for historians of the papacy. The Duchesne edition contains a helpful introduction and useful explanatory notes. See also Loomis (D0592).

D0444 Dufourcq, Albert. L'Avenir du Christianisme. 10 vols. Paris: Bloud et Cie, 1908-[1954].

Beginning with a comparative study of paganism and Judaism and then providing a roughly chronological treatment of church history, this Roman Catholic work is noted for its concise treatment, clear arrangement and wealth of data presented without embellishment. Each chapter is accompanied by a bibliography, but there is no index. This is one of the better Catholic reference histories for students of all persuasions. See also Fliche (D0473) and Mourret (D0632).

D0445 Dumeige, Gervais, ed. Histoire des Conciles Oecuméniques. Vol. 1- .

Paris: Editions de l'Orante, 1962- .

Volumes in this set are prepared by specialists and include excellent bibliographies for further study. See also Hefele (D0528).

D0446 Durnbaugh, Donald F. The Believers' Church: The History and Character of Radical Protestantism. New York: Macmillan Company, 1968.

D0447 Durnbaugh, Donald F., comp. and ed. The Brethren in Colonial America: A Source Book on the Transplantation and Development of the Church of the Brethren in the Eighteenth Century. Elgin, Ill.: Brethren Press, [1967].

This sequel to Durnbaugh's earlier volume (D0448) covers the period of the American colonies to the end of the Revolutionary War. Doctrinal and devotional literature, travels, early establishments, movements and historical developments are all represented in the collection. See also Sappington (D0692).

D0448 Durnbaugh, Donald F., comp. and ed. European Origins of the Brethren: A Source Book on the Beginnings of the Church of the Brethren in the Eighteenth Century; a Two-Hundred-Fiftieth Anniversary Volume. Elgin, Ill.: Brethren Press, 1958.

Based on materials found in more than 100 libraries in six countries, this collection includes source materials on the Church's formation, expansion, emigration and early development. It covers history as well as doctrine and theology. See also Sappington (D0692) and Durnbaugh's other works (D0447, D0449).

D0449 Durnbaugh, Donald F. Guide to Research in Brethren History. [Elgin, Ill.]: Church of the Brethren Historical Committee, 1968.

D0450 Eberhardt, Newman C. A Summary of Catholic History. 2 vols. St. Louis, Mo.: Herder, 1961-1962.

The first volume in this comprehensive history covers the ancient and medieval periods to 1453; the second carries the survey forward to the 1980s. Eberhardt presents historical data clearly and in some detail. Subject indexes and appendixes appear in each volume, and there is a substantial bibliography in volume 2. This work adequately fills the gap between single volume histories and such larger works as Jedin (D0548).

D0451 Eberhardt, Newman C. A Survey of American Church History. St. Louis, Mo.: B. Herder Book Company, 1964.

This usefully compact survey covers North and South American Catholic history in chronological sequence. A bibliography and a subject index are provided. Based on Eberhardt's Summary of Catholic History (D0450), this volume is suitable for basic reference requirements of less advanced students. See also McAvoy (D0594).

D0452 Edwards, I.E.S.; Gadd, C.J.; and Hammond, N.G.L., eds. The Cambridge Ancient History. 3rd ed. Vol. 1- . Cambridge: Cambridge University Press, 1970- .

Like the previous edition (D0379), this is the standard history of the

ancient world and forms an invaluable reference work on places and
periods relevant to biblical history. Each volume contains chapters by
individual scholars, and the table of contents for each volume lists the
chapters and their subdivisions to assist reference. There are also lists
of maps, tables and figures; there are extensive bibliographies arranged
by chapter at the end of each volume and a general index. This is un-
doubtedly the fullest and most useful guide to ancient history generally
and an important source of data for biblical studies. See also Bengtson
(D0352).

D0453 Ehler, Sidney Z., and Morrall, John B., eds. Church and State through
the Centuries: A Collection of Historic Documents with Commentaries.
Westminster, Md.: Newman Press, 1954.

Arranged chronologically, this 625 page collection contains selections
from a wide range of documents dealing with church-state relations.
Roman Catholic in focus, it includes useful introductions to individual
documents and to eras. There are numerous references to full editions
of the materials. This is a very worthwhile collection for the less advanced
student and is adequately indexed for reference purposes. See also Mercati
(D0620) and Tierney (D0736).

D0454 Ellard, Gerald. A Litany of Heroes and Saints: Notable Biographies
and Lives of Saints for Students of Church History. Milwaukee, Wisc.: Bruce
Publishing Company, 1961.

D0455 Ellis, John Tracy. American Catholicism. 2nd ed. The Chicago History
of American Civilization. Chicago, Ill.: University of Chicago Press, 1969.

This 322 page survey of American Catholic history provides a basic but
sound introduction for the beginner. Bibliographical notes, suggested
readings and a subject index are provided. See also Hennesey (D0529)
and McAvoy (D0594).

D0456 Ellis, John Tracy. Documents of American Catholic History. Rev. ed.
2 vols. Chicago, Ill.: Henry Regnery Company, 1967-1968.

First published in 1956, this useful source book reproduces documents
from 1493 to the date of publication. Volume 1 covers the church in
the Spanish colonies to 1866; volume 2 covers 1866 to the 1960s. This
collection is particularly useful for those who are unfamiliar with Roman
Catholic pronouncements and provides a good introduction to the history
of Roman Catholicism in America. See also Shearer (D0709).

D0457 Elton, Geoffrey Rudolph. England, 1200-1640. The Sources of History:
Studies in the Uses of Historical Evidence, vol. 1. Ithaca, N.Y.: Cornell
University Press; London: Hodder and Stoughton, 1969.

Intended to introduce students to the variety of primary source materials
available for the advanced study of English history, Elton covers narratives,
official records (both church and state), lesser authorities, private materials,
law, books and writings, non-documentary sources. Each chapter discusses
the various types of materials very clearly, providing essential information
on origins, content, use and significant variations. Numerous examples
and footnotes are provided, together with an index of materials and sources.
Elton is a most worthwhile starting point for the beginning researcher.

DA33²
R487

D0458 Elton, Geoffrey Rudolph. Reform and Reformation: England, 1509-1558. The New History of England. Cambridge, Mass.: Harvard University Press, 1977.

See also Dickens (D0433), Elton (D0460), Hughes (D0543) and Parker (D0655).

D228
B4
1966b

D0459 Elton, Geoffrey Rudolph. Reformation Europe, 1517-1599. London: William Collins Sons and Company, [c. 1963]; Cleveland, Ohio: Meridian Books [1964]; New York: Harper and Row, [1966].

This is a scholarly, readable account which covers intellectual, political, social and economic aspects. It is a standard work for undergraduate students. See also Bainton (D0330), Hillerbrand (D0537) and Sykes (D0730).

CB359
R4C
1963x

D0460 Elton, Geoffrey Rudolph. Renaissance and Reformation, 1300-1648. Ideas and Institutions in Western Civilization, vol. 3. New York: Macmillan Company, 1963.

See also Dannenfeldt (D0420), Dickens (D0431), Major (D0601) and Spitz (D0716).

D0461 Emmison, Frederick George. Archives and Local History. London: Methuen and Company, 1966.

For the student without experience in using archives Emmison provides a usefully detailed introduction to the field, especially from an English viewpoint. The 112 pages cover aids in using local archives, local repositories, visiting repositories, transcripts of selected illustrations, extracts from archives, selected pamphlets and articles. By far the largest section is that devoted to the use of local archives, and this contains many valuable pointers. The work is well illustrated and includes an index. See also Stephens (D0719).

D0462 Emmison, Frederick George. How to Read Local Archives, 1500-1700. Helps for Students of History, no. 82. London: Historical Association, 1967. Reprint. London: Historical Association, 1973.

Suitable primarily for advanced students embarking on research which requires the use of English manuscript sources, Emmison seeks to show how to read later pre-italic handwriting ("secretary hand"). It consists primarily of illustrations of documents in the original handwriting with transcriptions on opposite pages. Included are vestry minutes, church-wardens' accounts and similar documents of interest to church historians. Explanatory text is minimal, so this is essentially a preparatory workbook. See also Newton (D0641).

D0463 English Historical Documents. Vol. 1- . London: Eyre Methuen, 1953- .

DA26
E55

Expected to be in thirteen volumes, this important collection of documents seeks to provide representative materials on all aspects of English history from 500 to 1914. Each volume covers a specific historical period and includes an extensive introduction to the collection plus numerous bibliographies for further study. Early documents are reproduced in English translation from the original language. While not intended primarily for the church historian, this series includes much that is relevant to ecclesiastical affairs and serves as an excellent resource guide. See also Great Britain. Public Record Office (D0502).

D0464 Eubel, Conrad, ed. Hierarchia Catholica Medii Aevi sive Summorum Pontificum, S.R.E. Cardinalium, Ecclesiarum Antistitum Series ab Anno 1198 usque ad Annum 1605 Producta e Documentis Tabularii Praesertim Vaticani Collecta, Digesta, Edita. 2nd ed. 7 vols. Monasterii: Sumptibus et Typis Librariae Regensbergianae; Patavia: "Il Messagero di S. Antonio", 1913-1968.

This work provides a chronological listing of popes and of bishops of the Catholic Church arranged alphabetically by diocese. The index of modern diocesan names provides ready access to the Latin name listing of entries. In addition information is provided on diocesan history, boundaries and main sources of data. This is a useful handbook and chronology for students of Roman Catholic history. See also Gams (D0485).

D0465 Ewing, William, ed. Annals of the Free Church of Scotland, 1483-1900. 2 vols. Edinburgh: T. and T. Clark, 1914.

See also Lamb (D0566).

D0466 Fargues, Paul. Histoire du Christianisme. 5 vols. Bibliothèque d'Etudes Religieuses. Paris: Fischbacher, 1929-1939.

Written from the Protestant viewpoint and covering the entire span of Christianity, this history is arranged chronologically and, within periods, by topic. Numerous sources are cited, and these citations offer useful guidance on European historical literature. Although dated, Fargues retains factual reference value for those who lack access to the larger English language histories or who wish to have French Protestant views on a particular topic. For a French work written from the Roman Catholic viewpoint see Boulenger (D0364).

D0467 Farrar, Frederic William. Lives of the Fathers: Sketches of Church History in Biography. 2 vols. New York: Macmillan and Company; Edinburgh: Adam and Charles Black, 1889.

This popular but scholarly work treats the fathers from St. Ignatius to St. John Chrysostom, dealing with their lives, thought, character and contribution to the church. Although less critical than one might find useful today, Farrar remains a good work for beginners and for basic reference needs, if this drawback is kept in mind.

D0468 The Fathers of the Church: A New Translation. Vol. 1- . Wilmington, N.C.: Consortium Press, 1947- .

BR60
P3
A6
Projected in 100 volumes and published under various imprints (including Catholic University of America Press), this series represents a comprehensive attempt to provide contemporary English translations of the writings of the fathers. Each volume includes an introduction, a general index and a scriptural index. It is less technical than Quasten (D0676), containing few footnotes and shorter introductions.

D0469 Fellowships and Grants of Interest to Historians. Washington, D.C.: American Historical Association, Institutional Services Program, [1977]-, annual?

For the researcher seeking project funding this list, which is arranged by name of fund or agency, provides current details of requirements for eligibility, amounts and terms of grants, application procedures, deadlines and similar facts.

D0470 Ferm, Robert L., ed. Issues in American Protestantism: A Documentary History from the Puritans to the Present. Garden City, N.Y.: Anchor Books, 1969.

277.3
P358

This volume illustrates major issues of American Protestant history by using documents of the period, together with introductory remarks on the selections. Bibliographical notes conclude each of the sections. Arrangement is chronological, with themes indicated for the various periods. This contains most useful material for students seeking easy access to primary sources. See also Gaustad (D0488), Handy (D0520), Miller (D0626) and Smith (D0712).

D0471 Ferm, Vergilius Ture Anselm. Pictorial History of Protestantism: A Panoramic View of Western Europe and the United States. New York: Philosophical Library, 1957.

This 368 page volume contains selected pictures with text covering historical and denominational material. Its main interest is as a collection of generally old pictures of persons and places relevant to the historian of Protestantism. An index is provided.

D0472 Fink, Karl August. Das Vatikanische Archiv: Einführung in die Bestände und Ihre Erforschung. 2. Aufl. Rome: W. Regensberg, 1951.

First published in 1943, this is an essential reference tool for the historian using Vatican archives. The introduction provides valuable details on the history and organization of the archives, while the main part of the work consists of a list of the various archive groups together with brief notes on inventories and bibliography, as well as a list of published registers, accounts and reports.

D0473 Fliche, Augustin, and Martin, Victor, eds. Histoire de l'Eglise depuis les Origines jusqu'à Nos Jours. 20 vols. Paris: Bloud et Gay, 1934-1949.

270
P621

This substantial history of the church from its origins to the mid-nineteenth century provides somewhat uneven coverage of the field. Some volumes are particularly detailed and objective and provide useful bibliographical information. Others reflect a narrow Roman Catholic interpretation of history and should be consulted with caution. All of the volume authors are Roman Catholic specialists. See also Dufourcq (D0444) and Mourret (D0632).

D0474 Flick, Alexander Clarence. The Decline of the Medieval Church. 2 vols. London: K. Paul, Trench, Trübner and Company, 1930. Reprint. 2 vols. Burt Franklin Bibliography and Reference Series, no. 133. New York: Burt Franklin, [1967].

BR362
P58

This detailed study of the medieval church from the end of the thirteenth century provides a wealth of material for the student. Sources are indicated in each volume. There are detailed tables of contents. See also Oakley (D0647).

D0475 Flindall, Roy Philip, ed. The Church of England, 1815-1948: A Documentary History. London: SPCK, 1972.

This collection of 105 documents contains excerpts of a wide variety including speeches, letters, Acts of Parliament and missionary archives. It has been criticized for some disparity between the issues discussed in the introduction and the documents selected, and for a lack of good bibliographies.

D0476 Florilegium Patristicum, tam Veteris Quam Medii Aevi Auctores Complectens. Vol. 1- . Bonn: Petri Hanstein, 1906- .

D0477 Fochios, Michael James. For the Glory of the Father, Son and Holy Spirit: A History of Eastern Orthodox Saints. Translations from Megas Synaxaristēs and Vioi tōn Hagiōn. Ed. by Aristides Isidoros Cederakis. [Baltimore, Md.: Phanari Publications, 1974].

This 175 page collection of selected Russian writings deals with the lives and miracles of thirty-two well known saints in the Orthodox calendar.

D0478 Frankforter, A. Daniel. A History of the Christian Movement: The Development of Christian Institutions. Chicago, Ill.: Nelson-Hall, c. 1978.

This introductory work attempts to identify key events and to indicate patterns in the evolution of Christianity from the earliest history of the Christian movement to modern times. A select bibliography (pp. 277-298), a general index and a biblical reference index are included. This is a necessarily selective and interpretive treatment. See also Burke (D0374) and Manschreck (D0606).

D0479 Freeman-Grenville, Greville Stewart Parker. Chronology of World History: A Calendar of Principal Events from 3000 B.C. to A.D. 1973. Totowa, N.J.: Rowman and Littlefield, 1975.

This 753 page chronology presents data in tabular form. The first five columns present historical matters under geographical headings which vary to reflect historical changes. The sixth column treats religion and culture in all geographical areas and is particularly useful in presenting a rapid overview of major historical developments and events. The index covers individuals, places and events. See also Grun (D0509).

D0480 Fremantle, Anne Jackson, ed. A Treasury of Early Christianity. New York: Viking Press, 1953.

Similar in many ways to Stevenson (D0722), this 625 page collection contains documents arranged in the following sections: the Christian ideal; the martyrs; the testimony of the pagans; the testimony of the Christians; and a selection of poetry. A bibliography (pp. 619-622) and an index are provided. This work allows easy access to selected sources for the student of early Christianity. See also Ayer (D0328) and Kee (D0554).

D0481 Frend, W.H.C. The Early Church. Knowing Christianity. Philadelphia, Pa.: J.B. Lippincott Company; London: Hodder and Stoughton, 1965.

This 288 page history is intended as a nontechnical account suitable for the layman, although it is perhaps not as easy to read as an introductory work might be. It is particularly useful on biographical treatment of important figures of the period. See also Bainton (D0332), Chadwick (D0395), Conzelmann (D0408), Davies (D0422) and Wand (D0749).

D0482 Funk, Franz Xaver von. A Manual of Church History. Trans. by Luigi Cappadelta. 2 vols. London: Kegan Paul, Trench, Trübner, 1910. Reprint. New York: AMS Press, 1973.

D0483 Galbraith, Vivian Hunter. An Introduction to the Use of the Public Records. Oxford: Clarendon Press, 1934. Reprint. London: Oxford University Press, 1952.

This practical guide to the main types of records in Britain is a useful introduction to the field for beginners. It includes information on how to procure records, how to use them and the various ways in which they can be used. A bibliography lists numerous publications for more detailed study. For those about to embark on research in English church history this is an excellent survey of primary documentation.

D0484 Gallais, Pierre; Plumail, Bernadette; and Riou, Yves-Jean, eds. Répertoire International des Médiévalistes. Publications du Centre d'Etudes Supérieures de Civilisation Médiévale, no. 3. Poitiers: Université de Poitiers, Centre d'Etudes Supérieures de Civilisation Médiévale, 1965.

This enlargement of a 1960 publication by M.T. d'Alverney entitled Répertoire des Médiévalistes Européens lists more than 3500 medievalists from around the world. For each individual it includes name, position, address, specialization and publications. There are indexes of places of residence and of subject interests. Gallais is now in need of updating and has little current reference value. See also Labande (D0564).

D0485 Gams, Pius Bonifacius. Series Episcoporum Ecclesiae Catholicae, Quotquot Innotuerunt a Beato Petro Apostolo. 2. Aufl. Leipzig: K.W. Hiersemann, 1931. Reprint. Graz: Akademische Druck- und Verlagsanstalt, 1957.

This volume provides a geographical listing of the bishops of every diocese in the Roman Catholic Church from St. Peter to 1885. Dates of installation and death are provided for each bishop. The work is indexed by names of bishops. See also Eubel (D0464).

D0486 Gardiner, Samuel Rawson, ed. The Constitutional Documents of the Puritan Revolution, 1625-1660. 3rd ed. Oxford: Clarendon Press, 1906. Reprint. Oxford: Clarendon Press, [1958].

This collection of 105 documents is intended for those studying the constitutional or political history of the period indicated. They are arranged in five parts, organized chronologically. An index facilitates access to this useful compendium.

D0487 Garrison, Winfred Ernest, and De Groot, Alfred Thomas. The Disciples of Christ, a History. St. Louis, Mo.: Christian Board of Publication, 1948. Reprint. St. Louis, Mo.: Christian Board of Publication, 1954.

This 592 page work attempts to provide a comprehensive history of the Disciples of Christ. It covers precursors of the movement in Scotland and

America, the "founding fathers", and subsequent developments in the movement. It presents considerable detail for the researcher. See also Harrell (D0525) and Tucker (D0740).

D0488 Gaustad, Edwin Scott, ed. A Documentary History of Religion in America. Vol. 1- . Grand Rapids, Mich.: Wm. B. Eerdmans Publishing Company, 1982- .

This skilfully edited selection of primary sources shows the range and depth of American religion, and introductory sections provide their historical contexts. This is a valuable source book for the researcher. See also Handy (D0520) and Smith (D0712).

D0489 Gaustad, Edwin Scott. Historical Atlas of Religion in America. Rev. ed. New York: Harper and Row, 1976.

This new edition of a standard work provides, by maps, charts, tables and text, an excellent guide to the expansion and development of churches in America. The first part covers 1650-1800; the second, colonial and noncolonial denominations for 1800-1975; the third, noncolonial bodies for 1800-1975; the fourth, non-Christian religions in America and special aspects of American religions. Appendixes contain data on denominations in 1650, 1750, 1850 and 1950. In each main section Gaustad provides a brief history of each denomination and uses maps and charts to exemplify growth. Although the statistics must reflect the difficulties inherent in obtaining such information in many cases, this work does an admirable job in making figures readily available for those interested in the historical development of American denominations. There are indexes of authors and titles, places, religious bodies, names and subjects. A bibliography is also provided.

D0490 Gaustad, Edwin Scott. A Religious History of America. New York: Harper and Row, 1966.

This 421 page work describes the role of religion in American life, emphasizing national rather than denominational history. The book is clear and concise, with useful statistics, illustrations, excerpts from original documents, an excellent bibliography and a chronology. It is suitable for the student and provides very readable treatment for the nonspecialist. See also Ahlstrom (D0319), Handy (D0519), Hudson (D0541) and Mead (D0614).

D0491 Gebhardt, Bruno. Handbuch der Deutschen Geschichte. 9. Aufl. Hrsg. von Herbert Grundmann. Vol. 1- . Stuttgart: Union Deutsche Verlagsgesellschaft, 1970- .

First published in 1891-1892, this extremely thorough handbook is arranged by period and subject. It provides an excellent, factual reference guide on all topics and periods of German history and includes much bibliographical information. For advanced students and scholars of the German church and related historical subjects Gebhardt is an essential reference work. See also Bithell (D0361) and Grotefend (D0508).

D0492 Gee, Henry and Hardy, William John. Documents Illustrative of English Church History, Compiled from Original Sources. London: Macmillan and Company, 1896. Reprint. London: Macmillan and Company, 1914.

Arranged chronologically and covering the period between 314 and 1700, Gee is a standard collection of documents on British ecclesiastical history. Reprinted on several occasions, it retains significant reference value because of the inclusion of some texts not readily available elsewhere. See also Haddan (D0515) and Powicke (D0668).

D0493 Giry, Arthur. Manuel de Diplomatique: Diplomes et Chartes, Chronologie Technique, Eléments Critiques et Parties Constitutives de la Teneur des Chartes, les Chancelleries, les Actes Privés. Paris: Hachette et Cie, 1894. Reprint. Paris: F. Alcan, 1925.

Widely recognized as a standard in its field, this manual is aimed at those wishing to study and identify medieval documents, registers, decrees, charters, acts and similar writings. Bibliographical footnotes, treatment of chronology and other items make Giry an invaluable guide for the beginning graduate student of medieval history. See also Boüard (D0363), Bresslau (D0368) and Prou (D0670).

D0494 Glorieux, Palémon. Pour Revaloriser Migne: Tables Rectificatives. Cahier Supplémentaire aux Melanges de Science Religieuse 9 (1952). Lille: Facultés Catholiques, 1952.

This carefully compiled volume indicates many corrections concerning the authors of various works in Migne's Series Latina (D0624).

D0495 Goldie, Frederick. A Short History of the Episcopal Church in Scotland. 2nd ed. Edinburgh: St. Andrews Press, 1976.

First published in 1951, this 182 page history traces the development of Scottish Episcopalianism from the Reformation to the present, indicating major events in the growth, persecution and role of this denomination. Also included are comments on the problems faced by the church today. For students of the Anglican Communion and of Scottish church history this is a useful but very basic introduction.

D0496 Goodspeed, Edgar Johnson. A History of Early Christian Literature. Rev. and enlarged by Robert McQueen Grant. Chicago, Ill.: University of Chicago Press, [1966].

This brief guide of 214 pages covers ante-Nicene noncanonical Christian literature, including (in this revised edition) insights gained from discoveries such as Qumran and from recent research. A select bibliography (pp. 203-210) and indexes of ancient and modern authors are included. See also Krüger (D0563).

D0497 Graf, Georg. Geschichte der Christlichen Arabischen Literatur. 5 vols. Studi e Testi, nos. 118, 133, 146-147, 172. Vatican City: Biblioteca Vaticana, 1944-1953. Reprint. Vatican City: Biblioteca Vaticana, 1960.

Although containing a great deal of valuable and often indispensible information, this massive undertaking should be used with caution, as it suffers in particular from a lack of detailed, scientific linguistic understanding and from a failure to appreciate the critical problems involved in interpreting Christian Arabic literature. The four main volumes treat writings to the end of the nineteenth century, concentrating especially on the fifteenth through nineteenth centuries. The final volume is a detailed index to the entire work. See also Ceillier (D0394), Labriolle (D0565), Monceaux (D0629) and Schanz (D0697).

D0498 Graffin, René. Patrologia Syriaca, Complectens Opera Omnia SS. Patrum, Doctorum Scriptorumque Catholicorum Quibus Accedunt Aliorum Acatholicorum Auctorum Scripta Quae ad Res Ecclesiasticas Pertinent Quotquot Syriace Supersunt, Secundum Codices Praesertim Londinenses, Parisienses, Vaticanos. 3 vols. Paris: Firmin-Didot et Cie, 1894-1926.

Designed to complement Migne (D0623, D0624), this collection contains texts in Syriac and Latin from writers up to 320 A.D. A concordance is included in volume 3 and an index is provided. See also Graffin's Patrologia Orientalis (D0499) and Corpus Scriptorum Christianorum Orientalum (D0411).

D0499 Graffin, René; Nau, F.; and Saxe, Max, eds. Patrologie Orientalis. 26 vols. Paris: Firmin-Didot et Cie, 1907-1949.

Intended to complement Migne (D0623, D0624), this collection covers the same range of languages as the Corpus Scriptorum Christianorum Orientalum (D0411) but on a more selective basis. These languages include, among others, Arabic, Armenian, Coptic and Ethiopian. Each page includes the original text, a Latin translation plus a French, English or Italian translation. Variants and notes are also provided on the same page. Graffin is thus a useful working tool both for those seeking texts in the original languages and for those requiring accurate translations. See also Graffin's Patrologia Syriaca (D0498).

D0500 Grant, Robert McQueen, ed. The Apostolic Fathers: A New Translation and Commentary. 6 vols. New York: Thomas Nelson and Sons, 1964-1968.

This valuable set includes extensive introductory material, bibliographies and indexes in each volume. It is especially relevant as an introduction to the apostolic fathers for seminary students, and contains a wealth of information for scholars requiring these materials in English translation. Volume 1 is an introduction to the apostolic fathers; volume 2 covers I and II Clement; volume 3, Didache and Barnabas; volume 4, Ignatius; volume 5, Polycarp, Martyrdom of Polycarp, Fragments of Papias; and volume 6, the Shepherd of Hermas. For a substantial but earlier collection see Schaff (D0694, D0695).

D0501 Great Britain. Historical Manuscripts Commission. Record Repositories in Great Britain. 5th ed. London: HMSO, 1973.

This valuable guide to repositories is arranged geographically and covers only those places where record material has been systematically collected and where provision is made for its use by inquirers. Coverage ranges from government and parliamentary archives and national libraries to religious archives and libraries, colleges, universities, societies, commercial enterprises and public libraries. A basic index completes the volume, which has an obvious function in tracing manuscript collections.

D0502 Great Britain. Public Record Office. Rerum Britannicarum Medii Aevi Scriptores; or, Chronicles and Memorials of Great Britain and Ireland during the Middle Ages. 253 vols. London: Longmans, Green and Company, 1858-[1896].

The Rolls Series contains a significant collection of materials from papal, monastic and other sources related to the history of Britain from the Roman invasion to the time of Henry VIII. There are introductory notes on the lives of authors, sources of texts and related topics. All texts are thoroughly indexed to ease consultation. While not limited to ecclesiastical matters, this is an important collection for students of British church history. See also English Historical Documents (D0463).

D0503 Die Griechischen Christlichen Schriftsteller der Ersten Jahrhunderte. Bd. 1- . Berlin: Akademie Verlag, 1897- .

Issued by the Kommission für Spätantike Religionsgeschichte of the Deutschen Akademie der Wissenschaften and published until 1941 by J.C. Hinrichs, this is a most important collection of Greek patristic texts. Each text in Greek is complemented by a substantial introduction in German. Indexes are also in German. Overall the series exhibits a high degree of philological accuracy and is the most complete collection of its kind. The series is an invaluable resource for scholars of patristic literature. No volumes were published between 1942 and 1952. See also Texte und Untersuchungen (D0734).

D0504 Grimm, Harold John. The Reformation Era, 1500-1650. 2nd ed. New York: Macmillan Company, 1973.

Including a detailed, classified bibliography of primary and secondary sources in various languages (pp. 617-656), this general survey of the Reformation provides a thorough treatment suitable for undergraduate students. Four main sections cover Europe on the eve of the Reformation; the Reformation in Germany; the spread of Protestantism and revival of Catholicism; and religious conflicts and consequences. A detailed table of contents, an index and maps add to its reference value. See also Bainton (D0333), Chadwick (D0398) and Hillerbrand (D0534).

D0505 Grisar, Hartmann. History of Rome and the Popes in the Middle Ages. English trans. ed. by Charles Louis Dessoulay. 3 vols. London: Kegan Paul, Trench, Trübner and Company, 1911-1912.

This translation of Geschichte Roms und der Päpste im Mittelalter (Freiburg im Breisgau: Herder, 1898-1901) presents the history of the medieval papacy against a background of Roman history and civilization. It thus usefully places the papacy within a wider historical context, showing how the institution evolved and related to its environment. For factual data and interesting interpretive insights Grisar is a valuable guide for students of the medieval papacy. Ssee also Ranke (D0680), Schmidlin (D0701) and Seppelt (D0707).

D0506 [no entry]

D0507 Grotefend, Hermann. Taschenbuch der Zeitrechnung des Deutschen Mittelalters und der Neuzeit. 10. Aufl. Hrsg. von Theodor Ulrich. Hannover: Hahnsche Buchhandlung, 1960.

This is an acceptable condensation of Grotefend's Zeitrechnung des Deutschen Mittelalters (D0508) but often lacks the detail sought by church historians. Therefore, it should be used only for very basic needs or when the fuller compendium is not available. See also Bithell (D0361) and Gebhardt (D0491).

D0508 Grotefend, Hermann. Zeitrechnung des Deutschen Mittelalters und der Neuzeit. 3 pts. in 2 vols. Hannover: Hansche Buchhandlung, 1891-1898.

This chronology of medieval Germany is particularly useful for church historians. The first volume contains a glossary of terms and several tables; the second volume contains calendars dealing with dioceses in Germany, Switzerland and Scandinavia, with religious orders and with saints of the period. For factual chronological data and related information Grotefend is a very important time saver. See also Bithell (D0361) and Gebhardt (D0491). For an abridgement consult the preceding entry (D0507).

D0509 Grun, Bernard. The Timetables of History: A Horizontal Linkage of People and Events. Based on Werner Stein's "Kulturfahrplan". New York: Simon and Schuster, c. 1975.

Similar in content to Freeman-Grenville (D0479), this chronology uses a topical arrangement and covers history, politics; literature, theater; religion, philosophy, learning; visual arts; music; science, technology; and daily life in eight parallel columns. Religion and philosophy are treated adequately for basic reference purposes.

D0510 Gunneman, Louis H. The Shaping of the United Church of Christ: An Essay in the History of American Christianity. New York: United Church Press, c. 1977.

This 257 page discussion by a founder of the United Church of Christ describes how this union was created. It covers from the 1930s to the time of publication. Appendixes include a chronology and the Basis of Union.

D0511 Gwatkin, Henry Melvill. Early Church History to A.D. 313. 2 vols. London: Macmillan and Company, 1909. Reprint. 2 vols. [New York: AMS Press, 1974].

This narrative traces the growth of Christianity in the context of general history of the time. It includes selected references after each chapter, and an index is provided in volume 2. Intended for the general reader as well as the theological student, this is now a somewhat dated work. See also Bright (D0370), Kidd (D0558) and McGiffert (D0596).

D0512 Haag, Eugène, and Haag, Emile. La France Protestante; ou, Vies des Protestants Français Qui Se Sont Fait un Nom dans l'Histoire depuis les Premiers Temps de la Reformation jusqu'à la Reconnaissance du Principe de la Liberté des Cultes par l'Assemblée Nationale. 10 vols. Paris: J. Cherbuliez, 1846-1859.

This collection on French Protestantism contains biographical sketches of varying length on figures of some significance in the history and thought of this often overlooked group in European religious history. Extensive bibliographies of primary materials accompany many of the articles, which tend to be factual and descriptive rather than interpretive. The final volume contains "pieces justificatives" and includes texts of edicts, laws and other source materials relating to French Protestantism. A subsequent edition (Paris: Sandoz, 1877-1888) was never finished and reached only volume 6.

D0513 [no entry]

D0514 Habig, Marion Alphonse. Saints of the Americas. Huntington, Ind.:
Our Sunday Visitor, 1974.

This 384 page volume provides biographical sketches of forty-five Latin
American saints. It is aimed at the general reader and includes a certain
amount of inaccurate information. Nevertheless, for the historian with
some knowledge of the field this can serve as a useful reference guide.

D0515 Haddan, Arthur West, and Stubbs, William, eds. Councils and Ecclesiastical Documents Relating to Great Britain and Ireland; Edited after Spelman
and Wilkins. 3 vols. Oxford: Clarendon Press, 1869-1871. Reprint. 3 vols.
Oxford: Clarendon Press, 1964.

Based on Wilkin's Concilia Magnae Britanniae, this massive collection
of British ecclesiastical documents in Latin presents a wide range of
source materials on all aspects of church life from the earliest period,
with particular emphasis on the middle ages. Sections are arranged chronologically, topically and regionally, with a chronological sequence followed
in each section. The extensive table of contents compensates somewhat
for the lack of indexes. Detailed notes and references to sources accompany each document, making this an excellent collection of source materials for reference purposes. For a continuation see Powicke (D0688); see
also Gee (D0492).

D0516 Halphen, Louis. Initiation aux Etudes d'Histoire du Moyen Age. 3e éd.
Ed. by Y. Renouard. Paris: Presses Universitaires de France, 1952.

As an introductory manual to the study of medieval history, Halphen
is a good starting point for students about to embark on advanced research
in the period. Special attention is paid to the use of historical documents,
manuscripts and archives. Although written in French, this work is helpful
for those working on the medieval history of any European country. See
also Paetow (D0178) and Quirin (D0677).

D0517 Hamer, Philip May, ed. A Guide to Archives and Manuscripts in the
United States. Comp. for the National Historical Publications Commission.
New Haven, Conn.: Yale University Press, 1961.

This guide provides information on the holdings of some 1300 American
archives and manuscript collections. These are listed in inventory form
and for each depository include dates of coverage plus references to
related publications issued by the respective societies or archives. There
is a collection of notes on bibliographical guides and an index of subjects
and names. For those using primary sources on American church history
this is a useful starting point for tracing materials.

D0518 Hamilton, John Taylor, and Hamilton, Kenneth Gardiner. History of
the Moravian Church: The Renewed Unitas Fratrum, 1722-1957. [Bethlehem,
Penn.: Moravian Church in America, Board of Christian Education, 1967].

This 723 page successor to Hamilton's A History of the Church Known
As the Moravian Church includes a substantial section of notes (pp. 654-
675), a brief bibliography (pp. 676-679) and an index, as well as maps
and illustrations. It provides a useful source for the student.

D0519 Handy, Robert T. A History of the Churches in the United States and Canada. Oxford History of the Christian Church. Oxford: Clarendon Press, 1976; New York: Oxford University Press, 1977.

>   Containing a substantial bibliography (pp. 428-449), this 471 page history in the Chadwick series (D0396) provides a detailed overview of North American church history for the beginner and much reference detail for advanced students. The twelve chapters cover events from 1650 to the present; Canada is well treated in this survey, as are individual denominations. The work is very thoroughly indexed. See also Ahlstrom (D0319), Brauer (D0367), Gaustad (D0490), Hudson (D0540) and Mead (D0614).

D0520 Handy, Robert T., ed. Religion in the American Experience: The Pluralistic Style. Columbia, S.C.: University of South Carolina Press; New York: Harper and Row, 1972.

>   Emphasizing institutional aspects of American religious life, Handy seeks to show the pluralism of religion in America by providing documentary evidence of various European traditions, of tensions and the search for unity and of indigenous American churches. The thirty-three documents span the period from the seventeenth through the mid-twentieth centuries. Handy provides brief introductions to the documents, which are well chosen to reflect the theme of this work. See also Ferm (D0470), Gaustad (D0488), Miller (D0626) and Smith (D0712).

D0521 Harcup, Sara E., comp. Historical, Archaeological and Kindred Societies in the British Isles: A List. London: University of London, Institute of Historical Research, 1965.

>   This alphabetical listing provides the name, date of founding, address and publications for about 850 societies. There is a topographical index and a basic list of subjects (including religion). Local societies often undertake research and issue publications on very specific topics (parish registers, etc.) which can be of interest to church historians; this makes Harcup a useful, if somewhat dated, compendium.

D0522 Harder, Johannes. Kleine Geschichte der Orthodoxen Kirche. Munich: Christian Kaiser Verlag, 1961.

>   Aimed at the student unfamiliar with Eastern Orthodoxy, this basic survey covers oriental, East European and Russian branches of the denomination. Each chapter discusses the main features of Orthodoxy as seen in the region or country, providing summary information in a clear and uncomplicated fashion. See also Atiya (D0326), Neale (D0638) and Schmemann (D0700).

D0523 Harnack, Adolf von. The Expansion of Christianity in the First Three Centuries. Trans. and ed. by James Moffatt. 2 vols. New York: G.P. Putnam's Sons; London: Williams and Norgate, 1904-1905. Reprint. Freeport, N.Y.: Books for Libraries Press, [1972].

>   Also published in a largely unchanged second edition as The Mission and Expansion of Christianity in the First Three Centuries, this detailed study is arranged in four main sections; these are largely chronological and consist of a series of topical chapters on aspects of Christian expansion to 300 A.D. The text is scholarly and incisive, including much interpretive

material which is cogently argued and well footnoted. Much use is made of primary sources, and the editor has tried to include English translations or explanations wherever possible. Indexes treat NT passages, general subjects and authors, geographical terms. This is a valuable survey and reference work for advanced students of early Christian history and the NT period. See also Lietzmann (D0586).

D0524 Harper, Howard V. Profiles of Protestant Saints. New York: Fleet Press Corporation, 1968.

After a brief introduction on saints and Protestantism, this volume contains chapters on individuals (Luther, Calvin, Wesley through to Bonhoeffer and Schweitzer). It is a readable source of biographical data for those interested in key figures of Protestantism.

D0525 Harrell, David Edwin. A Social History of the Disciples of Christ. 2 vols. Atlanta, Ga.: Publishing Systems, 1966-1973.

Published under different imprints, these two volumes cover this American denomination from its beginnings to 1866 and from 1866 to 1900, detailing the diverse social thought of the movement. The work is based on extensive research into primary documentation, and indicates various currents of thought within the movement. See also Garrison (D0487) and Tucker (D0740).

D0526 Hauck, Albert. Kirchengeschichte Deutschlands. 8. Aufl. 5 vols. in 6. Berlin: Akademie Verlag, 1954.

This work was first published by J.C. Hinrichs of Leipzig between 1887 and 1929.

D0527 Hector, Leonard Charles. The Handwriting of English Documents. 2nd ed. London: Edward Arnold Publishers, 1966.

Intended to introduce students to problems associated with handwritten documents, this excellent primer covers writing equipment, languages, abbreviations, conventional written usage, handwriting from the conquest to 1500 and from 1500 onwards. An interesting collection of plates includes transcripts, and there is a helpful table of "confusibilia" for the beginner. A bibliography and an index complete the work. For the student unfamiliar with medieval English documents relevant to church history this is an essential prerequisite to using such primary source materials. See also Denholm-Young (D0429), Emmison (D0462), Martin (D0609) and Newton (D0641).

D0528 Hefele, Karl Joseph von. Histoire des Conciles d'après les Documents Originaux. Nouvelle traduction. 11 vols. in 22. Paris: Letouzey et Ané, 1907-1952.

This massive history treats provincial and ecumenical councils of the Catholic Church in great detail. Although dated in many respects, Hefele remains a standard work which is valuable for the wide range of information it contains. It is based on the German original and treats events up to 1854. An earlier English version, A History of the Councils of the Church from the Original Documents (Trans. and ed. by Henry Nutcombe Oxenham). 5 vols. Edinburgh: T. and T. Clark, 1876-1896), covers the councils only to 787. See also Dumeige (D0445).

D0529 Hennesey, James J. American Catholics: A History of the Roman Catholic Community in the United States. New York: Oxford University Press, 1981.

This history treads a middle path between the traditional approach (what the bishops achieved, etc.) and more recent historiography (focusing on individual Catholic experiences at a local level). It contains a wealth of information, and is especially strong on minority groups and developments in the western United States. Bibliographical references and an index add to its reference value. See also Ellis (D0455) and McAvoy (D0594).

D0530 Hertling, Ludwig von. A History of the Catholic Church. Trans. by Anselm Gordon Biggs. Westminster, Md.: Newman Press, 1957.

See also Hughes (D0544), McSorley (D0600) and Neill (D0639).

D0531 Heussi, Karl. Kompendium der Kirchen Geschichte. 13. Aufl. Tübingen: J.C.B. Mohr (Paul Siebeck), 1971.

See also Aubert (D0327) and Schmidt (D0702).

D0532 Heussi, Karl, and Mulert, Hermann. Atlas zur Kirchengeschichte: 66 Karten auf 12 Blättern 3. Aufl. Tübingen: J.C.B. Mohr, 1934. Reprint. Tübingen: J.C.B. Mohr (Paul Siebeck), 1937.

Covering the period from 390 A.D. to 1900, this atlas provides clear maps of the church's situation in various countries and at various stages of its development. See also Jedin (D0549) and Littell (D0588).

D0533 Heyer, Friedrich. The Catholic Church from 1648-1870. Trans. by D.W.D. Shaw. A History of the Christian Church. London: Adam and Charles Black, 1969.

This translation of Die Katholische Kirche vom Westfälischen Frieden bis zum Ersten Vatikanischen Konzil compresses a vast amount of material into 255 pages. It includes coverage of Catholicism in North America and of the Uniate Churches of Eastern Europe and the Near East. The translator has restricted footnotes to those refering to works readily available in English speaking countries, and has added a short list of English books on the period.

D0534 Hillerbrand, Hans Joachim. Christendom Divided: The Protestant Reformation. Theological Resources. New York: Corpus Books; London: Hutchinson and Company, 1971.

This 344 page study distinguishes three different uses of "reformation": theological, religious and political. The first main part of the work concentrates on the theological reformation, discussing Luther, Zwingli, Calvin and various radical movements in three chapters. The second part deals with the political reformation, paying particular attention to Germany and England but also touching upon events elsewhere in Europe. Substantial notes (pp. 306-319), a detailed bibliography (pp. 321-336) and an index conclude the work, which may be regarded as a sound introduction to the subject and a useful reference work for beginners. See also Bainton

(D0333), Chadwick (D0398) and Grimm (D0504).

BR30/
H68
1968

D0535 Hillerbrand, Hans Joachim, ed. The Protestant Reformation. Documentary History of Western Civilization. New York: Walker and Company; New York: Harper and Row; London: Macmillan and Company, 1968.

This 290 page collection of selected writings by Luther, Zwingli, the Anabaptists, Calvin and English reformers opens with a general introduction to the Reformation, which is especially helpful for the beginner. The documents also have their own introductions, setting context and explaining significance. Both general and specific introductory sections include bibliographies of related works. See also Kidd (D0556) and Spitz (D0715).

270.6
H652

D0536 Hillerbrand, Hans Joachim. The Reformation: A Narrative History Related by Contemporary Observers and Participants. New York: Harper and Row, 1964.

Published in Britain as The Reformation in Its Own Words (London: SCM Press, [1963]), this presentation of documents in translation provides quite a good picture of the Reformation as viewed by contemporaries. The documents are selected for their narrative rather than interpretive value. Illustrations accompany the text.

D0537 Hillerbrand, Hans Joachim. The World of the Reformation. New York: Charles Scribner's Sons, 1973.

Placed within a broad interpretive frame of reference, this survey of Reformation history provides particularly useful material on the interaction between religion and politics. As such it is useful for the undergraduate student; it does not attempt to provide profound theological interpretation. There is a select bibliography which has been criticized for its unevenness; there are no footnotes, and quotation of source material is slight. See also Bainton (D0330), Elton (D0459) and Sykes (D0730).

D0538 Holder-Egger, Oswald, and Zeumer, Karl. Indices Eorum Quae Monumentorum Germaniae Historicorum Tomis Hucusque Editis Continentur. Hannover: Hahnsche Hofbuchhandlung, 1890.

For accurate and rapid consultation of the Monumenta Germaniae Historica (D0630) this 254 page index is an essential reference tool. See also Pertz (D0659).

BR60
M5X

D0539 Hopfner, Theodorus, comp. Patrologiae Cursus Completus Accurante I.P. Migne. Index Locupletissimus. 2 vols. Paris: Librairie Orientaliste Paul Gouthner, 1928-1936. Micro-reprint. [Tumba: International Documentation Center, n.d.]

This is a useful index to Migne's Series Graeca (D0623). See also Cavallera (D0391).

D0540 Hudson, Winthrop Still. American Protestantism. The Chicago History of American Civilization. Chicago, Ill.: University of Chicago Press, 1961.

277.3
H88

In 198 pages this introductory volume examines three periods of American Protestantism: the colonial; 1787-1914; and "post-Protestant". Treatment is concise, with some interesting interpretive insights. See also Brauer

(D0367), Gaustad (D0490), Handy (D0519) and Mead (D0614).

D0541 Hudson, Winthrop Still. Religion in America: An Historical Account of the Development of American Religious Life. 2nd ed. New York: Charles Scribner's Sons, 1973.

This highly regarded study of American religious history covers the period from 1607 to the present in roughly equal parts. Factual data and scholarly interpretation are substantiated clearly and judiciously. Both primary and secondary sources are cited in the footnotes, and a brief bibliography of paperback works precedes the index. Hudson is an interesting study well suited to less advanced students and of some reference value to more knowledgeable readers, especially those interested in Protestantism. See also Ahlstrom (D0319), Olmstead (D0650), Gaustad (D0490) and Mead (D0614).

D0542 Hughes, Philip. A History of the Church. [2nd ed.] 3 vols. New York: Sheed and Ward, [1949-1950?].

Originally published in 1934, this popularly written introduction to church history for the beginner is a fairly discursive but adequately detailed survey. The particular strength of the three volumes is the analysis of ecclesiastical history in relation to Christian origins and to religious movements to the time of Luther. The first volume focuses on the early church in relation to its secular environment, while the second emphasizes the impact of the church on its environment. The third volume concentrates on internal efforts at reform from St. Thomas Aquinas to Luther. For those interested in a traditional Roman Catholic view of church history Hughes is a worthwhile compendium. Both a bibliography and an index are provided. See also Bihlmeyer (D0360).

D0543 Hughes, Philip. The Reformation in England. Rev. [5th] ed. 3 vols. in 1. New York: Macmillan Company; London: Burns and Oates, 1963.

The three volumes in this standard Roman Catholic view of the English Reformation cover "the King's proceedings", "religio depopulata", "true religion now established". The treatment throughout is scholarly and factual, providing reasonably detailed coverage for beginning and intermediate students. Footnotes, bibliographies and indexes are contained in each volume, as well as extremely detailed tables of contents. See also Dickens (D0433), Elton (D0458) and Parker (D0655).

D0544 Hughes, Philip. A Short History of the Catholic Church [New ed.] With a final chapter by Edward Elton Young Hales. London: Burns and Oates, 1967.

Originally published in 1939 as A Popular History of the Church, this work tells the story of the Roman Catholic Church in a popular, non-technical fashion from the point of view of a devout Roman Catholic. It is succinct and fairly comprehensive. See also Hertling (D0530), McSorley (D0600) and Neill (D0639).

D0545 Imbart de la Tour, Pierre. Les Origines de la Réforme. 2e éd. Rev. et augm. d'une bibliographie critique par J. de Pins. Vol. 1- . Melun: Librairie d'Argences, 1948- .

First published in 1905-1935, this history of the Reformation provides a somewhat different approach in being a Roman Catholic interpretation which views the whole era from the viewpoint of France. Thie is an interesting and fruitful perspective, especially for those used to a more Germanic Protestant perspective. However, Imbart treats all non-French reformers in a single volume, which is rather inadequate. A critical bibliography is included, but there are no indexes. See also Todd (D0738).

D0546 Jacobus de Varagine. The Golden Legend; or, Lives of the Saints As Englished by William Caxton. Trans. by F.S. Ellis. 7 vols. London: J.M. Dent and Company, 1900.

This medieval collection of hagiographical legends is based on folklore of the period. As such, it is not a scholarly collection but is useful for historians of popular belief and legends.

D0547 Jedin, Hubert. Ecumenical Councils of the Catholic Church: An Historical Outline. Trans. by Ernest Graf. New York: Herder and Herder, 1960.

This 253 page translation of Kleine Konziliengeschichte provides a brief historical outline of the twenty ecumenical councils of Roman Catholicism. A short bibliography (pp. 240-250) covers the history and sources of conciliarism as well as each council treated in the text. This is a scholarly and competent work for those who require basic historical information. See also Raab (D0547) and Margull (D0608).

D0548 Jedin, Hubert, and Dolan, John Patrick, gen. eds. The History of the Church. 10 vols. New York: Crossroad Publishing Company; London: Burns and Oates, 1965-1980.

Begun as Handbook of Church History, this translation of Handbuch der Kirchengeschichte (2. Aufl. 7 vols. in 10. Freiburg im Breisgau: Herder, 1973-1979) is a substantial, scholarly history prepared from a Roman Catholic viewpoint. The overall aim of the series is to provide an objective account of principal events and leading figures in church history. Each volume is thoroughly documented and contains a bibliography for each chapter together with a full index. Jedin is a sound introduction to the literature, sources and developments of church history, serving also as a suitable reference work for intermediate and advanced students. See also Fliche (D0473), The Christian Centuries (D0400) and Daniel-Rops (D0419).

D0549 Jedin, Hubert; Latourette, Kenneth Scott; and Martin, Jochen, eds. Atlas zur Kirchengeschichte: Die Christlichen Kirchen in Geschichte und Gegenwart; 257 Mehrfarbige Karten und Schematische Darstellungen, Kommentare, Ausführliches Register. Unter Mitwirkung zahlreicher Fachgelehrter bearb. von Jochen Martin. Kartographische Bearbeitung: Hans E.F. Quast. Freiburg im Breisgau: Herder, [1970].

The 152 pages of maps in this atlas provide very full cartographic coverage of church history. The maps are accompanied by brief commentaries on events, developments and changes, and each section of commentary is followed by bibliographical references. Both the maps and text are well prepared and reflect the ecumenical approach of the compilers. A detailed index concludes the work, which is one of the better historical atlases. See also Heussi (D0532) and Littell (D0588).

D0550 John, Eric, ed. The Popes: A Concise Biographical History. Historical surveys by Douglas Woodruff. Biographical articles by J.M.W. Bean and others. New York: Hawthorn Books; London: Burns and Oates, 1964.

This concise history presents brief and factual historical data on each papal reign from St. Peter to Paul VI. The work is well indexed (pp. 483-496) for reference purposes. John is a very useful compendium for data on papal history; for a detailed historical survey see the encyclopedic work by Pastor (D0656).

D0551 Jones, Putnam Fennell. A Concordance to the "Historia Ecclesiastica" of Bede. Mediaeval Academy of America Publication, no. 2. Cambridge, Mass.:Mediaeval Academy of America for the Concordance Society, 1929.

This concordance lists the occurrences of all significant words in Historia Ecclesiastica. Each word is listed under its first grammatical form, and enough text is quoted to identify the usage; this feature makes Jones as much an index as a concordance.

D0552 Jong, Jan de. Handboek der Kerkgeschiedenis. 4. druck. Herzien en verbeterd R.R. Post. 4 vols. Utrecht: Dekker, van de Vegt, 1945-1949.

This Roman Catholic manual covers the early church, middle ages, 1517-1789, 1789-1949. Each volume is very detailed and comprehensive for a work of this sort, and de Jong attempts to be objective and analytical in his commentary. There are numerous quotations from primary sources, helpful tables and lists and valuable bibliographies. For those unable to read Dutch, Jedin (D0548) is a comparable English language work. See also Albers (D0320).

D0553 Jung, Kurt Michael. Weltgeschichte in Einem Griff. Vergleichende Zeittafeln der Politischen Geschichte Deutschlands, Europas und der Welt Gegenübergestellt der Entwicklung von Soziologie, Wirtschaft und Kultur, von der Urzeit bis zur Gegenwart. Ein Chronologisches Nachschlagewerk mit 508 Zeitgenössischen Bildern, 66 Geschichtskarten zu den Epochen und Ausführlichen Sachs- und Namenregister. [Berlin: Safari Verlag, 1968].

Published in an earlier edition as Weltgeschichte in Stichworten, this chronology uses parallel columns to indicate important events in German, European, world, social, economic and cultural history. As Jung focuses particularly on German history and covers all historical periods, it is most useful as a guide to events to Germany during the Reformation era. For more general coverage see Peters (D0660).

D0554 Kee, Howard Clark. The Origins of Christianity: Sources and Documents. Englewood Cliffs, N.J.: Prentice-Hall, 1973.

Intended in part as an accompaniment to Kee's Understanding the New Testament, this is a comprehensive collection of historical and literary documents dealing with political, social, cultural and religious conditions and ideas of the early Christian world. The volume includes a number of more recently unearthed documents regarding both pagan and Jewish religious developments. See also Ayer (D0328), Fremantle (D0480) and Stevenson (D0722).

D0555 Ker, Neil Ripley, ed. The Parochial Libraries of the Church of England:

Report of a Committee Appointed to Investigate the Number and Condition of Parochial Libraries Belonging to the Church of England; with an Historical Introduction, Notes on Early Printed Books and Their Care and an Alphabetical List of Parochial Libraries, Past and Present. London: Faith Press in conjunction with the College of the Faith, 1959.

Particularly useful for the researcher and bibliophile is the list of libraries in this work, which includes a brief description of the contents and history of each library. Also provided is a list of medieval manuscripts belonging to parish churches either in the past or in the present (i.e., 1950s). See also Cox (D0414) and Tate (D0732).

D0556 Kidd, Beresford James, ed. Documents Illustrative of the Continental Reformation. Oxford: Clarendon Press, 1911. Reprint. Oxford: Clarendon Press, 1967.

Containing contributions in English, Latin and French, this 742 page compendium covers Lutheran and Reformed aspects of the Reformation. A detailed table of contents includes dates of the various documents. Presentation is by geographical area where appropriate. This is an invaluable collection of primary source material for students and scholars. See also Hillerbrand (D0535) and Spitz (D0715).

D0557 Kidd, Beresford James, ed. Documents Illustrative of the History of the Church. 3 vols. Translations of Christian Literature, Series VI: Select Passages. New York: Macmillan Company; London: SPCK, 1920-[1941].

Containing selected documents in translation, these three volumes cover the period to 313, 313-461, 500-1500. Each volume is well indexed and contains a broadly representative selection of extracts from conciliar documents, letters, laws, chronicles, monastic writings and other sources. See also the two collections by Stevenson (D0722), which are based on Kidd. See also Ayerst (D0329), Barry (D0345) and Bettenson (D0354).

D0558 Kidd, Beresford James. A History of the Church to A.D. 461. 3 vols. Oxford: Clarendon Press, 1922.

The three volumes in this classic history of the early church cover the period to 313, 313-408, 408-461. They are especially valuable for students in providing copious references to original sources and to sources in English translation. Each volume contains an informative table of contents and an index. See also Bright (D0370), Gwatkin (D0511) and McGiffert (D0596).

D0559 Kirch, Konrad, comp. Enchiridion Fontium Historiae Ecclesiasticae Antiquae, Quod in Usum Scholarum Collegit. 9. ed. Quod auxit et emendavit Leo Ueding. Barcelona: Herder, 1965.

D0560 Kirsch, Johann Peter, ed. Kirchengeschichte. Unter Mitwirkung von Andreas Bigelmain et al. 4 vols. Freiburg im Breisgau: Herder, 1930-1933.

Although providing some coverage of Orthodoxy and Protestantism, this is essentially a history of the Roman Catholic Church. Each volume is by a different author, but all are notable for their objective and balanced treatment of key issues, developments and controversies. Excellent bibliographies and indexes give each volume added reference value. For students able to read German Kirsch is a useful source of information, as well as a standard text. See also Alzog (D0323) and Bihlmeyer (D0360).

D0561 Kraft, Heinrich. Clavis Patrum Apostolicorum: Catalogum Vocum in Libris Patrum Qui Dicuntur Apostolici Non Raro Occurrentium. Adinvante Ursula Früchtel. Münich: Kösel Verlag, 1963.

This key to the writings of the Greek and Latin fathers lists authors alphabetically and provides references to sources. Greek terms are defined in Latin and German, while Latin terms are defined only in German. A full list of sources is included. As a concordance to the apostolic fathers, Kraft is more adequate than Edgard Johnson Goodspeed's Index Patristicus Sive Clavis Patrum Apostolicorum Operum ex Editione Minore Gebhardt Harnack Zahn, Lectionibus Editionum Minorum Funk et Lightfoot Admissis (Leipzig: J.C. Hinrichs Buchhandlung, 1907).

D0562 Krüger, Gustav, ed. Handbuch der Kirchengeschichte für Studierende. In Verbindung mit Gerhard Ficker et al. 4 vols. Tübingen: J.C.B. Mohr, 1909-1912. Reprint. Tübingen: J.C.B. Mohr, 1923-1931.

Covering the early church, middle ages, Reformation and Counter-Reformation, modern times up to the early twentieth century, this substantial history makes use of the best Protestant and Roman Catholic scholarship but does reflect a continental Protestant view of events. See also Baur (D0348).

D0563 Krüger, Gustav. History of Early Christian Literature in the First Three Centuries. Trans. by Charles Ripley Gillett. New York: Macmillan Company, 1897.

This volume is intended as a basis for lectures and as a students' handbook. It covers in detail primitive Christian and gnostic literature, patristic literature, legends, martyrologies, etc., including geographical areas where appropriate. Footnotes and an index are included in this scholarly nineteenth century work. See also Goodspeed (D0496).

D0564 Labande, Edmond-René, and Leplant, Bernadett. Répertoire International des Médiévalistes. 2 vols. Publications du Centre d'Etudes Supérieures de Civilisation Médiévale, no. 5. Poitiers: Université de Poitiers, Centre d'Etudes Supérieures de Civilisation Médiévale, 1971.

Replacing the similar directory prepared by Gallais (D0484), this work lists some 4800 medievalists from around the world. For each scholar the entry provides basic biographical data, titles of publications and notes on work in progress. The four indexes deal with geographical locations, specializations, reviews and collections, those deceased since 1964. As a current guide Labande is now somewhat dated, but it does provide an initial source of information in a field with strong theological links.

D0565 Labriolle, Pierre Champagne de. History and Literature of Christianity from Tertullian to Boethius. Trans. by Herbert Wilson. New York: A.A. Knopf; London: Kegan Paul, Trench, Trübner and Company, 1924.

This translation from the French provides scholarly coverage of the history of Christian literature to the end of the sixth century. A critical bibliographical essay precedes each chapter. The studies of authors are thorough, and indexes and tables are included. A revised and enlarged third edition of the French exists: <u>Histoire de la Littérature Latine Chrétienne</u> (3e éd. rev. et augm. par Gustav Bardy. 2 vols. Paris: Belles Lettres, 1947). For a companion volume see Puech (D0672); see also Ceillier (D0394), Graf (D0497), Monceaux (D0629) and Schanz (D0697).

D0566 Lamb, John Alexander, ed. <u>Fasti [of the United Free Church of Scotland], 1900-1929.</u> Edinburgh: Oliver and Boyd, 1956.

This compendium includes biographical data on clergy of the United Free Church of Scotland with indexes of congregations and ministers. See also Ewing (D0465) and Small (D0711).

270.8
L359

D0567 Latourette, Kenneth Scott. <u>Christianity in a Revolutionary Age: A History of Christianity in the Nineteenth and Twentieth Centuries.</u> 5 vols. New York: Harper and Brothers, 1958-1962; London: Eyre and Spottiswoode, 1959-1963. Reprint. 5 vols. Westport, Conn.: Greenwood Press, 1973.

Continuing Latourette's earlier history (D0568), this work brings the discussion down to 1960 and provides a very comprehensive survey of theological and ecclesiastical trends plus an analysis of Christian influence in the secular sphere. Latourette provides encyclopedic but brief coverage of all major traditions throughout the world, presenting information factually and concisely. Each volume is well indexed, and some bibliographical data are provided. For a single volume work on the modern period see Vidler (D0743).

D0568 Latourette, Kenneth Scott. <u>A History of Christianity.</u> Rev. ed. 2 vols. New York: Harper and Row, 1975.

This standard history of the development of Christianity ranks with Walker (D0748) in its widespread acceptance as a sound introductory handbook. The first volume covers church history to 1500; the second, 1500 to 1975. Each volume includes chapter bibliographies of relevant works plus a supplementary bibliography of post-1950 publications. The index to the entire work appears in each volume. See also Bainton (D0331).

D0569 Latreille, André; Delaruelle, E.; and Palanque, J.R. <u>Histoire du Catholicisme en France.</u> 3 vols. Paris: Editions Spes, 1957-1962.

These volumes present an analysis of many aspects of Roman Catholic life in France during the early period, the medieval era, and the modern period. Bibliographies are provided in each volume. For a more specific work see Viénot (D0744).

944
L413

D0570 Lavisse, Ernest, ed. <u>Histoire de France depuis les Origines jusqu'à la Révolution.</u> 9 vols. in 18. Paris: Hachette, 1900-1911.

Long regarded as the standard reference history in its field, Lavisse is the most detailed and substantial guide for users at all levels. While the slight anti-clerical bias common to much French historical writing is somewhat evident in this work, most of the chapters are relatively objective and contain a wealth of historical detail. The critical bibliographies, although dated, retain much value for reference purposes.

283
L565

D0571 Le Neve, John. <u>Fasti Ecclesiae Anglicanae, 1066-1300.</u> Rev. and expanded ed. Comp. by Diana E. Greenaway. Vol. 1- . London: Athlone Press in association with the University of London, Institute of Historical Research, 1968- .

> This and the following two series (D0572, D0573) correct and greatly expand the 1854 edition prepared by T. Duffus Hardy. Volumes are arranged by diocese and list bishops, deans, precentors, chancellors, treasurers, subdeans, archdeacons, prebendaries and similar ecclesiastical dignitaries. The lists are arranged by office, and there are indexes of persons and places. The beginning of each volume includes a list of references. Le Neve is indispensible for students of English church history and is a very accurate listing of ecclesiastical personalities.

D0572 Le Neve, John. Fasti Ecclesiae Anglicanae, 1300-1541. New and expanded ed. Comp. by Joyce M. Horn et al. 12 vols. London: Athlone Press in association with the University of London, Institute of Historical Research, 1962-1967.

> See the preceding entry (D0571) for a description of contents. This series follows the same format and pattern, covering dignitaries from 1300 to 1541.

D0573 Le Neve, John. Fasti Ecclesiae Anglicanae, 1541-1857. Comp. by Joyce M. Horn et al. Vol. 1- . London: University of London, Institute of Historical Research, 1969- .

> Like the two preceding series in format and arrangement, this collection of volumes covers Anglican dignitaries in various dioceses between 1541 and 1857. See also Stubbs (D0726).

D0574 Leclercq, Henri. Manuel d'Archéologie Chrétienne depuis les Origines jusqu'à VIIIe Siècle. 2 vols. Paris: Letouzey et Ané, 1907.

> This useful handbook of archeological studies covers much material of value to students of early church history, including catacombs, buildings, monuments, sculpture and related arts. Both a general bibliography and subject bibliographies are provided. Leclercq is well indexed and retains value as an introductory archeological handbook despite its age. Few later works have covered the same topic in such detail. See also Marucchi (D0611).

D0575 Léonard, Emile G. A History of Protestantism. Trans. by Joyce M.H. Reid and R.M. Bethell. Ed. by Harold Henry Rowley, Vol. 1- . London: Thomas Nelson and Sons, 1966- ; Indianapolis, Ind.: Bobbs-Merrill, 1968- .

> This translation of Histoire Générale du Protestantism (3 vols. Paris: Presses Universitaires de France, 1961-1964) covers the period from Protestant origins to 1564, from the establishment of Protestantism to the end of the seventeenth century, and the eighteenth and nineteenth centuries. While Léonard clearly exhibits a marked dislike of Calvinism and somewhat sketchy understanding of the medieval background of the Reformation, this does provide an interesting alternative to less critical surveys. The bibliographies, while not always up to date, are extremely comprehensive and list many European works not recorded elsewhere. For studies of Calvinism and radical Protestantism see McNeill (D0598) and Durnbaugh (D0446).

D0576 Leslie, James Blennerhassett. Ardfert and Aghadoe Clergy and Parishes: Being an Account of the Clergy of the Church of Ireland in the Diocese of Ardfert and Aghadoe from the Earliest Period, with Historical Notices of the Several Parishes, Churches, etc. Dublin: Church of Ireland Printing and Publishing Company, 1940.

For works complementary to this and to the following titles by Leslie see Cotton (D0413) and Swanzy (D0727).

D0577 Leslie, James Blennerhassett. Armagh Clergy and Parishes: Being an Account of the Clergy of the Church of Ireland in the Diocese of Armagh from the Earliest Period, with Historical Notices of the Several Parishes, Churches, etc. Dundalk: W. Tempest, 1911.

D0578 Leslie, James Blennerhassett. Clogher Clergy and Parishes: Being an Account of the Clergy of the Church of Ireland in the Diocese of Clogher from the Earliest Period, with Historical Notices of the Several Parishes, Churches, etc. Enniskillen: [Fermanagh Times], 1929.

D0579 Leslie, James Blennerhassett. Derry Clergy and Parishes: Being an Account of the Clergy of the Church of Ireland in the Diocese of Derry from the Earliest Period, with Historical Notices of the Several Parishes, Churches, etc. Enniskillen: [Fermanagh Times], 1937.

D0580 Leslie, James Blennerhassett. Ferns Clergy and Parishes: Being an Account of the Clergy of the Church of Ireland in the Diocese of Ferns from the Earliest Period, with Historical Notices of the Several Parishes, Churches, etc. Dublin: Church of Ireland Printing and Publishing Company, 1936.

D0581 Leslie, James Blennerhassett. Ossery Clergy and Parishes: Being an Historical Account of the Clergy of the Church of Ireland in the Diocese of Ossery from the Earliest Period, with Historical Notices of the Several Parishes, Churches, etc. Enniskillen, [Fermanagh Times], 1933.

D0582 Leslie, James Blennerhassett. Raphoe Clergy and Parishes: Being an Account of the Clergy of the Church of Ireland in the Diocese of Raphoe from the Earliest Period, with Historical Notices of the Several Parishes, Churches, etc. Enniskillen: [Fermanagh Times], 1940.

D0583 Leslie, James Blennerhassett, and Swanzy, Henry Biddell. Biographical Succession Lists of the Clergy of the Diocese of Down. Enniskillen: Fermanagh Times, 1936.

D0584 The Library of Christian Classics. 26 vols. Philadelphia, Pa.: Westminster Press, 1953-1969.

This widely used collection contains selections from the writings of early church fathers (e.g., Clement, Jerome) through the close of the sixteenth century (e.g., Calvin, Luther, Anabaptists). In most cases new English translations have been made, and there are excellent introductions and helpful explanatory notes. Each volume is well indexed. The series is useful both for reference purposes and for background reading.

D0585 Liebman, Seymour B. The Inquisitors and the Jews in the New World: Summaries of Procesos: 1500-1810, and Bibliographical Guide. Coral Gables,

Fla.: University of Miami Press, [1975] c. 1974.

Arranged geographically and then alphabetically by name of accused persons, this guide contains case summaries and locations of documents for each individual.

D0586 Lietzmann, Hans. A History of the Early Church. Trans. by Bertram Lee Woolf. 2nd and 3rd eds. 4 vols. London: Lutterworth Press, [1955].

Available in various imprints, this particular version presents the third edition of volumes 1 and 2 and the second edition of the final two volumes. The volumes cover the beginnings of the Christian church; the founding of the church universal; from Constantine to Julian; and the era of the church fathers. This is an important work which concentrates on the history of ideas, and contains useful aids such as chronological tables, bibliographies and indexes. For the student of the period this provides a wealth of information. See also Harnack (D0523); for an earlier Roman Catholic work see Duchesne (D0442).

D0587 Lindsay, Thomas Martin. A History of the Reformation. 2 vols. New York: Charles Scribner's Sons, 1906-1907; Edinburgh: T. and T. Clark, 1907-1908. Reprint. 2 vols. Freeport, N.Y.: Books for Libraries Press, 1972.

Available in many reprints, some of the earlier ones being labeled "second edition", this work aims to describe the Reformation in its social context. Volume 1 describes the eve of the Reformation and the movement itself under the guidance of Luther, covering intellectual, social and religious aspects. Volume 2 examines the Reformed Churches, the Anabaptist and Socinian movements and the Counter-Reformation in the sixteenth century. There are many references to primary source material, particularly at the beginning of each chapter. Volume 1 includes an index and chronological summary and volume 2 a map. Although dated, this is a thorough study suitable for use by students of history and theology. See also Seebohm (D0705).

D0588 Littell, Franklin Hamlin. The Macmillan Atlas History of Christianity. Cartography by E. Hausman. Prepared by Carta, Jerusalem. New York: Macmillan Company, [1976].

This excellent atlas is an extremely valuable complement to other compilations focusing on political or geographical issues. It concentrates on intellectual, ethical and expansionist aspects of Christianity and attempts to map doctrinal developments, social teachings and missions from the church's beginnings to the present. Each of the 197 maps is accompanied by a brief explanatory text. See also Heussi (D0532) and Jedin (D0549).

D0589 Livingston, James C. Modern Christian Thought from the Enlightenment to Vatican II. New York: Macmillan Company, [1971].

This 523 page survey covers the major intellectual movements in modern Christian thought from Locke and Voltaire to Teilhard, Rahner and Vatican II. It clearly presents the historical context, the principal ideas, and selections from individual thinkers to illustrate the ideas. It is suitable as a textbook for college or seminary courses, although it needs supplementing on the contemporary period. See also Creed (D0416).

D0590 Loetscher, Lefferts Augustine. A Brief History of the Presbyterians. 3rd ed. Philadelphia, Pa.: Westminster Press, c. 1978.

This is an updated edition of a 1938 work written as part of the church school curriculum for young Presbyterians. Early chapters cover the ideas of Luther and Calvin and the growth of Protestant groups in Europe, while chapters 6-15 trace developments among Presbyterians in America through to the late 1960s. This is valuable as a brief (205 pp.) introduction for students of Presbyterian church history. See also Thompson (D0735).

D0591 Lonsway, Jesse William, and Pembleton, Aaron. The Episcopal Lineage of the Hierarchy in the United States, Revised 1790-1963. 2nd ed. Cincinnati, Ohio: Episcopal Lineage, 1965.

This brief work (46 pp.) traces the apostolic succession in the American Roman Catholic hierarchy. It contains approximately twenty tables and diagrams and several explanatory essays.

D0592 Loomis, Louise Ropes, trans. The Book of the Popes. Liber Pontificalis. Vol. 1- . Records of Civilization: Sources and Studies, no. 3. New York: Columbia University Press, 1916- . Reprint. New York: Octagon Books, 1965- .

Based on the Mommsen text in Monumenta Germaniae Historica (D0630), this translation is a standard reference work for students of papal history who are unable to cope with Duchesne (D0443) or other Latin versions of the Liber Pontificalis, which is a useful source of biographical information. The first volume covers the period to Gregory I.

D0593 Lord, Clifford Lee, and Lord, Elizabeth Sniffen Hubbard. Historical Atlas of the United States. Rev. ed. New York: Holt, [1953]. Reprint. New York: Johnson Reprint Corporation, 1969.

This complement to both Adams (D0317) and Paullin (D0658) contains 312 maps in four sections: general, colonial, 1775-1865, 1865-1950. The maps are limited to political and economic affairs for the most part so should be used for general inquiries rather than issues related to church history. There are indexes of subjects and of place names.

D0594 McAvoy, Thomas Timothy. A History of the Catholic Church in the United States. Notre Dame, Ind.: University of Notre Dame Press, 1969.

This 504 page history is a standard survey for students of Roman Catholicism. It is particularly useful on institutional aspects, tracing the development of the organized church from its beginnings in colonial Maryland through to the time of Vatican II. See also Eberhardt (D0451), Ellis (D0455) and Hennesey (D0529).

D0595 McConnell, James, comp. Fasti of the Irish Presbyterian Church, 1613-1840. Rev. by Samuel G. McConnell. 12 [i.e. 14] pts. Belfast: Presbyterian Historical Society, 1936-1951.

This collection is arranged in seven chronological parts, each with its own alphabetical sequence of names. Its appearance in fascicles plus lack of a consolidated index make it difficult to consult, but this is an important source of historical data on Irish Presbyterianism. See also

Reid (D0682).

D0596 McGiffert, Arthur Cushman. A History of Christianity in the Apostolic Age. Rev. ed. New York: Charles Scribner's Sons, 1900. Reprint. New York: Charles Scribner's Sons, 1938.

Reprinted several times, this scholarly treatment is particularly useful on theological aspects of Christianity in the age of the apostles. It includes a chronological table and an index. This is suitable for advanced students and scholars who are also aware of more recent approaches to the subject. See also Bright (D0370), Gwatkin (D0511) and Kidd (D0558).

D0597 Mackinnon, James. Luther and the Reformation. 4 vols. London: Longmans, Green and Company, 1925-1930.

Covering Luther's life, thought and impact from his early years, this study treats the following themes and periods: early life and religious development to 1517; the breach with Rome, 1517-1521; progress of the movement, 1521-1529; and vindication of the movement, 1530-1546. There is thorough documentation, and each volume contains a detailed, analytical table of contents and an index. See also Bergendorff (D0353).

D0598 McNeill, John Thomas. The History and Character of Calvinism. New York: Oxford University Press, 1954. Reprint. New York: Oxford University Press, 1967.

This study of Zwingli, Calvin and the spread of reformed Protestantism includes a reasonably up to date list of books for further study on central issues and developments in the field. Four parts treat the origins of Calvinism under Zwingli and then under Calvin, the expansion of reformed Protestantism in Europe and early America, and Calvinism through to the present.

D0599 [no entry]

D0600 McSorley, Joseph. An Outline History of the Church by Centuries (from St. Peter to Pius XII). [11th ed.] St. Louis, Mo.: B. Herder Book Company, 1961.

Each chapter of this 1174 page history covers approximately one century, discussing both political background and ecclesiastical affairs with other topics treated in subsections. Excellent bibliographies by period, appendixes and an index accompany the text, which is clearly and lucidly presented for the benefit of less advanced students. For those requiring basic information from a Roman Catholic viewpoint McSorley is one of the better single volume histories. See also Hertling (D0530), Hughes (D0544) and Neill (D0639).

D0601 Major, James Russell. The Age of the Renaissance and Reformation: A Short History. Philadelphia, Pa.: J.B. Lippincott Company, [1970].

This short history attempts to provide a synthesis rather than a factual account of various aspects of the complex period of the Renaissance and Reformation based on the author's interpretation, while encouraging students to place more specialized works in a larger setting. Eight chapters treat themes such as the Renaissance state; the cultural and religious renaissance; wars and the cessation of economic progress; and science, thought and art. A table of popes, rulers and regimes; a bibliography (pp. 333-350); an index and nine maps are included. See also Dannenfeldt (D0420), Dickens (D0431), Elton (D0460) and Spitz (D0716).

D0602 Manitius, Maximilianus. Geschichte der Lateinischen Literatur des Mittelalters. 3 vols. Munich: Beck, 1911-1931.

This standard history of medieval Latin literature includes in each volume a section on theological writing of the period. The volumes cover the period from Justinian to the tenth century, tenth century to the wars between church and state, events to the end of the twelfth century. While not a theological guide, Manitius provides a valuable, if somewhat brief, survey of Latin theological writing and its historical development.

D0603 Mann, Golo, and Heuss, A., eds. Propyläen Weltgeschichte: Eine Universalgeschichte. 12 vols. Berlin: Propyläen Verlag, 1960-1965.

This series of volumes provides an excellent survey of world history by an international group of scholars. Particularly strong is the coverage of the Renaissance and Reformation in volumes 6 and 7, which include maps, chronologies and name and subject indexes. Although written from a European viewpoint, these volumes are scholarly and objective in their interpretation of ecclesiastical affairs and their impact on wider events. See also Clio (D0404) and Ploetz (D0665).

D0604 Mann, Horace Kinder. The Lives of the Popes in the Early Middle Ages. 2nd ed. 18 vols. in 19. St. Louis, Mo.: B. Herder Book Company; London: Kegan Paul, Trench, Trübner and Company, 1925-1932. Reprint. 18 vols. in 19. Nedeln: Kraus Reprint, 1980.

This substantial historical survey covers the popes from Gregory the Great to Benedict XI. Each pope receives full biographical treatment, which is scholarly, critical and well documented. Appendixes provide the texts of major papal documents, and each biography includes an introduction to sources and contemporary political events. Each volume is thoroughly indexed for reference purposes. Mann is an indispensible guide to early papal history and should be used for advanced reference requirements. Although later volumes are entitled Lives of the Popes in the Middle Ages, Mann does stop at 1304; Pastor (D0656) begins with 1305 and admirably complements the chronologically earlier work. For coverage of the papacy to 891 see Duchesne (D0443).

D0605 Manross, William Wilson. A History of the American Episcopal Church. 2nd ed. New York: Morehouse-Gorham Company, 1950.

This balanced and very readable history treats the period from the beginning of the seventeenth century to the 1930s. It is particularly strong on early history of the church in the various colonies, and makes use of original sources and contemporary biographies. An extremely detailed analytical table of contents for the seventeen chapters, a bibliography and an index are provided, as well as a number of illustrations. See also Albright (D0321) and Addison (D0318).

D0606 Manschreck, Clyde Leonard. A History of Christianity in the World: From Persecution to Uncertainty. Englewood Cliffs, N.J.: Prentice-Hall, [1974].

This 378 pages covers theology, church history and secular history. Useful summaries for each chapter, a 10 page bibliography of primary and secondary sources provide helpful aids, especially for undergraduate students. This is suitable as a teaching aid where more specific analyses are not required. See also Burke (D0374) and Frankforter (D0478).

D0607 Manschreck, Clyde Leonard. Melancthon: The Quiet Reformer. New York: Abingdon Press, c. 1958. Reprint. Westport, Conn.: Greenwood Press, 1975.

The first full length (350 pp.) biography of Melanchton to appear in English, this study provides a balanced appraisal of the life and thought of a colleague of Luther. It also includes quite adequate information on the historical context. For students of the Reformation, especially in Germany, this is a valuable specialized study.

D0608 Margull, Hans Jochen, ed. The Councils of the Church: History and Analysis. Trans. by Walter F. Bense. Philadelphi, Pa.: Fortress Press, [1966].

This 528 page collection of essays by scholars representing the various Christian traditions presents some historical accounts as well as exploring the possibility of attaining Christian reunion by means of a council involving all Christian groups. The Orthodox, Anglican, Lutheran and Reformed theologies of council are described, and the final essay considers ecumenical councils past and present. See also Jedin (D0547) and Raab (D0678).

D0609 Martin, Charles Trice, comp. The Record Interpreter: A Collection of Abbreviations, Latin Words and Names Used in English Historical Manuscripts and Records. 2nd ed. London: Stevens and Sons, 1910. Reprint. Hildesheim: Georg Olms Verlag, 1969.

The nine sections in this useful handbook for those who use primary documents related to English history include abbreviation of Latin words used in English records, abbreviations of French words, glossary of Latin words found in records but not in classical authors, Latin place names in Britain, Latin names of bishoprics in Britain, Latin forms of English surnames, Latin Christian names and their English equivalent. Martin is of obvious value to the scholar. See also Denholm-Young (D0429) and Hector (D0527).

D0610 Marty, Martin E. Protestantism. History of Religion Series. New York: Harper and Row; London: Weidenfeld and Nicolson, 1972.

This wide ranging study is primarily descriptive in approach, focusing on religious and theological emphases, cultural expressions, etc. from the sixteenth century to the present. It is particularly valuable for the scholar and student because of the lengthy (100 pp.) annotated bibliography on many aspects of Protestant life and history. See also Leonard (D0575).

D0611 Marucchi, Orazio. Manual of Christian Archeology. Trans. and adapted by Hubert Vecchierello. Paterson, N.J.: St. Anthony's Guild Press, 1935. Reprint. Paterson, N.J.: St. Anthony's Guild Press, 1949.

Based on Eléments d'Archéologie Chrétienne (2e éd. 3 vols. Paris: Desclée, Lefebvre et Cie, 1902-1906), this manual was prepared particularly for use by undergraduates. It contains six parts: the foundations of Christian archeology; a brief synopsis of the persecutions; the ancient Christian cemeteries; Christian epigraphy; ancient Christian art; and Christian basilicas. The manual is based almost entirely on the Christian monuments of Rome. Footnotes, a bibliography (pp. 433-437) and an index are included. See also Leclercq (D0574).

D0612 Mas-Latrie, Louis. Trésor de Chronologie d'Histoire et de Géographie pour l'Etude et l'Emploi des Documents du Moyen Age. Paris: V. Palme, 1889. Reprint. Turin: Bottego d'Erasmo, 1962.

This valuable compendium includes perpetual calendars, historical chronologies, lists of saints and church fathers, popes, cardinals, archbishops and bishops, secular rulers and other items useful to the student of medieval history. The list of church fathers serves as a table of contents and index to Migne (D0623, D0624). While not always completely reliable, Mas-Latrie in general is a useful guide to medieval dates; the emphasis on France and ecclesiastical topics makes the volume a very worthwhile complement to the more general chronologies. See also Delorme (D0428) and Storey (D0724).

D0613 Mayer, Alfred. Annals of European Civilization, 1501-1900. London: Cassell, [1949].

Concentrating on the cultural history of Europe, Mayer in the first section (Annals) presents a chronological listing of major events. The second section (Summaries) treats these same events by subject, including the church. Here events are arranged chronologically within each topic, allowing students to trace historical developments quickly and briefly. There are indexes of names and places. See also Schieder (D0698).

D0614 Mead, Sidney Earl. The Lively Experiment: The Shaping of Christianity in America. New York: Harper and Row, [1963].

This 220 page volume contains nine essays on forces which have shaped American Christianity from the colonial period to about 1930. The book is readable and stimulating for those interested in American religious history. See also Gaustad (D0490), Handy (D0519), Hudson (D0541) and Ahlstrom (D0319).

D0615 Meer, Frederik van der. Atlas of Western Civilization. English version by T.A. Birrell. 2nd ed. Princeton, N.J.: Van Nostrand, [1960].

This 240 page atlas is concerned with developments of Western culture and civilization rather than with political and military history, and is of interest to those concerned with the former perspective. There are many photographs in addition to the maps. See also Muir (D0633), Rand McNally (D0679) and Shepherd (D0710).

D0616 Meer, Frederik van der. Augustine the Bishop: The Life and Work of a Father of the Church. Trans. by Brian Battershaw and G.R. Lamb. New York: Sheed and Ward, 1961.

This 679 page translation of Augustine de Zielzorger is a biographical study of St. Augustine, his milieu and work. Each of the four main parts (the church of Hippo Regius, the cultus, preaching, popular piety) discusses not only the personal development of Augustine and his functions within the church but also the society and culture in which he worked. Substantial use is made of literary sources and archeological evidence in presenting a detailed (but occasionally prosaic and sometimes verbose) study of the man in context. Meer is extensively footnoted (pp. 593-659), well indexed and contains interesting illustrations. For those seeking a straight-forward biography which does not dwell on Augustine as theologian or philosopher, this is a standard work. See also Brown (D0371).

D0617 Meer, Frederik van der. Shorter Atlas of Western Civilization. With the assistance of G. Lemmens. Trans. by Marian Powell. London: Thomas Nelson and Sons, 1967.

This 224 page atlas contains only nineteen maps but includes fairly thorough text and interesting illustrations suitable for general inquiries at a basic level. For the fuller version see van der Meer (D0615).

D0618 Meer, Frederik van der, and Mohrmann, Christine. Atlas of the Early Christian World. Trans. and ed. by Mary F. Hedlund and Harold Henry Rowley. London: Thomas Nelson and Sons, 1958.

First published as Atlas van de Oudchristelijke Wereld (Amsterdam: Elsevier Publishing Company, 1958), this work contains forty-two excellent color maps showing in detail parts of the Roman Empire, city plans, regions and dioceses. These data are complemented by 620 plates illustrating the first six centuries of Christian history and a text which treats the background of biblical history. The commentary includes a valuable description of church life (303-600 A.D.) and quotations from patristic writings and inscriptions are a notable feature in this section. The text accompanying the illustrations comprises a brief introduction to each period or area, an explanation of features illustrated and relevant quotations from early writings. Indexes of people and places provide easy reference to both text and maps. See also Pieper (D0662).

D0619 Menéndez Pidal, Ramón, ed. Historia de España. Vol. 1- . Madrid: Espasá-Calpe, 1935- .

This massive series on the history of Spain consists of specialist volumes on specific periods. While the treatment is rather uneven, the church receives sound coverage in the relevant volumes, especially those dealing with the middle ages. For reference purposes the critical bibliographies in each volume are particularly valuable. This is a useful series for a wide range of reference needs.

D0620 Mercati, Angelo. Raccolta di Concordati su Materie Ecclesiastiche tra la Sante Sede e le Autorità Civili. 2 vols. Vatican City: Tipografia Poliglotta Vaticana, 1954.

This chronologically arranged collection contains the texts of all treaties made between the Roman Catholic Church and secular governments from 1098 to 1954. The first volume, originally published in 1919, covers 1098-1914; the second, supplementary volume treats 1915-1954. This is a handy and well indexed (by subject, pope and country) collection. However, for less advanced students introductions to each document would be a great help. See also Ehler (D0453) and Tierney (D0736).

D0621 Migne, Jacques Paul. Index Alphabeticus Omnium Doctorum, Patrum, Scriptorumque Ecclesiasticorum Quorum Opera Scriptaque vel Minima in Patrologia Latina Reperiuntur; [and] J.B. Pearson, Conspectus Auctorum Quorum Nomina Indicibus Patrologiae Graeco-Latinae a J.P. Migne, Editae Coninentur. Ridgewood, N.J.: Gregg Press, 1965.

The Index Alphabeticus is an extract from volume 218 of Patrologia Latina (D0624), and the Conspectus is a reprint of Pearson's work first published in 1882.

D0622 Migne, Jacques Paul, ed. Patrologiae Cursus Completus. Series Latina: Supplementum. Ed. by Gauthier Adalbert Hamman. 4 vols. Paris: Garnier, 1958-1971.

This supplement to Migne (D0624) is a volume-by-volume revision which summarizes recent scholarly opinion on the authorship, dates and related aspects of each work. It is extremely useful for bibliographical purposes, as references are provided to original studies; in addition new texts from authors under investigation and newly discovered materials are also added.

D0623 Migne, Jacques Paul. Patologiae Cursus Completus, Seu Bibliotheca Universalis Omnium SS. Patrum, Doctorum, Scriptorumque Ecclesiasticorum Series Graeca a S. Barnaba ad Photium. 161 vols. in 166. Paris: Migne, 1857-1866. Reprint. 60 vols. New York: Adler, 1965-1971. Micro-reprint. Washington, D.C.: Microcard Foundation, 1961.

This comprehensive collection of Greek patristic texts contains Latin and Greek versions in parallel columns. As with the Latin counterpart (D0624), all texts are reprints, often of uncritical editions of the originals. There is an excellent place index, and two additional indexes (D0391, D0539) usefully supplement the main set. Migne is being replaced by Corpus Christianorum: Series Graeca (D0409).

D0624 Migne, Jacques Paul. Patrologiae Cursus Completus, Seu Bibliotheca Universalis Omnium SS. Patrum, Doctorum, Scriptorumque Ecclesiasticorum Series Latina a Tertulliano ad Innocentium III. 221 vols. Paris: Migne, 1844-1880. Reprint. 146 vols. New York: Adler, 1965-1971.

Although gradually being replaced by Corpus Christianorum: Series Latina (D0410), this monumental set contains reprints of a wide range of Latin patristic texts. Unfortunately, Migne is based on uncritical editions of original texts and contains a significant number of serious misprints which require careful reading. The full subject indexes in volumes 218-221 are excellent and are bound to retain reference value long after the published texts have been superseded. Otherwise the critical approach adopted in Corpus Christianorum will make this the better series. For helpful attempts at correcting Migne see the following supplement by Hamman (D0622) and also Glorieux (D0494). See also Corpus Scriptorum Ecclesiasticorum Latinorum (D0412).

D0625 Milburn, Robert Leslie Pollington. Saints and Their Emblems in English Churches. Rev. ed. Oxford: Basil Blackwell, 1957.

This 283 page survey provides brief biographical sketches and an indication of the symbols associated with major saints in England. Location of portraits is often provided. The listing is alphabetical by names of saints, and an appendix presents an alphabetical listing of emblems. See also Baring-Gould (D0343).

D0626 Miller, Perry Gilbert Eddy, and Johnson, Thomas Herbert, eds. The Puritans. Rev. ed. Bibliographies rev. by George McCandlish. 2 vols. New York: Harper and Row, [1963].

First published in 1938, this thematic consideration of primary source materials from the various epochs of early American Puritanism offers views on all aspects of religion and society. The nine chapters are numbered consecutively throughout the two volumes, and focus on topics such as the theory of the state and of society; manners, customs and behavior; biographies and letters; and education. Illustrations, maps, notes, bibliographies (pp. 777-818) and an index are provided in this valuable collection. See also Ferm (D0470), Gaustad (D0488), Handy (D0520) and Smith (D0712).

D0627 [no entry]

D0628 Mirbt, Karl. Quellen zur Geschichte des Papsttums und der Römischen Katholizismus. 5. Aufl. Tübingen: J.C.B. Mohr, 1934.

This 650 page collection contains the Latin texts of some of the more important sources for the history of the papacy and of Roman Catholic doctrine. For each text the source is indicated, and an index is provided. As a collection of primary source materials, Mirbt is a standard reference volume for students of papal history who require Latin versions of these materials.

D0629 Monceaux, Paul. Histoire Littéraire de l'Afrique Chrétienne depuis les Origines jusqu'à 1'Invasion Arabe. 7 vols. Paris: E. Leroux, 1901-1923.

This specialized study of early Christianity in North Africa covers Tertullian, Minucius Felix, St. Cyprian, St. Augustine and Donatism. It is an excellent guide to an important era and area in the early history of the church and should be consulted by advanced students requiring detailed information on this subject. See also Ceillier (D0394), Labriolle (D0565), Rose (D0687) and Schanz (D0679).

D0630 Monumenta Germaniae Historica: Inde ab Anno Christi Quingentesimo usque ad Annum Millesimum et Quingentesimum. 32 vols. in 34. Hannover: Impensis Bibliopolii, 1826-1934.

Covering 500-1517, this massive collection contains complete texts of medieval authors, documents of councils and related ecclesiastical and civil documents from German Europe. As a collection of sources, this is an indispensible guide for advanced students and scholars. The indexes by Pertz (D0659) and Holder-Egger (D0538) are essential guides to the contents of this series. See also Tarouca (D0731).

D0631 Moorman, John Richard Humpridge. A History of the Church in England. 3rd ed. London: Adam and Charles Black, 1973.

This standard introductory history of the English church consists of twenty-two chapters in four parts: Roman and Anglo-Saxon period, middle ages, Reformation and after, industrial age. Each chapter is subdivided into topical sections indicated in the detailed table of contents. Throughout the survey Moorman presents facts clearly and with adequate detail for the student new to Anglican history. The full index of names and subjects (pp. 437-460) is a helpful reference tool. For coverage of more specific periods see Carpenter (D0389, D0390); see also Workman (D0747).

D0632 Mourret, Fernand. A History of the Catholic Church. Trans. by Newton Thompson. [9 vols.] St. Louis, Mo.: B. Herder Book Company, 1930-[1945].

This translation of Histoire Générale de l'Eglise (9 vols. Paris: Bloud et Cie, 1920-1928) is a Roman Catholic apologia which surveys the entire history of the church from this standpoint. Mourret is thorough but often misleading and inaccurate in detail. Daniel-Rops (D0419) is less biased, but Mourret contains more reference features and better indexes in each volume. This set should be used with caution by those with some knowledge of Catholic church history. See also Dufourcq (D0444) and Fliche (D0473).

D0633 Muir, Ramsay. Muir's Historical Atlas: Ancient, Medieval and Modern. 10th ed. Ed. by Reginald Francis Treharne and Harold Fullard. New York: Barnes and Noble, 1964; London: G. Philip, 1965 [c. 1964].

The two sections in this atlas cover ancient and classical history and medieval and modern history. Each of the two parts is separately indexed and presents cartographic details at a level most useful for the beginning student, especially those interested in medieval history. See also van der Meer (D0615), Rand McNally (D0679) and Shepherd (D0710).

D0634 Muratori, Lodovico Antonio, ed. Rerum Italicarum Scriptores: Raccolta degli Storici Italiani del Cinquecento al Millecinquecento. Nuova ed. Riveduta, ampliata e corr. con la direzione de Giosuè Carducci. Vol. 1- . Città di Castello: S. Lapi, 1900- .

This collection of documents on Italian history between 500 and 1500 contains a significant amount of material from papal, monastic and other ecclesiastical sources. It is, therefore, a useful collection of source materials but is limited in usefulness to those who know Latin.

D0635 Musurillo, Herbert Anthony. The Acts of the Christian Martyrs: Introduction, Texts and Translations. Oxford Early Christian Texts. Oxford: Clarendon Press, 1972.

This is an excellent edition of parallel Greek or Latin texts with English translation, covering twenty-eight acts of the early martyrs. A scholarly introduction precedes the texts. Notes accompany both introduction and texts, and an index is provided.

D0636 Musurillo, Herbert Anthony, ed. and trans. The Fathers of the Primitive Church. New York: New American Library, 1966.

This 272 page work contains a collection of documents in English translation. See also Bettenson (D0355), Staniforth (D0717) and Wiles (D0759).

D0637 Narbey, C., ed. Supplément aux Acta Sanctorum pour des Vies de Saints de l'Epoque Mérovingienne. 2 vols. Paris: Le Soudier, 1899-1912.

This is a supplement to Carnandet (D0388).

D0638 Neale, John Mason. A History of the Holy Eastern Church. 3 vols. in 5. London: J. Masters, 1847-1873. Reprint. 3 vols. in 5. New York: AMS Press, 1976.

See also Atiya (D0326), Harder (D0522), Schmemann (D0700) and Zananiri (D0767).

D0639 Neill, Thomas Patrick, and Schmandt, Raymond H. History of the Catholic Church. Milwaukee, Wisc.: Bruce Publishing Company, 1957.

This history covers its broad subject field from the beginnings of Christianity to the mid-twentieth century; it does not attempt to provide in depth treatment of theological issues. Selected readings in English are listed at the end of each chapter, and a bibliography of more scholarly w o r k s in various Western languages is provided (pp. 666-670). Review aids for students are included, and an index is provided, together with lists of ecumenical councils and of popes. This is suitable as an introductory work for students. See also Hertling (D0530), Hughes (D0544) and McSorley (D0600).

D0640 The New Cambridge Modern History, 14 vols. Cambridge: Cambridge University Press, 1957-1970.

Intended to succeed The Cambridge Modern History (D0381), this substantial series concentrates on political history in Western Europe. Each volume is extremely detailed and presents factual data in a very compressed form. However, for reference purposes it is far less adequate than the original series, as there are neither detailed footnotes nor bibliographies. For the latter one must consult Roach (D0196).

D0641 Newton, K.C. Medieval Local Records: A Reading Aid. Helps for Students of History, no. 83. London: Historical Association, 1971.

This 28 page book provides guidance on reading medieval local records, particularly those written in Court Hands scripts (those used in central courts of law from the twelfth century onwards and used for the majority of central and local records). Plates of twelve documents are provided with a transcript, translation and notes on each. A brief bibliography provides guidance to further study on this specialist area. See also Emmison (D0462).

D0642 Nichols, James Hastings. History of Christianity, 1650-1950: Secularization of the West. New York: Ronald Press Company, [1956].

This comprehensive 493 page history of the modern church contains considerable detail, and is particularly concerned with theological aspects. It is of interest to seminary students and teachers. See also Wand (D0750).

D0643 Nicolas, Nicholas Harris. The Chronology of History; Containing Tables, Calculations and Statements for Ascertaining the Dates of Historical Events and of Public and Private Documents from the Earliest Period to the Present Time. New ed. London: Longman, Brown, Green and Longmans, [1838]. Reprint. London: Longman, Orme, Grown, Green and Longmans, 1840.

Although dated in many respects, Nicolas provides useful information on chronological problems associated with such topics as the papacy, dates of councils and other areas relevant to church history. See also Peters (D0660) and Steinberg (D0718).

D0644 Norwood, Frederick Abbott. The Story of American Methodism: A History of the United Methodists and Their Relations. Nashville, Tenn.: Abingdon Press, 1974.

In 448 pages Norwood treats the history of American Methodism under four main sections: "ancestral heritage", "pioneer development", "settled institution", "ecumenical transformation". There are bibliographical references in the notes and an index. The development of the histories of each of the constituent bodies of the United Methodist Church as well as other Methodist groups is of particular interest to the historian of this denomination. See also Burke (D0373).

D0645 Nunn, Henry Preston Vaughan. An Introduction to Ecclesiastical Latin. 3rd ed. With an appendix of Latin Hymns. Eton: Aldon and Blackwell, 1951. Reprint. Oxford: Basil Blackwell, 1963.

PA2823
N4
1951

This standard grammar of ecclesiastical Latin for beginners assumes only basic prior knowledge of the conjugations of Latin verbs and the declensions of Latin nouns. It is divided into two main parts: the first (syntax) presents a summary of syntactical rules for the various parts of speech in a straightforward manner (pp. 8-113); the second (extracts from ecclesiastical writers) consists of a selection of passages from some of the principal authors of the period with notes drawing attention to the appropriate sections of the syntax. These extracts supplement the examples in the first part, which are taken largely from the Vulgate NT, and provide more extended samples of medieval Latin writing. There is an index of texts quoted and an appendix of Latin hymns (pp. 159-190) for additional translation practice. This is a sound introduction to the subject and, although lacking a detailed topical index, a useful reference grammar. See also Strecker (D0725).

D0646 [no entry]

D0647 Oakley, Francis. The Western Church in the Later Middle Ages. Ithaca, N.Y.: Cornell University Press, 1979.

This 345 page account treats the late medieval church on its own terms rather than as a prelude to the Reformation. It includes discussion of forms of piety, theological and doctrinal developments, heresies, reform movements and spirituality. This is a balanced survey which provides stimulating insights. See also Flick (D0474).

D0648 O'Hanlon, John. Lives of the Irish Saints, with Special Festivals and the Commemoration of Holy Persons, Compiled from Calendars, Martyrologies and Various Sources Relating to the Ancient Church History of Ireland. 9 vols. and 7 parts of vol. 10. New York: Benziger Brothers; Dublin: J. Duffy and Sons, 1875-1903.

Published under various imprints and never completed (covering only through October), this is a significant guide to Irish hagiography. The work is arranged according to the church calendar and provides extensive biographies of the saints under their feast days. Unfortunately, there is no index, so one must use other reference works to locate the relevant date for a given saint. See also Baring-Gould (D0343).

D0649 Olin, John C., comp. The Catholic Reformation: Savanarola to Ignatius Loyola; Reform in the Church, 1495-1540. New York: Harper and Row, 1969. Reprint. Westminster, Md.: Christian Classics, 1978.

This collection of documents from a wide range of sources contains the text of fifteen items dealing with the Catholic Reformation. An index of names is provided. For a handbook see Dickens (D0432).

D0650 Olmstead, Clifton E. History of Religion in the United States. Englewood Cliffs, N.J.: Prentice-Hall, 1960.

Covering the history of American religion from colonial beginnings to the recent past, Olmstead's 628 page survey clearly analyzes the intellectual, cultural, political and socio-economic forces which have shaped and been shaped by various religious institutions. The work brings together significant scholarly research in this field and includes a brief bibliography and an index. For students at various levels this is a worthwhile reference survey. See also Ahlstrom (D0319), Hudson (D0541), Gaustad (D0490), Mead (D0614) and Smith (D0712).

D0651 Olson, Adolf. A Centenary History As Related to the Baptist General Conference of America. Chicago, Ill.: Baptist Conference Press, 1952.

See also Baker (D0336) and Torbet (D0739).

D0652 Ortiz de Urbina, Ignatio. Patrologia Syriaca. Rome: Pont. Institutum Orientalium Studiorium, 1958,

This 250 page specialized study covers heretical, orthodox, anonymous and some post-patristic writers. Detailed bio-bibliographies are provided. For a collection of relevant documents see Graffin (D0498).

D0653 Owen, Dorothy M. The Records of the Established Church in England; Excluding Parochial Records. Archives and the User, no. 1. [Cambridge]: British Records Association, 1970.

In many ways an updating of Purvis (D0674), this 64 page handbook describes in general terms the various types of ecclesiastical records under four main headings: diocese, archdeaconry and peculiar jurisdictions; province; national church; capitular bodies. Within each category Owen analyzes the specific types of records, their content and likely use. The work concludes with an extremely useful list of the locations of records and an index of terms.

D0654 Ozment, Steven E. The Age of Reform (1250-1550): An Intellectual and Religious History of Late Medieval and Reformation Europe. New Haven, Conn.: Yale University Press, 1980.

This 458 page volume surveys the intellectual landscape of the late medieval world (scholasticism, mysticism, interrelations of states, church councils and papacy, etc.) and the varieties of reform of the Reformation period (Luther, Calvin, Zwingli, Knox, etc.). There are useful footnotes, but no bibliography is provided. This work usefully links late medieval and Reformation intellectual and religious history in a stimulating account suitable for graduate students and scholars.

274.2
F243

D0655 Parker, Thomas Maynard. The English Reformation to 1558. The Home University Library of Modern Knowledge, vol. 217. New York: Oxford University Press, 1950.

This brief survey of 200 pages is a scholarly but popularly written account. It focuses on the history of England during the Reformation, with special reference to religious policy, rather than on primarily theological aspects. See also Dickens (D0433), Elton (D0458) and Powicke (D0667).

BX955
P35
1898

D0656 Pastor, Ludwig Friedrich August von. The History of the Popes from the Close of the Middle Ages, Drawn from the Secret Archives of the Vatican and Other Original Sources. Trans. and ed. by Frederick Ignatius Antrobus et al. 40 vols. London: J. Hodges, 1891-1953. Reprint. 40 vols. Nedeln: Kraus Reprint, 1980.

Following Mann (D0604) chronologically, this translation of Geschichte der Päpste (16 vols. Freiburg im Breisgau: Herder, 1886-1933) covers the popes from 1304 to 1799. For each pope von Pastor provides a lengthy and thoroughly documented biography based on original sources in the Vatican archives. Lengthy bibliographies are provided and are particularly useful in listing works most often cited in the text. Each volume is thoroughly indexed, and there are numerous appendixes dealing with ancillary topics. Although not without its faults, this is a scholarly work which is widely regarded as an indispensible guide to papal history. See also Seppelt (D0707) and Schmandt (D0699).

284
P323

D0657 Pauck, Wilhelm. The Heritage of the Reformation. Rev. ed. Glencoe, Ill.: Free Press, 1961; London: Oxford University Press, [1968].

Written within the tradition of theological liberalism, this volume discusses the Reformation, Protestantism and liberalism, stressing the heritage of the past together with the need to respond to demands of the present. Notes and an index are provided. An analysis of the contribution to Protestant thought of Barth and Harnack is included.

G201
51
P3
1932x

D0658 Paullin, Charles Oscar. Atlas of the Historical Geography of the United States. Ed. by John Kirtland Wright. Carnegie Institution of Washington Publication no. 401. Washington, D.C.: Carnegie Institution of Washington; New York: American Geographical Society, 1932.

Widely regarded as the most useful general atlas of American history, Paullin provides detailed maps and text on a wide range of subjects. Churches are treated in a section which also covers colleges and universities for 1773-1890. For basic cartographic information on this field and on politics, society, economics and many other topics this is a reference work whose value has not yet been equalled in any other general atlas. Paullin is well indexed for reference purposes. See also Adams (D0317) and Lord (D0593).

D0659 Pertz, Georg Heinrich. Inhaltsverzeichnisse der Zehn Ersten Bände der "Monumenta Germaniae". Hannover: Hahnische Hofbuchhandlung, 1848.

This useful index covers the first eight volumes of scriptores and the first two volumes of leges. For a complete index to Monumenta Germaniae

Historica (D0630) see Holder-Egger (D0538).

D0660 Peters, Arno. Synchronoptische Weltgeschichte. [New ed.] 2 vols. Munich: Universum Verlag, 1965-1970.

The synoptic tables in this chronological guide show developments in social history, politics, religion, philosophy and other areas. It allows the student to make comparisons quickly and accurately, whether on Europe or other regions. The chronological strips are particularly well planned and easy to read, which is unusual in works of this sort. Volume 1 contains the chronological tables; volume 2, topical lists. See also Nicolas (D0643) and Steinberg (D0718).

D0661 Phillips, Walter Alison, ed. History of the Church of Ireland from the Earliest Times to the Present Day. 3 vols. London: Oxford University Press, 1933-1934.

Compiled under the auspices of the General Synod of the Church of Ireland, this standard history of Irish Anglicanism covers the Celtic church, medieval and Reformation eras and modern period. Each volume includes a useful bibliography and index, and volume 3 contains a list of the succession of Irish bishops. While written from an official standpoint, Phillips is reasonably factual and accurate. See also Cotton (D0413).

D0662 Pieper, Karl. Atlas Orbis Christiani Antiqui (Atlas zur Alten Missions- und Kirchengeschichte). Düsseldorf: L. Schwann, [1931].

The multilingual introduction to this work includes German, French and English texts. See also van der Meer (D0618).

D0663 Pitra, Jean Baptiste, ed. Analecta Sacra Spicilegio Solesmensi Parata. 4 vols. Paris: Typis Tusculanis, 1876-? Reprint. 4 vols. Farnborough, Hampshire: Gregg Press, 1966.

This continuation of Pitra's earlier collection (D0664) contains Greek hymns, writings of the ante-Nicene fathers, and other items. Indexes are provided in each volume.

D0664 Pitra, Jean Baptiste. Spicilegium Solesmense Complectens Sanctorum Patrum Scriptorumque Ecclesiasticorum Anecdota Hactenus Opera, Selecta e Graecis Orientalibusque et Latinis Codicibus. 4 vols. Paris: F. Didot Fratres, 1852-1858. Reprint. 4 vols. Graz: Akademische Druck- und Verlagsanstalt, 1962-1963.

This collection contains texts of Greek and Latin patristic writings not found in other collections such as Migne (D0623, D0624). Also included are writings on Greek canon law and hymns. Indexes for subjects, names and definitions of terms are provided in each volume.

D0665 Ploetz, K. Auszug aus der Geschichte. 26. Aufl. Würzburg: A.G. Ploetz Verlag, c. 1960.

This 1707 page survey presents a systematic overview of history in six main periods, which are arranged geographically and then chronologically. Philosophy and religion are among the areas covered briefly but succinctly. The excellent author and subject index (pp. 1624-1707) contains entries

on all items treated in the text. This is a good reference volume for check-
ing basic facts. See also Mann (D0603).

D0666 Powell, Ken G., and Cook, Chris. English Historical Facts, 1485-1603.
Totowa, N.J.: Rowman and Littlefield; London: Macmillan and Company,
1977.

This rather eclectic compendium presents a wide variety of lists, chronologies and general background information on the history of Tudor England.
Ten topical chapters cover government, law, religion, war, economics,
population, Ireland and Scotland. There is also a brief section on biography
(pp. 206-220) plus a short bibliography (pp. 221-228). While the treatment
of historical factors and events related to most topics is clear and quite
helpful for basic reference purposes, the lack of an index detracts notice-
ably from the usefulness of this volume. For a complementary chronology
see Powicke (D0669).

D0667 Powicke, Frederick Maurice. The Reformation in England. London:
Oxford University Press, [1958]. Reprint. London: Oxford University Press,
[1961].

Originally a contribution to a larger volume on European civilization,
this 136 page essay provides a concise account of the Reformation, including the medieval background, through to the Elizabethan church.
A detailed table of contents is provided, but there is no index. There
are some footnotes, and a list of books and papers available only after
the work was completed is provided. See also Parker (D0655).

D0668 Powicke, Frederick Maurice, and Cheney, Christopher Robert, eds.
Councils and Synods, with Other Documents Relating to the English Church.
1 vol. in 2. Oxford: Oxford University Press, 1964.

Planned as a continuation of Haddan (D0515), this work appears to have
resulted only in the second volume, which covers 1205-1313. The first
part treats 1205-1265; the second, 1265-1313. In each part relevant documents are printed in Latin without translation but with introductory
remarks and copious footnotes. Part 1 includes a list of printed books
and articles cited, while part 2 contains an index of manuscripts and
a general index. Powicke is an important collection of source materials
for advanced students of English medieval church history. See also Gee
(D0492).

D0669 Powicke, Frederick Maurice, and Fryde, E.B., eds. Handbook of British
Chronology. 2nd ed. Royal Historical Society Guides and Handbooks, no.
2. London: Royal Historical Society, 1961.

This detailed and thorough chronology consists of a series of lists covering
rulers, officers of state, archbishops and bishops, higher nobility, parlia-
ments, provincial and national councils of the church to 1536. Particularly
valuable is the listing of bishops, which is arranged chronologically within
each diocese and treats all episcopal office holders down to the 1950s.
Name, date of consecration, accession and death or translation are included
for each individual. The list of English church councils provides date
of meeting, place, reference, nature of assembly; references include
both major manuscript sources and printed collections. The introductions
to each section provide valuable notes on chronology. Powicke has obvious

reference value for students and scholars of English church history. For a complementary handbook see Powell (D0666).

D0670 Prou, Maurice. Manuel de Paléographie Latine et Française. 4e éd. Refondue avec la collaboration de Alain de Boüard. Paris: A. Picard, 1924.

For students beginning to read medieval documents in Latin or French this introductory manual is a most helpful guide to texts, handwriting, medieval language and other important topics. Especially useful is the dictionary of Latin and French abbreviations (pp. 303-474). See also Boüard (D0363) and Giry (D0493).

D0671 Prümm, Karl. Religionsgeschichtliches Handbuch für den Raum der Altchristlichen Umwelt, Hellenistisch-Römische Geistesströmungen und Kulte mit Beachtung des Eigenlebens der Provinzen. Anastatischer Neudruck. Rome: Päpstliches Bibelinstitut, 1954.

Prümm covers the entire background of religion in the classical world. Culture, society and provincial life generally in both Hellenic and Roman times are treated in a series of concise, clearly written chapters which include detailed notes and bibliographies. Author and subject indexes complete the work, which is a notable reference guide to the socio-cultural milieu of classical religions.

D0672 Puech, Aimé. Histoire de la Littérature Grecque Chrétienne depuis les Origines jusqu'à la Fin du IVe Siècle. 3 vols. Paris: Société d'Edition "Les Belles Lettres", 1928-1930.

Planned as a companion to Labriolle (D0565), this work follows a similar style.

D0673 Pugh, Ralph Bernard. How to Write a Parish History. 6th ed. London: Allen and Unwin, 1954.

This revision of John Charles Cox's How to Write the History of a Parish is a sound and highly reliable guide for the nonprofessional historian and student interested in preparing a parish history. While using many examples based on English resources, Pugh has applications in a much wider context. It is well documented and adequately indexed.

D0674 Purvis, John Stanley. An Introduction to Ecclesiastical Records. London: St. Anthony's Press, [1953].

This 96 page guide deals succinctly and thoroughly with the types of records likely to be found in English diocesan record offices. It covers archepiscopal and episcopal registers, visitation reports, records of ecclesiastical courts and similar categories of material. Purvis provides a valuable introduction to primary documentation for research students. See also Owen (D0653).

D0675 Quasten, Johannes. Patrology. 3 vols. Utrecht: Spectrum; Westminster, Md.: Newman Press, 1950-1960.

This very complete guide to the literature of the early church is more thorough than Altaner (D0004). It contains valuable summaries of the theology of the fathers, quotations from key texts and extensive bibliographies which list critical editions, translations into modern languages and articles and monographs on the writings discussed. Volume 1 deals with the beginnings of patristic literature; volume 2, with ante-Nicene literature after Irenaeus; volume 3, with Greek patristic literature from Nicea to Chalcedon. The French translation, Initiation aux Pères de l'Eglise (Trans. by J. Laporte. 3 vols. Paris: Editions du Cerf, 1955-1963) also contains extended bibliographies. This is the most thorough of the modern guides to patrology and is a particularly significant reference work, providing an excellent introduction to early Christian literature for users at various levels. See also Bardenhewer (D0342), Cayré (D0393) and Tixeront (D0737).

D0676 Quasten, Johannes; Burghardt, Walter J.; and Lawler, Thomas C., eds. Ancient Christian Writers: The Works of the Fathers in Translation. No. 1- . Westminster, Md.: Newman Press, 1946- .

This major series of English translations of patristic texts attempts to assist theological understanding and to be philologically precise. Each volume includes an introduction, a new translation and extensive scholarly notes and indexes. Bibliographies of other modern translations in a number of languages are provided. See also The Fathers of the Church (D0468).

D0677 Quirin, Karl Heinz. Einführung in das Studium der Mittelalterlichen Geschichte. 3. Aufl. Braunschweig: G. Westermann, 1964.

Including a bibliography (pp. 292-363), this handbook provides detailed information on the location, use and value of source materials in medieval history. Like Halphen (D0516) and Paetow (D0178) this work is a good starting point for students about to undertake advanced research. Quirin provides some data on German medieval history not found in similar guides.

D0678 Raab, Clement. The Twenty Ecumenical Councils of the Catholic Church. London: Longman, Green and Company, 1937. Reprint. Westminster, Md.: Newman Press, 1959.

Similar to Jedin (D0547), this 226 page guide is a basic source of information on the councils of the Roman Catholic Church. For each it provides dates, historical background and immediate reasons for being called, as well as sessional proceedings. An index is included. See also Margull (D0608).

D0679 Rand McNally and Company. Rand McNally Atlas of World History. Ed. by Robert Roswell Palmer. Contributing eds.: Knight Biggerstaff et al. Chicago, Ill.: Rand McNally and Company, [1965].

This 216 page collection of some seventy-five colored and fifty monochrome maps also contains textual comment and a name index. It is most thorough in its treatment of North American and European history (particularly for the nineteenth and twentieth centuries). See also van der Meer (D0615), Muir (D0633) and Shepherd (D0710).

D0680 Ranke, Leopold von. History of the Popes, Their Church and State. Rev. ed. Trans. by E. Fowler. 3 vols. New York: Colonial Press; New York: P.E. Collier and Son, [1901]. Reprint. 3 vols. New York: Frederick Unger Publishing Company, [1966].

This is a classic treatment of the popes in their historical context. See also Grisar (D0505), Schmidlin (D0701) and Seppelt (D0707).

D0681 Ranke, Leopold von. History of the Reformation in Germany. Trans. by Sarah Austin. Ed. by Robert A. Johnson. 2 vols. New York: E.P. Dutton and Company; London: G. Routledge and Sons, 1905. Reprint. 2 vols. New York: Frederick Unger Publishing Company, [1966].

This scholarly and detailed work by a leader of the modern scientific school of German historians contains a wealth of material based on extensive research. A bibliography, chronological table and an index are provided. This is suitable for the more advanced student who is interested in a now somewhat dated work for its historical value as well as for factual content.

D0682 Reid, James Seaton. History of the Presbyterian Church in Ireland; Comprising the Civil History of the Province of Ulster, from the Accession of James the First, with a Preliminary Sketch of the Progress of the Reformed Religion in Ireland during the Sixteenth Century, and an Appendix, Consisting of Original Papers. New ed. with additional notes by William Dool Killen. 3 vols. Belfast: W. Mullan, 1867.

See also McConnell (D0595).

D0683 Reorganized Church of Jesus Christ of Latter-Day Saints. Board of Publication. The History of the Reorganized Church of Jesus Christ of Latter-Day Saints. Vol. 1- . Independence, Mo.: Herald House, 1967- .

D0684 Ridley, Jasper Godwin. John Knox. New York: Oxford University Press; Oxford: Clarendon Press, 1968.

Arranged chronologically and dealing in part with Knox's intentions and motives, this 596 page study provides a thorough treatment based on recently discovered material and older sources. Footnotes, an excellent bibliography and six appendixes on technical points are included. This is an important biography for students of Knox.

D0685 Roberts, Alexander, and Donaldson, James, eds. Ante-Nicene Christian Library: Translations of the Fathers down to A.D. 325. 24 vols. Edinburgh: T. and T. Clark, 1867-1872.

Reprinted on various occasions and available in America as The Ante-Nicene Fathers: Translations of the Writings of the Fathers down to A.D. 325 (Rev. and chronologically arranged by Arthur Cleveland Coxe. 10 vols. Buffalo, N.Y.: The Christian Literature Publishing Company, 1885-1896. Reprint. 10 vols. Grand Rapids, Mich.: Wm. B. Eerdmans Publishing Company, 1956), this basic collection of writings by the apostolic fathers in English translation is arranged with subject indexes in each volume as well as a general index. There are numerous notes and scriptural references. A bibliographical synopsis is also provided. Although less comprehensive than Schaff (D0694, D0695) and less scholarly than Quasten (D0676) in terms of notes and explanatory devices, the collection remains useful when these alternatives are not available. See also Grant (D0500).

D0686 Rondet, Laurence-Etienne, ed. Table Générale des Matières Contenues dans les XIV Volumes de "L'Histoire Générale des Auteurs Sacrés et Ecclésiastiques". 2 vols. Paris: L. Vivès, 1868-1869.

For users of Ceillier (D0394) this is an indispensible index.

D0687 Rose, Herbert Jennings. A Handbook of Latin Literature from the Earliest Times to the Death of St. Augustine. 3rd ed. Reprinted, with a supplementary bibliography by E. Courtney. New York: E.P. Dutton Company; London: Methuen and Company, 1966.

See also Ceillier (D0394), Labriolle (D0565), Monceaux (D0629) and Schanz (D0697).

D0688 Rouët de Journel, Marie Joseph, comp. Enchiridion Patristicum: Loci SS. Patrum, Doctorum Scriptorum Ecclesiasticorum. 24. ed. Barcelona: Herder, 1969.

This 817 page collection of 2290 quotations from the church fathers is arranged chronologically, with a classified index and an alphabetical index of subjects, authors and titles. The texts are in Latin or Greek with Latin translations. Willis (D0762) provides an English version of this material.

D0689 Rousset, Paul. Histoire des Croisades. Bibliothèque Historique. Paris: Payot, 1957.

See also Runciman (D0690) and Setton (D0708).

D0690 Runciman, Stephen. A History of the Crusades. 3 vols. Cambridge: Cambridge University Press, 1951-1954. Reprint. Cambridge: Cambridge University Press, 1955-1962.

This is a standard work, containing a wealth of information for students and researchers. Each volume contains a discussion of sources and a bibliography, as well as maps, plates and an index. See also Rousset (D0689) and Setton (D0708).

D0691 Sandall, Robert; Wiggins, Arch S.; and Coutts, Frederick Lee. The History of the Salvation Army. 6 vols. London: Thomas Nelson and Sons; London: Hodder and Stoughton, 1947-1973.

This detailed official history of the Salvation Army is published under various imprints (vol. 6 by Hodder and Stoughton) and covers the organization from its beginnings to the 1950s. Volumes 1, 2 and 4 are devoted to the period from 1865 to 1904; volume 5 covers 1904-1914; volume 6 treats the period from 1914 to 1946; volume 3 is subtitled "1883-1953: Social Work and Reform". Each volume includes a bibliography, an analytical index and numerous illustrations.

D0692 Sappington, Roger Edwin, comp. and ed. The Brethren in the New Nation: A Sourcebook on the Developmnent of the Church of the Brethren, 1785-1865. Elgin, Ill.: Brethren Press, c. 1976.

Following the two earlier volumes by Durnbaugh (D0447, D0448), this collection of source materials uses letters, diaries, records, minutes and doctrinal writings to show the activities and growth of the Brethren in the eighteenth and nineteenth centuries.

D0693 Schaff, Philip. History of the Christian Church. 7 vols. in 8. New

York: Charles Scribner's Sons, 1888-1910. Reprint. Grand Rapids, Mich.: Wm. B. Eerdmans Publishing Company, 1960.

This extensive and detailed Protestant treatment of church history up to the time of Calvin and the Reformation makes extensive use of primary sources for each period. The chapters are clearly written and well arranged for reference purposes. Indexes of names and subjects accompany each volume. To balance Schaff's interpretation one should consult newer Protestant surveys and multivolume Roman Catholic works, especially Chadwick (D0396) and Jedin (D0548).

D0694 Schaff, Philip, et al. eds. A Select Library of the Nicene and Post-Nicene Fathers of the Christian Church. [First Series]. 14 vols. New York: Christian Literature Company, 1886-1890. Reprint. Grand Rapids, Mich.: Wm. B. Eerdmans Publishing Company, 1956.

The first and second series (D0695) together contain English translations of important writings by the Greek and Latin fathers. The first series treats writings up to and including the principal works of St. Augustine and St. John Chrysostom. Notes to the texts contain supplementary information on persons, places and events, and there are full references to sources and authorities. Entries are arranged chronologically by author, and each volume is well indexed. Numerous reprints are available. For a newer work see Grant (D0500).

D0695 Schaff, Philip, et al. A Select Library of the Nicene and Post-Nicene Fathers of the Christian Church. Second Series. 14 vols. New York: Christian Literature Company, 1890-1900. Reprint. Grand Rapids, Mich.: Wm. B. Eerdmans Publishing Company, 1961.

Published under various imprints and available in several reprints, this second series contains chief works in translation of the fathers from Eusebius to John of Damascus and from St. Ambrose to St. Gregory the Great. As such, it updates the first series (D0694), including early church histories, theological treatises and creedal statements of many ecumenical councils. Each volume includes indexes of subjects and biblical texts. The set also contains valuable notes and references to sources and authorities. The final volume has indexes of authors, names, words, places and subjects. Taken together, the twenty-eight volumes of these two series are a thorough Protestant attempt to provide source materials on the fathers, but overall Quasten (D0676) is more accurate and provides a better critical apparatus. For a newer work see Grant (D0500).

D0696 Schaff, Philip; Potter, H.C.; and Jackson, Samuel M., gen. eds. The American Church History Series, Consisting of a Series of Denominational Histories Published under the Auspices of the American Society of Church History. 13 vols. New York: Christian Literature Company, [1893-1897].

This series consists of separate histories of major denominations by various authors. Although rather dated and somewhat uneven in treatment, these volumes are useful reference sources for students at various levels. Each of the volumes includes a bibliography on the denomination discussed, while volume 12 contains a bibliography of American church history from 1820 to 1893. See also Sweet (D0729).

D0697 Schanz, Martin von; Hosius, Carl; and Krüger, Gustav, eds. Geschichte der Römischen Literatur bis zum Gesetzgebungswerk des Kaisers Justinian. 4th ed. 4 vols. in 5. Handbuch der Altertumswissenschaft, 8. Abt. Munich: C.H. Beck, 1914-1935.

This general history of Roman literature includes Christian Latin writings in its coverage. It is now quite dated (with only the first two volumes in a fourth edition). See also Ceillier (D0394), Labriolle (D0565), Monceaux (D0629) and Rose (D0687).

D0698 Schieder, Theodor, ed. Handbuch der Europäischen Geschichte. Vol. 1- . Stuttgart: Union Verlag, 1968- .

Projected in seven volumes, this valuable compendium deals with European history from late antiquity to the present. Each volume is devoted to a specific period, including both a general survey of the era and individual country studies. The bibliographies are especially useful for more advanced students seeking information on continental European titles. Although Schieder touches upon ecclesiastical affairs only marginally, this is a good reference work for those who require information on secular affairs. See also Mayer (D0613).

D0699 Schmandt, Raymond Henry, ed. The Popes through History. Vol. 1- . London: Burns and Oates, 1961- .

This series of biographies covers the lives of significant popes who have had a particular impact on the history of the church. Each of the volumes published to date is scholarly and dispassionate in content and includes both a bibliographical essay and an index. Although the series will not cover all popes, it should provide up to date and historically objective guides to those individuals treated. For more traditional and less detailed works on all of the popes to 1799 see von Pastor (D0656) or Seppelt (D0707).

D0700 Schmemann, Alexander. The Historical Road of Eastern Orthodoxy. Trans. by Lydia W. Kesich. New York: Holt, Rinehart and Winston, [1963].

This scholarly though popularly written history covers the period from the beginnings of Eastern Christianity to developments in Russian Orthodoxy in the period after Peter the Great. There are a few footnotes and only a rare mention of recent Western publications; it depends heavily on Russian Orthodox sources. There is no index. Although commended for rendering Eastern Orthodoxy more intelligible to the outsider, this study has been criticized for omitting certain issues such as the development of sectarian movements, and modern developments in Christian Orthodoxy in Greece, the Near East, Western Europe and the Americas. See also Atiya (D0326), Harder (D0522) and Neale (D0638).

D0701 Schmidlin, Joseph. Papstgeschichte der Neuesten Zeit. 2. Aufl. 4 vols. Munich: Josef Kösel und Friedrich Pustet, 1933-1939.

This history of the modern papacy covers 1800-1846, 1846-1903, 1903-1936 and 1922-1939. Each volume includes an introduction to the literature and sources. Schmidlin's analysis of events, trends and personalities is detailed, scholarly and thorough. Volume 2 exists in a second edition; the others have not been revised. See also Grisar (D0505), Ranke (D0680) and Seppelt (D0707).

D0702 Schmidt, Kurt Dietrich, and Wolf, Ernst, eds. Die Kirche in Ihrer Geschichte: Ein Handbuch. Vol. 1- . Göttingen: Vandenhoeck und Ruprecht, 1961- .

See also Aubert (D0327) and Heussi (D0531).

D0703 Schwartz, Eduard, ed. Acta Conciliorum Oecumenicorum. Issu atque mandato Societatis Scientiarum Argentoratensis. 4 vols. in 25. Berlin: Walter de Gruyter und Kompagnie, 1914-1940.

Covering the ecumenical councils of Ephesus, Chalcedon and Constantinople, this collection of conciliar documents has particular reference value because of its excellent indexing and generally full treatment of these councils. Schwartz is widely recognized as an indispensable compendium of source materials on the third, fourth and fifth councils and should be used by all historians who require accurate data on the conciliar texts. See also Stevenson (D0721) and Turner (D0741).

D0704 Scott, Hew. Fasti Ecclesiae Scoticanae: The Succession of Ministers in the Church of Scotland from the Reformation. New ed. Rev. and continued to the present time under the superintendence of a committee appointed by the General Assembly. 9 vols. Edinburgh: Oliver and Boyd, 1915-1961.

Arranged by synods and presbyteries, with parishes listed alphabetically under presbyteries, this compilation records the lives, writings and families of clergy in the Church of Scotland. The first seven volumes cover 1560-1914 and include valuable bibliographies of local and parish histories. Volume 8 is a supplementary listing for 1914-1928 together with addenda and corrigenda for 1560-1949; volume 9 covers 1929-1954. There are indexes of parishes and ministers, but a cumulative index has not been published.

D0705 Seebohm, Frederic. The Era of the Protestant Revolution. 2nd ed. With notes on books in English relating to the Reformation by George Park Fisher. New York: Charles Scribner's Sons, 1903. Reprint. New York: AMS Press, [1971].

This work provides a detailed analysis in three parts of the state of Christendom, the Protestant revolution, and its results. An analytical table of contents and references are provided. This is suitable for the student who is willing to supplement a dated approach with the results of modern historical scholarship. See also Lindsay (D0587).

D0706 Sellers, Robert Victor. The Council of Chalcedon: A Historical and Doctrinal Survey. London: SPCK, 1953.

Concentrating on the historical background of Chalcedon but also dealing with its theological significance, this 361 page survey provides a thorough treatment of early Christian doctrine of the period. It is historically accurate and makes good use of the sources. Sellers is suitable for the graduate student and the theologian.

D0707 Seppelt, Franz Xaver. Geschichte der Päpste von den Anfängen bis zur Mitte des Zwanzigsten Jahrhunderts. 2. Aufl. Vol. 1- . Munich: Kösel Verlag, 1954- .

Covering papal history to 1799 in the five available volumes, this work deals objectively and clearly with issues, personalities and events. Each volume includes a detailed bibliography and an index. As a scholarly and detailed guide to papal history, Seppelt serves as an excellent reference source where the greater biographical detail of von Pastor (D0656) is not required. See also Grisar (D0505), Ranke (D0680) and Schmidlin (D0701).

D0708 Setton, Kenneth Meyer, ed. A History of the Crusades. Vol. 1- . Philadelphia, Pa.: University of Pennsylvania Press, 1955- .

Projected in six volumes (with genealogies and bibliography in the final volume), this detailed and scholarly treatment of the crusades should supersede Runciman (D0690) for reference purposes. Each volume consists of clearly organized and well presented chapters on specific crusades and aspects thereof; scholarly footnotes add greatly to the critical apparatus accompanying Setton's factual and interpretive data. A gazetteer, chronology and analytical index complete each volume. This is an indispensible set for the advanced student and scholar. See also Rousset (D0689).

D0709 Shearer, Donald Cornelius, ed. Pontificia Americana: A Documentary History of the Catholic Church in the United States (1784-1884). New York: J.F. Wagner, 1933.

This collection of papal documents focuses on the Roman Catholic Church in America for the years indicated. Each document is presented in Latin, but useful introductions and brief summaries are provided in English. There is an adequate index. Shearer is an obvious starting point for historians seeking papal materials on American church history. See also Ellis (D0456).

D0710 Shepherd, William Robert. Historical Atlas. 9th ed. New York: Barnes and Noble, 1964. Reprint. New York: Harper and Row, 1973.

Long a standard atlas for students of history, this collection covers 1450 B.C.-1964 A.D. The ninth edition includes all seventh edition maps plus a supplement bringing the work up to date. The index covers both the original section and the supplementary maps. As a guide to ancient, medieval and modern history in general Shepherd usefully complements ecclesiastical collections by providing data on largely secular areas, including politics, society and diplomacy. See also van der Meer (D0615), Muir (D0633) and Rand McNally (D0679).

D0711 Small, Robert. History of the Congregations of the United Presbyterian Church from 1733 to 1900. 2 vols. Edinburgh: D.M. Small, 1904.

This work includes biographical notices of clergy. See also Lamb (D0566) and Ewing (D0465).

D0712 Smith, Hilrie Shelton; Handy, Robert T.; and Loetscher, Lefferts A. American Christianity: An Historical Interpretation with Representative Documents. 2 vols. New York: Charles Scribner's Sons, [1960-1963].

This collection of sources and interpretation covers 1607-1820 in volume 1 and 1820-1960 in volume 2. The source documents account for 60 per cent of the content and illustrate the various themes and periods of American church history from an ecumenical standpoint. Each chapter includes numerous footnotes and an annotated bibliography. Both volumes contain concise tables of contents and subject indexes. The 286 documents are useful both for background reading and for reference. See also Ahlstrom (D0319), Gaustad (D0488, D0490), Hudson (D0541), Mead (D0614) and Olmstead (D0650).

D0713 Sources Chrétiennes: Textes, Traductions, Introductions et Notes. Vol. 1- . Paris: Editions du Cerf, 1941- .

This extensive series of more than 160 volumes contains Greek and Latin patristic texts with French translations. Writings of Gregory of Nyssa, Clement of Alexandria, St. John Chrysostom, Aelred of Riévaulx and Shepherd of Hermas are included. Introductions, notes and indexes are provided. This is a valuable source for some writings not available elsewhere.

D0714 Southern, Richard William. Western Society and the Church in the Middle Ages. The Pelican History of the Church, vol. 2. Harmondsworth: Penguin Books, 1970.

Covering the eighth to the sixteenth centuries in seven chapters, Southern first sketches the main features of the middle ages and then deals in turn with the papacy, relations between Rome and Constantinople, bishops and archbishops, religious orders. Throughout the work there is a strong emphasis on ecclesiastical development and social change; the author attempts to avoid doctrinaire discussion and favors factual accounts of developments. This is a highly readable and well documented survey for beginning students and a useful reference volume for more advanced users. Charts and maps, a list of popes and an index provide additional reference value. See also Deanesly (D0424).

D0715 Spitz, Lewis William, ed. The Protestant Reformation. Sources of Civilisation in the West. Englewood Cliffs, N.J.: Prentice-Hall, [1966].

This volume contains a selection of statements dating from 1501-1559 made by the reformers. They are presented in five sections: the humanist critics; Luther's evangelical breakthrough; Zwingli and the radicals; Calvin's ecclesiastical reform; the English reformation. A reading list is included. This provides easy access for students to primary sources of the Reformation period. See also Hillerbrand (D0535) and Kidd (D0556).

D0716 Spitz, Lewis William. The Renaissance and Reformation Movements. Rand McNally History Series. Chicago, Ill.: Rand McNally Company, [1971].

This generally accurate and readable work of 614 pages covers the Renaissance in chapters 1-11 and the Reformation in chapters 12-21. Illustrations, maps and bibliographies are included. It is especially useful on intellectual history and biographical detail. See also Dannenfeldt (D0420), Dickens (D0431), Elton (D0460) and Major (D0601).

D0717 Staniforth, Maxwell, trans. Early Christian Writings: The Apostolic Fathers. Harmondsworth: Penguin Books, 1968.

See also Bettenson (D0355), Musurillo (D0636) and Wiles (D0759).

D0718 Steinberg, Sigfrid Henry. Historical Tables, 58 B.C.-A.D. 1972. 9th ed.

New York: St. Martin's Press; London: Macmillan and Company, 1973.

This very useful chronology of world history is arranged by period in six columns, including politics, economics, religion and culture. It is an extremely helpful work for the student who wishes to relate ecclesiastical history to other spheres of activity. See also Nicolas (D0643) and Peters (D0660).

D0719 Stephens, W.B. Sources for English Local History. Manchester: Manchester University Press, 1973. Reprint. Manchester: Manchester University Press, 1975.

This 260 page guide to published and unpublished source materials includes a general introductory section and individual chapters on population and society, local government and politics, economics, industry and trade, agriculture, education and religion. The treatment of sources is geared primarily to the needs of undergraduates and beginning research students interested in local history. The section on religion deals clearly and succinctly with basic information sources and various types of documentation. See also Emmison (D0461) and Tate (D0732).

D0720 Stephens, William Richard Wood, and Hunt, William, eds. A History of the English Church. 8 vols. in 9. London: Macmillan and Company, 1910-1931.

For many years a standard in its field, Stephens is a collection of volumes on specific periods of English church history. Each is by a specialist and relies heavily on both original sources and modern writers. Coverage extends beyond the traditional aspects of ecclesiastical history to include popular religion, learning and art as related to the church. Each volume includes maps, chronological tables and a detailed index; in addition each chapter contains a list of sources. Although somewhat dated, Stephens remains useful as a general guide to English church history. See also Dickinson (D0434).

D0721 Stevenson, James, ed. Creeds, Councils and Controversies: Documents Illustrative of the History of the Church, A.D. 337-461. Based upon the collection edited by the late B.J. Kidd. New York: Seabury Press; London: SPCK, 1967.

This successor to volume 2 of Kidd's compilation is a standard collection of major documents which includes sources and a brief commentary for each text. The commentaries provide helpful historical notes and details on content and authenticity. Biographical and chronological tables plus an index add to the reference value of Stevenson. See also A New Eusebius (D0722), Schwartz (D0703) and Turner (D0741).

D0722 Stevenson, James, ed. A New Eusebius: Documents Illustrative of the History of the Church to A.D. 337. Based upon the collection edited by the late B.J. Kidd. New York: Macmillan Company; London: SPCK, 1957.

Like the previous entry (D0721), this compilation is a standard collection of early Christian texts. Arranged chronologically, it provides extracts in English and contains helpful historical commentaries. The notes on sources (pp. 397-407) and index are useful for reference purposes. See also Ayer (D0328), Fremantle (D0480) and Kee (D0554).

D0723 Stier, Hans-Erich, et al., eds. Grosser Atlas zur Weltgeschichte: Vorzeit; Altertum, Mittelalter, Neuzeit. Unter Mitarbeit von Ekkehard Aner et al. [New ed.] Braunschweig: Georg Westermann Verlag, 1968.

First published in 1956 as Westermanns Atlas zur Weltgeschichte, this atlas treats pre- and ancient history, medieval history and modern history in roughly equal parts. The more than 400 maps are colored and provide excellent cartographic detail for a wide range of reference needs. See also Bayerischer Schulbuch Verlag (D0349).

D0724 Storey, R.L. Chronology of the Medieval World, 800 to 1491. General ed.: Neville Williams. New York: David McKay; London: Barrie and Jenkins, 1973.

Geared more to secular events than the chronology of Mas-Latrie (D0612), this compilation is essentially a listing of political events to which religious, intellectual and artistic developments are appended. Political events are listed on the left; other events, on the right. The detailed index covers persons, places, subjects, literary and artistic works, occupations. See also Delorme (D0428).

D0725 Strecker, Karl. Introduction to Medieval Latin. 4. unveränderte Aufl. English trans. and rev. by Robert B. Palmer. Dublin/Zürich: Weidmann, 1967.

This translation of Einführung in das Mittellatein is an introductory handbook to medieval Latin philology for students with knowledge of classical Latin. Not a grammar, it consists of a series of brief chapters on word formation, morphology, syntax, various literary forms (poetry, literary prose), collections of texts, paleography and related topics. In every case the discussion builds upon knowledge of classical Latin, pointing out differences, changes and variations. It is a useful introduction and guide to sources for more advanced students. Those seeking a grammatical guide should consult Nunn (D0645).

D0726 Stubbs, William. Registrum Sacrum Anglicanum: An Attempt to Exhibit the Course of Episcopal Succession in England from the Records and Chronicles of the Church. 2nd ed. With an appendix of Indian, colonial and missionary consecrations, collected and arranged by E.E. Holmes. Oxford: Clarendon Press, 1897.

See also le Neve (D0573).

D0727 Swanzy, Henry Biddall. Succession Lists of the Diocese of Dromore. Ed. by James Blennerhassett Leslie. Belfast: R. Caswell and Son, 1933.

Not simply a succession list, Swanzy provides biographical accounts of all Anglican clergy of the Diocese of Dromore, thereby supplementing other works by Leslie (D0576-D0583). See also Cotton (D0413).

D0728 [no entry]

D0729 Sweet, William Warren. Religion of the American Frontier. 4 vols. New York: H. Holt and Company, 1931-1939. Reprint. 4 vols. New York: Cooper Square Publishers, 1964.

Published under various imprints and never completed according to the original outline, Sweet presents wide ranging source materials on the Baptists from 1783 to 1830, the Presbyterians from 1783 to 1840, the Congregationalists from 1783 to 1850 and the Methodists from 1783 to 1840. To complement the extensive collection of documents on these denominations each volume includes a detailed introduction and a useful bibliography. The source materials are arranged topically for ease of reference. See also Schaff (D0729).

D0730 Sykes, Norman. The Crisis of the Reformation. The Christian Challenge Series. London: J. Heritage, 1938. Reprint. London: Geoffrey Bles, 1958.

This brief study of the Reformation in relation to related economic and political developments examines Lutheran, Calvinist and Anglican churches from the standpoint of their theology, worship and polity. It contains neither bibliography nor index. See also Bainton (D0330), Elton (D0459) and Hillerbrand (D0537).

D0731 Tarouca, Carlo da Silva, ed. Fontes Historiae Ecclesiasticae Medii Aevi in Usum Scholarum. Vol. 1- . Rome: Universitatis Gregorianae, 1930- .

This multivolume compilation consists of chronologically arranged excerpts from various authors and documentary sources. It includes references to complete texts and an index of names. The texts deal with all aspects of medieval church history. See also Monumenta Germaniae Historica (D0630).

D0732 Tate, William Edward. The Parish Chest: A Study of the Records of Parochial Administration in England. 3rd ed. Cambridge: Cambridge University Press, 1969.

Prepared mainly for those doing research in local history, this study of civil and ecclesiastical documents in parish archives in England includes numerous examples of these records, relates them to the laws and conditions which gave rise to them and to society of the period. The five chapters on ecclesiastical records treat the various types of parish registers, accounts and related categories; the six chapters on civil records cover vestry minutes, constables' accounts, poor law administration, highway maintenance, agricultural enclosures and miscellaneous records. There are numerous cross references and notes (pp. 283-306) plus appendixes dealing with major statutes and local record offices in England. A glossary and general index add greatly to the reference value of Tate, which is essential reading for any historian engaged in the use of primary source materials on English church history. See also Cox (D0414) and Ker (D0555).

D0733 Testimonia: Schriften der Altchristlichen Zeit. In Verbindung mit Theodor Klausner. Hrsg. von Eduard Stommel und Alfred Stuiber. Vol. 1- . Düsseldorf: Patmos Verlag, 1960- .

These volumes provide Latin texts and German translations. See also Bardenhewer (D0340) and Texte und Untersuchungen (D0734).

D0734 Texte und Untersuchungen zur Geschichte der Altchristlichen Literatur. Vol. 1- . Berlin: Akademie Verlag, 1883- .

Issued by the Kommission für Spätantike Religionsgeschichte of the Deutschen Akademie der Wissenschaften and initially published under the imprint of J.C. Hinrichs, this work consists of four series: fifteen volumes issued between 1822 and 1897, fifteen volumes issued between 1897 and 1906, fifteen volumes issued between 1907 and 1924, a current series of volumes begun in 1929. The first series includes indexes in volume 15. See also Bardenhewer (D0340), Die Griechischen Christlichen Schriftsteller (D0503) and Testimonia (D0733).

D0735 Thompson, Ernest Trice. Presbyterians in the South. 3 vols. Richmond, Va.: John Knox Press, 1963-1973.

Covering 1607-1861, 1861-1890, 1890-1972, these volumes offer a thoroughly researched and well documented account of the development of Presbyterianism in the southern United States. The work is perhaps least strong on doctrinal issues. It is suitable for lay readers and ministers. See also Loetscher (D0590).

D0736 Tierney, Brian. The Crisis of Church and State, 1050-1300; with Selected Documents. Englewood Cliffs, N.J.: Prentice-Hall, 1964.

This 212 page volume contains selected extracts from pamphlets, letters, treatises, etc. of the period, together with useful comments. However, it lacks an index and contains only a brief booklist. It has also been criticized for neglecting major narrative sources. See also Ehler (D0453) and Mercati (D0620).

D0737 Tixeront, Joseph. A Handbook of Patrology. Authorized trans. based upon the 4th French ed. by S.A. Raemers. 5th ed. St. Louis, Mo.: B. Herder Book Company, 1934. Reprint. St. Louis, Mo.: B. Herder Book Company, 1951.

Reprinted on several occasions, this Roman Catholic work surveys three main periods: the beginning and growth of early Christian literature (the first three centuries); "the golden age of patristic literature" (313-461); the period of decline (461-750). There are many subsections, particularly following geographical origins (Greek, Latin, Syrian, etc.). Bibliographical data are included in the introductory section. See also Bardenhewer (D0342), Cayré (D0393) and Quasten (D0675).

D0738 Todd, John Murray. Reformation. Garden City, N.Y.: Doubleday and Company, 1971; London: Darton, Longman and Todd, 1972.

This 377 page work examines the Protestant Reformation of the sixteenth century from a Roman Catholic perspective. It treats the counter-Reformation only incidentally. A bibliography is appended and apt references to authorities are made in the text. This work contains material of interest to both Roman Catholic and Protestant readers. See also Imbart de la Tour (D0545).

D0739 Torbet, Robert George. A History of the Baptists. Rev. ed. Valley Forge, Pa.: Judson Press, [1963]; London: Carey Kingsgate Press, [1966, c. 1963].

This work concentrates on the history of the American Baptists, providing much factual information. Readers seeking information on Baptist history elsewhere or on Baptist contributions to Protestantism more generally will need to supplement Torbet; Benedict (D0351) provides a suitable although dated account. See also Baker (D0336) and Olson (D0651).

D0740 Tucker, William Edward, and McAllister, Lester G. Journey in Faith: A History of the Christian Church (Disciples of Christ). St. Louis, Mo.: Bethany Press, 1975.

Including a substantial bibliography (pp. 463-488), this survey of the history of the Disciples of Christ combines chronological and thematic approaches to cover the period from the early nineteenth century to the present. The book contains considerable detail, and is suitable for students. See also Garrison (D0487) and Harrell (D0525).

D0741 Turner, Cuthbert Hamilton, ed. Ecclesiae Occidentalis Monumenta Iuris Antiquissima. Canonum et Conciliorum Graecorum Interpretationis Latinae. Post Christophorum Iustel et al. 2 vols. in 3. Oxford: Clarendon Press, 1907-1939.

First issued in seven parts, this valuable collection indexes the canons of all ecumenical councils up to the Council of Antioch in 431 A.D. It is based on major collections of documents available in the early twentieth century, most of which are still available in large libraries. See also Schwartz (D0703) and Stevenson (D0721).

D0742 The Victoria History of the Counties of England. Vol. 1- . London: Oxford University Press for the University of London, Institute of Historical Research, 1901- .

Published under various imprints, this massive series is indispensible for the student of local ecclesiastical history. Each county is treated very thoroughly, usually in several volumes, with chapters on political, ecclesiastical, social and economic history, architecture, arts, industry, biography and folklore. While some of the early volumes suffer from a lack of professionalism, there are few inaccuracies and much important data in every volume. Footnotes are useful for their indication of sources, but individual volumes are not indexed, nor are the tables of contents as detailed as they should be. The General Introduction by Ralph B. Pugh (London: Oxford University Press, 1970), on the other hand, contains indispensible finding aids: list of volumes, detailed lists of contents, index of article titles and author index. For advanced students and scholars interested in local church history this is a key reference work.

D0743 Vidler, Alexander Roper. The Church in an Age of Revolution: 1789 to the Present Day. The Pelican History of the Church, vol. 5. Harmondsworth: Penguin Books, 1971.

For the earlier period see Cragg (D0415); for a more detailed coverage of the modern period see Latourette (D0567).

D0744 Viénot, John. Histoire de la Réforme Française. 2 vols. Paris: Librairie Fischbacher, 1926.

Treating the reform movement in France from its origins to the Edict of Nantes in volume 1 and from the Edict to its revocation in volume 2, this work provides a now dated account. For a more general study of Catholicism in France see Latreille (D0569).

D0745 [no entry]

D0746 Volz, Carl A. The Church of the Middle Ages: Growth and Change from 600 to 1400. Church in History Series. St. Louis, Mo.: Concordia Publishing House, [1970].

> This straightforward historical account treats the period chronologically. An index and an appendix of selected readings are included, and the text contains many quotations. This is more appropriate for the general reader or beginning student. See also Baldwin (D0339).

D0747 Wakeman, Henry Offley. An Introduction to the History of the Church of England from the Earliest Times to the Present Day. Rev. by S.L. Ollard. 12th ed. London: Rivingtons, 1955.

> Also available in a reprint of the ninth edition (St. Clair Shores, Mich.: Scholarly Press, 1970), this classic introduction contains thorough but readable treatment of the Church of England from 200 A.D. to the twentieth century. An index is included, as well as notes on several issues (such as papal supremacy, and the dissolution of the religious houses). See also Moorman (D0631).

D0748 Walker, Williston. A History of the Christian Church. 3rd ed. Rev. by Robert T. Handy. New York: Charles Scribner's Sons, 1970.

> First published in 1918, Walker is one of the most widely respected single volume histories of the church. Treatment is in seven periods from the beginnings to the gnostic crisis, through to modern Christianity. An excellent classified bibliography (pp. 559-583), an index and seven maps complete this standard textbook which has been revised to take account of modern developments. See also Bainton (D0331) and Latourette (D0568).

D0749 Wand, John William Charles. A History of the Early Church to A.D. 500. With comparative tables and three maps. 3rd ed. London: Methuen and Company, 1957.

> This volume provides a sound treatment of the early church, and includes examination of aspects such as church life and worship, monasticism, and divergence between East and West. A select booklist (pp. 264-268), additional notes and an index add to the work's reference value. See also Bainton (D0332), Chadwick (D0395), Conzelmann (D0408), Davies (D0422) and Frend (D0481).

D0750 Wand, John William Charles. A History of the Modern Church from 1500 to the Present Day. London: Methuen, 1971.

> This 325 page general survey provides a broadly chronological treatment, but devotes separate chapters to particular themes as appropriate (e.g., pietism and Methodism, the Oxford movement, reunion movements). A select bibliography (pp. 290-293), lists of principal events, 1509-1929, and of popes and archbishops of Canterbury, an index and two maps are included. See also Nichols (D0642).

D0751 Watkin, Edward Ingram. Roman Catholicism in England from the Reformation to 1950. The Home University Library of Modern Knowledge. London: Oxford University Press, 1957.

This 244 page introductory history contains six chapters which cover the period chronologically. A select bibliography (pp. 235-239) and an index are provided. This is suitable for the beginning student. See also Bossy (D0362).

D0752 Weis, Frederick Lewis. The Colonial Clergy and the Colonial Churches of New England. Publications of the Society of the Descendants of the Colonial Clergy, no. 2. Lancaster, Mass.: American Antiquarian Society, 1936.

Like Weis' other works (D0753-D0755), this guide lists colonial clergy known to have been associated with the geographical area indicated. It provides only very brief biographical data but must be regarded as an important source of information on early American church history in view of the paucity of more adequate guides.

D0753 Weis, Frederick Lewis. The Colonial Clergy of Maryland, Delaware and Georgia. Publications of the Society of the Descendants of the Colonial Clergy, no. 5. Lancaster, Mass.: American Antiquarian Society, 1950.

Focusing on the three colonies indicated, this provides the same type of information as the 1936 compilation by Weis (D0752) and serves a similar purpose.

D0754 Weis, Frederick Lewis. "The Colonial Clergy of the Middle Colonies, New York, New Jersey and Pennsylvania", Proceedings of the American Antiquarian Society 66, part 2 (1957): 167-351.

This provides the same type of data as the original work by Weis (D0752) for the colonies indicated. It has also been reprinted as a monograph (Worcester, Mass.: American Antiquarian Society, 1957).

D0755 Weis, Frederick Lewis. The Colonial Clergy of Virginia, North Carolina and South Carolina. Publications of the Society of the Descendants of the Colonial Clergy, no. 7. Boston, Mass.: American Antiquarian Society, 1955.

For these three colonies this provides basic but significant biographical data on the clergy. See also Weis' 1936 and other compilations (D0752-D0754).

D0756 Wentz, Abdel Ross. A Basic History of Lutheranism in America. Philadelphia, Pa.: Muhlenberg Press, [1955].

This 430 page study contains six parts, each of which treats a time span in the life of the American nation, up to the modern ecumenical movement. A selective bibliography and an index add to the reference value of this work by an eminent Lutheran historian. See also Wentz's earlier work (D0757).

D0757 Wentz, Abdel Ross. The Lutheran Church in American History. 2nd ed. Philadelphia, Pa.: United Lutheran Publication House, [c. 1935].

Intended as a readable account for the beginning student, this volume contains six parts which deal with chronological periods from 1625 to the present. There is a detailed table of contents, but neither index nor bibliography. The volume does not attempt to be comprehensive; rather it is a stimulating interpretation that contains much useful material.

See also Wentz's later work (D0756).

D0758 Wilbur, Earl Morse. A History of Unitarianism. 2 vols. Cambridge, Mass.: Harvard University Press, 1945-1952.

The two volumes cover Socianism and its antecedents and the developments in Transylvania, England and America from the sixteenth century to the beginning of the twentieth. Each volume contains a pronouncing table, an index of abbreviations and a general index. THis is an excellent source for students interested in the Socinian-Unitarian movement.

D0759 Wiles, Maurice Frank, and Santer, Mark, eds. Documents in Early Christian Thought. Cambridge: Cambridge University Press, 1975.

This valuable introduction to the sources of early Christian thought seeks to collect writings from the early fathers on all main areas of doctrine. The topical arrangement covers such areas as God, Christ, Holy Spirit, sin and grace, tradition and scripture, sacraments. Each section opens with a very brief introduction to the topic, and there are numerous footnotes. However, an index is not provided. Wiles is a useful collection for students of the history of doctrine. See also Kee (D0554), Bettenson (D0355), Musurillo (D0636) and Staniforth (D0717).

D0760 Williams, George Hunston. The Radical Reformation. Philadelphia, Pa.: Westminster Press; London: Weidenfeld and Nicolson, 1962.

This 924 page study provides a synoptic view of the rise of radical sects in the sixteenth century. A particular strength is the use of many contemporary documents which have been overlooked in other studies. Three useful indexes are provided. This substantial work contains much of interest to the specialist as well as the student.

D0761 Williams, Glanmor. The Welsh Church from Conquest to Reformation. Cardiff: University of Wales Press, 1962.

This history of the church in Wales from the eleventh to the sixteenth century consists of fourteen admirable chapters on politics, religious literature, scholarship, secular clergy, monastic houses, popular belief and similar topics. The discussion is scholarly and detailed, providing clear insights into trends and events of the period. Footnotes, a detailed bibliography (pp. 567-582) and thorough index complete the work. Appendixes treat clerical income, monastic numbers and bequests to religious houses. Williams is the most detailed work in its field and serves as an excellent reference history.

D0762 Willis, John Randolph, ed. The Teachings of the Church Fathers. New York: Herder and Herder, 1966.

Based on Rouët de Journal (D0688), this collection comprises 2290 quotations from the church fathers up to 594 A.D. Arrangement is by subject, with references to complete texts. An index is provided. The collection presents a useful outline of Catholic doctrine as presented by patristic writings.

D0763 Wiltsch, Johann Elieser Theodor. Handbook of the Geography and Statistics of the Church. Trans. by John Leitch. 2 vols. London: T. Bosworth,

1868.

This is a translation of <u>Handbuch der Kirchlichen Geographie und Statistik von den Zeiten der Apostel bis zu dem Anfange des Sechszehnten Jahrhunderts</u> (2 vols. Berlin: H. Schultze. Reprint. 2 vols. in 1. Wiesbaden: M. Sandig, 1970).

D0764 [no entry]

D0765 Winsor, Justin, ed. <u>Narrative and Critical History of America</u>. 8 vols. Boston, Mass.: Houghton Mifflin Company, 1884-1889. Reprint. 8 vols. New York: AMS Press, 1967.

The eight volumes in this older general history cover early explorations and settlements, the growth of the colonies and the United States, French and Spanish America, manuscript sources and important printed works. While much of the text is now outdated, the excellent bibliographical references give Winsor continuing reference value for advanced students interested in early American history. Missions and ecclesiastical history are treated adequately. See also Commager (D0407).

D0766 Woolley, Davis C. <u>Guide for Writing the History of a Church</u>. Nashville, Tenn.: Broadman Press, [1969].

See also Baker (D0335).

D0767 Zananiri, Gaston. <u>Histoire de l'Eglise Byzantine</u>. Paris: Nouvelles Editions Latines, [1954].

See also Neale (D0638).

E. Missions/Ecumenism

MISSIONS/ECUMENISM: BIBLIOGRAPHIES

E0001 Althaus, Hans Ludwig. Literaturschau zu Fragen der Weltmission. Stuttgart: Evangelischer Missionsverlag, 1971.

See also Hering (E0026).

E0002 American Theological Library Association. Bibliography of Church Union in Canada. Toronto: American Theological Library Association, 1959.

E0003 Amistad Research Center. Author and Added Entry Catalog of the American Missionary Association Archives, with References to Schools and Mission Stations. 3 vols. Westport, Conn.: Greenwood Publishing Corporation, 1970.

> This catalog of 105,000 items (mainly letters and similar documents) from the American Missionary Association collection lists materials of value in studying the history of the Association and its activities in America. It also contains valuable data relating to the abolition of slavery, underground movements, education of blacks and similar topics relevant to nineteenth century negro history. All items in the Catalog have been microfilmed and are available in this form in selected American libraries. See also Missionary Research Library (E0041).

E0004 Anderson, Gerald H., comp. Bibliography of the Theology of Missions in the Twentieth Century. 3rd ed. New York: Missionary Research Library, 1966.

> This 119 page classified bibliography lists more than 1500 books and articles dealing with biblical studies, history, Christianity and relations with non-Christian religions, theory of missions and other areas related to missiology as viewed from a theological standpoint. Within each section material is arranged alphabetically by author, and there are some annotations. Anderson is a broadly representative guide to publications on an important period in the development of missiology. See also Hartley (E0025).

E0005 Anderson, Gerald H., ed. Christianity in Southeast Asia: A Bibliographical Guide; an Annotated Bibliography of Selected References in Western Languages. New York: Missionary Research Library, 1966.

> This 69 page bibliography includes an introduction as well as the bibliography which is organized geographically. Selection of materials took account of availability and of language (only Western language works are included), and tends to be Protestant in focus. Brief annotations are provided, and there is an author index.

E0006 Bachmann, E. Theodore. "Doctoral Dissertations on Mission", International Bulletin of Missionary Research 7 (1983): 98-134.

> This bibliography lists 934 doctoral dissertations on mission related subjects accepted at theological schools and universities in North America from 1945 to 1981. Entries are listed alphabetically by author, and there is a subject index. The majority of entries relate to Third World issues, contexts and concerns of Christianity. This is an invaluable guide for both scholars and advanced students. See also Person (E0047).

E0007 Bent, Ans Joachim van der. The Whole Oikoumene: A Collection of Bibliographies of the Works of Philip A. Potter. Geneva: World Council of Churches, 1980.

> See also De Groot (E0018).

E0008 Bibliografìa Missionaria. Vol. 1- . Rome: Pontificia Università Urbiana, Pontificia Biblioteca Missionaria della S. Congregazione per l'Evangelizzatione dei Popoli, 1935- ; annual.

> Initially published as part of Guida della Missione Cattoliche and since 1937 as a separate title, this annual bibliography is arranged according to geographical region and includes indexes of authors and subjects. Basic bibliographical data are provided for each entry, and brief abstracts are included for a few of the more important items. This service includes books in its coverage but is of particular value for its comprehensive treatment of missiological serials from around the world, both scholarly and popular. Coverage is quite up to date and provides users with a unique guide to materials on all aspects of missiology. See also International Review of Mission (E0029) and Neue Zeitschrift für Missionswissenschaft (E0044).

E0009 A Bibliography on Catholic-Protestant Understanding. Packard Manse Papers. Stoughton, Mass.: Packard Manse, 1960?

> This 19 page bibliography was compiled as a project of the Packard Manse study on Catholic-Protestant understanding. It contains alphabetically arranged, numbered entries with bibliographical details and brief (approximately three lines) annotations.

E0010 Brandreth, Henry Renaud Turner. Unity and Reunion: A Bibliography. 2nd ed. With supplement. London: Adam and Charles Black, 1948.

> In 158 pages Brandreth presents a classified and annotated listing of primary and secondary literature in English on reunion since the beginning of the nineteenth century. The focus of the 1200 entries is the visible reunion of a divided Christendom rather than cooperative ventures in

various areas. It includes an index of authors and a brief subject index. See also Crow (E0017), Senaud (E0054) and World Council of Churches (E0062).

E0011 Brownlee, Margaret. The Lives and Work of South African Missionaries: Bibliography. 3rd impression. School of Librarianship Bibliographical Series. Cape Town: University of Cape Town Libraries, 1969.

For a more general bio-bibliography see Missionary Research Library (E0042).

E0012 The Bulletin of the Scottish Institute of Missionary Studies. No. 1- . Aberdeen: University of Aberdeen, Scottish Institute of Missionary Studies, 1967- ; irregular.

Approximately one issue per annum of The Bulletin is devoted to a survey of current books on missions in the widest sense, covering the Christian mission, other world religions, relationship to the saeculum, ministry, pastoralia. Each survey is arranged first by subject, then geographically, with cross references from subject entries to geographical entries. The reviews vary considerably in detail, but all provide at least a basic guide to contents and conclusions. Most of the entries are quite current, and the coverage extends to works in most European languages and to both Protestant and Roman Catholic missions. This is a useful complement to the International Review of Missions (E0029), which contains an annotated bibliography on all types of materials. See also Missionalia (E0040).

E0013 Byrnes, Paul A., comp. Current Periodicals in the Missionary Research Library: A Subject List. New York: Missionary Research Library, 1972.

For an alphabetical list see Ma (E0038).

E0014 Center for Research Libraries. Church Missionary Society Archives Relating to Africa and Palestine, 1799-1923: Index to Records on Microfilm at the Center for Research Libraries. Chicago, Ill.: Center for Research Libraries, 1968.

See also Missionary Research Library (E0041).

E0015 Chao, Jonathan T'ien-en. A Bibliography of the History of Christianity in China (a Preliminary Draft). CGST Research Project, no. 3. Waltham, Mass.: Faculty-in-Preparation, China Graduate School of Theology, 1970.

See also Chu (E0016), Pfister (E0048) and Price (E0049).

E0016 Chu, Clayton H. American Missionaries in China: Books, Articles and Pamphlets Extracted from the Subject Catalog of the Missionary Research Library. Issued by the Committee on American Far Eastern Policy Studies, Department of History, Harvard University. 3 vols. Research Aids for American Far Eastern Policy Studies, no. 2. Cambridge, Mass.: distributed by Harvard University Press, 1960.

See also Chao (E0015), Pfister (E0048) and Price (E0049).

E0017 Crow, Paul A., Jr. The Ecumenical Movement in Bibliographical Outline. New York: National Council of the Churches of Christ in the USA, Department of Faith and Order, 1965.

Confined primarily to English language works, this classified bibliography includes chapters on bibliographies, reference works, periodicals, surveys, introductions, the modern conciliar movement, church unions and union schemes, denominational ecumenism, biographies, evangelical critics. Crow updates both Brandreth (E0010) and Senaud (E0054) and is similar to the European work by Lescrauwaet (E0037). Unfortunately, few Vatican II materials are included, and there are no annotations. For a partial successor see Rouse (E0154).

E0018 De Groot, Alfred Thomas. <u>An Index to the Doctrines, Persons, Events, etc. of the Faith and Order Commission, World Council of Churches; Given in the English Language Editions, Official, Numbered Publications, 1910-1948; and Check List, Faith and Order Commission Official, Numbered Publications: Series I, 1910-1948; Series II, 1948-1970.</u> [3rd ed.] Geneva: World Council of Churches, 1970.

For an alphabetical subject index to World Council of Churches documents and list of reports see P. Beffa <u>et al.</u> eds. <u>Index to the World Council of Churches' Official Statements and Reports, 1948-1978</u> (Geneva: World Council of churches, 1978). See also van der Bent (E0007).

E0019 Delfs, Hermann. <u>Ökumenische Literaturkunde.</u> Hrsg. von D.F. Siegmund-Schultze. Schriften des Ökumenischen Archivs Soest, Bd. 3. Soest: Westfälische Verlagsbuchhandlung Maker und Jahn, 1966.

This 579 page bibliography consists of 100 sections in three main parts. The first covers ecumenical beginnings; the second treats dogmatic and theological aspects of ecumenism in the various Christian traditions; the third deals with countries and regions (mainly Europe). Each section is further subdivided into specific topics, and there is a detailed index of authors and subjects. This is a very thorough and comprehensive bibliographical guide to literature of all periods and traditions. See also Crow (E0017) and Siegmund-Schultze (E0055).

E0020 Domínguez, Olegario. <u>Bibliografía Misional Hispanoamericana 1948.</u> Cuadernos de Cultura Misional, no. 1. Burgos: Instituto Español de Misiones Extranjeras, Biblioteca ID, [1949].

See also Santos Hernández (E0053).

E0021 Ebisawa, Arimichi. <u>Christianity in Japan: A Bibliography of Japanese and Chinese Sources.</u> Vol. 1- . Tokyo: Committee on Asian Cultural Studies, International Christian University, 1960- .

Volume 1 was published in connection with a research project on Christianity in Asia, and covers the period 1543-1858. It includes books and manuscripts written in Japan and China, with titles translated into English. Books are arranged in chronological order. In addition to the main bibliography (pp. 3-131) the volume contains a list of libraries and sources, a table of Japanese and Chinese era names, and indexes of titles, authors/translators/compilers and subjects. See also Ikado (E0027) and Laurès (E0036).

E0022 <u>The Ecumenical Review: The Quarterly of the World Council of Church-</u>

es. Vol. 1- . Geneva: World Council of Churches, 1948/1949- ; quarterly.

Although not a proper indexing or abstracting service by any means, The Ecumenical Review regularly contains both book reviews and a listing of the contents of significant ecumenical journals. This journal covers not only inter-church relations but also social and political issues of interest to the church at an international level. As each volume lists the contents of 100 journal issues in these areas, this is a useful current awareness service. Both the journals and book reviews appear within a year of publication, making this a very up to date guide. See also Journal of Ecumenical Studies (E0033) and Okumenische Rundschau (E0046).

E0023 Facelina, Raymond. Evangelization and Missions: International Bibliography 1972 Indexed by Computer/Evangelisation et Mission: Bibliographie Internationale 1972 Etablie par Ordinateur. RIC Supplément, no. 5. Strasbourg: CERDIC Publications, 1973.

See also Masson (E0039).

E0024 Geoghegan, Abel Rodolfo. Bibliografía sobre Ludovico A. Muratori y Su Obra sobre las Misiones Jesuíticas del Paraguay, 1743-1749. Buenos Aires: n.p., 1960.

E0025 Hartley, R.W., comp. and ed. Bibliography on the History and Theology of Missions from the Collection in Leigh College Library, Enfield, N.S.W., Australia. Leigh College Library Bulletin, no. 15. Enfield, New South Wales: Leigh College Library, 1969.

See also Anderson (E0004).

E0026 Hering, Hollis W., comp. Recommended Titles on Missions and Related Subjects. New York: Committee of Reference and Counsel, [Protestant Foreign Missions Conference of North America], 1925.

This 29 page bibliography is issued under the auspices of the Missionary Research Library. See also Althaus (E0001).

E0027 Ikado, Fujio, and McGovern, James R., comps. A Bibliography of Christianity in Japan: Protestantism in English Sources (1859-1959). Tokyo: Committee on Asian Cultural Studies, International Christian University, 1966.

See also Ebisawa (E0021) and Laurès (E0036).

E0028 International Bulletin of Missionary Research. Vol. 1- . Ventnor, N.J.: Overseas Ministries Study Center, 1950- ; quarterly.

Originally the Missionary Research Library's Occasional Bulletin until its merger with Gospel in Context in 1977, this useful serial includes both special bibliographies and lists of theses. There are cumulative indexes for vols. 1-5 and 6-8. For special issues see Bachmann (E0006), Person (E0047) and Price (E0049); see also Missionalia (E0040) and Bulletin of the Scottish Institute of Missionary Studies (E0012).

E0029 International Review of Mission. Vol. 1- . Geneva: World Council of Churches, Commission on World Mission and Evangelism, 1912- ; quarterly.

Originally entitled International Review of Missions, this scholarly journal includes in each issue a "Bibliography on World Mission and Evangelism", which is arranged by subject and by geographical region to suit most approaches. The Christian mission broadly interpreted is the focus of this section, which treats periodical articles, books, reports and dissertations. The bibliographical citations are complete and often provide abstracts as well. This bibliography is international both in focus and in the resources on which it draws, thereby complementing the Bulletin of the Scottish Institute of Missionary Studies. For those interested in Christian mission vis-à-vis world religions or in society, pastoralia, ministry and their relationships this is an indispensible survey. Annual indexes are provided. See also Bibliografía Missionaria (E0008) and Neue Zeitschrift für Missionswissenschaft (E0044).

E0030 Internationale Okumenische Bibliographie/International Ecumenical Bibliography/Bibliographie Oecuménique Internationale/Bibliografía Ecuménica Internacional. Vol. 1- . Munich: Christian Kaiser Verlag; Mainz: Matthias Grünewald Verlag, 1962/1963- ; irregular.

This multilingual bibliography lists books, dissertations and articles from some 600 journals dealing with various aspects of the ecumenical movement. The subject divisions into which entries are arranged reflect the historical, denominational, organizational and theological factors in ecumenism. Under the various headings entries are listed alphabetically by author and include full bibliographical information plus abstracts in a majority of instances. A classified table of contents, instructions for use and list of periodical abbreviations precede the main listing; an author index, a full German subject index and abbreviated subject indexes in the other three languages of the compilation complete each volume. Despite its international coverage and thorough treatment of material, the IOB no longer appears either with any regularity or with any degree of currency; because of this serious failure, those interested in current treatment of ecumenical literature must consult such selective guides as The Ecumenical Review (E0022) or Journal of Ecumenical Studies (E0033). See also Oecumene (E0045).

E0031 Istina. Vol. 1- . Paris: Centre d'Etudes "Istina", 1954- ; quarterly.

Focusing especially on relations between Orthodoxy and Roman Catholicism, this ecumenical journal contains articles, documents and brief book reviews in each issue; less regular is the Chronique Oecuménique des Périodiques, which surveys a substantial number of periodicals not treated by other indexing services. Each Chronique is arranged in four sections: biblical, theological and Jewish studies; relations with Eastern churches; Anglicanism and Protestantism; ecumenism and the study of religion. In each section the articles are provided with brief abstracts and appear to be listed within two years of their publication. Because of its Eastern focus and treatment of less well known titles, Istina is a useful indexing journal but should be used in conjunction with the Journal of Ecumenical Studies (E0033) to ensure broad coverage.

E0032 Jackson, Herbert C., ed. Judaism, Jewish-Christian Relations and the Christian Mission to the Jews: A Selected Bibliography. New York: Missionary Research Library, [1966].

E0033 Journal of Ecumenical Studies. Vol. 1- . Philadelphia, Pa.: Temple

University, 1964- ; quarterly.

Aside from the articles, reviews and summary of ecumenical events, this journal includes a substantial collection of abstracts in each issue. These abstracts are of articles from a wide range of ecumenical and other theological journals, usually published within the preceding twelve months. The entries are arranged by country of origin and then by periodical title, and the abstracts themselves are brief but adequately detailed. For those who wish to keep up with current articles rather than undertake a systematic survey this is a helpful service. See also Istina (E0031), which has a narrower confessional focus than the broad inter-church and inter-faith coverage of this journal. See also Ecumenical Review (E0022) and Okumenische Rundschau (E0046).

E0034 Lambeth Palace. Library. Christian Unity: The Anglican Initiative; Catalogue of an Exhibition of Books and Manuscripts Held in the Library of Lambeth Palace. London: SPCK, 1966.

E0035 Landis, Benson Young. Doctoral Dissertations Relevant to Ecumenics. New York: World Council of Churches, [1965].

This bibliography contains a representative but not exhaustive list of titles of doctoral dissertations relevant to ecumenics, mainly completed since 1940. Titles are, with a few exceptions, confined to United States institutions and authors. The listing is intended to assist students, especially those selecting topics for dissertations, teachers and others interested in this field. See also World Council of Churches (E0061).

E0036 Laurès, John. Kirishtan Bunko: A Manual of Books and Documents on the Early Christian Mission in Japan; with Special Reference to the Principal Libraries in Japan and More Particularly to the Collection at Sophia University, Tokyo. With an Appendix of Ancient Maps of the Far East, Especially Japan. 3rd ed. Monumenta Nipponica Monographs, no. 5. Tokyo: Sophia University, 1957.

First published in 1940, this 536 page bibliography lists all types of printed materials and manuscripts dealing with missionary activity in Japan from its earliest days to the first fifty years after the reopening of the country to outsiders. Prepared from a Roman Catholic viewpoint, Laurès is especially strong on works related to this tradition. It is arranged by publisher, with "doubtful" items listed separately. An author/title/subject index is provided. See also Ebisawa (E0021) and Ikado (E0027).

E0037 Lescrauwaet, Josephus Franciscus. Critical Bibliography of Ecumenical Literature. Bibliographia ad Usum Seminariorum, vol. 7. Nijmegen: Bestel Centrale V.S.K.B., 1965.

This annotated, classified bibliography lists 351 works on the history, doctrine and practice of various churches in the ecumenical movement and on the movement itself. The focus tends to be European. Works listed are generally available and in print. An index of authors and anonymous works is provided. Published at the same time as the similar work by Crow (E0017), this guide is slightly longer. Its detailed annotations reflect a post-Vatican II Roman Catholic perspective. See also Puglisi (E0050) and Sutfin (E0058). For a very specific bibliographical contribution on ecumenism see Marine Buhler, Les Unions Chrétiennes de Jeunes

Gens et le Mouvement Oecuménique: Bibliographie Analytique et Selective (Geneva: n.p., 1966).

E0038 Ma, John T., comp. Current Periodicals in the Missionary Research Library, Alphabetical List and Index. 2nd ed. New York: Missionary Research Library, 1961.

For a subject list see Byrnes (E0013).

E0039 Masson, Joseph. Bibliographie Missionaire Moderne: Choix Classé de 1400 Titres et Notes d'Histoire. Tournai: Casterman, 1945.

This 184 page bibliographical introduction provides information on basic and popular works dealing with Roman Catholic missions and closely related topics. See also Facelina (E0023), Rommerskirchen (E0051), Streit (E0057) and Vriens (E0060).

E0040 Missionalia. Vol. 1- . Pretoria: South African Missiological Society, 1973- .

This review journal provides abstracts, covering some 700 works per annum, and following the classification system used in the International Review of Mission bibliography on world mission (E0029). See also Bulletin of the Scottish Institute of Missionary Studies (E0012).

E0041 Missionary Research Library. Dictionary Catalog of the Missionary Research Library (New York). 17 vols. Boston, Mass.: G.K. Hall and Company, 1967.

Established in 1914 and located at Union Theological Seminary since 1929, the Missionary Research Library is one of the world's largest collections of material on Christian missions and related topics. The Catalog contains 273,000 photolithographed cards for approximately 100,000 individual items, including books, reports, pamphlets, articles and archive materials on the history and theory of missions, non-Christian religions, environment of missions, international affairs. Entries are under author, title and subject, allowing for a variety of approaches. Although somewhat dated in coverage, this is an essential bibliographical tool for advanced study. See also Amistad Research Center (E0003) and Center for Research Libraries (E0014).

E0042 Missionary Research Library. Missionary Biography: An Initial Bibliography. New York: Missionary Research Library, 1965.

See also Brownlee (E0011).

E0043 Missionary Research Library. Selected List of Books and Pamphlets Added to the Collection. No. 1- . New York: Missionary Research Library, 19--?; irregular.

See also the collection's main catalog (E0041).

E0044 Neue Zeitschrift für Missionswissenschaft/Nouvelle Revue de Science Missionaire. Vol. 1- . Immensee: Association for Promoting Mission Studies, 1945- ; quarterly.

With text in English, French, German and Italian, this quarterly includes both review and bibliographical sections. See also <u>Bibliografía Missionaria</u> (E0008) and <u>International Review of Mission</u> (E0029).

E0045 <u>Oecumene</u>. Vol. 1- . RIC Supplément, nos. 31-34. Strasbourg: CERDIC Publications, 1977- ; irregular.

Published approximately annually under the direction of Marie Zimmermann, this computer indexed bibliography includes books, pamphlets and articles from around the world on specific ecumenical subjects or questions studied in an ecumenical context. The volumes contain a selection of abstracts from more than 1400 periodicals and 3000 books scanned annually, together with a multilingual keyword index in English, French, German, Italian and Spanish. The first volume covers 1975 and 1976, containing 1758 titles and 534 keywords; the second covers 1977 and contains 813 titles and 299 keywords; the third lists 3058 titles and 354 keywords for 1978-1980 publications. Citations are arranged numerically and provide adequate bibliographical details on a wide range of materials. This series has a strong European bias and is reasonably current, providing a useful service for those with advanced interests in ecumenical topics. See also <u>Internationale Okumenische Bibliographie</u> (E0030).

E0046 <u>Okumenische Rundschau</u>. Vol. 1- . Frankfurt am Main: Verlag Otto Lembeck, 1952- ; quarterly.

Covering all aspects of ecumenism as well as international social, political and economic issues of importance to the church, this journal regularly includes both a <u>Zeitschriftenschau</u> and a collection of book reviews. The listing of periodical articles covers some 120 items annually but in no particular order, while the review section treats more than five dozen titles and arranges them by subject. Some of the articles are annotated, and the reviews are always descriptive and critical. Concentrating particularly on German publications, this is a useful complement to the <u>Ecumenical Review</u> (E0022) and is more comprehensive than either the <u>Journal of Ecumenical Studies</u> (E0033) or <u>Internationale Okumenische Bibliographie</u> (E0030).

E0047 Person, Laura. <u>Cumulative List of Doctoral Dissertations and Masters Theses in Foreign Missions and Related Subjects As Reported by the Missionary Research Library in the "Occasional Bulletin", 1950 to 1960</u>. New York: Missionary Research Library, 1961.

This listing covers doctoral dissertations (pp. 1-12) and masters' theses (pp. 13-36) separately. An index of universities, seminaries and schools, and a subject index are provided. Some of the items (which are numbered) include brief annotations provided by those reporting them. Where abstracts are known to be available this is indicated. See also Bachmann (E0006).

E0048 Pfister, Aloys. <u>Notices Biographiques et Bibliographiques sur les Jésuites de l'Ancienne Mission de Chine, 1552-1773</u>. 2 vols. Variétés Sinologiques, nos. 59-60. Shanghai: Imprimerie de la Mission Catholique, 1932-1934. Reprint. 2 vols. in 1. Reprint Series: Chinese Materials Center, no. 59. San Francisco, Calif.: Chinese Materials Center, 1976.

See also Chao (E0015), Chu (E0016) and Price (E0049).

E0049 Price, Francis Wilson. <u>Selected Bibliography of Books, Pamphlets and Articles on Communist China and the Christian Church in China.</u> Occasional Bulletin, vol. 9, no. 8. New York: Missionary Research Library, 1958.

See also Chao (E0015), Chu (E0016) and Pfister (E0048).

E0050 Puglisi, James J. <u>A Workbook of Bibliographies for the Study of Interchurch Dialogues.</u> Rome: Centro Pro Unione, 1978.

This updating and expansion of Ehrenstrom and Gassman's <u>Confessions in Dialogue</u> (Geneva: World Council of Churches, 1975) deals with official international, regional and national dialogues in progress among various churches. Fifty-two dialogues are treated, each in two parts. The first lists information of a directory nature, including sponsors, meetings held, dates, subjects, key personnel. The second is a bibliography of reviews, books, pamphlets, articles and dissertations on the particular dialogue published before 1978. See also Lescrauwaet (E0037) and Sutfin (E0058).

E0051 Rommerskirchen, Johannes, and Dindinger, Giovanni. <u>Bibliografía Missionaria.</u> 23 vols. Rome: Unione Missionaria del Clero in Italia, 1935-1959.

This large bibliography lists books and periodical articles from 1933 in classified arrangement without annotations (although some notes on contents are included). Each volume contains subject and author indexes, with a cumulation every four years. This supplements Streit (E0057). See also Masson (E0039) and Vriens (E0060).

E0052 Ronda, James P., and Axtell, James. <u>Indian Missions: A Critical Bibliography.</u> Bibliographical Series - The Newberry Library, Center for the History of the American Indian. Bloomington, Ind.: Indiana University Press for The Newberry Library, 1978.

Aimed at both students and scholars, this critical bibliography deals with the breadth of mission writing and understanding about white-Indian relations from the earliest period to the 1970s. Protestant and Catholic mission activity, goals of missions, methods of conversion and Indian responses are all dealt with. Basic works are recommended for the beginner. This is a sound contribution to a field not well covered elsewhere.

E0053 Santos, Hernández, Angel. <u>Bibliografía Misional.</u> 2 vols. Misionología, vol. 3. Santander: Editorial Sal Terrae, 1965.

See also Domínguez (E0020).

E0054 Senaud, Auguste. <u>Christian Unity, a Bibliography: Selected Titles Concerning International Relations between Churches and International Christian Movements (from a Larger Bibliography).</u> Geneva: World's Committee of YMCAs, 1937.

This classified, chronological listing of nearly 2000 books and articles includes material on various aspects of the ecumenical movement in various Christian traditions and groups. There is an author/subject index. Annotations are not provided. See also Brandreth (E0010), Crow (E0017) and World Council of Churches (E0062).

E0055 Siegmund-Schultze, Friedrich, ed. <u>Inventarverzeichnis des Okumenischen</u>

Archives in Soest (Westfalen). Soester Wissenschaftliche Beiträge, Bd. 22. Soest: Westfälische Verlagsbuchhandlung, 1962.

See also Delfs (E0019).

E0056 Smalley, William Allen. Selected and Annotated Bibliography of Anthropology for Missionaries. Rev. ed. Occasional Bulletin from the Missionary Research Library, vol. 11, no. 1. New York: Missionary Research Library, 1962.

See also Tippett (E0059).

E0057 Streit, Robert, and Dindinger, Johannes. Bibliotheca Missionum: Veröffentlichen des Internationalen Instituts für Missionswissenschaftliche Forschung. Hrsg. von P.J. Rommerskirchen und P.N. Kowalsky. 29 vols. in 31. Freiburg im Breisgau: Herder, 1916-1974.

Published under various imprints, this is the most detailed Roman Catholic bibliography of missions available. Each volume is devoted to specific regions and periods, covering both East and West from the earliest days to 1970. It includes voyages, relations, official documents and many other types of materials. The entries include full bibliographical details, critical annotations, references to sources and locations of copies in European libraries wherever possible. Each volume includes indexes of authors, persons, subjects and places. This work is the starting point for all research on Roman Catholic missions, providing details of over 30,000 relevant titles. See also Masson (E0039), Rommerskirchen (E0051) and Vriens (E0060).

E0058 Sutfin, Edward J., and Lavanoux, Maurice. A Selected, Annotated Bibliography on Ecumenical and Related Matters. Haverford, Pa.: Catholic Library Association, 1967.

This 56 page bibliography, reprinted from Liturgical Arts Magazine, covers a wide variety of topics, providing long and critical annotations. See also Lescrauwaet (E0037) and Puglisi (E0050).

E0059 Tippett, Alan Richard, comp. Bibliography for Cross-Cultural Workers. South Pasadena, Calif.: William Carey Library, [c. 1971].

See also Smalley (E0056).

E0060 Vriens, Livinius; Disch, Anastasius; and Wils, J. Critical Bibliography of Missiology. Trans. by Deodatus Tummers. Bibliographia ad Usum Seminariorum, vol. E.2. Nijmegen: Bestelcentrale der V.S.K.B., 1960.

This brief bibliography contains 206 entries on Roman Catholic missions and work in the mission field. Arrangement is by subject (e.g., mission theory, law, history, missiography) and critical annotations are provided. There are introductions to each type of literature, and an index of authors and anonymous works is provided. See also Masson (E0039), Rommerskirchen (E0051) and Streit (E0057).

E0061 World Council of Churches. Doctoral Dissertations and Ecumenical Themes: A Guide for Teachers and Students. Geneva: World Council of Churches, 1977.

This 70 page guide consists of two sections. The first suggests themes which await substantive research, listing topics of concern to the ecumenical movement generally and specific topics suggested for investigation by staff members of the World Council of Churches. This section ends with a list of leaders in the ecumenical movement on whom little has been written. The second section is an alphabetical author listing of completed dissertations which are available in the Ecumenical Center library in Geneva. This is an obvious starting point for students choosing research topics in ecumenism. See also Landis (E0035).

E0062 World Council of Churches. Ecumenical Book Shelf. 5 vols. New York: World Council of Churches, 1950-1969.

See also Brandreth (E0010), Crow (E0017) and Senaud (E0054).

E0063 World Council of Churches. Library. Classified Catalog of the Ecumenical Movement. 2 vols. Boston, Mass.: G.K. Hall and Company, 1972.

This reproduction of catalog cards from the Council's library contains 11,000 titles on ecumenism mainly in English; it is arranged according to a modified Dewey classification. Entries cover the history of the ecumenical movement, history of the World Council of Churches, publications of national and regional church councils, materials on various union negotiations, documentation relating to Vatican II, all aspects of ecumenical theology and biographies of individuals of importance in the ecumenical movement. An alphabetical index of authors and editors is provided. Containing nearly 1000 pages, this is the most representative bibliography on ecumenism, although the works by Crow (E0017) and Lescrauwaet (E0037) are quite useful and probably more widely available. See also the supplement (E0064).

E0064 World Council of Churches. Library. Classified Catalog of the Ecumenical Movement. First Supplement. Boston, Mass.: G.K. Hall and Company, 1981.

This is a supplement to the previous entry (E0063).

MISSIONS/ECUMENISM: DICTIONARIES

E0065 Birkeli, Fridtjov, et al., eds. Norsk Misjonsleksikon. Utg. med tilslutning fra Norsk misjonsråd og de misjoner dette representerer. 3 vols. Stavanger: Nomi, 1965-1967.

E0066 Dwight, Henry Otis; Tupper, H. Allen; and Bliss, Edwin Munsell, eds. The Encyclopedia of Missions: Descriptive, Historical, Biographical, Statistical. Ed. under the auspices of the Bureau of Missions. 2nd ed. New York: Funk and Wagnalls Company, 1904. Reprint. Detroit, Mich.: Gale Research Company, 1975.

This encyclopedia is somewhat uneven in coverage, providing not very thorough treatment of mission activity by various denominations. It also contains appendixes (a directory of foreign missionary societies, list of Bible versions, statistical tables, etc.), although maps included in the first edition have been omitted in the second.

E0067 Goddard, Burton L., ed.-in-chief. The Encyclopedia of Modern Christian Missions; the Agencies. Associate ed.: William Nigel Kerr and William L. Lane. Camden, N.J.: Thomas Nelson and Sons, 1967.

Prepared by staff of the Gordon Divinity School, this 743 page compilation concentrates primarily on Protestant foreign missions, but there are survey articles on Roman Catholic and Orthodox agencies and societies as well. The articles are reasonably detailed and clearly written, and the work is indexed by subject, place and denomination. Goddard is a suitable reference tool for a range of needs, from basic to advanced. However, a certain amount of the data provided on more than 1400 agencies, organizations and societies is now somewhat out of date, so the work must be used with caution.

E0068 Gründler, Johannes. Lexikon der Christlichen Kirchen und Sekten unter Berücksichtigung der Missionsgessellschaften und Zwischenkirchlichen Organisationen. 2 vols. Vienna: Herder, 1961.

E0069 Littell, Franklin H., and Walz, Hans Hermann, eds. Weltkirchen Lexikon: Handbuch der Okumene. Im Auftrag des Deutschen Evangelischen Kirchentages. Unter Beratung von Georges Florovosky et al. Stuttgart: Kreuz Verlag, 1960.

This ecumenical dictionary includes accounts of Christianity throughout the world by countries, biographies of church leaders, and articles on church history and theological terms, mostly followed by bibliographies with German, English and French titles. More than 400 European and American contributors provided material. The dictionary shows a Protestant bias in the understanding of ecumenism, particularly a German Protestant approach.

E0070 Neill, Stephen Charles; Anderson, Gerald H.; and Goodwin, John, eds. Concise Dictionary of the Christian World Mission. Nashville, Tenn.: Abingdon Press; London: United Society for Christian Literature, Lutterworth Press, 1971.

International and ecumenical in scope, this excellent source of information covers all facets of missions. Brief signed articles by more than 200 specialists treat the spread of Christianity in various countries, as well as topics relating to missionary work and biographies of missionary leaders. There are also entries for the missions of Islam and Buddhism, giving the work additional comparative value. Bibliographies are appended to most entries, and there are numerous cross references. Neill is an indispensible reference work in its field.

MISSIONS/ECUMENISM: HANDBOOKS

E0071 Agenzia Internationale Fides. Le Missioni Cattoliche Dipendenti della Sacra Congregazione de Propagande Fide: Storia, Geografia, Statistica. Rome: Consiglio Superiore della Pontificia Opera della Propagazione delle Fide, 1950.

This directory of bishops, seminaries, schools and other institutions includes brief histories of each territory as well as statistics. An index is provided. The work is now out of date. See also Alfaro (E0072).

E0072 Alfaro, Carlos. Guía Apostolica Latinoamericana. Barcelona: Editorial Herder, 1965.

This 591 page directory of Latin American Roman Catholic organizations dedicated to apostolic activities includes organizations of the hierarchy and the laity. Names, addresses, officers, history, purposes and publications of both national and international organizations are covered. Indexes of names, organizations and subjects are supplied. See also Agenzia Internationale Fides (E0071).

E0073 Anderson, Gerald H., and Stransky, Thomas F., eds. Evangelization. Mission Trends, no. 2. New York: Paulist Press, c. 1975.

This volume contains a selection of twenty-two essays, as well as conclusions from recent major assemblies. The essays are presented under four headings: mandate and meaning of evangelization; priorities and strategies; common faith and divided witness; and new perspectives on other faiths and ideologies.

E0074 Anderson, Gerald H., ed. The Theology of the Christian Mission. New York: McGraw-Hill Book Company; London: SCM Press, 1961.

This volume contains twenty-five essays by contributors (including reprints of writings by Barth, Tillich and Cullmann) on such aspects of Christian mission as the biblical basis, history, theory and Christianity and other faiths. It represents a wide diversity of ecclesiastical traditions and theological outlooks. A 22 page bibliography of materials in English, French and German is provided. While individual contributions vary in quality, the volume as a whole contains valuable material on Christian mission. See also Bassham (E0075), Bosch (E0086) and Margull (E0133).

E0075 Bassham, Rodger C. Mission Theology, 1948-1975: Years of Worldwide Creative Tension - Ecumenical, Evangelical and Roman Catholic. Pasadena, Calif.: William Carey Library, c. 1979.

Including an excellent bibliography (pp. 371-427), this 434 page study considers major issues in contemporary missiology: the development of ecumenical, conservative evangelical and Roman Catholic mission theology, various tensions, etc. Thoroughly researched and objectively presented, this is a useful work for students of missions and of ecumenism. See also Anderson (E0074), Bosch (E0086) and Margull (E0133).

E0076 Baum, Gregory. Progress and Perspectives: The Catholic Quest for Christian Unity. New York: Sheed and Ward, 1962.

This 245 page volume examines the ecumenical movement as seen from within the Roman Catholic Church. It is popular in tone, and makes simple but accurate use of scripture. It is particularly concerned with the possibility of the worship and liturgy of the church being the source for new rapport. See also Baum (E0077), Boyer (E0087) and Sartory (E0158).

E0077 Baum, Gregory. That They May Be One: A Study of Papal Doctrine

(Leo XIII - Pius XII). Westminster, Md.: Newman Press; London: Bloomsbury
Publishing Company, 1958.

See also Baum (E0076).

E0078 Bavinck, Johan Herman. An Introduction to the Science of Missions.
Trans. by David Hugh Freeman. Philadelphia, Pa.: Presbyterian and Reformed
Publishing Company, 1960.

> This comprehensive exposition of Christian missionary thought shows
> a keen awareness of contemporary problems as well as a broad historical
> perspective. Translated from the Dutch, it includes reference notes but
> lacks an index. It contains much useful material for theological students
> and for clergy concerned with the church's responsiblity in missions.
> See also Niles (E0141).

E0079 Beach, Harlan Page, and Fahs, Charles H., eds. World Missionary Atlas;
Containing a Directory of Missionary Societies, Classified Summaries of
Statistics, Maps Showing the Location of Mission Stations throughout the
World, a Descriptive Account of the Principal Mission Lands and Comprehen-
sive Indices. New York: Institute of Sociological and Religious Research,
c. 1925.

> This successor to earlier works entitled World Atlas of Christian Missions
> and World Statistics of Christian Missions sets out to present the status
> of Christian missions throughout the world in the 1920s. It does not cover
> mission work within Europe or (with a few exceptions) home missions
> in North America. Explanatory notes and a section on statistics are in-
> cluded in addition to the maps. See also Despont (E0107) and Freitag
> (E0113).

E0080 Beaver, Robert Pierce. Ecumenical Beginnings in Protestant World
Mission: A History of Comity. New York: Thomas Nelson and Sons, 1962.

> This study of the origins of ecumenism in the mission field is relevant
> to students of church history and of missions. It is well documented and
> carefully researched, providing definitive treatment of its subject. See
> also McNeill (E0129).

E0081 [no entry]

E0082 Bell, George Kennedy Allen. Documents on Christian Unity. Series 1-4.
4 vols. London: Oxford University Press, 1924-1958.

> Each series in the collection covers a limited period (1920-1924, 1924-1930,
> 1930-1948, 1948-1957) and is designed to illustrate the growth of ecu-
> menism around the world. This is a key collection of source materials
> for historians of the ecumenical movement.

E0083 Bent, Ans Joachim van der. Major Studies and Themes in the Ecumenical
Movement, 1948-1980. Geneva: World Council of Churches, 1981.

> This survey is divided into two parts: major studies by various World
> Council units; themes of numerous ecumenical assemblies, conferences
> and consultations. There are alphabetical indexes to major studies and to
> themes. The guide is designed particularly as a quick reference for students

of ecumenism and as a source of appropriate themes for organizers of ecumenical gatherings. Suggestions for further reading are provided.

E0084 Bishop, Crawford Morrison. Missionary Legal Manual. Chicago, Ill.: Moody Press, [1965].

E0085 Blauw, Johannes. The Missionary Nature of the Church: A Survey of the Biblical Theology of Mission. Foundations of the Christian Mission. New York: McGraw-Hill Book Company; London: Lutterworth Press, 1962. Reprint. Grand Rapids, Mich.: Wm. B. Eerdmans Publishing Company, 1974.

This 182 page survey of biblical scholarship on subjects related to OT, NT and intertestamental periods provides a useful account of the foundations of missions. It includes notes and an extensive bibliography. The focus is on continental scholarship. See also Peters (E0146).

E0086 Bosch, David J. Witness to the World: The Christian Mission in Theological Perspecitve. New Foundations Theological Library. Atlanta, Ga.: John Knox Press, 1980.

This 277 page study of the mission of the church in the world includes discussion of the biblical foundation of mission and theological developments in missiology. This is an insightful work for those concerned with theological aspects of mission activities. See also Anderson (E0074), Bassham (E0075) and Margull (E0133).

E0087 Boyer, Charles. Christian Unity. Trans. by Jill Dean. The Twentieth Century Encyclopedia of Catholicism, vol. 138. Section 14: Outside the Church. New York: Hawthorn Books, 1962.

See also Baum (E0076).

E0088 Brasio, Antonio Duarte, ed. Monumenta Missionaria Africana. Vol. 1- . Africa Occidental.2. série. Lisbon: Divisão de Publicações e Biblioteca, Agência Geral do Ultramar, 1958- .

See also Groves (E0118) and Northcott (E0142).

E0089 Brown, Robert McAfee. The Ecumenical Revolution: An Interpretation of the Catholic-Protestant Diaologue. Garden City, N.Y.: Doubleday and Company, 1967; London: Burns and Oates, 1969.

This 388 page study provides sound treatment of the history of the ecumenical movement and discusses Protestant and Roman Catholic approaches separately. An index and a bibliography are included. The author's theological liberalism is evident in the approach adopted.

E0090 [no entry]

E0091 Buker, Raymond B., and Ward, Ted, comps. The World Directory of Mission Related Educational Institutions. South Pasadena, Calif.: William Carey Library, [c. 1972].

See also Smith (E0164).

E0092 Cavert, Samuel McCrea. The American Churches in the Ecumenical

Movement, 1900-1968. New York: Association Press, 1968.

This work concentrates on the Federal (National) Council of Churches, providing an objective account by someone who has participated actively in the developments of which he writes. Containing a wealth of detail, this is a standard account of the ecumenical movement in America during the period covered. See also Cavert's other work (E0093).

E0093 Cavert, Samuel McCrea. Church Cooperation and Unity in America; a Historical Review, 1900-1970. New York: Association Press, [1970].

This 400 page survey covers mission, religious education, higher education, social tasks, evangelism, race relations, women in the church, international affairs and other cooperative areas in American Christianity. A valuable bibliography (pp. 354-396) is provided. See also Cavert's other work (E0092).

E0094 Cavert, Samuel McCrea. On the Road to Christian Unity: An Appraisal of the Ecumenical Movement. New York: Harper and Row, 1961.

This 192 page study appraises the ecumenical movement from its official beginnings early in the twentieth century up to the eve of the Third Assembly of the World Council of Churches. The author, who has been closely identified with the movement, provides an understanding account, with awareness of the problems to be overcome. See also Rouse (E0154) and Tavard (E0166).

E0095 Champagne, Joseph Etienne. Manuel d'Action Missionaire. Ottawa: Scholasticat Saint Joseph, [1947].

See also De Reeper (E0104, E0105), Pío María de Mondreganes (E0148) and Walsh (E0176).

E0096 Cook, Harold R. Highlights of Christian Missions: A History and Survey. Chicago, Ill.: Moody Press, 1967.

See also Kane (E0121).

E0097 Cook, Harold R. An Introduction to Christian Missions. 15th ed. Chicago, Ill.: Moody Press, c. 1971.

See also Kane (E0122), Lindsell (E0129) and Verkuyl (E0173).

E0098 Costas, Orlando E. The Church and Its Mission: A Shattering Critique from the Third World. Wheaton, Ill.: Tyndale House Publishers, [1974].

Expressing a strongly evangelical Protestant viewpoint, this 313 page study deals with broad subjects such as God's mission, the church's nature, and church tensions. While sympathetic to the ethical emphases of liberation theology, Costas is critical of its theological aberrations. This is a stimulating introduction to the contemporary mission scene. See also Costas' later works (E0099, E0100).

E0099 Costas, Orlando E. The Integrity of Mission: The Inner Life and Outreach of the Church. San Francisco, Calif.: Harper and Row, c. 1979.

This 114 page work examines Christian world mission as a unitary whole.

It is more modest in scope and more popular in tone than Costas' earlier works (E0098, E0100).

E0100 Costas, Orlando E. Theology of the Crossroads in Contemporary Latin America: Missiology in Mainline Protestantism, 1969-1974. Amsterdam: Rodopi, 1976.

Based on a doctoral dissertation, this study provides an accurate account of the period in the life of the churches under consideration and of ecumenical efforts in Latin America. While it raises critical questions about ecumenical efforts, this book has been criticized for neglecting key contextual factors such as Marxism. See also Costas' earlier work (E0098).

E0101 Davey, Cyril James. The March of Methodism: The Story of Methodist Missionary Work Overseas. New York: Philosophical Library, [1951].

E0102 De Groot, Alfred Thomas. Church Unity: An Annotated Outline of the Growth of the Ecumenical Movement. Fort Worth, Tex.: Texas Christian University, 1969.

This brief guide is in the form of nineteen annotated lists of, for example, denominational agencies for unity; Bible societies; ecumenical institutes; and various cooperative endeavors. It is international in scope, although there is somewhat more emphasis on North American activities. There is no index. See also World Council of Churches (E0177).

E0103 Delacroix, D., ed.-in-chief. Histoire Universelle des Missions Catholiques d'après la Conception Originale de J.L. Françoisprismo. 4 vols. Paris: Grund, [1956-1959].

See also Descamps (E0106), Lesourd (E0126) and Vaulx (E0172).

E0104 De Reeper, John. A Missionary Companion: A Commentary on the Apostolic Faculties. Westminster, Md.: Newman Press; Dublin: Browne and Nolan, 1952.

See also Champagne (E0095), Pío María de Mondreganes (E0148), Walsh (E0176) and the following entry (E0105).

E0105 De Reeper, John. The Sacraments on the Missions: A Pastoral Theological Supplement for the Missionary. 2nd ed. Dublin: Browne and Nolan, [1962].

See also Champagne (E0095), Henry (E0119), Pío María de Mondreganes (E0148), Walsh (E0176) and the preceding entry (E0104).

E0106 Descamps, Edouard Eugène François. Histoire Générale Comparée des Missions. Paris: Plon, 1932.

See also Delacroix (E0103), Lesourd (E0126) and Vaulx (E0172).

E0107 Despont, Joseph. Nouvel Atlas des Missions. Paris: Oeuvre de la Propagation de la Foi, 1951.

This 59 page atlas covers mission territories, showing national and diocesan boundaries and providing history and statistics. An index is included, and five supplements appear in some copies. Freite (E0113) provides more up to to date coverage of mission territories. See also Beach (E0079).

E0108 Directory of Foreign Missions: Missionary Boards, Societies, Colleges, Cooperative Councils and Other Agencies of the Protestant Churches of the World. [Ed. 1-]. New York: International Missionary Council, 1933- .

Initially published as Directory of World Missions, this guide provides detailed articles, statistics and indexes. It is limited to Protestant missionary societies. Arrangement is geographical, according to where societies have their headquarters, although there is a separate section for international organizations. An index of societies and a list giving denominational grouping are included.

E0109 Drummond, Richard Henry. A History of Christianity in Japan. Christian World Mission Books. Grand Rapids, Mich.: Wm. B. Eerdmans Publishing Company, 1971.

This comprehensive study of Japanese Christianity, which includes bibliography and full indexes, covers from the sixteenth century to the present, treating Roman Catholic, Protestant and Orthodox activities. Biographical studies are included where appropriate in this well documented study.

E0110 Flachsmeier, Horst R. Geschichte der Evangelischen Weltmission. Geissen: Brunnen Verlag, [c. 1963].

This work on foreign missions is in two parts: the first examines the growth of missions from the time of the earliest missionaries to the present; the second reviews historical developments in the mission field. A chronological table, some bibliographical references and an index conclude the volume. The author, a medical missionary of the Methodist Church in Germany, is writing mainly to inform the local churchgoer of aspects of mission worldwide. See also Hünerman (E0120).

E0111 Fouyas, Methodios. Orthodoxy, Roman Catholicism and Anglicanism. London: Oxford University Press, 1972.

This is a useful background study of 280 pages, including a bibliography (pp. 260-272).

E0112 Freitag, Anton. Mission und Missionswissenschaft. Steyler Missionsschriftenreihe, nr. 4. Kaldenkirchen: Steyler Verlagsbuchhandlung, [1962].

See also Seumois (E0162).

E0113 Freitag, Anton. The Twentieth Century Atlas of the Christian World: The Expansion of Christianity through the Centuries. In collaboration with Heinrich Emmerich and Jakob Buijs. Rev. and up-to-date trans. New York: Hawthorn Books, [1963, i.e. 1964].

Published in Britain as The Universe Atlas of the Christian World: The Expansion of Christianity through the Centuries (London: Burns and Oates for Associated Newspapers, [1963]), this translation of Atlas du Monde Chrétien (Paris: Elsevier, [1959]) includes numerous photographs and twenty-nine color maps plus text. The text covers the history of Roman Catholic missions and of some Protestant ones, and the maps illustrate the spread of Christianity at various points in history. The index covers text, illustrations and notes. This is a suitable atlas for students of Catholic mission history. See also Beach (E0079) and Despont (E0107).

E0114 Friars of the Atonement. Ecumenism around the World: A Directory of Ecumenical Institutes, Centers and Organizations/L'Oecuménisme à travers le Monde: Directoire des Instituts, Centres et Organisations Ecuméniques. Rome: Friars of the Atonement, Centro pro Unione, 1971?

This somewhat dated but still relevant directory lists more than 300 ecumenical bodies in a continental and country arrangement. Each entry contains the usual directory information, which in itself can be very useful if current; in this compilation one should rely mainly on name and address of a particular center, as other factors may have altered since 1971. There is an index of countries and an appendix of bulletins, newsletters and reviews produced by the named institutions.

E0115 Glover, Robert Hall. The Progress of World-Wide Missions. Rev. and enlarged by J. Herbert Kane. New York: Harper and Row, 1960.

This 502 page study summarizes the expansion of world missions from the apostolic age to the early nineteenth century, and analyzes missionary activity in all countries outside Europe, North America, Australia and New Zealand. Statistical charts and a substantial (21 pp.) classified bibliography are included. This is a standard reference work which is concise and easy to use. See also Neill (E0139) and, for a more substantial history, Latourette (E0125).

E0116 Goodall, Norman. Ecumenical Progress: A Decade of Change in the Ecumenical Movement, 1961-71. London: Oxford University Press, 1972.

This 134 page sequel to the following entry (E0117) brings up to date the account of progress, including aspects such as stronger representation in the movement of Eastern Orthodoxy, and changes in the position of the Roman Catholic Church regarding ecumenism. Appendixes treat the structure of the World Council of Churches and other topics. See also Villain (E0174).

E0117 Goodall, Norman. The Ecumenical Movement: What It Is and What It Does. New York: Oxford University Press, 1961.

This 240 page study, by one who has been closely involved in the ecumenical movement, concentrates on the history of the movement and its organizational structures, but also examines goals and problems faced. It is suitable for the general reader seeking basic, nontechnical information. Appendixes include an annotated bibliography, extracts from selected documents and membership lists for the World Council of Churches and the International Missionary Council. See also the sequel (E0116) and Villain (E0174).

E0118 Groves, Charles Pelham. The Planting of Christianity in Africa. 4 vols. London: Lutterworth Press, 1948-1958. Reprint. 4 vols. London: Lutterworth Press, 1964.

Published under the auspices of Selly Oak Colleges in Birmingham, this survey is written from a Protestant viewpoint and follows a chronological arrangement. Volume 1 covers the first century to 1840; succeeding volumes treat shorter periods (1840-1878, 1878-1914, 1914-1954) in some detail. There are numerous footnote references which serve as valuable starting points for further study. See also Brasio (E0088) and Northcott (E0142).

E0119 Henry, Antonin Marcel. A Mission Theology. Trans. by Albert J. LaMothe, Jr. Themes of Theology. Notre Dame, Ind.: Fides Publishers, 1963.

See also De Reeper (E0105), Santos Hernández (E0157) and Schmidlin (E0160).

E0120 Hünerman, Wilhelm. Geschichte der Weltmission: Lebensbilder Grosser Missionare. Vol. 1- . Lucerne: Rex Verlag, 1960- .

See also Flachsmeier (E0110).

E0121 Kane, J. Herbert. A Global View of Christian Missions from Pentecost to the Present. Grand Rapids, Mich.: Baker Book House, [1971].

Including a useful bibliography (pp. 557-576), this 590 page historical survey is in two parts: missions through the ages; missions around the world (subdivided into thirteen geographical areas). Maps and an index are included. This provides the student with easy geographical and historical reference on the status of Christian mission in any country. See also Cook (E0096).

E0122 Kane, J. Herbert. Understanding Christian Missions. Grand Rapids, Mich.: Baker Book House, 1974.

See also Cook (E0097), Lindsell (E0127) and Verkuyl (E0173).

E0123 Keen, Rosemary. A Survey of the Archives of Selected Missionary Societies. London: Historical Manuscripts Commission, 1968.

Limited to member groups of the Conference of British Missionary Societies with headquarters in or near London, this mimeographed guide is arranged alphabetically by society and provides information on four types of material: home archives, dealing with central administration and work in Britain; overseas archives, covering foreign departments of societies; auxiliaries, treating unofficial papers and archives of miscellaneous content; periodicals and printed papers. There are indexes of countries and names. Now somewhat dated, this remains a good starting point for students of mission history. See also Marchant (E0131).

E0124 Lambert, Bernard. Ecumenism: Theology and History. Trans. by Lancelot C. Sheppard. New York: Herder and Herder; London: Burns and Oates, 1967.

This substantial study of 533 pages first appeared in French in 1962. Its main emphasis is on principles of ecumenism rather than history of the movement, although it contains much historical information. It shows a good balance of theology, spirituality and psychology, and provides useful expositions of Catholic and Reformed theology. It would have been valuable if the English translation had contained an updated bibliography. See also Mascall (E0135) and Villain (E0175).

E0125 Latourette, Kenneth Scott. A History of the Expansion of Christianity.

7 vols. New York: Harper and Brothers, 1937-1945; London: Eyre and Spottis-woode, 1938-1947. Reprint. 7 vols. Grand Rapids, Mich.: Zondervan Publishing House; London: Paternoster Press, 1971.

> This important survey of mission history is an encyclopedic guide which remains the most complete work of its kind on missions from their beginnings to the present. There are full bibliographies with brief annotations for each country to the 1940s, and an appendix treats developments to 1970. Each volume is indexed and includes useful maps. Latourette is the standard guide to mission history and serves as a valuable reference tool for beginners and advanced students. For less ambitious surveys see Glover (E0115) or Neill (E0139).

E0126 Lesourd, Paul. Histoire des Missions Catholiques. Paris: Librairie de l'Arc, 1937.

> This 491 page introductory survey is arranged by century and country, providing basic facts, dates and statistics on the development of Roman Catholic missions. See also Delacroix (E0103), Descamps (E0106) and Vaulx (E0172).

E0127 Lindsell, Harold. A Christian Philosophy of Missions. Wheaton, Ill.: Van Kampen Press, [1949].

> See also Cook (E0097), Kane (E0122) and Verkuyl (E0173).

E0128 Mackay, John A. Ecumenics: The Science of the Church Universal. Englewood Cliffs, N.J. Prentice-Hall, 1964.

> Including a bibliography (pp. 267-288), this work is in four main sections: the science of ecumenics; the church and the purpose of God; the function of the Church Universal; the church and the world. The author writes after many years' personal involvement in ecumenical affairs. See also Sartory (E0158).

E0129 McNeill, John Thomas. Unitive Protestantism: The Ecumenical Spirit and Its Persistent Expression. [Rev. ed.] Richmond, Va.: John Knox Press, 1964.

> This 352 page study examines the theological resources and developments within Protestantism of the movement towards unity from the time of the Reformation. The revised edition has been updated and enlarged from the original of 1930. See also Beaver (E0080).

E0130 March, Arthur W., comp. Directory of Protestant Medical Missions. New York: Missionary Research Library, 1959.

> This directory supplies information about the work of Protestant medical missions in Asia, Africa, Latin America and the Pacific at the end of the 1950s. The questionnaire used to collect data is reproduced at the beginning of the directory, which also provides statistics, a directory of leprosy missions, and a list of hospitals and their addresses.

E0131 Marchant, Leslie Ronald. A Guide to the Archives and Records of Protestant Christian Missions from the British Isles to China, 1796-1914. Nedlands: University of Western Australia Press, [1966].

See also Keen (E0123).

E0132 Missions Advanced Research and Communication Center. Christianity across Cultures: A Survey of Available Research. Monrovia, Calif.: Missions Advanced Research and Communication Center, 1970.

This 60 page guide is intended to provide information on work being done to spread Christianity to various cultures. It lists the findings of the 1969 MARC survey in a KWIC (Keyword in Context) index. In addition there are suggestions for further research and a section on using these survey lists. The substantial bibliography (pp. 33-50) is especially useful.

E0133 Margull, Hans Jochen. Theologie der Missionarischen Verkündigung. Stuttgart: Evangelisches Verlagswerk, [1959].

See also Anderson (E0074), Bassham (E0075) and Bosch (E0086).

E0134 Mary Just. Digest of Catholic Mission History. World Horizon Reports, no. 20. Maryknoll, N.Y.: Maryknoll Publications, 1958.

This brief account covers from early Christian times to the era of world-wide missionary expansion (with the final three chapters covering expansion by geographical area). At the end of the book are dates of missionary significance, suggestions for further reading (pp. 109-124) and an index. The study is of interest to those concerned with the missionary activity of a particular denomination. See also Schmidlin (E0159).

E0135 Mascall, Eric Lionel. The Recovery of Unity: A Theological Approach. London: Longmans, Green and Company, 1958.

This book is based on the conviction that the problem of Christian unity is fundamentally a theological one, that the theological issues are more profound than commonly recognized, and that theological unity ought to be sought for its own sake. In ten chapters it surveys various issues such as the liturgy, church and ministry, and church and papacy. A bibliography (pp. 234-238) and an index are included. See also Lambert (E0124).

E0136 Mission Handbook: North American Protestant Ministries Overseas. Ed. 1- . Prepared and ed. for the Missionary Research Library. Monrovia, Calif.: Missions Advanced Research and Communication Center, 1953- .

Originally published by the Missionary Research Library under such titles as Check List of Foreign Missionary Agencies in the United States , North American Protestant Foreign Missionary Agencies and Directory of North American Protestant Foreign Missionary Agencies, this useful compendium regularly includes basic statistical information on both church related and independent mission agencies. Also provided are special articles on current issues, lists of schools and professors of missiology. The work is well indexed and provides essential data for those interested in the present state of Protestant missions. See also Parker (E0143).

E0137 Moffett, Samuel Hugh. The Christians of Korea. New York: Friendship Press, [1962].

This 174 page survey of Korean Christianity includes informative statistics, a judicious selection of facts about the background in Korea, and a bibliography. It is particularly appropriate for group study of mission activities in Asia. See also Shearer (E0163).

290
N413

E0138 Neill, Stephen Charles. Christian Faith and Other Faiths: The Christian Dialogue with Other Religions. London: Oxford University Press, 1961.

This 241 page study contains valuable descriptions of the major living religions together with suggestions for Christian dialogue with them. It is based on the Moorhouse Lectures delivered in Melbourne in 1960, and displays a sympathetic but concise treatment of the various faiths. See also Samartha (E0155) and Stowe (E0165).

BV2500
N4

E0139 Neill, Stephen Charles. Christian Missions. The Pelican History of the Church, vol. 6. Baltimore, Md.: Penguin Books, [1964]; Grand Rapids, Mich.: Wm. B. Eerdmans Publishing Company, [1965, c. 1964].

This is a full historical survey of missions during their first seventeen centuries and includes an analysis of modern missions since the time of William Carey. Somewhat fuller treatment is given to the nineteenth and twentieth centuries than to earlier periods. Footnotes and a selected bibliography add to the reference value of this comprehensive, objective and readable work. See also Latourette (E0125) and Payne (E0144).

E0140 Neill, Stephen Charles. The Story of the Christian Church in India and Pakistan. Christian World Mission Books. Grand Rapids, Mich.: Wm. B. Eerdmans Publishing Company, [1970].

This 83 page popular survey of Christianity in the Indian subcontinent covers nineteen centuries; it provides useful background on the socio-political context, and a concise outline of the story of Christianity, with particular emphasis on India rather than Pakistan. See also Richter (E0152) and Thomas (E0169).

E0141 Niles, Daniel Thambyrajah. Upon the Earth: The Mission of God and the Missionary Enterprise of the Churches. Foundations of the Christian Mission: Studies in the Gospel and the World. New York: McGraw-Hill Book Company, [1962].

See also Bavinck (E0078).

BR1360
NC

E0142 Northcott, William Cecil. Christianity in Africa. Philadelphia, Pa.: Westminster Press; London: SCM Press, [1963].

Aimed largely at the beginner, this 125 page work provides introductory treatment of Christianity in Africa in eight short chapters. Suggestions for further reading (p. 121) and an index are included. See also Brasio (E0088) and Groves (E0118).

E0143 Parker, Joseph I., ed. Interpretative Statistical Survey of the World Mission of the Christian Church; Summary and Detailed Statistics of Churches and Missionary Societies, Interpretative Articles and Indices. New York: International Missionary Council, 1938.

More adequate for statistical data than Beach (E0079), this 323 page compendium contains statistical tables in part 1 (pp. 13-225) and twenty-seven interpretive articles on topical and geographical subjects in part 2 (pp. 237-311). Four indexes are provided. The tables include data on staff, finance, educational and medical activities and philanthropic concerns. See also Mission Handbook (E0136).

E0144 Payne, Ernest Alexander. The Growth of the World Church: The Story of the Modern Mission Movement. London: Edinburgh House Press, 1955.

This study examines the way in which the Christian religion has spread in the last 250 years, concentrating on the work of British missionary societies and some of their leading figures. A selected bibliography (pp. 167-169) and an index are included. This is a suitable introductory work for the student. For a broader survey see Neill (E0139).

E0145 Person, Laura. A Directory of Professors of Missions in the United States and Canada. New York: Missionary Research Library, 1955.

See also Schwartz (E0161).

E0146 Peters, George W. A Biblical Theology of Missions. Chicago, Ill.: Moody Press, [1972].

In three sections this conservative study examines biblical foundations of missions, biblical delineations of missions, and biblical instruments and dynamics of missions. Notes, a bibliography of books and periodicals, and scripture and subject indexes are included. The work is of particular interest to conservative students concerned with theological aspects of mission activities. See also Blauw (E0085) and Peters (E0147).

E0147 Peters, George W. A Theology of Church Growth. Contemporary Evangelical Perspectives. Grand Rapids, Mich.: Zondervan Publishing House, c. 1981.

This evangelical approach takes account of recent missiological trends in the World Council of Churches and other moves for unity, and calls for more scriptural accountability. It provides a conservative interpretation of the subject. See also Peters (E0146).

E0148 Pío María de Mondreganes. Manuel de Misionología. 3. ed. Publicada por el Consejo Superior de Misiones. Madrid: Ediciones España Misionera, 1951.

See also Champagne (E0095), De Reeper (E0104, E0105) and Walsh (E0176).

E0149 Price, Francis Wilson. Protestant Churches of Asia, the Middle East, Africa, Latin America and the Pacific Area. New York: Missionary Research Library, 1959.

E0150 Read, William R.; Monterroso, Victor M.; and Johnson, Harmon A. Latin American Church Growth. Church Growth Series. Grand Rapids, Mich.: Wm. B. Eerdmans Publishing Company, 1969.

This rather basic work reviews the history and spread of Protestantism in the various regions of Latin America. A bibliography (pp. 387-417), maps and an index supplement the text, which often lacks details sought by researchers and advanced students. For a statistical survey see Taylor (E0167).

E0151 Rétif, Louis, and Rétif, André. The Church's Mission in the World.

Trans. by Reginald F. Trevett. The Twentieth Century Encyclopedia of Catholicism, vol. 102. Section 9: The Church and the Modern World. New York: Hawthorn Books, 1962.

This study examines contemporary issues relevant to mission activities (migration, modern consciousness, etc.); the church and contemporary movements; and "a new missionary era". A select bibliography is included, but there is no index. This is an interesting Roman Catholic interpretation of the situation in the early 1960s. For an earlier view see Schmidlin (E0160).

E0152 Richter, Julius. A History of Missins in India. Trans. by Sydney H. Moore. New York: Fleming H. Revell Company; Edinburgh: Oliphant, Anderson and Ferrier, 1908.

See also Neill (E0140) and Thomas (E0169).

E0153 Richter, Julius. A History of Protestant Missions in the Near East. New York: Fleming H. Revell Company; Edinburgh: Oliphant, Anderson and Ferrier, 1910. Reprint. New York: AMS Press, 1970.

This classic history of Protestant missions is arranged by countries and covers the period to the beginning of the twentieth century. Statistical tables and an index are included.

BX 6.5
R 62

E0154 Rouse, Ruth; Neill, Stephen Charles; and Fey, Harold Edward, eds. A History of the Ecumenical Movement. 2nd ed. with rev. bibliography. 2 vols. Philadelphia, Pa.:Westminster Press; London: SPCK, 1967-1970.

Superseding the single volume work published in 1957, this set covers 1517-1968. The volume by Fey, covering 1948-1968, was published as The Ecumenical Advance: A History of the Ecumenical Movement. In both volumes each section is by a specialist and provides a succinct survey of events, topics and movements in ecumenism. Both volumes contain substantial bibliographies and detailed indexes. This is an excellent modern treatment of the movement. For an earlier bibliography see Crow (E0017); for smaller works see Cavert (E0094) and Tavard (E0166).

E0155 Samartha, Stanley J., ed. Living Faiths and the Ecumenical Movement. Geneva: World Council of Churches, 1971.

Focusing on the history and theology of Christian relations with other faiths, this 184 page collection of thirteen essays is designed to indicate the state of contemporary discussions on ecumenism and to draw attention to fundamental issues on the nature and purpose of the dialogue among different faiths. Many of the articles had appeared previously in the journals of the World Council of Churches. For another volume of essays on ecumenism see Geoffrey Fillingham Nuttall and Owen Chadwick, eds. From Uniformity to Unity, 1662-1961 (London: SPCK, 1962). See also Neill (E0138) and Stowe (E0165).

E0156 Sánchez Vaquero, José. Ecumenismo: Manuel de Formación Ecuménica. Salamanca: Universidad Pontificia, Centro Ecuménico Juan XXIII, [1971].

E0157 Santos Hernández, Angel. Misiologia: Problemas Introductorios y Ciencias Auxiliares. Santander: Editorial Sal Terrae, 1961.

This 570 page study consists of the first two parts of a larger work. See also Henry (E0119) and Schmidlin (E0160).

E0158 Sartory, Thomas A. The Ecumenical Movement and the Unity of the Church. Trans. by Hilda C. Graef. Westminster, Md.: Newman Press, 1963.

This 289 page study by a Roman Catholic examines the historical develop-ment of the ecumenical movement, as well as "systematic" aspects (the church and the churches, the church and eschatology, the frontiers of the church, etc.). A bibliography is included. This work may be supple-mented by accounts by those who have been closely involved inside the ecumenical movement. See also Baum (E0076, E0077) and Mackay (E0128).

E0159 Schmidlin, Joseph. Catholic Mission History. Trans. by Thomas J. Kennedy and William Hall Robertson. Ed. by Matthias Braun. Techny, Ill.: Mission Press, 1933.

This 862 page translation of Katholische Missionsgeschichte (Kaldenkirchen: Missionsdrück, 1925) provides a survey of Roman Catholic mission activity from the time of Christ. There is a general bibliography and critical bibliographies for each chapter. An extensive index, which covers the bibliographies, is provided. See also Mary Just (E0134).

E0160 Schmidlin, Joseph. Catholic Mission Theory. Trans. by Matthias Braun. Techny, Ill.: Mission Press, 1931.

This 544 page translation of Katholische Missionslehre im Grundriss provides a guide to the literature and sources of missiology and to its aims and methods. It is now dated in view of the Vatican II decree on missions. See also Henry (E0119) and Santos Hernández (E0157); for a later inter-pretation see Rétif (E0151).

E0161 Schwartz, Glenn, ed. American Directory of Schools and Colleges Offering Missionary Courses. South Pasadena, Calif.: William Carey Library, c. 1973.

See also Person (E0145).

E0162 Seumois, André V. Introduction à la Missiologie. Neue Zeitschrift für Missionswissenschaft, Supplementa 3. Schöneck-Beckenried: Administration der Neuen Zeitschrift für Missionswissenschaft, 1952.

This 491 page volume includes excellent bibliographical data on post-1903 missiology. See also Freitag (E0112).

E0163 Shearer, Roy E. Wildfire: Church Growth in Korea. Church Growth Series. Grand Rapids, Mich.: Wm. B. Eerdmans Publishing Company, [1966].

This 242 page study covers the major Protestant churches in Korea but concentrates on the Presbyterian Church. Eleven chapters provide background on Korea and a historical and analytic survey of church growth from the early nineteenth century to the 1960s. A bibliography (pp. 229-236) is included, as well as some interesting statistical material. See also Moffett (E0137).

E0164 Smith, C. Stanley, and Thomson, Herbert F., comps. Protestant Theological Seminaries and Bible Schools in Asia, Africa, the Middle East, Latin America, the Caribbean and Pacific Areas. Ed. by Frank W. Price. MRL Directory Series, no. 12. New York: Missionary Research Library, 1960.

> This directory is based on responses to a questionnaire sent in 1959 to institutions in the geographical areas stated in the title. These data are presented by country within regional divisions. A supplementary list drawn from reports, directories, etc. follows the main listing. Details include name and address of institution, date of establishment, staffing, students, entrance requirements, courses and library facilities. This is a useful handbook covering nearly 600 overseas seminaries and Bible schools. See also Buker (E0091).

E0165 Stowe, David M. When Faith Meets Faith. New York: Friendship Press, 1963. Reprint. New York: Friendship Press, 1967.

> This nontechnical work for the general reader contains ten chapters, including descriptions of Hinduism, Buddhism, Judaism, Christianity, Islam. Notes and suggestions for further reading are included. See also Neill (E0138) and Samartha (E0155).

E0166 Tavard, Georges Henri. Two Centuries of Ecumenism: The Search for Unity. Trans. by Royce W. Hughes. New York: New American Library, [1962].

> Published in Britain without the subtitle (London: Burns and Oates, 1960), this translation of Petite Histoire du Mouvement Oecuménique provides a concise (239 pp.) history of the modern ecumenical movement with special reference to the development of Roman Catholic ecumenism. It is intended primarily for a Catholic readership, but includes adequate treatment of Protestant ecumenism. The volume lacks an index. See also Cavert (E0094) and Rouse (E0154).

E0167 Taylor, Clyde Willis, and Coggins, Wade T., eds. Protestant Missions in Latin America: A Statistical Survey. Washington, D.C.: Evangelical Foreign Missions Association, 1961.

> This presentation of basic statistics on Protestant work in Latin America uses data for 1960, with some comparative figures from the 1930s. Organization is alphabetical by country. A directory of missionary agencies, and regional comparisons are included. See also Read (E0150).

E0168 Thiessen, John Caldwell. A Survey of World Missions. [3rd] rev. ed. Chicago, Ill.: Moody Press, [1961].

E0169 Thomas, Paul. Christians and Christianity in India and Pakistan: A General Survey of the Progress of Christianity in India from Apostolic Times to the Present Day. London: Allen and Unwin, [1954].

> This review of Christian history in the Indian subcontinent treats the three main branches of the church in a readable and sympathetic style. The 260 pages provide a condensed account, including particularly valuable material on the generally neglected period between St. Thomas and the arrival of the Portuguese. Little attention is given to Pakistan, so the title is somewhat misleading. See also Neill (E0140) and Richter (E0152).

E0170 United States Catholic Mission Council. <u>Handbook</u>. Washington, D.C.: United States Catholic Mission Council, 1960- ; biennial.

This compendium provides statistical data on the numbers of missionaries sent overseas by American Roman Catholic religious orders and other agencies. A geographical index is included in each edition. See also <u>United States Catholic Overseas Missionary Personnel</u> (E0171).

E0171 <u>United States Catholic Overseas Missionary Personnel</u>. Washington, D.C.: Mission Secretariat, 1960- ; irregular.

The statistical summaries in this report deal with numbers of American missionaries sent overseas by Roman Catholic religious orders and other groups. A geographical index is provided in each issue. See also United States Catholic Mission Council (E0170).

E0172 Vaulx, Bernard de. <u>History of the Missions</u>. Trans. by Reginald F. Trevett. The Twentieth Century Encyclopedia of Catholicism, vol. 99. Section 9: The Church and the Modern World. New York: Hawthorn Books, [1961].

In three parts this Roman Catholic study traces mission activity from the death of Christ to the discovery of the new world, from then to Gregory XVI, and from Gregory XVI to Benedict XV. A select bibliography is included; there is no index, but the table of contents is quite detailed. See also Delacroix (E0103), Descamps (E0106) and Lesourd (E0126).

D0173 Verkuyl, Johannes. <u>Contemporary Missiology: An Introduction</u>. Trans. and ed. by Dale Cooper. Grand Rapids, Mich.: Wm. B. Eerdmans Publishing Company, [c. 1978].

This 414 page translation of <u>Inleiding in de Nieuwere Zerdingswetenschap</u> concentrates on Asia, Africa, Latin America, the Caribbean and Pacific areas. It is intended as an introductory treatment, although it contains a wealth of detail on historical aspects; biblical foundations; goals, purposes and means; contemporary theological trends; and ideologies in developing countries. A guide to the literature on black theology and on theological developments in Asia, Africa and Latin America, and a survey of ecumenical organizations in all the geographical areas covered are valuable elements. Each section is followed by a bibliography, and there is an index of persons. See also Cook (E0097), Kane (E0122) and Lindsell (E0127).

E0174 Villain, Maurice. <u>Introduction à l'Oecuménisme</u>. 2e éd. Eglise Vivante: Série Etudes. Tournai: Castermann, 1959 [c. 1958].

See also Goodall (E0116, E0117).

E0175 Villain, Maurice. <u>Unity: A History and Some Reflections</u>. Trans. by J.R. Foster from the 3rd French ed. Baltimore, Md.: Helicon Press, 1963.

This study provides a summary of the history of the ecumenical movement and treatment of the various denominations within the context of moves for unity. Although written by a Roman Catholic this work is not uncritical of that church in relation to ecumenism. See also Lambert (E0124).

E0176 Walsh, Maurice B. <u>Mission Faculties: A Commentary on the Decennial Faculties Granted by the Sacred Congregation of Propaganda Fide, 1961-1970</u>.

Washington, D.C.: Mission Secretariat, [c. 1960].

See also Champagne (E0095), De Reeper (E0104, E0105) and Pío María de Mondreganes (E0148).

E0177 World Council of Churches. Ecumenical Terminology/Terminologie Oecuménique/Okumenische Terminologie/Terminologia Ecuménica. Rev. ed. Geneva: World Council of Churches, 1975.

Published in a second edition (1967) as Ecumenical Glossary, this multilingual work is in two parts. The first includes a chronological table of major ecumenical events from 1910 to 1975, with a list of world and regional assemblies and conferences and their themes, and also information on the World Council of Churches and its associated bodies. The second section gives a representative selection of current ecumenical vocabulary, listed alphabetically, with translations into the other three languages. Indexes are provided in English, French, German and Spanish, and a bibliography is included. This is intended as an aid to translators, interpreters and participants at ecumenical meetings. See also De Groot (E0102).

F. Religious Orders

RELIGIOUS ORDERS: BIBLIOGRAPHIES

F0001 Acta Ordinis Fratrum Minorum. Vol. 1- . Rome: Curia Generalis Ordinis, 1882- ; bimonthly.

Following a collection of texts and documents relating to the order, each issue of Acta includes a bibliographical section which lists books relevant to the order, titles of periodicals with lists of contents, titles of periodicals with volumes and parts received. Although reasonably up to date, this compilation is very limited in its coverage and normally lists only a few books in each issue; the bibliographical detail provided for periodicals and books is very incomplete. Therefore, this should be used sparingly except by those with a strong interest in the order of Friars Minor. See also Donato da S. Giovanni (F0026) and Felice da Mareto (F0028).

F0002 Adams, Eleanor Burnham. A Bio-Bibliography of Franciscan Authors in Colonial Central America. Publications of the Academy of American Franciscan History. Bibliographical Series, vol. 2. Washington, D.C.: Academy of American Franciscan History, 1953.

This 97 page bio-bibliography contains information on the lives and writings of Franciscans during the Spanish colonial period in Central America. The listing of entries is quite thorough, and descriptive annotations are included. See also Adasiewicz (F0003), Asencio (F0009), Marcellino da Civezza (F0040) and Zulaica Garate (F0061).

F0003 Adasiewicz, Leo, and Bilinski, Donald, comps. Catalog of Books in the Academy of American Franciscan History Library.

This short catalog of an important Franciscan library contains many items by Franciscans active in Spanish America during the colonial era. It is especially useful for students of history and missions, although other subjects are also represented. See also Adams (F0002), Asencio (F0009), Marcellino da Civezza (F0040) and Zulaica Garate (F0061).

F0004 Albareda, Anselmo Mariá. Bibliografia de la Regla Benedictina. Montserrat: [Imprenta del Monestir de Montserrat], 1933.

This 660 page bibliography opens with a detailed introduction to the Benedictine rule, a bibliography of related literature and facsimiles of title pages. The bibliography proper lists in chronological order 902 editions published between 1489 and 1929; locations are given for each item. There are indexes of translators, commentators, editors, printers and booksellers. See also Lama (F0037), Le Cerf (F0038) and Monte Cassino (F0041).

F0005 Ambrogio di S. Teresa. Bio-Bibliograrhia Missionaria Ordinis Carmelitarum Discalceatorum (1584-1940). Rome: Apud Curiam Generalitiam, 1940.

This is a 495 page bio-bibliography of the Discalced Carmelites. For Carmelite bibliographies see Bartolommeo da S. Angelo (F0013), Benno (F0014) and Villiers de St. Etienne (F0058).

F0006 Archivum Bibliographicum Carmelitanum. Vol. 1- . Rome: Edizioni dei Padri Carmelitani Scalzi, 1951- ; irregular.

Each volume of Archivum normally contains a Bibliographia Carmeli Teresiani, which treats books, serials, reviews and documents dealing with any aspect of Carmelite history, thought or life. The thousand or so entries in each volume (4500 in the combined vols. 19-22) are arranged in a single alphabetical sequence of authors, persons or places and topics, and entries are repeated under headings as necessary, thus avoiding the need for indexes. A list of journals scanned is not provided but the 25,000 entries to date clearly show that coverage is wide ranging and comprehensive. As with many European guides of this kind, the date of publication and dates of coverage are both rather delayed; but as the only full bibliography in its field, this drawback must be accepted. For students of Carmelite monasticism this compilation is clearly indispensible. See also Benno (F0014) and Carmelus (F0018).

F0007 Archivum Franciscanum Historicum. Vol. 1- . Grottaferrata (Rome): Collegio S. Bonaventura, 1908- ; quarterly in two parts annually.

This serial includes a bibliographical section entitled Notae Bibliographicae, which contains detailed notes on books and articles dealing with all aspects of Franciscana. Up to 200 entries per annum are included for items from around the world; most reviews are in French and provide critical, evaluative comments on relatively recent publications. There is an author index but no subject index, and the entries are not classified. This is a useful supplement to Bibliographia Franciscana (F0016), which is more comprehensive but less up to date.

F0008 Archivum Historicum Societatis Iesu. Vol. 1- . Rome: Archivum Historicum Societatis Iesu, 1932- ; semiannual.

Covering all aspects of Jesuit history, each issue of this specialized journal contains a substantial bibliographical section, which is divided into seven main sections. An index at the beginning of the section clearly outlines the topical distribution of entries, which include books, articles, dissertations and series. Coverage is multilingual and geographically international, giving this work the breadth and depth required by the subject matter. There is an author index to the bibliographical section. In addition each issue contains articles, reviews and news items, all of which are indexed. For students of Jesuit history this work is an indispensible bibliography because of its thorough and up to date coverage. See also Index Bibliographicus Societatis Iesu (F0034).

F0009 Asencio, José. Cronistas Franciscanos. Colección de la Revista "Estudios Historicos". Cuadernos, no. 1. Guadalajara: Impr. Gráfica, 1944.

This very brief (38 pp.) bio-bibliography is arranged geographically by province and covers both Franciscans and Capuchins active in Mexico until the early twentieth century. Biographical and bibliographical notes are very brief and sometimes inaccurate. An author index is provided. See also Adams (F0002), Adasiewicz (F0003), Marcellino da Civezza (F0040) and Zulaica Garate (F0061).

F0010 Augustiniana: Revue pour l'Etude de Saint Augustin et de l'Ordre des Augustins. Vol. 1- . Heverlee-Louvain: Institut Historique Augustinien, 1951- ; semiannual.

The regular "Bibliographie Historique de l'Ordre de Saint Augustin" is a useful source of data about publications related to this order.

F0011 Backer, Augustin de; Backer, Aloys de; and Carayon, Auguste. Bibliothèque de la Compagnie de Jésus. Nouvelle éd. par Carlos Sommervogel. 12 vols. Brussels: O. Schepens; Paris: A. Picard, 1890-1932. Reprint. Louvain: Editions de la Bibliothèque S.J., 1960.

This very detailed bibliography on the Jesuits contains a main author listing in the first eight volumes, anonymous works in the ninth volume, a classified index in volume 10 and supplementary listings by Ernest M. Rivière and Pierre Bliard in the final two volumes. In addition to detailed bibliographical citations this compilation includes interesting historical notes on events and personalities connected with particular works. Baker is indispensable for students of Jesuit history and thought. See also Bangert (F0012), Polgár (F0046) and Sommervogel (F0053).

F0012 Bangert, William V. A Bibliographical Essay on the History of the Society of Jesus: Books in English. Study Aids on Jesuit Topics, no. 6. St. Louis, Mo.: The Institute of Jesuit Sources, 1976.

This 75 page bibliography is a narrative guide to approximately 400 English language books on Jesuit history. Each entry is annotated, but overall Bangert is too selective except for beginners interested in basic Jesuit history in Europe, the Americas and elsewhere. See also Polgár (F0046) and Backer (F0011).

F0013 Bartolommeo da S. Angelo. Collectio Scriptorum Ordinis Carmelitarum Excalceatorum Utruisque Congregationis et Sexus; Cui Accedit Supplementum Scriptorum Ordinis Qui Aut Obliti Fuerunt Aut Recentius Vixerunt, Auctore et Collectore P.F. Henrico M. a SS. Sacramento. Accedunt Insuper Catalogus Episcoporum, Index Praepositorum Generalium et Prospectus Provinciarum et Coenobiorum Ordinis. 2 vols. in 1. Savonae: A. Ricci, 1884.

This Carmelite bibliography contains bio-bibliographies of male and female members of the order from its origins to 1884. Entries are listed according to first names of authors and cover both printed books and manuscripts. See also Villiers de St. Etienne (F0058).

F0014 Benno, A.S. Joseph. Bibliographia Carmelitana Recentior. 3 vols. Rome: Ephemerides Carmeliticano, 1946-1949.

This predecessor of Archivum Bibliographicum Carmelitanum (F0006) lists a wide range of books and articles on the Carmelites. Although not complete by any means, Benno is an important bibliography for its period in view of the dearth of other bibliographical guides on the Carmelites during the 1940s.

F0015 Bertrand, Louis. Bibliothèque Sulpicienne; ou, Histoire Littéraire de la Compagnie de Saint-Sulpice. 3 vols. Paris: A. Picard et Ses Fils, 1900.

This chronological listing covers the seventeenth, eighteenth and nine-teenth centuries. It provides lengthy biographical sketches of individual Sulpicians and bibliographies of both published and unpublished works. Each volume is individually indexed, and the final volume includes a supplement. Bertrand is the major bibliographical guide to this religious order.

F0016 Bibliographia Franciscana. Vol. 1- . Rome: Istituto Storico dei Fratri Minori Cappuccini, 1942- ; annual.

This annual bibliographical supplement to Collectanea Franciscana lists books, periodical articles and Festschriften dealing with Franciscan history and the life and work of St. Francis of Assisi. Each volume, which in fact spans several of the annual supplements, is arranged in broad categories with very specific subdivisions. The numbered entries provide standard bibliographical details and occasional content notes. The present volume covering works published between 1964 and 1973 has appeared in four annual supplements to date, which indicates that this service is much less up to date than it should be. In addition the rather unusual classification scheme and lack of subject indexes mean that use of the bibliography can be somewhat frustrating. Nevertheless, this is the most complete listing of Franciscan materials available and must be consulted by all advanced workers in this field. In the first twelve volumes of Collectanea Franciscana (1931-1942) the bibliography appeared as an integral part of the periodical. Since then it has been produced as a separately paginated supplement. See also Archivum Francis-canum Historicum (F0007) for a less comprehensive but more up to date service.

F0017 Bouton, Jean de la Croix. Bibliographie Bernardine, 1891-1957. Commis-sion d'Histoire de l'Ordre de Citeaux. Etudes et Documents, no. 5. Paris: P. Lethielleux, 1958.

Continuing Janauschek's work on the Cistercians (F0035), Bouton lists an additional 1075 books and articles in chronological order. There are indexes of authors and geographical locations. This is a very useful updating of the earlier work and provides details on many important Cistercian publications.

F0018 Carmelus: Commentarii ab Instituto Carmelitano Editi. Vol. 1- . Rome: Institutum Carmelitanum, 1954- ; semiannual.

Covering all aspects of the Carmelite Order, from history to education and psychology, this serial in the second issue each year includes a subject bibliography. Arranged by thirteen main subjects and subdivided as necessary, the bibliography covers books, articles and theses, all with full bibliographical citations. While this compilation does not pretend to be up to date, it does provide very broad coverage on all areas related to the Carmelites and should be regularly consulted by students of this order. See also Archivum Bibliographicum Carmelitanum (F0006).

F0019 Cěrnik, Berthold Otto. Die Schriftsteller der Noch Bestehenden Augustinerchorherrenstifte Osterreichs von 1600 bis auf den Heutigen Tag. Unter Mitwirkung der reg. lat. Chorherren: Johannes Chrysostomus Miterrutzner et al. Vienna: H. Kirsch, 1905.

Limited to Augustinians in the Austrian Empire, this bibliography is arranged chronologically and lists the known writings of each member of the order. Indexes cover subjects and persons. See also Ossinger (F0043).

F0020 Cistercian Studies. Vol. 1- . Chimay: Collectanea Cisterciensia, 1966- ; quarterly.

Focusing on the Cistercian Order and on the monastic life, this scholarly journal contains in most issues a bulletin of monastic spirituality. The bulletin is essentially a book review section, often with a particular theme, and the reviews are both detailed and critical. However, there is very often a five year delay in the coverage of titles, so for bibliographical needs of a more current nature one should consult Citeaux (F0021) and Collectanea Cisterciensia (F0022). Cistercian Studies complements these other compilations by providing very detailed coverage of important English language materials.

F0021 Citeaux: Commentarii Cistercienses. Vol. 1- . Achel: Abbaye Cistercienne, 1950- ; quarterly.

Following a series of scholarly articles on the Cistercian Order, each issue of Citeaux contains a conspectus bibliographicus. This usually focuses on a specific subject with subdivisions by place and individual as required. The bibliography covers a wide range of journals, many of which are not indexed elsewhere, and the abstracts are always very informative. Although often dated in its coverage, this section provides a useful service for those interested in the Cistercians and related monastic topics. See also Cistercian Studies (F0020) and Collectanea Cisterciensia (F0022).

F0022 Collectanea Cisterciensia: Revue de Spiritualité Monastique. Vol. 1- . Chimay: Collectanea Cisterciensia, 1934- ; quarterly.

Like the other journals devoted to the Cistercians, Citeaux (F0021) and Cistercian Studies (F0020), this serial contains a series of scholarly articles; this is followed by a news bulletin and usually by a bulletin of monastic spirituality. This last section is a bibliography arranged largely by period, each of which is treated annually rather than in every issue. Within sections arrangement is by person or place, and there is an annual name index. Both books and articles dealing with the Cistercians and related topics are included, always with a detailed review or abstract. The coverage is fairly up to date and lists a number of French and Italian publications not indexed by Cistercian Studies (F0020) or similar services. For those interested in current treatment of monastic topics in serials this is a very useful abstracting service.

F0023 Constable, Giles. <u>Medieval Monasticism: A Select Bibliography</u>. Toronto Medieval Bibliographies, no. 6. Toronto: University of Toronto Press, 1976.

This bibliography of some 1000 books and articles provides a broad over- view of medieval monasticism by subject. Coverage includes history, economics, daily life, rules, government, education and related topics. The annotations are brief and factual. Constable is suitable for beginning students of monastic life and history. See also St. John's University (F0050).

F0024 Dessubré, M. <u>Bibliographie de l'Ordre des Templiers (Imprimés et Manuscrits)</u>. Bibliothèque des Initiations Modernes, 5. Paris: E. Nourry, 1928. Reprint. Nieuwkoop: B. de Graaf, 1966.

This alphabetical author listing covers written works of the Templars from all regions. Annotations summarize the author's thesis or opinion, and Bibliothèque Nationale (Paris) classifications are provided for some works. Dessubré provides fairly thorough coverage of a very specific category of materials but should not be regarded as a complete bibliog- raphy of works by the Templars.

F0025 Dirks, Servatius. <u>Histoire Littéraire et Bibliographique des Frères Mineurs de l'Observance de St. François en Belgique et dans les Pays Bas</u>. Anvers: Typographie van Os de Wolf, 1886.

This 456 page bibliography focuses on Franciscans in Belgium and the Low Countries who died between 1473 and 1886. The biographical notes and bibliographies provide much useful information on a significant sector of this order. The chronological arrangement of names is sup- plemented by a name index. See also Troeyer (F0055-F0057).

F0026 Donato da S. Giovanni in Persiceto. <u>Biblioteca dei Fratri Minori Cappuccini della Provincia de Bologna (1535-1946)</u>. Budrio: Montanari Fratelli, 1949.

This complement to Felice da Mareto (F0028) is a thorough bio-bibliog- raphy of Capuchins in the province of Bologna. Brief biographical sketches and some portraits are supplemented by annotated bibliographies of writings. There are author and editor indexes. See also <u>Acta Ordinis Fratrum Minorum</u> (F0001).

F0027 Facelina, Raymond and Zimmermann, Marie. <u>Religious Life: Inter- national Bibliography, 1972-June 1973, Indexed by Computer/Vie Religieuse: Bibliographie Internationale, 1972-Juin 1973, Etablie par Ordinateur</u>. RIC Supplément, no. 8. Strasbourg: CERDIC Publications, 1973.

This 42 page bibliography contains 607 items.

F0028 Felice da Mareto. <u>Biblioteca dei Fratri Minori Cappuccini della Provin- cia Parmense</u>. Sottogli auspice della deputazione di storia patria per le Provincie Parmensi. Modena: Societa Tip. Modense, 1951.

Similar to Donato da S. Giovanni (F0026) in scope, this 451 page bibliog- raphy provides brief biographical sketches, full bibliographies and portraits of Capuchins in the province of Parma. Locations are indicated for most titles, which cover works by and about this group. The arrangement by religious name is supplemented by full indexes. See also Acta Ordinis Fratrum Minorum (F0001).

F0029 François, Jean. Bibliothèque Générale des Ecrivains de l'Ordre de Saint Benoît, Patriarche des Moines d'Occident: Contenant une Notice Exacte des Ouvrages de Tout Genre, Composés par les Religieux des Diverses Branches, Filiations, Réformes et Congrégations de Cet Ordre, sous Quelque Dénomination Qu'elles Soient Connues, avec les Dates du Temps où Ces Ouvrages Ont Paru; et les Eclaircissements Nécessaires pour en Faire Connaître les Auteurs. 4 vols. Bouillon: Société Typographique, 1777-1778. Reprint. 4 vols. Louvain: Bibliothèque S.J., 1961.

This substantial eighteenth century attempt to list publications by Benedictines is an important source of information on writings up to that time by members of this order. Together with Kapsner (F0036) it provides an excellent bibliographical guide to theological, historical and spiritual works by a group significant in many areas of church life. In addition to writings François provides biographical notes on the authors, many of whom are not treated elsewhere. See also Monte Cassino (F0041).

F0030 Gilmont, Jean François, and Daman, Paul. Bibliographie Ignatienne, 1894-1957: Classement Méthodique des Livres et Articles Concernant Saint Ignace de Loyola, Sa Vie, les Exercices Spirituels, les Constitutions, Ses Autres Ecrits et Sa Spiritualité. Museum Lessianum Section Historique, no. 17. Paris: Desclée de Brouwer, 1958.

Arranged by subject, the 2872 books and articles in this bibliography deal with the life, works and teachings of St. Ignatius. Although annotations are lacking, the citations are full and accurate. Author and subject indexes are provided. Gilmont continues the coverage of St. Ignatius begun as part of the Monumenta Historica Societatis Iesu in 1894.

F0031 Golubovich, Gerolamo. Biblioteca Bio-Bibliografica della Terra Santa e dell'Oriente Francescano. Vol. 1- . Quaracchi: Collegio di S. Bonaventura; Cairo: Centre d'Etudes Orientales de la Custodie Franciscaine, 1906- .

This detailed guide to the Franciscans in the Middle East covers their lives and publications in four series, consisting of annals, documents (two sequences) and studies. No volumes have appeared in recent years.

F0032 Goovaerts, André Léon. Ecrivains, Artistes et Sauvants de l'Ordre de Prémontré: Dictionnaire Bio-Bibliographique. 4 vols. Brussels: Société Belge de Librairie, 1899-1920.

Issued in parts, this is an alphabetical listing of notable members of the Norbertines. For each individual biographical details plus works by and about are listed. The first two volumes contain the main sequence, while the last two contain the second and third series, which are additions and corrections. There is no index.

F0033 Harmer, Mary Fabian. Books for Religious Sisters: A General Bibliography. Washington, D.C.: Catholic University of America Press, 1963.

This select bibliography lists and annotates nonprofessional works for nuns, covering both religious and cultural literature in the classified arrangement. An author index is provided.

F0034 Index Bibliographicus Societatis Iesu. Vol. 1- . Rome: n.p., 1938- ; annual.

This bibliography lists books and articles published during the preceding year by Jesuits of all regions. Entries are arranged by author, and there is a subject index. Annotations are not provided. This compilation is useful as an updating of Sommervogel (F0053). For works about rather than by Jesuits see Archivum Historicum Societatis Iesu (F0008).

F0035 Janauschek, Leopold. Bibliographia Bernardina; Qua Sancti Bernardi, Primi Abbatis Claravallensis, Operum cum Omnium tum Singulorum, Editiones ac Versiones, Vitas et Tractatus de Eo Scriptos Quotquot Usque ad Finem Anni MDCCCXC Reperire Potuit Collegit et Adnotavit. Vindobonae: in Commissis apud A. Hölder, 1891.

This Cistercian bibliography of 558 pages provides a chronological listing of 2761 printed books and 129 manuscripts. Janauschek includes references to major authorities and to libraries where copies of works, many of them extremely rare, were to be found at the time of compilation. The work is well indexed. See also Bouton (F0017).

F0036 Kapsner, Oliver Leonard. A Benedictine Bibliography: An Author-Subject Union List. Comp. for the Library Science Section of the American Benedictine Academy. 2nd ed. 2 vols. American Benedictine Academy Library Science Studies, no. 1. Collegeville, Minn.: St. John's Abbey Press, 1962.

Essentially a union list of publications held by North American Benedictine libraries, this compilation treats 13,428 books, manuscripts, theses and music by Benedictines. The first section is arranged by author; the second, by subject. There are no annotations, but notes are provided on the contents of substantial series. Locations are given for each entry. This is a comprehensive guide to the thought, history and literature of the Benedictines but should not be treated as a definitive bibliography for advanced students. See also François (F0029) and Monte Cassino (F0041).

F0037 Lama, Carl von. Bibliothèque des Ecrivains de la Congrégation de Saint-Maur, Ordre de Saint-Benoît en France. Ouvrage publié avec le concours d'un Bénédictin de la Congrégation de France de l'Abbaye de Solesmes. 2e éd. Munich: Carl van Lama; Paris: V. Palme, 1882.

Focusing on an important Benedictine congregation, this bio-bibliography covers writings by members from 1620 to 1830. Together with Le Cerf (F0038) it provides excellent coverage of a house significant in the history of the Benedictines.

F0038 Le Cerf de la Viéville, Philippe. Bibliothèque Historique et Critique des Auteurs de la Congrégation de St. Maur. Où l'On Fait Voir Quel A Eté Leur Caractère Particulier, Ce Qu'Ils Ont Fait de Plus Remarquable; . et Où l'On Donne un Catalogue Exact de Leurs Ouvrages et une Idée Générale de Ce Qu'Ils Contiennent. The Hague; P. Grosse, 1726.

This bio-bibliography deals with Benedictines of the Congregation of St. Maur up to the early eighteenth century. Full descriptions of their lives and works provide valuable insights into the work of an important Benedictine house. See also von Lama (F0037).

F0039 McCoy, James Comly. Jesuit Relations of Canada, 1632-1673: A Bibliography. Paris: A. Rau, 1937. Reprint. Burt Franklin Bibliography and Reference Series, vol. 456. New York: Burt Franklin, 1972.

Listing 132 items, McCoy notes the first printed edition of each work and provides accurate bibliographical citations, title page reproductions, locations in libraries and references to English translations printed in Thwaites (F0096). This is a useful bibliography for students of early Canadian church history and missions. See also Walter (F0060).

F0040 Marcellino da Civezza. Saggio di Bibliografia, Geografica, Storica, Etnografica Sanfrancescana. Prato: R. Guasti, 1879.

Although covering only slightly more than 800 writers, this Franciscan bio-bibliography lists many items of interest to historians of the church in Spanish America. Excerpts, reprints, biographical notes and full bibliographies are provided for each author. See also Adams (F0002), Adasiewicz (F0003), Asencio (F0009) and Zulaica Garate (F0061).

F0041 Monte Cassino [Monastery]. I Registi dell'Archivo. A cura di Tommasso Domenico Leccisotti. Vol. 1- . Ministerio dell'Interno Publicazioni degli Archivo di Stato, 54- . Rome: Ministerio dell'Interno, 1964- .

This classified bibliography lists the contents of an important Benedictine archive, which contains much primary source material on church history and theology in general. Each entry includes a brief annotation and indication of location. An index is provided for each volume. See also Albareda (F0004), François (F0029) and Kapsner (F0036),

F0042 Morgan, John H. Aging in the Religious Life: A Comprehensive Bibliography, 1960-75. Wichita, Kans.: Institute on Ministry and the Elderly, 1977.

This brief bibliography lists a representative selection of books and articles which treat the problems of aging in religious orders. It also includes a handful of more general publications on aging and how to deal with it.

F0043 Ossinger, Johann Felix. Bibliotheca Augustiniana, Historica, Critica et Chronologica, in Qua Mille Quadrigenti Augustiniani Ordinis Scriptores Eorumque Opera tum Scripta, Quam Typis Edita Inveniuntur, Simulque Reperitur, Quo Saeculo Vixerint, et de Plurimus Quo Anno Obierint Nec Non Cuius Nationis, Patriae, Provinciae et Coenobii Fuerint Quos e Variis, et Plusquam Ducentis ac Septuaginta Octo Scriptoribus Tam Exteris, Quam Huius Ordinis, e Diversis Bibliothecis, Catalogis, atque Manuscriptis Collegit, et in Ordinem Alphabeticum Secundum Cognomen, et Nomen e Religione Impositum Redegit. Vindelicorum: Ingolstadii et Augustae, 1768. Reprint. Turin: Bettega d'Erasmo, 1963.

This classic bibliography of early Augustinians lists all known works together with sources of biographical information for each member. Brief biographical notes are also provided. See also Cĕrnik (F0019) and Perini (F0044).

F0044 Perini, David Aurelio. <u>Bibliographia Augustiniana, cum Notis Biographicus. Scriptores Itali</u>. 4 vols. Florence: Tipografia Sordomuti, 1929-1938.

This bibliography of Italian Augustinian authors is arranged alphabetically and provides a brief biographical sketch plus list of manuscripts and printed works for each individual. All fields are covered, making Perini valuable as a guide to Augustinian intellectual life in Italy. See also Ossinger (F0043).

F0045 Pigault, Gérard. <u>Christian Communities/Communautés Chrétiennes: International Bibliography, 1972-June 1974, Indexed by Computer</u>. RIC Supplément, no. 16. Strasbourg: CERDIC Publications, 1974.

F0046 Polgár, László. <u>Bibliography of the History of the Society of Jesus</u>. Sources and Studies for the History of the Jesuits, no. 1. St. Louis, Mo.: St. Louis University; Rome: Jesuit Historical Institute, 1967.

More detailed and complete than Bangert (F0012), this 207 page bibliography is a selective guide to literature on all aspects of Jesuit history. The selection is wide ranging and broadly representative of the field, providing a sound starting point for those about to undertake advanced research on the Jesuits. Entries are arranged chronologically, and there is an index. See also Backer (F0011).

F0047 Quétif, Jacques. <u>Scriptores Ordinis Praedicatorum Recensiti Notisque Historicis et Criticis Illustrati, Opus Quo Singulorum Vita, Praeclaresque Gesta Referuntur, Chronologia Insuper, Sèu Tempus Quo Quisque Floruit Certo Statuitur: Fabulae Exploduntur; Scripta Genuina, Dubia, Supposititia Expenduntur, Recentiorum de Iis Judicium Aut Probatur, Aut Emendatur: Codices Manuscripti, Variaeque e Typis Editiones, et Ubi Habeantur Indicantur</u>. 2 vols. Paris: J.B.C. Ballard et N. Simart, 1719-1721. Reprint. 2 vols. in 4. Burt Franklin Bibliographical and Reference Series, no. 16. New York: Burt Franklin, 1959-1961.

Limited in coverage to Dominicans who died between 1701 and 1749, this extensive compilation includes brief biographical notes plus full bibliographies of works for each author. Arrangement is chronological, and the lack of an author index makes consultation unnecessarily time consuming.

F0048 Ravasi, Ladislaus R. <u>Fontes et Bibliographia de Vocatione Religioso et Sacerdotali</u>. Mediolani: Edizioni Fonti Vive, 1961.

This 139 page classified bibliography of books and articles is devoted to religious vocations in the Roman Catholic Church. The references are limited almost exclusively to European titles, and very few of them are English language works. Ravasi does not include an index and is of use only to those who wish selected bibliographical references to pre-1960 publications.

F0049 <u>Revue Bénédictine. Supplément: Bulletin d'Histoire Bénédictine</u>. Vol. 1- . Maredsous: Abbaye de Maredsous, 1907- ; quarterly.

Issued less frequently than quarterly, this supplement to the <u>Revue Bénédictine</u> appears in fascicles with author and subject indexes in the final issue of each volume. The bibliography itself covers both books and articles on Benedictine history and is arranged into four main subjects (St. Benedict and the Rule, generalities, history of monasteries, biographies) with subdivisions as necessary. Although the treatment of this specific subject appears to be quite comprehensive and despite the accurate citations, the very delayed appearance of issues and indexes is a serious flaw in an otherwise important guide. See also Kapsner (F0036).

F0050 St. John's University. Library. Checklist of Manuscripts Microfilmed for the Monastic Manuscript Microfilm Library. Vol. 1- . Collegeville, Minn.: St. John's University Library, 1967- .

Arranged by country, this catalog lists all manuscripts which have been microfilmed as part of this extensive undertaking. Each item includes manuscript codex number and project number of the microfilm. As such, it serves not as a full bibliography but rather as a basic finding list for advanced students of monasticism. See also Constable (F0023).

F0051 Santiago Vela, Gregorio de. Ensayo de una Biblioteca Ibero-Americana de la Orden de San Augustin: Obra Basada en el Catálogo Bio-Bibliográfico Augustiano del p. Bonifacio Moral. 8 vols. Madrid: Imprenta del Asilo de Huerfános del S.C. de Jesús, 1913-1931.

This detailed bio-bibliography covers Augustinians who were born or served in Latin America up to the early years of this century. It is the only substantial work on the topic and is very important for students of Latin American ecclesiastical or monastic history.

F0052 Smet, Joachim, and Toelle, Gervase, comps. Catalog of the Carmelitana Collection, Whitefriars Hall. [Washington, D.C.: Whitefriars Hall, 1959].

This 381 page bibliography is a classified listing of nearly 250 works either about or by Carmelites. An author index is provided. Although limited in scope, this is a useful supplement to such older Carmelite bibliographies as Bartolommeo da S. Angelo (D0013) and Villiers de St. Etienne (F0058).

F0053 Sommervogel, Carlos. Dictionnaire des Ouvrages Anonymes et Pseudonymes Publié par des Religieux de la Compagnie de Jésus depuis Sa Fondation jusqu'à Nos Jours. Paris: Librarie de la Société Bibliographique, 1884.

This 1398 page bibliography is arranged alphabetically by title and provides full information, including author whenever possible, for each entry. Because many earlier Jesuit publications were issued anonymously or under pseudonyms, this is a major time saver for librarians and others interested in determining the authorship of Jesuit works. See also Backer (F0011) and Tavagnutti (F0054).

F0054 Tavagnutti, Mario Sigismondo. Bibliotheca Catholica Societatis Jesu: Verzeichniss der Wichtigsten uber den Order und Einzelne Mitglieder der Gesellschaft Jesu von 1830 bis 1891 Sowohl Apologetischen, Biographischen und Historischen, als auch die Pädagogische und die Missionsthätigkeit Umfassenden, von Katholischer Seite Erschienenen Werke, Predigten und Andachtsbücher, mit einem Autoren- und einem Stichwort-Register. Katholisch-Theologische Bücherkunde der Letzten Fünfzig Jahre, Bd. 6. Vienna: Drescher und Compagnie, 1891.

See also Sommervogel (F0053).

F0055 Troeyer, Benjamin de. <u>Bio-Bibliographia Franciscana Neerlandica</u> <u>Saeculi XVI.</u> 2 vols. Nieuwkoop: B. de Graaf, 1969-1970.

Covering biographies in the first volume and bibliographies in the second, Troeyer includes both primary and secondary sources in its treatment of the Dutch Franciscans in the sixteenth century. Each volume is provided with an index. See also Dirks (F0025) and the following two entries (F0056, F0057).

F0056 Troeyer, Benjamin de. <u>Instrumentum ad Editiones Neerlandicas Fran-</u> <u>ciscanas Saeculi XVI Indagandas.</u> Sint Truiden: Archief der Paters Minder-broeders, 1967.

See also Troeyer's other works (F0055, F0057).

F0057 Troeyer, Benjamin de, and Mees, Leonide. <u>Bio-Bibliographia Franciscana</u> <u>Neerlandica ante Saeculum XVI.</u> 3 vols. Nieuwkoop: B. de Graaf, 1974.

Volume 1 of this bibliographical guide to the Dutch Franciscans contains the biographical entries (auctores editionem qui scripserunt ante saeculum XVI); volume 2 contains the pars bibliographica devoted to incunabula, and volume 3 contains the pars bibliographica covering illustrationes incunabulorum. The work includes references to manuscripts, printed works and writings about the authors. Library locations, primarily in Europe, are given for the incunabula and manuscripts. See also Dirks (F0025) and the preceding entries (F0055, F0056).

F0058 Villiers de St. Etienne, Cosme de. <u>Bibliotheca Carmelitana: Notis</u> <u>Criticis et Dissertationibus Illustrada.</u> 2 vols. Aurelianis: Rousseau-Montau, 1752. Reprint. With a preface and supplement by Gabriel Wessles. 2 vols. in 1. Rome: Collegii S. Alberti, 1927.

Like Bartolommeo da S. Angelo (F0013) this compilation is a bio-bibliog-raphy of Carmelite authors. The original collection covers individuals up to the mid-eighteenth century, and the supplement by Wessles lists an additional seventy authors.

F0059 Wadding, Luke, and Sbaralea, G.G. <u>Scriptores Ordinis Minorum, Quibus</u> <u>Accessit Syllabus Illorum Qui ex Eodem Ordine pro Fide Christi Fortiter</u> <u>Occubuerunt, Priores Atramento, Posteriores Sanguine Christianam Religionem</u> <u>Asseruerunt.</u> Editio novissima. 4 vols. Bibliotheca Historico-Bibliographica, 1-4. Rome: Attilio Nardecchia, 1906-1936.

This substantial collection consists of bio-bibliographies of the Franciscans and covers many of the more notable members of the order. Brief bio-graphical notices and detailed bibliographies are provided for each in-dividual. The initial volume was prepared by Wadding in 1650; the three supplementary volumes are by Sbaralea. See also <u>Bibliographia Franciscana</u> (F0016).

F0060 Walter, Frank Keller, and Doneghy, Virginia, comps. <u>Jesuit Relations</u> <u>and Other Americana in the Library of James F. Bell: A Catalogue.</u> Minne-apolis, Minn.: University of Minnesota Press, [1950].

In this catalog "relations" refers to letters, reports and other documents written by early Jesuit missionaries in North America. Walter lists an indispensible collection of sources for the advanced student of early American and Canadian church history and is particularly valuable for those interested in the historical study of Roman Catholic missions. The sources themselves are printed in Thwaites (F0096). See also McCoy (F0039).

F0061 Zulaica Garate, Román. Los Franciscanos y la Imprenta en México en el Siglo XVI: Estudio Bio-Bibliografico. Mexico: D.F.P. Robredo, 1939.

This bio-bibliography of Franciscans in sixteenth century Mexico is arranged chronologically. Many of the entries include extensive annotations on content, and all are bibliographically accurate. An author index is provided. See also Adams (F0002), Adasiewicz (F0003), Asencio (F0009) and Marcellino da Civezza (D0040).

RELIGIOUS ORDERS: DICTIONARIES AND HANDBOOKS

F0062 Annuaire des Instituts de Religieuses en France. [Ed. 1-]. Paris: Service National des Vocations Françaises, 1959- ; irregular.

This directory of French religious orders contains the addresses of main houses and related foundations, as well as descriptions of the work of each order.

F0063 Anson, Peter Frederick. The Call of the Cloister: Religious Communities and Kindred Bodies in the Anglican Communion. [4th] ed. Rev. and ed. by A.W. Campbell. London: SPCK, 1964.

This standard reference work provides a list of all known Anglican religious communities throughout the world together with a brief history of each one. A full bibliography and an appendix of communities arranged by date of foundation are also provided. Somewhat dated for current reference requirements, Anson nevertheless is a valuable source of information for historians of the monastic movement. See also Church of England (F0068).

F0064 Anson, Peter Frederick. The Religious Orders and Congregations of Great Britain and Ireland. Worcester: Stanbrook Abbey Press, 1949.

This predecessor of Directory of Religious Orders (F0075) is arranged in separate sections for men and women. In each the arrangement of orders and congregations is alphabetical, and details are given on history, activities, location of communities and habit. Each part is provided with an index. Although no longer useful as a current directory, Anson does provide reference data on religious orders in the British Isles.

F0065 Bangert, William V. A History of the Society of Jesus. St. Louis, Mo.: The Institute of Jesuit Sources, 1972.

This 558 page history of the Jesuits covers the period from the fifteenth century to the Society's thirty-first General Congregation in 1966. It is a scholarly and comprehensive account which incorporates research findings of recent years, and provides a sympathetic approach to the history of the Society. See also Brodrick (F0067) and Clancy (F0069).

F0066 Braunfels, Wolfgang. Monasteries of Western Europe: The Architecture of the Orders. Trans. by Alastair Laing. 3rd ed. London: Thames and Hudson, 1972; Princeton, N.J.: Princeton University Press, 1973 [c. 1972].

This guide to monastic architecture in Western Europe is notable for its excellent illustrations, photographs and floor plans. Entries are arranged by such categories as major orders, types of orders and periods; this arrangement is less than satisfactory for most reference requirements, but patience is more than adequately repaid with detailed information on all forms and periods of architecture. See also Knowles (F0086).

F0067 Brodrick, James. The Origins of the Jesuits. London: Longmans, Green and Company, 1940. Reprint. London: Longmans, Green and Company, 1947.

This history of the origin of the Jesuits is not intended to provide an exhaustive account; rather it is a preliminary to a more scholarly, detailed treatment. An index is provided. See also Bangert (F0065) and Clancy (F0069).

F0068 Church of England. Advisory Council on the Relation of Bishops and Religious Communities. Guide to the Religious Communities of the Anglican Communion. [New ed.] New York: Morehouse-Gorham Company; London: A.R. Mowbray and Company, 1955.

This 140 page guide covers both men's and women's communities in Britain, America and elsewhere. Basic information, now somewhat dated for current reference requirements, is provided for each community. There are indexes of communities and of geographical locations. See also Anson (F0063).

F0069 Clancy, Thomas H. An Introduction to Jesuit Life: The Constitutions and History through 435 Years. Study Aids on Jesuit Topics, no. 3. St. Louis, Mo.: Institute of Jesuit Sources, 1976.

See also Bangert (F0065) and Brodrick (F0067).

F0070 Code, Joseph Bernard. Great American Foundresses. New York: Macmillan Company, 1929. Reprint. Essay Index Reprint Series. Freeport, N.Y.: Books for Libraries, 1968.

Also published as The Veil Is Lifted (Milwaukee, Wisc.: Bruce Publishing Company, 1932), this biographical work contains historical sketches of the lives of sixteen women who founded religious orders in America. The 1932 version has the advantage of useful bibliographical listings for each foundress. See also Dehey (F0074).

F0071 Cottineau, L.H. Répertoire Topo-Bibliographique des Abbayes et Prieurés. 3 vols. Mâcon: Protat Frères, 1935-1970.

This combined dictionary and bibliography is arranged by geographical location. For each abbey and priory Cottineau provides brief historical notes, location with reference to larger places, variant form of name, order to which the house belongs and detailed bibliography. Included are houses of all periods and in all countries, medieval as well as modern. For historians this is a particularly useful work and one in which the bibliography deserves updating in a new edition.

F0072 Coulton, George Gordon. Five Centuries of Religion. 4 vols. Cambridge Studies in Medieval Life and Thought. Cambridge: Cambridge University Press, 1923-1950.

These volumes treat medieval monasticism in a series of related narratives: St. Bernard, his predecessors and successors; the friars; "getting and spending"; the final days of medieval monasticism. The text is somewhat discursive and anecdotal, but the factual data make Coulton an interesting complement to Knowles (F0083-F0086) and other more scholarly surveys. The bibliographies, although very dated, are useful for advanced students of this subject.

F0073 Cowan, Ian Borthwick, and Easson, David Edward. Medieval Religious Houses, Scotland. With an Appendix on the Houses in the Isle of Man. 2nd ed. London: Longman Group, 1976.

This companion volume to Knowles (F0086) and Gwynn (F0078) is arranged by religious order; under each it lists alphabetically by place each foundation established by an order. The entries include brief notes on the establishment, size, nature, income and fate of the houses. A full index of religious houses accompanies the listing, which is an excellent source of detailed historical information on medieval monasticism in Scotland.

F0074 Dehey, Elinor Tong. Religious Orders of Women in the United States: Catholic; Accounts of Their Origin, Works and Most Important Institutions, Interwoven with Histories of Many Famous Foundresses. Rev. ed. [Hammond, Ind.: W.B. Conkey Company, c. 1930].

Now dated for its directory content but still useful for historical purposes, Dehey covers some 200 of the larger Roman Catholic women's orders in the United States. The biographical notes on foundresses are particularly helpful for students of this field. See also Code (F0070).

F0075 Directory of Religious Orders, Congregations and Societies of Great Britain and Ireland. Glasgow: J.S. Burns, 1955- ; annual.

This alphabetical listing of Roman Catholic orders in the British Isles includes a brief outline of the history and major activities of each society. There is an alphabetical index of priests, brothers and nuns belonging to the various orders. This is both a useful directory and a sound guide for basic historical inquiries. For an earlier guide see Anson (F0064).

F0076 Dugdale, William. Monasticon Anglicanum: A History of the Abbies and Other Monasteries, Hospitals, Friaries and Cathedral and Collegiate Churches, with Their Dependencies, in England and Wales; also of All Such Scotch, Irish and French Monasteries, As Were in Any Manner Connected with the Religious Houses in England. Originally published in Latin by Sir William Dugdale. New ed. enriched with a large accession of materials now first printed from leiger books, chartularies, rolls and other documents preserved in the national archives, public libraries and other repositories;

the history of each religious foundation in English being prefixed to its respective series of Latin charters. By John Caley, Henry Ellis and Bulkeley Bandinel. 6 vols. in 8. London: Hurst, Rees, Orme and Brown, 1817-1830. Reprint. 6 vols. in 8. London: T.G. March, 1849.

First published in the late seventeenth century, this monumental collection of charters, annals and similar documents is a fundamental compendium which deals with all aspects of the medieval English church. It includes historical summaries of the various religious houses and is of particular value for those interested in the foundation of monasteries in Britain. The English translations are useful for less advanced students without knowledge of Latin. See also Knowles (F0083-F0086).

F0077 Gibson, Mary, ed. Directory of Secular Institutes with Foundations in the U.S.A. Prepared by the National Center for Church Vocations in collaboration with the U.S. Conference of Secular Institutes. Washington, D.C.: United States Catholic Conference, 1975.

This brief directory of secular institutes or lay religious societies provides basic information on fifteen establishments with American membership. It is limited to those with Roman Catholic affiliation. See also McCarthy (F0091) for fuller but less up to date information.

F0078 Gwynn, Aubrey Osborn, and Hadcock, Richard Neville. Medieval Religious Houses: Ireland; with an Appendix to Early Sites. Harlow, Essex: Longmans, Green and Company, 1970.

First published in 1957, this companion to Knowles (F0086) lists more than 1000 Irish religious houses, cathedrals, hospitals, colleges and military orders for the period 1111-1600. The appendix lists sites of earlier date. Establishments are arranged by order and then by geographical location. There is an attempt to provide basic factual data on numbers, history and dates for each foundation. There is an index of places and of alternate names or spellings. A detailed bibliography of works on Irish monasteries is also included. See also Cowan (F0073).

F0079 Heimbucher, Max Josef. Die Orden und Kongregationen der Katholischen Kirche. 3. Aufl. 2 vols. Paderborn: Ferdinand Schöningh, 1933-1934.

First published in 1896-1897, this updated condensation of Hélyot's Histoire des Ordres Religieux provides brief historical treatment of major religious orders, biographies of important members, some statistical data and other relevant information. Volume 1 covers Benedictines, Dominicans and Franciscans; volume 2, Carmelites, Jesuits, Sulpicians and other smaller orders. The bibliographical information is particularly valuable and gives Heimbucher much of its continuing usefulness. See also Hélyot (F0080) and Kapsner (F0082), both of which cover more religious orders but without adequate bibliographical treatment.

F0080 Hélyot, Pierre. Dictionnaire des Ordres Religieux; ou, Histoire des Ordres Monastiques, Religieux et Militaires, et des Congrégations Séculières de l'Un et de l'Autre Sexe, Qui Ont Eté Etablies jusqu'à Présent. 4 vols. Paris: J.P. Migne, 1859-1863.

In the absence of an equally comprehensive later work on Roman Catholic religious orders, Hélyot remains a useful history of the various types of orders and congregations. Arranged alphabetically by name of order, each volume provides quite substantial histories of orders to the mid-nineteenth century. A supplement by Marie-Léandre Badiche provides histories of congregations omitted by Hélyot and of societies established after the work was first compiled. The major drawback is the insubstantial bibliographical coverage, but otherwise this remains the most useful encyclopedic history in its field. See also Heimbucher (F0079), Kapsner (F0082) and Pelliccia (F0094).

F0081 Holub, William, coordinating ed. Ministries for the Lord: A Resource Guide and Directory of Church Vocations for Men, 1979-1980 ed. New York: Paulist Press, 1978.

This successor to The Guidepost: Religious Vocational Manual for Young Men is aimed at those who wish to test their vocation in Roman Catholic religious orders. It includes a brief history, description of work and names and addresses of vocation directors for each order. See also Mc-Carthy (F0091).

F0082 Kapsner, Oliver Leonard, ed. Catholic Religious Orders: Listing Conventional and Full Names in English, Foreign Language, and Latin, also Abbreviations, Date and Country of Origin and Founders. 2nd ed. Collegeville, Minn.: St. John's Abbey Press, 1957.

First published in 1948 and intended primarily for librarians, this valuable dictionary lists 1777 religious orders, congregations, societies and military orders, both existing and defunct. Cross references from variant forms, a glossary of related terminology and an index of founders are all included. Particularly useful for non-Catholics is the inclusion of abbreviations of orders in the cross references. See also Hélyot (F0080) and Ooms (F0093).

F0083 Knowles, David. The Monastic Order in England: A History of Its Development from the Times of St. Dunstan to the Fourth Lateran Council, 940-1216. 2nd ed. Cambridge: Cambridge University Press, 1963.

First published in 1940, this detailed historical account of English monastic life during its formative period is based on contemporary sources and provides a wealth of factual data on the origins, development and expansion of early medieval monasticism. The 780 pages include a bibliography (pp. 727-748) and bibliographical references in additional notes (pp. 749-759), as well as a full index. For advanced students this work and the companion set (F0084) remain indispensible reference sources. See also Coulton (F0072).

F0084 Knowles, David. The Religious Orders in England. 3 vols. Cambridge: Cambridge University Press, 1948-1959. Reprint. 3 vols. Cambridge: Cambridge University Press, 1961-1962.

This companion to The Monastic Order in England (F0083) covers 1216-1304 in volume 1, the end of the medieval period in volume 2 and the Tudor era in volume 3. The balanced treatment, historical accuracy and broad coverage make this a standard reference set for advanced students. Volume 3 includes a bibliography, an index and an series of appendixes. See also Coulton (F0072) and Dugdale (F0076).

F0085 Knowles, David; Brooke, Christopher Nugent Lawrence; and London, Vera C.M., eds. The Heads of Religious Houses, England and Wales, 940-1216. Cambridge: Cambridge University Press, 1972.

This listing of abbots, priors and other heads is arranged by order and then alphabetically by house, with a separate section for women's houses. For each entry the editors provide dates of accession and death plus basic career details. The bibliography lists manuscripts and published sources of relevant information, and the detailed introduction discusses the means of unearthing such data together with comments on their accuracy and usefulness. There are indexes of names and of houses.

F0086 Knowles, David, and Hadcock, Richard Neville. Medieval Religious Houses, England and Wales. New ed. London: Longmans, Green and Company, 1971; New York: St. Martin's Press, 1972 [c. 1971].

This expansion of the 1953 edition lists several thousand monasteries, hospitals and secular colleges in England and Wales. Houses are grouped by religious order, and each entry provides details on history, numerical size, wealth, architectural remains and documentary sources. The appendixes, index of monasteries and excellent introduction add to the reference value of this work, which is admirably suited to students of British church history and monasticism. See also the companion works by Gwynn (F0078) and Cowan (F0073).

F0087 Koch, Ludwig. Jesuiten-Lexikon: Die Gesellschaft Jesu Einst und Jetzt. Paderborn: Verlag Bonifacius-Druckerie, 1934. Reprint with corrections and supplement. 2 vols. Louvain-Heverlee: Verlag der Bibliothek S.J., 1962.

This concise work of some 2200 entries covers the history, activities and institutions of the Jesuits. Bibliographical references accompany each article. Koch is an excellent and accurate guide for basic inquiries and is the only work of its kind devoted to the Jesuits.

F0088 Lexau, Joan M., ed. Convent Life: Roman Catholic Religious Orders for Women in North America. New York: Dial Press, 1964.

This collection contains both a series of brief essays on convent life and work in American Catholic houses plus a detailed index of orders which gives the names and addresses of mother houses in America. See also McCarthy (F0090). Both works are now dated in terms of current directory information.

F0089 Lexicon Capuccinum, Promptuarium Historico-Bibliographicum Ordinis Fratrum Minorum Capuccinorum (1515-1950). Rome: Biblioteca Colegii Internationalis S. Laurentii Brundusini, 1951.

This wide ranging dictionary on the Capuchins covers major figures, provinces, monasteries, historical events, publications, missions and similar material. The articles are detailed and scholarly, with bibliographies for further study.

F0090 McCarthy, Thomas Patrick. Guide to the Catholic Sisterhoods in the United States. 5th ed. Washington, D.C.: Catholic University Of America Press, 1964.

McCarthy contains brief descriptions of approximately 380 religious orders in the United States. History, statistics, apostolic work and dress are covered in the single page articles. Indexes of variant forms of names, initials and affiliated houses are provided. Although dated as a current guide in view of post-Vatican II changes, this is a valuable source of historical information on Roman Catholic religious orders for both men and women. See also Lexau (F0088).

F0091 McCarthy, Thomas Patrick. Total Dedication for the Laity: A Guide-book to Secular Institutes. Boston, Mass.: St. Paul Editions, 1964.

This directory of secular institutes or societies describes the purposes, history, formation and membership requirements of twenty Roman Catholic societies based in the United States. For more current information see Gibson (F0077); see also Holub (F0081).

F0092 Molette, Charles. Guide des Sources de l'Histoire des Congrégations Féminines Françaises de Vie Active. Paris: Editions de Paris, 1974.

Published with the assistance of the Centre National de Recherche Scientifique, this work is arranged in two main sections: introduction historique, sources et bibliographie. The latter part (pp. 107-379) lists nearly 400 religious congregations alphabetically by name of the order, indicating address, publications and bibliographical references to writings about the order and its members. There are indexes of names, of places and of societies. This is an important guide for students of monastic history.

F0093 Ooms, Herwig. Repertorium Universale Siglorum Ordinum et Institutum Religiosorum in Ecclesia Catholica. Bibliographica Belgica, 45. Brussels: Commission Belge de Bibliographie, 1959.

For each Roman Catholic religious order Ooms lists the full Latin name together with names in other languages, date and place of foundation, name of founder. This is a most useful guide to an area in which appellation is frequently confusing. See also Kapsner (F0082).

F0094 Pelliccia, Guerrino, and Rocca, Giancarlo, eds. Dizionario degli Istituti di Perfezione. Vol. 1- . Rome: Edizione Paoline, 1974- .

This detailed encyclopedic successor to Hélyot (F0080) contains signed articles in alphabetical sequence on the history and structure of some 4000 Roman Catholic religious societies and orders, on Eastern and Western monasticism and on religious institutions of non-Catholic traditions. There are also many biographical articles on founders of religious orders, as well as entries on the terminology of the religious life, of monastic architecture and similar fields. Most entries have bibliographies for further reference, and indexes are planned for the concluding volume. This is a significant guide to monasticism for students at all levels.

F0095 Schmitz, Philibert. Histoire de l'Order de Saint Benoît. 6 vols. Maredsous: Editions de Maredsous, 1942-1949.

This substantial history of the Benedictines provides a detailed, chronological analysis of the origins, development and activities of the order from its origins to the twentieth century. Although volumes 2 and 5 on the civilizing influence of the Benedictines lack objectivity, the other volumes

are reasonably objective and scholarly, providing much valuable information for students of monastic history.

F0096 Thwaites, Reuben Gold, ed. <u>The Jesuit Relations and Allied Documents,
Travels and Explorations of the Jesuit Missionaries in New France, 1610-
1791: The Original French, Latin and Italian Texts with English Translations
and Notes.</u> 73 vols. Cleveland, Ohio: Burrows Brothers, 1896-1901. Reprint.
73 vols. in 36. New York: Pageant Book Company, 1959.

This valuable collection of source materials on early North American
church history consists of letters, reports, papers and other documents
prepared by early Jesuit missionaries. Each document includes an introduction, bibliographical notes and an English translation. The final two
volumes contain indexes. See also Walter (F0060).

F0097 Walz, Angelus Maria. <u>Compendium Historiae Ordinis Praedicatorum.</u>
Editio altera recognita et aucta. Rome: Pontificium Athenaeum Angelicum,
1948.

This is a 733 page history of the Dominicans.

F0098 Wessels, Gabriel, ed. <u>Capitulorum Generalium Ordinis Fratrum B.V.
Mariae de Monte Carmelo.</u> 2 vols. Rome: apud Curiam Generalitim, 1914-1934.

This useful reference work on the Carmelites covers 1318-1593 in the
first volume and 1598-1902 in the second.

Author Index

Byrne, T.S., D0323
Byrnes, J.J., C0697
Byrnes, P.A., E0013

Cadbury, H.J., D0365, D0366
Cadden, J.P., D0378
Caenegem, R.C. van, D0057
Cahen, L., D0179
Cahn, Z., C0375
Caird, J., C0376
Cairns, E., D0301
Calcagno, F.S., C0377
Caley, J., F0076
Callan, C.J., C0378
Calvez, J.-Y., C0379
Calvin, J., C0380
Cameron, J.K., D0025
Cameron, K.W., D0382
Cameron, R.M., D0383
Campbell, T.J., D0384, D0385
Campenhausen, H. von, D0386, D0387
Cannon, W.R., C0381
Cantelar Rodriguez, F., D0102
Cappadelta, L., D0482
Cappelli, A., D0258, D0305
Carayon, A., F0011
Carbone, C., C0228
Carducci, G., D0634
Carmody, J., C0382
Carnandet, J.B., D0388
Carol, J.B., C0383
Caron, P.,D0059, D0060
Carpenter, S.C., D0389, D0390
Carruth, G., D0259
Cary, M., D0260
Case, A.T., C0048
Case, S.J., D0061
Cassilly, F.B., C0384
Castelot, J.J., C0609
Catholic Students Mission Crusade, C0385
Cauwenbergh, E. van, D0252
Cavallera, F., C0301, C0386, D0391
Cave, A., C0387
Cave, R.C., D0392
Cavert, S.M., E0092-E0094
Cayre, F., D0393
Cederakis, A.I., D0477
Ceillier, R., D0394
Center for Reformation Research, D0063-D0066
Center for Research Libraries, E0014
Cernik, B.D., F0019

Chabot, I.B., D0411
Chadwick, H., D0395, D0396
Chadwick, O., D0067, D0396-D0399, E0155
Champagne, J.E., E0095
Chao, J.T., E0015
Chatfield, C., C0054
Chaussin, L., D0347
Cheetham, S., D0310
Cheney, C.R., D0668
Chenu, M.D., C0388
Cheruel, P.A., D0261
Chevalier, C.U.J., C0049, D0068
Childs, J.M., C0389
Chirat, H., C0218
Choquette, D., C0050
Christ, K., D0069
Christie, I.R., D0051, D0070
Chu, C.H., E0016
Church of England. Advisory Council on the Relation of Bishops and Religious Communities, F0068
Church of England. National Assembly. Joint Board of Studies, C0051
Clancy, T.H., F0069
Clark, G., D0402
Clark, G.K., D0403
Clarke, W.N., C0390
Clarkson, J.F., C0391
Claus, H., C0019
Claxton, J.H., D0197
Clouser, K.D., C0052
Cobb, J.B., C0393
Cochran, T.C., D0237
Code, J.B., F0070
Coffey, P., C0746
Coggins, W.T., E0167
Cohen, A.A., C0501
Cohn, M., C0053
Cole, S.G., D0405
Collins, J.D., C0394
Collins, W.J., C0558
Collison, R.L., D0262
Comite Francais de Sciences Historiques, D0072
Commager, H.S., D0406, D0407
Committee for a New England Bibliography, D0073
Cone, J.H., C0396
Congar, Y.M.J., C0397
Conn, H.M., C0398
Constable, G., F0023
Conway, J.D., C0399
Conzelmann, H., D0408
Cook, B.W., C0054

Title Index

Abortion, C0078
Abortion and Euthanasia, C0052
Abortion in Context, C0061
Abbreviations Latines Medievales, D0305
Achievement of Jacques and Raissa Maritain, C0069
Acta Conciliorum Oecumenicorum, D0703
Acta Ordinis Fratrum Minorum, F0001
Acta Sanctorum Quotquot Toto Orbe Coluntur, D0316
Acta Sanctorum Quotquot Toto Orbe Coluntur (Carnandet), D0388
Acts of the Christian Martyrs, D0635
Actualidid Bibliografica de Filosofia y Teologia, C0001
African Theology, C0067
Afro-American History, D0203
Agape and Eros, C0610
Age of Humanism and Reformation, D0431
Age of Reform (1250-1550), D0654
Age of the Fathers, D0370
Age of the Reformation, D0330
Age of the Renaissance and Reformation, D0601
Aging in the Religious Life, F0042
Allgemeine Philosophische Bibliographie, C0035
America: History and Life, D0007, D0203
American Catholic Thought on Social Questions, C0307
American Catholicism, D0455
American Catholics, D0529
American Christianity, D0712
American Church History Series, D0696
American Churches in the Ecumenical Movement, 1900-1968, E0092
American Directory of Schools and Colleges Offering Missionary Courses, E0161
American Episcopal Clergy, D0382
American Historical Review, D0009
American History, D0121
American Missionaries in China, E0016
American Protestantism, D0540
Analecta Bollandiana, D0010
Analecta Sacra Spicilegio Solesmensi Parata, D0663
Ancient Christian Writers, D0676
Anglo-Norman England, 1066-1154, D0006
Anglo-Saxon and Celtic Bibliography, 450-1087, D0045
Annals of European Civilization, 1501-1900, D0613
Annals of the Free Church of Scotland, 1843-1900, D0465
Annee Philologique, D0011
Annee Theologique Augustinienne, C0165
Annotated Bibliography of Luther Studies, 1967-1976, C0030

1850-1900, C0095
Bibliografia Mariana, C0021
Bibliografia Misional, E0053
Bibliografia Misional Hispano-
americana 1948, E0020
Bibliografia Missionaria, E0008
Bibliografia Missionaria (Rommers-
kirchen), E0051
Bibliografia Origeniana, 1960-1970,
D0094
Bibliografia Regionata delle Reviste
Filosofiche Italiane, C0096
Bibliografia sobre Ludovico A.
Muratori, E0024
Bibliografia Storica Internazionale,
1940-1947, D0180
Bibliografia Teologica Comentada,
C0022
Bibliografia Teologica en Lingua
Portuguesa, C0173
Bibliographia Augustiniana,C0006,F0044
Bibliographia Augustiniana, seu
Operum Collectio, C0136
Bibliographia Bernardina, F0035
Bibliographia Calviniana, C0064
Bibliographia Carmelitana Recentior,
F0014
Bibliographia de Vita, Operbus et
Doctrina Johannis Duns Scoti,
C0175
Bibliographia Franciscana, F0016
Bibliographia Internationalis Spiritual-
itatis, C0023
Bibliographia Logica, C0170
Bibliographia Patristica, D0030
Bibliographia Philosophica, 1934-1945,
C0041
Bibliographia Synodorum Partic-
ularium, D0199
Bibliographical Essay on the History
of the Society of Jesus, F0012
Bibliographical Guide to the History
of Christianity, D0061
Bibliographical Index of Five English
Mystics, C0174
Bibliographie Annuelle de l'Histoire
de France, D0031
Bibliographie Annuelle des Travaux
Historiques, D0159
Bibliographie Bernardine, F0017
Bibliographie Chronologique de la
Litterature de Spiritualite, C0058
Bibliographie Critique d' Origene,
D0076
Bibliographie Critique de la Philos-
ophie Grecque, C0202

Bibliographie de Cartographie
Ecclesiastique, D0138
Bibliographie de l'Humanisme des
Anciens Pays-Bas, C0070
Bibliographie de l'Ordre des Tem-
pliers, F0024
Bibliographie de la Philosophie,
C0093
Bibliographie de la Philosophie:
Bulletin Trimestriel, C0024
Bibliographie de la Reforme, D0025
Bibliographie de la Reforme,
1450-1648, D0139
Bibliographie der Fest- und Gedank-
schriften fur Personlichkeiten,
C0063
Bibliographie der Inquisition, D0220
Bibliographie des Sciences Theolog-
iques, C0083
Bibliographie des Taufertums,
1520-1630, D0126
Bibliographie Generale des Travaux
Historiques, D0160
Bibliographie Generale des Travaux
Historiques et Archeologiques,
D0101
Bibliographie Historischer Zeit-
schriften, 1931-1951, D0153
Bibliographie Ignatienne, 1894-1957,
F0030
Bibliographie Internationale de
l'Humanisme et de la Renais-
sance, C0025
Bibliographie Internationale des
Travaux Historiques, D0136
Bibliographie Karl Rahner: 1924-
1969, C0033
Bibliographie Karl Rahner: 1969-
1974, C0032
Bibliographie Missionaire Moderne,
E0039
Bibliographie Oecumenique Inter-
nationale, E0030
Bibliographie Philosophie, C0026
Bibliographie Philosophique de
Saint Albert le Grand (1931-1960),
C0179
Bibliographie Thomiste, C0122
Bibliographie zum Studium des
Neuern Geschichte, D0026
Bibliographie zur Alteuropaischen
Religionsgeschichte, 1954-1964,
D0053
Bibliographie zur Deutschen Ge-
schichte, D0032
Bibliographie zur Deutschen Ge-

Subject Index

C0631, C0633, C0634, C0645, C0662, C0666, C0671, C0672, C0687, C0697, C0699, C0702, C0710, C0723
Seventh-Day Adventist, C0353
USA, C0445

Teilhard de Chardin
 bibliographies, C0117, C0154, C0155
 dictionary, C0231
 handbooks, C0405, C0602
theologians
 directory
  USA, C0500
theology
 bibliographies, C0001, C0007, C0046, C0051, C0083, C0153, C0158, C0166, C0178, C0188
  Africa, C0067
  Austria, C0074
  Germany, C0074, C0105
  history of, C0007
  Latin America, C0022
  see also development theology; theology, liberation, Third World
  liberation, C0004, C0066
  see also theology, Africa; development theology; theology, Latin America, Third World
  Lutheran, C0169
  medieval, C0075
  methodology, C0188
  Netherlands, C0020
  Portugal, C0173
  Protestant, C0063, C0065, C0112, C0201
  see also theology, Reformed
  Reformed, C0029
  see also theology, Protestant
  Roman Catholic, C0074, C0105
  South Africa, C0036
  Switzerland, C0074
  Third World, C0004, C0071
  see also theology, Africa; development theology; theology, Latin America, liberation
 dictionaries, C0217, C0220, C0224, C0227, C0230, C0240, C0249-C0252, C0262, C0284, C0291, C0293, C0304
  Roman Catholic, C0209, C0229, C0263, C0279-C0281, C0299
 grammar
  German, C0587
 handbook
  liberation, C0396

vocabularies
 German, C0269, C0330
 see also entries for individual theologians
theology of hope
 see eschatology
Thirty-Nine Articles
 handbook, C0706
Thomism
 bibliographies, C0038, C0045, C0122, C0133, C0207
 dictionary, C0292
 index, C0160
 see also Aquinas; scholasticism; Summa Theologica
trinity
 handbook, C0729

Unitarianism
 handbook, D0758
United Church of Christ, history of
 bibliography, D0146
 handbook, D0510
United Free Church of Scotland
 handbook, D0566
urban-industrial mission
 bibliography, C0102

Vatican Archives
 bibliographies, D0019, D0049
 handbook, D0472
 see also archives

war and peace
 bibliographies, C0054, C0085, C0141, C0205
 handbook, D0327
Wesley, Charles
 bibliographies, C0010, C0077
Wesley, John
 bibliographies, C0010, C0077, C0177
 handbooks, C0328, C0381, C0675
Wittgenstein, Ludwig
 bibliography, C0110
women, and Reformation
 handbook, D0334
World Council of Churches
 bibliography, E0018
worship
 see liturgy

youth
 handbook, C0460

Zwingli, U.
 bibliography, D0236

About the Authors

THE REVEREND G. E. GORMAN is Lecturer in Librarianship at the Ballarat College of Advanced Education (Australia). He is the author of *The South African Novel in English* and *Guide to Current National Bibliographies in the Third World, Theological and Religious Reference Materials: General Resources and Biblical Studies* and editor of *Library Acquisitions Practice and Theory* and other journals and book series. His articles have appeared in *Communio Viatorum, Journal of Religious History, Modern Churchman, International Social Science Journal,* and elsewhere.

DR. LYN GORMAN has been a tutor or administrator at the University of New England (Australia), the Institute of Development Studies at the University of Sussex, and Brighton Polytechnic. Her articles have appeared in the *Army Journal, European Studies Review, International Social Science Journal,* and *Die Dritte Welt*. She is coeditor of *The Second Enlargement of the EEC,* cofounder of Library, Information and Publishing Consultants and currently works as a freelance editor and information consultant.